The Integrated Learning Approach

For the Student

The Big Picture
Each chapter begins with a building block visual that highlights the focus of the chapter and systematically ties the chapters together. These chapter opening visuals emphasize how information systems are planned and developed.

Learning Objectives
Numbered learning objectives at the beginning of each chapter provide a framework for systematic learning.

Chapter Summaries
Directly linked to the chapter opening learning objectives, a numbered summary provides a concise review of the chapter.

End-of-Chapter Learning Activities
Chapters close with a plentiful selection of testing material that appeals to various learning styles. Multiple choice exercises reinforce basic content knowledge. To promote critical thinking and the application of key IS concepts to real world events, each chapter concludes with

Group Exercises

Field Exercises

Individual Exercises

Web/Internet Exercises

Real World Case Problems

www.jessup-valacich.com
Some of the exciting features of our Web page include
- Additional exercises
- Current cases
- Scavenger hunts
- Links to Web addresses of companies discussed in the book

Interactive Edition
 A discovery-based learning tool, the Interactive Edition provides a searchable HTML version of the entire book, study guides, note-taking tools, and electronic review questions.

For the Instructor

Test Bank
Organized by the main text's numbered learning objectives, the Test Bank and computerized test bank contain 3,000 multiple choice, fill-in, true or false, and short essay questions. A correlation table appears at the beginning of each chapter to clearly identify which questions support each numbered learning objective. Instructors can systematically design exams based on the numbered learning objectives they want to emphasize.

Instructor's Resource Manual
Designed as a flexible teaching tool, the Instructor's Resource Manual includes classroom ideas and projects organized around the main text's numbered learning objectives. Instructors can customize their class based on the learning objectives to maximize student learning. Tips on when to present PowerPoint images and videos will also assist the instructor in motivating students.

Video Cases
Developed and filmed exclusively for *Information Systems Foundations*, these five videos visually bring to life the role of information systems in well-known and respected companies, including Lands' End, Oracle, and Andersen Consulting.

Cases and Case Problems

Part 1: Information Systems Foundations: The Big Picture

Chapter 1: Information Systems Overview
An Information System Gone Awry: Denver International Airport

An Information System That Works: Federal Express

Ethical Perspective: Information Systems Code of Ethics

International Perspective: Global Competitiveness

IT Spending in '98: Full Speed Ahead

Social Security Gets It Right

Part 2: Information Systems Essentials

Chapter 2: Information Systems Hardware
The Birth of the Mouse

IBM at the Olympics

Allstate Insurance

Apple Macintosh

Information Systems Foundations

Leonard M. Jessup
Joseph S. Valacich

que
E&T

INFORMATION SYSTEMS FOUNDATIONS

Leonard M. Jessup

Joseph S. Valacich

Copyright © 1999 by Que ® Education and Training

Library of Congress Catalog Number: 98-066784

ISBN: 1-57676-415-6

Trademark Acknowledgments

IBM is a registered trademark of International Business Machines Corporation. Apple, Macintosh, and Mac are registered trademarks of Apple Computer Incorporated. Microsoft Access, MS-DOS, Windows, Windows 95, Windows 98, Windows Explorer, Windows NT, Microsoft Internet Explorer, Microsoft Network, Microsoft Word, Excel, and Microsoft are registered trademarks of Microsoft Corporation. Lotus 1-2-3 and Notes are registered trademarks of Lotus Development Corporation. America Online is a registered service mark of America Online, Incorporated. Intel is a registered trademark and Pentium is a trademark of Intel Corporation. Novell and NetWare are registered trademarks of Novell, Inc. in the United States and other countries.

All terms mentioned in this book that are known to be trademarks or service marks have been appropriately capitalized. Que Education and Training cannot attest to the accuracy of this information.

http://www.queet.com

Credits

Publisher:
Robert Linsky

Executive Editor:
Randy Haubner

Director of Product Marketing:
Susan L. Kindel

Managing Editor:
Caroline Roop

Senior Developmental Editor:
Lena Buonanno

Senior Editor:
Dayna Isley

Copy Editors:
Margo Catts
Leah Williams

Book Designer:
Louisa Klucznik

Cover Designer:
Nathan Clement

Team Coordinator:
Ken Schmidt

Indexer:
Chris Wilcox

Production Team:
Betsy Deeter
Becky Stutzman

Contents at a Glance

Table of Contents

These sections appear at the end of each chapter.

Approach

The field of information systems is changing so quickly that the only constant we can count on is change itself. Hardware keeps getting better and cheaper, new software is being developed to take advantage of the better hardware, telecommunications equipment steadily improves, and organizations are quickly adopting new technology. As a result of this pace, teaching people about information systems and training them for careers in this field has become increasingly challenging.

Given the dynamic nature of information systems, and given that it is difficult to find introductory information systems textbooks that are both up-to-date and student-friendly, we wrote *Information Systems Foundations* with two primary goals in mind. First, we not only wanted readers to learn about information systems, but we also wanted them to feel as excited as we do about the field and about the amazing opportunities available in this area. Second, we don't want to spoon-feed readers the technical terms and the history of information systems and then stop there. Instead, we want readers to understand exactly what modern organizations are doing today with information systems and, more importantly, where things are headed.

Audience

Information Systems Foundations is aimed primarily for the undergraduate introductory information systems course. This course is typically offered in the junior year of four-year undergraduate programs and in the second year at two-year institutions. The introductory information systems course comprises a diverse audience of students intending to major in many different areas, such as accounting, economics, finance, marketing, management, operations, personnel, and information systems. The introductory information systems course may even be attended by students majoring in areas outside of business. Therefore, this book has been written to appeal to a diverse audience.

Information Systems Foundations can also be used for the introductory course offered at the graduate level—for example, in the first year of an MBA program.

Key Features

As authors and teachers of information systems, we understand that motivating students to take an interest in the field is a key component in helping them assess the true value of the field and its impact on their everyday lives. We have therefore devised a unique pedagogy treatment that shows how today's professionals are using information technology to help modern organizations become more efficient and competitive. Our focus is on the application of technology to real world, contemporary situations.

Our case treatment, end-of-chapter material, and boxed features are all aimed at interesting business majors and information systems majors in our field. The latest technology tools, including the Internet and electronic commerce, are integrated in each chapter.

Cases: A Four-Tiered Approach

Descriptive Cases

Each chapter includes between four and six brief cases, which are identified by a margin icon.

```
A BRIEF CASE
```

These cases are descriptive in nature and are an integral part of the narrative. They are not boxed off and segregated from the body of the chapter. Companies discussed include Starbucks Coffee, Pepsi, American Express, Eddie Bauer, Microsoft, and Federal Express. To keep material current, we feature the Web addresses of the companies in the end-of-chapter reference section.

Case Problems

To test and reinforce chapter content, we present two real world case problems at the end of each chapter. Sources for these cases include *Information Week*, *Business Week*, *CIO Magazine*, and various Web sites. A brief article adaptation is followed by a series of questions to test students' understanding of key concepts presented in the chapter. Topics include the Compaq-Digital deal, the Year 2000 problem, and electronic commerce.

Customized Case Videos

In today's rapidly evolving technological environment, being current is key. We are pleased to provide two means of delivering current, real world case material. First, a set of five videos is available free to adopting instructors. Companies presented are Lands' End, Oracle, Lotus, Pillsbury, and Andersen Consulting. These case videos were developed by Beverly Amer of Northern Arizona to support our book. A case reading and discussion guide for these videos appears in the Instructor's Resource Manual.

Web Cases

New cases and discussion questions are posted frequently on our Web page: http://www.jessup-valacich.com.

Real World Chapter Opening Scenarios

Our goal for the chapter openers is to immediately spark the students' interest in the topic covered in the chapter. How does information systems affect students' lives? How do they purchase concert tickets online? How does their school use databases to store grades and transcripts? Our chapter opening scenarios pique students' interest by relating to their immediate interests and concerns. A photo or illustration is included with each scenario. We return to the chapter opening scenario to elaborate and highlight key content within the chapter. We also provide an end-of-chapter exercise directly related to the scenario.

End-of-Chapter Evaluation and Test Material

Our end-of-chapter material is designed to accommodate various teaching and learning styles. It promotes learning beyond the book and the classroom. Elements in this concluding section include the following:

- Review questions

    Test students' understanding of basic content

- Group exercises

    Promote team activities and presentations

- Field exercises

    Ask students to investigate a company IS system or interview an employee at that company

- Internet exercises

    Promote Web investigation

- Scenario exercise

    Ask students to complete an exercise based on the chapter opening scenario

- Real world case problems

    Summarize a journal article and ask students to respond to three questions related to that article

International Coverage

Each chapter includes a full-page international perspective special feature that is designed to support the content of the chapter. Topics presented include international software piracy, IS in South Africa, cross-cultural JAD teams, and global outsourcing. A set of discussion questions is included with each international topic.

Ethical Coverage

Each chapter includes a full-page ethical perspective special feature that is designed to support the content of the chapter. Topics presented include cyberterrorism, information ownership, and managing in a wired world. The feature closes with a set of discussion questions.

Interviews

We are fortunate to have 14 interviews of information systems professionals in our book. This feature is designed to alert business and information systems majors to the career opportunities that exist for those who appreciate and understand IS. Each interview includes an "Advice to Students" section and a "Critical Success Factors" section. The interviews provide students with real world, practical exposure to people of various backgrounds working in this dynamic field. Among our interviewees are Robert Ridout of DuPont, Wanda Miles of Oracle, Butch Winters of EDS, and R.W. Ransdell of IBM.

Pedagogy

In addition to our use of cases, chapter openers, and end-of-chapter exercises, we provide a list of learning objectives to lay the foundation for the chapter. The end-of-chapter summary repeats and briefly discusses each learning objective. A list of references, including Web references and selected readings, closes each chapter.

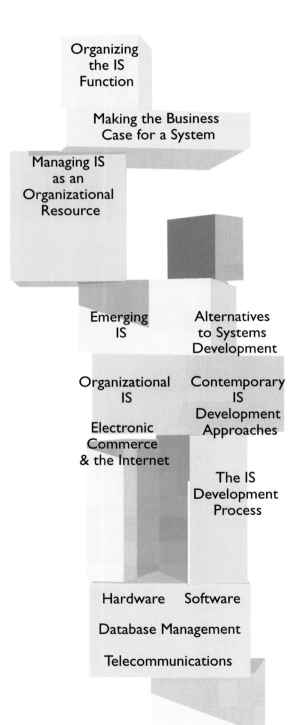

Organization

The content and organization of this book are based on our own teaching experience, as well as on feedback from reviewers and colleagues in the field. Each chapter builds on the others to reinforce key concepts and allow for a seamless learning experience. Essentially, the book has been structured to answer six fundamental questions:

1. What are information systems?

2. Why are information systems so important and interesting?

3. Why should I care about this field?

4. Now that you have my attention, what is this all about?

5. How do we build and manage information systems?

6. Now that I'm a believer, how can I develop and manage an IS?

To answer these questions in order, we structured the book into five parts, which are highlighted in "the big picture." Each part in the book features a big picture building block visual that highlights the focus of the chapters within that part and explains how that part relates to the previous parts. Each chapter also begins with a big picture visual that highlights the chapter content and how it relates to previous chapters. These chapter and part opening visuals emphasize how information systems are planned and developed.

Part 1, "Information Systems Foundations: The Big Picture," consists of Chapter 1, "Information Systems Overview." In this chapter, we present the "big picture" of information systems and demonstrate how they serve as the building blocks for all successful organizations. We highlight how organizations can use leading-edge information systems to operate more efficiently, provide high-quality goods and services, and, more importantly, gain or sustain a competitive advantage over their rivals.

FIGURE P.2

The big picture…

Part 2, "Information Systems Essentials," includes Chapter 2, "Information Systems Hardware"; Chapter 3, "Information Systems Software"; Chapter 4, "Database Management"; and Chapter 5, "Telecommunications." In this part, we present the building blocks of all information systems.

Part 3, "Information Systems in Practice," includes Chapter 6, "Electronic Commerce and the Internet"; Chapter 7, "Organizational Information Systems"; and Chapter 8, "Emerging Information Systems." This part highlights what types of systems companies are using and to what advantage.

Part 4, "Information Systems Development," includes Chapter 9, "The Information Systems Development Process"; Chapter 10, "Contemporary Information Systems Development Approaches"; and Chapter 11, "Alternatives to Systems Development." The focus of this part is on how information systems are built or purchased through outsourcing.

Part 5, "Information Systems Management," includes Chapter 12, "Managing Information Systems as an Organizational Resource"; Chapter 13, "Making the Business Case for a System"; and Chapter 14, "Organizing the Information Systems Function." This part highlights the skills required to manage large, complex information systems in modern organizations.

Print Supplements

We have worked closely with our supplement authors and Que Education & Training to create a teaching and learning package that meets the needs of today's classroom. A comprehensive Instructor's Resource Manual and an extensive Test Bank are designed to maximize teaching ease and flexibility.

Instructor's Resource Manual

Prepared by David VanOver of the University of Idaho, the Instructor's Resource Manual (IRM) uses the Integrated Learning Approach. Each numbered learning objective from the parent text appears in the IRM margin to highlight where each learning objective is reinforced. Instructors can customize their classes and maximize stu-

dent learning based on the numbered learning objectives. Other features of the IRM include the following:

- Conversion guide for users of competing texts
- Course syllabi
- Overview of each chapter
- Classroom ideas to generate discussion
- Solutions to exercises and problems in the book
- Tips on when to integrate videos and PowerPoint material

The IRM is available in both print and electronic form.

Test Bank

Prepared by Gary Margot and David Lifer of Ashland University, the Test Bank, like the IRM, implements the Integrated Learning Approach. Each learning objective number from the parent text appears next to each test bank question. A correlation table at the beginning of each Test Bank chapter clearly identifies which questions support each learning objective. This format allows instructors to systematically design exams based on the numbered learning objectives they want to emphasize. The Test Bank contains 3,000 questions, which appear in the following forms:

- Multiple choice
- Fill in the blank
- True or false
- Short essay

Solutions and a page reference from the main text are also included. Each question is coded by level of difficulty. This test bank is also available in computerized form.

Technology Supplements

Our technology teaching and learning package motivates students about the field of information systems and provides them with the tools to investigate current, real world topics.

Information Systems Foundations Interactive Edition CD-ROM

Que Education & Training created the *Information Systems Foundations* Interactive Edition CD-ROM to provide students with a unique, discovery-based learning tool. The Interactive Edition provides interactive multimedia explorations of key textbook topics, video cases, seamless integration of the World Wide Web, personalized study guides and note-taking tools, and electronic review exercises with emailable results. The Interactive Edition also includes a searchable HTML version of the entire textbook.

Video Cases

Five video cases were custom-produced exclusively for *Information Systems Foundations* by Beverly Amer of Northern Arizona University and Aspenleaf Productions, Inc. Written cases and accompanying student video materials on CD-ROM, provide students with the opportunity to do further exploration of the issues raised in the videos. Several links to the Web and additional materials are available on the CD-ROM.

These innovative and stimulating cases focus on such topics as: (1) the role of information systems in business, (2) data warehousing and data management, (3) groupware and collaborative work, (4) systems development approaches, and (5) the functions of a world-class MIS department. The companies selected are well-known and respected organizations that have interesting and valuable lessons for today's MIS students. Companies filmed are as follows:

- Part 1—Lands' End
- Part 2—Oracle
- Part 3—Lotus
- Part 4—Andersen Consulting
- Part 5—Pillsbury

www.jessup-valacich.com: An Integrated and Active Web Site

The www.jessup-valacich.com Web site provides supplemental exercises, current cases with discussion questions, demo software, Web projects, Web scavenger hunts, and links to the Web addresses of companies discussed in the book.

QueTest by inQsit

The finest Web-based testing system available! QueTest by inQsit (developed by Ball State University) utilizes the World Wide Web and Web technologies to present questions, record answers, and return customized graded results. QueTest uses Smart Wizards to help you create your tests and has a variety of question types that can be selected at will or at random. QueTest supports proctored tests, transference of existing test questions, and test item analysis!

Information Systems Foundations QuePresents

QuePresents is a CD-ROM packed with a library of PowerPoint 97 presentations that are designed to enhance your classroom presentations. These presentations include a variety of materials used by the author team in their classrooms. QuePresents can be used as is or customized to meet the needs of your students.

For more information about Que E&T's extraordinary teaching and learning resources, please contact your local Macmillan Computer Publishing representative. You may also contact us on the Web at http://www.queet.com

Application Manuals

Que Education & Training offers a variety of computer lab applications manuals that can be used in conjunction with *Information Systems Foundations* to provide your students with the tools they need to succeed in your class and beyond.

Series	Essentials	Learn	MOUS Essentials	SmartStarts
Applications	Windows 3.1/95/98	Windows 95/98	Windows 95/98	DOS/Windows 3.1/95/98
Level B = Beginning I = Intermediate A = Advanced	B, I, A for all Win95 and higher	B	Proficient and Expert	B–I
Course Length	8–12 contact hours	6–8 contact hours	8–12 contact hours	12–24 contact hours
Features	4 color (most first levels). Project orientation teaches problem solving. Step-by-step approach and oversized screen shots. End-of-chapter exercises combine skill assessment and application. All first-level Office 97 books include Screen ID and Challenge exercises.	4 color. Screen shots show results of steps taken. Learn On-Demand software.	4 color. Microsoft-approved for MOUS Program. Included appendix on certification process.	2 color. Skills focus emphasizes practical knowledge. Material is organized around objectives. End-of-chapter exercises integrate material from earlier exercises.
Learning Tools	Why would I do this? Jargon Watch. If You Have Problems. Inside Stuff. Running marginal glossary. Lesson objectives.	Completed screen shots at chapter opener. In Depth, Caution, and Shortcuts.	Why would I do this? If You Have Problems. Inside Stuff. Required activities and MS Test Notes give students guidelines and tips for preparing for the certification exams.	Objectives and end-of-chapter summaries. Running marginal glossary. "Notes." Running cases.

continues

Series	Essentials	Learn	MOUS Essentials	SmartStarts
Resources	Instructor's Manual with data disks. Annotated Instructor's Editions (Office 97 apps only). QueTest (Office 97 apps only). Virtual Tutor CD-ROM.	Annotated Instructor's Editions. QueTest. Learn On-Demand.	Annotated Instructor's Edition.	Instructor's Manual with data disk.

Que E&T also offers custom publishing that is as easy as 1,2,3 through our **Quest Custom Publishing Program**. Please contact your local Macmillan Computer Publishing representative for more details. To obtain the name of your representative, call 1-800-428-5331. You may also contact us on the Web at http://www.queet.com.

Acknowledgments

Although only our two names will be listed as the authors for this book, this was truly a team effort that went well beyond the two of us. Que E&T has been an outstanding publishing company to work with. They are innovative and adaptive, they do not hesitate to spend resources where needed, and they've treated us like "VIPs."

Among the many amazingly helpful people at Que E&T, there are two people who we wish to thank specifically. The first is Randy Haubner, our executive editor. From the inception of this project over two years ago, Randy has been a constant source of motivation, vision, and guidance. The second is Lena Buonanno, our development editor. Lena took our original, rough chapter drafts and helped us shape them into the finished, professional product you see now. Her attention to detail, her pursuit of excellence, and her thoughtfulness and tact in dealing with us are unsurpassed.

There is one other person who was intimately involved in this project, without whom we could not have finished on time. Lee Freeman, a doctoral student in the Kelley School of Business at Indiana University, contributed to the end-of-chapter materials, references, interviews, case studies, international and ethical features, and much more. We literally couldn't have done it without you, Lee.

There are a number of other people who conducted background research and helped craft early drafts of chapters. They are Andrew Urbaczewski, Brad Wheeler, and Anne Massey; all of the Kelley School of Business at Indiana University; and Mike Morris of the Air Force Institute of Technology. Similarly, Jeff Butterfield of Western Kentucky University contributed much of the innovative content you see on the book's Web site.

A fine group of people helped with the supplements. We thank Beverly Amer of Northern Arizona University for producing the innovative video cases. David VanOver of the University of Idaho developed the Instructor's Guide. Gary Margot and David Lifer of Ashland University developed the Test Bank. Jane Mackay of Texas Christian University helped craft and shape many of the end-of-chapter case problems. In addition, a number of people helped with reviews of drafts of this book throughout its life.

Most importantly, we thank our families for their patience and assistance in helping us complete this book. Len's wife, Joy, helped craft the international insets and tested early drafts of chapters in her introductory information systems course. Joe's wife, Jackie, proofread and helped reshape drafts of every chapter through the entire revision phase. You both were not only patient with us as we spent long hours working on this book over the course of two years, but you were also instrumental in helping us finish the project and produce an excellent book. Finally, we thank our children. Len's beautiful new baby, Jamie, and Joe's beautiful children, Jordan and James, were the true inspiration for this book.

Reviewers

We are indebted to the many reviewers who have provided us with positive feedback as well as sound revision recommendations on our approach, content, and pedagogy.

Beverly Amer, Northern Arizona University

Robert Bostrom, University of Georgia

Michael Godfrey, California State University at Long Beach

Ellen D. Hoadley, Loyola University

Robert T. Keim, Arizona State University

Edward Kaplan, Bentley College

Mohammed B. Khan, California State University at Long Beach

Wafa Khorsheed, Eastern Michigan University

Jane Mackay, Texas Christian University

Gary L. Margot, Ashland University

Srinivasan Rao, University of Texas at San Antonio

Lora Robinson, Saint Cloud State University

A.B. Schwarzkopf, University of Oklahoma

Robert VanCleave, Univesity of Minnesota

Jack VanDeventer, Washington State University

Connie E. Wells, Nicholls State University

Vincent Yen, Wright State University

Dale Young, Miami University

About the Authors

Leonard M. Jessup

Leonard M. Jessup is an Associate Professor of Information Systems and Chairperson of the Technology Committee for the Kelley School of Business at Indiana University. Professor Jessup received his BA in Information and Communication Studies in 1983 and his MBA in 1985 from California State University, Chico, where he was voted Outstanding MBA Student. He received his PhD in Organizational Behavior and Management Information Systems from the University of Arizona in 1989. He is a member of the Association for Information Systems and Alpha Iota Delta, Program Co-Chair for the Association for Information Systems 1997 Americas Conference, Associate Editor for the *Management Information Systems Quarterly,* and a member of the editorial board for *Small Group Research.* He was voted the Outstanding Faculty Member in the College of Business Administration at California State University, San Marcos, and he received a Teaching Excellence Recognition Award in the Kelley School of Business at Indiana University. With his wife, Joy L. Egbert, he won Zenith Data System's annual Masters of Innovation award. With Joseph S. Valacich, he co-edited *Group Support*

IU Photographic Services. Photographer: Paul Riley

Systems: New Perspectives for Macmillan Publishing Company. He teaches in various areas of management and management information systems and has published, presented, and consulted on electronic commerce, computer-supported collaborative work, computer-assisted learning, and on related topics. His research has appeared in journals such as *MIS Quarterly, Management Science,* and *Decision Sciences.* He has helped create and has worked for a number of small, high-tech start-up firms.

Joseph S. Valacich

Joseph S. Valacich is an Associate Professor of Information Systems and is the George and Carolyn Hubman Distinguished Professor in Information Systems for the College of Business and Economics at Washington State University, Pullman. He received his BS in Computer Science and MBA from the University of Montana. He received his PhD in Management Information Systems from the University of Arizona. He is a member of the Institute for Operations Research and Management Sciences (INFORMS) and the Association for Computing Machinery (ACM). He is also a charter member of the Association for Information Systems (AIS). Dr. Valacich worked in the information systems field as a programmer, systems analyst, and technical product manager prior to his academic career. In 1992, Alpha Kappa Psi gave one of his articles the Distinguished Publication in Business Communications award. In 1993, The Academy of Management named one of his articles the Best Article in Information Systems. Professor Valacich served on the ACM, AIS, and Association of Information Technology Professionals (formerly DPMA) joint national task force to design IS '97: Model Curriculum and Guidelines for Undergraduate Degree Programs in Information Systems. He is currently serving on the joint ACM-AIS task force designing the curriculum for master of science information systems programs. He was awarded the Outstanding Faculty Service Award from the Washington State University College of Business and Economics in 1997, the Sanjay Subhedar Faculty Fellow from the Indiana University School of Business in 1996; and the Exceptional Inspiration and Guidance

Award from the Indiana University School of Business Doctoral Student Association in 1995. He is Vice-Chairperson of ICIS 1999 in Charlotte. His current research interests include technology-mediated group decision-making, electronic commerce, the diffusion of technology in organizations, and distance learning. Dr. Valacich serves on the editorial board of *Small Group Research* and is an Associate Editor for *MIS Quarterly*. His past research has appeared in publications such as *MIS Quarterly, Information Systems Research, Management Science,* and *Academy of Management Journal*. With Leonard M. Jessup, he co-edited *Group Support Systems: New Perspectives* for Macmillan Publishing Company in 1993. Professor Valacich is a co-author with Jeffery A. Hoffer and Joey F. George of the best-selling *Modern Systems Analysis and Design, Second Edition*, published by Addison Wesley Longman.

PART I

Information Systems Foundations:
The Big Picture

Chapter 1:   *Information Systems Overview*

Part 1 consists of Chapter 1, *Information Systems Overview*. In this chapter, we present the "big picture" of Information Systems and demonstrate how they serve as the building blocks for all successful organizations. We highlight how organizations can use leading-edge information systems to operate more efficiently, to provide high-quality goods and services and, more importantly, to gain or sustain a competitive advantage over their rivals.

We begin by defining information systems and describing the evolution of computing. Next, we explain the technology, people, and organizational components of an information system. We also discuss how information systems can be used to automate, informate, and support business strategy.

As you read Chapter 1, try to see the "big picture." We use a chapter opening image called "the big picture" to provide you with an overview of what information systems are. This image is integrated throughout the book to serve as a starting point and foundation for each chapter.

Information Systems
Management

Information
Systems
in Practice

Information
Systems
Development

Information Systems
Essentials

Scenario: Fleetwood Mac Tickets Online

Imagine that you're sitting at your computer writing a paper on your word processor. You decide to check your email and find a new message from an online ticket service that you've just started doing business with. You open the message and find out that the megaband of the 1970s, Fleetwood Mac, is back on tour again (see Figure 1.1). With your permission, this ticket service tracks your purchases with them, so they know your tastes in music. You recently bought the Beatles Anthology release from them, and they know that you like retro rock groups that pop back onto the music scene. Part of their service is to inform you of upcoming events and album releases that might be of interest to you.

You jump right over to your Internet World Wide Web browser and click on your saved bookmark for the ticket service. After you reach their Web site, you log in with your user ID and password. You are greeted by name and asked whether you enjoyed your recent purchase of the Beatles Anthology. The service then asks whether you're at their site to follow up on the Fleetwood Mac information. This is a very personal service! You click "yes" and are taken into their concert category. (They also deal with sporting events, theater events, and just about everything else for which you can buy a ticket.). For fun, you check out their Top 25 Concerts list, which is tabulated in real time from online information requests. Sure enough, Fleetwood Mac is at the top of the list. You better get your tickets fast.

You click the onscreen map to indicate where you live and are shown the venues near you where Fleetwood Mac will be playing. You choose one of the venues and are shown the onscreen schematic that displays the seating arrangement at that particular venue. You are asked whether you want seats in front, as you have chosen in the past. You say yes and are shown a schematic of the concert hall, with the front seats highlighted. The price and availability of these seats are flashing at the bottom of your screen. The seats are a bit expensive, so you check out the prices and availability of other seats in the hall. While you're checking out other seats, you notice that several of the seats in the front have just been purchased. You immediately click on a block of available seats down in front and click on the order button.

You are asked whether you would like to use the same VISA account again, and your VISA number is posted for you to verify. Everything you do at this Web site is encrypted, or coded, so that it is nearly impossible for anyone to steal your credit card number. In any event, giving your credit card at this Web site is a lot safer than giving it to a stranger over the phone. You choose to pick up the tickets at the "will call" window on the night of the concert. After the

FIGURE 1.1

Fleetwood Mac, megaband of the 1970s, on tour in 1997.

ticket purchase is complete, the agency's database is immediately updated so that other people won't be able to buy tickets for your seats.

You are asked whether you would like to buy any Fleetwood Mac goodies for the concert. You say yes so that you can at least browse through their online gift shop. You don't see anything you want to purchase, but you check out the background information on Fleetwood Mac. You follow a link to the home page for a Fleetwood Mac fan club near you and have fun checking out some old pictures of the band. You always got a kick out of the outfits that Stevie Nicks wore. You remember that you recently lost your Fleetwood Mac Rumours compact disc, so you go back to the gift shop and check the price. The price isn't bad, so you make a mental note to come back later and order it.

You click back to the home page of the ticket service and choose to exit. They say thanks and goodbye and ask for your feedback on their service for that day. You type in a line or two of comment about your service with them this time and then return to your word processor. Your purchase of Fleetwood Mac concert tickets online took about 10 minutes, starting from the moment you read the ticket service's email message.

What you did not notice is that while this online ticket service was offering its products and making a sale, it was simultaneously performing several other processes—initiating the printing and distribution of the tickets you ordered, updating its inventory and accounting systems as a result of your transaction, learning about its products and its Web site from the path that you took through the Web, and learning from your written feedback how to improve service to you. This online ticket service is an integrated, enterprise-wide information system, but that doesn't matter much to you. You might even take it for granted that their products are good and their prices are low—they have to be. What matters most to you is that their service is fast and easy. In fact, the online ticket service is the key to the company's success. It provides the company with a critical competitive advantage over their rivals.

Introduction

Many organizations today are using the World Wide Web to conduct business in much the same manner as that described in the preceding scenario. Our scenario is a good example of the many ways that an organization can use leading-edge information systems to conveniently provide high-quality goods and services and, more importantly, gain or sustain a competitive advantage over their rivals.

In this chapter, we provide an overview of information systems. Our objective is to help you gain an understanding of what information systems are and how they have evolved to become an increasingly important part of virtually all modern organizations. After reading this chapter, you will be able to do the following:

1. Understand what the term *information systems* (IS) means.

2. Describe the evolution of computing.

3. Explain the technology, people, and organizational components of an information system.

4. Discuss how information systems can be used to automate, informate, and strategically support business activities.

5. Describe information systems' critical, strategic importance to the success of modern organizations.

To achieve these objectives, we provide an overview of key IS-related terms and issues and explain the importance of understanding how information systems can be used to help organizations be more productive and competitive. In terms of our guiding framework (see Figure 1.2), this chapter *is* The Big Picture—an overview of what information systems are and why it is important for you to know about them. In subsequent chapters, we break down each piece of The Big Picture and provide you with the essential information needed to gain a thorough and comprehensive understanding of information systems.

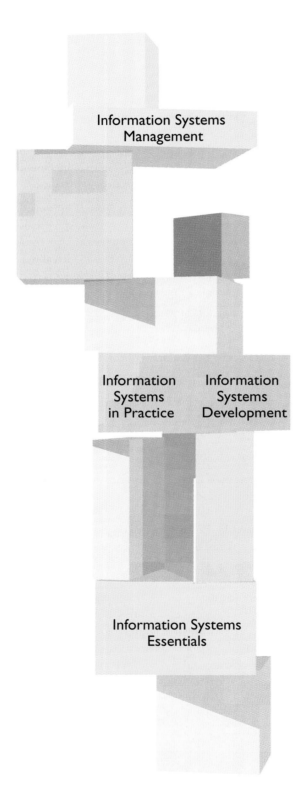

Information Systems
Management

Information
Systems
in Practice

Information
Systems
Development

Information Systems
Essentials

Information Systems Defined

Information systems, such as the online ticket service that we described in the opening scenario, are combinations of hardware, software, and telecommunications networks that people build and use to collect, create, and distribute useful data for organizations. In Figure 1.3, we show these components of information systems and their interrelationships. Information systems are used within organizations to process sales transactions; manage loan applications; and help financial analysts decide where, when, and how to invest. They are also used to help product managers decide where, when, and how to market their products and related services and to help production managers decide when and how to manufacture products. Information systems can also help us in a wide variety of other situations. They enable us to get cash from ATM machines, communicate by live video with people in other parts of the world, buy concert tickets, and much more. So much for standing in line all night to buy concert tickets the following morning!

This book focuses on information systems, the field that encompasses a variety of people involved in the development, use, management, and study of computer-based information systems in organizations. In Figure 1.4, we show the essential ingredients of the definition of IS. Because of the great diversity and rapid changes in the field of IS, several other terms are used to describe the field. These alternative terms include management information systems, data processing management, systems management, business computer systems, computer information systems, and just systems. For better or worse, the term IS seems to be the most commonly used; therefore, we'll stick with the term *information systems* and the acronym *IS*. Next, we describe how the information systems field has evolved to become one of the most important components of modern organizations and one of the most dominant aspects of our economy.

FIGURE 1.2

The big picture: focusing on information sytems overview.

The Rapid Rise in the Development and Use of Technology

Computers are the core component of IS. Perhaps nothing as important has happened to and for businesses over the past decade as the advent of powerful, relatively inexpensive, easy-to-use computing systems. To see this phenomenon, you need only look around your university or place of work. At your university, you may be registering for classes online, using email to communicate with fellow students and your instructors, and completing assignments on networked personal computers. At work, you are probably using a personal computer and email. Your paychecks are probably generated by computer and automatically deposited in your checking account via high-speed networks. Chances are you see a lot more technology now than you did just a few short years ago, and most likely, this technology is a more fundamental and important part of your learning and work than ever before.

One characteristic of this industry is the rapidity with which things change. More than 90 percent of the $25 billion in revenue earned by computer chip manufacturing giant Intel in 1997 came from products that did not even exist in 1996 (McHugh, 1998). Now that is change!

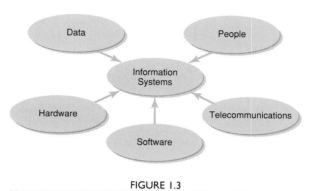

FIGURE 1.3

The components of an information system.

Information systems are combinations of
hardware, software, and telecommunications networks
which
people build and use
to
collect, create, and distribute useful data,
typically in
organizational settings.

FIGURE 1.4

The essential ingredients of the definition of IS.

Many of the hot companies in the world today are in the computer industry, and they are experiencing greater than 30 percent sales growth every year. This growth rate is amazing when you consider that the median growth rate for all industries in the U.S. in 1997 was 7.9 percent (McHugh, 1998). Microsoft had a growth rate of more than 36 percent in 1997, with sales at more than $12 billion. Oracle grew around 33 percent, with sales at more than $6 billion. Cisco Systems grew more than 45 percent, with sales of almost $7 billion. These are just a few of the many, many computer-related companies that are growing rapidly and achieving record sales. Not long ago, the computer industry was a relatively minor player in the world's economy; today, it has become the 800-pound gorilla!

The business-computing phenomenon has been chronicled well in the popular business press. We're not necessarily talking about magazines such as *InformationWeek* or *PC Computing*, which naturally always publish stories about computing. Take a look instead at a purely business-oriented publication, such as some recent issues of *BusinessWeek* magazine. In recent years, nearly every issue has included at least one important story about technology in business in addition to the "Technology & You" weekly column.

The cover story in nearly every other weekly issue of *BusinessWeek* in 1997 and 1998 has been about technology or has had a technological component. Figure 1.5 shows some recent *BusinessWeek* covers that concern technological issues. Some of these cover stories have been about the direct use of technology in business, with titles such as "Annual Buying Guide on Computers," "The Software Revolution," "Reinventing the Store,"

Reprinted from December 22, 1997,
February 9, 1998, and February 23,
1998 issues of BusinessWeek by special
permission. ©1997, 1998 by The
McGraw-Hill Companies.

FIGURE 1.5

Three BusinessWeek *covers with stories related to technology.*

"Internet," "Intranets," and so on. In addition, many recent *BusinessWeek* cover stories have featured companies such as Intel, Compaq, Microsoft, IBM, Sun, and Apple. Other cover stories have recommended the best industries and companies to invest in. The companies in the computing and telecommunications industries have continually been one of the bright spots in terms of sustained growth and value in these articles (Smith, Bremner, and Edmondson, 1996). Anyone following the stock market recently has experienced the fever over stocks such as Netscape, Sun, or Cisco Systems (see Figure 1.6 for more information on Cisco's rise). Technology is hot!

If you are in business, going into business in some capacity, or simply interested in some aspect of business, then you should know about technology. As we will discuss throughout this book, technology is being used to radically change how business is conducted—from the way that products and services are produced, distributed and accounted for, to the ways that they are marketed and sold. To be the best you can be in business today—even if your area is finance, accounting, or marketing—technology is critical.

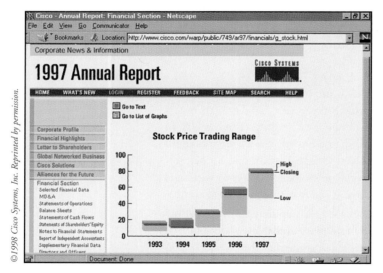

FIGURE 1.6

Graph of Cisco Systems' phenomenal growth in stock value.

IS Past and Present

You just read about how information systems technology has evolved to become a big part of modern organizations and our economy. Next, we provide a quick summary of how all this occurred and review additional details on the components of a modern information system.

The Evolution in Computing

The information systems field has rapidly evolved over the past 50 years (see Figure 1.7). This evolution is highlighted by several key developments that begin or end particular eras of computing. Although the date when one era begins or ends could be debated, at least five clearly distinct eras of computing can be defined:

- Mainframe
- Minicomputer
- Personal computer
- Interpersonal computing
- Internetworking

Each era has been marked by major events. Naturally, some of these eras of computing overlap. Nonetheless, we define each era as the time when specific types of technologies and applications dominated the information systems field.

The mainframe era of computing had its beginnings with the introduction of ENIAC (Electronic Numerical Integrator and Calculator), the first electronic digital computer, in 1946, and UNIVAC (Universal Automatic Computer), the first general-purpose computer, in 1951 (see Figure 1.7). The introduction of these rather large, complex, expensive computers influenced the early years of IS. Throughout the 1950s and 1960s, organizations relied primarily on mainframe computers sold by IBM and other firms— large, general-purpose computers capable of performing many tasks simultaneously while hundreds, even thousands, of people use them at the same time. Mainframe computers were used for transaction processing and related business applications. Given their size and cost, mainframe computers were nearly always kept locked away in safe, separate computer facilities.

The minicomputer era began in the late 1960s and continued throughout the 1970s and 1980s (see Figure 1.7). During this time, the world witnessed the development and tremendous sales growth of minicomputers made by Digital Equipment Corporation, Data General Corporation, and others. A minicomputer is a medium-sized computer that was meant to be a smaller, less expensive alternative to the mainframe. Compared to mainframes, minicomputers were much less expensive to buy and operate, making computing accessible to more than just the largest organizations.

The industry then shifted from these early computing eras to the personal computer era (see Figure 1.7). A personal computer fits on a desktop, is most often used by a single user, and is far less expensive than either mainframes or minicomputers. Early precursors to modern personal computers, such as the MITS Altair, were available as early as 1975, and the Apple I was introduced in 1976. However, many argue that the real beginning of the personal computer industry came in 1981, with the highly successful introduction of the IBM PC. Much of the success of the personal computer has been fueled by Microsoft pioneer Bill Gates' goal to put a computer on every desk and in every home.

In the late 1980s computing once again shifted, this time from the personal computing era to what Steve Jobs, cofounder of Apple Computers, called the interpersonal computing era (see Figure 1.7). Suddenly, organizations were using computer networks to connect their personal computers together and to the company's mainframe and minicomputers. Companies such as Banyan, Novell, and Artisoft flourished.

In the 1990s, we've seen another shift in computing in organizations. We have now moved from the interpersonal computing to the internetworking era (see Figure 1.7). In this new era of computing, people in organizations are integrating their disparate computers and networks into seamless, responsive enterprise-wide information systems. This integration is enabling customers' direct access into an organization's systems, connecting one organization's enterprise-wide systems to the systems of other organizations, and connecting everything to the Internet—the global network of networks. The objective is to put valuable data at everyone's fingertips and to enable electronic commerce in a variety of forms.

FIGURE 1.7

The evolution of computing.

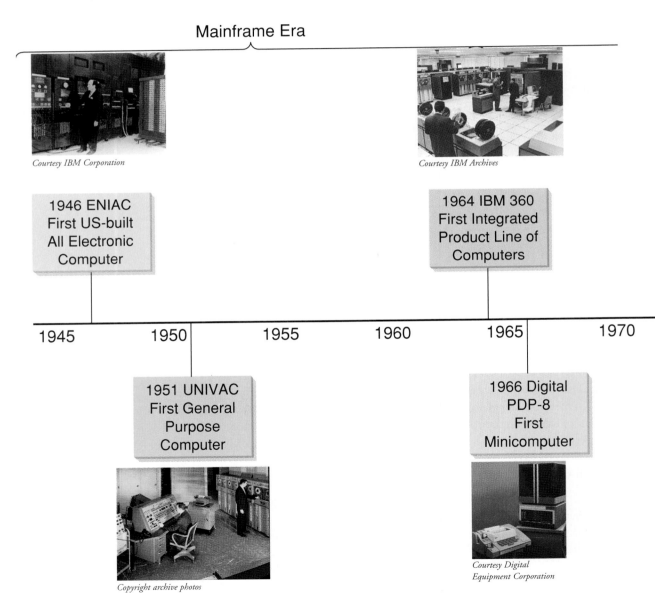

In this internetworking era, software companies such as Netscape and hardware companies such as Sun Microsystems have flourished. Netscape produces software to enable users to easily and quickly browse and access content on the Internet. Sun produces workstation computers, which are versatile, multi-user computers (typically using a version of the UNIX operating system) that have quickly become the servers forming the backbone of the Internet. Workstations come in a variety of sizes and prices, but they are generally somewhere in between personal computers and minicomputers in terms of their power and price.

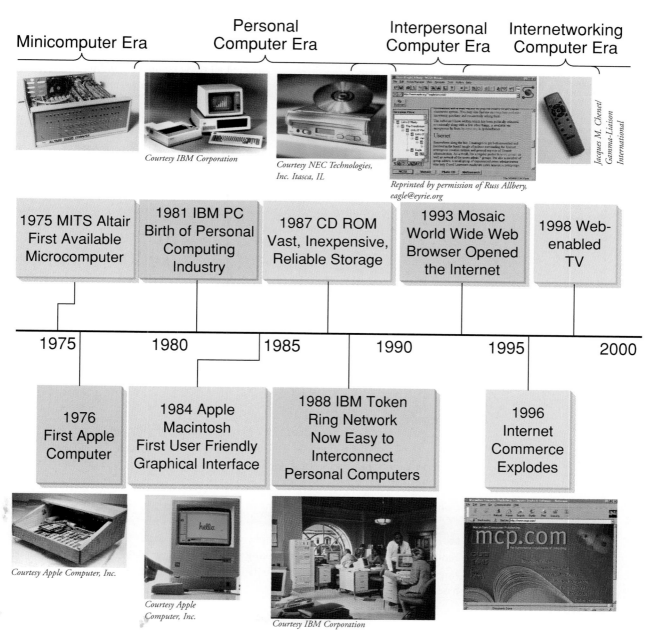

Minicomputer Era | Personal Computer Era | Interpersonal Computer Era | Internetworking Computer Era

Courtesy IBM Corporation

Courtesy NEC Technologies, Inc. Itasca, IL

Reprinted by permission of Russ Allbery, eagle@eyrie.org

Jacques M. Chenet/ Gamma-Liaison International

1975 MITS Altair First Available Microcomputer

1981 IBM PC Birth of Personal Computing Industry

1987 CD ROM Vast, Inexpensive, Reliable Storage

1993 Mosaic World Wide Web Browser Opened the Internet

1998 Web-enabled TV

1975 — 1980 — 1985 — 1990 — 1995 — 2000

1976 First Apple Computer

1984 Apple Macintosh First User Friendly Graphical Interface

1988 IBM Token Ring Network Now Easy to Interconnect Personal Computers

1996 Internet Commerce Explodes

Courtesy Apple Computer, Inc.

Courtesy Apple Computer, Inc.

Courtesy IBM Corporation

IS Today

As you can see, times have changed in IS since the early mainframe days. Today, when you talk about the technology side of IS, you're not just talking about mainframes anymore—although mainframe computers still play a vital role in IS planning and implementation for some large organizations. In most organizations today, the field of IS encompasses a diverse range of computing and networking technologies, from super-computers, mainframes, and minicomputers to workstations, personal computers, and personal digital assistants (as illustrated in Figure 1.8). The IS field also ranges from local area networks to wide area networks and wireless data communication. It includes a wide variety of useful peripheral devices as well, such as scanners and laser printers. The task of connecting all these computers and devices together has become almost more important than the computers themselves. What's interesting about this technology side of IS is not necessarily that so many more, better technologies are available, but that in many cases, the technology rests in the hands of the users and not the IS personnel.

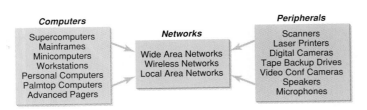

FIGURE 1.8

The technologies of IS come in a variety of flavors.

In addition to the changes to the technology side of IS, the people of IS are changing as well. Many more women are in IS positions than there were just a few short years ago. Also, it is now more common for an IS professional to be a polished, professional systems analyst, dressed in a sharp business suit—someone who can talk fluently about both business and technology. Similarly, today's systems programmers are well-trained, high-ly skilled, valuable professionals who garner high wages and play a pivotal role in helping firms be successful. For example, today good programmers with skills in SAP R/3 (Systems, Applications, and Products in Data Processing, Release 3) are so valuable that some organizations are willing to pay $150,000 a year to get them. In short, times have changed for IS. The people have changed, and the technology has changed. IS is an important field and a growing profession. For an example, read how the career of one IS professional evolved.

The Technology Side of IS

Let's break down the definition of IS we discussed earlier in the chapter and think about each part of that definition. We'll begin by discussing the core of IS—the computer-based information system. In Part 2, we'll talk more about the nuts and bolts of computer-based systems.

Computer-based information systems are a type of technology. **Technology** is any mechanical and/or electrical means to either supplement or replace manual operations or devices. In this basic sense, some sample machine technologies include the heating and cooling system for a building, the braking system for an automobile, and a laser used for surgery. In Figure 1.9, we show the relationship between technologies and computer-based information systems.

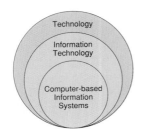

FIGURE 1.9

Venn diagram depicting the relationship between technologies and computer-based information systems.

We use the term **information technology** to refer to any use of machine technology that is controlled by or uses information in some important way. For example, one type of information technology is a programmable robot on the shop floor of a manufacturing firm that receives component specifications and operational instructions from a computer-based database.

On one level, we could argue that any technology makes use of information in some fundamental way, as does each of the three examples of basic technology listed earlier. However, information technologies, such as programmable manufacturing robots, use relatively more information and in a relatively more sophisticated way. You might think that we are splitting hairs with the difference between technologies and information technologies. While the difference is subtle, it is important. Information technologies use machine technologies as building blocks and then combine them and integrate them with computing and networking technologies. A technology such as a mechanical drill press is nice, but it's even better when combined with a computer database that instructs that drill press when and how to act.

Information technologies and information systems are similar. Remember that we defined an information system as a combination of hardware, software, and telecommunications networks that people build and use to collect, create, and distribute data. Information systems are computer-based information systems that contain current data. Their ultimate goal is to provide information to users in a way that helps them to do things. An example of an information system would be the computer-controlled drill press that we described earlier, combined with other shop floor equipment in such a way that a person could monitor and control each piece of equipment from a separate, possibly remote, computer.

Other examples of information systems include a series of integrated electronic spreadsheets used for a budget, an order-fulfillment system for managing customers' purchases, or a set of linked pages on the World Wide Web. You may be asking,"Does my PC at work or school count as part of the company's or university's IS?" Our answer is, yes—exactly! IS includes personal, group, organizational, interorganizational, and even global computing systems.

The People Side of IS

The information systems field includes a vast collection of people who develop, maintain, manage, and study information systems. The career opportunities for a person with IS training have never been better, and they will continue to improve over the next ten years (King, 1998). *Money Magazine* calls being a systems analyst—a common IS career—one of the best jobs in the world today (Marable, 1995).

The U.S. Department of Commerce is predicting huge labor shortages for people with skills in using, designing, developing, and managing information systems. A recent edition of *CIO magazine*—a leading journal for IS executives—dedicated an entire issue to the IS staffing crisis. *Computerworld* reported that more than 350,000 technology-related jobs were unfilled in 1998 (King, 1998). Furthermore, the Commerce Department predicts that this labor shortage for IS workers is only going to increase over the next decade. Even if you don't plan to pursue an IS-related career, you should be interested in this shortage. For example, because virtually all industries heavily rely on IS professionals, not just computer hardware and software companies, the shortage in skilled workers may have a big impact on the economy. The U.S. Bureau of Labor Statistics has reported that high demand for technology-related workers and escalating salaries could lead to inflation in the economy and lower corporate profits over the next decade (Hoffman, 1998).

The field of IS includes those in organizations who design and build systems, those who use those systems, and those responsible for managing those systems. In Table 1.1, we list some of these types of careers and the salaries you might earn in various IS positions. The people who help develop and manage systems in organizations include systems analysts, systems programmers, systems operators, network administrators, database administrators, systems designers, systems managers, and chief information officers. Throughout this book, we'll talk more about these various people and what they do.

Table 1.1 Some of the types of people in IS.

Some IS Activities	Typical Careers	Salary Ranges
Develop	Systems analyst	$40,000–$80,000+
	Systems programmer	$50,000–$80,000+
	Systems consultant	$50,000–$100,000+
Maintain	Database administrator	$75,000–$100,000+
	Webmaster	$40,000–$75,000+
Manage	IS director	$75,000–$100,000+
	Chief information officer	$100,000–$200,000+
Study	University professor	$50,000–$100,000+
	Government scientist	$50,000–$100,000+

Another significant part of the IS field comprises the people who work in IS consulting firms such as IBM, Electronic Data Systems (EDS), and Andersen Consulting. These consultants advise organizations on how to build and manage their systems and, more recently, sometimes actually build and run systems for those organizations. The systems consulting and systems integration areas are red hot. Companies such as IBM, which have traditionally been hardware/software companies, are now doing a lot of systems consulting and related work. Similarly, companies such as Andersen, which specializes in offering systems consulting and/or systems integration (such as EDS), are doing very well.

Another very large group of people in the IS field is made up of university professors throughout the world who conduct research on the development, use, and management of information systems. These IS academic researchers typically work in a school or college within a university, such as a School of Business.

Non-academic researchers who conduct research for agencies such as the Department of Defense or for large corporations such as IBM, Xerox, Hewlett-Packard, and AT&T face almost unlimited opportunities. These professionals generally conduct more applied research and development in the information systems field. For example, a researcher for a major computer manufacturer might be developing a new computer product or examining ways to extend the life of a current product by integrating leading-edge components with the older architecture. Other groups involved in the IS field include "headhunter" agencies that help IS professionals find jobs and publishers who bring you IS books (such as this one!) and magazines. You get the picture—the field is big and diverse!

The Organizational Side of IS

The last part of our IS definition is the term organization. Information systems are used in all types of organizations—professional, social, religious, educational, and governmental. In fact, the U.S. Internal Revenue Service launched its own site on the World Wide Web (shown in Figure 1.10). The IRS Web site was so popular that approximately 220,000 users visited it during the first 24 hours and more than a million in its first week—even before the Web address for the site was officially announced!

We've now covered each part of our definition of IS, shown again in Figure 1.11. We've talked about the great diversity of people in the IS field and the wide variety of functions they perform. In the next section, we focus on how information systems can be applied within organizations.

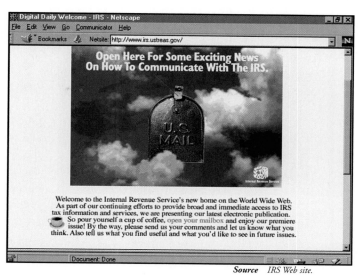

Source   *IRS Web site.*

FIGURE 1.10

The Web site of the U.S. Internal Revenue Service.

The Dual Nature of Information Systems

Now that we have a working definition of IS, let's talk more about why information systems are so important and interesting. Technology is often like a sword—you can use it effectively as a competitive weapon to win, but as the old saying goes, those who live by the sword sometimes die by the sword.

Information systems are combinations of
hardware, software, and telecommunications networks
which
people build and use
to
collect, create, and distribute useful data,
typically in
organizational settings.

FIGURE 1.11

A representation of the definition of IS, as shown in Figure 1.3.

An Information System Gone Awry: The Denver International Airport

A BRIEF CASE

What happens when an information system is implemented poorly? Perhaps the most notable example of an information system gone wrong in recent years is the automated baggage-handling system for the new, $4.2-billion Denver International Airport (DIA), which is shown in Figure 1.12.

Like the newly constructed DIA, the new underground, automated baggage-handling system for the airport was intended to be amazing. This information system would not only coordinate the automated check in and routing of all luggage for all customers throughout the airport, but it would also enable airport employees to monitor the flow of baggage and literally locate bags anywhere in the airport. The system, which cost $200 million, included the following features:

■ 21 miles of steel track

■ 4,000 independent "telecars" that would route and deliver luggage among the counters, gates, and claim areas of 20 different airlines

Ron Coppock/Gamma-Liaison

FIGURE 1.12

The $4.2-billion Denver International airport.

- 100 networked computers
- 5,000 electric eyes
- 400 radio receivers
- 56 bar-code scanners

Due to software glitches, the system opened, damaged, and misrouted cargo, forcing airport authorities to leave the system sitting idle for nearly a year (Gibbs, 1994). Because of this and other delays, the airport was not opened and was literally wasting away, at a cost of $1.1 million a day in interest and operating costs, for quite some time.

The DIA story has a happy ending, or beginning, as it were. The automated baggage system is now operational for United Airlines, while other carriers at DIA still use standard baggage-handling methods. The airport is now operational, making money and winning awards. Indeed, the baggage-handling system is one of many ways that this organization is attempting to be innovative and to outdo the competition. However, the airport is still useful as an example of how a problematic information system can adversely affect the performance of an organization.

A BRIEF CASE — An Information System That Works: Federal Express –

Just as there are examples of information systems gone wrong, there are many examples of information systems gone right. For example, take Federal Express's innovative use of information systems (see Figure 1.13).

FIGURE 1.13

The Web site for Federal Express.

FedEx, the world's largest express transportation company, delivers more than 2 million items to over 200 countries each business day. FedEx uses extensive, interconnected information systems to coordinate more than 110,000 people, 500 aircrafts, and more than 35,000 vehicles worldwide.

To improve its services and sustain a competitive advantage, FedEx now offers services on the World Wide Web. Customers can now visit the FedEx Web site and track a FedEx package anywhere in the world, find out about FedEx's delivery options and costs, and download FedEx's popular FedExShip PC-based software to prepare packages, verify them online, and print barcoded shipping documents. FedEx plans to soon offer as part of their Web site a digitized map of the world linked to their underlying tracking system, which will show customers the exact location of their packages at any point in time and at any part of the world. These and other information systems assure FedEx a position of dominance in the shipping business for many years to come.

Information Systems for Competitive Advantage

The DIA and Federal Express systems are both good examples of information systems' use for a couple of reasons. First, these two examples are typical of large, complex, new information systems for large organizations—systems that are so large in scale and scope that they are difficult to build and can make or break an organization. It is important to handle the development of such systems the right way the first time around.

Second, each of the choices made in developing these new systems was **strategic** in its intent. These systems weren't developed solely because managers in these organizations wanted to do things faster or because they wanted to have the latest, greatest technology. These systems were developed strategically to help organizations gain or sustain some **competitive advantage** (Porter, 1980), or an edge over rivals. Let's not let this notion slip by us—technology is an enabler of strategic, competitive advantage.

Although we described information systems' uses at two relatively large organizations, using information systems for competitive advantage also occurs in small firms. In fact, information systems can be used to enable firms of all types and sizes to gain or sustain a competitive advantage over their rivals.

IS for Automating: The First Step

You can view and use information systems in many ways, as summarized in Figure 1.14, but we believe that the strategic perspective is the most important. Let's first talk about some other points of view and see how they can and should build up to the strategic perspective.

One simple way to view information systems is in terms of **automating**. Someone with this perspective thinks of technology as a way to continue doing the same things he has been doing in an organization, but to do them faster and, perhaps, more cheaply with the help of technology. Let's look at a typical example.

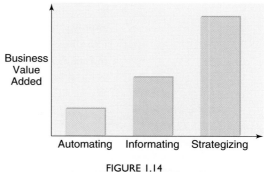

FIGURE 1.14

The business value added from automating, informating, and strategizing mentalities toward IS.

A person with an **automating mentality** would take an existing loan application screening process and automate it with technology. The individual might have someone input information about the loan applications (or perhaps the entire loan application) into a computer database so that those involved in decision making for the loans could process the applications faster, easier, and with fewer errors. The use of this technology would probably save some time, paper, and, subsequently, money. Better yet, the individual could even have customers complete the loan application online, saving even more time and money. In Figure 1.15, we show how long the automated process takes. On a larger scale, such a transition from a manual to an automated process might enable the organization to remove or better deploy employees, leading to further cost savings.

① Applicant Completes Loan Application and Submits It	1.5 Days
② Employee Checks Application for Errors	2.5 Days
③ Employee Inputs Application Data into System	2.5 Hours
④ Computer Performs Initial Screening Process	2.3 Seconds
⑤ Committee Decides on Any Loans for Over $100,000	30 Days
⑥ Applicant Notified	1 Hour

Switch to online loan application for both in-store and remote customers

2 hours

FIGURE 1.15

Information technology helps managers improve the loan approval process.

Many of the significant early gains from computing in organizations came from automating previously manual processes. While nothing is actually wrong with this view and this use of information systems, it is a bit shortsighted. Much more can be done with technology than is being exploited in this instance. In the next section, we'll explain what else can be done.

IS for Informating: The Second Step

Another way to view and use information systems was described cleverly by Shoshana Zuboff (1984) as **informating**. Zuboff explained that a technology informates when it provides information about its operation and the underlying work process that it supports. In other words, the system not only helps us to automate but also to learn to improve its day-to-day operation.

The **informating mentality** builds on the automating mentality because it recognizes that information systems can be used as a vehicle for organizational learning and change as well as for automation. In a useful 1993 article in *Harvard Business Review*, David Garvin described a **learning organization** as one that is "skilled at creating, acquiring, and transferring knowledge, and at modifying its behavior to reflect new knowledge and insights." Figure 1.16 shows how a computer-based loan processing system can help a manager plan more effectively. The processing system tracks types of loan applications by date, month, and season and notifies the manager of trends so that the manager can improve the efficiency and effectiveness of the application process. The manager plans accordingly for the timely ordering of blank application forms, "just-in-time" staffing and training of personnel in the Loan department, and better management of funds used to fulfill loans.

FIGURE 1.16

A computer-based loan processing system enables the manager to improve the efficiency and effectiveness of the application process.

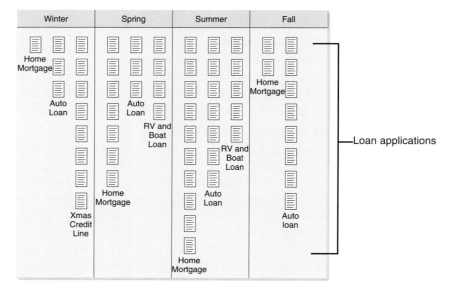

For example, let's return to our automating example with the computer-based loan application processing system. In addition to using the automated system to process loans faster and easier and save costs, the organization could use it to learn a great deal about the business process involved. Using an informating approach might allow those working on the system to track and learn about the types of applications filed by certain types of people at certain times of the year, the patterns of the loan decisions made, or the loan applications and the subsequent performance of those loans. In short, this new system creates data about the underlying business process that can be used to better monitor, control, and change that process.

A combined automating and informating approach, in the long run, is more effective than an automating approach alone. If the underlying business process supported by technology is inherently flawed, an informating use of the technology might help you detect the problems with the process and change it. For example, in our loan processing example, an informating use of technology may help us to uncover a pattern among the loans accepted that enables us to distinguish between low- and high-performing loans over their lives and, subsequently, change the criteria for loan acceptance.

If, however, the underlying business process is bad, and you are using technology only for automating, you are more likely to continue with a flawed or less-than-optimal business process. In fact, such an automating use of the technology may mask the process problems. With a computer-based loan application processing system, you cannot readily "see" the process or the data unless informating aspects are built into the system. You might eventually take the process for granted and conclude that the system works. You might find yourself saying that it's faster and easier this way, things are fine, or tell others to just let the system do its thing.

If the technology acts as a magnifier, it may cause the process to become exponentially bad. For example, with a bad underlying set of loan acceptance criteria, a person might manually review four applications in a day and, because of the problematic criteria used, inadvertently accept two "bad" applications per week on average. If you automated the same faulty process, with no informating aspects built in, the system might help to review twelve applications per day, with six "bad" applications accepted per week on average. The technology would serve only to magnify the existing business problems. Without informating, it is more difficult to uncover bad business processes underlying the IS application. Worse, you might subsequently choose to automate (that is, spend even more time and money) additional bad-business processes.

IS as Strategic Enabler: The Final Step

We've described the automating and the informating approaches toward using information systems. Now, let's talk about using information systems strategically.

Using information systems strategically occurs when a person thinks of ways to use the technology as an enabler of **organizational strategy** and competitive advantage. Fundamental to this approach is the assumption that the use of information systems ought to fundamentally support the mission and strategy of the organization. Let's talk about these concepts of organizational strategy and planning and then see how they fit with information systems.

FIGURE 1.17

Five generic organizational strategies.

Courtesy Thompson, A.A. and Strickland, A.J. III, 1995. Strategic Management: Concepts and Cases, *8th Edition, Homewood: Richard D. Irwin, Inc.*

When senior managers conduct **strategic planning**, they form a vision of where the organization needs to be headed, convert that vision into measurable objectives and performance targets, and craft a strategy to achieve the desired results. In Figure 1.17, we show some common organizational strategies. An organization might decide to pursue a low-cost leadership strategy, as does K-Mart or Packard-Bell. Alternatively, an organization might decide to pursue a differentiation strategy, whereby it tries to provide better products or services than its competitors, as does Porsche, Nordstrom, or IBM. It also might target a particular segment of consumers, as did Apple for many years with its focus on home and educational computing. Still other organizations might pursue a middle-of-the-road strategy of being the best-cost provider, offering good quality products and services at reasonable prices, as does Wal-Mart.

A person with a strategic approach tries to find ways information systems can be used to achieve the organization's chosen strategy. This individual undoubtedly wants to take advantage of any benefits that come from automating and informating, but he/she also looks for strategic benefits and ways to help the organization gain or sustain a competitive advantage. An organization has a competitive advantage whenever it has an edge over rivals in attracting customers and defending against competitive forces (see Porter, 1985, for a useful discussion on the concept of competitive advantage). For most businesses, it is not enough to simply aim to make money. Each business must have a clear vision, one that focuses their investments in resources such as information systems and technologies to help achieve competitive advantage.

Sources of Competitive Advantage

Some sources of competitive advantage include the following:

■ Having the best-made product on the market

■ Delivering superior customer service

■ Achieving lower costs than rivals

■ Having a proprietary technology

■ Having shorter lead times in developing and testing new products

■ Having a well-known brand name and reputation

■ Providing customers more value for their money

Each of these sources of competitive advantage can be gained or sustained through the effective use of information systems. For example, rental car agencies compete fiercely with each other to provide the best cars, the best service, and the best rates. It's a constant competitive battle. Companies find it difficult to differentiate themselves, so they discover clever ways to use information systems to improve customer service.

Avis-Rent-A-Car

In order to sustain a competitive advantage over rivals in the area of customer service, Avis-Rent-A-Car customer service representatives wait for the customer out in the lot, armed with specially designed, hand-held computers and printers either strapped around their waists or over their shoulders. With this "Avis Roving Rapid Return" service (shown in Figure 1.18), the representative inputs the license number of the car on the portable computer when he sees the customer driving in to return a car. Inputting this information brings up the customer's rental contract. As the customer gets out of the car, the representative inputs the mileage and the fuel level, while a second attendant retrieves the customer's luggage and places it on the curb. By the time the customer has exited the car and stood next to her luggage, the representative has already printed the customer's receipt (if she had previously paid by credit card). The representative hands it to the customer immediately with a smile and a "Thank you!" The service encounter for the customer is fast and pleasant. That's using technology for competitive advantage! In Table 1.2, we show how Avis's computer-supported process compares with the traditional rental car service encounter.

© Michael Newman/Photoedit

FIGURE 1.18

Avis Roving Rapid Return.

Table 1.2 The Avis airport computer-supported service encounter versus the traditional airport rental car service encounter.

	Traditional Rental Car Return Service Encounter	Avis's Computer-Based Service Encounter
	Return car to lot attendant, get bags from another attendant, walk inside and wait in line to settle contract with another attendant, walk out, and board a shuttle.	Return car to lot attendant, grab receipt and bags, and board shuttle.
Elapsed time	5–10 minutes	2–3 seconds
Number of people to interact with	2–3 people	1–2 people
Average number of steps customer takes	60–75 steps	5–10 steps
Relative efficiency	Low	High

Not all uses of information systems for competitive advantage are necessarily as exotic as Avis's use of hand-held computers. An organization might simply be using a more common technology, such as a shared computer database, but in a strategic way. Let's look again at our computer-based loan application processing example.

A person with a strategic approach would like a loan processing application for its automating and informating benefits, as discussed earlier. In addition, however, this person would have chosen this application in the first place because people in his organization have agreed that three achievements are absolutely critical to the strategy and success of the organization—processing loan applications faster and better, proactively re-engineering this particular business process, and better integrating this process with other business processes. This person likes the loan processing system because it adds value to the organization in the short term AND matches the organization's strategy. In short, this system has been deemed essential to the long-term survival of the firm.

Alternatively, a person with a strategic approach might have determined that the loan application processing system might not be a good fit with the organizational strategy, even though the system is likely to add value to the organization in other ways. For example, the managers of this organization may have determined that in order to suc-ceed, they must grow and generate new products and services. They should deploy their assets and invest in technologies in ways that achieve these objectives. In this situation, the loan application processing system might still provide automating and informating benefits, but it would provide little or no direct strategic value. Indeed, spending money, time, and other resources on such a system would be foolish if growing and generating new business were paramount. An elaborate loan system would do this organization lit-tle good if, overall, they lost out to rivals and ultimately went out of business.

The online ticket service in the chapter opening scenario is another good example of how an organization can use an information system to achieve a competitive advantage over rivals. The online ticket system enables customers to buy tickets quickly and easily, which is critical in the ticket industry. In addition, the system enables the organization to market, sell, and manage the ticket-selling process efficiently (automating), as well as to learn from customers' behaviors at their Web site, their purchase patterns, and their written online feedback (informating). This system does everything that it should: automating, informating, and enabling strategy.

IS and Value Chain Analysis

One popular way organizations can determine how information systems are strategical-ly important to their long-term survival is through **value chain analysis** (Porter, 1985; Shank and Govindarajan, 1993). Think about an organization as a big input/output process. At one end, supplies are purchased and brought into the organization (see Figure 1.19). Those supplies and resources are then integrated in some way to create products and services, which are marketed, sold, and then distributed in many ways to customers. Finally, some future service is provided after the initial sale of these goods and services. Throughout this process, there are opportunities for people and groups in the organization to add value to the organization—by bringing in supplies in a more effective manner, improving products, selling more products, and so on. This process is known as the value chain within an organization.

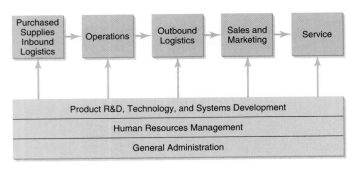

FIGURE 1.19

A sample generic organizational value chain.

Value chain analysis is the process of analyzing an organization's activities to determine where value is added to products and/or services and the costs that are incurred for doing so. Because IS can automate many activities along the value chain, value chain analysis has become a very popular tool for applying IS for competitive advantage. In value chain analysis, you first think about and then draw the value chain for your organization by fleshing out each of the activities, functions, and processes where value is or should be added. Next, determine the costs—and the factors that drive costs or cause them to fluctuate—within each of the areas in your value chain diagram. You then **benchmark** (compare) your value chain and associated costs with those of other organizations, preferably your competitors. You can then make changes and improvements in your value chain to either gain or sustain a competitive advantage.

The Role of Information Systems in Value Chain Analysis

The use of information systems has become one of the primary ways that organizations are making changes and improvements in their value chains. In Figure 1.20, we show a sample value chain and some ways that information systems can be used to improve productivity. For example, many organizations now use Electronic Data Interchange (EDI), a set of standards and methods for connecting businesses together electronically (for example, connecting a business with its suppliers) so that they can exchange orders, invoices, and receipts online in real time. Using EDI is one proven way to use information systems to improve the front end of the organizational value chain.

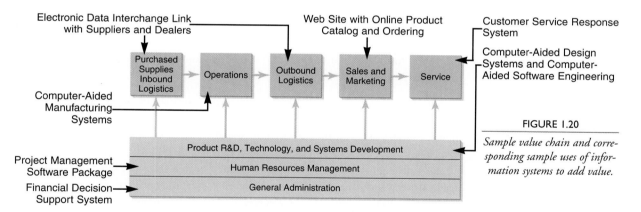

FIGURE 1.20

Sample value chain and corresponding sample uses of information systems to add value.

One of the more innovative ways to use information systems to improve the back end of the value chain, the service after the sale, is to provide service to customers online in real time. For example, owners of McLaren's $850,000 F1 Supercar plug into the car an accompanying modem kit that enables McLaren engineers to diagnose the car and make adjustments to it over the phone lines in real time (see Figure 1.21). That may sound exotic and restricted to those few individuals who can afford an $850,000 automobile, but this method is also being used by computer companies and others to diagnose and maintain their customers' products remotely and, in some cases, to download new software products.

Gamma-Liaison

FIGURE 1.21

The McLaren F1 supercar.

The Technology/Strategy Fit

You might be asking, if any information system helps to do things faster and better and helps save money, who cares whether or not it matches the company's strategy? Good question. One answer is that most organizations are typically faced with many different, valuable systems that could be built, but due to constraints on time, money, and other resources, they cannot all be built simultaneously. When you manage an organization, you can't afford to do everything, so you must prioritize the list of alternative, proposed systems and choose to build those that add the most value—those that give the biggest bang for the buck. In other words, you should choose systems that help automate and informate, as well as have strategic value. In most cases, you don't want systems that don't match the strategy, even if they offer automating and informating benefits.

For example, you probably don't want a system that helps differentiate your products based on high quality when the organizational strategy is to be the overall industry low-cost leader. For example, creating an expensive computer-aided design system would probably add exorbitant costs to the process and would likely defeat the strategy of spending less in the production of products and, subsequently, selling products at the lowest possible prices.

In any event, it simply makes good business sense to have a clear organizational strategy and to have systems that fit well with the strategy. Building systems solely because they help you to do things faster and improve business processes—without having a clear sense of their strategic value—is not a sensible practice. It's like being out on the ocean in a powerfully motored boat without knowing your destination or why you want to reach it. Your competitors know where they should be going and will, undoubtedly, beat you to the finish line. Furthermore, if you are unknowingly headed for trouble, your powerful, fast motor will only hasten your trip.

Organizations that have a combined automating, informating, and strategic approach first get a clear sense of the overall mission and strategy of the organization. Next, they lay out a clear plan for using information systems that support the overall organization plan. These two plans—one for the organization and the other for the information systems—are tightly coupled. All decisions about, and actions on, information systems are driven by these dual plans. Essentially, we want you to start thinking strategically about information systems. As you can see, there is a lot more to the field of IS than bits, bytes, and hackers.

Everyone Must Think Strategically for Every Technology Decision

Managing technology well has become a strategic necessity, and managing technology for competitive advantage is the way to do it. Thinking this way requires systems personnel to see the big picture and to be long-term, critical thinkers. They must also know the business side and the technology side of the organization. Furthermore, systems personnel must see technology as a means to serve the business's ends, rather than seeing technology as an end in itself. This kind of strategic thinking isn't just for the chief information officer and other high-ranking information systems managers. This kind of thinking is absolutely essential for everyone in the organization, including personnel from marketing, operations, finance, human resources, or accounting—not just the systems analysts and programmers.

In order to be successful, everyone who participates in business decisions that involve technology must have a strategic mindset. Even if we're only talking about the purchase of a new PC in an organization, we shouldn't be concerned only with what microprocessor it has or how large the hard disk is. Instead, we should think first about how this technology is used to help add value, and second about what technical specifications will be needed to accomplish the task effectively.

Talking with...

Robert R. Ridout, CIO and Vice-President of Information Systems at DuPont

Educational Background

B.S. in Mathematics (computer science concentration), College of William and Mary

Job Description

Mr. Ridout is responsible for the stewardship of information systems and information technology globally for DuPont. DuPont's worldwide IS organization consists of 23 strategic business units and 7 functional units, all networked to a small, centralized component at headquarters. Mr. Ridout is also responsible for leading and managing the newly formed DuPont IT Alliance (a 10-year, $4-billion deal with Computer Sciences Corporation and Andersen Consulting, providing DuPont's businesses with access to the "best of the best" in information technology). He also oversees a distributed organization of 1,200 DuPont IT professionals.

Critical Success Factors

An intimate understanding of the businesses within DuPont and their strategic directions and key business drivers. A keen ability to articulate the competitive advantage of IT services and solutions in order to achieve competitive advantage in the marketplace. Open, honest, and frequent communications with executive and senior management in the company. The ability to sense the external technology and business environments and to create and communicate vision and direction for the corporation. The ability to motivate and lead a network of people from around the world.

Advice to Students

Make the most of your college experience—study hard, look for opportunities to broaden yourself, and always be receptive to new opportunities and ideas. Whatever your profession, take the time to learn the larger business perspective and how your job relates to the strategy and goals of your firm. Be self-reliant and chart your own path for success. Plan your own career paths and development areas. Always strive for excellence. Hone your communication skills, both verbal and written. These are critical for your success, and you should always work towards perfecting your ability to communicate with people at all levels, internal and external to your company. Stay abreast of the latest technology trends and keep focused on how these technologies can add business value. Always be respectful toward others. Your success will be dependent on your ability to provide leadership and vision to an increasingly diverse and global workforce.

ETHICAL PERSPECTIVE: THE NEED FOR A UNIFIED INFORMATION SYSTEMS CODE OF ETHICS

Given that computers and information systems are now a fundamental part of doing business, opportunities for misusing and abusing information, computers, and systems now abound. For example, an organization that manages your credit card transactions might sell data on your purchasing behavior to another organization that has information from a survey you filled out about your lifestyle. This new information might then be sold to a third organization, which uses the information to market to you via the mail some specialty products or services they believe you are likely to be interested in. Alternatively, purchasing data about someone with a name similar to your own may appear in your credit report, causing you to wrongly be denied a loan.

This new wired world we live in causes us to ask some important new ethical questions. Who owns information, particularly information about us? Which information should be private, and who should be given access to which information? Who is responsible for the accuracy of information? Should guidelines be set for how business organizations and business professionals use information, computers, and information systems, and if so, what should these guidelines be? Academic and business leaders have suggested and supported the idea of an information systems code of ethics to be adhered to by all.

Currently, computer-related professional organizations throughout the world have written codes of ethics for their members, including the Association for Computing Machinery, the Australian Computer Society, the Canadian Information Processing Society, the Institute for Electrical and Electronics Engineers, and the International Programmers Guild. The codes differ in minor ways. Some are more general, while others are more specific. Some emphasize different ethical issues than do others. Furthermore, there is no unified code of ethics for all computer-related professionals, and there is no code of ethics for the information systems profession in particular.

Information systems professionals "meet frequently in professional conferences, read and contribute to professional publications, and share a professional jargon," so they should also have a uniform and coherent code of ethics. Such a uniform code could provide guidance to professionals on acceptable conduct and could help raise awareness and consciousness of important ethical issues. Some people also believe that a code would go a long way toward promoting a positive public image of information systems professionals worldwide. The public would be assured that the profession is concerned about the welfare of society, employers, clients, and sister organizations. Perhaps more importantly, the new unified code would be without regard to national borders, a must in this age of borderless networking.

ISWorld Net, the Web site for information systems academics, has a Professional Ethics page, which is intended to provide a forum for discussing issues concerning the practice of the information systems profession (http://csrc.lse.ac.uk/iswnet/profact/ethics.htm). The philosophy of a code of ethics is summarized on that Web page as follows: "The real challenge is not to indulge in a never-ending debate on the feasibility or necessity of having a code of ethics, but rather, to be able to capture the essence of our profession to be shared and provide as a guiding light to the many more people who are already or who would one day be part of this profession."

Some governmental policy makers believe that a formal unified code of ethics for the information systems profession is paramount. "Many [European Union] member states perceive the need now for some discipline, some kind of regulatory framework or code of ethics," says the Italian telecommunications minister at a meeting of the EU's culture and telecommunications ministers. It remains to be seen whether or not a unified code is developed and ratified. One thing is certain: As technology continues to advance rapidly, new information systems ethical issues arise every day.

Questions for Discussion

1. Do you believe that there is a need for a unified information systems code of ethics? Why or why not?

2. What are some other advantages of having a unified code? What are some of the disadvantages, limits, and barriers to a unified code?

3. How could such a unified code be made to cope with the fast pace of technological development around the globe?

Sources   Oz, Effy. 1992. Ethical standards for information systems professionals: A case for a unified code. MIS Quarterly, December, 16:4:423–433. Wall Street Journal, May 3, 1996, B5B

INTERNATIONAL PERSPECTIVE: GLOBAL COMPETITIVENESS

The U.S. isn't the only player in the IS game; the competition to produce and use computer-based knowledge and the means of transferring it is fierce from Thailand to Israel and from France to Chile. Companies around the globe plan to use IS as part of their strategy to obtain a competitive edge over rivals, and governments are pushing technology use as a means of bringing their countries into competition on the world market. Newspapers and journals abound with evidence of these trends, as countries in Europe open their markets and relax rules and as competition in corporate networks and mobile phone services multiplies at a furious pace. Business alliances in Italy, Germany, and France have made investments in the billions in an effort to introduce competition to the formerly monopolized communications markets. Even developing nations, among them Chile and the Philippines, have opened previously state-owned communications enterprises to competition in order to secure critical investment and to help push them into the global information economy.

Use of technology also increases the possibilities for expansive growth. The days of privileged information may be waning—no longer will connections and human networks be the sole source of a business's success in Japan or Hong Kong. In addition, the explosion of electronic commerce via the Internet is causing a rush to enter the global market. The savings and the opportunities available through the electronic exchange of goods and services have the potential to support the creation of thousands of new businesses and to encourage the expansion of local businesses around the world.

The globalization of IS and the need to stay competitive are changing not only the way companies worldwide do business, but also the ways in which companies are run. Tasks are being simplified, the Internet is giving companies access to international regulatory information at the touch of a key, and Japanese companies and their American subsidiaries around the world can meet without plane tickets being purchased. To conduct business successfully with videoconferencing, electronic mail, and other forms of electronic (and often instantaneous) communication, businesses in both the East and West must learn to adapt to a variety of management styles and learn a new language of communication.

In fact, as companies join global networks and do business with those in other countries, new employment opportunities abound. The successful employee in the age of instant global communication may be the one who can function well in a variety of cultural and linguistic spheres. Lack of multicultural representatives in an era of global contact could cause businesses to lose their competitive edge. Having women lead a videoconference with Saudi businessmen or making a cultural gaffe while communicating with a Japanese customer could have major financial repercussions.

Technology is also changing people's lives as governments strive to help their economies compete. In India, for example, only a very small percentage of the village population has access to a telephone or a phone line. With government support aimed at economic development on a monumental scale, over 15 million additional telephones throughout the country are expected to be connected by the year 2000.

Embassies and foreign ministries are joining the information revolution, allowing governments to obtain critical policy-making information instantaneously. This quick access results in changes in diplomatic strategies, giving governments less time and less secrecy in which to act; however, it also provides needed economic data in areas such as import and export and changes in trade law. As technology is employed to assist in economic development, it also encourages individuals to seek and share information. Communist countries, such as China, have found that they now have less control over their populations because the Internet allows access to formerly inaccessible information and enables people to broadcast to the world in ways that were not possible before. With the Internet, it's far easier for Taiwanese political activists to compete for the world's attention than ever!

Questions for Discussion

1. Can companies from different countries really compete with each other in terms of information technology, given that the basic telephone wiring infrastructures within countries are vastly different from one another—with some countries far ahead of others?

2. What role should information technology play in the growth and expansion of a company internationally?

3. How can you best prepare yourself to use information technology to enable your future employer's strategy and competitive advantage?

Summary

1. **Understand what the term information systems (IS) means.** Information systems are combinations of hardware, software, and telecommunications networks, which people build and use to collect, create, and distribute useful data typically in organizational settings. Information systems also used to represent the field in which people develop, use, manage, and study computer-based information systems in organizations. IS is a huge, diverse, growing field that encompasses many different people, purposes, systems, and technologies.

2. **Describe the evolution of computing.** Computing technology has evolved over the past fifty years. Over this time, five distinct computing eras have occurred. During the mainframe computer era, which spanned from the 1940s to the 1970s, the dominant technology was the large, general-purpose computer that supported hundreds of users. The minicomputer era extended from the late 1960s to the 1980s. Like mainframes, minicomputers could support a large number of users, but they were much less expensive to buy and operate and much easier to program than mainframes. Minicomputers helped to bring computer technology into smaller organizations. The personal computer era began in the early 1980s. The introduction of the IBM PC was the era's most significant event. The hallmark of the era was the low-cost computer that made its way onto the desktops of many homes and offices. The interpersonal computing era began in the late 1980s, as networking technology interconnected large and small computers. Human-to-human communication through electronic mail, bulletin boards, and chat rooms became a dominate computing application. The internetworking computing era began in the mid- to late-1990s with the development of the Internet's World Wide Web browsing tool, Mosaic. The dominant application in this current era of computing is interconnecting enterprise-wide networks and information systems into a seamless, worldwide network to support communication and commerce.

3. **Explain the technology, people, and organizational components of an information system.** Information systems combine hardware, software, and telecommunications networks that people build and use to collect, create, and distribute useful data in organizations. The technology part of information systems is the hardware, software, and telecommunications networks. The people who build, manage, and use information systems make up the people component. Finally, information systems reside within organizations, so they are said to have an organizational component. Together, these three aspects form an information system.

4. **Discuss how information systems can be used to automate, informate, and strategically support business activities.** Automating business activities occurs when information systems are used to do a business activity faster or more cheaply. IS can be used to help automate. It can also be used to improve aspects of an operation in order to gain dramatic improvements in the operation as a whole. When this occurs, technology is said to informate because it provides information about its operation and the underlying work process that it supports. Using information systems strategically occurs when the technology is used to enable organizational strategy and competitive advantage.

5. **Describe information systems' critical, strategic importance to the success of modern organizations.** Using information systems to automate and informate business processes is a good start. However, information systems can add even more value to an organization if they are conceived, designed, used, and managed with a strategic approach. To apply information systems strategically, you must understand the organization's value chain and be able to identify opportunities in which you can use information systems to make changes or improvements in the value chain to gain or sustain a competitive advantage.

Key Terms

Information systems

Technology

Information technology

Strategic

Competitive advantage

Automating

Automating mentality

Informating

Informating mentality

Learning organization

Strategic mentality

Organizational strategy

Strategic planning

Value Chain analysis

Benchmark

Review Questions

1. What is "Information Systems"?

2. Describe the types of people in the field of IS.

3. How is "information technology" different than generic "technology"? Provide examples of each.

4. List some sources of competitive advantage.

5. What is "automating," and what does it mean to have an automating mentality?

6. What is "informating," and how is it different than automating?

7. What is a "learning" organization? Describe how an organization can learn.

8. What is a "strategic mentality," and why is it important?

9. List the five generic organizational strategies.

10. Describe the role that information systems can play in value chain analysis.

11. Explain the phrase "technology/strategy fit." What can happen if there is not a good technology/strategy fit?

Problems and Exercises

 Individual   **Group**   **Field**   **Web/Internet**

1. Match the following terms to the appropriate definitions.

   _____ Information systems

   _____ Strategic

   _____ Competitive advantage

   _____ Informating

   _____ Strategic mentality

   _____ Organizational strategy

   _____ Strategic planning

   _____ Value chain analysis

a. Using technology in such a way that it provides information about its operation and the underlying work process that it supports

b. Analyzing an organization's activities to determine where value is added to products and/or services and the costs that are incurred for doing so, as well as comparing the activities, added value, and costs of the organization to those of other organizations in order to make improvements in the organization's operations and performance

c. Important in or essential to a planned series of activities for obtaining a goal or desired result

d. Combinations of hardware, software, and telecommunications networks that people build and use to collect and create useful data and then disseminate that data to those who need it

e. When an organization has an edge over rivals in attracting customers and defending against competitive forces

f. A person with this mentality recognizes the importance of technology for automating and informating but believes that technology is primarily an enabler of organizational strategy and competitive advantage

g. The process whereby members of an organization form a vision of where the organization needs to be headed (that is, the organization's mission), develop measurable objectives and performance targets for that vision, and craft a strategy for achieving the vision, objectives, and targets

h. An overall game plan for how an organization will achieve its primary mission

2. Imagine that you had to explain to a five-year-old child what the field of information systems is. Write down your explanation in terms that the five-year-old child would best understand. Chances are, you will form an explanation that will be effective for adults as well.

3. Is the recent growth in information systems' development and use in organizations just a fad, or will information systems' use in organizations continue to be important and pervasive? Why? How do your fellow classmates feel about this? Do they agree with you?

4. Some people argue that the benefits provided by using information systems for competitive advantage are fleeting because rival firms can easily copy these same uses of information systems. Discuss this with a small group of classmates. Do you agree? Why or why not? Present some counterarguments.

5. Some people argue that simply automating with information systems is enough. They claim that trying to informate with technology is not necessary. What arguments and examples can you offer to persuade them that informating with information systems has value beyond merely automating?

6. To stop thinking about technology as a tool for automating and to develop an informating and strategic mentality toward information systems can be a difficult, radical change in perspective for some people. How difficult do you think it is to get people to make these paradigm shifts in the real world? Why? Do your classmates agree with you? What can be done to help them see the world differently?

7. Is it truly possible for organizations to learn? Why or why not?

8. Imagine an organization that deploys information systems with no rhyme or reason, for which the technology/strategy fit is nonexistent. Form a group of classmates and determine what this organization might look like. How is this organization using information systems? Is this organization likely to be successful? Why or why not?

9. Is the process of benchmarking an ethical activity? Why or why not?

10. Consider an organization that you are familiar with, perhaps one that you have worked for or have done business with. Describe the types of information systems

that this organization uses and whether or not they are useful. If there are ways that this organization should be using information systems but is not, describe how this organization might make better use of information systems.

11. Identify someone who works within the field of information systems, as an information systems instructor, professor, or practitioner (for example, as a systems analyst or systems manager). Find out why this individual got into this field and what he or she likes and dislikes about working within the field of MIS. What advice can he or she offer to someone entering the field?

12. Choose an organization and identify its strategy. You can determine this information by looking for clues in the organization's annual report, advertisements, and/or its site on the World Wide Web. Can you identify anything about this organization's information systems that suggest to you that their information systems are aligned well with their strategy? If so, describe the technology/strategy fit for this organization. If not, describe some ways that information systems could be used to best enable the organization's strategy.

13. Consider an organization you are familiar with that does not appear to use information systems strategically. List at least four reasons why information systems are not used strategically within this organization. Are these reasons justifiable? Why or why not? What are the implications for this organization if its members continue to deploy information systems in this way?

14. Interview a manager within an organization with which you are familiar. Perhaps this individual works where you work or at your university or college. Ask this person a series of questions to help you understand his or her perspective on information systems and their value. For example, ask what value information systems provide in his or her organization. When finished with the interview, review your interview notes and determine whether this person has an automating mentality, an informating mentality, a strategic mentality, or some combination of these perspectives toward information systems. Does this person appear to have a healthy, useful perspective toward information systems? Why or why not? If not, how could this person be helped to better understand the potential of information systems?

15. Form a small group of classmates. Choose an idea for a valuable new product or service that you could offer as part of a start-up firm. What will be your basic organizational strategy (for example, differentiation based on high quality, low cost leadership, and so on)? Describe four ways that you can use information systems to enable your strategy. Prepare a 10-minute class presentation on your organizational strategy and how you will use information systems in your firm.

16. Consider the scenario from the previous question and imagine that a new competitor has entered the market and is doing exactly what you are doing. How can you use information systems to gain or sustain a competitive advantage over this rival firm? How easily can this rival firm copy your use of information systems for competitive advantage? What other steps can you take to sustain your competitive advantage?

17. Search the World Wide Web for several organizations that you like or are interested in. Using only their home pages and related links, determine each company's organizational strategy and their information systems strategy. Can these be determined from the documentation available through the World Wide Web? Do you have a clear understanding of these organizations' approaches to information systems? Were your fellow classmates able to find any better information from their searches?

18. Consider the scenario that opened this chapter regarding the purchase of concert tickets from an online system. This system provided a competitive advantage over the ticket company's rivals. Identify additional systems that you as a customer can interact with that also provide some competitive advantage for the organization running the system. What are these competitive advantages? How many of these systems are Web-based?

Real World Case Problems

1. IT Spending in '98: Full Speed Ahead

After eight years of record economic expansion in the United States, economists still expect 1998 to repeat 1997. Even with the massive Asian currency collapse, IT investors are still spending high dollars. It is the complexity of business that is causing IT to make the investment to assist their customers in dealing with these issues.

A recent survey by *InformationWeek* and *VARBusiness* of 250 senior IT managers reports that IT spending will increase by 18 percent and that more than 70 percent of those managers will spend it through IT resellers. The Web will be used for purchasing PCs in 1998 by 25 percent of IT managers. Other expenditures on the agenda are as follows: training, with its direct correlation between application productivity and training; network storage for intranets and electronic business applications; Windows NT 5.0; Novell NetWare 5.0 upgrades; and network computer purchasing. However, the most important project looming ahead is the year 2000 conversion. This project is driving the cost of IT spending higher than ever. DHL Worldwide Express, the multinational package courier, plans to spend $25 million on the year 2000 problem during the next two years to fix their 20 million lines of programming code.

Approximately 29 percent of the year 2000 budgets will go toward testing the revitalized applications. "The biggest time-consumer is in the testing—testing end-to-end systems around the world to make sure everything works right," states Joseph Riera, CIO and senior VP of DHL Airways, Inc. In the future, managers are planning to decrease costs and make it easier to do business with DHL by creating better customer access through the company's Web site.

Other current issues include globalization and mergers, such as at Smith Barney, a domestic firm, and at Salomon Brothers, an international firm. Now Peter Remch, Vice President of Smith Barney, is faced with the issues of trading systems to support Europe's Euro currency. In the end, no matter what applications are completed, managers will still have key applications moved to the back-burner because IT money always runs out before all projects are completed.

a. What does it mean when so many companies continue to increase their spending on IT, even in the face of stock market drops and foreign currency collapses?

b. Is it a bad idea for DHL and other firms to be diverting so many IT resources to solve their Year 2000 problems? Why or why not? Remember, for systems in which years have been coded as two-digit numbers (for example, 85) rather than four-digit numbers (for example, 1985), in the year 2000 (a k a Y2K), the two digits "00" will be interpreted as the year 1900, causing miscalculations and potential systems crashes.

c. How important is it to firms such as Smith Barney to spend IT resources on systems to support the internationalization of the business, such as tweaking trading system software to support Europe's Euro currency? Why?

Source Weston, Rusty. 1998. *"IT Spending in '98: Full Speed Ahead."* InformationWeek, *January 5, 16–17.*

2. Social Security Gets It Right

The Social Security Administration's (SSA) sound management has led the way toward modernizing its vast data center and deploying a nationwide network of desktop work stations. The agency, which currently has more than 3.5 million lines of code and 25 million transactions per day, serves a large number of demanding clients.

The key to the SSA's success, states Greenwalt, a staffer for the Senate Governmental Affairs Committee, is that "they got out from under Health and Human Services and started approaching things like a company." SSA uses automation as a manufacturing function.

In 1996, a law was enacted that required federal agencies to have a CIO. In reality, it didn't change much at the SSA. The SSA already saw IT as critical to getting a major part of the work done. In many agencies, communication is near to impossible because the IT group is down several layers in the organization. However, at the SSA, the agency's deputies provide a business perspective and assist in IT acquisitions.

The SSA has adopted a conservative approach to modernization by not reinventing the wheel or making unnecessary changes. They have reduced their dependence on mainframes, converted 80-some applications to Windows NT servers, and decreased access time from several minutes to 30 seconds. The SSA's rollout of 60,000 workstations to 1,400 offices is about half done. They are also upgrading the communications network and are on target to meet their $280 million budget. All of this success is due to having a strategic plan.

a. Why have other U.S. federal agencies had such disastrous results in building, acquiring, and managing IT projects?

b. Why has the U.S. Social Security Administration been so successful in using IT?

c. How important is the successful use of IT to the Social Security Administration? What would happen—and with what repercussions—if their systems failed?

Source Cone, Edward. 1998. *"Social Security Gets It Right."* InformationWeek, *January 12, 48.*

References

Applegate, L.M., and R. Montealegre. 1995. Eastman Kodak Co.: Managing information systems through strategic alliances. Harvard Business School, 9-192-030.

Brady. 1998. Information from: http://www.whbrady.com/. Verified: Feb. 2, 1998.

Garvin, D. A. 1993. Building a learning organization. *Harvard Business Review* (July–August): 78–91.

Gibbs, W. W. 1994. Software's chronic crisis. *Scientific American,* September, 86–95.

Hoffman, T. 1998. Group targets software labor shortage. *Computerworld,* January 12, 96.

King. J. 1998. Nerdy image feeds labor crisis. *Computerworld,* January 12, 1; 96.

Marable, L.M. 1995. The fifty hottest jobs in America. *Money,* March, 114–116.

McHugh, J. 1998. Computers and software. *Forbes,* January 12, 122–128.

Porter, M. E. 1985. *Competitive strategy.* New York: Free Press.

Shank, J. K., and V. Govindarajan. 1993. *Strategic cost management.* New York: Free Press.

Smith, Bremner, and Edmondson. 1996. Be it ever so pricey, high tech is still hot. *BusinessWeek,* June 17, 100–101.

Zuboff, S. 1984. *In the age of the smart machine: The future of work and power.* New York: Basic Books, Inc.

Related Readings

Attewell, P. 1992. Technology diffusion and organizational learning: The case of business computing. *Organization Science*. 3(1): 1–19.

Boland, Tenkasi, and Te'eni. 1994. Designing information technology to support distributed cognition. *Organization Science* 5(3): 456–475.

Cohen, W.M. and D.A. Levinthal. 1990. Absorptive capacity: A new perspective on learning and innovation. *Administrative Science Quarterly* 35(1): 128–152.

Dowling, M.J. and J.E. McGee. 1994. Business and technology strategies and new venture performance: A study of the telecommunications equipment industry. *Management Science* 40(12): 1663-1677.

Huber, G.P. 1991. Organizational learning: The contributing processes and the literatures. *Organization Science* 2(1): 88–115.

Jarvenpaa, S.L. and B. Ives. 1993. Organizing for global competition: The fit of information technology. *Decision Sciences* 24(3): 547–580.

Macdonald, S. 1995. Learning to change: An information perspective on learning in the organization. *Organization Science* 6(5): 557–568.

Mata, Fuerst, and Barney. 1995. Information technology and sustained competitive advantage: A resource-based analysis. *Management Information Systems Quarterly* 19(4): 487–505.

Reich, B.H. and I Benbasat. 1996. Measuring the linkage between business and information technology objectives. *Management Information Systems Quarterly* 20(1): 55–81.

Sethi, V. and W.R. King. 1994. Development of measures to assess the extent to which an information technology application provides competitive advantage. *Management Science* 40(12): 1601–1627.

Stein, E.W. and V. Zwass. 1995. Actualizing organizational memory with information systems. *Information Systems Research* 6(2): 85–117.

Swanson, E.B. 1994. Information systems innovation among organizations. *Management Science* 40(9): 1069-1092.

Zhu, Priehula, and Hsu. 1997. When processes learn: Steps toward crafting an intelligent organization. *Information Systems Research* 8(3): 302-317.

PART 2

Information Systems Essentials

Part 2 provides you with the fundamental technical building blocks of all computer-based information systems—hardware, software, databases, and telecommunications networks and equipment.

In Chapter 2, *Information Systems Hardware*, we'll describe key elements of information systems hardware and the various types of computers that are being used in organizations today. We'll also explain how hardware has evolved, where it is headed, and why computer hardware has become so important to the success of modern organizations.

In Chapter 3, *Information Systems Software*, we'll describe the various types of systems, applications software, and programming languages, including how they work and how they are used. We'll also review the evolution of software, where it is headed, and why software has become so important to organizational success.

In Chapter 4, *Database Management*, we'll describe data, databases, and database management systems. We'll explain three emerging database trends: client/server computing, data mining, object-oriented databases, and integrating Web applications to organizational databases. We'll also show why these uses of databases have become absolutely critical to the functioning of most organizations.

In Chapter 5, *Telecommunications*, we'll describe the evolution and types of computer networks and networking fundamentals, including network services, transmission media, network topologies, and connectivity hardware for both local area and wide area networks. We'll also explain the role of the Open System Interconnect (OSI) model and network operating systems in enabling network communication. This chapter will help you understand the important role of telecommunications in organizations and what it means to thrive in a wired world.

Get ready for your ride through Part 2, "Information Systems Essentials." This is the most technical part of this book and is, as its name implies, "essential" before you can understand and appreciate other parts of this book.

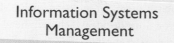

Information Systems
Management

Information   Information
Systems   Systems
in Practice   Development

Hardware   Software

Database Management

Telecommunications

Scenario: Take the PC Plunge

Purchasing personal computers is one of the most difficult decisions facing individuals and organizations today. It is difficult to determine how much computing power you need, how much you should pay, and what computer will run all the software necessary for the applications of today and tomorrow. Many computers are relatively obsolete soon after they are purchased. While the IRS allows computers to be depreciated over five years, many people replace their computers after as little as two years, and some even sooner! These "old" machines may work fine for most applications, but they are likely to be too slow to run the latest software packages that you or your company needs to use. How can you make an educated purchasing decision?

Your first step in answering this question is to understand the numerous options you face when making this decision. You need to consider many things. The first important choice is to determine the general type of computer to buy. Which general computer platform best suits your needs? In the realm of the personal computer, you generally have two choices—a Microsoft Windows-based computer or an Apple Macintosh-based computer. In making this decision, you are choosing between two different hardware architectures and two different operating systems, although these two platforms have been evolving closer and closer toward each other over the past several years.

You will need to resolve countless other questions as well. Where will you purchase? What type of microprocessor—the engine of the computer—do you need? Similarly, you need to decide on how much RAM—internal processing storage—and the size of the permanent storage. Most desktop computers come with at least one gigabyte of permanent storage, but if you plan to use lots of new software or store many large files—such as video clips—you'll probably want to have more. In addition to RAM and permanent storage, you must decide which peripheral components you want for your computer. For example, most computers today come with compact-disc drives to read software issued in CD-ROM format. What speed do you need for your computer's CD-ROM player? 8X speed? 16X speed? 24X speed? What type of monitor do you want? Do you want a standard 14″ or 15″ monitor, or a 17″ monitor? What kind of printer should you buy? Monochrome or full color, inkjet or laser? What type of keyboard and pointing device do you want? Do you want a standard keyboard or one that is ergonomically designed? Do you want to use a standard mouse, a trackball, or a joystick?

All of these questions confront you when you are making the purchasing decision for your personal computer. Needless to say, you have literally thousands of options to consider and are about to make a difficult decision, as depicted in Figure 2.1. It would be awful to choose a computer that didn't meet your needs, that didn't work, that quickly became obsolete, that was later proven in the market to be an inferior technology, or that was made by a manufacturer who went out of business soon after your purchase. Even worse, imagine that you were making the purchasing decision for a business and had to purchase hundreds—or even thousands—of personal computers. Buying computers is not easy.

The question of how to make an educated decision remains. Knowing the options well is a good place to start. In addition, many people buying for themselves or for organizations have followed the general rule of thumb that you should go with a dominant computer and manufacturer and purchase as much computer as you can afford. For example, the safe choice today would probably be a

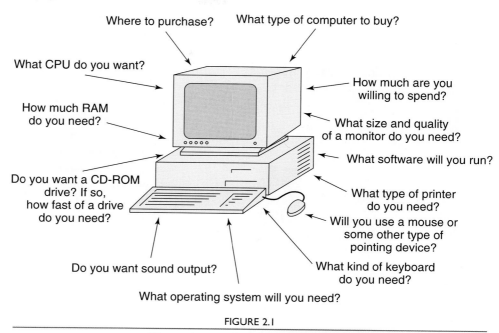

FIGURE 2.1

The questions you face when purchasing a PC.

Windows-based computer with an Intel microprocessor, manufactured by one of the more dominant computer makers—such as IBM, HP, Compaq, Packard Bell, Dell, or Gateway 2000—and loaded with the fastest CD-ROM player and microprocessor, the best monitor and printer, and as much RAM and hard drive space as you can afford. This way, you are more likely to bet on a winner that will remain current for a longer period of time.

Our goal in this scenario is to illustrate how complex, difficult, and important something as simple as selecting a personal computer can be. In the rest of this chapter, we remove some of the mystery surrounding information system hardware. After you understand what all the pieces are and how they work together to make a computer system, you will be better able to make informed purchasing decisions for you and your organization.

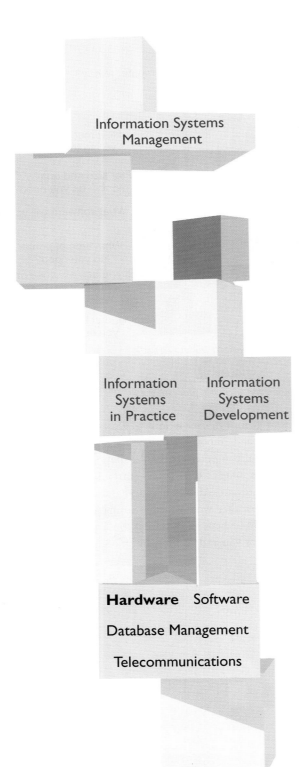

Information Systems
Management

Information
Systems
in Practice

Information
Systems
Development

Hardware Software

Database Management

Telecommunications

Introduction

As pointed out in the opening scenario, a broad range of options are available to you when you purchase a computer-based information system, and hardware is a central ingredient. Over the years, the price of hardware has become less expensive, making it possible for individuals and organizations of all sizes to take advantage of computer-based technologies. However, large computer systems can still easily cost more than a million dollars. Facing days of ever-shrinking budgets and a more competitive marketplace, organizations must take care to select the right hardware for the job or risk making a costly mistake. In order to make more informed decisions about IS hardware, you must have an understanding of what IS hardware is and how it works.

After reading this chapter, you will be able to do the following:

1. Understand the important role of information systems hardware in the success of modern organizations.

2. Describe key elements of information systems hardware.

3. List and describe the types of computers that are being used in organizations today.

4. Explain how hardware has evolved and where it is headed.

Given the importance technology plays in our lives, it is useful to understand the key underlying elements of IS hardware. Our approach in this chapter is not to bog you down with facts and jargon but to provide you with an overview. In terms of our guiding framework—The Big Picture—this is the first of four chapters focusing on the essential elements of information systems (see Figure 2.2).

FIGURE 2.2

The big picture: focusing on information systems hardware.

The Importance of Information Systems Hardware

As we discussed in Chapter 1, "Information Systems Overview," computer-based information systems are a key enabler for the competitive strategy and many day-to-day activities of nearly every modern organization. As a result, organizations have a strong motivation for acquiring the right equipment. As we showed in the opening scenario, making hardware choices is complicated. If an organization buys too little, its people may be idle while waiting for these under-powered systems to finish processing. If an organization buys too much, hardware may sit idle because it is unneeded or seldom used, while the firm incurs a large expense.

Phil Cantor/Superstock

Organizations need information systems hardware in today's rapidly changing and highly competitive global economy for numerous reasons. There is an increasing need for real-time information. For example, global financial markets change by the second. If your organization relies on this data, you must have the capability to capture, store, and route this information to the appropriate decision makers instantaneously (see Figure 2.3). Alternatively, let's suppose that you own a manufacturing company that manages their inventories using a Just-In-Time (JIT) approach. At this company, the levels of manufacturing supplies and finished goods, as well as the costs associated with managing these inventories, are kept to a minimum. Computer monitoring of inventories must instantly notify suppliers when additional raw materials are needed so that your manufacturing processes do not go idle. The exchange of real-time information is needed in countless other situations as well. Remote offices must be connected with home offices. Remote sales personnel must be able to process orders, check product availability, communicate with their supervisor, and so on. In all instances, computer hardware facilitates the exchange of real-time information. This is strong motivation for investing in IS hardware.

FIGURE 2.3

Wall Street trader analyzing rapidly changing data.

Key Elements of Information Systems Hardware

Information systems hardware is classified into three types: input, process, and output technologies (see Figure 2.4). Input-related hardware includes devices used to enter information into a computer. Process-related hardware transforms inputs into outputs. The central processing unit (CPU) is the device that performs this transformation, with the help of several other closely related devices that store and recall information. Finally, output-related hardware delivers information in a usable format to users. The focus of this section is to describe each of these three key elements of information systems hardware.

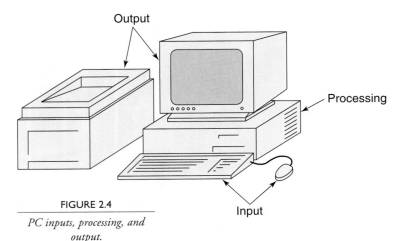

FIGURE 2.4

PC inputs, processing, and output.

Input: How Information Is Entered into an Information System

In order for information systems hardware to perform a task, data must be input into the system. As you will see, this can be done in many ways because different types of information can be entered more easily using one type of input device versus another. For example, keyboards are currently the primary means to enter text and numbers. Alternatively, architects and engineers often want to enter their designs and drawings into computers. Many special types of pointing devices have been developed to simulate the process of drawing or sketching on a sheet of paper. A great deal of research and development has been conducted to identify optimal ways to input various types of information and to build and sell new input devices. In this section, we describe some of the most commonly used input devices. To organize this discussion, we classify input methods into four general categories by the type of information being entered: entering original text/numbers, selecting and pointing, entering batch data, and entering audio and video. Table 2.1 summarizes the fundamental characteristics of each category.

Table 2.1   Methods of providing input to an information system.

Information Category	Representative Device(s)
Entering original text/numbers	Keyboard
Selecting and pointing	Mouse Trackball and joysticks Touch screen Light pen
Entering batch data	Scanners Bar code/optical character readers
Entering audio and video	Microphones and speakers Video and digital cameras MIDI

Entering Original Text/Numbers

One of the primary computer-based applications is the entry of text and numbers. The primary device used to support this type of input is the **keyboard**. Used first as the input method on typewriters, keyboard data entry is a mainstay of the computer industry. A recent advance in keyboard technology is the development of ergonomically correct keyboards, which are designed to reduce the stress placed on the wrists, hands, and arms when typing. Figure 2.5 shows a normal keyboard and the Microsoft Natural keyboard. When typing for long periods, some users develop aching, numbing, and tingling in their arms, wrists, or hands. These injuries are generally referred to as **repetitive stress injuries**. The broadened use of computers in the workplace and the associated injuries to workers, resulting in more sick days and insurance claims, has made the ergonomics of keyboards and employees' workstations much more important to organizations. In the bulleted list that follows Figure 2.5, we describe ways to reduce repetitive stress injuries.

2.5a Courtesy Apple Computer, Inc.

FIGURE 2.5

Normal keyboard (2.5a) versus MS Natural keyboard (2.5b).

2.5b Courtesy Microsoft Corporation

- Have an ergonomically designed workplace—desk, chair, monitor size and angle, keyboard height and position.

- Take frequent breaks from typing. When your wrists and fingers start to ache, take a break.

- Maintain a straight wrist position when typing. Don't let wrist bend up/down or left/right.

- Avoid resting on your wrists while typing. Keep your wrists elevated off the desk.

■ Use a light touch on the keys. Don't press harder on the keyboard to enter information than you need to press.

■ Maintain good health habits and exercise your arms, wrists, and hands.

Selecting and Pointing

In addition to entering text and numbers, **pointing devices** are used to select items from menus, to point, and to sketch or draw (see Figure 2.6). As with keyboards, you probably have used a pointing device, such as a mouse, when using a graphical operating environment (such as Microsoft Windows) or when playing a video game. Several of the most popular types of pointing devices are listed in Table 2.2.

Table 2.2   Selecting and pointing devices.

Device	Description
Mouse	Pointing device that works by sliding a small box-like device on a flat surface; selections are made by pressing buttons on the mouse.
Trackball	Pointing device that works by rolling a ball that sits in a holder; selections are made by pressing buttons located near or on the holder.
Joystick	Pointing device that works by moving a small stick that sits in a holder; selections are made by pressing buttons located near or on the holder.
Touch screen	A method of input for which you use your finger; selections are made by touching the computer display.
Light pen	Pointing device that works by placing a pen-like device near a computer screen; selections are made by pressing the pen to the screen.

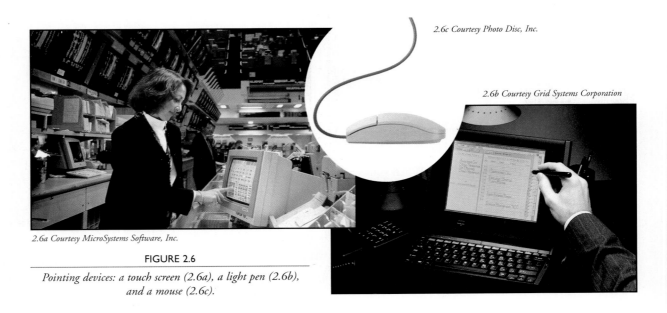

2.6c Courtesy Photo Disc, Inc.

2.6b Courtesy Grid Systems Corporation

2.6a Courtesy MicroSystems Software, Inc.

FIGURE 2.6

Pointing devices: a touch screen (2.6a), a light pen (2.6b), and a mouse (2.6c).

The Birth of the Mouse

Speaking of mice, although it is true that Apple Computer made the mouse popular in the 1980s, the real inventor of the mouse was Doug Engelbart. He invented it in the early 1960s while working for the Stanford Research Institute (SRI). It was not until the mid-1980s that Apple Computer contacted SRI to purchase the rights to the mouse—reportedly for only about $40,000! Dr. Engelbart is also credited as the original developer of hypertext and videoconferencing—all in the 1960s. Many of these discoveries were not widely known or diffused into mainstream computing for almost 30 years. (For more information on the birth of the mouse and Dr. Engelbart, visit http://www.superkids.com/aweb/pages/features/mouse/mouse.html or use a search engine and search for "Doug Engelbart." You are likely to come up with a lot of hits!)

Entering Batch Data

Along with keyboards and pointing devices, a third category of computer-based input is referred to as **batch input**. Batch input is most often used when a great deal of routine information needs to be entered into the computer. Two widely used batch data input devices are scanners and bar code/optical character readers. **Scanners** convert printed text and images into digital data. They range from a small handheld device that looks like a mouse to a large desktop box that resembles a personal photocopier, both of which are shown in Figure 2.7. Rather than duplicating the image on another piece of paper, the computer translates the image into digital information that can be stored or manipulated by the computer. Special **text recognition software** can convert handwritten text into the computer-based characters that form the original letters and words. Insurance companies, universities, and other organizations that routinely process large batches of forms and documents have applied scanner technology to increase employee productivity.

2.7a Courtesy Intermec Technologies Corp.

FIGURE 2.7

Handheld (2.7a) and flat-bed (2.7b) scanners.

2.7b Courtesy Hewlett-Packard Company

An extension of the general purpose scanner is the **bar code/optical character reader**. Like scanners, these devices use light to scan magnetic information on a package or document and then input this information into a computer. Figure 2.8 shows a sample bar code reader. For example, grocery stores use bar code readers as clerks pass the UPC (Universal Product Code) over a bar code reader implanted in the checkout stand. Banks use optical character readers to process batches of checks through their systems. The U.S. military uses bar codes to assist in inventorying bombs, ammunition, and other precious equipment. Needless to say, a broad range of organizations has gained significant benefits from applying scanner-related technologies to their day-to-day operations.

FIGURE 2.8

UPC bar code and check.

3700 62811

John Doe	0101
123 Main Street	12-345
Anywhere, USA 00000 ——19——	00

Pay to the
order of _____ $ [   ]

_____ DOLLARS

First National Bank
Downtown Branch
P.O. Box 456
Anywhere, USA 00000

Memo _____

⑆121000358⑆0101⑈01234⑈5678⑊⑈   ⑈000000 2765⑈

Audio and Video

An emerging method for entering information is through **audio input** devices. Audio-based input, which can be done in several ways, is helpful when a user's hands need to be free to do other tasks. A special form of controlling and manipulating audio input is through the Musical Instrument Digital Interface (MIDI). MIDI is a specification for using the computer to record, sample, mix, and play music. Musical instruments, amplifiers, and other equipment can be connected to a computer through a MIDI.

A final way in which information can be entered into a computer is through **video input**. For example, televisions and videocassette recorders can be connected to computers as input devices. Digital cameras have also been developed to quickly capture still images. Video input is widely used to assist in security-related applications, such as room monitoring and employee verification. Also, teleconferences can be held on your personal computer using simple video cameras, which cost less than $100 (see Figure 2.9).

FIGURE 2.9

Connectix QuickCam video camera.

QUICKCAM

QuickCam is a registered trademark of Connectix Corporation.

In manufacturing applications, high-resolution video cameras are used to evaluate the quality of products by taking a picture of a new product or part and comparing this image with one stored in a database. If the images match, the part passes a quality control inspection. If the images do not match, the part can be rejected without human intervention. Both audio and video input are expected to increase in popularity in the near future.

In this section, we have described numerous options for providing input to a computer. After information is entered into a computer, it can be processed, stored, and manipulated. In the next section, we describe the processing aspects of information systems hardware.

Processing: Transforming Inputs into Outputs

Computer input and output are easy for us to understand, yet the language computers use to process information is not easy for us to understand. The computer converts inputs into a language it understands, a language made up of special computer codes. This means that all text, numbers, sounds, and video must be converted into a common format that the computer can store and manipulate. The language of internal computer processing is in binary notation. Binary information is simply a series of 0s and 1s. Each 0 or 1 is referred to as a **bit** or binary digit. A combination of eight bits is typically referred to as a **byte**. For example, one keyboard character, such as the letter "A," is stored as a single byte of information.

To translate a word, number, or sound into a series of binary digits, the computer industry has developed internal computer language codes that represent and translate information. For example, the most widely used code for representing text and numbers is called **ASCII** (American Standard Code of Information Interchange, pronounced "as-key"). Table 2.3 shows the ASCII codes for representing the alphabet and the numbers 0–9. Standard codes for representing graphics, sounds, and video have also been developed. When you enter information into a computer, it automatically translates the information into binary.

Table 2.3   ASCII codes for alphabet and numbers.

Character	ASCII-8 Binary Code	Character	ASCII-8 Binary Code
A	1010 0001	S	1011 0011
B	1010 0010	T	1011 0100
C	1010 0011	U	1011 0101
D	1010 0100	V	1011 0110
E	1010 0101	W	1011 0111
F	1010 0110	X	1011 1000
G	1010 0111	Y	1011 1001
H	1010 1000	Z	1011 1010
I	1010 1001	0	0101 0000
J	1010 1010	1	0101 0001
K	1010 1011	2	0101 0010

continues

Table 2.3   Continued.

Character	ASCII-8 Binary Code	Character	ASCII-8 Binary Code
L	1010 1100	3	0101 0011
M	1010 1101	4	0101 0100
N	1010 1110	5	0101 0101
O	1010 1111	6	0101 0110
P	1011 0000	7	0101 0111
Q	1011 0001	8	0101 1000
R	1011 0010	9	0101 1001

Within the processing component of the computer, there are three key internal elements: primary storage, secondary storage, and the central processing unit (CPU), as depicted in Figure 2.10. When information is input to a computer, it is temporarily stored in primary storage before being permanently stored in secondary storage or being manipulated by the CPU. Likewise, when information is output from a computer, it is stored in primary storage before being sent to some output device, such as a video display or printer. For example, if you type a term paper on your PC, the characters you type are moved from the keyboard to the primary storage area (see Figure 2.10). This movement of characters is controlled by the CPU (and the operating system—see Chapter 3, "Information Systems Software," for a discussion of operating systems). When you save your work, these characters are copied from the primary storage to a secondary storage device, such as a floppy disk (see Figure 2.10). The CPU controls this movement of characters to the secondary storage. At some later date, when you decide to print a copy of your paper, you make this request by inputting commands to the processor. After they are input, these commands are stored in primary storage and interpreted by the CPU. After they are interpreted, the CPU instructs the secondary storage to recall your term paper and load it into primary storage. The CPU can send your term paper to the printer after it is loaded into primary storage (see Figure 2.10).

FIGURE 2.10

Computer components showing the path through primary storage, secondary storage, and the central processing unit.

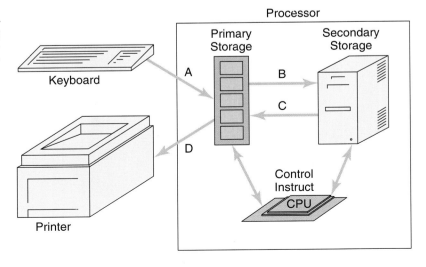

In sum, all input and output passes through primary storage. All information stored in secondary storage is moved to primary storage before being output or manipulated. The CPU is the "traffic cop" in the process. It interprets the meaning of commands. It translates input into binary information and binary information into information that can be understood by humans. CPU controls both input and output processes. Now that you have a general understanding of what happens during processing, we describe in detail each of these three processing components.

Primary Storage: Storage for Current Information

When a computer makes calculations or manipulates data in some way, it needs a place to store the information it is currently working on. This storage location is called **primary storage**, or simply memory. Memory is measured in bytes. Each byte is about one keyboard character (see Table 2.4). For example, a paper that you write for class may contain 30 thousand bytes (in computer lingo, 30 kilobytes or 30KB). A large software program may contain several million bytes (megabytes or MB). Databases containing billions of bytes of information (gigabytes or GB) make up IRS taxpayer records. Memory is very important to a computer's performance. Without enough memory, some programs may not run, and if they do run, they may run very slowly. Computers have different types of memory—each type having somewhat different characteristics and roles in information processing. We describe each in more detail in the sections that follow.

Table 2.4   Elements of computer storage.

Name	Number of Bytes	Description	Abbreviation
Kilobyte*	1,000*	One thousand bytes	KB
Megabyte	1,000,000	One million bytes	MB
Gigabyte	1,000,000,000	One billion bytes	GB
Terabyte	1,000,000,000,000	One trillion bytes	TB

*   A kilobyte is actually 1,024 bytes.

ROM (Read-Only Memory)

ROM is memory that cannot be changed by the processor or user of the computer, hence the name read-only. ROM is nonvolatile, meaning that it does not lose its instructions when the computer is powered off. Because of this characteristic, computer manufacturers typically use ROM to hold the instructions for starting the computer and for running predefined maintenance processes.

RAM (Random-Access Memory)

RAM is what we most commonly think of as memory. Unlike ROM, RAM is volatile and can be changed as you work on your computer. For example, when you load an application such as Microsoft Word to type a paper for class, both the application program and your paper are stored in RAM. If you turn the computer off without saving, you will lose your work. In essence, when the computer is turned off, RAM loses all its stored values and instructions. Therefore, anything in RAM that the user wants to reuse should be written to secondary storage. Many personal computers sold today are equipped with 16 megabytes (MB) of RAM, an amount needed to run popular operating systems such as Windows 95 and Windows NT. RAM is typically configured as a SIMM (single in-line memory module), which is simply a small circuit board that contains one or more RAM chips. A sample SIMM chip is shown in Figure 2.11.

FIGURE 2.11

A SIMM chip.

Courtesy IBM Corporation

Cache Memory

Cache memory is a special type of RAM that is extremely fast and expensive. Cache memory is used to store information that is used a lot by the CPU. Cache memory can dramatically boost the speed of a computer by storing commonly used instructions that would normally be stored on RAM or on a secondary storage device, such as a fixed disk. When these instructions are needed, the CPU can quickly retrieve them from the cache, rather than from some other, slower storage area. To compare the relative amounts of RAM and cache, a typical PC with 16MB of RAM may have only 256 or 512KB of cache memory.

Secondary Storage: Keeping Information for Later Use

Secondary storage archives data and programs so that they can be accessed as needed. Computer processing does us little good unless we can store the information for later use. Several technologies have evolved in the last 50 years for storing computerized data. Table 2.5 describes many storage methods and provides a comparison of their speed, method of access, and relative cost. We describe each of these secondary storage methods in the following sections.

Table 2.5 Comparing methods of secondary storage.

Type	Speed	Method of Data Access	Relative Cost/MB
Magnetic tape	Slow	Sequential	Low
Floppy disks	Slow	Direct	Low
Fixed disks	Fast	Direct	High
Compact discs	Medium	Direct	Medium
Optical disks	Fast	Direct	Medium

Magnetic Tape

Magnetic tape was one of the earliest methods of storing and retrieving computer-generated data. Just as with audio cassette tapes, data is written by magnetically rearranging the atoms on the tape. Tape uses **sequential data**

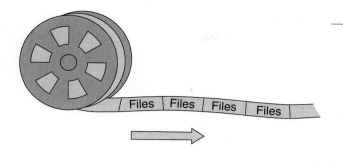

FIGURE 2.12

Sequential access of information.

access, meaning that if you want to access a particular piece of information, you must wind through the tape to get to the location of that information, as depicted in Figure 2.12. After that information is located, it can be read into the computer. Similarly, you must be very careful when writing to tape. If any information is stored where you are writing, you will overwrite that information—much like taping over a song on an audio tape. Magnetic tape is primarily used today for backing up large amounts of data, such as payroll records. It is rarely used as a primary means of secondary storage. While it is very cheap, it is also very slow because you have to move sequentially through the tape to write and retrieve information.

Floppy Disks

Floppy disks were the next widely used technique for providing secondary computer storage. A floppy disk is a small magnetic disk protected from dirt and dust by a plastic coating. A *read/write head*, which is positioned very close to the disk surface, reads or writes information to and from the disk while the disk is spinning, as depicted in Figure 2.13. Because the read/write head can move back and forth across the disk surface, information on the disk can be accessed directly. You don't need to read other data that was recorded before. This type of access—going directly to the spot on the disk where the desired information is stored—is called **direct data access** (or random access). Direct data access was a major breakthrough in secondary storage technology because it significantly enhanced the speed of storing and retrieving computer-based information. The first floppy disks available in the 1970s were eight inches across and stored less than a few hundred thousand bytes.

Today's floppy disks are typically 2.5 inches and can be formatted to hold 1.44MB or 2.88MB of information. Very high-capacity floppy drives, such as Iomega's ZIP Drive, store more than 100MB on a single disk! Until recently, floppy disks were the primary means to transfer information from one computer to another and to distribute retail software. As newer applications become more sophisticated and therefore larger, more applications are distributed using CD-ROMs, which are discussed in the next section.

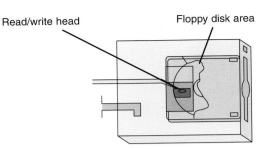

Read/write head   Floppy disk area

Fixed Disks

Fixed disks, also referred to as hard disks or hard drives, are an extension of the floppy disk technology, but they have much greater capacities and data transfer speeds. Therefore, fixed disks have become the most commonly used method for providing secondary storage. A typical fixed disk has several magnetic layers, called platters, that are located in a sealed, clean environment, as shown in Figure 2.14. Fixed disks have several read/write heads, one for reading and writing to each separate surface. Fixed disks also spin at very high speeds, and the read/write heads are positioned to be very close to (but not touching) the magnetic surface. Because fixed disks spin at a much higher rate and the sealed environment allows special high-storage capacity materials to be used, each platter has a huge storage capacity and a much faster data transfer rate than a floppy disk. A single fixed disk, for example, can hold hundreds or thousands of megabytes of information.

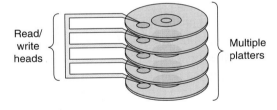

Read/
write
heads

Multiple
platters

CD-ROM (Compact Disc-Read-Only Memory)

CD-ROM is an increasingly popular method for distributing software and backing up information. Using the same technology as audio CD players, lasers burn information onto a compact disc by creating pits in the disc, as shown in Figure 2.15. Information is retrieved from the disk by having a special type of laser interpret the sequence of pits as data. CD-ROMs are typically a WORM (write-once, read-many) technology; after data is written to the disc, it cannot be changed.

CD-ROM

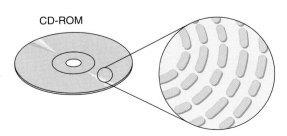

CD-ROMs are popular with software developers for distributing systems and data. The average CD-ROM holds 650MB of information—*the same amount it takes over 450 individual floppy disks to hold!* Like floppy and fixed disks, CD-ROMs provide direct access to information. The data transfer rates for CD-ROM technology are not as high as they are for a fixed disk, but they are still much faster than for a floppy. When CD-ROM disks are copied from a master disk with the same data pattern, they can cost manufacturers less than $1 each to produce. CD-R (CD-Recordable) drives have been available to the public in the last few years. These drives enable you to create CD-ROMs on your personal computer. CD-R drives are becoming increasingly inexpensive and can be found for less than $750. Blank recordable discs cost less than $10 each. Given that the cost of this storage is about one cent per megabyte, many companies are turning to CD-Rs for backup and archiving of data.

Optical Disks

Optical disks are an emerging technology born from research and development related to CD-ROMs. Like CD-ROM technology, optical disks provide direct access to data, with the added benefit of being able to be rewritten many times. Optical disks also have tremendous capacities. They often have more than one gigabyte (GB) on a single disk. The disks themselves are relatively inexpensive, often around $100 for a one-GB disk. Optical disk players, however, still cost over $1,000, making optical disks too costly to be widely used by individuals and organizations.

The Central Processing Unit: The Brain of the Computer

The final process component is the **central processing unit (CPU)**, where the computer calculates and manipulates data. The CPU, also referred to as the computer's main microprocessor, processor, or chip, is composed of millions of tiny transistors. These transistors arranged in complex patterns that allow the CPU to interpret and manipulate data. The inner workings of a CPU are very complex. For most of us, it is easiest to think of a CPU as being a "black box" where all the processing occurs. The CPU is a small device made of silicon. For example, the Intel Pentium II® CPU is about 2 square inches in surface area and less than .5 inch thick, as shown in Figure 2.16. Within these two square inches are more than 5 million transistors!

The number of transistors that can be packed into a modern CPU and the speed at which processing and other activities occur are remarkable. For example, the Intel Pentium II® can complete hundreds of mil-

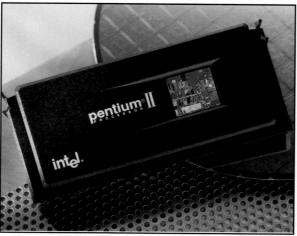

Courtesy Intel

FIGURE 2.16

The Intel Pentium II.

lions of operations every second. To achieve these incredible speeds, things must occur very rapidly within the computer, and the things that occur the fastest are inside the CPU (see Table 2.6). For example, it takes a fixed disk about 10 milliseconds to access information. Within a CPU, however, a single transistor can be changed from one state to another in about 10 picoseconds (one trillionth of a second). This means that activities occur inside the CPU about one billion times faster than they do in a fixed disk. The primary reason for this huge speed difference is that CPUs only operate on electronic impulses. Fixed disks have both electronic and mechanical activities occurring, such as the spinning disk and moving read/write head. Mechanical activities are extremely slow relative to electronic activities, which move at close to the speed of light!

Table 2.6   Elements of computer time.

Name	Fraction of a Second	Description	Example
Millisecond	1/1000	One thousandth of a second	Fixed disks access information in about 10–20 milliseconds.
Microsecond	1/1,000,000	One millionth of a second	A 200MHz CPU executes approximately 200 million operations in a second—or about 200 operations every microsecond.
Nanosecond	1/1,000,000,000	One billionth of a second	Most types of RAM used in PCs have access times (the time needed to read information from the RAM to the CPU) from 60–100 nanoseconds (lower is better). Most cache memory has access times of less than 20 nanoseconds.
Picosecond	1/1,000,000,000,000	One trillionth of a second	Inside a CPU, the time it takes to switch a circuit from one state to another is in the range of 5–20 picoseconds.

When you decide which computer to purchase, one of your primary considerations is its overall speed. Over the years, CPU manufacturers, such as Intel, Motorola, and Digital Equipment Corporation (DEC), have spent a considerable amount of effort defining how best to measure the performance of a computer. The easiest way to compare the performance of one computer to another is to contrast the number of instructions each can perform in a given period of time. Because CPUs operate at such high speeds, the unit of time for this comparison is typically only one second. Most modern computers can perform more than a million instructions in a second. This is quite a shift from the original "big iron" mainframe computers of the 1950s, 60s, and 70s, which took up many large rooms and processed fewer than one million instructions in a second.

Now that you understand more about how information is input into a computer and how it is processed, we can turn our attention to the third category of hardware—output technologies.

Output: How Information Is Displayed and Printed

After information is input and processed, it must be presented to the user. Although information can be entered into the computer in several different ways, our output choices are relatively simple. Computers can display information on a screen, print it, or emit sound. Details on how each of these types of devices operate are discussed in the sections that follow.

Video Output

Monitors are typically used to display information from a computer. They usually consist of a cathode ray tube (CRT), which is similar to a television, but with much higher resolution. Monitors can be color, black and white, or monochrome (meaning all one color, usually green or amber). Notebooks and other portable computers use liquid crystal display (LCD) or plasma screens because a CRT is too bulky for a portable device. The research and development of monitor technologies is focusing on creating lightweight, low-cost, high-resolution devices. Because display monitors are being embedded into a broad range of products and devices, such as automobiles, to display global positioning, route maps, and other relevant information, they must be sturdy, reliable, lightweight, and low in cost. Someday, all televisions and computers will use lightweight display panels that are similar to those used on notebook and laptop computers.

Paper-based Displays

Information can be printed in several different ways, as shown in Figure 2.17. A **plotter** is normally used for transferring engineering designs from the computer to drafting paper, which is often as big as 34"×44". Several pens are used by the plotter as it draws each of the lines individually. **Dot-matrix printers** are older, electric-typewriter-based technology for printing information to paper. Letters are formed using a series of small dots. Once the most commonly used type of printer, dot-matrix printers are now mostly found printing voluminous batch information, such as periodic reports and forms. **Inkjet printers** use a small cartridge to transfer ink onto paper. This process creates a typewriter-like image that can initially smear because the ink is wet when it is sprayed onto the paper. Inkjet printers can be designed to print both black and white and color. **Laser printers** are the most commonly used printers today. They use an electrostatic process to force ink onto the paper, literally "burning" the image onto the paper. The result is a high-quality image considered necessary for almost all business letters and documents. Laser printers can also produce color images, but high-end color laser printers can cost in excess of $10,000.

ETHICAL PERSPECTIVE: DESKTOP PUBLISHING AND COMPUTER CRIME

Personal computers. Desktop publishing software. Scanners. Color printers. These have become the tools of trade for a new form of computer crime involving the alteration of images and the creation of bogus documentation. Rapid advancements, decreased prices, and increased availability of hardware and software for desktop publishing and artwork have made it much easier for people to falsify images and documents or to simply create them out of thin air. Without much more than a PC, a scanner, and a good desktop publishing package or photo/video editing package, anyone can take an original image and modify it in nearly any way. The image created will be of professional quality.

Using this technology to manipulate the signature on a copy of a check, once thought to be a complex task, is now relatively easy. Sophisticated computer criminals can now use the technology to manipulate more complex images. It is now relatively easy to take a snapshot of a person and change the skin tones, eye color, hair color, and facial expressions. Even placing an image of one person's head on another person's body is a fairly easy task. Some useful purposes do exist for this technology. For example, department stores increasingly rely on this technology to show their customers the look of new clothes, hairstyles, or contact lenses. In addition, plastic surgeons are now using similar technology to show their patients the results of multiple potential surgeries inexpensively. The problems arise when this technology is used to make people look different than they really look without their knowledge and consent. How many times have you wondered whether or not the photograph on the cover of the tabloid sitting on the supermarket shelf was modified? Chances are that it was.

Similarly, the same technology allows the computer user to not only change simple colors on a photograph or an image, but to completely overhaul the image itself. Backgrounds can be exchanged and people can be deleted or added—creating an entirely new picture or image. These capabilities can be used toward positive, creative ends. For example, the last feature film you saw probably used computer-generated or computer-modified filming.

Unfortunately, these capabilities are often used illegally and unethically. A *New York Newsday* cover photograph in February of 1994 after the now infamous attack on Nancy Kerrigan showed figure skaters Kerrigan and Tonya Harding practicing together on the ice. However, they were not on the ice together, as they were in the digitally doctored image. This image caused much debate in journalistic corners about the "ultimate journalistic sin."

A similar form of this type of computer crime involves the use of high-resolution scanners and laser printers to create fake documentation, IDs, tickets, and even counterfeit money. Criminals can take the original image, scan it, modify it, and print electronically "forged" copies. Given its monetary implications and close ties to more traditional forms of forgery, this form of computer crime is much more closely watched by the police and the government than the doctoring of images.

The U.S. government has been constantly fighting the counterfeiters by producing increasingly complex currency and by making people aware of what to look for in counterfeit money. You may, for example, have recently used the new $100 bill, designed to be more difficult to counterfeit.

One of the difficulties with computer crimes of this nature is that the criminal only needs to purchase several components of completely legal technology and be able to use them. There is no crime in owning a computer, a scanner, a color printer, or desktop publishing software, and each is fairly easy to set up and use. Furthermore, in the technology realm, what is unethical isn't always illegal. The fight to stop computer crime is not easy or well-defined.

Questions for Discussion

1. The United States government recently began circulation of new $100 bills that are more difficult to scan and copy. However, this circulation came at a significant cost. The price for the technology and research was well over $750,000. Is the government's costly effort to keep our money tamper-resistant the best solution to money counterfeiting? Why or why not?

2. What should be done to either punish or stop people from committing these types of computer crimes? Why?

3. Do you believe that it is wrong to alter someone's personal photographic image without her consent? What if the person were famous?

Sources *February 17, 1994, New York Times, A12. Figures are from communication with Dale Servetnick, Staff Assistant at the Office of Public Correspondence of the U.S. Treasury Department. For specific information on the $100 bill, see the U.S. Treasury Department's home page at http://www.us.treas.gov/.*

INTERNATIONAL PERSPECTIVE: THE EVOLUTION OF THE ASIAN GIANTS

Indonesia, Legend, Mitac, Creative Technology—not familiar with the names of these high-tech companies? You don't have long to wait! These Asian businesses—located in Asian countries as disparate as Japan, the Philippines, Singapore, Korea, and Taiwan—are developing global strategies that are quickly providing them with a competitive advantage in the world marketplace. These companies are taking on new managerial styles, dividing into smaller units, and spreading throughout the globe as they strive to lead the world in the production of PCs and computer parts, telecommunications equipment, integrated circuits, and digital services. In partnership with the U.S. and other companies, Asian high-tech firms are quickly becoming technology powerhouses around the world.

A case in point is Texas Instruments' Thai partner, the Alphatec Group, packagers and testers of microchips. The group is undertaking massive expansion and expects to reach $4 billion in sales by the year 2000—making this achievement in an area of the world that is expected to be the second biggest market (after the U.S.) within the next several years. What is driving the success of Alphatec? Clifford (1996) attributes much of its success to the fact that its chair, Charn Uswachoke, received a good education and training in the U.S. and has many years of experience dealing with Western organizations and people. In addition, the ethnic Chinese community in Thailand, of which Uswachoke is a member, provides financial support to the group.

Developing high-tech industries in countries that do not yet have them is not that easy, however; many companies experience a scarcity of qualified employees, a lack of knowledge about the design and construction of physical plants, and inadequate IT infrastructures. Workers brought in from partner companies or hired as consultants from outside of the region risk area-specific diseases, culture-bound problems, and management style clashes, in addition to any number of other uncertainties.

Asian companies are being helped by the boom in technology use in Asia. Brull, Hof, Flynn, and Gross (1996) note projections that the Japanese alone will spend over $600 billion on telecommunications products and services by the year 2000, a 53 percent increase from 1993. In addition to the increase in chip exports to overseas buyers, this boom has had a major impact on Japan's Fujitsu, Ltd. Now the top computer manufacturer in Japan and second in the world after IBM, Fujitsu is branching out into Internet and multimedia and is putting the weight of its financial and technical capabilities behind this new venture. However, to break into markets overseas, where it has not been successful in the past, Fujitsu has had to change the way the business is run and the kind of products it markets. Changes include relaxing the strict Japanese standards of dress and conduct, allowing employees to make their own hours and work on their own projects, and hiring younger, Western-educated employees with cutting-edge views of what the future can be.

Many factors could stop the advance of these Asian companies in IT markets. If the chip market, for example, were to bottom out, many of the companies that have staked their fortunes in this area would be in trouble. For the time being, however, the IT companies would do well to keep an eye on their competitors in the East.

Questions for Discussion

1. What other factors have precipitated the rise of the Asian companies?

2. What factors could inhibit the continued success of these Asian companies?

3. What should U.S. companies do to maintain a strategic advantage?

Sources Brull, Hof, Flynn, and Gross. 1996. *Fujitsu gets wired.* BusinessWeek, March 18, 110–112.

Clifford, M. 1996. *The magical moneyman of Thailand.* BusinessWeek, Dec 25./Jan.1, 52.

FIGURE 2.17

A plotter (2.17a), a dot matrix (2.17b), an inkjet (2.17c), and a laser printer (2.17d).

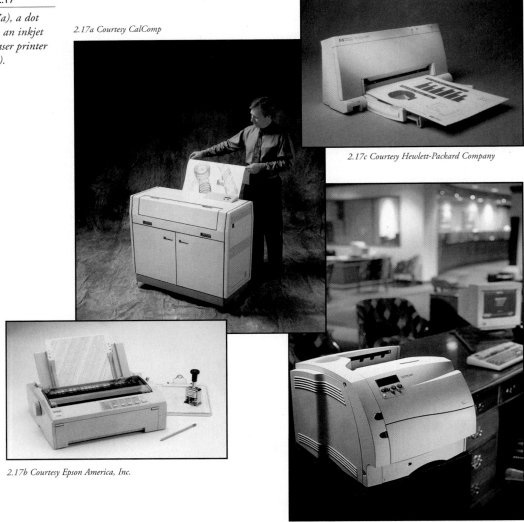

2.17a Courtesy CalComp

2.17c Courtesy Hewlett-Packard Company

2.17b Courtesy Epson America, Inc.

2.17d Courtesy Lexmark International

Audio Output

A computer can now also transmit audio as output. With the use of small specialized speakers and a *sound card*, stereo-quality sound can come from a computer. The computer translates digits into sound by sending data to a sound card that interprets this data into tones. The tones are then sent to the speakers for output. Musicians and composers often use this output to simulate a full orchestra when working on new or unfamiliar pieces of music.

Now that you have a fundamental understanding of how computer hardware works, we can discuss the types of computers that people and organizations typically use.

Types of Computers

We talked about the three basic hardware building blocks—input, process, and output technologies—that you would find in nearly every computer, large or small. In this section, we describe the many different types of computers that are made up of these three basic building blocks. Table 2.7 gives you a sneak preview of the types of computers we will discuss. Computers come in all shapes, sizes, degrees of power, and costs. We will present these computer types to you, beginning first with the fastest, biggest, and most costly computers, and ending with the slower, smaller, and cheaper computers.

Table 2.7 Relative comparison of types of computers.

Type of Computer	Performance	Memory (RAM)	Physical Size	Typical Cost Range
Supercomputer	1 to 100 GigaFLOPS*	100 to 2000GB	Like an automobile	$1,000,000 to over $20,000,000
Mainframe	Up to 1000 MIPS	Up to 2GB	Like a refrigerator	$1,000,000 to over $10,000,000
Minicomputer	250 to more than 500 MIPS	Up to 2GB	Like a file cabinet	$10,000 to over $100,000
Workstation	100 to 500 MIPS	32 to 64MB	Fits on a desktop	$5,000 to over $50,000
Microcomputer	100 to 300 MIPS	16 to 32MB	Fits on a desktop	$1,000 to over $5,000

GigaFLOPS, billions of floating point operations per second, and MIPS, millions of instructions per second, are both common metrics for computer speed ratings.

Supercomputers

The most powerful and expensive computers that exist today are called **supercomputers.** Figure 2.18 shows a Cray supercomputer, one of the more popular computers in this class. Supercomputers usually cost many millions of dollars. They are equipped with numerous very fast processors that work in parallel to execute several instructions simultaneously. These special-purpose computers are used by researchers and scientists to solve very complex problems that were literally unsolvable until these computational giants were created (Cray Research, 1998). For example, Sandia National Laboratories uses a supercomputer to model fallout from

Courtesy SiliconGraphics Computer Systems

FIGURE 2.18

The Cray supercomputer.

nuclear explosions and other nuclear phenomena. This particular machine has several gigabytes of RAM and the computational horsepower of more than 9,000 Pentium processors. Pharmaceutical companies, such as Eli Lilly and Dow Chemical, use supercomputers to design and evaluate new combinations of chemical elements in order to quickly identify promising prescription drugs and treatments. An extensive staff is usually required to operate and maintain supercomputers and to support the researchers and scientists using them.

Mainframes

The backbone of large corporate computing has historically been large, high-powered computers called **mainframes**. Figure 2.19 shows an IBM mainframe, one of the more popular computers in this class. These machines can be the size of a large refrigerator (and even larger), and they often cost several million dollars to purchase. In spite of their size and cost, however, a few companies even own more than one. While mainframe computers typically don't have the power and speed of supercomputers, mainframe computers are still very fast and are normally used for enterprise-wide computing. Many federal and state governments use mainframe computers to manage the massive amount of data generated by day-to-day governmental activities. Federal agencies, such as the Internal Revenue Service (IRS), have several mainframe computers to handle the massive databases related to individual and corporate payroll and tax information. Large corporations, such as Alamo Rent-A-Car, American Airlines, and Holiday Inn, use mainframes to perform repetitive tasks, such as processing reservations.

FIGURE 2.19

IBM mainframe.

Courtesy IBM Corporation

IBM at the Olympics

The company synonymous with mainframe computing is IBM, which has long dominated the mainframe market. Today, IBM provides many organizations with some of the most powerful mainframes ever created (see Table 2.8). For the 1996 Summer Olympics in Atlanta, IBM provided the Olympic Committee with the free use of an IBM System/390. This machine served as the heart of a networked computing environment used by 150,000 athletes, coaches, officials, media, and other members of the Olympic family during the 1996 Olympic Games. One key component of this system was the "Results System," which delivered real-time information to the broadcasters reporting on the games worldwide.

Table 2.8   Applications of IBM mainframe computers in organizations (IBM, 1998).

Organization	Application
Alamo Rent-A-Car	Customer reservation and car tracking system
American Airlines	Global customer reservation system (Saber)
Holiday Inn	Global reservation system
State governments	Payroll, individual and company taxes, motor vehicle licensing, division and offices of government, and so on
Universities	Student grades, course registrations, payroll, financial management, and so on

See IBM's World Wide Web home page (http://www.ibm.com) for more on how mainframe computers are being used.

Minicomputers

Minicomputers are scaled-down versions of mainframes. They were created when companies had needs for fast enterprise computers but did not need all the power of a mainframe or could not afford one. For example, a mid-sized business might use a minicomputer to process its payroll, to conduct online order entry, and to perform other tasks, but it might not have the funds or the workload to justify buying a mainframe computer. In this way, minicomputers have become integral to many smaller and mid-sized organizations. These computers usually cost tens to hundreds of thousands of dollars. As with mainframes, IBM is a leader in the minicomputer market, with its AS/400 model. Manufacturers such as Hewlett-Packard have done quite well in this portion of the market as well, however. The midrange market as a whole has been declining as workstations and microcomputers have become faster and have absorbed some of the functionality once required of minicomputers and mainframe computers.

Allstate Insurance

Allstate Insurance has had great success using minicomputers (IBM, 1998). Allstate has approximately 15,000 employees—and another 13,000 agents who link into their systems for support. On a typical day, their information systems must handle more than 30 million transactions. In the aftermath of a natural disaster, however, Allstate may see its already heavy workload increase by 50 percent. For example, in the first 12 days following Hurricane Andrew in 1992, Allstate received more than 7,000 claims per day from southern Florida alone.

In the face of disaster, most people expect from their insurance company exactly what they expect from the police or fire departments—an instant response, without excuses. To achieve this, Allstate uses several IBM minicomputers. These minicomputers, located in one of three data centers in different parts of the country, are linked together through high-speed data networks. Linking these smaller machines together allows Allstate to dynamically shift work between sites as workloads change. This strategy also allows Allstate to quickly add capacity to their system as needed. The design of using multiple, independent processors has allowed Allstate to take many of the peaks and valleys out of their systems response, leading to better customer service.

FIGURE 2.20

A Sun workstation.

Courtesy Sun Microsystems, Inc.

Workstations

Workstations are a relatively new class of computers. They have the power and operating systems of some minicomputers, but they typically fit on a desktop and can be placed nearly anywhere (rather than requiring their own closet or room). Many relatively new computer hardware companies, such as Silicon Graphics, Sun Microsystems, and DEC, are leaders in this market. Workstations are a special class of microcomputer (as is your PC). They have an extremely fast CPU (or multiple CPUs), large capacities of RAM and secondary storage, and video displays that are of a very high quality. Workstations generally cost between $5,000 and $50,000. Figure 2.20 shows a Sun Sparcstation, one of the more popular computers in this class. Workstations are often used by engineers to design new products with processing-intensive applications, such as computer-aided design (CAD); by financial analysts modeling stock market fluctuations; and by researchers working with large, complex, computational-intensive applications. For example, researchers at NASA are using workstations to study the effects of global warming on ocean surface temperatures. Workstations' sales have also seen a boost in recent years because they are often used as Web servers.

Microcomputers

Microcomputers, also referred to as personal computers, fit nicely on desktops, generally cost between $1,000 and $5,000, and are most commonly seen in homes and offices. Figure 2.21 shows Compaq personal computer, one of the popular computers in this class. Microcomputers can be relatively stationary desktop models or portable, notebook-sized computers that weigh about five pounds or less. High-end microcomputers can cost more than $10,000 and rival the power and speed of low-end workstations. These types of microcomputers are often used as network and Web servers. In the last few years, the popularity of microcomputers has exploded. Within organizations, microcomputers are the most commonly used computing technology for knowledge workers and are becoming almost as commonplace as the telephone. For individuals and families, more microcomputers than televisions are now sold in the United States each year. Clearly, the computer revolution was motivated by the microcomputer. Given the huge impact microcomputers have had on business and society, let's delve a bit deeper into the development and types of microcomputers for a moment.

FIGURE 2.21

The Compaq Presario 4240ES.

©1998 Compaq Computer Corporation

Apple Macintosh

From a computer hardware perspective, the microcomputer revolution was led by two firms: Apple and IBM. In 1984, Apple Computer developed the Macintosh (The "Mac," shown in Figure 2.22), which pioneered the idea of making computers easy to use through the use of a graphical user interface (GUI). Users no longer had to remember special words and commands to use the computer. GUI allowed them to see pictures and text and to choose their options with a mouse rather than typing those options with a keyboard. The GUI made the Macintosh very popular with K–12 schools and educators, among other users.

2.22b Courtesy Apple Computer, Inc.
Photo by John Greenleigh.

2.22a Courtesy Apple Computer, Inc.

FIGURE 2.22

An original Apple Macintosh (2.22a) and a recent PowerMac (2.22b).

Apple used a proprietary hardware architecture (based on the Motorola 68000 family of microprocessors) and a proprietary software operating system in the Mac. Therefore, you could purchase hardware and operating system software only from Apple. Similarly, your Mac could only be opened up and worked on by certified repair persons. Although this strategy allowed Apple to control the price and development of its hardware and software, it was not widely supported by the microcomputer marketplace. Many people wanted lots of choices of places and vendors from whom to buy computers and software, and they wanted competition among multiple vendors to breed low prices. Consequently, Apple decided in early 1996 to license the operating system and hardware architecture to other companies. Many computer experts feel that Apple retains only a relatively small (3 percent) share in the business marketplace as a direct result of its business strategies. Only time will tell if Apple can turn around its performance.

The most dominant microcomputer architecture is based on the original IBM personal computer (or just PC), which was developed in 1981. (See Figure 2.23). The road taken by the IBM PC is quite different than that taken by the Macintosh. Unlike Apple, IBM licensed its architecture to other companies in the mid-1980s. Many companies licensed the technology and produced "IBM-compatible" products. This resulted in a great deal of competition and rapid changes in the PC marketplace, leading to a general trend of lower prices and higher performance. Consequently, the PC-based architecture dominates the microcomputer marketplace today. The two most dominant players in this market are Intel and Microsoft; Intel is a dominant player because the architecture is based on the Intel family of microprocessors. Microsoft is a dominant player because most PCs run the Microsoft Windows operating system.

FIGURE 2.23

An original IBM PC (2.23a) with a recent IBM PC (2.23b).

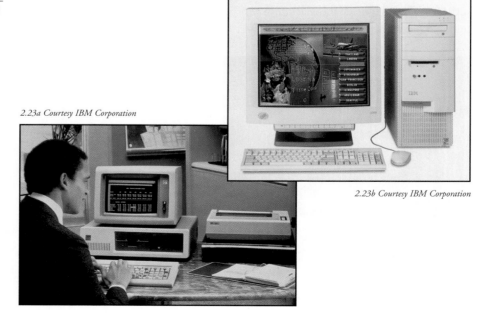

2.23a Courtesy IBM Corporation

2.23b Courtesy IBM Corporation

Apple Responds: The PowerPC

In an effort to combat the near monopoly of Intel and Microsoft in the microcomputer marketplace, old rivals Apple, IBM, and Motorola have introduced the PowerPC. The PowerPC is designed to run either the Macintosh operating system or PC-based operating systems (Apple, 1998). The Power Macintosh came to market in 1995, using the PowerPC processor and the Mac operating system. Since then, several other software vendors have made versions of their operating systems available on the PowerPC (for example, Windows NT and IBM AIX). Only time will tell if the PowerPC will have a significant impact on the microcomputer marketplace.

Portable and Handheld Computing

Two areas of the microcomputer marketplace that are rapidly taking off are portable and handheld computing. Portable computing devices, such as laptop and notebook computers, are becoming very common in business today, as shown in Figure 2.24. Many manufacturers have designed lightweight, rugged computers

©Allen McInnis/Gamma-Liaison International

FIGURE 2.24

A businesswoman using a notebook computer in the airport.

designed to travel with the businessperson either across town or around the world. These computers are equipped with flat display, and the entire system weighs in at between 5 and 10 pounds! Portable computers normally use a trackball or alternative pointing device integrated into the system rather than an external mouse. As the portability and expandability of these computers increases, many executives are choosing single, high-performance portable computers as their only PC rather than having both a desktop and a portable computer (see Table 2.9).

Table 2.9 Desktop versus portable computer tradeoffs.

Desktop Computer	Portable Computer
One location for use	Mobile—any location for use
Lower price	Higher price
Expandable	Very limited expandability
Better ergonomics—full size/high resolution color screen, large keyboard, and so on	Cramped ergonomics—small screen, limited color quality, small keyboard, awkward pointing device, and so on
Relatively easy to service/repair	Hard to service/repair

Handheld computers are very lightweight, ranging from about the size of a small calculator to the size of large billfold-style wallet. They function as electronic organizers, electronic mail readers, and monitors for remote systems. The Apple Newton, shown in Figure 2.25, is an example of a handheld computer. As the circuitry of microprocessors continues to shrink and their performance increases, more extremely lightweight and compact computers will be developed.

FIGURE 2.25

Apple Newton.

Courtesy Apple Computer, Inc. Photo by Frank Pryor.

Portable and handheld technologies are becoming very broadly used by organizational "road warriors," who spend days on the road, and by telecommuters, who work remotely from home. For example, portable computers can be equipped with a high-speed fax/modem linked via cellular phone to a central information bank. Such a configuration allows re-mote personnel to easily share information with the organization, customers, suppliers, and other relevant parties. These technologies have allowed organizations to distribute personnel around the world more easily and for less expense. In fact, many believe that mobile technologies are prompting a radical change in our conception of an office or of going to work. We now have the *virtual office*. It is likely that microcomputer technology will continue to influence what we do and how we do it for a long, long time.

Evolution of Information Systems Hardware

Over the last 50 years, information systems hardware has gone through many radical changes. In the World War II era, almost all business and government information systems consisted of file folders, filing cabinets, and document repositories. Huge rooms were dedicated to the storage of these records. After it was stored, information was often difficult to find, and corporate knowledge and history were difficult to maintain. Most information was known only by certain employees. If or when these employees left the firm, so did all the corporate knowledge. Needless to say, management and organizations needed a better way to keep track of information.

The solution to the information storage and retrieval problems facing organizations of the 1940s has been the modern digital computer. As briefly discussed in Chapter 1, computers have gone through many changes over the past 50 years. We described the evolution of computing eras and the dominant technology of each era. Shifts in computing eras were facilitated by fundamental changes in the way computing technologies worked. Each of these fundamental changes is referred to as a distinct generation of computing (see Table 2.10). In the sections that follow, we describe each of these generations.

Table 2.10 Generations of computing (Freed, 1995).

Generation	Defining Event	Computing Era	Major Characteristics/Events
1 (1946–1958)	Vacuum tubes	Mainframe era begins	ENIAC and UNIVAC were developed
2 (1958–1964)	Transistors	Mainframe era continues	UNIVAC was updated to use transistors
3 (1964–1990s)	Integrated circuits	Mainframe era ends; Minicomputer era begins and ends; Personal computer era begins	IBM 360—integrated circuits and general-purpose operating system; Microprocessor revolution: Intel, Apple Macintosh, IBM PC, MS-DOS
4 (1990s–present)	Multimedia	Personal computer era ends; Interpersonal computing era begins; Internetworking era begins	High-speed microprocessor and networks; High-capacity secondary storage; Low cost/ high performance integrating video, audio, and data

Source Freed, L. 1995. The history of computing. *Emeryville, CA: Ziff-Davis Press.*

The First Generation: Vacuum Tubes

Developed in 1946, the ENIAC was one of the first computers. It was the size of a room, and it had more than 18,000 vacuum tubes, as shown in Figure 2.26. ENIAC could perform approximately 5,000 additions or 500 multiplications in a minute, which was a huge accomplishment for the time. However, it was replaced by the UNIVAC from Sperry Corporation in 1950. UNIVAC also used vacuum tubes, and it, too, filled a large room. In order to operate, these computers needed to be kept in cool, air-conditioned rooms. If they got too hot, they would break. Some computers during this era were even water-cooled, as is a radiator in an automobile engine, in an attempt to help solve this overheating problem. In 1956, IBM invented the first magnetic disk storage to help replace tape storage devices.

FIGURE 2.26

ENIAC and a vacuum tube.

Courtesy Corbis-Bettman

Courtesy Corbis-Bettman

The Second Generation: Transistors

By 1958, the UNIVAC was being produced with transistors instead of vacuum tubes. Transistors generated less heat, were much smaller, worked faster, and were much more reliable than vacuum tubes. These first transistors were each slightly smaller than a dime. Today's computers also use transistor technology, but now there are several million transistors in a single microprocessor—which is itself just larger than a dime. The performance of UNIVAC by 1958 was significantly greater than that of first-generation machines, performing thousands of operations in a second.

The Third Generation: Integrated Circuits

In 1964, the IBM 360 (shown in Figure 2.27) used integrated circuits (IC) for the first time, as well as the first general-purpose operating system. These circuits were called integrated circuits because each IC, or chip, had multiple transistors on it. The development of ICs was a major breakthrough in speed and reliability. A general-purpose operating system allowed computers to be more easily programmed and to therefore more easily shift from one application to another. Prior to this point, computers were configured to run one application at a time. When a new application was desired, the computer had to be significantly reconfigured, often taking many hours, if not days. In short, operating systems transformed computers from *special-purpose* to *general-purpose* machines. During this period of time (1963, to be exact), DEC produced the PDP-5 line of minicomputers, which would be a staple in business computing for the next 20 years.

FIGURE 2.27

An IBM 360.

Courtesy IBM Archives

The next major IS hardware event occurred in 1971, when Intel developed the Intel 4004, the world's first microprocessor. Desktop computing could now be a reality. In 1975, the Altair 8800 was introduced as the first microcomputer. Two Harvard students, William Gates and Paul Allen, founded Microsoft when they wrote a version of the BASIC computing language for the Altair 8800. In 1976, Steve Jobs and Steve Wozniak built the first Apple computer in their garage. Together, they founded Apple Computers. Just five years later, in 1981, two events occurred that have profoundly influenced the development of computing ever since. First, IBM introduced the PC. Second, Microsoft acquired the rights to an operating system called Q-DOS from a small computer manufacturer, Seattle Computer Products. Within a short period of time, Q-DOS became PC-DOS. And the rest is history. In 1987, Microsoft wrote Windows 1.0 for the PC, and in 1989 Intel created the 486 processor. By the time Intel announced the Pentium processor in 1993, the "Wintel" (Windows/Intel) dynasty was off and running.

The third generation has evolved rapidly, as summarized in Table 2.11. The processors of 1995 are approximately 5,000 times faster than their 1971 counterparts. An analogy of the rapid evolution of computer performance as it relates to automobiles has been widely circulated on Internet bulletin boards and discussion groups. This analogy states that "if automotive technology had kept pace with computer technology over the past few decades, you would now be driving a car with a top speed of 10,000 miles per hour, that would weigh about 30 pounds, and would travel a thousand miles on a gallon of gas. Additionally, the sticker price of this car would be less than $50" (Anonymous). In response to all this goading, Detroit grumbles: "Yes, but would you really want to drive a car that crashes twice a day?" (Anonymous). Nonetheless, the evolution in computing is remarkable.

Table 2.11   Comparison of Intel CPU microprocessors (Intel, 1998).

Processor	Initial Year	Data Width	Number of Transistors	Clock Speed	Addressable Memory	MIPS
4004	1971	4bits	2,300	108KHz	640bytes	0.06
8088	1979	8bits	29,000	5–8MHz	1MB	0.33–.075
80286	1982	16bits	134,000	6–12MHz	16MB	0.9–2.66
80386	1985	32bits	275,000–855,000	20–33MHz	4GB	5–11.4
80486	1989	32bits	1.2–1.6 million	16–100MHz	4GB	13–70.7
Pentium	1993	64bits	2.1 million	60–166MHz	4GB	70.4–250
Pentium Pro	1995	64bits	5.5 million	150–300MHz	64GB	250–500
Pentium II	1997	64bits	7.5 million	233–400MHz	64GB	400

The data width roughly reflects the number of bits that can be manipulated by the CPU at one time (more is better). The clock speed of a computer is measured in hertz (Hz), which is similar to the revolutions per minute (RPM) within automobile engines. One cycle per second is therefore 1Hz; KHz=kilohertz (thousands of cycles); MHz= Megahertz (millions of cycles). Again, more is better. Addressable memory refers to how much RAM the CPU can effectively read and write to. As is often the case with computers, more is better.

The Fourth Generation and Beyond

Experts disagree over whether we are now in the third or fourth generation of computing hardware because integrated circuits are still the primary component of today's computers. Some experts feel that the microcomputer revolution that is currently occurring marks the beginning of the fourth generation of computing. In the fourth generation, radically new applications are being developed. One important development is multimedia, which is the integration of voice, video, and data in a standard microcomputer. Apple's HyperCard, introduced in 1987, was the first application to integrate voice, video, and data. Over the past few years, the use of CD-ROMs and faster CPUs has allowed developers to create and distribute multimedia applications. Doing so was not possible before, due to the large storage and processing requirements of video and sound data. Another multimedia application that is gaining popularity is interactive, desktop videoconferencing, as shown in Figure 2.28. Videoconferencing is becoming widely available through the use of the Internet. Software such as Cornell's CuSeeMe, low-cost video cameras, high-speed modems, and other network connections are freely available on the Internet. Currently, less than 5 percent of large businesses use desktop videoconferencing as a standard communication option for their employees. It is predicted, however, that this figure will increase to 15 percent by the year 2000 (Intel, 1998).

FIGURE 2.28

People using a desktop video-conferencing system.

©*Jon Feingersh/The Stock Market*

Computing technology is getting much faster, much smaller, much easier to use with a broader range of applications, and, most importantly, much less expensive. This evolution has had several implications for organizational computing. First, the end users of information are now empowered to do their own computing, called *end-user computing*. Individuals in organizations no longer have to wait for someone else to provide a report or to analyze some data. People are empowered to solve their own informational problems. Due to this empowerment, the IS department in many organizations no longer has to attend to the day-to-day computing needs of knowledge workers. This empowerment has thus freed up the IS staff in many organizations, enabling them to focus on broader, more strategic applications of technology. Individuals and families have also been empowered to buy their own computers. You can use your PC to write letters, analyze finances, surf the Web, and communicate with your friends and loved ones around the world. The concept of owning your own high-performance computer was unthinkable less than 30 years ago.

The evolution of computer-based technology has progressed from large, slow, unreliable machines—known as the "big iron"—to small, fast machines that can sit on every desktop. The most interesting aspect of this evolution of smaller, faster, cheaper technology is that most experts feel that it will continue. Given how much the computer hardware has evolved over the past 50 years, it is hard to imagine what will occur over the next 50 years. Hang on for the ride!

The Future of Information System Hardware

In this final section, we briefly look ahead at the future of information systems hardware. This discussion of future technology issues could be a book in itself, but we will limit our comments to just a few key issues. We can make one easy prediction about the future of information systems hardware: Computer technologies will continue to become smaller, faster, cheaper, and more pervasive.

—— Moore's Law: Smaller, Faster, Cheaper for How —— Much Longer?

A BRIEF CASE

The general trend in computing is for smaller, faster, and cheaper devices. But for how long can this trend continue? In the 1970s, Dr. Gordon Moore, then a researcher at Intel, hypothesized that computer-processing performance would double every 18 months. When Moore made this prediction, he did not limit it to any specified period of time. This bold prediction became known as "Moore's Law." Interestingly, Dr. Moore has been basically correct so far. Feature size—the size of lines on the chip through which signals pass—has been reduced from about the width of a human hair in the 1960s (20 microns—a micron is equal to one millionth of a meter), to the size of a bacterium in the 1970s (5 microns), to smaller than a virus today (.35 micron—the size of the feature width on an Intel Pentium Pro). Figure 2.29 shows this trend.

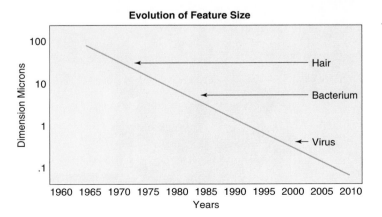

FIGURE 2.29

Shrinking feature size.

Reductions in feature size are the key determinant of processing performance, and each reduction in feature size leads to an equivalent increase in performance. At some point, however, the physical limits of miniaturization on silicon will be reached. In fact, until recently, many felt that Moore's prediction was in some jeopardy. Recent advances by researchers at IBM and Texas Instruments have resulted in the development of a feature width of .18 micron, however (*Scientific American*, August 1996). Experts believe this breakthrough will power the continued evolution of smaller, faster, and cheaper technology well into the 21st century.

With the continued improvements in computer chip technology, all kinds of innovative computers and computer uses are made possible and feasible. Read on to learn more about three specific applications—virtual reality, wearable computing, and smart cards—that are now available and are likely to become more pervasive in the near future.

Virtual Reality

Virtual reality (VR) uses computer programs, along with specialized viewing devices, to give users the impression that they are in an alternative world that is created by the computer. In this world, three-dimensional graphics, sound, and touch are being simulated. The goal of VR research is to develop computer-based environments that simulate **all** human senses—touch, smell, and hearing, and so on (see Figure 2.30). VR is applied in many ways other than the obvious applications for games and entertainment. The military uses VR to simulate combat conditions for troops and pilots—without risk to people or machines. In fact, the U.S. Marine Corps has modified the popular interactive game DOOM and adapted it to their own weapons, locations, and tactics for training. Doctors are using VR to simulate new procedures before trying them on humans. The U.S. Department of Energy in Richland/Hanford, Washington, uses VR to train workers who will be working in radioactive areas. Through VR technology, workers can be trained to maintain equipment in a realistic setting without being exposed to radioactivity. Many feel that the application of VR technologies is limitless and will be one of the hottest technology areas in the 21st century and beyond.

FIGURE 2.30

VR headgear.

©*Seth Resnick/Gamma-Liaison International*

Wearable Computing

Related to VR is wearable computing. Researchers at the Massachusetts Institute of Technology (MIT) are experimenting with computers that are strapped to people, like a tool belt, and used for processing information remotely. For example, it is envisioned that cellular telephones will soon be the size of wristwatches—in fact, the ability to make cellular calls will be a feature of your wristwatch! Voice commands for dialing will replace keypads. Others believe that special computers can be embedded on clothing to act as sensors and monitors, which would potentially be very useful for the elderly and individuals with physical or mental limitations. Business executives could have a computer in their pocket monitoring day-to-day events, keeping a calendar, and providing automatic and dynamic reminders of upcoming events and meetings. One researcher at MIT, Steve Mann, attaches a camera to his head and a computer to his side. He transmits images in real-time over a wireless network to his World Wide Web page to better understand how wearable computing might work and be used. (Curious? Visit Steve at http://www.mit.edu.)

Smart Cards

A more down-to-earth application of technology that is quickly coming down the track is the use of smart cards. Used already in many European countries, smart cards are a special type of credit card that has a small microprocessor and memory embedded into it. One smart card could serve as personal identification, credit card, automated teller machine (ATM) card, telephone credit card, transit pass, carrier of crucial medical information and insurance, and so on. The beauty of a smart card is that you would need only one card. This one card could substitute for all the credit and ID cards that currently fill your wallet or purse. Additionally, because of the technology embedded in the card, smart cards are much more resistant to tampering than current credit cards with magnetic strips. Most importantly, smart cards have large storage capacities, so they can engage in a sequence of questions with the holder to verify the validity of information and the identity of the card holder.

Talking with...

Marilyn McCoy Franklin, Senior Systems Engineer at Advanced Hardware Architecture, Inc.

Educational Background

B.S. in Zoology and B.S. in Computer Science, University of Idaho

Job Description

Ms. Franklin's main job is to design behavioral system environments for the integrated circuits (ICs) and to simulate and verify the IC design in this system. This involves modeling peripheral interface chips that talk to the IC, such as SCSI chips, DRAMs, microprocessors, and so on. After designing the IC and the chips interfacing it, she simulates the customer's environment

Bill Watts, Hot Shots Photography © 1998.

to verify that the chip functions as specified. This is all done in the software before the chip is fabricated. By thoroughly testing chips in this manner, she ensures that a high percentage of the chips work as specified straight from the fabricator, preventing costly returns.

Critical Success Factors

To be successful, you need to enjoy what you do. If you enjoy what you do, you'll have the drive to do your job well. It's also important that you can work well with others in a team environment. How others perceive you can greatly affect your career success. You also need to be flexible. Job requirements and needs can change drastically in engineering in order to keep up with the current technology.

Advice to Students

Be practical rather than idealistic in choosing a career. Can the career you've chosen support you? How hard is it to find a job in that field now and in the future? Any practical knowledge you can gain prior to graduating will ensure you a better chance of getting a job. Be aggressive in trying to find relevant jobs for your career prior to graduating because it can make a big difference in how employers perceive you. Especially good are the summer intern jobs.

Summary

1. **Understand the important role of information systems hardware in the success of modern organizations.** Nearly every modern organization uses computer-based information systems as a key enabler for their competitive strategy and many day-to-day activities. Computer-based information systems allow for the high-speed capturing, processing, storage, and routing of information to the appropriate decision maker. These capabilities allow organizations to more easily and more rapidly do business in our increasingly global economy.

2. **Describe key elements of information systems hardware.** Information systems hardware is classified into three types: input, process, and output technologies. Input-related hardware consists of devices used to enter information into a computer. Process-related hardware focuses on transforming inputs into outputs. The central processing unit (CPU) is the device that performs this transformation with the help of several other closely related devices that store and recall information. Finally, output-related hardware focuses on delivering information in a usable format to users.

3. **List and describe the types of computers that are being used in organizations today.** Computers come in all shapes, sizes, degrees of power, and costs. The five general classes of computers are supercomputer, mainframe, minicomputer, workstation, and microcomputer. A supercomputer is the most expensive and most powerful category of computers; it is primarily used to assist in solving massive research and scientific problems. A mainframe is a very large computer that is the main, central computing system for major corporations and governmental agencies. A minicomputer is a computer with a lower performance than mainframes but a higher performance than microcomputers. Minicomputers are typically used for engineering and mid-sized business applications. A workstation is a very high-performance microcomputer, typically used to support individual engineers and analysts in solving highly computational problems. A microcomputer is used for personal computing, small business computing, and as a workstation attached to large computers or to other small computers on a network.

4. **Explain how hardware has evolved and where it is headed.** Over the last 50 years, information systems hardware has gone through four distinct generations. The first generation of computing used vacuum tubes; during this period, computers were very slow and unreliable. The second generation of computing used transistors; during this period, computers became faster and significantly more reliable. The third generation of computing used integrated circuits or chips; during this period, computers became very powerful, much smaller, and much less expensive. The defining event for the current generation of computing, the fourth generation, is multimedia—the integration of video, audio, and data.

Key Terms

Keyboard

Repetitive stress injuries

Pointing devices

Mouse

Trackball

Joystick

Touch screen

Light pen

Batch input

Scanners

Text recognition software

Bar code/optical character reader

Audio input

Video input

Bit

Byte

ASCII

Primary storage

ROM—read-only memory

RAM—random-access memory

Cache memory

Secondary storage

Magnetic tape

Sequential data access

Floppy disks

Direct data access

Fixed disks

CD-ROM

Optical disks

CPU

Monitors

Plotter

Dot-matrix printers

Inkjet printers

Laser printers

Supercomputers

Mainframes

Minicomputers

Workstations

Microcomputers

Review Questions

1. Describe the four different categories of information that can be input into a computer.

2. What causes repetitive stress injuries?

3. How are bits and bytes related?

4. How do a computer's primary storage, secondary storage, ROM, and RAM interact?

5. Describe the differences between sequential data access and direct data access.

6. Compare and contrast the five different methods of secondary data storage.

7. What are the common measurements of a computer's processing speed?

8. Compare and contrast the five computer types presented in this chapter. How do they differ in size, memory, speed, cost, target users, and so on?

9. Summarize the history of the microcomputer from the perspective of Apple and IBM.

10. What role has Microsoft played in the evolution of information systems hardware?

11. Describe some of the emerging areas of information systems hardware for the 21st century.

Problems and Exercises

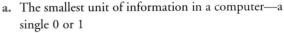

Individual   **Group**   **Field**   **Web/Internet**

1. Match the following terms to the appropriate definitions:

   _____ Trackball

   _____ Batch input

   _____ Bit

   _____ ROM

   _____ Cache memory

   _____ Sequential data access

   _____ Plotter

   _____ Workstation

a. The smallest unit of information in a computer—a single 0 or 1

b. A category of computer, based on a very high-performance microcomputer, that is typically used to support individual engineers and analysts in solving highly computational problems

c. A data access method in which information is accessed and stored in a sequence

d. A type of pointing device that works by rolling a ball that sits in a holder; selections are made by pressing buttons located near or on the holder

e. A type of primary memory that you cannot erase or add to—you can only read information from it

f. A paper-based output device that uses pens to draw information onto paper

g. A type of data input in which you enter a "batch" of information at one time

h. A type of primary memory that the CPU uses to store information it uses a lot

2. Imagine that you have decided it is time to purchase a new computer. Analyze your purchase options with regard to using this computer for personal productivity versus business productivity. What differences might your potential usage make on your hardware choices? Why?

3. Imagine that you have just informed your supervisor that you will need to purchase new computers for yourself and three fellow employees. Your supervisor states that she has heard in the news that computer prices are dropping constantly, and she feels that you should wait a bit before making this purchase. She adds that you can still be 100 percent effective with your current computer and software. Develop a counterargument explaining why you should make the purchase now instead of waiting. Will this be a hard sell? Why or why not?

4. In a small group of fellow classmates, explain why employers need to be concerned about repetitive stress injuries. How do these injuries affect productivity? How do they affect morale? Have any of the group members suffered from repetitive stress injuries?

5. Many people have a mental image of a joystick being good only for game playing. Provide reasons and examples to convince them that joysticks are a legitimate input device for modern computers. How are joysticks different from a mouse or a trackball?

6. What happens when a computer runs out of RAM? Can more RAM be added? Is there a limit? How does cache memory relate to RAM? Why is RAM so important in today's modern information systems world? Search the World Wide Web for RAM retailers. Compare their prices and options.

7. Do you feel that floppy disks will go the way of the dodo bird or the 8-track player sometime in the near future? Why or why not? How do your classmates feel? Support your reasoning with examples or scenarios and provide a summary for the rest of the class.

8. Back in the 1970s, today's microcomputer would have had enough computing power to send a rocket to the moon. Now, these microcomputers seem to be outdating themselves every two years. Will this era of continuous improvement end? When will it end, if it does? Why or why not?

9. Within a small group of classmates, discuss the implications of having more than one type of hardware platform within an organization. What might be the advantages? What are some of the disadvantages? Would your group recommend such a situation?

10. Interview an IS Manager within an organization that you are familiar with. Determine what issues played a role in the latest information systems hardware purchase this person made. How is the real world different, if at all, from the descriptions in the chapter?

11. Based on your experiences with different input devices, which do you like the best? Why? Which do you like the least? Why? How do your fellow classmates rate these and other input devices? Are their preferences due to the devices' design or usability, or are they based on the integration of the device with the entire information system?

12. The end of the chapter provides information on three possible products for the future. Of the three, which one(s) has had the most coverage in the popular press? Why do you think this is so? Which do you feel will have the broadest implementation the soonest? Why?

13. Choose an organization with which you are familiar that utilizes several different types of computers. Which types do they use? Which of the five categories of computers are being used at this company? Are there any plans to expand their computer usage to another category? Why or why not?

14. In simple language, explain what happens with the keystrokes that you type into a computer using a keyboard. Be sure to discuss memory, processing, and inputs. Draw any diagrams that may help you with this explanation.

15. In a small group, describe your experiences with IBM-compatible and Macintosh computers. Which did you use first? What about the others in the group? Which do you use now? If you have changed, why? What influences your computer-purchasing decisions?

16. As a group, choose a few of the computer hardware vendors—as illustrated in the scenario at the beginning of the chapter—that sell computers to the general public. These include Dell, Compaq, IBM, Gateway, Apple, and Packard Bell. Using their home pages, determine what options these vendors provide for input devices, processing devices, and output devices. Does it seem that this company has a broad range of choices for their customers? Is there something that you did not find available from this company? Present your findings in a 10-minute presentation to the rest of the class.

Real World Case Problems

1. Power Play: How the Compaq-Digital Deal Will Reshape the Entire World of Computers

Since coming to Compaq six years ago, CEO Eckhard Pfeiffer has regularly sent shockwaves through the PC business. In 1992, he forced competitors to react quickly or lose business by slashing PC prices by 32 percent. Last year, he again slashed prices, announcing a line of home computers priced below $1,000. On January 26, 1998, Pfeiffer created another shakeup—reaching every corner of the $700-billion computer world—by announcing that he and Digital CEO Robert Palmer had concluded four days of negotiations, with the outcome being a record-breaking $8.7-billion acquisition. The deal was the largest in computer industry history, creating a computer giant of $37.5 billion in revenues, second only to IBM in computer sales.

This acquisition has propelled Compaq from the upstart, wild, woolly PC generation into the high-tech big-league companies that supply the world's most complex and critical information systems. Compaq now has the ability to sell everything, from $649 handheld computers to super-powerful $2-million fail-safe computer servers. In addition, Compaq has the use of Digital's 22,000-strong service and consulting staff.

Compaq's timing was strategic. Customers are now changing from mainframes to powerful servers that are tied to banks of PCs and buying new equipment to help fend off problems caused by the year 2000. Compaq now has the ability to offer solutions to low-cost, powerful, computing systems and has the staff to install and maintain the systems. They have the ability to deliver low-cost PC economics into the high-end computing markets that were previously dominated by IBM, Hewlett-Packard, and Sun Microsystems. Compaq spends $.15 for every $1 in sales, compared to $.24 and $.27 for Hewlett-Packard and IBM, respectively. Even Dell Computer Corporation and Gateway 2000 can no longer assume business as usual. Compaq increased the stakes by adding service and support.

Compaq, the largest seller of Windows software and Intel chips, may now be on a par with Microsoft Corporation and Intel Corporation in setting the agenda. Eighty-seven percent of PCs run Windows and 89 percent use Intel's processor, called Wintel. These three companies now have the ability to handle complex computing jobs, from financial databases to inventory management. In the past, customers were attracted to Compaq's low pricing but would often use a service provider such as Digital. They now have the best of both worlds.

a. Was it a good idea for Compaq to acquire Digital? Why or why not?

b. If you were at the helm of IBM, what would your next move be? What if you were at the helm of Microsoft?

c. To rephrase the title of the article, "How will the Compaq-Digital deal reshape the entire world of computers?" What's your forecast?

Source   1998. *Power Play: How the Compaq-Digital deal will reshape the entire world of computers,* BusinessWeek, *February 9, 91–97.*

2. Let's Talk! Speech Technology Is the Next Big Thing in Computing

At IBM's T. J. Watson Research Center, excitement abounds. Scientists have been trying since the 1960s to develop a software program that can recognize what people say, and they have done so—with 95 percent accuracy. However, last summer IBM beat most of its competitors to the market with a snazzy, affordable, speech program called ViaVoice Gold. The program translates spoken sentences into text on a computer screen and lets users open Windows programs by voice command.

Already at Watson Research Center, scientists have begun to work on the next generation of voice technology, which will have a dramatic impact on how we live and work. At the center, a researcher may be testing an automated airline ticket reservation system by asking the computer for flight information. In a speech lab, a researcher may be accessing a database full of digitized CNN news clips using nothing but spoken words. Others may be accessing 3D images of molecules, cylinders, and topographic maps on a wall-sized display by motioning or speaking to images.

With these models, IBM is moving toward the dream of scientists the world over: machines that understand "natural language"—sentences as people actually speak them, unconstrained by special vocabulary or context. Previously, start-up companies have sold specialized speech-recognition programs, but these programs had small vocabularies, required speaker training, and demanded unnatural pauses between words. MIT, Carnegie Mellon, SRI, and Lucent Technologies are also racing to get their products out to industry.

Speech may very well be the bridge between humans and technology. Few people enjoy mouse-clicking through Internet sites, memorizing commands, or searching files that are hardly ever used. In addition to being tedious, these kinds of processes are not open to those who lack digital skills or education. "Speech is not just the future of Windows, but the future of computing itself," states Microsoft CEO, Bill Gates.

a. What are some of the useful applications of systems employing natural language capabilities?

b. Will people be willing to use these systems, or will they prefer traditional methods of inputting data into computers?

c. What are some tasks and/or situations in which systems using natural languages just don't make sense?

Source   1998. *Let's talk! Speech technology is the next big thing in computing,* BusinessWeek, *February 23, 61–72.*

References

Apple, 1998. Information from: www.apple.com. Verified: January 28, 1998.

Cray Research, 1998. Information from: www.cray.com. Verified: January 8, 1998.

Datamation, 1996. Videoconferencing to take off, May 1. Information from: www.datamation.com. Verified: January 29, 1998.

Freed, L. 1995. *The history of computing.* Emeryville, CA: Ziff-Davis Press.

IBM, 1998. Information from: www.ibm.com. Verified: January 29, 1998.

Intel, 1998. Information from: www.intel.com. Verified: January 29, 1998.

Related Readings

Amini, M.M., and R.E. Schooley. 1993. Supercomputing in corporate America. *Information and Management* 24(6): 291–303.

Bailey, D.H. 1997. Onward to Petaflops computing. *Communications of the ACM* 40(6): 90–92.

Briggs, Dennis, Beck, and Nunamaker. 1993. Whither the pen-based interface? *Journal of Management Information Systems* 9(3): 71–90.

Burgess, Ullah, Van Overen, and Ogden. 1994. The PowerPC 603 microprocessor. *Communications of the ACM* 37(6): 34–42.

Coll, Zia, and Coll. 1994. A comparison of three computer cursor control devices: Pen on horizontal tablet, mouse and keyboard. *Information and Management* 27(6): 329–339.

Harris, A.L., and D.S. Dave. 1994. Effects of computer system components on the price of notebook computers. *Information and Management* 27(3): 151–160.

Hillis, W.D., and L.W. Tucker. 1993. The CM-5 connection machine: A scalable supercomputer. *Communications of the ACM* 36(11): 30–40.

Kennedy, Bender, Connolly, Hennessy, Vernon, and Smarr. 1997. A nationwide parallel computing environment. *Communications of the ACM* 40(11): 62–72.

Khanna, T., and M. Iansiti. 1997. Firm asymmetries and sequential R&D: Theory and evidence from the mainframe computer industry. *Management Science* 43(4): 405–421.

Moore, G.E. 1997. The microprocessor: Engine of the technology revolution. *Communications of the ACM* 40(2): 112–114.

Peak, D.A., and M.H. Azadmanesh. 1997. Centralization/decentralization cycles in computing: Market evidence. *Information and Management* 31(6): 303–317.

Peleg, Wilkie, and Weiser. 1997. Intel MMX for multimedia PCs. *Communications of the ACM* 40(1): 24–38.

Sites, R.L. 1993. Alpha AXP architecture. *Communications of the ACM* 36(2): 33–44.

Scenario: Fast Cash at an ATM

Think about how you use an Automated Teller Machine (ATM). Typically, you place your ATM card into the slot, enter your Personal Identification Number (PIN), and press the Enter button (or some other button that confirms that the number you entered is correct). You then press a button to choose to *withdraw* money and another button to choose to withdraw from your *checking* account. You then enter the amount you want to withdraw and press the Enter (or "correct") button. The ATM you are using might have a Fast Cash button, which you can press to be issued $40 or $50 immediately. You then take your cash, card, and receipt. If you were transferring money from your savings account to your checking account, the process would be just as easy, perhaps even faster. You would choose a button to *transfer* money from savings to checking, enter the amount, and confirm it. That's it!

Now think about what is happening behind the scenes when you use an ATM to get cash. Is there a teller back there shuttling your money back and forth and keeping records as you push buttons on the ATM? Hardly. Your ATM transaction generates data to tell the bank to do something with your account. For example, the machine tells the bank to check whether you have enough money in your account for it to give you cash or to transfer $100 from your savings account to your checking account. Your PIN, your request, and the balances in your checking and savings accounts are all pieces of information that serve as the raw material for your bank. As in traditional manufacturing, the raw material must be processed. The processing done in a financial institution for an ATM transaction is all information oriented. When you transfer $100 from savings to checking, the bank subtracts the $100 from your savings account and adds it to your checking account by manipulating a series of numbers associated with your bank accounts. No physical currency has been moved from one vault in the bank to another. Rather, the bank has used and manipulated information to accomplish your transaction, as shown in Figure 3.1. The bank's outputs are also information oriented. The ATM machine prints out a slip of paper showing you the date and time of your request and showing that $100 was, in fact, transferred from your savings account to your checking account. At the end of the month, your bank statement shows the ATM transaction processed earlier that month and gives you current balances on both your checking and savings accounts.

The bank services that we have just discussed—an ATM transaction and a bank statement—are forms of information. Therefore, it should not be surprising that small banks spend over double the U.S. company average of 4 percent of their budgets on information technology, and large banks may spend up to 16 percent, a total that adds up to tens of billions of dollars across the whole industry each year. Overall, about $150 billion each year is spent in the U.S. on information technology (Fishauf, 1994). At the heart of all of this information technology is software—sets of instructions that control the operations of computer hardware. In our ATM example, software instructs the ATM to ask you for your PIN number, verifies that your PIN number is correct, checks whether there is enough

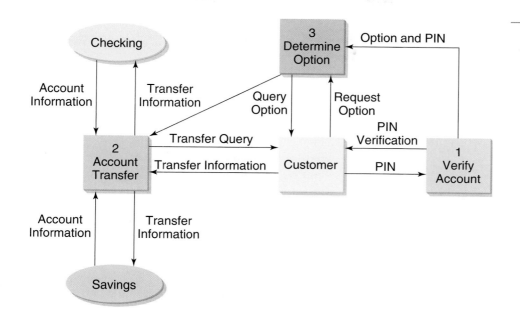

FIGURE 3.1

Data flow diagram of
account-to-account transfer.

money in your account, and so on. Software drives the entire ATM process, as it does all other information technology uses.

Companies such as your bank remain successful by providing innovative services. Increasingly, a key component in providing innovative services such as ATM machines is the use of information technologies. These advanced information technologies are always useless unless software guides the hardware to perform the desired service. In this chapter, we talk more about this essential component of information systems.

Introduction

A key component of all information systems is software. Hardware and software form a tightly coupled system; that is, hardware and software operate together to perform operations or tasks desired by users. Without software, the biggest, fastest, most powerful computer in the world is nothing more than a fancy paperweight. It relies on software to run programs, solve problems, and presentinformation to its user(s).

After reading this chapter, you will be able to do the following:

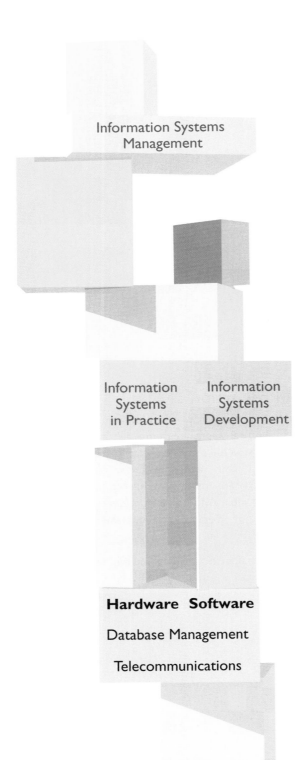

1. Understand the importance of information systems software for today's organizations.

2. Describe the common functions of systems software.

3. Explain the various types of application software.

4. Describe the characteristics of various types of programming languages.

5. Discuss the evolution of computer software.

Information technologies such as the ATM in the opening scenario are playing an increasingly larger role in our lives. Given this increasing role, it is useful to better understand information systems (IS) software. In terms of our guiding framework—The Big Picture—this is the second of four chapters focusing on the essential elements of information systems (see Figure 3.2). We begin by discussing the importance of information systems software to the success of modern organizations.

The Increasing Importance of Software to Organizations

Today's organizations rely on information systems more than ever before. This reliance is due in large part to the rapidly expanding capabilities of modern hardware and software systems, which enable organizations to process increasing amounts of information quickly, cheaply, and efficiently. For today's organizations, information systems are no longer a luxury that helps them perform their job; they are a necessity. Virtually every major company in the U.S. today has a World Wide Web site for selling products and supporting customers. Just a few short years ago, no company had a Web site. Needless to say, a lot has

FIGURE 3.2

The big picture: focusing on information systems software.

changed over the past few years. This growth and importance of information systems has been evident throughout the 1990s and is likely to increase in the 21st century.

An increasingly large percentage of the money spent on information technology is spent on software, as shown in Figure 3.3. In the 1960s, for example, computer hardware was relatively rare and therefore expensive. Software costs were only a small percentage of the costs associated with using information technology. This situation has reversed itself today. In today's business environment, it is not uncommon for software costs to exceed 75 percent of the cost of information systems. Software has become a very large investment for any organization, with most companies spending from 5 to more than 20 percent of their annual revenues on information systems.

Several trends explain this shift in technology spending. First, as outlined in the previous chapter, advances in hardware technology have allowed hardware manufacturers to produce even more capable machines at lower costs. Therefore, organizations are able to buy more computers without a large increase in their investments. In today's businesses, it is not unusual for almost every employee to have a computer (or sometimes, more than one) on his desk. Second, today's software is increasingly complex and takes more time to develop. Because of this development time, which includes updating software so that it can run efficiently on new hardware, software costs are more expensive. Finally, because of the demand for skilled programmers, salaries for those employees have increased, resulting in higher software costs. Needless to say, information systems in general, and software in particular, are big business.

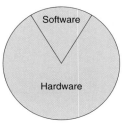

1960s–1970s

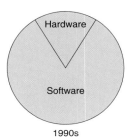

1990s

FIGURE 3.3

Shift from hardware costs exceeding software costs in the 1960s to the opposite in the 1990s.

The History of Microsoft

A BRIEF CASE

Microsoft Corporation, founded in 1975 by William H. Gates and Paul G. Allen, is today the largest software company in the world, with sales of more than $12 billion and 22,000 employees (see Figure 3.4). Table 3.1 provides a brief summary of some of the major events that have shaped Microsoft's history (Microsoft, 1998). Over the past two decades, Microsoft has outgrown five separate headquarters. The current corporate headquarters is located in Redmond, Washington—the Microsoft Corporate Campus—which has numerous interconnected buildings, giving it a university look and feel. Because of Microsoft's growth, several additional buildings seem to always be under construction. Today, Microsoft markets a broad range of products for personal computing: personal productivity tools, development tools and languages, systems software, hardware peripherals, books, and multimedia applications.

Microsoft's latest slogan is "Where do you want to go today?" This question can easily be turned back to Microsoft. In fact, they have answered their own question. Microsoft has developed their own version of a World Wide Web browser to compete with Netscape Navigator (we discuss this competition in more detail later in the chapter). In addition to Internet Explorer, Microsoft has numerous software applications for creating and manipulating Web pages. The company has forged alliances with banks and other financial institutions in order to set standards for managing digital cash. The Microsoft

FIGURE 3.4

*Microsoft employee and sales
growth (Microsoft, 1998).*

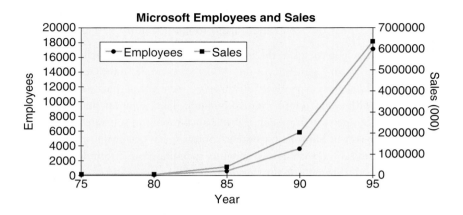

Wallet, which is now available, can be used to make purchases via the Internet without
the user having to give credit card numbers or other sensitive information. It acts as a
virtual credit card linked to real money. Microsoft is obviously continuing to develop
and explore new applications and new technologies in their never-ending desire to place
a computer on every desk. As Microsoft continues to grow and help evolve the computer industry, they will continue to turn today's important discoveries into tomorrow's
practical standards.

Table 3.1   Key events in the history of Microsoft (Microsoft, 1998).

Year	Event
1975	BASIC language interpreter developed for Altair
1981	MS-DOS and IBM PC are wed
1982	MS-DOS licenses to 50 computer hardware companies
1985	Windows 1.0 released
1990	Windows 3.0 released
1993	Windows NT released
1994	MS Office becomes number one in product category
1995	Windows 95 and Internet Explorer released
1996	MS-NBC 24-hour news, talk, and information network is established
1998	Windows 98 released

Even though software costs continue to grow, organizations should not be deterred from
this investment. Today's software is extremely capable, allowing organizations to operate
in an environment that is increasingly fast-paced and complex. In fact, software remains
one of the best investments a business can make. Software can help businesses plan and
execute their strategy. As we described in Chapter 1, "Information Systems Overview,"
companies that are able to use information systems to improve their competitive position may thrive where others fail in today's information age.

The SABRE GROUP

In an attempt to improve its position in the airline industry, American Airlines led the travel industry into the computer technology age in the late 1950s with the first true computer reservations system, the Magnetronic Reservisor. That seed grew into the Semi-Automated Business Research Environment—SABRE—in 1963. This mainframe system was able to process 84,000 telephone calls per day. Today, the system can handle over 20 million equivalent calls, which are now processed electronically. That reservation system has grown into a network of over 30,000 travel agencies, 3 million online consumers, and numerous corporations, which are all accessing real-time travel information over the Internet, 24 hours a day, 7 days a week, 52 weeks a year (see Figure 3.5).

Courtesy of The Sabre Group

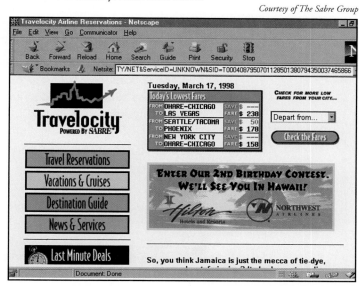

To run this massive reservation system, American Airlines built the world's largest privately owned computer system in Tulsa, Oklahoma. SABRE gave American Airlines a big competitive advantage; in fact, the airline industry argued that SABRE gave American Airlines an "unfair" competitive advantage because many travel agents used SABRE for booking flights and AA flights were often the first on the list of available flights. As a result, AA was forced to change the way the software

FIGURE 3.5

Screen from online travel system.

worked and to operate SABRE as an independent corporation, The SABRE Group, under the AA parent company, AMR Corporation. This reorganization was completed in 1996. Today, The SABRE Group owns and manages this system, as well as the next generation of systems used throughout AMR. An estimated $40 billion in travel products and services is purchased through the SABRE system each year. In October 1996, 18 percent of the equity of The SABRE Group was sold in an initial public offering that raised nearly $500 million; the remaining 82 percent of the company is under AMR control. Although no longer a part of American Airlines, SABRE is a key reason AA grew into one of the world's most successful airlines and why AMR corporation is so profitable (for more information, see SABRE, 1998).

Companies can also take advantage of systems and software *internally*. That is, they can use software to help them re-engineer or rightsize the organization. For example, consulting companies often use one type of software, groupware, to draw on common expertise in the firm. By sharing information through groupware, managers are able to access the status of projects instantly and consultants are able to be more responsive to client needs. This kind of efficiency may enable the firm to hire fewer consultants each year. Hiring fewer consultants results in fewer costs for relocating and training new personnel. Rightsizing does not have to mean that people lose their jobs. In this example, rightsizing simply means hiring fewer new people each year, while pooling expertise. This expertise is distributed throughout the company, to everyone's benefit.

New software and systems are often used to help standardize procedures and share expertise. For example, General Motors recently selected SAP R/3 (Systems, Applications, and Products in Data Processing) financial software to help manage their worldwide financial resources (SAP, 1998). Until recently, GM's four major regions of business—North America, South America, Europe, and Asia Pacific—used different financial methods and systems. Standardizing on SAP will allow information integration never before possible. Training employees to use the new software effectively is fundamental to GM's success. An added benefit of providing new skills to employees is that many find these new skills stimulating, giving them an added sense of their importance to the organization. Thus, this training leads to increased productivity.

As you can see, software can help provide innovative services and new ways to do business. However, the term "software" can often be confusing because it is used in many different ways. The next section describes different types of software and details their place in today's organizations.

Key Information Systems Software Components and Issues

Before you can understand how information systems software operates to manipulate data and instruct hardware, it is important to distinguish between "data," "information," "knowledge," and "wisdom," terms that are often erroneously used interchangeably. **Data** is raw material, recorded, unformatted information—such as words and numbers. Data has no meaning in and of itself. For example, if I asked you what 465889724 meant or stood for, you could not tell me. However, if I presented the same data as 465-88-9724 and told you it was located in a certain database, in John Doe's file, in a field labeled "SSN," you might rightly surmise that the number was actually someone named John Doe's social security number.

Data formatted with dashes or labels is more useful. It is transformed into **information**, which can be defined as a representation of reality. In the previous example, 465-88-9724 was used to represent and identify an individual person, John Doe. Information relies on context cues, such as a particular question or label (as in the previous example) that is familiar to the recipient. Let's draw on the ATM scenario earlier in the chapter. A raw list of all the transactions at a bank's ATM machines over the course of a month would be fairly useless *data*. However, a table that divided ATM machine users into two categories—bank customers and non–bank customers—and compared the two groups' use of the machine—such as, their purpose for using the ATM machines and the times and days on which they use them—would be incredibly useful *information*. A bank manager could use this information to recruit new customers.

Knowledge is needed to understand relationships between different pieces of information. For example, you must have knowledge to be aware that each individual only has one social security number and can be uniquely identified by that social security number. Knowledge represents some form of accumulated information. It is a body of governing procedures, such as guidelines or rules, that are used to organize or manipulate data in order to make it suitable for a given task.

Finally, **wisdom** can be thought of as accumulated knowledge. Wisdom goes beyond knowledge in that it represents broader, more generalized rules and schemas for understanding a specific domain or domains. Wisdom allows you to apply concepts across different types of problems or understand how to apply concepts from one domain to new situations. Understanding that a unique individual identifier, such as a social security number, can be applied in certain programming situations to single out an individual record in a database is the result of accumulated knowledge. Wisdom can be gained though academic study, personal experience, or, ideally, both.

Understanding the distinctions between data, information, knowledge, and wisdom is important because all are used in the study, development, and use of information systems—information systems software in particular. Information systems **software** can be defined as a program or set of programs that controls the operation of computer hardware, along with any documentation that accompanies that program. A program is simply a set of coded instructions that are read and executed by a computer. **Computer programs**, which are written in programming languages, direct the hardware circuitry to operate in a predefined way. **Documentation**, the set of books and/or instructions that accompanies the computer program, is designed to assist the user in successfully operating the computer program. Documentation often includes instructions for how to install and operate the program, as well as troubleshooting tips for common problems. Traditionally, documentation has been provided in the form of books and manuals. However, software companies are increasingly including online documentation— electronic documentation embedded within the program itself—in addition to or sometimes as an alternative to more traditional, external forms.

The two basic types of information systems software are systems software and application software. In the next section, we discuss systems software and how it supports the overall operation of the computer hardware.

Systems Software

Systems software is the collection of programs that forms the foundation for the basic operations of the computer hardware. Systems software, or the **operating system**, as it is sometimes called, performs and coordinates the interaction between hardware devices (for example, the CPU and the monitor), peripherals (for example, printers), and application software (for example, a word processing program), as shown in Figure 3.6.

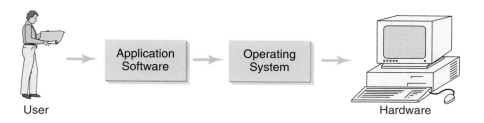

User → Application Software → Operating System → Hardware

FIGURE 3.6

Operating systems coordinate the interaction between users, application software, and hardware.

Operating systems are generally written in assembly language, a very low-level computer programming language that allows the computer to operate as quickly and efficiently as possible. The operating system is designed to insulate you from this low-level language and make computer operations as unobtrusive as possible. Essentially, the operating system performs all of the day-to-day (and nanosecond to nanosecond!) operations that we often take for granted when operating a computer. Just as our brain and nervous system control our bodies' breathing, heartbeat, and senses without our conscious realization, the systems software controls the computer's basic operations transparently.

Common Systems Software Functions

Many tasks are common to almost all computers. These include getting input from a keyboard or mouse, reading and/or writing data from a storage device (such as a hard disk drive), and presenting information to you via a monitor. Each of these tasks is performed by the operating system, just as a manager of a firm oversees people and processes (as depicted in Figure 3.7).

FIGURE 3.7

A manager (OS) overseeing the operations of many different departments: file management, disk management, and peripherals.

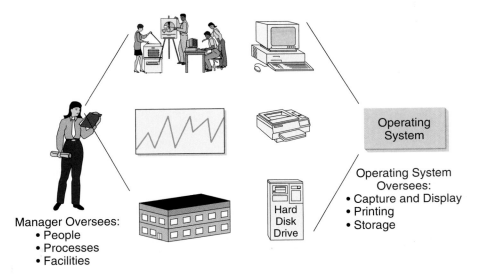

Manager Oversees:
• People
• Processes
• Facilities

Operating System

Operating System Oversees:
• Capture and Display
• Printing
• Storage

Hard Disk Drive

For example, let's say you want to copy a word processing file from a floppy disk onto your computer. Many of today's operating systems make this very easy for you. Using an operating system with a graphical user interface (GUI), such as Microsoft Windows, you simply drag an icon of the word processing file you want to copy onto an icon of your hard disk. With a few clicks of your mouse, the file on the floppy disk has been copied to your hard drive. Seems easy, right? Thanks to the operating system, copying the file *is* relatively easy. However, underlying the icons and simple dragging operations is a complex set of coded instructions that tells the electronic components of the computer that you are transferring a set of bits and bytes located on the floppy disk to a location on your internal hard disk. Imagine if you had to program those sets of instructions every time you wanted to copy a file from one place to another. Productivity would grind to a halt! Therefore, the operating system manages and executes these types of system operations so that you can spend your time on more important tasks.

The operating system performs many different tasks, including the following:

- Booting (or starting) your computer
- Reading programs into memory
- Managing memory allocation to those programs
- Managing where programs and files are located in secondary storage
- Maintaining the structure of directories and subdirectories
- Formatting disks
- Controlling the computer monitor
- Sending objects to the printer

The operating system is typically stored on disk, and a portion of it is transferred into temporary memory when the computer starts up. After the operating system is in memory, it can go about its task of managing the computer and providing an **interface** for you. It is through this interface that you interact with the computer. Many people refer to the interface as the "dialogue" between the user and the computer. One type of interface is a **command-based interface**. This type of interface requires you to type text commands into the computer to perform some basic operation. You could type the command "DELETE File1" to erase the file with the name "File1." Many mainframe computers use a command-based user interface. For example, a specific job control language (JCL) is used to control how jobs are run on large mainframe computers. MS-DOS (Microsoft–Disk Operating System) is also an example of an operating system using a command-based user interface.

Today, the most common type of interface for the PC is called a **graphical user interface** (GUI). The GUI uses pictures and icons as well as menus to send instructions back and forth from the user to the computer system. Because GUIs enable users to avoid inputting sometimes arcane commands into the computer, most people consider them easier to use and learn than other user interfaces. As a result, they are popular. Some of the benefits of GUIs are listed in the bulleted list that follows. Examples of systems software using a GUI are Windows 95 and 98, Windows NT, and the Macintosh OS. Figure 3.8, a modification of Figure 3.6, shows how the GUI links the application and systems software by presenting information to the users in a common way.

- ■ Intuitive
- ■ Consistency
- ■ Flexibility
- ■ Ease of use
- ■ Ease of learning
- ■ Undo
- ■ Linking
- ■ Embedding

FIGURE 3.8

GUI links software applications and systems software.

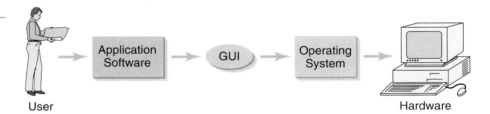

User   Hardware

Types of Operating Systems

Just as there are many kinds of computers, there are many different kinds of operating systems. In general, these operating systems—whether for large mainframe computers or for small notebook computers—perform similar operations. Obviously, large multi-user supercomputers are more complex than small desktop systems; therefore, the operating system must account for and manage that complexity. However, the basic purpose of all operating systems is the same.

> **A BRIEF CASE** ── **The Roots of MS-DOS** ──

Interestingly, some confusion has surrounded the origins of Microsoft's MS-DOS, the most widely used operating system in the history of computers. MS-DOS is arguably the product that catapulted Microsoft into the software giant it is today. When IBM decided to enter the microcomputer market with the IBM PC in the early 1980s, they needed an operating system. Because IBM's focus was on hardware, they contracted with Microsoft to deliver the operating system and some programming language compilers. Microsoft did not have an operating system, but they were aware that a small hardware company, Seattle Computer Products, had developed an operating system called Q-DOS (Quick and Dirty Operating System) that could be relatively easily modified to run on the IBM PC. This operating system was not written to run on the Intel 8088, the CPU used in the IBM PC, but for a close cousin, the Intel 8086. On July 27, 1981, Microsoft purchased Q-DOS and turned it into MS-DOS with the help of the original author of the software, former Seattle Computer engineer, Tim Patterson. The purchase price for Q-DOS, including sole ownership rights for it, was around $50,000! That purchase was a key reason why Microsoft has emerged as the leading producer of microcomputer software and, as a result, Bill Gates has become the richest person in the world. Sadly, Seattle Computer Products no longer exists. Tim Patterson is still an employee at Microsoft. To show that it really is a small world, Joe Valacich, one of the authors of this book, took his first job after finishing his undergraduate degree in computer science with Seattle Computer Products in 1983. At that time, Seattle Computer focused on designing and manufacturing add-on boards for the IBM PC and designing a high-performance computer system called the Gazelle. In the remainder of this section, we describe some popular operating systems.

MVS/ESA (Multiple Virtual Storage/Enterprise Systems Architecture). This is a proprietary operating system used on large IBM mainframe computers. MVS/ESA has high reliability and multilevel security for enterprise-wide systems management. It has the capability to effectively support massive transactions.

UNIX. This is a multi-user, multitasking operating system that is available for a wide variety of computer platforms. UNIX was developed in 1969 at Bell Labs. It is an open operating system, which means that people and organizations are free to copy, modify, adapt, or write application software for it. It is most commonly found on workstation-class computers made by vendors such as Sun Microsystems, Digital Equipment Corporation, Hewlett-Packard, and Silicon Graphics, although versions of UNIX run on other hardware platforms, such as personal computers and supercomputers. Many vendors have developed their own versions of UNIX—for example, IBM's AIX and HP's HP-UX.

MS-DOS. (Microsoft–Disk Operating System). This is a command-based operating system used on IBM-compatible PCs. The first version of MS-DOS was introduced in 1981, and the operating system is still being used today. However, newer GUI-based operating systems have been developed, which have replaced MS-DOS as the most common operating system found on today's PCs.

OS/2. An operating system developed by IBM for powerful PCs that was introduced in 1988. OS/2, which features a graphical shell, has many powerful functions. OS/2 can run applications written for MS-DOS, Windows, or OS/2.

Windows. Developed by Microsoft, Windows was originally simply an operating system shell designed to present a graphical interface to MS-DOS. However, newer versions of Windows, such as Windows 95 and 98, are independent, fully functional operating systems that do not require MS-DOS to operate (see Figure 3.9). Windows NT is a more industrial-strength version of Windows that is typically used for high-end computer servers and workstations in organizational networks.

Daniel Sheehan/Gamma Liaison International

FIGURE 3.9

Bill Gates and the Windows 98 introduction.

Macintosh OS. The Macintosh OS was the first commercially popular graphics-based operating system, making its debut in 1984. The Macintosh OS is used in Apple Macintosh personal computers. The graphical user interface used in the Macintosh OS was developed based on research conducted by XEROX PARC (Palo Alto Research Center) that was designed to improve the usability of computers. The Macintosh OS refined and made popular some truly unique technical breakthroughs that had been developed earlier at XEROX PARC, such as icons, menus, and the mouse. Today, the principles embodied in the Macintosh OS have been incorporated into all major GUI-based operating systems, such as Windows 95 and 98. Figure 3.10 shows how you would copy a file within three different operating systems environments: MS DOS, MS Windows, and the Macintosh.

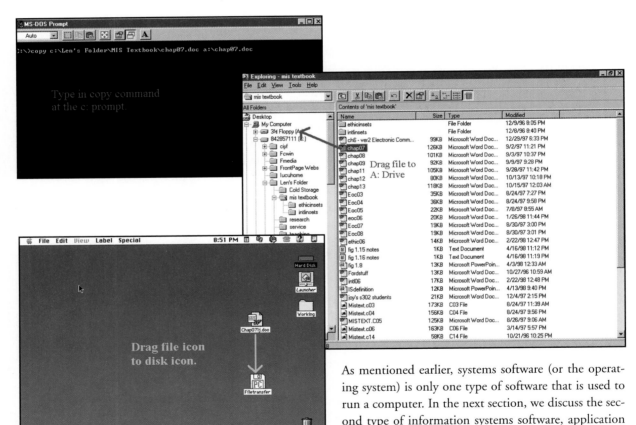

As mentioned earlier, systems software (or the operating system) is only one type of software that is used to run a computer. In the next section, we discuss the second type of information systems software, application software, that is used in today's information systems.

Application Software

FIGURE 3.10

Copying a file using different operating systems, MS-DOS, Windows, and Macintosh.

Unlike systems software, which manages the operation of the computer, **application software** performs a specific task, such as writing a business letter or manipulating a series of forecasts to come up with the most efficient allocation of resources for a project. The application program interacts with the systems software (which, in turn, interacts with the computer hardware) to accomplish the job.

- Accounts receivable
- Accounts payable
- Cash-flow analysis
- Desktop publishing
- General ledger
- Inventory control
- Order entry

- Payroll
- Purchasing
- Receiving
- Resource planning
- Shipping
- Stock and bond management
- Tax planning and preparation

The two basic types of application software are those 1) developed specifically by or for a particular organization (called customized or proprietary software) and 2) those purchased off-the-shelf, which can be used by a variety of people and/or organizations to meet their specific needs (called commercial software). These two types of software will be discussed next.

Customized Application Software

Customized application software is developed based on specifications provided by a particular organization. This software may be developed in-house by the company's own IS staff or it may be contracted, or outsourced, to a specialized vendor charged with developing the software to the company's contractual specifications. Customized application software has two primary advantages:

1. *Customizability*—Because the software is customized, it can be specifically tailored to meet unique user requirements. For example, suppose a retailer needs a kiosk in its store to help shoppers locate specific products. Many shoppers may not be familiar with computers and may be intimidated by operating a keyboard or a mouse. With customized software, the company could develop a touch screen input interface, with which users could simply point at objects in a catalog. The computer could then process this information and tell the user that, for example, women's shoes are located on the first floor in the southeast corner and provide a map of the store. The retailer-specific touch screen is one example of how customized software might be used to meet user (shopper) needs.

2. *Problem specificity*—With customized software, the company pays only for the things specifically required for its users or tasks. For example, company- or industry-specific terms or acronyms can be included in the program, as can unique types of required reports. Such specificity is not possible in off-the-shelf programs that are targeted to a general audience. This is important because customized application software can provide a good value; the user gets exactly what she needs and nothing else.

Off-the-Shelf Application Software

After reading our previous discussion, you might assume that customized application software is automatically the best way to go. This is not the case. Off-the-shelf software programs are very common in organizations today. **Off-the-shelf application software** is typically used to support common business processes that do not require any specific tailoring. Advantages of the off-the-shelf application software include the following:

1. *Lower cost*—Because off-the-shelf applications are developed for more general markets, the development company is able to distribute its development costs across a larger customer base and therefore reduce the cost for individual customers.

2. *Faster procurement*—Customized software takes a notoriously long time to develop. Because it is designed to meet specific requirements, a lengthy process of understanding specific user and task needs, programming, testing, and maintenance is required for customized applications. Off-the-shelf programming, on the other hand, can simply be purchased and installed by users.

3. *High quality*—Many off-the-shelf programs are of high quality. Software development has become a highly competitive industry; therefore, companies that produce shoddy products are often forced out of the marketplace by higher-quality competitors. In addition, developers have access to a large customer base and can ensure that their product continues to meet customer needs through continual research and testing. As customers identify flaws in the software, the company can upgrade their product to ensure that any problems are rectified for future users.

4. *Lower risk*—Developing customized software in house requires a large amount of resources (personnel, time, and financial), and this may be the first time the software application has ever been used. Therefore, you can always depend on a number of unknowns in the software's performance and in the time of its delivery. Existing off-the-shelf application software is relatively easy to evaluate through in-house testing, talking with other customers, or from software reviews in the popular and trade press.

Combining Customized and Off-the-Shelf Applications Software

It is possible in some cases to combine the advantages of customized and off-the-shelf software. In these cases, companies may be able to purchase off-the-shelf software and then modify it for their own use. For example, a retailer may want to purchase an off-the-shelf inventory management program and then modify it to account for the specific products, outlets, and reports it needs to conduct its day-to-day business. In some cases, the company selling the off-the-shelf software makes these customized changes for a fee. Other vendors, however, do not allow their software to be modified. Oracle Applications and SAP are two very popular off-the-shelf application software suites that provide a set of customizable, wide-ranging business modules.

Examples of Information Systems Application Software

Application software is often categorized according to its design. Another useful way to categorize application software is by the type of application or task it supports. The two task-oriented categories for application software are large, business-oriented systems and office automation or personal productivity tools. Applications in the former category are purchased or developed by the organization to support the central, organization-wide operations of the company. Those in the latter category are tools primarily used to support the daily work activities of individuals and small groups. We'll describe each type of application software in the following sections and give some examples.

Business Information Systems

Business information systems are applications developed to perform the organization-wide operations of the firm. For example, most organizations have payroll applications to process their payrolls. A payroll application may take as inputs the individual time sheets completed by managers each week. These time sheets can be in the form of computerized sheets that can be read by optical scanners. Time sheets can be fed through the optical scanner to create a file of time sheet data, organized by employee (probably by using social security numbers, as mentioned earlier in the chapter). After the time sheet data is sorted by employee, it can be processed. That is, the application software can look at the pay rate for each employee, as well as the number of regular and overtime hours worked by each employee, to come up with a gross pay figure. Next, the application can consider the federal, state, and local taxes that must be deducted from the employee's gross pay. After all deductions are calculated, the application arrives at a net pay figure. This amount is what is actually paid to the employee.

At this point, the application has taken all time sheets, organized and sorted them by employee, and calculated gross pay, deductions, and net pay for each employee. These figures form a payroll master file. The payroll master file is created and backed up, perhaps on a tape drive on a mainframe computer. Next, the application must process checks so that they can be distributed to employees. To do this, the payroll application may create a check and register file. The check file might include the date, the employee's name, the social security number, and the net pay for the employee. The register file contains all of the previous elements, along with the time period, gross pay, and deductions for that time period for the employee's records. The check file is sorted by department, and checks are printed. Registers (a record of the checks printed) are also sorted and printed for distribution to employees.

This may not seem to be a complex process to conduct for only two or three employees. However, consider a large governmental organization, such as the Department of Defense, which must process and account for millions of employees' checks. Suddenly, a relatively simple process becomes a potential information-processing nightmare. Fortunately, very sophisticated application software exists, which can easily handle these very large data-intensive operations.

The same holds true for virtually any business operation you can think of. The "Mom and Pop" general store of the early 1900s may have been able to manage its inventory in the back of a notebook or on a handwritten ledger, but the "Mom and Pop" general store of the 21st century cannot afford to forego the benefits of computerizing operations. In particular, the mega-retailers of today, such as JC Penney, Sears Roebuck and Company, and Lands' End, must manage millions of pieces of merchandise and millions of transactions on a daily basis. These businesses rely on inventory management, order processing, billing, and shipping applications to conduct their operations. Without sophisticated, large-scale business application software, these businesses could not survive.

Office Automation/Personal Productivity Application Software

The second major type of application software is often grouped into a category called **office automation** or **personal productivity software**. Individuals or groups who want to accomplish a wide range of tasks typically use this type of software. Many of the large, well-known software companies, including Microsoft, Netscape, and Lotus, produce office automation software. Table 3.2 outlines some of the more popular personal productivity tools.

Table 3.2   Some examples of popular personal productivity tools.

Tool	Examples
Word Processor	Microsoft Word, Corel WordPerfect, Lotus AmiPro
Spreadsheet	Microsoft Excel, Lotus 1-2-3
Database management system	Borland Paradox, Microsoft Access, Borland dbase, Microsoft FoxPro
Presentation software	Microsoft PowerPoint, Software Publishing Corporation Harvard Graphics
PC-based email	Lotus cc:Mail, Microsoft Mail, Novell Groupwise
Web browser	Netscape Navigator, Spyglass Mosaic, Microsoft Internet Explorer

A BRIEF CASE

Microsoft Office

Microsoft Office 97's success should give you an idea of just how popular personal productivity software tools are becoming. It is the fastest selling business application ever. During 1997, Office 97 sold more than 20 million licenses, at an average rate of more than 60,000 per day (Microsoft, 1998). Microsoft Office provides the user with a suite of personal productivity software tools (see Table 3.3). In the past, many organizations purchased one tool from software vendor A and a second from software vendor B. Microsoft's strategy has been to bundle several popular tools into a single integrated suite of tools. This integration makes installation and ongoing maintenance much easier.

For example, suppose a company chooses to purchase a word processor from software vendor A, a spreadsheet from software vendor B, and an electronic mail system from vendor C. To install this software would require three separate installation activities. Software tends to evolve and change, so vendors often release new versions of their software on at least a yearly basis. In this scenario, each upgrade to the software requires the installation of the new version. Imagine that users have more than three types of software, but five or ten different packages from five or ten different vendors. Imagine also that an organization has thousands of PCs to upgrade and maintain. Note that many organizations keep commonly used software tools such as word processors on a common server that all users can access to ease installation and maintenance. Microsoft's strategy of having a suite of commonly used tools bundled on a single CD-ROM makes things much easier to install and maintain, no matter how and where the software is stored by the organization. As a result, other software companies are finding themselves at a big disadvantage. None have as broad a suite of tools as Microsoft. The result of this competitive advantage is that Microsoft Office has become the standard personal productivity software at increasing numbers of organizations, such as the World Bank, Chrysler Corporation, Dell Computer Corporation, and countless others. In the following sections, we describe several categories and examples of these tools and take a closer look at six types of personal productivity software.

Table 3.3 Personal productivity tools in Microsoft Office 97 Professional.

Tool Name	Primary Function
Word	Word processing for document preparation and desktop publishing
Excel	Spreadsheet for analyzing and organizing data
Outlook	Electronic mail and calendar for communication and personal schedules
PowerPoint	Presentation software to create graphics and presentation slides
Access	Database management system to store and report data

Word Processing. Word processing software is probably the most widely known and used type of personal productivity software. Although the purpose of word processing software has always been to produce a wide range of documents—from business letters to reports—today's word processors bear little resemblance to their predecessors of five or ten years ago. Today's word processors have incorporated powerful desktop publishing features that allow you to produce sophisticated layouts of your documents (see Figure 3.11). Today's word processors also enable you to import or create graphics, charts, or tables. Some even enable you to link charts or tables embedded in their word processing document to spreadsheets or graphics programs so that when a table is updated in a spreadsheet, that same table is automatically updated in the word processing document.

Courtesy FileMaker Inc.

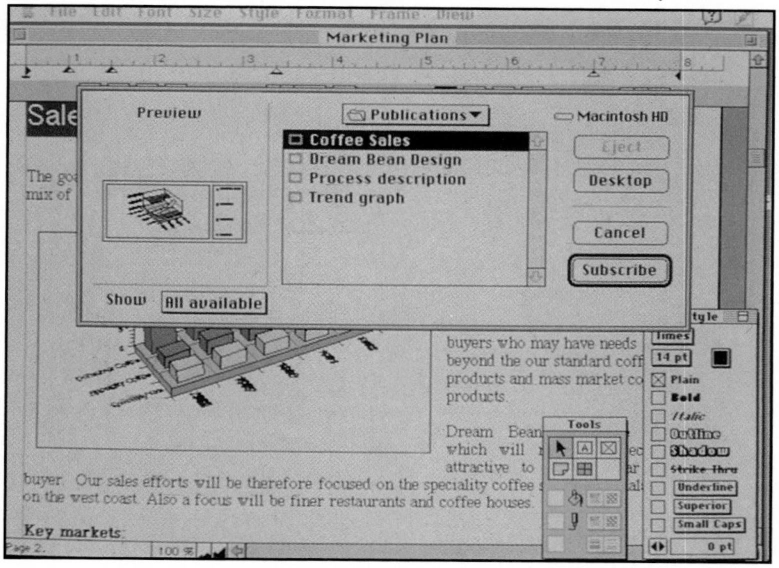

FIGURE 3.11

A document created with a word processor.

Spreadsheets. Spreadsheets are important personal productivity tools for today's managers. Just as word processors allow you to work with and manipulate text, spreadsheets allow you to do the same with numbers. Spreadsheets are wonderfully adept at automatically calculating standard math operations. For example, finding the average of a series of numbers in a column, such as the average sales for a given period of time or region, is very simple to do with a spreadsheet. Spreadsheets can also be used to generate a wide variety of graphs to help present and summarize data. This capability makes them powerful forecasting tools that are invaluable for spotting and analyzing trends. Like word processors, today's spreadsheets offer many powerful features, including sophisticated statistical analysis, the capability to write macros (a type of programming that allows you to customize spreadsheets to automate routine tasks), and optimization routines, which walk you through a series of questions in order to arrive at a problem solution. Figure 3.12 shows a spreadsheet document.

FIGURE 3.12

A document created with a spreadsheet.

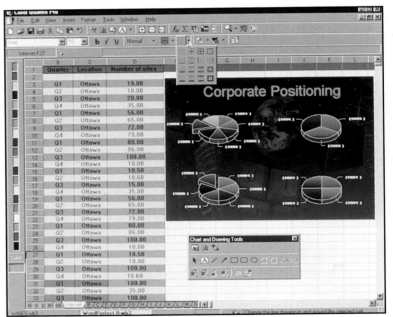

Courtesy Corel Corporation

Database Management Systems (DBMS). A database management system is designed to help us store and manipulate data in all formats—text, numerical data, or, in some cases, whole documents, graphics, or photos. Database systems are used on virtually all types of computers, from mainframes to PCs. They run some of the most powerful business-oriented applications that are used in organizations today. However, some PC-based database management systems fall into the personal productivity category. Database management systems enable you to view, manipulate, and summarize vast volumes of rich data in meaningful ways. Today's database systems offer graphical user interfaces and facilities for helping you formulate queries (see Figure 3.13) Powerful form generation features allow users to customize input forms that are used to enter data into the database and output forms (for example, preformatting a standard company report). We'll talk more about this important type of software in the next chapter.

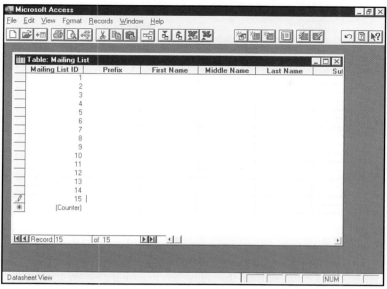

FIGURE 3.13

Database screen shot.

Presentation Software. Presentation software is used for creating graphics and presentations. For example, sales teams can create presentations that help sell the company's products to prospective clients. The presentation might be presented using 35mm slides or overheads. An audio-visual tool that simply projects the screen images from a notebook computer onto a large 6-foot wide screen could also be used. Presentation software offers sophisticated layout options that enable you to create professional-looking presentations. Presentation software allows you to enter text or bulleted statements into an outline. It then takes that outline and generates titles, headings, and subheadings on eye-pleasing backgrounds. You can also import or link slides with spreadsheet or word processing documents so that any updates in one automatically update the other. Today's presentation software also offers you the option of specifying unique transitions between slides (for example, having one slide fade out and then be replaced by another or having the slide appear to drop off the bottom of the screen while the next slide appears to slides down from the top). Presentation software makes these operations relatively simple for you to create, so you can generate impressive, attention-grabbing displays (see Figure 3.14).

FIGURE 3.14

A salesperson giving a presentation.

Electronic Mail. An innovation for many offices is electronic mail, or email (see Figure 3.15). These packages allow you to send electronic mail messages and files to others via a computer network. When attached to a network, all users have their own electronic mailboxes, in which they can send and receive messages. Electronic mail offers advantages over traditional (postal) mail, phone calls, or memos because it is often cheaper and faster to use. Newer electronic mail software features graphical user interfaces. With this software, you can compose messages offline, which the computer sends at a designated time.

FIGURE 3.15

Diagram of an email message being sent between two users over a network.

Internet and World Wide Web Browser Software. An even newer innovation for most offices is the use of the international Internet network and the World Wide Web (see Chapter 6, "Electronic Commerce and the Internet," for more information). Growth in the use of the Internet and World Wide Web has skyrocketed over the last few years. The Internet links people and networks from all over the world, allowing those at one location to send messages and access computers thousands of miles away, perhaps even on another continent. The World Wide Web is a graphical portion of the Internet that allows you to navigate through linked pages to other sites (called home pages). A relatively new type of office automation software is becoming a standard tool in many organizations—World Wide Web browsing software, or browsers. These browsers allow you to easily navigate a series of linked pages on the Web. Browser software also lets you view and download files, bookmark some of your favorite or commonly used Web pages for easy and immediate access later on, and connect to various Web search engines that allow you to look for information about a topic you are interested in.

A BRIEF CASE

Browser War

Web browsers have become an increasingly important tool for organizations. One of the most interesting ongoing developments in the software industry relates to the antitrust allegations by the U.S. Department of Justice (DOJ) against Microsoft for their Web browser, Internet Explorer (IE). At the root of this controversy is whether Microsoft's inclusion of IE with Windows 95 violated a 1995 consent decree in which the company agreed not to "tie" products to the operating system. In these proceedings, the DOJ has argued that bundling IE with Windows 95 is a violation of the decree (Ziff-Davis, 1998). Microsoft has argued that the browser is a part of the operating system and is therefore allowed under the consent decree. The issue gets even messier with the release of Windows 98, the recently released version of Microsoft's popular operating system, which was released in 1998. Windows 98 completely integrates the Web browser into the operating system. This issue will likely be a long-fought battle because it involves much more than Web browsers. It hits at the root of the multibillion dollar software market. Some in the software industry are arguing that because Microsoft controls a substantial part of the microcomputer operating system market, any bundling of nonoperating system applications with the operating system gives Microsoft an unfair competitive

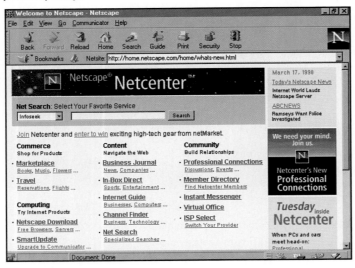

FIGURE 3.16

A Netscape screen showing a home page.

advantage over other software companies. Opponents of Microsoft fear that while today it is browsers, tomorrow it will be application programs and development tools. Such expansion would shut many companies out of the software business. Figure 3.16 shows a Netscape screen shot.

Programming Languages

All of the application software previously discussed is based on some programming language. A programming language is the computer language used by the software vendor to write application programs. For application software such as spreadsheets or database management systems, the underlying programming language is invisible to the user. However, programmers in an organization's information systems group and, in some instances, end users, can use programming languages to develop their own specialized applications. Many different types of programming languages exist, each with its own strengths and weaknesses. Some of the popular languages used in businesses today are included in Table 3.4.

Table 3.4 Some common programming languages.

Language	Application	Description
Ada	General purpose	Named after Ada, the Countess of Lovelace, who long ago envisioned computing machines. Ada is the Department of Defense's standard system development language for a broad range of applications.
BASIC	General purpose	Beginner's All-Purpose Symbolic Interaction Code. BASIC is a relatively simple language that has evolved into a very powerful language for developing systems with graphical user interfaces.
C/C++	General purpose	Third in a series (that is, Version C) of programming languages developed at AT&T Bell Labs. C is a very complex and powerful language that is used for a broad range of system- and application-level programming. C++ is an object-oriented extension of C.
COBOL	Business	Common Business Oriented Language. COBOL is the most widely used language for developing large data processing applications. Despite being challenged by newer languages, COBOL remains a popular alternative for many businesses.
FORTRAN	Scientific	Formula Translator. FORTRAN is used primarily for developing scientific and engineering applications. Like COBOL, it remains a popular language.
Java	World Wide Web	Java is an object-oriented programming language developed at Sun Microsystems. It is quickly becoming the programming language for the Internet.

Compilers and Interpreters

Programs created using programming languages must be translated into code—called assembly or **machine language**—that the hardware can understand. Most programming languages are translated into machine languages through a type of systems program called a **compiler**, as depicted in Figure 3.17. The compiler takes an entire program written in a programming language, such as C, and converts it into a completely new program in machine language that can be read and executed directly by the computer. Use of a compiler is a two-stage process. First, the compiler translates the computer program into machine language, and then the machine language program is executed.

FIGURE 3.17

How a compiler does its job.

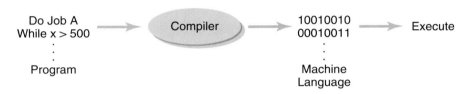

Some programming environments don't compile the entire program into machine language. Instead, each statement of the programming code is converted into machine language and executed one statement at a time, as depicted in Figure 3.18. The type of program that does the conversion and execution is called an **interpreter**. In sum, programming languages can be implemented by using either a compiled or an interpretive method.

FIGURE 3.18

How an interpreter does its job.

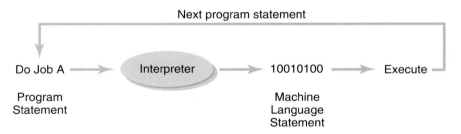

The Evolution of Information Systems Software

Information systems software continues to evolve. To understand where software may be headed in the future, it is useful to first understand where it came from.

Generations of Programming Languages

Like the evolution of IS hardware (see Chapter 2, "Information Systems Hardware"), the evolution of software can be described in terms of generations. In the following sections, we describe five generations of software.

First Generation: Machine Language

As you can imagine, the first generation of programming languages was quite crude by today's standards. Initially used in the 1940s, the first generation of programming languages was called machine languages. This is because programmers wrote their code in binary code, telling the computer exactly which circuits to turn on and which to turn off. As described in the previous chapter, binary code is written as a series of 1s and 0s, called bits. These bits are combined in order to turn the electronic circuits on and off and to perform operations on the computer. For example, a program statement in machine language that is used to simply add two numbers together might take several lines of code. More complex operations required thousands or hundreds of thousands of lines of code. Hobbyists who in 1975 bought the widely available first "personal" computer, the MITS Altair 8800 (which had to be assembled piece by piece, with some soldering required!), were forced to interact with their new computer by flipping toggle switches up and down on the front panel to program commands bit by bit. Now that's hacking!

Machine language is considered a low-level language. It is very unsophisticated and therefore very difficult to write. Because it is so difficult, very few programs are actually written in machine language. Programmers rely on higher-level languages instead. Still, all higher-level programs must eventually be translated into machine language by the computer before being executed.

Second Generation: Assembly Language

Assembly language, which is one step up from machine language, was first developed in the early 1950s. In assembly language, the binary code of 1s and 0s was replaced by symbols that are easier to understand. Letters were used to stand for a series of binary statements. For example, the letter "A" could be used to "Add" two numbers instead of relying on several lines of code. Because second-generation languages and those that followed relied on symbols instead of binary code, they are often called **symbolic languages**.

As mentioned previously, programs written in assembly language still must be converted into machine language by an **assembler** in order to run.

Third Generation: High-level Languages

Take a look again at Table 3.4. The languages listed in this table are all high-level languages, or third-generation languages. FORTRAN, the first third-generation language, was developed in the mid-1950s by IBM. These types of programs use symbols in their code, which are then translated into machine language. The difference between these high-level languages and second-generation languages is that the high-level languages use English-like words and commands. Continuing with our example, a third-generation programming language might use the English word "add" or the instruction "VARIABLE 3 = VARIABLE 1 + VARIABLE 2" to specify an addition operation. This is much easier to understand than its alternatives, using 1s and 0s in machine language or using the letter "A" in assembly language. A statement written in a high-level language usually translates into several machine language instructions. High-level languages are much easier to program than lower-level languages because they require fewer steps to achieve the same operation.

Different high-level languages are more appropriate for different types of tasks. Looking at Table 3.4, you can see that some high-level languages are better for scientific, or math-oriented applications. Other languages, such as COBOL, may be better for handling the large numbers of files that are common in business applications. Programmers must fully understand the tasks that are to be accomplished with the new application in order to choose the best programming language for those tasks.

Fourth Generation: Outcome-oriented Languages

As you might expect, fourth-generation languages are an even higher-level breed of language than third-generation languages. First developed in the 1970s, fourth-generation languages are even more like English, and they tend to focus on the desired output instead of the procedures required to get that output (as is the case for third-generation languages). Fourth-generation languages (4GLs) are often used to write and execute queries of a database. For example, the widely used database query language called Structured Query Language (SQL) is considered a fourth-generation language (see Figure 3.19).

```
SELECT LAST FIRST
FROM CUSTOMER
WHERE CREDIT_LIMIT = 100

DIEHR GEORGE
JANKOWSKI DAVID
HAGGARTY JOSEPH
JESSUP JAMIE
VALACICH JAMES
VALACICH JORDAN
```

FIGURE 3.19

Several lines of SQL, a 4GL language.

```
BEGINNING WITH THE LAST NAME ON THE FOL-
LOWING LIST OF CUSTOMERS, FIND CUSTOMERS
WHO HAVE A CREDIT LIMIT OF $100.

DIEHR GEORGE
JANKOWSKI DAVID
HAGGARTY JOSEPH
JESSUP JAMIE
VALACICH JAMES
VALACICH JORDAN
```

FIGURE 3.20

The same code used in Figure 3.19 as it would appear in a natural language.

4GLs enable users to ask computers to provide certain information using sentence-like statements in English. For example, Figure 3.19 shows a 4GL statement that can be used to print a certain variable if that variable is greater than $100.00. If it is not greater than $100.00, then the computer prints another variable, Y.

Fifth Generation: Natural Languages

Fifth-generation languages (5GLs), although they are still not widespread, are being used in some expert system or artificial intelligence applications. 5GLs are called natural languages because they allow the user to communicate with the computer using true English sentences. For example, Hewlett-Packard and other software vendors have developed tools for document search and retrieval and database queries that let the user query the documents or database with English-like sentences. These sentences are then automatically converted into the appropriate commands (in some cases Structured Query Language) needed to query the documents or database and produce the result for the user. In some cases, if the system doesn't understand exactly what the user wants, it can ask for clarification. The same code shown in Figure 3.19 might appear as shown in Figure 3.20 if a natural language were used.

Although 5GL languages are not common and are still being further developed, they have been used to forecast the performance of financial portfolios, help diagnose medical problems, and estimate weather patterns.

What's next after 5GL? Will the 6GL be a computer system that we simply talk to and instruct what to do, as we would another human? We might simply ask it if the accounts payable ledger exceeds $100.00. Even better, we might ask it to pay any existing bills under $100.00 and notify us whenever a bill for over $100.00 comes in. Perhaps the system could, over time, grow to know us and infer meaning from what we say or don't say. We might someday simply say, "Take care of the payables," and the system would automatically know what we meant from past experience, handle the payables accordingly, and then say, "Next time, say please."

While we haven't quite perfected the type of 6GL that we describe, programming languages continue to evolve. One new characteristic for describing programming languages is whether or not they are object-oriented. Next, we introduce object-oriented and visual programming languages.

Object-oriented Languages

Object-oriented programming languages are among the newest types of programming languages (see Satzinger and Orvik, 1996). Instead of separating variables, procedures, and data, as in traditional programming languages, object-oriented programs group all pieces together into "objects." An example of an object might be employee identification and payroll information and a set of corresponding rules for calculating monthly payroll for a variety of job classifications and tax rules. This process of grouping the data and instructions together into a single object is called **encapsulation**. By encapsulating the instructions and data together, programs are easier to maintain because the things that are grouped together are protected or isolated from other parts of the program. A programmer can go in and make major changes to object B without having any of those changes ripple throughout the program and affect object A.

A second characteristic of object-oriented languages is **inheritance**, which means that all lower-level, or children, nodes in an inheritance hierarchy inherit the characteristics of the parent node. For example, if engineers within a firm are determined to be part of the parent class called employees, they would automatically inherit any of the properties defined for the employee class, such as the property that all employees have a unique, nine-digit identification number. In traditional programming languages, data and processing steps are not coupled together, and lower-level procedures don't always inherit properties of a higher level one. As a result, reusing code is possible but much more complex, time-consuming, and error-prone than it is for object-oriented languages. In other words, after an object is created, it can be much more easily plugged into a number of different applications. Just as a radio made by Pioneer can be plugged into several different cars, an object can be plugged into several different applications.

Object-oriented languages are currently among the most popular languages, and their use continues to grow. C++ is an object-oriented enhancement of the original C programming language. Smalltalk, developed by Xerox, is also gaining strength in the business market. You can also see elements of object-oriented programming in Visual Basic and in multimedia authoring tools, such as Asymetrix Toolbook.

In addition to being object-oriented, programs and programming languages can also be **event-driven**. Unlike programs written in procedural programming languages, programs written with the event-driven approach do not follow a sequential logic. The programmer does not determine the sequence of execution for the program. The user can press certain keys and click on various buttons and boxes presented to her. Each of these user actions can cause an *event* to occur, which triggers a program procedure that the programmer has written. Programming languages, which are object-oriented, tend to also be useful for event-driven programming, as is Microsoft's Visual Basic. In addition to being object-oriented and event-oriented, programming languages are also visual.

Visual Programming Languages

As mentioned earlier in this chapter, today's system and application software often makes use of graphics through graphical user interfaces. Although the heavy use of graphics makes GUI applications easy to use (hopefully, anyway), it also makes them very difficult to program. In order to help programmers develop these graphical environments for their applications, visual programming languages have been created.

Visual programming languages make programming easier and more intuitive. They allow the programmer to create the graphics-intensive applications that today's business users demand. For example, to make a button appear for the user on a particular screen at a particular point in time, a programmer using a visual programming language only needs to bring up the screen where the button is to appear, choose the button from a palette of choices, drag and drop the button to the proper location, size and style the button with a few mouse clicks, and click on the button's pop-up menu to set the properties that will control its behavior (see Figure 3.21). To accomplish the same tasks with a traditional programming language was much more difficult and time-consuming, and it required far more expertise. We would have had to describe in many, many painstaking lines of programming code exactly which pixels on the screen were to be colored in to make the button appear, what colors were to be used, and exactly how the button was to behave when clicked. Programs such as Visual Basic or Visual C++ (a visual derivative of the object-oriented C++) are popular examples of visual programming languages.

As you can see, the development of programming languages is an ongoing process of change and innovation. These changes often result in more capable and complex systems for the user. The final

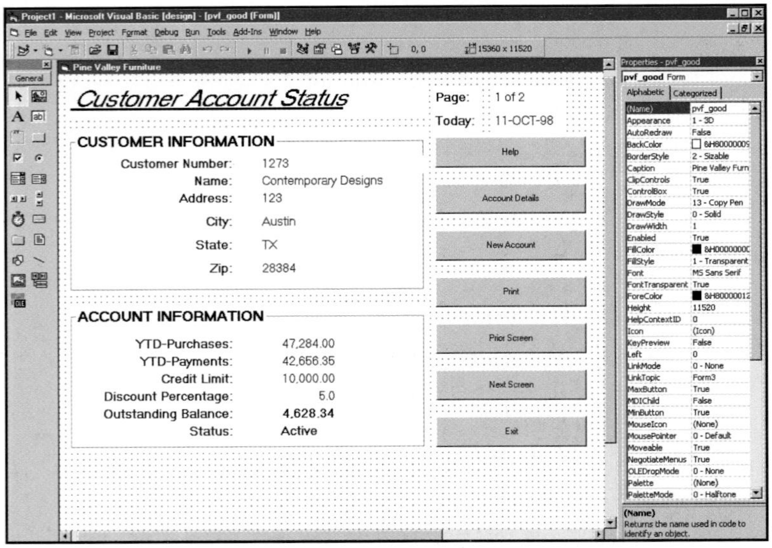

Screen shot reprinted by permission of Microsoft Corporation.

FIGURE 3.21

Visual Basic development environment.

section of this chapter explores trends that can be seen in the software developed by today's programmers.

Emerging Trends in Software

Writing a trends section in any information systems book is dangerous because today's trend can quickly become tomorrow's history. However, it is worth mentioning a couple of recent developments that may significantly change how we think about software and, ultimately, computing.

Merging of Hardware and Software

Although it has been useful to think of hardware and software as separate, independent, distinct components of information systems, the line between the two is becoming more and more blurred.

For example, many small computers have been developed that contain software directly programmed into the computer itself (usually coded into a microchip). These computers are designed to perform a single task or set of tasks easily and efficiently. Have you ever signed for a package from Federal Express? Today, when you sign for a package, your signature is recorded electronically on a computer tablet and is communicated to a central set of computers that track each and every package in the Federal Express system. This clipboard makes it possible for you to call a carrier (or even better, to access their World Wide Web site), enter a package tracking number, and find out the location of that package. Federal Express's automated clipboard is a good example of an application where the software is embedded with the hardware (the computer tablet and stylus).

Also, some of today's automobiles contain sophisticated on-board computer hardware/software that manages, corrects, and diagnoses all systems in the automobile, from oxygen flow to whether the taillights are operating properly. Computer chips monitor all of these operations. Are these chips hardware? Yes. Are they software? Yes. You can see that the distinction between hardware and software is becoming a little murkier than it once was. Computer chips with complex on-board software are finding their way into more and more devices throughout our homes and offices—for example, home appliances, credit cards, and door locks.

Integrated Telecommunications

In information systems today, a system's hardware and software are almost always tied to some form of telecommunications. In fact, as in the preceding section, a system's telecommunications capabilities are almost inseparable from the hardware/software itself.

Returning to our Federal Express example, once you sign for a package, that information is communicated (probably via satellite) to the company's central computers. As mentioned earlier, automobiles also make heavy use of hardware/software systems, including an integrated telecommunications system. Have you ever seen an automobile that had a built-in map system that could plot and track your route to a given destination? While this system currently exists mainly in today's very expensive luxury cars, such systems will probably be commonplace within the decade. These systems make use of a Global Positioning System (or GPS) to track where your car is in relation to your intended destination, as shown in Figure 3.22. In GPS systems, a chip in your car communicates with a GPS satellite to plot your position anywhere on the earth and can compare the information about your current location with your desired destination. On-board systems then figure out how to reconcile those differences and plot that information on a map. GPS systems are standard equipment on today's aircraft and ships and will likely become common in tomorrow's automobiles, bicycles, or golf carts!

©Torin Boyd

FIGURE 3.22

A GPS system in a car.

Another example of an integrated software and telecommunications system is the simple voice mail systems offered by many vendors today. Callers can leave voice mail messages that can be stored on a computer and then retrieved later by the intended recipient. Like email, this integrated software/telecommunications system enables people to avoid the hassle of playing telephone tag all day just to deliver a short message to someone.

Similarly, touch-tone routing systems can be used to enable users calling into a company to get information automatically or can be routed to someone who can help them. For example, many financial institutions allow a user to get existing balances on accounts over the phone by simply entering her account number and a personal identification number (PIN). The user may then be presented with a number of choices (for example, hitting "1" to get a checking balance, "2" to get a savings balance, "3" to get current loan rates, or "4" to speak with a customer service representative). The goal of these systems is to permit greater access to the customer (customers can access information 24 hours a day), while relieving personnel strains for the financial institution.

Screen shot reprinted by permission from Microsoft Corporation.

The World Wide Web promises to revolutionize the intermingling of telecommunications and software. Software physically located in one place might be linked to other locations around the globe. For example, it is possible to conduct a teleconference over the Internet (see Figure 3.23). The teleconferencing software controls who gets to talk and controls the views that each user has. At the same time, it interfaces with sophisticated telecommunications systems in order to compress and decompress audio and visual images being sent from several locations. The user does not have to see or manage this process himself. If he did, no work could ever get done, because his attention would be focused on *how to communicate* rather than *the task at hand.* Today's software systems that integrate telecommunications allow the user to focus on business-related tasks, rather than on how to make the computer and/or telecom-

FIGURE 3.23

Screen shot from NetMeeting.

munications systems work. If these systems become widely used, and early evidence suggests that they will (Arnaut, 1998), companies will greatly reduce travel expenses.

One other interesting way that the Web is changing our notions of telecommunications and software is through the rising popularity of the Java programming language. Java is an object-oriented programming language that runs across multiple hardware platforms and operating systems. Java can be used to create small programming applications, called applets, that appear on Web pages in much the same way images do, except that, unlike images, applets can be dynamic and interactive. For example, applets could be used to create animations, figures, or even areas on the user's screen where she can respond by clicking a mouse or by inputting text. An applet might contain a game that the user can play on her computer (Lemay and Perkins, 1996).

You use Java to write and compile the applet and then link the applet to your Web page. When a Web user views your page with the embedded applet, his Web browser downloads the applet to his local system and executes it (see Figure 3.24). In a sense, Java allows you to write and dynamically ship little programs back and forth across the Internet that other people can use quite easily and quickly without knowing they have downloaded and are running a special piece of software. Let's apply this to the banking scenario from the beginning of the chapter. The bank we described might choose to enable customers to do some of their banking via the Web. The bank could easily write a Java application that, when a customer visited the bank's Web site and clicked on the right button, would automatically download itself on the customer's computer, launch itself, and enable the customer to quickly and easily set the parameters for a loan—such as the loan amount, number of months until payoff, and the interest rate. The same Java program could then automatically calculate and present the payment amount for the customer on her Web browser.

These are just some of the emerging trends in software. As you read this chapter, more trends are developing that will replace those mentioned here. Software remains an exciting and innovative area where capabilities continue to grow at unprecedented rates. Stay tuned!

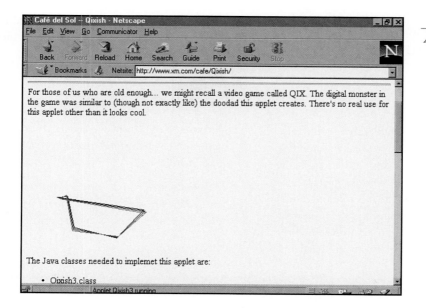

FIGURE 3.24

An applet on a browser screen.

ETHICAL PERSPECTIVE: VENI, VIDI, VICI—I CAME, I SAW, I HACKED

When you hear the term "computer hacker," you might imagine a techno-geek, someone who sits in front of her computer all day and night attempting to break the ultra-super secret security code of one of the most sophisticated computer systems in the world, perhaps a computer for the U.S. Military, a Swiss bank, or the CIA. While this fits the more traditional profile for a computer hacker, there is no clear profile today. More and more people have the skills, tools, and the motive to hack into a computer system. A modern-day hacker could be a disgruntled, middle-aged, white-collar worker sitting at a nice desk on the fourteenth floor of the headquarters building of a billion-dollar software manufacturer.

Computer hackers, also known as crackers, have been around for decades. For the most part, we associate hackers with their pranks and crimes involving security systems and viruses. Hackers have caused the loss of billions of dollars' worth of stolen goods, repair bills, and lost goodwill with customers. The premise for the movie *War Games* is based on this more traditional notion of the "typical" young hacker whose prank goes awry. However, many companies are beginning to take advantage of this highly technical and computer-literate community in their own research and development, as exemplified in the movie *The Net*.

In an attempt to create the perfect software program, companies are hiring hackers to find the bugs in the software prior to its release to the public. These companies may be manufacturing anything—from a new release of a software game, to a serious business application, to security software for banks. In some cases, the hackers have been formerly convicted and are now using their programming expertise to help the firms battle against other hackers. These firms essentially contract with the hackers to attempt to break into their systems, steal data, copy files, and otherwise cause havoc. These firms reason that they would rather have a contracted hacker attempting to break in, modify, or steal their software than another, unknown hacker. If there are weaknesses in the software, the contracted hacker can help the firm identify and address them before the product is released for general use. As you can imagine, using hackers in this way requires a lot of trust from the firms. However, such a relationship between firm and hacker can be quite beneficial.

A similar successful practice has been the use of the general public to find bugs and loopholes in early versions of software. These beta versions of software are made available to the public, who are asked to report any bugs, loopholes, errors, and so on while using the software. The manufacturer uses the information from these pseudoconsultants to fix the software before final release. This process is far cheaper than using in-house or contracted experts, yet it is not as efficient or as extensive. Software producers, such as Microsoft and Netscape, have made very good use of this practice. In addition to being a vehicle for improving the software, this practice also has the strategic marketing value of prebuilding market share before the final release of a software package.

Still, hackers with negative intentions do exist, and they continue to cause problems for companies and government organizations. Efforts to thwart hackers have increased. New hardware solutions, such as passkey microchips, work for only one user at a time. There are new software solutions, such as better encryption algorithms. Finally, there are new organizational solutions, such as the use of internal emergency response teams. Like the Computer Emergency Response Team at Carnegie Mellon, many businesses and government agencies are now staffing their own teams. The government has also announced plans for a "hacker SWAT team" that would remain on alert for large-scale national emergencies. As long as there are smart people with the capabilities to hack into systems and the motivation to do harm, other smart people will continue to devise technological and organizational solutions to thwart them.

Questions for Discussion

1. Can former criminals really be trusted to put forth their best efforts for these software manufacturers?

2. Do you feel the media generates too much hype regarding hacking and hackers? Or is the danger legitimate?

3. Are you concerned about hackers cracking the security codes on the computer programs at your bank and accessing your account and other sensitive information?

Source Kerr, Deborah. 1998. Hacker stoppers? Companies bought $65 million worth of network-intrusion tools last year but capabilities still lag what's promised. InformationWeek, April 20, 140-144.

INTERNATIONAL PERSPECTIVE: SOFTWARE PIRACY ACROSS INTERNATIONAL BORDERS

A major international issue businesses deal with is the willingness (or unwillingness) of governments and individuals to recognize and enforce the ownership of intellectual property—in particular, software copyright. Piracy of software and other technologies is widespread internationally. The Business Software Alliance (BSA) points to countries such as China, Thailand, Turkey, Indonesia, Iran, Saudi Arabia, and Kuwait as those with the highest percentages of illegal software.

In the United States, $2,876,922,400 worth of illegal software was pirated in 1994. Roughly 35 percent of all of the software in use in the country is running from illegal copies, which is only the tip of the iceberg. The BSA estimates that in 1994, U.S. companies lost $101,000,000 from pirated software in Saudi Arabia alone. Around 90 percent of all of the software in the kingdom is illegal. China is another country notorious for software piracy, with a rate of 90 percent of all software in the country pirated. It is said that Chinese companies can take one legitimate software purchase and churn out enough copies to satisfy the entire country's needs.

An ethical problem? Perhaps in part, but there are other perspectives that business people must acknowledge and deal with as well. In part, the problem stems from countries' differing concepts of ownership. Many of the ideas about intellectual property ownership stem from long-standing cultural traditions. For example, the concept of individual ownership of knowledge is traditionally a strange one in countries such as Saudi Arabia, where knowledge is meant to be shared. Plagiarism doesn't exist in a country where words belong to everyone. By the same token, piracy does not exist either. This view is gradually changing, and the Saudi Patent Office recently granted its first patents.

In other cases, there are political, social, and economic reasons for piracy. In many other countries, software publishers are simply not catering to the needs of consumers, who often simply do not have the funds to purchase software legitimately. This is true in many areas of South America and other regions with low per capita income. It is particularly true of students and other members of university communities, whose needs are critical in some areas.

In China, these and other forces come into play. Although the Chinese government claims to enforce treaties, only a handful of intellectual property cases in China have ever been decided in favor of foreign companies. One of the few was brought by the Walt Disney Company, which won a $77,000 judgment against Chinese companies that were producing books based on Disney films. In an era of high growth and little internal policy, treaties, although given lip service, are difficult to enforce.

The Chinese might be resistant to following copyright laws for several reasons. Kenneth Ho (1995) notes that historically, the Chinese (along with many other cultures) have had a strong emphasis on learning by copying. Ho notes that copying well is regarded as a compliment to the originator of the work. In addition, for many Chinese individuals, the concept of ownership of intellectual property is not only foreign, but something that goes against the notion of the value of the society over the individual.

Other factors leading to piracy or infringement of intellectual property agreements throughout the world include lack of public awareness about the issue, lack of an industrial infrastructure that can produce legitimate software, and the increasingly high demand for computer and other technology products. The U.S. has repeatedly pressured and threatened other countries accused of pirating. It is interesting to note, however, that few of these cultural and economic explanations are valid in the U.S. but that we lead the world in the sheer volume of illegal software in use. Businesses that operate in glass offices should surely not throw stones.

Questions for Discussion

1. How can businesses accommodate the cultural perspectives of other groups while remaining competitive?

2. Should American businesses address the needs of the economically and technologically poor around the world? If so, in what ways?

3. How can the high volume of pirated software in the U.S. be explained?

Sources   Ho, Kenneth. 1995. A study into the problem of software piracy in Hong Kong and China. London School of Economics and Political Science. See http://pluto.houston.com.hk/hkgipd/piracy.html

Talking with...

Patrick Casey, Senior Systems Analyst at Interart Distribution, Inc.

Education

B.A., Indiana University; M.B.A., Indiana University

Job Description

Mr. Casey is responsible for the analysis and design of new and/or existing data systems. He coordinates resources, schedules, and communication for the implementation of new systems or major enhancements to existing systems. Mr. Casey is also responsible for applications development of critical modules for large systems.

Critical Success Factors

Technical competence is, of course, a must. On that foundation, seek to see things through the eyes of your customers. Avoid speaking of IT issues in techno-babble, but phrase them—and see them—as much as possible through the lens of business objectives and user deliverables. Make your objectives concrete and measurable (in God we trust; everyone else is required to provide facts).

Advice to Students

Be objective, not ego-protective. Understand your role—and the role of your projects—in the "big picture." Regularly reassess the usefulness of operations. Don't accept criticism; welcome it!

Summary

1. **Understand the importance of information systems software for today's organizations.** As the use of computer-based systems has continued to rise, software has become a larger percentage of an organization's total technology costs. Because software gives life to the information system hardware, it has become the key enabler for today's business strategies, allowing businesses to compete in today's dynamic environment and facilitating re-engineering, or rightsizing, business operations in order to become as efficient as possible.

2. **Describe the common functions of systems software.** Systems software is the collection of programs that form the foundation for the basic operations of the computer hardware. Systems software, or the operating system, performs many different tasks. Some of these tasks include booting your computer, reading programs into memory, managing memory allocation to those programs, managing where programs and files are located in

secondary storage, maintaining the structure of directories and subdirectories, formatting disks, controlling the computer monitor, and sending objects to the printer. The systems software manages the dialogue you can have with a computer using either a command-based or graphical interface. A command-based interface requires that text commands be typed into the computer, while a graphical user interface (GUI) uses pictures and icons as well as menus to send instructions back and forth from the user to the computer system.

3. **Explain the various types of application software.** You can find a large number of computer software applications. Some, which are called customized application software, are developed specifically for a single organization. This kind of software is tailored to an organization's unique requirements. Off-the-shelf application software is not customized to the unique needs of one organization but is written to operate within many organizations. In

general, off-the-shelf software is less costly, faster to procure, of higher quality, and less risky than customized software. Business information systems are applications developed to perform the firm's organization-wide operations, such as payroll or inventory management. Office automation or personal productivity software is designed to support activities such as word processing and electronic mail.

4. **Describe the characteristics of various types of programming languages.** A programming language is the computer language used by programmers to write application programs. In order to run on a computer, programs must be translated into binary machine language. Programming languages are translated into machine languages through special types of programs, which are called compilers and interpreters.

5. **Discuss the evolution of computer software.** There have been five generations of programming software. The first generation used machine language, which told the computer exactly which circuits to turn on and which to turn off. The second generation used assembly language, which used symbols to represent a series of binary statements. Assembly language made it much easier to write programs. The third generation used high-level languages, such as FORTRAN, COBOL, C, and Java. The difference between these high-level languages and second-generation languages is that the high-level languages use English-like words and commands, making it even easier to write programs than it was with the assembly language. Fourth-generation languages are called outcome-oriented languages because they contain even more English-like commands and tend to focus on what output is desired instead of the procedures required to get that output. Again, these languages made it even easier to program. Fifth-generation languages are called natural languages because they allow the user to communicate with the computer using true English sentences.

Although not part of this generational evolution, object-oriented programming and visual programming are relatively new enhancements to programming languages. Object-oriented languages group together data and their corresponding instructions into manipulatable objects. Visual programming languages use a graphical interface that allows programs to be visual objects for the applications that need a graphical interface. Both object-oriented and visual programming languages are making it easier for programmers to develop today's complex software systems. While it has been useful to think of hardware and software as separate, independent, distinct components of information systems, the line between the two is becoming increasingly blurred. In the future, the distinction between hardware and software will continue to blur.

Key Terms

Data

Information

Knowledge

Wisdom

Software

Computer programs

Documentation

Systems software

Operating system

Interface

Command-based interface

Graphical user interface

Application software

Customized application software

Off-the-shelf application software

Business information systems

Office automation or personal productivity software

Machine language

Compiler

Interpreter

Symbolic languages

Assembler

Object-oriented programming languages

Encapsulation

Inheritance

Event-driven

Visual programming languages

Review Questions

1. Compare and contrast the terms "data," "information," and "knowledge."

2. Describe the two basic types of information systems software.

3. Describe at least four different tasks performed by an operating system.

4. What is the difference between a command-based interface and a graphical user interface?

5. Describe the similarities and differences among at least three major operating systems in use today.

6. List some of the advantages of using off-the-shelf application software.

7. Describe how office automation software differs from business information systems.

8. Describe the six major types of office automation software outlined in this chapter.

9. Explain the differences between a compiler and an interpreter.

10. What does the term "4GL" mean and how does it differ from "3GL" and "5GL"?

11. Describe several examples of technology that have incorporated the trend of merging hardware and software.

Problems and Exercises

◆ **Individual**   ◆ **Group**   ☞ **Field**   ◐ **Web/Internet**

1. Match the following terms to the appropriate definitions:

_____ Information

_____ Computer program

_____ Systems software

_____ Graphical user interface

_____ Customized application software

_____ Business information systems

_____ Compiler

_____ Object-oriented programming languages

a. Translates the computer program into machine language, which is then executed by the computer

b. An interface that enables the user to select pictures, icons, and menus in order to send instructions to the computer

c. Data formatted in such a way that it has additional value

d. Applications developed to perform the organization-wide operations of the firm

e. The collection of programs that performs and coordinates the interaction among hardware devices, peripherals, and application software

f. A set of coded instructions written in a programming language that directs the hardware circuitry to operate in a predefined way

g. Programming languages that group together data and their corresponding instructions into manipulatable objects

h. Software developed based on specifications provided by a particular organization

2. Imagine that your boss has just told you that "this piece of software is useless because all it does is store numbers and text." How would you explain the usefulness of this software application to your boss so that he would understand its importance to the company? Be sure to use terms such as "data," "information," "software," and so on.

3. Discuss the following in a small group of classmates. Many long-time computer users have grown up with command-based interfaces to the computer's operating system. Based on what you know about resistance to change from Chapter 2, outline a detailed explanation of the advantages of moving to a graphical user interface (GUI) so that these long-time users will be convinced to make the switch.

4. As a group, discuss the implications for an organization of having more than one operating system. What might be the advantages? What are some of the disadvantages? Would you recommend such a situation? Can you find organizations using the World Wide Web that specifically mention their utilization of multiple operating systems in their information system architecture? Do these organizations comment on this arrangement or simply mention its existence? Prepare a 10-minute presentation to the rest of the class of your findings.

5. Imagine that you are in charge of procuring software applications for your division of a company. You are in need of a powerful business information systems software application that will control most of the accounting and bookkeeping functions. Based on your current knowledge of the intricacies of the accounting profession and its practices, would you be more likely to purchase this application as a customized software application or an off-the-shelf software application? Why did you select this choice? What would make you choose the other option?

6. Do you feel that 5GL programming languages will lead to the 6GL "proposals" mentioned in this chapter? Why or why not? Discuss this idea with some of your classmates. What would you like to see as a part of the next generation of programming languages?

7. Based on the information within this chapter and others within this textbook, discuss the importance of a single decision to purchase one software application over another—for example, purchasing Microsoft Excel instead of Lotus 1-2-3. Who will be affected? How will they be affected? What changes might occur because of the purchase?

8. Interview an IS manager within an organization with which you are familiar. Determine the extent to which this person gets the data, information, knowledge, and wisdom needed to get the job done effectively. Does she obtain this information from IS sources? If not, how could IS be used to help?

9. In a small group of classmates, discuss the following. Based on your own experiences with computers and computer systems, what do you like and dislike about different operating systems that you have used? Were these uses on a professional or a personal level, or both? Who made the decision to purchase that particular operating system? Did you have any say in the purchase decision?

10. Choose an organization with which you are familiar that utilizes a variety of different software applications. Are these software applications customized applications, off-the-shelf applications, or a combination of the two? Talk with some of the employees to determine how they feel about using customized versus off-the-shelf software applications.

11. Search the World Wide Web for organizations that specialize in creating customized software applications for their clients. What specific product categories do these organizations specialize in, if any? Were you able to find any pricing information directly from their home pages?

12. Have the off-the-shelf software applications you've experienced met your requirements? Were you able to perform the functions and routines that you needed? Did the software meet your expectations? Would you have bought this type of software if you knew then what you know today?

13. Form a small group and describe your experiences with programming languages. Have you utilized them professionally? Based on the definitions in this chapter, with what generation of languages were you working? Were you aware of this designation prior to reading this chapter?

14. Choose an organization with which you are familiar that does a lot of in-house programming and utilizes a variety of different programming languages. Determine the generation level of these languages. Are the same personnel programming most (or all) of the languages, or are different personnel programming for each of the languages? Is this assignment of programmers intentional or unintentional?

15. Choose an organization with which you are familiar that utilizes a variety of different software applications. As a group of classmates, determine whether these software applications are from the same vendor or different vendors. Does this organization have compatibility problems between applications? Are there any plans underway to solve these compatibility problems? Who is trying to solve the problems, the programmers and end users or management?

16. Imagine that you and a friend are at a local ATM machine getting some cash from your account to pay for a movie. The ATM machine doesn't seem to be working. It is giving you an error message every time you press any button. Is this most likely a software-related problem or a hardware-related problem? Why? Use the information in this chapter and in the previous chapter to help you make your decision.

Real World Case Problems

1. ZAP! How the Year 2000 Bug Will Hurt the Economy

Robert Cowie, CIO of Genzyme Corporation, the biotech giant, realized early in 1996 that nearly every major system in the company would be unable to handle dates in the next century—the Year 2000 problem. If left uncorrected, the production equipment, the research and development computers, and the computers handling order taking and billing would all fail on or before January 1, 2000. Cowie is fortunate; thanks to an early start, the systems in his firm will all be repaired well ahead of the deadline.

Organizations that are not ready for the year 2000 are in for a serious awakening. Already the Securities &

Exchange Commission has been strongly encouraging companies to report the effect of the Year 2000 problem on their earnings. Although many believe the issue has generated too much hype, the Year 2000 problem is starting to have a significantly negative impact on the U.S. economy. A recent analysis by Standard & Poor's DRI shows the growth rate in 1999 to be 0.3 percentage points lower as companies divert resources to solve the problem. The Year 2000 problem could also cut one half a percentage point off growth in 2000 and in 2001. This growth reduction is the same size as the economic damage from the turmoil in East Asia. The total cost of the Year 2000 problem could be as high as $119 billion in lost economic output between now and 2001. Inflation will increase and productivity growth will be lower than it otherwise would have been. Instead of creating or installing new productivity-enhancing systems, every company is diverting money and staff toward fixing the Year 2000 problem.

Management consulting firms have added approximately 200,000 new workers over the past two years. Additionally, programmers' wages are dramatically increasing due to the need to correct this problem. Some businesses are doomed to have computer failures in 2000. A December 1997 survey by Howard Rubin at Hunter College found that two out of three companies did not have detailed plans to address the Year 2000 problem. Even the Federal Reserve is under pressure to raise interest rates, which would further run the risk of increasing the post–2000 slowdown.

   a. Is this just a bunch of hype promoted by consulting companies, or is the Year 2000 problem real? Why?

   b. What are some of the types of firms and systems that are likely to be adversely affected by this problem?

   c. Robert Cowie, CIO of Genzyme Corporation, fixed his firm's Year 2000 problems early. What are the implications of NOT fixing the problem on time?

Source   1998. *Zap!: How the Year 2000 bug will hurt the economy.* BusinessWeek, *March 2, 93–97*

2. Java for the Enterprise: Faster, Easier to Manage, More Scalable

In 1997, Sun Microsystems announced its eagerly awaited Enterprise JavaBeans specification—the industry's first server-specialized component model. Oracle also announced another Java milestone—the vendor's entire suite of client/server applications, Oracle Applications 10.7 NCA, was delivered as an all-Java package. These all-Java products and technologies were designed to push Java further into the mainstream.

Mike Anderson, director of application services at Home Depot, a $20-million home improvement chain center, says that they have been building mission-critical applications that he plans to implement throughout their 700 locations nationwide. These applications include inventory replenishment, human resource systems for training, job applicant requirements and benefits, and a virtual office for remote store managers.

Sabre Technologies and the Ralston Purina Company will both be using Java for cross-platform benefits. Sabre's Qik-Access product, which includes easy-to-use airline reservations, airport departure control, and travel agency systems, was written in C++ and is on more than 100,000 PCs using OS/2, Windows, and DOS. Rewriting the program in Java allows customers to use network computers and other thin clients to gain Sabre access to the smaller customers in the marketplace.

Ralston Purina will follow similarly with Packview, a Java-based manufacturing application for managing managers' schedules and equipment for packing rooms. Packview, as with Qik-Access, will run on multiple platforms. Applications that were once written in C or C++ can now be handled by JavaBeans. Companies can use JavaBeans to increase their flexibility in creating applications on the Internet; however, JavaBeans is still in the first draft—not in the final stage.

   a. How important is Sun's unveiling of its Enterprise JavaBeans specification and Oracle's delivery of its products as all-Java packages? Why?

   b. Why are firms such as Home Depot and Ralston Purina so attracted to Java?

   c. Should firms and universities still spend resources on training people to program in languages such as C, C++, Visual Basic, and COBOL?

Source   Levin, Rich. 1997. *Java for the enterprise.* InformationWeek, *December 8, 18–20.*

References

Arnaut, G. 1998. No frills, just service with a screen. *New York Times*, January 26, C5.

Fishauf, L. 1994. The Information Age in charts. *Fortune*, April 4, 75.

Fitzgerald, M. 1990. 'When' is now at Sears. *Computerworld*, October 8, 67.

Lemay, L., and C. L. Perkins. 1996. *Sams Teach Yourself Java in 21 Days*. Indianapolis, Indiana: Sams Publishing.

Microsoft, 1998. Information from: www.microsoft.com. Verified: February 7, 1998.

SABRE, 1998. Information from: www.amr.com. Verified: February 7, 1998.

SAP, 1998. Information from: www.sap.com. Verified: February 7, 1998.

Satzinger, J. W., and T. U. Orvik. 1996. The object-oriented approach: Concepts, modeling, and system development. Danvers, Massachusetts: boyd & fraser publishing company.

Ziff-Davis, 1998. Information from: www.sap.com. Verified: February 7, 1998.

Related Readings

Druschel, P. 1996. Operating system support for high-speed communication. *Communications of the ACM* 39(9): 41–51.

Dumas, J., and P. Parsons. 1995. Discovering the way programmers think about new programming environments. *Communications of the ACM* 38(6): 45–56.

Gentner, D., and J. Nielson. 1996. The anti-Mac interface. *Communications of the ACM* 39(8): 70–82.

Glass, R.L. 1997. The next date crisis and the ones after that. *Communications of the ACM* 40(1): 15–17.

Glass, R.L. 1997. The ups and downs of programmer stress. *Communications of the ACM* 40(4): 17–19.

Glass, R.L. 1997. Cobol—A contradiction and an enigma. *Communications of the ACM* 40(9): 11–13.

Kekre, Krishnan, and Srinivasan. 1995. Drivers of customer satisfaction for software products: Implications for design and service support. *Management Science* 41(9): 1456–1470.

Kim, J., and F.J. Lerch. 1997. Why is programming (sometimes) so difficult?: Programming as scientific discovery in multiple problem spaces. *Information Systems Research* 8(1): 25–50.

Klepper, R., and D. Bock. 1995. Third and fourth generation language productivity differences. *Communications of the ACM* 38(9): 69–79.

Nachenberg, C. 1997. Computer virus–antivirus coevolution. *Communications of the ACM* 40(1): 46–51.

Rudnicky, Hauptmann, and Lee. 1994. Survey of current speech technology. *Communications of the ACM* 37(3): 52–57.

Wiebe, Hirst, and Horton. 1996. Language use in context. *Communications of the ACM* 39(1): 102–111.

Scenario: Databases at Your School

Whether you realize it or not, databases are likely a significant part of your everyday life at your university, college, or community college. When you first registered for classes, you probably filled out what seemed to be an endless mountain of paperwork. You probably gave information about yourself, such as your social security number, your permanent home address, your temporary address at school, your high school's name and location, your GPA, your placement test scores, and your intended major. You might have also given similar information about your parent or legal guardian. Many years ago, this information sat in file cabinets, and retrieving it was a long and arduous process.

For example, as recently as the early 1980s, student records at many universities sat in manila folders in row after row of filing shelves. When a particular student record was needed, a student assistant was asked to "search the stacks" for the record. After it was found, the manila folder containing the record was removed, and a marker was left in its place to let others know that a record had been taken. Finally, the record was carried to the person who needed it. Universities now store records in electronic databases. When implemented well, these databases help us use information more effectively and efficiently than we could if the information were stored manually.

Think for a moment about how information about you on campus is created, stored, and used. When you registered for classes, you were probably assigned a student identification number, either your social security number or a special matriculation number. This number stays with you as long as you have interaction with your school. For example, when you register for classes, you do so with your ID number. Grades are assigned by student ID number, bills are sent out by student ID number, and books checked out

from the library are assessed against your student ID number. You get the idea. If the university has implemented their databases well, you should only have to change your address once with the university, and then all subsequent bills, grades, and overdue book notices will automatically follow you to your new, updated address. In effect, the databases keep track of the fact that you appear in them in many different places and situations.

In much the same manner, you will not receive your grades or diploma if you have an outstanding parking ticket, library fine, or other debt to the university. The databases keep track of all of your information, and they can be designed to alert personnel in one part of the university, such as the registrar's office, about significant events that have happened to you in other parts of the university, such as the library (see Figure 4.1). The existence of your records in these databases, and the usefulness of the databases to people at the school, doesn't stop when you graduate. Universities that keep strong relationships with their alumni can continue to use and update information about their graduates in their databases. This enables them to know precisely where you are and what you're up to—and when you last donated money to the school!

Business organizations make similar use of information and databases. The only difference is that businesses manage other types of information. In any event, educational institutions, business firms, governmental agencies, and nearly all other types of organizations have made use of the power of computer-based databases to manage data and provide information to people when and where they need it. In this chapter, we discuss such databases and the systems we use to create and manage them.

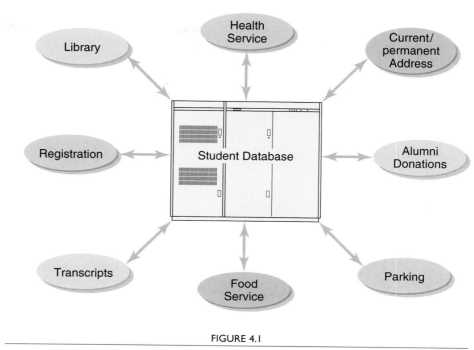

FIGURE 4.1

Types of information gathered in the student database.

Introduction

In the first three chapters of this book, we have learned about computers and their role in the workplace. In Chapters 2, "Information Systems Hardware," and 3, "Information Systems Software," we discussed computer hardware and software, but we did not discuss in detail how the computer stores and processes the information that is vital to the success of the firm. Databases and database management systems store this key information.

You may hear people in organizations refer to their information as mission-critical corporate data. They use and rely on their information every day. Whether this information is about customers, products, invoices, suppliers, markets, transactions, or competitors, an organization would be in dire straits without it. In large organizations, this information is stored in databases that can be billions (giga-) or trillions (tera-) of bytes in size. If an organization lost this data, it would have difficulty pricing and selling its products or services, cutting payroll checks for its employees, and even sending out mail. To say that an organization's data is mission critical is not an overstatement.

After reading this chapter, you will be able to do the following:

1. Describe why databases have become so important to modern organizations.

2. Describe what database and database management systems are and how they work.

3. Explain four emerging database trends: client/server computing, object-oriented databases, data mining, and integrating Web applications.

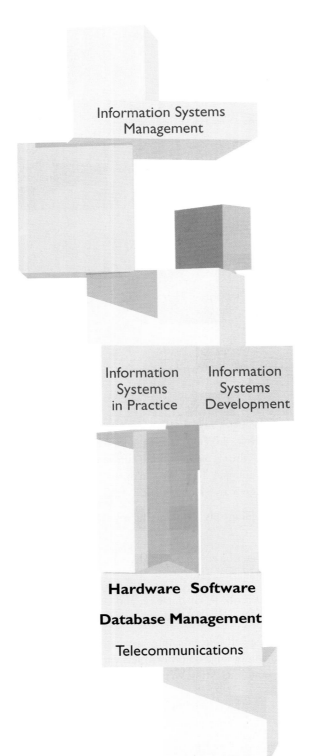

Information Systems
Management

Information
Systems
in Practice

Information
Systems
Development

Hardware Software

Database Management

Telecommunications

Information technologies, such as the ATM in the opening scenario of the last chapter, are playing an increasingly larger role in your lives. Given this increasing role, it will be useful to further your understanding of IS software. In terms of our guiding framework—The Big Picture—this is the third of four chapters focusing on the essential elements of information systems (see Figure 4.2). We begin by discussing the importance of information systems software to the success of modern organizations.

Database Management for Strategic Advantage

As we discussed in the introduction, an organization's **databases** are often their lifeblood. Let's think about why these databases, technology unknown to the business world 50 years ago, are so vital to organizations today.

Increasingly, we are living in an information age. Information once taken for granted or never collected at all is now used to make organizations more productive and competitive. Stock prices in the market, potential customers who meet our criteria for our products' target audience, and the credit rating of wholesalers and customers are all types of information—data that is organized and presented in a manner that makes it useful for us. Think about this book you are reading, which is in itself information. Also think about the other information sources used in its creation. The publishers had to know available authors capable of writing this book. The publishers also had to have information on you, the target audience, in order to determine that it was valuable to write this book and to suggest a writing style and collection of topics. Market information had to be used to set a price for the book, and information on reliable wholesalers and distribution partners had to be used to get the books from the publisher to you, the consumer.

FIGURE 4.2

The big picture: focusing on database management.

In addition to using databases to create this book, the publisher also uses databases to keep track of the book's sales, to determine royalties for the authors, to set salaries and wages for employees, to pay employees, to prospect for new book opportunities, to pay bills, and to perform nearly every other function in the business. For example, to determine royalties for authors on books sold, information must be collected from hundreds of bookstores and consolidated into a single report. Large publishers, such as Macmillan Computer Publishing, must regularly do this for thousands of books! Needless to say, the publisher could not effectively function without the use of computer databases.

Other types of organizations use databases to support their operations as well. Indeed, the process of using databases to create and sell this book are quite similar to the way other types of organizations use databases to create and sell their products. For example, the process of producing the Lands' End clothing catalog and marketing and selling their products to us is heavily database dependent. Companies such as Lands' End not only use databases to design and create their catalogs, but they also heavily depend on those databases containing information about us and our purchasing behavior. Some of these companies even produce tailor-made catalogs and other mailings for specific individuals based on the purchasing information stored in corporate databases.

NOVUS Financial

A BRIEF CASE

For a more specific example of the value of database systems, consider NOVUS Financial Corporation, a part of Dean Witter, Discover & Co. NOVUS offers a variety of consumer loans—everything from auto and boat loans to home mortgages. To stay ahead in today's competitive world of money lending, NOVUS realized it needed to make some changes in its information management systems. To be successful, NOVUS has to work fast, be flexible, and deliver the best customer service it can. The company's inflexible, outdated mainframe-based system made these goals impossible to achieve. To realign its information management systems for a better competitive advantage, NOVUS chose database products from Oracle Corporation.

In creating their new system, NOVUS wanted an environment that would satisfy customer service requests with one phone call. All of NOVUS's customer service functions are centralized in Sioux Falls, South Dakota, where more than 100 customer service professionals handle address changes and payment tracking. In the past, customer data was so spread out and inaccessible that follow-up calls to customers were inevitable. Users are delighted with the new database system's power and ease of use. Customer service representatives can access and share account information on a single screen without having to re-key the account number. NOVUS has also integrated all of their loan-related modules—customer, asset, vendor, and sales producer—so that all data is completely accessible across modules. This new database system has enabled NOVUS to improve customer service, improve the productivity of the customer service and developer staffs, reduce technology expenses, enable faster product time-to-market, and reduce paper flow. In other words, this database system is giving NOVUS a competitive advantage (see Oracle, 1998 for more on the success of NOVUS).

U.S. Airways

In a similar way, the fifth largest airline in America, U.S. Airways—with 2500 jet flights per day—is using an IBM database system to better manage its in-flight meal and video services. By analyzing upgrade, no-show, and cancellation patterns, U.S. Airways can more accurately predict how many meals are needed on each flight. Unused meals are a significant cost for airlines. Additionally, the database allows managers to understand which beverages are being carried but not being ordered. Like the food and beverages data, the number of headsets ordered for in-flight movies is also being analyzed and compared with the demographics of the passengers. Through this analysis, U.S. Airways is better able to provide movies that the majority of their customers really want to watch. When more passengers enjoy the in-flight movie, headset sales and customer satisfaction increase. Using this approach to managing their in-flight services, U.S. Airways paid for their investment in their database system within two months of use. Their long-term goal is to someday have a system that allows all customers to enjoy their favorite meal or drink and to be able to watch their favorite movie when flying U.S. Airways (for more information, see IBM, 1998).

As illustrated in these examples, database management systems have become an integral part of the total information systems solution for many organizations. Database management systems allow organizations to easily retrieve, store, and analyze information. Yet, it was not always this easy. Next, we describe how information was managed prior to computer-based database management systems.

Databases Before the Use of Computers

Think about what it would mean to have volumes of important information but to not have computers. All of the information mentioned in the previous examples needs to be collected, stored, analyzed, and updated, and it is easiest to do so using computers. If this book were priced using old manufacturing cost data written down several years ago, you would probably be very happy with the low price of your book, but the publisher would probably soon go out of business. If the list of wholesalers were stored on a blackboard that could be smudged or erased easily, you would find that it wouldn't be a very effective method over the long term. In order to manage data in the past, many people, lots of storage space, and painstaking care were needed. Data was kept in books, ledgers, card files, folders, and file cabinets—or sometimes simply in people's heads! Response times were long, and the process was labor intensive. Reported data was often incomplete or incorrect as a result.

Computers are used to automate much of the data processing done today. You can use computers to receive data electronically, store it, update it with new data feeds, and analyze numerical data using complex algorithms. Many uses for and analysis of data required in business today would have been impossible just a few years ago, particularly for large organizations with terabyte databases. Databases store the data, procedures are run against the database to analyze the data, and the data from them can be displayed as information. All of these tasks can be done relatively quickly and easily with the help of computers. Figure 4.3 highlights how computers help us store data efficiently.

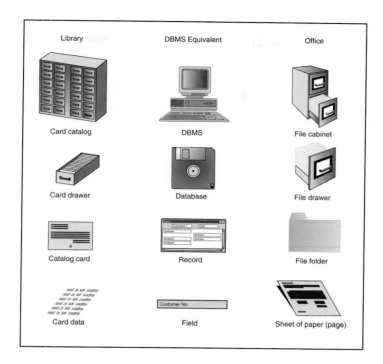

FIGURE 4.3

Computers make the process of storing and managing data much easier.

The Database Approach

To understand databases, we must familiarize ourselves with the terminology. In Figure 4.3, we compare some of the terminology with their equivalents in a library or a business office. Today, we use **database management systems** (DBMS) to interact with the data in databases. A DBMS is a software application with which you create, store, organize, and retrieve data from a single database or several databases. Microsoft Access is an example of a popular DBMS for personal computers. In the DBMS, such as Access, the individual database is a collection of related records and other files about entities. An **entity** is something you collect data about, such as people or classes (see Figure 4.4). We often think of entities as **tables**, where each row is a record and each column is a field. Each record consists of many **fields**, which are individual pieces of information. For example, a person's last name or social security number might be a field. A **record** is a collection of related fields within a single entity.

Before there were DBMSes, organizations used the file processing approach or another comparative approach to electronically store and manipulate data. Data was usually kept in a long, sequential computer file, which was often stored on tape. In addition, information about entities often appeared in several different places throughout the information system, and the data was often stored along with, and sometimes embedded within, the programming code that used the data. The concept of separately storing information about entities in nonredundant databases had not yet been envisioned, so files often had repetitive data about a customer, supplier, or another entity. When someone's address changed, it had to be changed in every file where that information occurred, an often tedious process. Similarly, if the programming code were changed, the corresponding data typically had to be changed along with it. This was often no better than the pen-and-paper approach to storing data.

Field Types

ID Number	Last Name	First Name	Street Address	City	State	Zip code	Major
209345	Vance	James	1242 N. Maple	Bloomington	Indiana	47401	Recreation
213009	Haggarty	Joe	3400 E. Longvi	Bloomington	Indiana	47405	Business Management
345987	Borden	Chris	367 Ridge Roa	Bloomington	Indiana	47405	Aeronautical Engineering
457838	Jessup	Mike	12 Long Lake	Bloomington	Indiana	47401	Computer Science
459987	Chan	Virginia	8009 Walnut	Bloomington	Indiana	47405	Sociology
466711	Monroe	Lisa	234 Jamie Lan	Bloomington	Indiana	47401	Pre-Medicine
512678	Austin	John	3837 Wood's E	Bloomington	Indiana	47401	Law
691112	Sherwin	Jordan	988 Woodbridg	Bloomington	Indiana	47404	Political Science
910234	Moore	Larry	1234 S. Grant	Bloomington	Indiana	47403	Civil Engineering
979776	Dunn	Pat	109 Hoosier Av	Bloomington	Indiana	47404	Psychology
983445	Pickett	Steve	989 College	Bloomington	Indiana	47401	Sports Science

Field

Record
(One Row)

FIGURE 4.4

This sample data table for the entity student includes eight fields and eleven records.

It is possible for a database to only consist of a single file or table. However, most non-trivial databases managed under a DBMS consist of several files, tables, or entities. The power and sophistication of the DBMS allow the tables to be joined, or linked, where there are similarities and to operate as a single database. A DBMS can manage hundreds, or even thousands, of tables simultaneously. These tables are linked as part of a single system. The value of the database approach is best evidenced with these large, complex sets of interrelated databases. The DBMS helps us manage the tremendous volume and complexity of interrelated data so that we can be sure that the change is automatically carried for every instance of that data if, for example, a student or customer address is changed. Such a change literally ripples out through all parts of the system where that data might occur. Using the DBMS prevents unnecessary and problematic redundancies of the data, and the data is kept separate from the programming code in applications. The database need not be changed if a change is made to the code in any of the applications. It is easy to see why the database approach now dominates nearly all of computer-based information systems used today.

Key Database Issues and Activities

In this section, we describe the database approach in more detail. We discuss the key issues and activities involved in the design, creation, use, and management of databases. We start by describing how people use databases, beginning with the entry of data.

Entering and Querying Data

Several tasks are performed using a database. Some of these tasks can be done by data entry clerks or managers; others require skilled database administrators and programmers. The general trend has been toward using DBMS software that is easy to use, enabling end users to create and manage their own database applications. At some point for all database applications, data must somehow be entered into the database.

Data gets into the database through data entry. A clerk or other data entry professional creates records in the database by entering data. This data may come from telephone conversations, preprinted forms that must be filled out, historical records, electronic files, or other means of getting data (see Figure 4.5A). Data entry is usually not performed by entering data into the database files as the computer sees them. Today, most applications enable us to use a *graphical user interface* (GUI) to create a **form**, which typically has blanks where the user can enter the information or make choices, each of which represents a field within a database record (see Figure 4.5B). This form presents the information to the user in an intuitive way so that the user can easily see and enter the data. The form might be online or printed, and the data could even be entered directly by the customer rather than by a data entry clerk. Forms can be used to add, modify, and delete data from the database.

Application For Employment — Pine Valley Furniture

Personal Information

Name: Date:

Social Security Number:

Home Address:

City, State, Zip

Home Phone: Business Phone:

U.S. Citizen? If Not, Give Visa No. & Expiration:

Position Applying For

Title: Salary Desired:

Referred By: Date Available:

Education

High School (Name, City, State):

Graduation Date:

Business or Technical School:

Dates Attended: Degree, Major:

Undergraduate College:

Dates Attended: Degree, Major:

Graduate School:

Dates Attended: Degree, Major:

Pine Valley Furniture

References

Form #2019
Last Revised:9/15/95

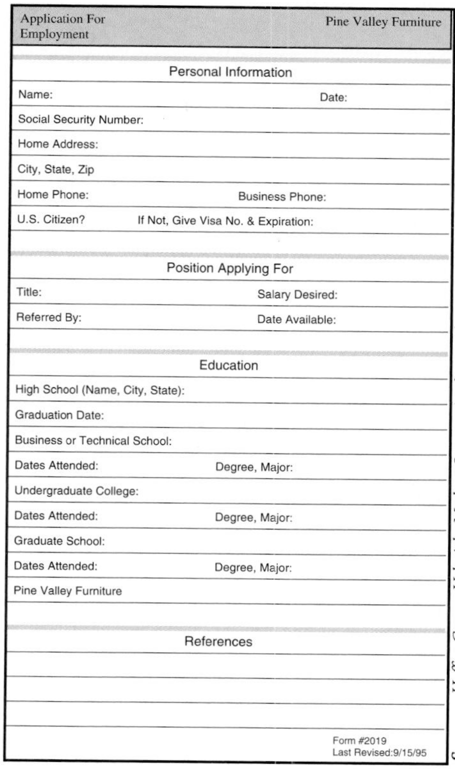

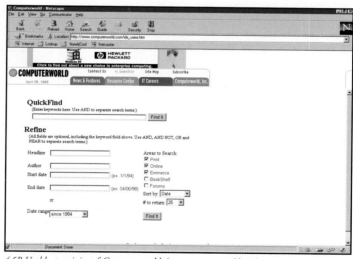

Source *Hoffer, George, Valacich, Modern Systems Analysis and Design (Figure 12.7 from page 475). © 1996 Benjamin/Cummings Publishing Company. Reprinted by permission of Addison Wesley Longman.*

FIGURE 4.5A

Preprinted form.

4.5B Used by permission of Computerworld *(www.computerworld.com)*

FIGURE 4.5B

Form A is an example of a preprinted form, while form B is an example of a computer-based entry form.

Querying the database is how we get information from it. To complete this task, we must have a way of interfacing with the database, usually through a form of query language. **Structured Query Language** (SQL) is the most common language used to interface with databases. Figure 4.6 is an example of a SQL statement used to find students who made an "A" in a particular course. These grades are sorted by student ID number.

```
SELECT DISTINCTROW STUDENT_ID, GRADE
FROM GRADES
WHERE GRADE = "A"
ORDER BY STUDENT_ID;
```

FIGURE 4.6

This sample SQL statement would be used to find students who earned an "A" in a particular course and to sort that information by student ID number.

Writing SQL statements requires a lot of time and practice, especially when dealing with complex databases with many entities or when writing complex queries with multiple integrated criteria—such as adding numbers while sorting on two different fields. Many DBMS packages have a simpler way of interfacing with the databases—using a concept called **query by example** (QBE). QBE capabilities in a database enable us to fill out a grid, or template, in order to construct a sample or description of the data we would like to see. Modern DBMS packages let us take advantage of the drag-and-drop features of a GUI to quickly and easily create a query. Conducting queries in this manner is much easier than typing the corresponding SQL commands. In Figure 4.7, we provide an example of the QBE grid from Microsoft's Access desktop DBMS package.

Screen shot reprinted by permission from Microsoft Corporation.

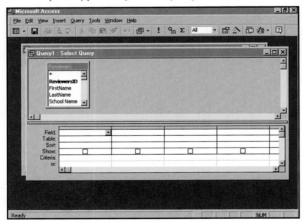

FIGURE 4.7

This screen capture from Microsoft Access shows the QBE grid that a user would fill out to describe the data he wants to see.

Creating Database Reports

In addition to ways to interactively query a database, most DBMS packages include a report writer feature. A **report** is a compilation of data from the database that is organized and produced in printed format. Reports are typically produced on paper, but they can be presented to users onscreen as well. Report writers, a special component accessed with the DBMS, are used to take data from the database to be manipulated (aggregated, transformed, or grouped) and displayed for the users in a useful format.

An example of a report is a quarterly sales report for a restaurant, as shown in Figure 4.8. Adding the daily sales totals, grouping them into quarterly totals, and displaying the results in a table of totals creates such a report. However, reports are not limited to text and numbers. Report writers enable us to create reports using any data in the databases at whatever level we choose. For example, we could add breakdowns of the data that show the average daily sales totals by days of the week to the restaurant report. Furthermore, this report could easily be improved by adding graphics. Perhaps we could show the quarterly sales totals in a bar chart. Each of these reports could be presented to the user either on paper or online. We could even create automatic links between the underlying sales data located in the database and the fields on the report in which the underlying data is used. In this way, the reports could be automatically updated every time they are produced.

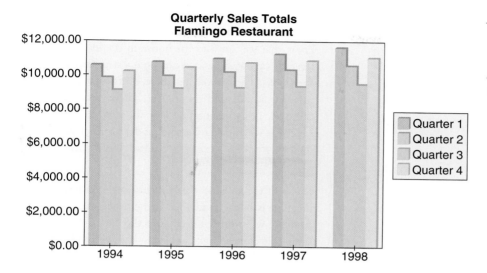

FIGURE 4.8

The quarterly sales report could either show text and numbers or a bar chart and could include the level of detail captured by the database data.

Book-of-the-Month Club

A BRIEF CASE

Database reports are making a big impact at the Book-of-the-Month Club (BOMC), the oldest and largest mail-order book club in the U.S., with more than 3.5 million members. Since its inception in 1926, the BOMC has shipped over 570 million books! Recently, the BOMC switched from a proprietary mainframe system to an Oracle database system. Using the new system, customer service representatives can be trained to use the system in about three days—versus 20 with the old system. Because the new system uses a database that can produce reports easily, the BOMC can analyze their data in ways never before possible. Reports are generated on the kinds of books being bought and the type of people ordering them. As a result, the BOMC has been able to fine-tune their acquisition strategy and marketing efforts. In addition to sophisticated analysis, the system provides customers who contact service representatives with very rapid response times. A customer's record can be recalled from the database in less than two seconds. Online reports provide complete information for the service representative, which helps to provide the best possible customer service. The Oracle database reporting environment is helping the company achieve its goal of becoming an unrivaled customer service organization—providing the books customers want with rapid response to questions. (For more information on BOMC, see Oracle, 1998).

Data Structure

The best database in the world is no better than the data it holds. Conversely, all the data in the world does you no good if it is not organized in a manner in which there are few or no redundancies and in which you can retrieve, analyze, and understand it. Therefore, the organizational database really has two parts, the data and the structure of that data.

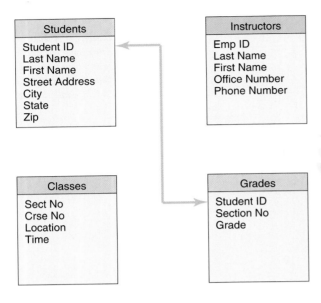

FIGURE 4.9

The attributes for and links among the four entities—students, instructors, classes, and grades.

Let's refer back to the library example in Figure 4.3 to better understand what the structure of data means. We know that we can find the books in the library based on the card catalog. The card catalog is a structure for finding the books. Each book has three cards, one each for the title, the author, and the subject. These classifications are a model, or representation, for the data in this system. Likewise, we must have a data model for databases. A **data model** is a representation of entities and their relationships in the real world.

Much of the work in creating an effective organizational database is in the modeling. If the model is no good, the database will not be effective. If the database is relatively small, the effects might not be so bad. However, in a corporate database, there are many entities, perhaps hundreds or thousands. In this case, the implications of a poor data model can be catastrophic. A poorly organized database is difficult to maintain and process—thus defeating the purpose of having a database management system in the first place. For example, think back to the scenario we used to open this chapter. We talked about the use of data at a school and mentioned several types of entities—students, instructors, classes, and grades. Each of these entities has attributes, which appear as fields in the database. Attributes of students might be their last names, first names, middle initials, and student ID numbers. Each of the other entities has attributes as well. Figure 4.9 shows attributes and links among four entities.

For the entity students, each student is represented as a record (or row) in the student table, and the attributes that describe each student appear as fields in each student record. The DBMS can sort an entity based on the information in a field. To do so, the field must be labeled as a *key*. The DBMS can sort that data in an ascending or descending order.

For the DBMS to distinguish between entities correctly, each instance of an entity must have one unique attribute. In our example, each student must be uniquely identified. A name alone will not work because students may have the exact same name. We must create and use a unique identifier in the database, which is called the **primary key**. For example, the student ID number is the primary key in the student table because no two students can have the same student ID number. The primary key can also be a combination of two or more attributes, called a combination primary key. An example of this might be the grades entity shown in Figure 4.9. The combination of student ID number and section number uniquely refers to an individual student and the semester she took the particular class because she may have taken the class more than once.

Data Type

Each field, or attribute, in the database needs to be of a certain type. For example, a field may contain text, numbers, or dates. This **data type** helps the DBMS organize and sort the data, complete calculations, and allocate storage space.

After the data model has been created, there needs to be a format for entering the data in the database. A **data dictionary** is a document—sometimes published as an online, interactive application—prepared by the designers of the database to aid individuals in data entry. The data dictionary explains several pieces of information for each attribute, such as the name of the field, whether or not it is a key or part of a key, the type of data expected in the field (dates, alphanumeric, numbers, and so on), and valid values for a field. Some data dictionaries include information such as why the data item is needed, how often it should be updated, and on which forms and reports the data appears.

One powerful use of data dictionaries is to enforce business rules. Business rules, such as who has authority to update a piece of data, are captured by the designers of the database and included in the data dictionary to prevent illegal or illogical entries from entering the database. For example, a validation check for a warehouse might be that the date the order was shipped could not be before the date the order was placed. The designers of the database for this business process would capture this rule in the data dictionary and prevent invalid ship dates from being entered into the database.

Database Management Systems Approaches

Now that we have discussed data, data models, and the storage of data, we need a mechanism for joining entities that have natural relationships with one another. For example, there are several relationships among the four entities we described previously—students, instructors, classes, and grades. Students are enrolled in classes. Likewise, instructors teach multiple classes and have many students in their classes in a semester. It is important to keep track of these relationships. We might, for example, want to know which courses a student is enrolled in so that we can notify her instructors that she will miss courses because of an illness. The three main DBMS approaches, or models, for keeping track of these relationships among data entities are hierarchical, network, and relational.

The Hierarchical Model

The **hierarchical database model** was the first model designed to join entities. DBMS packages that have followed this model refer to entities in a parent-child relationship. Records in parent entities can have many child records, but each child can have only one parent. Referring to our school example, a department (parent) can offer many courses (children), but each course belongs to only one department. This relationship, also called a *one-to-many relationship,* is very common in databases for organizations. However, forcing this parent-child relationship on data may be too restrictive and demanding for many databases. We sometimes also find pieces of data that have different relationships to each other, in which it is not always clear which is the parent and which is the child.

To better understand this problem, think back to our student example (see Figure 4.10). A student can be enrolled in many different courses at one time, and a course can have

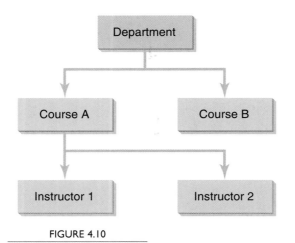

FIGURE 4.10

This hierarchical model depicts departments as parents of courses and courses as parents of instructors.

many different students enrolled at any one time. We do not necessarily have a one-to-many relationship here, and it is not clear which entity should be the parent and which should be the child. These types of problems can make the hierarchical model inadequate for many applications.

The Network Model

The **network database model** is much more flexible than the hierarchical model. With this model, there can be multiple children and parents. An example of this is a course with many sections (see Figure 4.11). Several different instructors could teach the sections of that course. One section of a course could even be team-taught by multiple instructors. Furthermore, the same instructor could teach multiple sections of a course and even more than one type of course. This relationship, also called a *many-to-many relationship*, is easier to represent with the network model than with the hierarchical model.

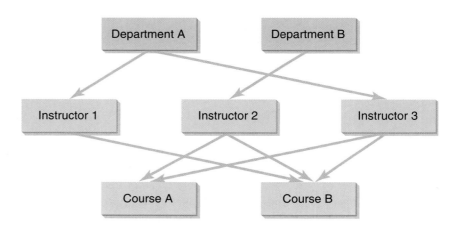

FIGURE 4.11

This network model depicts multiple parent-child relationships among entities.

The network model's flexibility is also its weakness. As the size and complexity of the databases in the organization become greater, so do the complexity and confusion in the model. In organizations with hundreds or thousands of entities, many of which have complex one-to-many and many-to-many relationships with one another, the network model quickly becomes too cumbersome for the database management system to manage effectively.

The Relational Model

The most common DBMS approach in use today is the **relational database model**. A DBMS package using this approach is often referred to as a relational DBMS, or RDBMS. With this approach, the DBMS views and presents entities as two-dimensional tables, with records as rows and fields as columns. Like a mathematical union operation, tables can be joined when there are common columns in the tables. The uniqueness of the primary key, as mentioned earlier, tells the DBMS which records should be joined with others in the corresponding tables. This structure supports very powerful data manipulation capabilities and linking of inter-related data. Database files in the relational model can be thought of as being three-dimensional in that a database has rows (one dimension), columns (a second dimension), and can contain a row of data in common with another file (a third dimension). This three-dimensional database is potentially much more powerful and useful than traditional, two-dimensional, "flat file" databases (see Figure 4.12).

Department Records

Department No	Dept Name	Location	Dean
Dept A			
Dept B			
Dept C			

Instructor Records

Instructor No	Inst Name	Title	Salary	Dept No
Inst 1				
Inst 2				
Inst 3				
Inst 4				

FIGURE 4.12

With the relational model, we represent these two entities, department and instructor, as two separate tables and capture the relationship between then with a common column in each table.

A good relational database design eliminates unnecessary data duplications and is easier to maintain than a poor design, in which most of the effort is expended in correctly identifying the entities, their attributes, and the relationships between those entities. The relational DBMS supports one-to-many relationships, many-to-many relationships, and one-to-one relationships between entities. To design a database with clear, nonredundant relationships, you perform a process called normalization.

Normalization

To be effective, databases usually must be efficient. Developed in the 1970s, **normalization** is a technique to make complex databases more efficient and more easily handled by the DBMS (Date, 1990). To better understand the normalization process, let's return to the scenario in the beginning of this chapter. Think about your report card. It looks like nearly any other form or invoice. Your personal information is usually at the top, and each of your classes is listed, along with an instructor, a class day and time, the number of credit hours, and a location. Now think about how this data is stored in a database back at the school. Imagine that this database is organized so that in each row of the database, the student's identification number is listed on the far left. To the right of the student ID are the student's name, local address, major, and phone number. In addition, the row contains course and instructor information, as well as a final course grade (see Figure 4.13). Notice that there is redundant data for students, courses, and instructors in each row of this database. This redundancy means that this database is not well organized. If, for example, we want to change the phone number of an instructor who has hundreds of students, we have to change this number hundreds of times.

Student ID#	Student Name	Campus Address	Major	Phone	Course ID	Course Title	Instructor Name	Instructor Location	Instructor Phone	Term	Grade
A121	Joy Egbert	100 N. State Street	MIS	555-7771	MIS 350	Intro. MIS	Van Deventer	T240C	555-2222	F'98	A
A121	Joy Egbert	100 N. State Street	MIS	555-7771	MIS 372	Database	Hann	T240F	555-2224	F'98	B
A121	Joy Egbert	100 N. State Street	MIS	555-7771	MIS 375	Elec. Comm.	Chatterjee	T240D	555-2228	F'98	B+
A121	Joy Egbert	100 N. State Street	MIS	555-7771	MIS 448	Strategic MIS	Chatterjee	T240D	555-2228	F'98	A−
A121	Joy Egbert	100 N. State Street	MIS	555-7771	MIS 474	Telecomm	Gilson	T240E	555-2226	F'98	C+
A123	Larry Mueller	123 S. State Street	MIS	555-1235	MIS 350	Intro. MIS	Van Deventer	T240C	555-2222	F'98	A
A123	Larry Mueller	123 S. State Street	MIS	555-1235	MIS 372	Database	Hann	T240F	555-2224	F'98	B−
A123	Larry Mueller	123 S. State Street	MIS	555-1235	MIS 375	Elec. Comm.	Chatterjee	T240D	555-2228	F'98	A−
A123	Larry Mueller	123 S. State Street	MIS	555-1235	MIS 448	Strategic MIS	Chatterjee	T240D	555-2228	F'98	C+
A124	Mike Guon	125 S. Elm	MGT	555-2214	MIS 350	Intro. MIS	Van Deventer	T240C	555-2222	F'98	A−
A124	Mike Guon	125 S. Elm	MGT	555-2214	MIS 372	Database	Hann	T240F	555-2224	F'98	A−
A124	Mike Guon	125 S. Elm	MGT	555-2214	MIS 375	Elec. Comm.	Chatterjee	T240D	555-2228	F'98	B+
A124	Mike Guon	125 S. Elm	MGT	555-2214	MIS 474	Telecomm	Gilson	T240E	555-2226	F'98	B
A126	Jackie Judson	224 S. Sixth Street	MKT	555-1245	MIS 350	Intro. MIS	Van Deventer	T240C	555-2222	F'98	A
A126	Jackie Judson	224 S. Sixth Street	MKT	555-1245	MIS 372	Database	Hann	T240F	555-2224	F'98	B+
A126	Jackie Judson	224 S. Sixth Street	MKT	555-1245	MIS 375	Elec. Comm.	Chatterjee	T240D	555-2228	F'98	B+
A126	Jackie Judson	224 S. Sixth Street	MKT	555-1245	MIS 474	Telecomm	Gilson	T240E	555-2226	F'98	A−
...	...	...	...	...	...	...	...	...	...	...	...

FIGURE 4.13

Database of students, courses, instructors, and grades with redundant data.

Elimination of data redundancy is a major goal and benefit of using data normalization techniques. After the normalization process, the student data is organized into five separate tables (see Figure 4.14). This reorganization helps simplify the ongoing use and maintenance of the database and any associated analysis programs.

Student Table

Student ID#	Student Name	Campus Address	Major	Phone
A121	Joy Egbert	100 N. State Street	MIS	555-7771
A123	Larry Mueller	123 S. State Street	MIS	555-1235
A124	Mike Guon	125 S. Elm	MGT	555-2214
A126	Jackie Judson	224 S. Sixth Street	MKT	555-1245
...	...	...	...	...

Class Table

Course ID	Course Title
MIS 350	Intro. MIS
MIS 372	Database
MIS 375	Elec. Comm.
MIS 448	Strategic MIS
MIS 474	Telecomm
...	...

Teaching Assignment

Course ID	Term	Instructor Name
MIS 350	F'98	Van Deventer
MIS 372	F'98	Hann
MIS 375	F'98	Chatterjee
MIS 448	F'98	Chatterjee
MIS 474	F'98	Gilson
...	...	...

Instructor Table

Instructor Name	Instructor Location	Instructor Phone
Chatterjee	T240D	555-2228
Gilson	T240E	555-2226
Hann	T240F	555-2224
Valacich	T240D	555-2223
Van Deventer	T240C	555-2222

Enrolled Table

Student ID#	Course ID	Term	Grade
A121	MIS 350	F'98	A
A121	MIS 372	F'98	B
A121	MIS 375	F'98	B+
A121	MIS 448	F'98	A−
A121	MIS 474	F'98	C+
A123	MIS 350	F'98	A
A123	MIS 372	F'98	B−
A123	MIS 375	F'98	A−
A123	MIS 448	F'98	C+
A124	MIS 350	F'98	A−
A124	MIS 372	F'98	A−
A124	MIS 375	F'98	B+
A124	MIS 474	F'98	B
A126	MIS 350	F'98	A
A126	MIS 372	F'98	B+
A126	MIS 375	F'98	B+
A126	MIS 474	F'98	A−
...	...	...	...

FIGURE 4.14

Organization of information on students, courses, instructors, and grades after normalization.

Associations

The associations, or relationships, among entities in our data structures help determine whether a database is well designed. The three types of associations among entities are one-to-one, one-to-many, and many-to-many. Table 4.1 summarizes each of these three associations and how they should be handled in database design.

Table 4.1 Rules for expressing associations among entities and their corresponding data structures.

Relationship	Example	Instructions
One-to-One	Each team has only one home stadium, and each home stadium has only one team.	Place the primary key from each table in the table for the other entity as a foreign key.
One-to-Many	Each player is on only one team, but each team has many players.	Place the primary key from the entity on the one side of the relationship as a foreign key in the table for the entity on the many side of the relationship.
Many-to-Many	Each player participates in games, and each game has many players.	Create a third entity/table and place the primary keys from each of the original entities together in the third table as a combination primary key.

To better understand how associations work, consider Figure 4.15, which shows four tables—Home Stadium, Team, Player, and Games—for keeping track of the information for a basketball league.

To obtain meaningful information from these tables, we must be able to create relationships between them. For example, the Home Stadium table lists the stadium name and capacity but not the city in which the stadium is located. Only through making an association with the Team table can we obtain this information. For example, if each team has only one home stadium, and each home stadium has only one team, we have a one-to-one relationship between the team and the home stadium entities. In situations in which we have one-to-one relationships between entities, we place the primary key from one table in the table for the other entity as a foreign key (see section A. in Figure 4.16). We can choose in which of these tables to place the foreign key of the other. After doing this to the team entity, we can identify which stadium is the home for a particular team.

Home Stadium

Stadium ID	Stadium Name	Capacity	...

Team

Team ID	Team Name	Location

Player

Player ID	Player Name	Position

Games

Team ID (1)	Team ID (2)	Date	Final Score

FIGURE 4.15

Associations keep track of the information for a basketball league.

When we find a one-to-many relationship—for example, each player plays for only one team, but each team has many players—we place the primary key from the entity on the one side of the relationship, the team entity, as a foreign key in the table for the entity on the many side of the relationship, the player entity (see section B. in Figure 4.16). In essence, we take from the one and give to the many, kind of a Robin Hood strategy. When we find a many-to-many relationship (for example, each player plays in many games, and each game has many players), we create a third, new entity—in this case, the Player Statistics entity and corresponding table. We then place the primary keys from each of the original entities together into the third, new table as a new, combination primary key (see section C. in Figure 4.16).

A. One-to-one relationship: Each team has only one home stadium, and each home stadium has only one team.

Team

Team ID	Team Name	Location	Stadium ID

B. One-to-many relationship: Each player is on only one team, but each team has many players.

Player

Player ID	Player Name	Position	Team ID

C. Many-to-many relationship: Each player participates in many games, and each game has many players.

Player Statistics

Team 1	Team 2	Date	Player ID	Points	Minutes	Fouls

FIGURE 4.16

Tables used for storing information about several basketball teams, with fields added in order to make associations.

You may have noticed that by placing the primary key from one entity in the table of another entity, we are creating a bit of redundancy. We are repeating the data in different places. We're willing to live with this bit of redundancy, however, because it enables us to keep track of the inter-relationships among the many pieces of important organizational data that are stored in different databases. By keeping track of these relationships, we can quickly answer questions such as, "Which players on the SuperSonics played in the game on February 16 and scored more than 10 points?" In a business setting, the question might be, "Which customers purchased the 1998 forest green Ford Explorer XLTs with four-wheel-drives from Thom Roberts at the Roberts' Ford dealership in Bloomington, Indiana during the first quarter of 1998, and how much did each of them pay?" This kind of question would be useful in calculating the bonus money Thom should receive for that quarter or in recalling those specific vehicles in the event of a recall by the manufacturer.

You now have an understanding of the importance of creating simple, clear data structures for your database. If you decide to take more information systems courses, you will likely have opportunities to learn more about these concepts and techniques. For now, you know the basics that will help you understand the databases you will use in your career.

Recent Developments Affecting Database Design and Use

As is true for all computing and information systems, there are constantly new developments that have important implications for how we design, create, use, and manage databases in organizations. For example, the move to relational DBMS packages and the development of powerful personal computer-based DMBS packages fundamentally changed the way databases are used and enabled many more people to build them. In the next section, we discuss four more recent developments: client/server computing, object-oriented databases, data mining, and Web links to organizational databases.

Databases and Client/Server Computing

Database applications in organizations have become so large and complex and serve so many different purposes and people that they sometimes do not run efficiently on any one computer. **Client/server architecture** was designed to help solve this problem. In a client/server architecture, the application is divided into two parts (see Figure 4.17). The database itself resides on a powerful computer, called a **database server**. The programs used to manipulate the database reside on a user's desktop computer, called a client. In other words, you can retrieve data from the server by running an application at your desktop computer. This client application usually consists of forms, reports, and other visual tools to aid you in modifying data in the database and in displaying it onscreen or in a printout. Table 4.3 highlights popular DBMS packages.

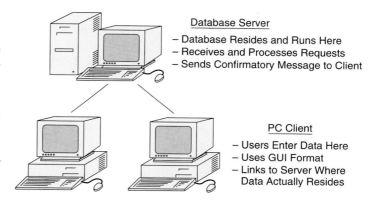

Database Server
– Database Resides and Runs Here
– Receives and Processes Requests
– Sends Confirmatory Message to Client

PC Client
– Users Enter Data Here
– Uses GUI Format
– Links to Server Where
  Data Actually Resides

FIGURE 4.17

With the client/server approach to databases, the data actually resides on a server, while users enter data and perform other database functions from their own client computers.

Table 4.2   Some popular DBMS packages.

Desktop	Midrange	Mainframe
Access	SQL Server	Informix
Paradox	Rdb	Oracle
Approach	RMS	Sybase
dBASE	CA-Ingres	DB2

Object-Oriented Databases

Some databases have begun to embrace the object-oriented design techniques used in programming. For many of the same reasons that object-oriented programming is popular, **object-oriented databases** (OODBs) are becoming popular. OODBs treat tables, queries, and other components as generic, reusable objects that can be mixed and matched and used in many different applications (Norman, 1996). Modularity and the opportunity for relatively quick and easy reuse of objects is appealing to organizations investing a great deal of time and money into their databases. Fortunately, for the most part, the OO languages, such as C++ or Smalltalk, carry over easily to OODBs.

OODBs are not meant to replace the relational data model; the paradigm used in OODBs supports the relational model. Objects can relate to objects much as entities relate to entities. Using OODBs is better than using the relational model, however, because OODBs can handle complex, user-defined data types. Recall the data types supported by the relational model; they are limited to text, floating-point numbers, integers, and dates. OODBs also support the encapsulation of both data and the methods used to manipulate the data, whereas the models we discussed earlier separate the data from the procedures used to act upon them. Objects can also inherit data and methods from other objects, something not possible in traditional database designs.

While many popular database management systems have object-oriented characteristics, full-fledged OODBs are still somewhat experimental. OODB vendors are primarily small start-up companies that have yet to gain a large amount of market share. Examples of OODBMs on the market today include Illustra, MATISSE, and Total ORDB. For any OODB to be successful, it must be compatible with SQL. SQL has been the standard for data manipulation since the 1970s. Any technology that requires programmers to learn a completely different way of interacting with it will have difficulty gaining acceptance. As it is, object-orientation is so different from traditional ways of writing software that it is difficult to get developers to embrace the technology. Although there are many perceived advantages of OODBs, there are also still very few success stories related to them. The theoretical foundation is exciting, but not yet widely accepted, unlike the relational model.

Data Mining

To support more effective information management, many large organizations are using **data mining**. This is a method used by large firms to sort and analyze information to better understand their customers, products, markets, or any other phase of their business for which data has been captured. With data mining tools, you can graphically drill down from summary data to more detailed data, sort or extract data based on certain conditions, and perform a variety of statistical analyses, such as trend analysis, correlation analysis, forecasting, and analysis of variance. Data mining is also referred to as online analytical processing (OLAP). It is very closely related to the IS academic research area, decision support systems (see Chapter 7, "Organizational Information Systems"). Some of the software tools for data mining include ProBit and Pilot Software's Decision Support Suite. Sales of software, hardware, and services for data mining are expected to grow from $2 billion in 1995 to $8 billion in 1998 (Foley, 1996). In order to effectively mine data, special types of databases, called data warehouses and data marts, are created.

Data Warehouses

Many large organizations are building **data warehouses**, which integrate multiple, large databases and other information sources into a single repository. This repository is suitable for direct querying, analysis, or processing. Much like a physical warehouse for products and components, the data warehouse involves the physical storage and distribution of data on computer-based information systems. The data warehouse appears to the user as a virtual storehouse of valuable data from the organization's disparate information systems and, perhaps, from other external sources. It supports the online analysis of sales, inventory, and other vital business data that has been culled from operational systems. The purpose is to put key business information into the hands of more decision makers, and the driving force is the need for data access. Table 4.3 lists some sample industry uses of data warehouses. Data warehouses can involve hundreds of gigabytes, even terabytes, of data. They usually run on fairly powerful mainframe computers, and can cost millions of dollars.

Data warehouses represent more than just big databases. An organization that successfully deploys a data warehouse has committed to pulling together, integrating, and sharing critical corporate data throughout the firm.

Table 4.3   Sample industry uses of data warehousing (adapted from: Boar, 1998).

Uses of Data Warehousing	Representative Companies
Retail	
Analysis of scanner check-out data	Wal-Mart
Tracking, analysis, and tuning of	Kmart
sales promotions and coupons	Sears
Inventory analysis and redeployment	Osco/Savon Drugs
Price reduction modeling to "move"	Casino Supermarkets
the product	W. H. Smith Books
Negotiating leverage with suppliers	Otto Versand Mail Order
Frequent buyer program management	
Profitability analysis	
Product selections for granular	
market segmentation	
Telecommunications	
Analysis of the following:	AT&T
Call volumes	Ameritech
Equipment sales	Belgacom
Customer profitability	British Telecom
Costs	Telestra Australia
Inventory	Telecom Ireland
Purchasing leverage with suppliers	Telecom Italia
Frequent buyer program management	
Banking and Finance	
Relationship banking	Bank of America
Cross-segment marketing	Bank One
Risk and credit analysis	Merrill Lynch
Merger and acquisition analysis	CBOE
Customer profiles	CNA
Branch performance	

Source   Copyright © 1998, NCR Corporation. Used with permission.

Data Marts

Rather than storing all enterprise data in one monolithic database, many organizations have created multiple **data marts**, each containing a subset of the data for a single aspect of a company's business—for example, finance, inventory, or personnel. Data marts have been popular among small and medium-sized businesses and among departments within larger organizations, all of which were previously prohibited from developing their own data warehouses due to the high costs involved.

Data marts typically contain tens of gigabytes of data, as opposed to the hundreds of gigabytes in data warehouses. Therefore, they can be deployed on less powerful hardware with smaller disks. The differences in costs between different types of data marts and data warehouses can be significant. The cost to develop a data mart is typically less than $1 million, while the cost for a distributed data mart can approach $10 million. The cost for an enterprise-wide data warehouse can exceed $10 million (Foley & DePompa, 1996). With this amount of money on the table, the data mart business is heating up. For example, Informatica, which bills itself as "the enterprise data mart company," estimates that data mart software sales will grow 351 percent between 1995 and 1998, from $153 million to $690 million. Companies such as Computer Associates, NCR Corp., Sybase, Software AG, Red Brick Systems, and others are coming out with new products and services that make it easier and cheaper to deploy these scaled-down data warehouses.

Many organizations that cannot afford a data warehouse first built themselves a data mart. This may not be an optimal decision. Some experts believe that users should create enterprise data warehouses first and then build data marts as highly summarized subsets of the warehouse. These experts believe that doing so helps keep the data clean and nonredundant, which helps maintain its integrity. In any event, large organizations often deploy a data warehouse and multiple data marts. For example, Merck-Medco Managed Care Inc., a subsidiary of Merck & Co. in Montvale, New Jersey, runs both a 500-GB data warehouse and six smaller data marts.

Linking Web Site Applications to Organizational Databases

A recent database development is the use of databases to create links between sites on the Web to organizational databases. For example, many companies are enabling users of their Web site to view product catalogs, check inventory, and place orders—all actions that ultimately read and write to the organizations' databases.

The applications on the Web site are created using Hypertext Markup Language (HTML) editors and other Web development tools, such as SoftQuad HotMeTaL, Netscape LiveWire Pro, and Microsoft FrontPage. They are managed with Web server software, such as NCSA HTTPd, Netscape Commerce Server, and Microsoft Internet Information Server. Using these tools, it is easy to create interactive forms that users can access on the Web. These forms pass data from the form to the database, and vice versa. To shuttle data, queries, and other information back and forth between Web applications and databases, developers create common gateway interface (CGI) scripts in PERL, Microsoft VBScript, or programming languages, such as C (Hermann, 1996). The databases are created using standard DBMS packages, such as Microsoft Access or Oracle, and they can be housed on nearly any hardware platform.

This evolution in computing provides users with easy, fast access to an organization's processes and data. Many companies are using Web-based interfaces to databases in order to greatly improve customer service. We will talk more in Chapter 8, "Emerging Information Systems," about the implications of using such technologies to improve customer contact. As you might expect, security is critical with applications like this. Any time you let people or data into critical organizational databases, you must ensure the safety and integrity of those databases. Organizations that link Web sites to back-end databases are careful to use *firewall* applications, which act much like physical firewalls in monitoring the kinds of data traffic that are passed back and forth and in blocking unwanted data traffic.

CNN Interactive   A BRIEF CASE

An example of successfully linking a large corporate database with a Web interface can be found at CNN Interactive. CNN Interactive provides a free, online custom news service to hundreds of thousands of subscribers around the world. Using the World Wide Web, the site delivers up-to-the-minute news from over 100 sources and offers more than 2,000 categories of customized news options, ranging from sports and health to recreation, pop culture, crime, and consumer issues. On a typical week, 20,000 new articles are stored. CNN Interactive uses an Oracle database to dynamically build personalized news pages for hundreds of thousands of daily users. These pages are updated every 15 minutes to deliver the most current information. This application is only made possible by the sophisticated database system, which manages the vast amount of changing information and automatically builds the customized Web pages (for more information, see Oracle, 1998).

Effective Management of Databases

We've come full circle in this chapter. We first explained why databases are so important to organizations and then described how databases are developed and used. We can now talk more about how organizational databases can be managed effectively. Of the many roles taken in managing organizational databases, none is more important than that of the **database administrator** (DBA). The DBA is responsible for the development and management of the organization's databases. The DBA works with the *systems analysts* (described in great detail in later chapters), programmers, and data modelers to design and implement the database.

Along with these technical tasks, the DBA must also work with users and managers of the firm on more managerial and organizational issues relating to the database. For example, the DBA must properly implement the relevant business rules and validity checks on the database data, as set forth by managers. The DBA is also responsible for implementing some security features, such as designating who can look at the database and who is authorized to make changes. The DBA should not make these decisions unilaterally; rather, these are business decisions made by organizational managers that the DBA merely implements.

In a later chapter, you learn more about the systems analysis and design process. For now, you should know that the process of database development for an organization can be very complex. It usually involves a team of systems personnel, users of the database, and managers. Together, they determine the form and function of the database. In some organizations, the DBA is a specific job, while in others, people with other job titles perform DBA functions. Although you may not find someone with the DBA title, you can be sure that someone is fulfilling the DBA functions—either formally or informally—if the organization is using computer databases well.

ETHICAL PERSPECTIVE: DATABASE PROPRIETORSHIP AND INFORMATION OWNERSHIP

It happens to all of us. Nearly every day in the mail, we receive unwanted solicitations from credit card companies, department stores, magazines, or charitable organizations. Many of these envelopes are never opened. We ask the same question over and over again: "How did I get on another mailing list?" Your name, address, and other personal information were most likely sold from one company to another for use in mass mailings. You probably did not give anyone permission to buy or sell information about you, but that is not a legal issue, or a matter of concern, for some firms.

Who owns the computerized information about people—the information that is stored in thousands of databases by retailers, credit card companies, and marketing research companies? The answer is that the company that maintains the database of customers/subscribers legally owns the information and is free to sell it. Your name, address, and other information are all legally kept in a company database to be used for the company's future mailings and solicitations. However, the company can sell its customer list or parts of it to other companies who want to do similar mailings. This is where the problems begin. For instance, LL Bean, the outdoor and apparel retailer, can sell names and addresses from its customer database to companies looking for a similar customer base or buying pattern. Of course, LL Bean would not sell parts of their list to competitors. The list is to be used only once and can be used again only with repayment of the initial fee. Still, many people are concerned that these companies have full ownership of this purchasing and demographic data.

There are limits, however, to what a company can do with such data. For example, if a company stated at one time that its collection of marketing data, including demographic (who am I and where do I live) and psychographic (what are my tastes and preferences) data, was to be used strictly internally as a gauge of its own customer base and then sold that data to a second company years later, would be unethically and illegally breaking their original promise.

Companies collect data from credit card purchases (by using a credit card, you indirectly allow this) or from surveys and questionnaires, which obtain demographic and psychographic data. By filling in a survey at a bar, restaurant, supermarket, or mall, you are implicitly agreeing that this data can be used as the company wishes (within legal limits, of course).

What is even more problematic is the combination of this survey data with transaction data from your credit card purchases. How do you know who is accessing these databases? This is an issue that each company must address at both a strategic/ethical level (is this something that we should be doing?) and at a tactical level (if we do this, what can we do to ensure the security and integrity of the data?). The company needs to ensure proper hiring, training, and supervision of employees who have access to the data, as well as to implement the necessary software and hardware security safeguards.

Do you want to stop receiving junk mail? To have your name added to the Direct Marketing Association (DMA) Pander File—the list of names that are never to be included in junk mailings or database selling—write to the Direct Marketing Association, Mail Preference Service, PO Box 9008, Farmingdale, New York, 11735-9008. Provide your name and address, and you should notice a reduction after about 90 days. For more information, you may call the DMA at 1-212-768-7277 during regular business hours.

Questions for Discussion

1. Is having your name included on the Pander File enough? Should other legal measures be taken to ensure the confidentiality of information about us? Why or why not?

2. What other ethical issues concerning property and information ownership have you heard about or encountered?

3. Right now, there are no laws or FTC regulations concerning the use of names on company databases. The DMA is a self-regulated group with its own policies. Does this make you feel any less comfortable about the use of your name and information?

INTERNATIONAL PERSPECTIVE: INFORMATION AND ECONOMIC POVERTY—GLOBAL HAVES AND HAVE NOTS

Today, the Internet enables us to tap into vast and varied stores of information around the globe. Unfortunately, not everyone around the world has equal access to these global data stores. Just as there have been economic haves and have nots, in this wired world, there are those who now live in information poverty.

In mid-1995, about 70 percent of all computers (single and multi-user) connected to the Internet worldwide were located in the U.S. (Holderness, 1995). Holderness contrasts that statistic with a statistic from this past April, when Vietnamese academics announced the first dozen text-only connections in the country. In many countries, the possibility of Internet access does not mean that there are users who are able and technology that is capable of taking the opportunity. While the Internet reaches into well over 100 countries now, nearly half the world's population is without telephones and, thus, has no Internet access.

Internet users in some developing countries spend up to 25 times what those in the U.S. spend to make connections that are not only slower and more precarious, but also do not have advanced capabilities, such as graphics and sound. This trend seems to be leading not only to information poverty in some parts of the world, but to increasing economic poverty, as the developing countries—rich in natural resources—are excluded de facto from world trade and world information.

Holderness implies that access to and the instant transfer of data will change commerce and the way that humans communicate. It seems that it is already doing so. Kaljee (online) notes that "Clearly the technological revolution that took place once the benefits of access to the Internet became clear to the general public has been limited to the developed countries only." (See http://www.sas.upenn.edu/African_Studies/ASA/Marcel_Kaljee.html) He claims that the move away from using the Internet for mostly personal email and research to major advertising campaigns and other focused marketing is creating new markets, from which the developing countries are excluded. The factors that excluded developing countries from global trade in the past—trade restrictions and lack of physical infrastructure, such as roads—are not major hindrances on the information superhighway. Now that the Internet is attracting such a large number of consumers and businesses worldwide, people in these developing countries need to get connected.

Kaljee notes that the Internet systems that do exist in these developing countries are antiquated by U.S. standards. Mobile telecommunications exist in some developing countries. Packet radio networks, which can be used to broadcast packets of data via radio waves, reach into some areas that are without phone lines (and where phones will not be feasible for quite some time). Satellite telecommunications are employed in some areas, but mostly for broadcast—and then not to the rural areas. ISDN (Integrated Services Digital Network) phone lines have been introduced in only a few areas.

Developed countries should assist developing countries in gaining greater access to the Internet for many reasons. Holderness (1995) suggests that the poorer countries are not receiving such help for the same reasons that they should. He claims that access in developing countries could help the problem of "brain drain" there; outstanding academics could be recognized as part of a borderless Internet-based academe without having to travel to the U.S. or the U.K. He also notes that the lack of information access makes countries in the Southern Hemisphere even more dependent on those in the North and increases the distance between information haves and have nots, not only on a global scale, but within countries as well. In times when information is money, access to information seems closely guarded by those who have it.

An economic system seems to be developing in accessing global information sources, such as the Internet. How this system will shape the future of the global economy is purely speculative, but perhaps some balance can eventually be reached by the time that the currency is solely informational and the infrastructure is purely technology based.

Questions for Discussion

1. Who should be initiating and funding the development of IS in developing countries? Why?

2. Predict what the world will look like in 50 years if the information gap continues to increase.

3. In your opinion, what is likely to happen with respect to developing countries going online? In what kind of time frame?

Sources *Holderness, M. 1995. Falling through the net. New Statesman and Society 8 (Oct. 13): 24. Kaljee, M. Feeder. Roads close the information gap: low cost public e-mail systems for access to the information highway. Available online at http://www.sas.upenn.edu/African_Studies/ASA/Marcel_Kaljee.html.*

Talking with...

Marty Schick, Senior Database Analyst at Indiana University

Educational Background

B.A. in History, Rollins College; M.B.A., Butler University

Job Description

Marty Schick is primarily responsible for the maintenance and support of all DB2 databases that are used to support Indiana University's administrative needs. She also has the primary responsibility for data modeling activities performed by the Database Administration Team. She has secondary responsibility for Sybase Databases, which exist on a variety of UNIX platforms. Sybase Databases are used in support of the university's administrative systems.

Critical Success Factors

A key factor to success in the information systems world today is to develop a good customer service orientation. Customers can be clients from an external department that you support, co-workers, or fellow team members. Time management is also a crucial factor in succeeding in the information systems world. Identifying and prioritizing tasks ensures that the most value is received for time invested. Another critical success factor is to be flexible. The information systems world is changing on a daily basis. You must be willing to learn new technologies to keep pace with the environment.

Advice to Students

Pursue a well-rounded education. By being exposed to many different aspects of the business and technical world, you can learn how businesses function, as well as how to be a provider of information technology services. Understanding the functionality of businesses is critical to providing quality information services.

Summary

1. **Describe why databases have become so important to modern organizations.** Databases often house mission-critical organizational data, so proper design and management of the databases is critical. If designed and managed well, the databases can be used to transform raw data into information that helps people do their jobs faster, cheaper, and better, which ultimately helps customers and makes the firm more competitive.

2. **Describe what database and database management systems are and how they work.** A database is a collection of related data organized in a way that facilitates data searches. A database contains entities, fields, records, and tables. Entities are things about which we collect data, such as people, courses, customers, or products. Fields are the individual pieces of information about an entity, such as a person's last name or social security number, that are stored in a database cell. A record is the collection of related fields about an entity; usually, a record is displayed as a database row. A table is a collection of related records about an entity type; each row in the table is a record and each column is a field. A database management system is a software application with which you create, store, organize, and retrieve data from a single database or several databases. Data is typically entered into a database through the use of a specially formatted form. Data is retrieved from a database through the use of queries and reports. The data within a database must be

adequately organized so that it is possible to effectively store and retrieve information. The three main approaches to structuring the relationships among data entities are the hierarchical database model, the networked database model, and the relational database model. The most widely used approach today is the relational database model.

3. **Explain four emerging database trends: client/server computing, object-oriented databases, data mining, and integrating Web applications with organizational databases.** Client/server database environments allow large and complex database systems to be divided into two parts. The database itself resides on a powerful computer, called a database server. The programs used to manipulate the database reside on a user's desktop computer, called a client. Object-oriented databases (OODBs) treat tables, queries, and other components as generic, reusable objects that can be mixed and matched and used in many different applications. OODBs are not meant to replace the relational data model, but to support and extend the relational model by allowing the storage of more complex, user-defined data types, such as sound and video. Objects within an OODB can also inherit data and methods from other objects, something not possible in traditional database designs. Data mining is a popular application of database technologies in which information stored in organizational databases, data warehouses, or data marts is sorted and analyzed to improve organizational decision making and performance. A data warehouse is the integration of multiple, large databases and other information sources into a single repository or access point that is suitable for direct querying, analysis, or processing. A data mart is a small-scale data warehouse that contains a subset of the data for a single aspect of a company's business—for example, finance, inventory, or personnel.

Many organizations are allowing employees and customers to access corporate databases management systems via the World Wide Web. These capabilities are allowing greater flexibility and innovative products and services.

Key Terms

Databases	Query by example	Normalization
Database management systems	Report	Client/server architecture
Entity	Data model	Database server
Tables	Primary key	Object-oriented databases
Fields	Data type	Data mining
Record	Data dictionary	Data warehouses
Form	Hierarchical database model	Data marts
Querying	Network database model	Database administrator
Structured Query Language (SQL)	Relational database model	

Review Questions

1. Explain the difference between a database and a database management system.

2. List some reasons why record keeping with physical filing systems is less efficient than using a database on a computer.

3. Describe the relationship among the following terms: entity, field, record, and table.

4. Describe the key, combination key, and primary key within an entity.

5. How do SQL and query by example relate to each other?

6. Describe the differences in the use of parent and child designations in the hierarchical and network DBMS models.

7. What is the purpose of normalization?

8. In a client/server architecture, what aspect of the database has been separated from the data itself (that is, what aspects of the database are on the client and what aspects are on the server)?

9. Describe from a business standpoint some of the potential opportunities for combining database applications with the World Wide Web.

Problems and Exercises

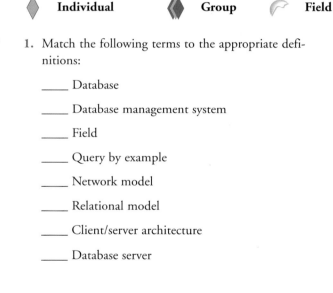 **Individual**   **Group**   **Field**   **Web/Internet**

1. Match the following terms to the appropriate definitions:

    _____ Database

    _____ Database management system

    _____ Field

    _____ Query by example

    _____ Network model

    _____ Relational model

    _____ Client/server architecture

    _____ Database server

a. Individual pieces of information about an entity, such as a person's last name or social security number, which are stored in a database cell

b. The part of a client/server database system running on a server that provides database storage and access to client workstations

c. A collection of related data organized in a way that facilitates data searches

d. A DBMS approach in which entities can have multiple parent-child relationships

e. A software application with which you can create, store, organize, and retrieve data for one or many databases

f. A distributed processing system in which a client application that needs data or software gets it from a server that is a source for some or all of the needed data or software

g. The capability of a DBMS to enable us to request data by simply providing a sample or a description of the types of data we would like to see

h. A DBMS approach in which entities are presented as two-dimensional tables that can be joined together with common columns

2. Imagine that a fellow student has seen an announcement for a job as a database administrator for a large corporation, but is unclear about what this title means. Please explain to your friend in very clear wording the role of a database administrator.

3. How and why are organizations without extensive databases falling behind in competitiveness and growth? Is this simply a database problem that can be fixed easily with some software purchases? In a small group, search the World Wide Web for stories or news articles that deal with the issue of staying competitive by successfully managing data. How are these stories similar to each other? How are they different? Prepare a 10-minute presentation to the class on your findings.

4. In a group of classmates, discuss the implications that the current downsizing, reorganizing, and redefining of organizations and their functions may have for the employees previously responsible for managing the extensive filing systems within their organizations. Would their computer literacy make a difference? Does everyone in the group agree? Why or why not?

5. Why would it matter what data type is used for the fields within a database? How does this relate to programming? How does this relate to queries and calculations? Does the size of the database matter?

6. Discuss the issue of data accuracy, based on what you have learned from the chapter. Does a relational model handle accuracy issues any better than a hierarchical or network model? Does a computer database handle accuracy issues better than a filing system? Who (or what) is ultimately responsible for data accuracy?

7. As a group, argue for and against the following statement: Using a database is faster than manually searching for information. Provide clear reasons and/or examples for your arguments. What conclusions can you draw from this discussion?

8. Have several classmates interview a database administrator within an organization with which they are familiar. To whom does this person report? How many employees report to this person? Is there a big variance in the responsibilities across organizations? Why or why not?

9. Consider an organization with which you are familiar. Describe the organization's approach to database management. What job positions exist to handle these responsibilities? Is there a database administrator? How long has the current database (or set of databases) been in effect?

10. Interview an IS Manager within an organization with which you are familiar. Determine what types of databases are currently in use (hierarchical, network, or relational). What are these databases used for (that is, what type of data do they store)? Who uses the databases and how do they use them (for queries, reports, and so on)?

11. Based on your understanding of a primary key and the following sample grades table, determine the primary key field(s) that would best satisfy all the necessary requirements.

STUDENT ID	COURSE	GRADE
100013	Visual Programming	A-
000117	Telesystems	A
000117	Introduction to MIS	A

12. Based on your previous work and/or professional experiences, describe your experiences with database systems. Were they relational databases or another type? Discuss your experiences with other classmates. What role did you play in utilizing the database and the data within it? How are the experiences of your classmates different?

13. Search the World Wide Web for an organization's home page that utilizes a link between the home page and their own database. Describe the data that the browser enters and the possible uses for this data within the organization. Can you retrieve company information, or can you only send information to the company? How is the data displayed on the home page?

14. Select an organization with which you are familiar that utilizes "flat file" databases for their database management. Determine whether they should move to a relational database. Why would you make this recommendation? Is it feasible to do so? Why or why not?

15. Discuss the following in a small group. Using the scenario outlined at the beginning of this chapter, consider how you have dealt with the database(s) at your educational institution. Have you filled out a lot of paperwork that was then entered by someone else? Did you actually do some of the data entry for your account? What kind of information were you able to retrieve about your account? From where was the database administered? Were you able to access it online?

Real World Case Problems

1. Anatomy of a Failure: The Inside Story of a Fatally Flawed Data Warehouse Project

In 1995 the CEO of a company we'll name Close Call Corporation was playing golf with a software vendor. Close Call's CEO knew he needed to make drastic technology changes to transform his business and that these changes needed to be made quickly. Beginning with $200 in the 1970s, his teleservices company was now worth over $100 million. He was intent on selecting the most direct path to get the double-digit growth he wanted when the vendor offered advice.

Close Call's telemarketing and catalog sales business units had been operating totally independently. The company

had gone public, and the rapid growth was putting pressure on its old proprietary system. The vendor convinced the CEO that a data warehouse could be up and running in four months and would provide a unified solution for the business units.

With 1996 reporting to be a pennant year, the timing couldn't have been more disastrous. Not only did the company expand from 6 to 116 call centers, but it also implemented new, open switching systems in new centers for automatic dialing and call routing and needed to update the internal management system for human resources and internal audit. The CEO assured everyone 1996 would be memorable—but unfortunately, it was not memorable for the reasons he had hoped.

The positive culture was a thing of the past. The CEO believed all he had to do was hire the right consultant. This time he faced an IS staff already stretched to the limit. The CEO set deadlines and a budget before the project team was on board. Then five consultants with experience were hired. Inside the organization, the users didn't understand the analytical environment, and therefore, didn't know what they were missing that could have helped them with their job. They saw no value in the new system. The lack of demand for this system foretold the outcome of the users' effort and commitment. The scope of the project became scaled down to a pilot, and the time frame was pushed back. The CEO stuck to his guns, but he never did understand the enormity of the project. From the onset, the data warehouse lacked a clearly defined business objective. The users had certainly never asked for any system with greater analytical abilities. Finally, things started to fall apart. The MIS director never reached out to the business users, and each user group wanted the other group to spend time on it.

a. Why are data warehouses and other large-scale systems that cut across the organization so difficult to implement?

b. Does Close Call Corporation really need a data warehouse? Why or why not?

c. What would you recommend that Close Call Corporation do next? Why?

Source   Paul, Lauren Gibbons. 1997. The anatomy of a failure: The inside story of a fatally flawed data warehouse project. CIO Enterprise (November 15): 55–60.

2. Survival of the Fastest: Facing a Competitive Threat from Upstart Rivals, State Street Global Advisors Had to Build a New Customer Service System for Retirement Plan Transactions—and Do It Quickly

State Street Global Advisors (SSGA), a caretaker of corporate retirement plans, was responsible for managing retirement plans for about 2 million employees of 120 corporations. The biggest challenge that SSGA faced in managing these plans was to reallocate assets from stock funds to bonds or vice versa, based on the market performance. The availability of the technology had reduced the transaction time from 6 weeks to 24 hours. Aggressive mutual fund companies focused on capturing the retirement plan business were driving the customer service standards even higher. SSGA realized the increasing importance of improving the efficiency of its transaction process if it was to remain a major player in the marketplace. SSGA's business strategy hinged on its ability to act as an extension of its clients' benefits department. The company decided to build a client/server workflow customer service system because the customer service center played a key role in attracting and retaining customers. The company spent $15 million over five years on building this workflow customer service system.

Prior to automating the process, the customer service reps were involved with a lot of paperwork and spent time answering phone calls. This process was prone to mistakes, and the company had spent a considerable amount of time correcting the mistakes. Moreover, when investors wanted to reallocate the assets, SSGA would have to wait until the first of a new month to perform the transaction. The reps had to memorize the rules of each retirement plan because they varied from company to company.

At present, the use of database technology has simplified and increased the efficiency of the customer service department's activities. SSGA's customer service center system revalues assets every day and allows representatives to compile transactions in less than 24 hours. Almost all of the necessary information, including the rules for each plan, is available online, which helps the reps answer customer inquiries promptly without having to put callers on hold. The system also has a sophisticated help function tailored for each individual plan. This function informs the representative whether or not the participant is eligible to enroll in a plan. The representatives no longer have to memorize the nuances of every plan and hence can provide service to more companies. Previously, reps serviced employees of half a dozen companies. Now, each rep handles 14 to 15 plans on average.

The use of the system has enabled the representatives to perform transactions accurately 99.8 percent of the time. It has also increased the efficiency of the workers and helped them to better serve the customers. As a result, customer satisfaction has increased and has contributed to the company moving from tenth in its industry to third.

The project challenged SSGA's IT department with an ambitious time frame and unfamiliar technology. To ensure the success of the system, SSGA involved its customer service reps in the design of the prototype and listened to users' suggestions. Companies that underestimated the impact that faster customer service would have on the industry and failed to take action are out of business now. SSGA, by accurately sensing the movement of the market and responding quickly to it, grew to be an industry leader.

a. How was database technology used for this new system? How important is the database in this case?

b. Summarize the benefits gained from the customer service system. Is this enough to convince even the most skeptical CFO that a project like this is worth the money?

c. What can other firms learn from State Street's use of database technology?

Source   Fabris, Peter. 1998. Survival of the fastest. CIO Enterprise (February 1): 56–58.

References

Boar, B. 1998. Understanding data warehousing strategically. NCR white paper at http://www.3ncr.com/product/whitepapers/bboar1.htm. Information verified: April 7, 1998.

Date, C. J. 1990. *An introduction to database systems.* New York: Addison-Wesley Publishing Company, Inc.

Foley, J. 1996. Data dilemma. *InformationWeek,* June 10, 14–16.

Foley, J. and B. DePompa. 1996. Data marts: Low cost, high appeal. *InformationWeek,* March 18, 20–21.

Hermann, E. 1996. *Sams Teach Yourself CGI Programming with PERL in a Week.* Indianapolis, Indiana: Sams.net Publishing.

IBM, 1998. Information from: www.ibm.com. Verified: February 7, 1998.

Norman, R. 1996. Object-oriented systems analysis and design. Upper Saddle River, New Jersey: Prentice Hall, Inc.

Oracle, 1998. Information from: www.oracle.com. Verified: February 7, 1998.

Related Readings

Brachman, Khabaza, Kloesgen, Piatetsky-Shapiro, and Simoudis. 1996. Mining business databases. *Communications of the ACM* 39(11): 42–48.

Cerpa, N. 1995. Pre-physical database design heuristics. *Information and Management* 28(6): 351–359.

Chan, Wei, and Siau. 1993. User-database interface: The effect of abstraction levels on query performance. *Management Information Systems Quarterly* 17(4): 441–464.

Clark, G.J. and C.T. Wu. 1994. DFQL: Dataflow query language for relational databases. *Information and Management* 27(1): 1–15.

Clifford, Croker, and Tuzhilin. 1996. On data representation and use in a temporal relational DBMS. *Information Systems Research* 7(3): 308–327.

Kulkarni, V.R. and H.K. Jain. 1993. Interaction between concurrent transactions in the design of distributed databases. *Decision Sciences* 24(2): 253–277.

Leitheiser, R.L. and S.T. March. 1996. The influence of database structure representation on database system learning and use. *Journal of Management Information Systems* 12(4): 187–213.

Premerlani, W.J. and M.R. Blaha. 1994. An approach for reverse engineering of relational databases. *Communications of the ACM* 37(5): 42–49.

Ram, S. and S. Narasimhan. 1994. Database allocation in a distributed environment: Incorporating a concurrency control mechanism and queuing costs. *Management Science* 40(8): 969–983.

Ram, S. 1995. Deriving functional dependencies from the entity-relationship model. *Communications of the ACM* 38(9): 95–107.

Segev, A. and J.L. Zhao. 1994. Rule management in expert database systems. *Management Science* 40(6): 685–707.

Storey, V.C. and R.C. Goldstein. 1993. Knowledge-based approaches to database design. *Management Information Systems Quarterly* 17(1): 25–46.

Weber, R. 1996. Are attributes entities?: A study of database designers' memory structures. *Information Systems Research* 7(2): 137–162.

Scenario: Video Conferencing Lessens the Need for Travel

Brand-X Foods is one of the nation's leading manufacturers of canned food products. Brand-X has its own nationally known brands and also manufactures store brands for many large food store chains. The food products industry is very competitive and all food manufacturers vie for limited store shelf space and prime product locations. Research has found, for example, that product location within a store—eye level versus bottom shelf—can influence sales by more than fifty percent! Needless to say, a critical success factor for Brand-X is to make sure its products occupy prime shelf location in as many stores as possible.

Mary Shide, a product manager for Brand-X, stays in close contact with countless stores and product buyers over a four-state region. Her job is to promote Brand-X products and to help secure prime shelf locations for Brand-X products. To do this, Mary works very closely with store "buyers"—the people in individual stores or chains who are responsible for buying products and placing them into stores.

Over the years, the job of a product manager has radically changed. Just a few years ago, most communication between product managers and buyers was face-to-face. During this time, product managers spent most of their time on the road, going from store to store to meet with store managers and buyers. Although face-to-face meetings are still needed, product mangers travel far less today, staying in touch with buyers and store managers through the use of electronic mail, faxes, and, of course, the telephone. Product managers use these communication technologies to not only talk with buyers and store managers, but also to send new prices, promotions, or other product information that might help to stimulate sales.

Brand-X's largest customer, Nicholls Food Stores, has been a big supporter of electronic communication between manufacturers like Brand-X and their buyers. On a recent trip to Nicholls' headquarters, Mary met with the vice president in charge of buying, Patty Nicholls, to hear her plans for expanding the role of technology in assisting and improving product buying and support.

"Mary, Nicholls Foods has long been using the Internet to send email and data between our stores and manufacturers like Brand-X. We are currently testing desktop video conferencing (DVC) using the Internet so that managers at headquarters can stay in better contact with store managers around the country. Like you, I spend a considerable amount of my time traveling to our stores. We believe that DVC will provide significant benefits to our organization. I will be able to meet face-to-face with my store managers without ever having to leave my office! Our early testing has gone better than expected. Consequently, we are considering using DVC with other organizational activities and are curious to see whether Brand-X would be willing to join in our testing of this technology."

"Doesn't video conferencing require hundreds of thousands of dollars and a dedicated meeting facility?" asked Mary.

"Oh, no," replied Patty. "This is *desktop* video conferencing; it's much cheaper."

"Well, what do you have in mind, Patty?"

"Well Mary, you know better than anyone the value of our meetings. Unfortunately, our schedules preclude meeting more than once a month or so. We believe that if we could find a way to meet more regularly, we could be more effective in our sales and promotional efforts. Our idea is to use DVC to support these meetings. If we can cut out travel time, we will easily be able to expand the frequency of our meetings and *still* save a significant amount of time due to a vast reduction in travel."

Courtesy of Intel

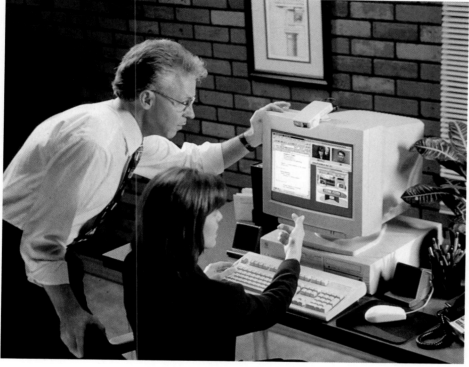

FIGURE 5.1

A desktop video conferencing system.

"That sounds exciting, Patty. So tell me, just how expensive is something like this to get off the ground? I still imagine it would be a lot," replied Mary.

"That's the best part about this. Desktop video conferencing is done right on your personal computer, in your office, using the Internet (see Figure 5.1). We all have Internet connections and personal computers on our desks, so there is no added cost for that. What you need to do is to add a sound card to your PC, some speakers and a microphone, a small camera, and some software. In total, no more than a few hundred dollars worth of equipment that you can buy at any computer store!"

"This is unbelievable! Does it really work? What about picture and voice quality?" asked Mary.

"I would say that the voice quality is excellent and I would rate the picture quality as being very good," answered Patty. "In addition, I would have to add that you still see a bit of jerkiness when someone moves around on the screen. It's not as smooth as a television broadcast, but it's pretty good, considering how inexpensive it is."

"Sounds good," replied Mary. "I'd like to see it in action."

"Let me show you," offered Patty.

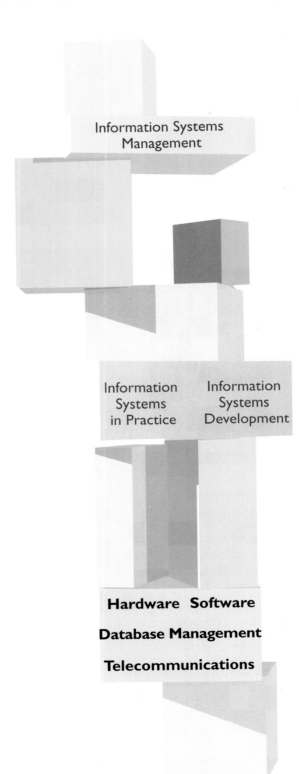

Information Systems
Management

Information
Systems
in Practice

Information
Systems
Development

Hardware Software

Database Management

Telecommunications

Introduction

Everywhere we look today, we see businesses and institutions, both public and private, that demand more speed to market, more flexibility, accelerated global expansion, and more customer and supplier integration. Like the two organizations described in the opening scenario, people and enterprises want to connect to other people and enterprises around the world. This desire has driven the rapid development of telecommunications-based information technologies. These technologies enable people and enterprises to share information across time and distance, and they can lower boundaries between markets and cultures. The telecommunications revolution is changing the way we live and work, and how we communicate with each other. Businesses facing increasingly volatile competitive environments use technology to rapidly develop, gather, store, and disseminate information about their products and processes across boundaries of time and distance. This chapter introduces telecommunications concepts, key technologies, and applications. This discussion provides you with a solid foundation for understanding how computers are connected across a room or across the world.

After reading this chapter, you will be able to do the following:

1. Understand the role of telecommunications in organizations.

2. Describe the evolution and types of computer networks.

3. Understand networking fundamentals, including network services, transmission media, network topologies, and connectivity hardware for both local area and wide area networks.

4. Explain the role of the Open System Interconnect (OSI) model and network operating systems in enabling network communication.

FIGURE 5.2

The big picture: focusing on telecommunications.

Telecommunications technologies, like the desktop video conferencing system described in the opening scenario, are taking an ever-larger place in your life. Understanding how this technology works and where this technology is going, as part of your wider understanding of IS hardware, software, and databases, will complete your understanding of the "essential" elements of information systems (see Figure 5.2). The discussion begins with a description of the expanding role that telecommunications is playing in organizations. This is followed by a presentation of many of the concepts fundamental to a basic understanding of telecommunications and computer networking.

The Role of Telecommunications in Organizations

People around the world are finding that networks——Local Area Networks (LANs), Wide Area Networks (WANs), and the Internet—are highly effective tools for communication across and among enterprises and people. The following sections briefly examine a few telecommunications-based applications that individuals and organizations are using.

Work Group Communication

Using technology-mediated communication is a common part of day-to-day business communication. Two commonly used technologies for this communication are electronic mail and video conferencing. Arguably, one of the most pervasive uses of a network is for sending electronic mail, or *email*. The biggest benefits of email are that it nearly eliminates "telephone tag" and enables widespread work groups to ignore time zones and office hours. The greater the number of people in an organization who use email, with its capability to store information and deliver it when a recipient is ready to receive it, the less they are controlled by the constraints of real-time communication.

Video conferencing, like that described in the chapter-opening scenario, provides video-audio connections between people in two physically separate locations. Basic video conferencing systems enable groups to see and hear each other. In more advanced systems, remote teams can use application and data-sharing tools to jointly make changes to the same document, such as a spreadsheet or diagram (refer to Figure 5.1). CU-SeeMe is an example of a basic Internet-based video conferencing tool that supports multiparty video conferencing over the Internet. Microsoft's NetMeeting supports video, audio, and application sharing.

Emerging Business Applications

Everywhere businesses and institutions look today, they see the need for more speed to market, more flexibility, accelerated global expansion and competitiveness, and a greater need for customer and supplier integration. Because networks can support interactivity and transport rich content, they are redefining the nature of commercial transactions and can also level the playing field for small businesses. Networks also enable organizations to reshape the how, where, and when of their operations by bringing employees, customers, and suppliers together in entirely new ways. Two existing, evolving, and increasingly important telecommunications-based applications are electronic commerce and electronic data interchange (EDI).

Electronic Commerce

Electronic commerce includes EDI (described in the following section) and other company-to-company commerce, as well as direct-to-the-customer commerce using concepts such as at-home shopping via interactive TV or the World Wide Web (see Figure 5.3). Increasingly, as new services and application tools are developed, the Internet is becoming a means to conduct electronic commerce. Order taking, order verification, invoicing, and electronic funds payments are becoming a reality for both large and small businesses. Chapter 6, "Electronic Commerce and the Internet," describes in more detail what businesses are doing in the area of electronic commerce.

Courtesy of Peapod.

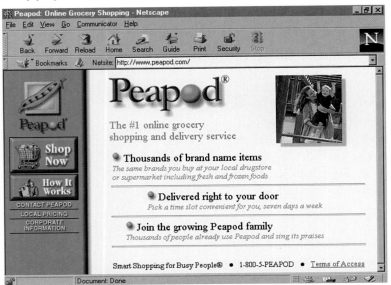

Electronic Data Interchange (EDI)

The use of telecommunications technologies to directly transfer business documents between organizations is called **electronic data interchange**

FIGURE 5.3

Internet-based shopping is growing rapidly.

(EDI). Using EDI, trading partners (suppliers, manufacturers, customers, and so on) establish computer-to-computer links that enable them to exchange data electronically. For example, a company using EDI may send an electronic purchase order, rather than a paper request, to a supplier. The paper order may take several days to arrive at the supplier, whereas an EDI purchase order takes a few seconds. EDI is fast becoming the standard by which organizations will communicate with each other in the world of electronic commerce.

A BRIEF CASE

EDI at Walgreens

Walgreens Corporation uses EDI to save time and money (see Washington, 1998). Using EDI, Walgreens can easily combine the invoices from more than 2,100 of their specialty and drug stores into a single statement and forward this to a supplier such as Hallmark Corporation. On a recent exchange, Walgreens sent an invoice containing more than 66,000 records with payment authorizations to Hallmark. When Hallmark received the invoice, its EDI system not only verified the correctness and completeness of the order, but also was able to notify Walgreens' bank to transfer payment to Hallmark's bank. This transaction was sent and verified, and payment was exchanged in a matter of minutes. Before EDI, the processing of 66,000 records would have taken several weeks to prepare, send, and resolve. It is easy to see that telecommunications applications like EDI are radically changing the way organizations are able to do business. Walgreens uses a proprietary EDI network to which its suppliers must also subscribe. To save even more money, many organizations are using the Internet for sending EDI information.

Building Blocks of Telecommunication

Human communication involves the sharing of information and messages between individuals: senders and receivers. The sender of a message forms the message in his brain and **codes** the message into a form that can be communicated to the receiver—through voice, for example. The message is then transmitted along a communication pathway to the receiver. The receiver, using her ears and brain, then attempts to **decode** the message, as shown in Figure 5.4. This basic model of human communication helps us to understand telecommunication or computer networking.

Messages, Senders, and Receivers

Computer networking is the sharing of information or services. As with human communication, all computer networks require three things:

- Senders and receivers that have something to share

- A pathway or transmission media to send the message

- Rules or protocols so that senders and receivers can communicate

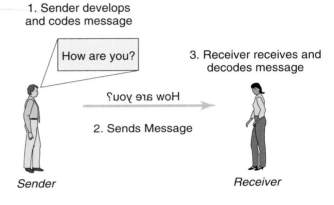

1. Sender develops and codes message

How are you?

Sender

How are you?

2. Sends Message

3. Receiver receives and decodes message

Receiver

FIGURE 5.4

Communication requires senders and receivers.

The easiest way to understand computer networking is through the human communication model. Suppose you are planning to study a semester abroad in Europe. To do this, you need information about schools that accept exchange students. Of course, you assume these schools will want to know about you. The first requirement for a network—information to share—has now been met. Now, suppose you start your search by writing a letter (coding your message) and fax it to all the schools you can identify. You have met the second requirement—a means of transmitting the coded message. The fax is the pathway or transmission media used to contact the receiver. **Transmission media** refers to the physical cable used to carry network information. At this point, though, you may run into some difficulties. Not all the receivers of your faxed letter may be able to understand what you've written—decode your message—because they speak other languages. Although you have contacted the receiver, you and the receiver of your message must meet the third requirement for a successful network: You must establish a language of communication—that is, establish the rules or protocol governing your communication. Protocols define the procedures that different computers follow when they transmit and receive data. You both might decide that English will be the communication protocol. Here, we can see that having a pathway does not ensure that communication will occur—the message must be understood for communication to really take place. This communication session is illustrated in Figure 5.5.

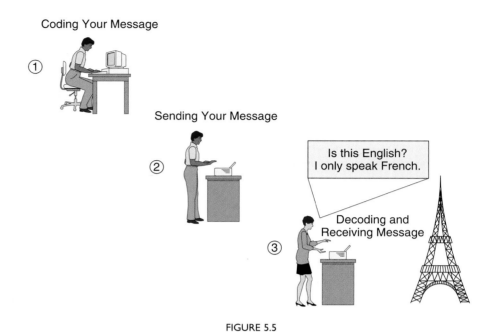

FIGURE 5.5

Coding, sending, and decoding a message.

Computer Networks

There are many similarities between human communication (that is, human-to-human) and the operation of computer networks. A fundamental difference between human and computer communication is that human communication consists largely of words, whereas computer communication consists of bits, the fundamental information units of computers, as depicted in Figure 5.6. Fortunately, virtually all types of information can be transmitted on a computer network—business information, art, music, film—although each type of information has vastly different requirements for effective transmission, as described in Table 5.1. The process of converting a photograph or a song into digital information, or bits, is called **digitizing**. After information is converted into bits, it can be given a passport to travel across **networks**—groups of computers and associated peripheral devices, connected by a communications channel that is capable of sharing files and other resources between several users. **Telecommunication** is the electronic transmission of all forms of information, including digital data, voice, fax, sound, and video, from one location to another over some type of network. Powerful new technologies are giving networks the **bandwidth**—the carrying capacity of telecommunications networks—needed to handle rich content, such as movies, medical records, or great works of art. These networks also work at speeds great enough to support interaction between users. Digital content and high-powered networks make the following possible:

- Distance learning—students learning from teachers that are not in the room with them

- Telemedicine—physicians in different hospitals consulting and examining medical records

- Telecommuting—employees working at home on a computer connected to the office, wherever that may be

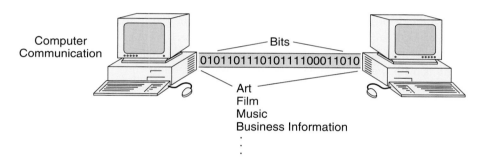

FIGURE 5.6

Human versus computer communication.

Table 5.1 Communication and storage requirements for different types of information.

Type of Information	Raw Size	Compressed Size
Voice		
Telephone	64KBps	16–32KBps
Teleconference	96KBps	32–64KBps
Compact disc	1.41MBps	63–128KBps
Data		
Single screen of text	14.4KB	4.8–7.2KB
Typed page, single-spaced	28.8KB	9.6–14.4KB
Faxed page (low to high resolution)	1.68–3.36MB	130–336KB
Super VGA screen image	6.3MB	315–630KB
Digital X-ray	50.3MB	16.8–25.1MB
Publication-quality photograph	230.4MB	23–46MB

continues

Table 5.1   Continued.

Type of Information	Raw Size	Compressed Size
Video		
Video telephony	9.3MBps	64–384KBps
Video teleconferencing	37.3MBps	384KBps–1.92MBps
CCITT multimedia	166MBps	1.7MBps
High definition television	1.33GBps	20–50MBps

Source   Table adapted from Business Data Communications, Second Edition by Stallings/VanSlyke. ©1997. Reprinted by permission of Prentice-Hall, Inc., Upper Saddle River, NJ.
Note: KB = Kilobytes; KBps = Kilobytes per second; MB = Megabytes; MBps = Megabytes per second; GBps = Gigabytes per second.

A BRIEF CASE ───── **Florida School for the Deaf and Blind** ─────

At the Florida School for the Deaf and Blind, telecommunications technologies open unseen doors for many students (see DOE, 1998). The K-12 residential school serves more than 600 students who are blind, deaf, or have special needs. When specially made computers were first introduced to students who are blind, staff members began experimenting with word-processing capabilities. Within a short time, they realized that computers provided a way for students who are blind to break out of their isolation and communicate with people in the community to whom they would not otherwise have access. In first grade, students who are blind are introduced to basic keyboarding skills. Usually by third grade, they begin learning how to use software to telecommunicate. They start by learning how to communicate with one another, then branch out to a local bulletin board within the community, which enables them to talk with other people outside the school. By the end of middle school, students become relatively fluent in the use of the network and can download files; and as experience with telecommunication increases, students begin using the Florida Information Resource Network, which gives them Internet access.

Students who are deaf use technology to develop language skills. These students tend to have trouble processing written language, but, through the use of animation, video, and other electronic media, students and teachers work cooperatively to enter new worlds of expression. For example, high school students, some of whom escaped from Cuba, are building a hypermedia presentation of life in Cuba. Through a cooperative effort, students who are deaf are planning, developing, and producing a multimedia expression of their experiences to share with others. Through telecommunication technology, a world of information that was previously inaccessible is being made available to these students. Computers and telecommunications are really making a difference with these students.

Computer networking provides the communication technologies that enable computers to share electronic information and capabilities, as they do with the students at the Florida School for the Deaf and Blind. Like human networks, computer networks require that entities have something to share, such as files or other resources, a pathway to contact other computers or networks, and rules or protocols for communication.

One of the most common means for individuals to use computer networking is through the use of a **modem** (MODulator / DEModulator) and standard dial-up telephone lines. Modems enable you to connect your PC to other PCs or computer networks with standard dial-up telephone lines. Because the dial-up telephone system was designed to pass the sound of voices in the form of analog signals, it cannot pass the electrical pulses—digital signals—that computers use. The only way to pass digital data over conventional voice telephone lines is to convert it to audio tones—analog signals—that the telephone lines can carry. Simply stated, a modem converts digital signals from a computer into analog signals so that telephone lines may be used as a transmission media to send and receive electronic information.

Suppose you are at home and you want to use your personal computer to send an electronic message through the Internet to a friend at another university. The modem attached to your PC converts your digital message into audio tones. The message is transmitted over the telephone lines to your university. The message then travels through the Internet from your university to your friend's university. Your friend also uses a modem to dial into her university to read your message, and a modem attached to your friend's computer at home converts the analog signals back to digital signals, which your friend's computer can understand, as shown in Figure 5.7.

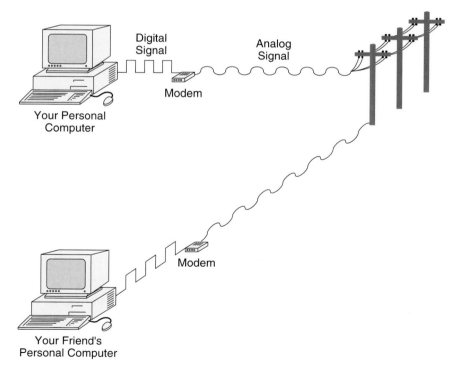

FIGURE 5.7

Modems convert digital communication to analog and analog to digital.

Evolution in Computer Networking

Since the beginning of the Information Age in the 1950s, people and enterprises have used computers to process data and information. This method of computing, depicted in Figure 5.8, remained largely unchanged through the 1970s. Very large centralized computers ("mainframes") were used to process and store data. During this era, people entered data on mainframes through the use of local input devices called terminals. These devices were often called "dumb" terminals because they did not conduct any processing or "smart" activities. This computing model is called **centralized computing**. The centralized computing model is not really a network because there is no *sharing* of information and capabilities. Rather, the mainframe provides all the capabilities and the terminals are only input/output devices. True computer networks evolved when organizations needed separate, independent computers to communicate with each other.

FIGURE 5.8

Centralized computing model.

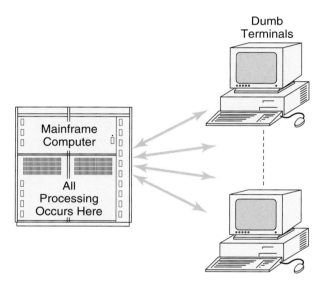

The introduction of personal computers in the late 1970s and early 1980s gave individuals control over their own computing. Organizations also realized that they could use multiple smaller computers to achieve many of the same processing goals of a single large computer. Separate computers could work on subsets of tasks rather than use one mainframe to perform all the processing. Achieving the goal of separate processing required computer networks, so that information and services could be easily shared between these distributed computers. The 1980s were characterized by an evolution to a computing model called **distributed computing**, shown in Figure 5.9, in which multiple types of computers are networked together to share information and services.

In the 1990s, a new computing model, called **collaborative computing**, has emerged. Collaborative computing is a synergistic form of distributed computing, in which two or more networked computers are used to accomplish a common processing task. That is, in this model of computing, computers are not simply communicating data but sharing processing capabilities. For example, one computer may be used to store a large employee database. A second computer may be used to process and update individual employee records selected from this database. The two computers collaborate to keep the company's employee records current, as depicted in Figure 5.10.

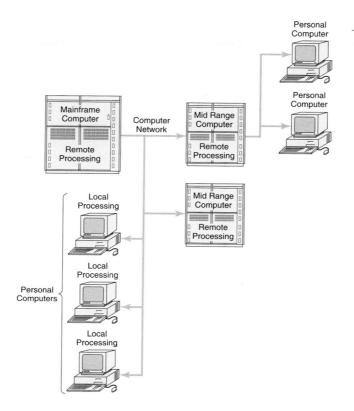

FIGURE 5.9

Distributed computing model.

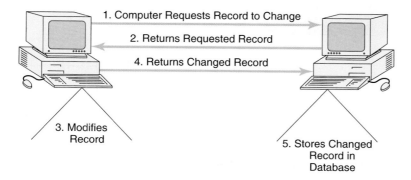

FIGURE 5.10

Collaborative computing model.

Computing networks today include all three computing models: centralized, distributed, and collaborative. The emergence of new computing models did not mean that organizations completely discarded older technologies. Rather, a typical computer network includes mainframes, minicomputers, personal computers, and a variety of other devices. Computer networks are commonly classified by size, distance covered, and structure. Today, the most commonly used classifications are a private branch exchange (PBX), local area network (LAN), or a wide area network (WAN). Each is described in the following sections.

Private Branch Exchange (PBX)

A **private branch exchange (PBX)** is a telephone system that serves a particular location, such as an office, providing connections from one extension to another, as well as a set of connections to the external telephone network. An organization can use a PBX to distribute integrated data and voice. In other words, a PBX network can connect computers and phone systems within an organization to the outside world by connecting to other PBXs or to outside networks, as shown in Figure 5.11. The main disadvantage of PBX networks is their limited bandwidth. In other words, because a PBX uses standard telephone lines, it cannot easily transport some types of information such as interactive video, digital music, or high-resolution pictures.

FIGURE 5.11

A private branch exchange (PBX) supports local phone and data communications, as well as links to outside phone and data networks.

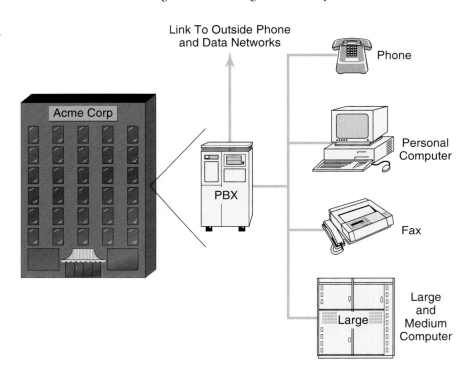

Local Area Network (LAN)

A **local area network (LAN)**, shown in Figure 5.12, is a data communications system that enables a number of independent computers to communicate directly with each other and other peripheral devices, such as a printer. LAN-based communications may involve the sharing of data, software applications, or other resources between several users. LANs typically do not exceed tens of kilometers in size, and are normally contained within a single building or a limited geographical area. In addition, they tend to use only one kind of transmission media or cabling.

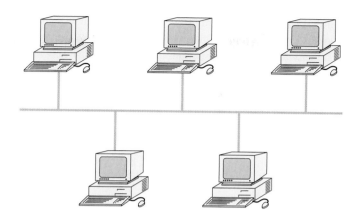

FIGURE 5.12

A local area network (LAN).

Wide Area Network (WAN)

A **wide area network (WAN)** connects users across much larger distances than a LAN. WANs are, in fact, used to interconnect two or more LANs. Different hardware and transmission media are often used in WANs because they must efficiently cover large distances. Two specific types of WANs are "enterprise networks" and "global networks."

Pepsi's Enterprise Network

A BRIEF CASE

An **enterprise network** connects all the LANs of a single organization that may, for example, have locations across the U.S., as shown in Figure 5.13. When consumers reach for a Pepsi beverage on a store shelf, they may not give much thought to how it got there. But delivering a Pepsi product to the consumer is a complex and information-intensive activity, with data collected at multiple points in the manufacturing and distribution processes. For Pepsi, like any consumer-goods company, a critical business challenge is to ensure that these processes deliver the right products to the right place at the right time. Pepsi's enterprise network connects nearly 330 manufacturing, distribution, and sales sites around the U.S. and Canada. The Pepsi enterprise network transports sales data that help marketing managers identify buying trends and make faster decisions regarding product distribution. For example, sales data help managers identify regions where certain products are not selling well, and move any excess inventory to areas where those products are in demand. Sales data also help Pepsi managers make decisions about products before they reach the freshness date and must be pulled from the shelf and discarded. (For more information, see HP, 1998.)

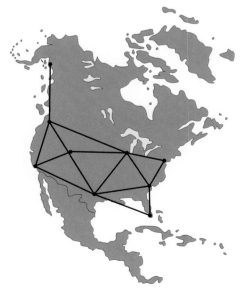

FIGURE 5.13

An enterprise network.

A **global network** spans multiple countries and may include the networks of several organizations. An example of a global network is the **Internet,** the world's largest computer network, consisting of thousands of individual networks supporting millions of computers and users in over 60 countries. Chapter 6 provides a detailed discussion of the Internet.

An emerging trend is the use of medium-speed WANs called **value-added networks (VANs)**, designed for the transfer of data by many organizations simultaneously. VANs are private, third-party managed networks that are economical because they are shared by multiple organizations. Customers do not have to invest in dedicated network equipment; rather, they subscribe for services. VANs can provide good communication service for multiple organizations because they use packet switching. *Packet switching* maximizes the use of a transmission line by transmitting packets of digital data from many customers simultaneously over a telephone line or a single communication channel. Delays in transmission are avoided because short messages sent by one customer do not have to wait while another customer is sending a long message. Rather, long messages are divided into smaller *data packets* that are independently sent and then reassembled at their proper destination. In essence, customers whose computers share a network take turns using the transmission line to send data packets.

Now that you have an understanding of the general types of networks, it's time to examine some of their fundamental components. This discussion is divided into three areas: networking fundamentals, connectivity hardware, and connectivity software. These three sections help you understand how software and hardware work together to form different types of networks.

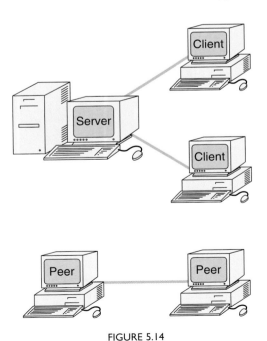

FIGURE 5.14

Servers, clients, and peers.

Networking Fundamentals

Telecommunications advances have enabled individual computer networks—constructed with a variety of hardware and software—to connect together in what appears to be a single network. Networks are increasingly being used to dynamically exchange relevant, value-adding knowledge and information throughout global organizations and institutions. The following sections take a closer look at the fundamental building blocks of these complex networks and the services they provide.

Servers, Clients, and Peers

In networking, a distinction is made between servers, clients, and peers, as depicted in Figure 5.14. A **server** is any computer on the network that makes access to files, printing, communications, and other services available to users of the network. Simply put, servers only provide services. A server typically has a more advanced microprocessor, more memory, a larger cache, and more disk storage than a single-user workstation. A **client** is any device, such as a user's workstation or PC on the network; or any software application, such as a word-processing application, that uses the services provided by the server. Clients only request services. A client usually has only one user, whereas many different users share the server. A **peer** may both request and provide services. Whether or not a particular computer or device on the network is considered a server, client, or peer depends on the operating system that is running. The trend in recent years has been toward **server-centric networks**, in which servers and clients have defined roles. However, **peer-to-peer networks** that enable any computer or device on the network to provide and request services can be typically found in small offices and homes.

Network Services

Network services are the capabilities that networked computers share through the multiple combinations of hardware and software. The most common network services are file services, print services, message services, and application services. *File services* are used to store, retrieve, and move data files in an efficient manner, as shown in Figure 5.15a. For example, an individual user can use the file services of the network to electronically move a customer file to multiple recipients across the network. *Print services* are used to control and manage users' access to network printers and fax equipment, as shown in Figure 5.15b. Sharing printers on a network reduces the number of printers needed by the organization. *Message services* include the storing, accessing, and delivering of text, binary, graphic, digitized video, and audio data. These services are similar to file services, but they also actively deal with communication interactions between users and applications. Message services include, for example, electronic mail or the transfer of messages between two or more networked computers, as shown in Figure 5.15c. *Application services* run software for network clients and enable computers to share processing power, as shown in Figure 5.15d. Application services highlight the concept of

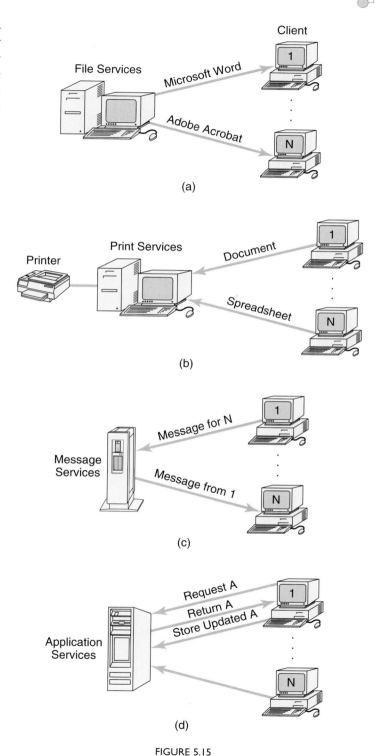

(a)

(b)

(c)

(d)

FIGURE 5.15

Networks can provide file, print, message, and application services.

client/server computing, in which processing is distributed between the client and server. Clients request information or services from the servers. The servers store data and application programs. For example, the physical search of database records may take place on the server, while a much smaller database application that handles the user-interface functions runs on the client.

When an organization decides to network its computers and devices, it must decide what services will be provided and whether these services will be centralized (a server-centric approach), distributed (a peer-to-peer approach), or some combination of both. These decisions ultimately affect the choice of the **network operating system**. An example of a network operating system is Novell's NetWare. The trend is toward the use of a specialized server—file server, print server, database server, or communications server—designated to perform some specific network function. For example, a communications server is equipped with specialized hardware and software that can accept telephone calls from remote users.

Transmission Media

In addition to having network services, every network uses some type of **transmission media**—the physical pathway to send data and information between two or more entities on a network. To send messages, computers send energy-based signals—electric currents using electromagnetic waves—to contact each other. These electromagnetic waves can be altered by semiconductor materials and are represented in two discrete or binary states—the 0s and 1s of a computer, known as bits. These bits are transmitted over physical pathways or media as computers communicate with each other.

When deciding which type of media to use in a network, an organization should consider bandwidth, attenuation, immunity from electromagnetic interference (EMI) and eavesdropping, the cost of the cable, and ease of installation. Bandwidth is the transmission capacity of a computer or communications channel, stated in megabits per second (Mbps), and represents how much binary data can be reliably transmitted over the medium in one second. For example, some networks have a bandwidth of 10Mbps; others have 100Mbps; others have even more. To appreciate the significance of these speeds, consider how long it would take to transmit a document consisting of about three million characters (the equivalent of about 24 million bits), which is about the length of this chapter. Assuming no other traffic is on the network, it would take about 2.4 seconds at 10Mbps. At 100Mbps, it would take about .24 seconds. In contrast, using a standard PC modem that transmits data at a rate of 28,800 bits per second (bps), it would take you nearly 14 minutes to transmit the same document. Needless to say, more bandwidth is clearly better!

In addition to bandwidth, a second key issue to consider is a medium's vulnerability to attenuation. **Attenuation** results from the tendency of the power of an electric signal to weaken as it is sent over increasing distance, as shown in Figure 5.16. In a network, an important concern is how far a signal can travel and still maintain its original properties or meaning. EMI (electromagnetic interference), occurs when such things as fluorescent lights, weather, or other electronic signals interfere with the original signal being sent. All media differ as to how immune they are to EMI.

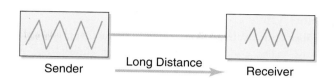

FIGURE 5.16

Signals weaken when sent over increasing distances.

Two forms of media are used in networks: cable and wireless media. Although wireless data communications is in increasing use, it is still in its infancy and is generally a much slower means of transmission than cable. For example, transferring an application such as Microsoft Word from a server to a client is six to ten times slower when using wireless media (PC Magazine, 1996). Nonetheless, wireless media have many useful applications. The following sections describe the characteristics of both cable and wireless media.

Cable Media

The most common forms of cable media are twisted pair, coaxial, and fiber optic.

Twisted Pair Cable

Twisted pair (TP) **cable** is made of two or more pairs of insulated copper wires twisted together. The cable may be *unshielded* (UTP) or *shielded* (STP). Telephone wire installations use UTP cabling. UTP is rated according to its quality; category 3 (Cat 3) and Cat 5 UTP are often used in network installations. UTP is cheap, easy to install, and has a capacity from 1 to 100Mbps at distances up to 100 meters. However, like all copper wiring, it has rapid attenuation and is very sensitive to EMI and eavesdropping—the undetected capturing of network information. Alternatively, STP is insulated cable wrapped in a foil shielding which helps to improve resistance to EMI and eavesdropping. As you might expect, the cost of STP is greater than UTP, and it is more difficult to install because it requires special grounding connectors to drain EMI. STP can support bandwidths up to 500Mbps at distances up to 100 meters. However, it is most commonly used to support networks running at 16Mbps. Like UTP, STP also has high attenuation rates.

Coaxial Cable

Coaxial (or "coax") **cable** contains a solid inner copper conductor, surrounded by plastic insulation and an outer braided copper or foil shield. Coax cable comes in a variety of thicknesses—thinnet coax and thicknet coax—based on resistance to EMI. Thinnet coax is less costly than STP or CAT 5 UTP; thicknet coax, however, is more expensive than STP or CAT 3 UTP. Coax is the simplest cable to install. The cable is cut and a connector, called a *T-connector,* is attached to the cable and each device. Coax cable is most commonly used for cable television installations and for networks operating at 10Mbps, although it can perform at higher rates. Its attenuation is lower than twisted pair cable and it is moderately susceptible to EMI and eavesdropping.

Fiber Optic Cable

Fiber optic cable is made of a light-conducting glass or plastic core, surrounded by more glass, called cladding, and a tough outer sheath. The sheath protects the fiber from changes in temperature, as well as from bending or breaking. This technology uses pulses of light sent along the optical cable to send data. Fiber optic cable is immune to EMI and eavesdropping, and has low attenuation. It is extremely powerful because it can support bandwidths from 100Mbps to greater than 2Gbps (gigabits per second). Additionally, distances from 2 to 25 kilometers are very common. However, it is relatively expensive compared to copper wire, primarily due to the cost and difficulties associated with installation and repair. Optical interfaces must be installed at both the input and output ends in order to convert the signals and light pulses to and from the optical fibers. Fiber optic cables are often used for high-speed **backbones**—the high-speed central networks to which many smaller networks can be connected. A backbone may connect, for example, several different buildings in which other, smaller LANs reside.

As you have read, a lot of differences exist among the types of cable media. Table 5.2 summarizes the key benefits and drawbacks of each cable medium. Table 5.3 makes a relative comparison of cable media across several criteria.

Table 5.2   Key benefits and drawbacks of different cable media.

Media	Key Benefit(s)	Drawback(s)
Twisted Pair	Inexpensive; Easy to install and reconfigure	Highly susceptible to EMI, eavesdropping, and attenuation; Unsuitable for high speeds
Coaxial	Higher bandwidth than twisted pair; Lower susceptibility to EMI, eavesdropping, and attenuation than twisted pair	More expensive than twisted pair; More difficult to install, reconfigure, and manage attenuation than twisted pair; Bulky
Fiber Optic	Very high bandwidth; Low attenuation and immune to EMI and eavesdropping	Expensive cable and hardware; Complex installation and maintenance

Table 5.3   Relative comparison of cable media.

Media	Expense	Speed	Attenuation	EMI	Eavesdropping
Twisted Pair	low to high	4–16Mbps	moderate to high	moderate	moderate to high
Coaxial	moderate	10Mbps	moderate	moderate	moderate
Fiber Optic	high	Up to 2Gbps	low	none	none

Wireless Media

Although doing so is not very common, LANs and WANs may be constructed by connecting workstations to a network by using **wireless media** rather than conventional cabling. Wireless media transmit and receive electromagnetic signals using methods such as infrared line of sight, high-frequency radio, and microwave systems.

Infrared Line of Sight

Infrared line of sight uses high-frequency light waves to transmit data on an unobstructed path between nodes on a network, at a distance of up to 24.4 meters. Infrared light is used in the remote controls for most audio/visual equipment such as your TV, stereo, and other consumer electronics equipment. Infrared systems may be set up as point-to-point systems, which require exact positioning of nodes; or broadcast systems, which are ideal for locally mobile devices. Infrared equipment is relatively inexpensive, but point-to-point systems require strict line-of-sight positioning. Installation and maintenance focuses on ensuring proper optical alignment between nodes on the network. In terms of capacity, point-to-point infrared systems can support up to 16Mbps at 1km, whereas broadcast systems support less than 1Mbps. Attenuation and susceptibility to EMI and eavesdropping are problematic, particularly when objects obstruct the light path, or when other environmental conditions such as smoke or high-intensity light are prevalent.

High-Frequency Radio

High-frequency radio signals can transmit data at rates of up to 10Mbps to network nodes anywhere from 12.2 to 39.6 meters apart, depending on the nature of any obstructions between them. The flexibility of the signal path makes high-frequency radio ideal for mobile transmissions. For example, most police departments use high-frequency radio signals that enable police vehicles to communicate with each other as well as the dispatch office. Today's technology has come a long way from the first mobile radio system introduced in 1928 by the Detroit Police Department. The first system was severely limited by distance and allowed communication in only one direction: from the dispatch office to police vehicles (hence the phrase "calling all cars"). This medium is, however, relatively expensive due to the cost of antenna towers and high-output transceivers. Installation is also complex and often dangerous due to the high voltages involved. Although attenuation is fairly low, this medium is very susceptible to EMI and eavesdropping.

Two common applications of high-frequency radio communication are pagers and cellular phones. A pager is a one-way, wireless messaging system that is commonly used to contact people on the move (see Table 5.4). In a business setting, there are countless uses for a pager. For example, if you travel a lot, your boss can easily contact you when you are away from the office. Or, when on vacation, you can learn the outcome of an important business deal. Pagers are also popular with families for notifying others of changes in plans, notifying parents when kids need to be picked up from school, or notifying teenagers when it's time to come home!

Table 5.4   Types of pagers.

Pager Type	Description	Advantages
Tone-only	User is alerted with an audible tone to call a predetermined phone number for a message	Simple
Numeric Display	User is alerted and number to call to call is displayed	Any phone number, storage of phone number, less chance of error or missing message
Alphanumeric Display	User is alerted and reads alphanumeric message	Same as numeric display, plus complete, accurate text message
Tone and Voice	User is alerted and receives a short voice message	User gets notification and message in single event, easier for caller and user

People on the move also use cellular phones. Unlike pagers, cellular phones provide two-way wireless communication. In a cellular system, for example, a city is divided into *cells* with a low-powered radio antenna/receiver in each cell; these cells are monitored and controlled by a central computer (see Figure 5.17). Any given cellular network has a fixed number of radio frequencies. When a call is initiated or received, a unique frequency is assigned to a caller for the duration of the call. As a person travels within the network, the central computer monitors the quality of the signal and automatically assigns the call to the closest cellular antenna. Only a few years ago, cellular phones were big, bulky, and expensive devices that were primarily used by businesses and the very wealthy. Today, much smaller and inexpensive cellular phones are widely used for both business and personal communication.

FIGURE 5.17

Cellular network.

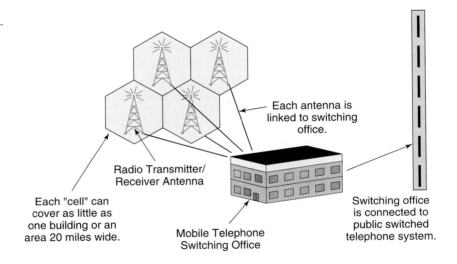

Each antenna is linked to switching office.

Radio Transmitter/ Receiver Antenna

Each "cell" can cover as little as one building or an area 20 miles wide.

Mobile Telephone Switching Office

Switching office is connected to public switched telephone system.

Microwave

Microwave data communication systems exist as terrestrial (earth-based) systems or satellite systems. Both are forms of radio transmissions that use high-frequency waves for line-of-sight communications. **Terrestrial microwave**, shown in Figure 5.18, typically uses antennas that require an unobstructed path or line of sight to other units. Terrestrial microwave systems are often used to cross inaccessible terrain or to connect buildings where cable installation would be expensive. The cost of a terrestrial microwave system depends on the distance to be covered. Typically, businesses lease access from service providers rather than invest in antenna equipment. Any kind of installation requiring a clear line of

FIGURE 5.18

Two forms of terrestrial microwave.

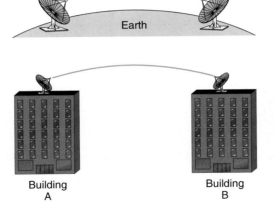

Earth

Building A

Building B

sight is difficult due to exacting conditions. Data may be transmitted at up to 10Mbps. Over short distances, attenuation is not a problem, but signals can be obstructed over longer distances by environmental conditions such as high winds and heavy rain. EMI and eavesdropping are significant problems with microwave communications.

Satellite microwave, shown in Figure 5.19, involves the transfer of signals between antennas located on earth and satellites orbiting the earth. Due to the long distances that must be traveled, satellite transmissions are subject to relatively long delays. On the other hand, satellite communication's greatest strength is that it can be used to access very remote and undeveloped locations on the earth. Such systems are extremely costly because their use and installation depends on space technology. Companies such as AT&T sell satellite services with typical transmission rates ranging from <1 to 10Mbps, although higher rates are possible. Like terrestrial microwave, satellite systems are prone to attenuation, and susceptible to EMI and eavesdropping.

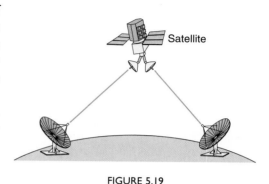

FIGURE 5.19

Satellite microwave.

As with cable media, there are a lot of differences between each type of wireless medium. Table 5.5 summarizes the key benefits and drawbacks of each wireless medium. Table 5.6 makes a relative comparison of wireless media across several criteria.

Table 5.5   Key benefits and drawbacks of different wireless media.

Media	Key Benefit(s)	Drawback(s)
Infrared line of sight	Easy to install and configure; inexpensive	Very limited bandwidth; line of sight required; environmental factors influence signal quality
High-frequency radio	Mobile stations; low attenuation	Frequency licensing; complex installation; high attenuation
Terrestrial microwave	Access remote locations or congested areas; high bandwidth; low attenuation	Frequency licensing; complex installation; environmental factors influence signal quality
Satellite microwave	Access remote locations; high bandwidth; earth stations can be fixed or mobile	Frequency licensing; complex installation; environmental factors influence signal quality; propagation delays

Table 5.6   Relative comparison of wireless media.

Media	Expense	Speed	Attenuation	EMI	Eavesdropping
Infrared line of sight	Low	Up to 16 Mbps	High	High	High
High-frequency radio	Moderate	Up to 10 Mbps	Low	High	High
Terrestrial microwave	Moderate	Up to 274 Mbps	Low	High	High
Satellite microwave	High	Up to 90 Mbps	Moderate	High	High

Network Topologies

Now that you have looked at different types of transmission media, the next issue to consider is how workstations can be connected together. **Network topology** refers to the shape of the network, how the wiring is laid out, and the physical and logical relationship of nodes on the network. The three common network topologies are star, ring, and bus.

Star Network

A **star network** is configured, as you might expect, in the shape of a star (shown in Figure 5.20A). That is, at the center of the star is a wiring hub or concentrator to which all the nodes or workstations are attached and through which all messages pass. A hub serves as a central point of connection between media segments. Active hubs amplify transmission signals so relatively longer cable lengths may be used. The workstations represent the points of a star. Star topologies are easy to lay out and modify. However, they are also the most costly because they require the largest amount of cabling. In addition, although it is easy to diagnose problems at individual workstations, star networks are susceptible to a single point of failure at the hub.

FIGURE 5.20A

Network topologies: the star network.

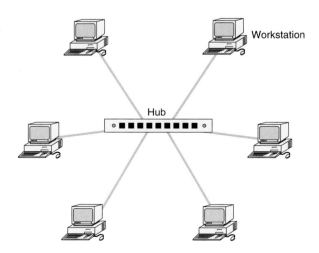

Ring Network

A **ring network** is configured in (yes, you guessed it) the shape of a closed loop or circle, with each node connecting to the next node, as shown in Figure 5.20B. In ring networks, messages move in one direction around the circle. As a message moves around the circle, each workstation examines it to see whether the message is for that workstation. If not, the message is regenerated and passed on to the next node. This regeneration process enables ring networks to cover much larger distances than star or bus networks can. Relatively little cabling is required, but, a failure of any node on the ring network can cause complete network failure. In addition, it is difficult to modify and reconfigure the network. Ring networks normally use some form of token passing media access control method to regulate network traffic, as is discussed in the "Network Access Control Methods" section.

Bus Network

A **bus network** is in the shape of an open-ended line (shown in Figure 5.20C) and, as a result, is the easiest to extend and has the simplest wiring layout. This topology enables all network nodes to receive the same message through the network cable at the same time. However, it is difficult to diagnose and isolate network faults. Bus networks use CSMA/CD for media access control (see "Network Access Control Methods," following).

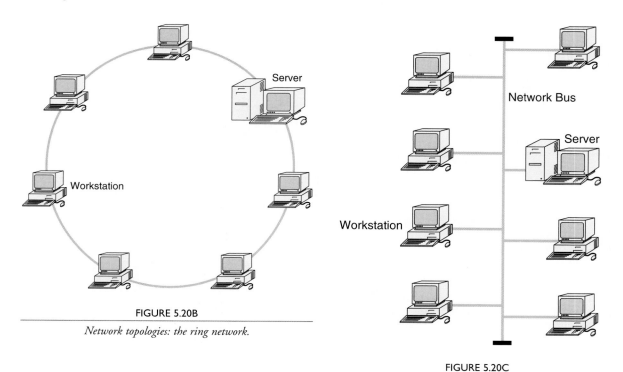

FIGURE 5.20B

Network topologies: the ring network.

FIGURE 5.20C

Network topologies: the bus network.

Network Access Control Methods

Network access control methods are the rules that govern how a given node or workstation gains access to the network to send or receive information. There are two general types of access control: distributed and random access. With distributed control, only a single workstation at a time has authorization to transmit its data. This authorization is transferred in a logical fashion from workstation to workstation. Under random control, any workstation can transmit its data by checking whether the medium is available. No specific permission is required. The following sections describe each type in more detail.

Distributed Access Control

The most commonly used method of distributed access control is called **token passing**. Token passing is an access method that uses a constantly circulating electronic token to prevent **collisions** (when two or more workstations simultaneously transmit messages onto the network) and give all workstations equal access to the network. A workstation must be in possession of the token before it can transmit a message on to the network. A workstation that receives the token and wants to send a message marks the token as busy, appends a message to it, and transmits both. The message and token are passed around the ring. Each workstation copies the message and retransmits the token/message combination. Ultimately, when it is received back at the originating workstation, the message is removed, the token is marked as free, and it is retransmitted, as depicted in Figure 5.21. Although token passing prevents collisions, it is a complex process.

FIGURE 5.21

Token ring operation.

Figure adapted from Business Data Communications, Second Edition by Stallings/VanSlyke. 1997. Reprinted by permission of Prentice-Hall, Inc., Upper Saddle River, NJ.

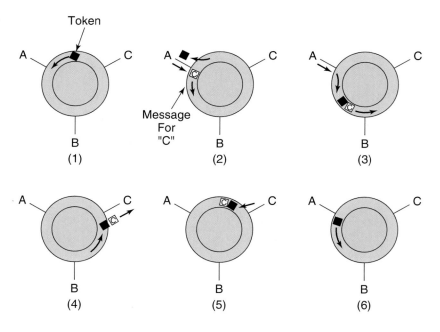

Random Access Control

The most commonly used method of random access control is called **CSMA/CD**—carrier sense multiple access/collision detection. In CSMA/CD each workstation "listens" to the network to determine whether a message is currently being transmitted. If the network is quiet, the workstation sends its message; otherwise, it waits. When a workstation gains access to the media and sends information onto the network, messages are sent to all workstations on the network; however, only the destination with the proper address is able to "open" the message. If two or more workstations try to send a message simultaneously, all workstations detect that a collision has occurred, and all sending is ceased. After a short random period of time, the workstations again try to send their messages. CSMA/CD provides very good media access performance when network traffic is light and there are few collisions. Performance deteriorates rapidly, however, under heavy traffic conditions.

Major Standards

Standards play a key role in the capability to interconnect networks. Consequently, the physical elements of networks—adapters, cables, and connectors—are defined by a set of standards that have evolved since the early 1970s. Standards ensure the interoperability and compatibility of network devices. The Institute of Electrical and Electronic Engineers (IEEE), acting as a coordination body, has established a number of telecommunications standards. The three major standards for LAN cabling and media access control are Ethernet, Token-Ring, and ARCnet (see Table 5.7). Each of the three standards combines physical and logical topologies, and media-access control techniques in different ways.

Table 5.7 Summary of major LAN standards.

Network Standards	Access Control	Topology	Typical Media	Speed
Ethernet	CSMA/CD	Bus	Coax or Twisted Pair	10–100 Mbps
Token Ring	Token Passing	Ring	Twisted Pair	4–16 Mbps
ARCnet	Token Passing	Star or Bus	Coax or Twisted Pair	2.5Mbps

ETHICAL PERSPECTIVE: PRIVACY—ELECTRONIC MAIL AND EMPLOYEE MONITORING

As time passes, more and more companies are providing electronic mail (email) capabilities to their employees. Many times, these firms are also providing access to the Internet, enabling employees to send email to anyone in the world who has an Internet connection. It makes good business sense, for a variety of reasons, to provide these kinds of communication capabilities to employees.

Of course, the intention is that these email airwaves will be used for business only, or at least that non-business email messages will be kept to a minimum. In fact, some companies choose to use only a local email system such as Microsoft Mail, and not provide the connection to other email systems or to the Internet. That's one way to solve the problem.

Many companies have decided to enable employees to have access to the Internet and other outside email systems and then periodically monitor the email messages that employees send. Monitoring employee behavior is nothing new, and it was to many businesses a natural extension to monitor email messages. However, monitoring of employee email has become quite controversial.

Messages sent and received in the workplace via email often contain personal information. Most companies accept this type of interaction as healthy and necessary. However, many companies feel that because they own the systems and network on which the email runs, and because the email is there for business purposes, they can monitor the email messages of employees using the system. In fact, several recent court case judgments have upheld corporations' rights to monitor their employees' email messages.

Surprisingly, there is little legal recourse for those who support email privacy. In 1986, the Electronic Communications Privacy Act (ECPA) was passed by Congress, but it offered far stronger support for voice mail than it did for email communications. This act made it much more difficult for anyone (including the government) to eavesdrop on phone conversations. Email privacy is, thus, much harder to protect. In addition, no other laws at the federal or state levels protect email privacy. However, some states, most notably California, have passed laws that define how companies should inform their employees of this situation and in which situations monitoring is legal.

Even so, this law is more of a guideline for ethical practice than a protection of privacy (Sipior and Ward, 1995).

Fortunately, ECPA and the court case judgments thus far on email monitoring suggest that companies must be prudent and open about their monitoring of email messages. Companies should use good judgment in monitoring email messages and should make public their policy about monitoring messages. One primary reason that employees perceive their email to be private is the fact that they are never told otherwise (Weisband and Reinig, 1995). In addition, employees should use email only as appropriate, based on their company's policy and their own ethical standards.

Given recent actions and rulings on the capture and usage of email messages over the Internet, it appears that email privacy is in jeopardy, in and out of business organizations. In what federal agents called the first-ever use of a court-approved wiretap for electronic mail, investigators have used a wiretap of email to break up a cellular phone fraud ring. The tap marks a milestone for law enforcement in cyberspace, and privacy experts have predicted that the use of such wiretaps will grow (Violino and Gilloly, 1996). As a general rule, we all need to realize that what we type and send via email in and out of the workplace is likely to be read by others for whom the messages were not intended. It is wise to generate only those email messages that would not embarrass us if they were made public.

Questions for Discussion

1. Do you believe that it is ethical to transmit personal email messages over company lines?

2. Do you feel that email should be protected by privacy laws such as the ECPA? Or are email messages company property?

3. Now that you know that email is not necessarily a private communication system, will this change your use of email in any way?

Sources Sipior, Janice C., and Burke T. Ward. 1995. *The ethical and legal quandary of e-mail privacy.* Communications of the ACM, *December, 48–54.*
Weisband, Suzanne P., and Bruce A. Reinig. 1995. *Managing user perceptions of e-mail privacy.* Communications of the ACM, *December, 40–47.*
Violino, B., and C. Gillooly. 1996. *Feds tap e-mail in bust—court-approved tactic raises privacy concerns.* InformationWeek, *January 8.*

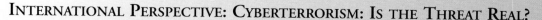

INTERNATIONAL PERSPECTIVE: CYBERTERRORISM: IS THE THREAT REAL?

One issue receiving a lot of attention recently is the threat of terrorism over the Internet. To most computer users, this kind of threat seems unlikely; however, the U.S. Department of Defense alone was attacked over 250,000 times, and 65 percent of these attacks were successful.

Smith (1996) describes a survey conducted by the CIA and other intelligence organizations seeking to understand the risk of an attack on "computers controlling U.S. telephones, the electric power grid, oil refineries, and other utilities." Although official results have not been made public, these agencies are searching for "evidence of any foreign intent to attack U.S. computers, any sign of foreign sponsorship for U.S.-based computer hacking activities, and for any indication that foreign organized crime figures are becoming involved in attacks on computers at U.S. financial institutions." Although no specific examples were mentioned, Smith notes that the CIA lists cyberterrorism (or "computer warfare") as "the second most worrisome threat to U.S. national security—just below the threat posed by foreign chemical, nuclear, and biological arms." If it were declassified and more information were available, it would be given less attention.

Berman (1995) and other Internet users dismiss the threat of terrorism, claiming that posting messages on how to make bombs and hack computers is in itself a harmless act. He claims that "Though one can shout fire in an email message or on an Internet newsgroup, the likelihood that it will incite readers to imminent, criminal action is much reduced because the readers are dispersed around the country, and even around the world." Kreth (1994) alleges that the threat of terrorism via the Internet has been manufactured by governments around the world in an attempt to regulate the Internet.

Some Web users argue that we need cyberterrorism to keep us on our toes. The author of one "here's now" site claims: "Hackers keep our computer systems strong. It forces administrators to know their stuff and keep security, strengthening our society, which is so utterly dependent on computer systems. Imagine what serious damage could be done by a terrorist with access to easy information on a system that hasn't had to deal with any security issues" (Anonymous).

A related security issue is the developing battle between those who believe that Internet users are entitled to privacy, and the governments and agencies that fear what would happen if actions take place behind "closed (electronic) doors." May notes that the U.S. government is fighting privacy by attempting to restrict encryption (S.266, never passed), to require encryption key registration, and with the Digital Telephony Bill ($10,000 a day fines). Kreth claims that "To reassert [the government's] 'leash,' encryption has become the new modus operandi, a potentially chilling federal freon-blast of executive privilege to protect the State and the Union from wild-eyed Hezbolah, Shiites, and seventeen-year-old hackers with digitized videotape of the next Rodney King or Dolores Huerta police beating. The government has a keen interest in shaping public opinion, as we witnessed during the Iran/Contra hearings, the conveniently forgotten S&L crisis, and the Persian Gulf war."

Many other nations have already instituted strict policies on the private use of encryption. May reports, "France outlaws private crypto, though enforcement is said to be problematic...Third World countries often have bans on crypto, and mere possession of random-looking bits may mean a spying conviction and a trip to the gallows. There are also several reports that European nations are preparing to fall in line behind the U.S. on key escrow—Norway, Netherlands, and Britain." Germany and Russia are also leaning toward cooperating with the U.S. government on encryption issues.

Questions for Discussion

1. In your opinion, is the threat of cyberterrorism real?

2. In what ways are you vulnerable to cyberterrorism or to invasions of privacy? In what ways are you protected?

3. What can your business or organization do to combat this threat, real or imagined?

Sources Berman, J. 1995. Testimony of Jerry Berman, executive director, Center for Democracy and Technology before the Senate Judiciary Committee Subcommittee on Terrorism, Technology and Government Information. Available online at http://www.cdt.org/policy/terrorism/internet_bomb.test.html.
Kreth, W. 1994. The obliteration of "scarcity." Available online at http://www.arts.ucsb.edu/~speed/speedPast/1.1/kreth.html.
May, Tim. Policy: Clipper, key escrow, and digital telephony: crypto laws outside the U.S. cyphernomicon 9.7. Available on line at http://www.oberlin.edu/~brchkind/cyphernomicon/chapter9/9.7.html.
1996. Parade Magazine. A new worry. Terrorism in cyberspace. Sept. 29, 14.
Smith, J. 1996. Deutch lists computer break-ins, terrorism as high-priority potential threats to national security. The Washington Post. April, A19. Available online at http://www.mainkey.com/netresor/www/july96wn.htm.

Connectivity Hardware

Stand-alone computers can be physically connected to create LANs and WANs in a variety of ways. In a network, each device or computer must be connected to the medium or cable segment. Transmission media connectors, network interface cards, and modems are used to accomplish this. After individual devices are connected to the network, multiple segments of transmission media can be connected to form one large network. Repeaters, hubs, bridges, and multiplexers are used to extend the range and size of the network. These devices are summarized in Table 5.8.

Table 5.8 Key components of a local network.

Component	Description
Transmission media connectors	Include T-connectors for coax cable and RJ-45 connectors (similar to a phone jack) for twisted pair cable. The appropriate connector is attached to each length of cable and plugged into a network interface card.
Network Interface Cards (NICs)	A PC expansion board that plugs into a computer and works with the network operating system to control the flow of information between the computer and the network. Each NIC has a unique identifier (determined by the manufacturer) that is used to identify the address of the computer on the workstation.
Modems (MODulator/DEModulators)	Enable computers to transmit information over telephone lines by converting the digital signals used in computers and the analog signals used in telephone systems.
Repeaters	Used to amplify or regenerate the electronic signal. A repeater moves data from one media segment to another and effectively extends the length of the cabling.
Hubs	Used as a central point of connection between media segments. Like repeaters, hubs enable the network to be extended to accommodate additional workstations. Hubs are commonly used in 10BaseT networks.
Bridges	Network devices that forward traffic between network segments. However, unlike repeaters, bridges determine the physical location of the source and destination computers. They are used to divide an overloaded network into separate segments and prevent unnecessary intrasegment traffic. Bridges can also connect segments that use different wiring or network protocols (see below).
Multiplexers (MUX)	Devices used to share communications circuits among a number of users. Sometimes a transmission media provides more capacity than a single signal can occupy. To efficiently use the entire media bandwidth, multiplexes are installed to transmit several signals over a single channel.

Organizations use the components summarized in Table 5.8 to construct a LAN by attaching individual computers and media segments into one network. Many times organizations want to connect users and/or networks in different geographical areas. Distributed LANs, interconnected by WANs, are needed to exchange data and information across an organization. The WAN, however, appears transparent to the user because information stored in a computer at another location appears to be locally available. **Internetworking** connectivity hardware—routers, brouters, CSUs (channel service units), and gateways—provide businesses with the freedom to locate their operations in different places, while at the same time running them as integrated units. These technologies are summarized in Table 5.9.

Table 5.9 Key components for internetworking.

Component	Description
Routers	Intelligent devices used to connect two or more individual networks. When a router receives a signal, it looks at the network address and passes the signal or message on to the appropriate network.
Brouters	Devices that combine both routing and bridging functions.
Channel Service Units (CSUs)	Devices that act as a "buffer" between the LAN and a public carrier's WAN. CSUs ensure that all signals placed on the public line are appropriately timed and formed. CSUs must be certified by the FCC.
Gateways	Shared connections between a LAN and a larger system, such as a mainframe or a large packet-switched network whose communications protocols are different. Gateways perform protocol conversions so that different networks can communicate, even though they "speak" different languages.

Connectivity Software

The previous sections have examined how networks are constructed. It's time now to consider the role of software in making networks operate. The first role, the OSI model, focuses on network protocols that define the rules of communication on and between networks. The needs of organizations to interconnect devices that use different protocols have driven the industry to an open system architecture, in which different protocols can communicate with each other. The International Standards Organization (ISO) defined a networking model called the Open Systems Interconnection (OSI) that divides computer-to-computer communications into seven connected layers. A second important software role relates to software that controls the network: the network operating system. Both of these important software roles are described as follows.

The OSI Model

Protocols enable two computers to communicate, even if they have different architectures and operating systems. The **OSI model** is a protocol that represents a group of specific tasks, represented in Figure 5.22 as successive layers, which enable computers to communicate data. Each successively higher layer builds on the functions of the layers below. For example, suppose you are using a PC, and connected to the Internet, running Windows, and you want to send a message to a friend who is connected to the Internet through a large workstation computer running UNIX—two different computers and two different operating systems. When you transmit your message, it is passed from layer to layer in the Windows protocol environment of your system. At each layer, a header is added that contains that layer's requests and information. Eventually, the data packages are transferred from the Windows' Layer 1 to the UNIX's Layer 1 over some physical medium. Upon receipt, the message is passed up through the layers in the UNIX application. At each layer, the corresponding header information is stripped away, the requested task is performed, and the remaining data package is passed on until your message arrives as you sent it, as shown in Figure 5.23.

FIGURE 5.22

The OSI model.

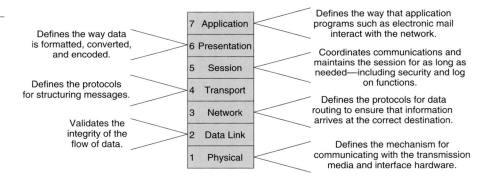

FIGURE 5.23

Message passing between two different computers.

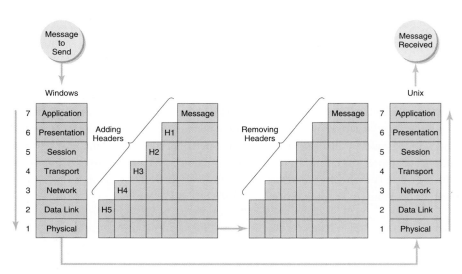

Although many protocols exist for computer networking, two of the most commonly used are Novell NetWare's IPX/SPX protocol and the internetworking protocol used by the Internet, called TCP/IP. What you need to remember is that protocols represent an agreement between different parts of the network on how data is to be transferred. Though you aren't supposed to see them and only a few people understand them, their effect on system performance can be spectacular.

Network Operating Systems

The network operating system (NOS) is the major piece of software that controls the network. In a typical client/server-architecture LAN, the NOS consists of two parts. The first and most complex part is the system software that runs on the file server. The system software coordinates many functions, including user accounts, access information, security, and resource sharing. The second and much smaller part of the NOS runs on each workstation connected to the network. In peer-to-peer networks, usually a piece of the NOS is installed on each attached workstation and runs on top of the local operating system. A recent trend has been the integration of the NOS into the workstation operating system itself. This is the approach used in Windows NT. Examples of client/server NOSs are Banyan Vines, Novell NetWare, and Microsoft LAN Manager. Peer-to-peer NOS include LANtastic, Personal NetWare, and Windows for Workgroups.

Remotely Managing AFS's Network

A BRIEF CASE

To give you an idea of what a NOS can do, consider AFS-USA, a non-governmental, nonprofit organization that manages an international exchange program for high school students. Overseeing more than 10,000 volunteers from coast to coast and a paid staff of 100 in New York City, AFS-USA uses Novell NetWare to manage its local area network (Novell, 1998). To effectively match students to sponsor families, ASF-USA needs up-to-the-minute information. Unfortunately, when AFS decided to interconnect its computers via a network, it did not have an information systems staff. Given its nonprofit status and the attendant responsibility to keep its overhead low, ASF-USA did not want to hire network professionals to manage its network. Consequently, ASF-USA hired Quality Technology Solutions, Inc. (QTS), in South Orange, New Jersey, to manage the network. Using Novell's remote network-management features in the NOS, QTS could remotely manage the AFS-USA network from its New Jersey offices. Novell's NOS that provides remote network management enables AFS-USA to focus on its primary mission of facilitating student exchange programs, not on its network, and keeps its overhead to a minimum.

Talking with...

Todd D. Taylor, Director of Technology/Chief Technology Officer at Washington State University

Educational Background

B.A. in Management and Management of Information Systems, Washington State University; M.B.A. in MIS, Washington State University

Job Description

Mr. Taylor provides access, training, and support for all information technology-related activities in support of the mission of the college. He is responsible for setting priorities; developing policy; and evaluating, assessing, and implementing both the technological infrastructure and the human infrastructure. He develops and oversees college information technology plans, and he implements and administers a college-wide infrastructure of information services. This includes the implementation and supervision of network servers; electronic mail;the Internet and intranet services; and the development of policies, procedures, and standards that facilitate and enhance the use of computer technology in the college environment.

Critical Success Factors

Every decision is made in the best interest of the organization. If it is not in the best interest, revisit the situation, choices, and decision. Internships really focus your academic motivation. Look for shortages or holes where you can add value. Then, determine your level of participation and proceed.

Advice to Students

Seize hidden opportunities. Take advantage of internships or hands-on training programs, both formal and informal. Learn technology, as it applies to your career and life. It will only help you. Don't sell yourself short. Really think about what you want to do, who you want to be, and where you want to go. Be the "professional" you, meaning you should be yourself, while keeping in mind that you must be professional in the business.

Summary

1. **Understand the role of telecommunications in organizations.** Applications such as electronic mail and video conferencing are rapidly changing the way business is conducted. Global networks are allowing organizations to streamline business operations in ways never before possible. Telecommunications technologies are becoming fundamental, not only for supporting day-to-day activities within most organizations, but they are also playing a growing role in the competitive strategy of more and more organizations. More than ever before, managers must understand these technologies to ride the information systems wave and to apply the right solutions to the right problems.

2. **Describe the evolution and types of computer networks.** Since the 1950s, three models of computing have been used. First, from the 1950s until the 1970s, the centralized computing model was dominant. In the centralized computing model, all processing occurs at a large central computer and users interact with the system through the use of terminals. From the late 1970s until the late 1980s, a distributed computing model was dominant. In this model, separate computers work on subsets of tasks and then pool their results by communicating on a network. In the 1990s, the collaborative computing model emerged. In this model, two or more networked computers work together to accomplish a common processing task. A private branch exchange (PBX) is a private telephone exchange, located in a single facility, which provides both voice and data communication. A local area network (LAN) is a group of computers at one location that share hardware and software resources. A wide area network (WAN) refers to two or more LANs from different locations that are linked together. An enterprise network is a WAN that connects all the LANs of a single location. Finally, a global network is a WAN that spans multiple countries and may include the networks of several organizations.

3. **Understand networking fundamentals including network services, transmission media, network topologies, and connectivity hardware for both local area and wide area networks.** In networking, a distinction is made between servers, clients, and peers. A server is a computer that stores information (programs and data) and provides services to users through a network. A client is any device or software application that makes use of the information or services provided by a server. Peers are two separate computers or devices on a network that request and provide services to each other. Servers and clients are combined to create server-centric networks. Peers are combined to create peer-to-peer networks. Networks provide file, print, message, and application services that extend the capabilities of stand-alone computers. Networks exchange information by using cable or wireless transmission media. Cable media include twisted pair, coaxial, and fiber optic. Wireless media include infrared line of sight, high-frequency radio, and microwave. The shape of a network can vary; the three most common topologies are star, ring, and bus configurations. Network access control refers to the rules that govern how a given workstation gains access to the network. There are two general types: distributed and random access. With distributed access, only a single workstation at a time has authorization to transmit its data. Under random access control, any workstation can transmit its data by checking whether the medium is available. In a network, each device or computer must be connected to the media or cable segment. To accomplish this, transmission media connectors, network interface cards, and modems are used. After individual devices are connected to the network, multiple segments of transmission media can be connected to form one large network. Repeaters, hubs, bridges, and multiplexers are used to extend the range and size of the network. Routers, brouters, CSUs (channel service units), and gateways are used to interconnect networks.

4. **Explain the role of the Open System Interconnect (OSI) model and network operating systems in enabling network communication.** The needs of organizations to interconnect devices that use different protocols have driven the industry to an open system architecture, in which different protocols can communicate with each other. The International Standards Organization (ISO) defined a networking model called the Open Systems Interconnection (OSI) that divides computer-to-computer communications into seven connected layers. Each successively higher layer builds on the functions of the layers below.

Hardware and software vendors can use networking standards such as OSI to build devices that can be more easily interconnected. The network operating system (NOS) is the major piece of software that controls the network. In a typical client/server-architecture LAN, the NOS consists of two parts. The first and most complex is the system software that runs on the file server. The system software coordinates many functions, including user accounts, access information, security, and resource sharing. The second and much smaller part of the NOS runs on each workstation connected to the network.

Key Terms

Electronic data interchange

Codes

Decode

Transmission media

Protocol

Digitizing

Networks

Telecommunication

Bandwidth

Modem

Centralized computing

Distributed computing

Collaborative computing

Private branch exchange (PBX)

Local area network (LAN)

Wide area network (WAN)

Enterprise network

Global network

Internet

Value-added networks

Server

Client

Peer

Server-centric network

Peer-to-peer network

Network services

Network operating system

Attenuation

Twisted pair cable

Coaxial cable

Fiber optic cable

Backbones

Wireless media

Infrared line of sight

High-frequency radio

Terrestrial microwave

Satellite microwave

Network topology

Star network

Ring network

Bus network

Token passing

Collisions

CSMA/CD

Internetworking

OSI model

Review Questions

1. What are the three components necessary for data communication?

2. Briefly describe how a modem operates within a computer.

3. Compare and contrast centralized, distributed, and collaborative computing.

4. How are local area networks, wide area networks, enterprise networks, and global networks related to each other?

5. Distinguish the following components of network computing: servers, clients, and peers.

6. What are the four major types of network services available on today's networks?

7. Describe the five aspects of transmission media to consider when implementing a network.

8. What are four common methods of wireless transmission media for networking? How do they differ from each other?

9. What is a network topology? Describe the three common topologies that are used today.

10. What is the purpose of the OSI model?

Problems and Exercises

◆ **Individual**

◈ **Group**

☞ **Field**

◗ **Web/Internet**

1. Match the following terms to the appropriate definitions:

_____ Transmission Media

_____ Distributed Computing

_____ Peer-to-Peer Network

_____ Network Operating System

_____ Attenuation

_____ Bus Network

_____ Token Passing

_____ Electronic Data Interchange

a. Networks in which computers may both request and provide services to each other

b. Computer-to-computer communication, in which information is exchanged using previously agreed-upon formats

c. A decrease in the power of an electric signal as it is sent over distance

d. The pathway used to send a message

e. A network access control method in which a token circulates around a ring topology and stations can transmit messages onto the network only when a non-busy token arrives at a station

f. Computing model, in which separate computers work on subsets of tasks and then pool their results by communicating on a network

g. A network topology, in which all stations are connected to a single open-ended line

h. A group of software programs that manages and provides the network services

2. Using terms such as digital, analog, dial-up telephone lines, and modem, explain how a file is sent from your computer to your friend's computer through the regular phone system. What happens when and where?

3. Discuss the differences between PBX networks and LANs. What are the advantages of each? What are possible disadvantages of each? When would you recommend one over the other?

4. Compare and contrast client-server and peer-to-peer networks. How do the computers and devices interact with each other in these networks? How does the term "client" relate to a peer-to-peer network? Is one type of network better than the other? Why?

5. Do you feel that the future of telecommunications rests in wireless media? Why or why not? If so, how long until wireless media becomes the standard? What is/will be the biggest obstacle to overcome? Compare your views with those of some of your classmates. How are they different, if at all?

6. As a small group of classmates, explain the differences in network access of a token passing scheme and a CSMA/CD scheme. Which has more control over the network? Why? Think of a situation in which each scheme would be the best choice for network access control.

7. Do you feel that desktop video conferencing, as described in the opening to this chapter, will become a reality for most businesses? Why or why not? What about the face-to-face, in-person meetings that have existed for centuries? Are certain industries or products more conducive to desktop video conferencing?

8. Based on your experiences with computer networks, select one situation and describe it. What type of topology was being used? What was the network operating system? Was the network connected to any other networks? How? As a user, did you care about any of this? Why or why not?

9. Choose an organization with which you are familiar that utilizes wireless media. What are the media? What types of data are being transmitted? Where is the data going? Does this organization utilize cable media as well? If so, compare and contrast the uses of wireless and cable media in this organization.

10. Interview an IS Manager within an organization with which you are familiar. Determine this person's feelings toward telecommunications media, networks, and protocols. What media does the organization utilize? Does this person feel that this is the best choice? What were the factors for choosing the media and network setup?

  11. Scan the popular press and search the World Wide Web for articles concerning emerging technologies for telecommunications. This may include new uses for current technologies or new technologies altogether. Discuss as a group the "hot" issues. Do you feel they will become a reality in the near future? Why or why not? Prepare a 10-minute presentation of your findings to the class.

 12. Choose an organization with which you are familiar that utilizes a client-server network. How many servers are on this network? How many clients? How many other devices? Before being a client-server network, what was it? Why the change? What network topology is being used?

 13. Based on your knowledge of networks, networking, hardware, and software, can you determine how the Internet works? Use the terms from this chapter and previous chapters to help you. The Internet will be discussed in great detail in Chapter 6.

14. In a group, each person should describe what type of network setup would be most appropriate for a small office with about 10 devices (computers, printers, servers), all within one building, and relatively close to one another. Be sure to talk about transmission media, network topology, hardware, and software. Did all group members come up with the same setup option? Why or why not? What else would you need to know to make a good recommendation?

15. Imagine that you were Mary Shide, product manager for Brand-X, as introduced in the opening of this chapter. Discuss in a small group the concerns you would have for Patty Nicholls of Nicholls Food Stores regarding the implementation of the desktop video conferencing. Why? How much will the speed of your own computer affect the transmission?

Real World Case Problems

1. Warp Speed Ahead: Soon, a Superfast Web. But first, a War Over Technology?

Starting in 1996, Michael Stepp, a federal government worker, participated in the trial of Bell Atlantic Corp.'s digital subscriber line (DSL) that sends data over basic copper telephone lines more than 30 times faster than today's fastest modems. He searched the Web at rapid speed and even told his wife that they would only buy a house in the DSL area. However, the latter did not happen.

Nowadays, telephone, cable, and satellite companies are investing billions of dollars in new technologies that will link users to the Internet at lightning speeds. Companies such as US West, Inc. and @Home Corporation have increased their service to as many as 10 million and 4.5 million people, respectively. By 2001 nearly 80 percent of households will have fast access at hand, an increase from 15 percent today.

The foot dragging of telephone and cable companies to provide high-speed access appears to be over. Competition has forced them to provide access or lose customers. Internet access is a $6.5 billion business that is expected to double in the next four years. Each camp is pushing technology that plays with its strength. Phone companies want DSL, as it works over the phone lines, whereas the cable companies are pushing cable modems connected to the existing TV cable networks.

The cable companies are ahead by a nose, but the phone companies are starting to catch up. On January 26, 1998, the Regional Bell Operating Companies (RBOC) banded with Microsoft, Intel, and Compaq Computer to get a DSL standard called "DSL lite" to make the technology easier for the consumers to use. Microsoft is throwing its weight and money behind the cable and phone camps to get more bandwidth to homes. The feeling is that faster access will allow for jazzing up the Net and in turn, the larger audience will purchase more Microsoft products.

Of these options, cable is cheaper and is already served in a lot of homes. On the other hand, cable also shares pipelines in neighborhoods, allowing hackers to literally dig their way into the neighbor's computer files. Further, although cable modems can bring data to the home at a fairly fast rate, more than 80 percent of the cable modems have sluggish mechanisms for sending data back. DSL has the advantage of being fast in bringing and sending data to your computer, and DSL can serve as a second phone line.

a. Which of the three technologies—DSL, cable modems, or satellite—do you think will win out for the next evolution of the Information Superhighway? Why?

b. Why is a faster Internet better for companies like Microsoft and Intel?

c. What are the implications of having the Internet operate and be accessible at these faster speeds?

Source   1998. *Warp speed ahead.* BusinessWeek, February 16, 81–83.

2. Breaking the Mold: A Startup Called Level 3 Is Pumping Billions of Dollars into a New IP Network that Could Change the Way You Do Business

The former executives of local and long distance fiber carrier MFS Communications and its original holding company are reuniting to create the first business-focused, pure Internet Protocol (IP) local and long-distance carrier. With nearly $3 billion in financing, James Crowe, the founder of MFS, announced the formation of Level 3 Communications, a fiber carrier that will deliver services at $1/27$th the cost of today's traditional circuit-switched networks.

Level 3's strategy is not without risk. Although the researchers continually improve the voice-over-IP technology, business quality may not be in the near future. Some competitors have stated that Level 3's network is merely a concept. However, many believe that Crowe & Co. can execute. Crowe's former company, MFS, increased its market value more than any other company in a 33-month period and is now owned by World Com.

If Level 3 succeeds, new applications that converge video, data, and voice could be created. It is expected that data traffic will exceed voice transmission within the next three to five years. Level 3 could also lead to lower-cost applications that could make many vital legacy applications available to employees and businesses. Analysts estimate that there are $5 trillion worth of installed legacy systems that could lead to potentially gigantic business opportunities.

Level 3 would enable customers to develop applications that include both voice and data. For example, a marketing rep could send a picture of the product, a phone call, and the billing information all over a single line.

In the past, when traditional carriers thought the fiber-network would be cutting edge for 20 years, they didn't build physical accesses to the network, so they are now left in the lurch. Level 3's approach is easier, inexpensive, and faster to upgrade. Level 3 can design an open, back office system to support any customer's operations. Furthermore, the majority of the carriers' leaders are former MFS executives. Crowe's has the vision, experience, and money to accomplish it.

a. Will Level 3 succeed in deploying a pure Internet Protocol local and long-distance service network? Why or why not?

b. If you ran a more traditional Regional Bell Operating Company such as Ameritech or a traditional long-distance carrier such as AT&T, what would be your reaction to the Level 3 start-up? Why? What would you do next?

c. What are the implications for businesses of having a telecommunications infrastructure that is primarily digital rather than made of analog lines built for primarily voice traffic?

Source *Thyfault, Mary E. 1998. Breaking the mold.* InformationWeek, *January 19, 44–46.*

References

DOE. 1998. Information from: www.ed.gov/Technology/TeleComp/. Information verified: February 17, 1998.

HP. 1998. Information from: www.hp.com. Information verified: February 17, 1998.

Novell. 1998. Information from: www.novell.com. Information verified: February 17, 1998.

PC Magazine. 1996. IBM Corp. IBM wireless LAN entry. Information from: www.zzdnet.com. Information verified: February 17, 1998.

Stallings, W., and R. Van Slyke. 1994. *Business Data Communications.* 2d ed. New York: Macmillan.

Washington. 1998. Information from: www.wpc-edi.com. Information verified: February 17, 1998.

Related Readings

Bell, G., and J. Gemmell. 1996. On-ramp prospects for the information superhighway dream. *Communications of the ACM* 39(7): 55–61.

Coyne, K. P., and R. Dye. 1998. The competitive dynamics of network-based businesses. *Harvard Business Review* 76(1): 99–109.

Farber, D. J. 1997. Communications technology and its impact by 2010. *Communications of the ACM* 40(2): 135–138.

Giridharan, P. S., and H. Mendelson. 1994. Free-access policy for internal networks. *Information Systems Research* 5(1): 1–21.

Grover, V., and M. D. Goslar. 1993. The initiation, adoption, and implementation of telecommunications technologies in U.S. organizations. *Journal of Management Information Systems* 10(1): 141–163.

Imielinski, T., and B. R. Badrinath. 1994. Mobile wireless computing. *Communications of the ACM* 37(10): 18–28.

Kettinger, W. J. 1994. National infrastructure diffusion and the U.S. information superhighway. *Information and Management* 27(6): 357–368.

Kim, B. G., and P. Wang. 1995. ATM network: Goals and challenges. *Communications of the ACM* 38(2): 39–44, 109.

Laguna, M. 1994. Clustering for the design of SONET rings in interoffice telecommunications. *Management Science* 40(11): 1533–1541.

Lai, V. S. 1994. A model of ISDN (integrated services digital network) adoption in U.S. corporations. *Information and Management* 26(2): 75–84.

Lai, V. S. 1997. Critical factors of ISDN implementation: An exploratory study. *Information and Management* 33(2): 87–97.

Lee, Shi, and Stolen. 1994. Allocating data files over a wide area network: Goal setting and compromise design. *Information and Management* 26(2): 85–93.

Velter, R. J. 1995. ATM concepts, architectures, and protocols. *Communications of the ACM* 38(2): 30–38, 109.

PART 3

Information Systems In Practice

The purpose of Part 3 is to help you understand how organizations use various types of information systems to their advantage.

In Chapter 6, *Electronic Commerce and the Internet,* we describe what the Internet is and how it works, the TCP/IP networking protocol, basic Internet services, and the World Wide Web. We also explain electronic commerce and the differences between Internet-, intranet-, and Extranet-based electronic commerce.

In Chapter 7, *Organizational Information Systems,* we describe the operational, managerial, and executive levels of an organization. We then explain three types of information systems designed to support each of the unique levels of an organization–transaction processing systems, management information systems, and executive information systems. We also describe three types of information systems that span the organizational, managerial, and executive levels–decision support systems,

expert systems, and office automation systems. Finally, we explain the information system needs of each of the various functional areas of the firm

In Chapter 8, *Emerging Information Systems,* we explain why companies are continually looking for new ways to use technology for competitive advantage. We describe specific examples of emerging information systems, such as videoconferencing, groupware, and group support systems for supporting collaboration and virtual teams. We also describe how companies are using computer kiosks, telephone interfacing, and the Internet and Web to support improved customer contact and reach.

Get ready for Part 3, "Information Systems in Practice." This is a comprehensive tour of the types of information systems that organizations are using today. It's quite likely that in your next internship or in your job after graduation, you'll be using or even building systems like those you'll read about in this next part of the book.

Information Systems
Management

Emerging
IS

Organizational   IS
IS   Development

Electronic
Commerce
& the Internet

Hardware   Software

Database Management

Telecommunications

Scenario: Researching a Term Paper on the Net

Imagine that a professor in one of the courses in your major (for example, marketing, finance, accounting, education, commutations, and so forth) opened class by saying the following. "Today, I am going to assign your term project. For this project, I want you to write a paper on how the Internet is changing the way _____ professionals (fill in the blank with your degree program—for example, marketing) do their jobs. For this project, I want you to provide me two types of information. First, provide me with some background on the Internet. To help you organize this information, please provide at least the following information" (the professor puts up an overhead with the following bullet list):

Internet Background

- History of the Internet

- Demographics of Users (who, where, age, and so forth)

- Growth—historic and projections for the future

"For the first three to five pages of your paper, I would like you to summarize some of the key background information needed to understand the Internet. Don't get bogged down in the bits and bytes, just focus on the big picture. In addition to the text you write, use as many tables, graphs, or figures as you need to clearly explain the functions and capabilities of the Internet.

"In the second half of your paper, I want you to focus on the effects that the Internet is having and/or will have on _____ professionals" (again, fill in your degree program). To do this, imagine that you are working for the organization of your dreams. As an employee of this organization, analyze the impacts the Internet is having. Your analysis must contain at least the following information" (the professor now puts a second slide on the overhead):

How the Internet is Affecting _____ Professionals

- Short background on your organization

- How the Internet is changing day-to-day skill requirements and expectations of individuals

- How the Internet is changing the way the organization does business

- Projections for the future

"As with the first half of the paper, this part should be three to five pages of text with as many tables, graphs, or figures as you need to explain your results. Oh, yes, one more thing. *Use only the Internet itself to conduct your research for this paper!* Provide a bibliography with full Internet address for all the information you reference.

"Any questions?"

If it hasn't happened already, it is likely that one of your professors will assign a term paper much like the one described above. Perhaps not surprisingly, all the information you need to write a successful term paper such as this can be found on the Internet, with some digging and some patience. In fact, you'll probably find too much information! Powerful search facilities enable you to easily create complex queries, enabling you to find information on just about any subject (see Figure 6.1). Fortunately, all this work adds great value to your education. A term paper such as this would be very useful in helping you to learn more about the Internet and the role it will play in your career. Reports similar to this term project are very popular in the business world and are often written by consultants. These reports, called "white papers" or "briefings," describe some new technology or application. If your professors haven't given an assignment such as this, ask them to!

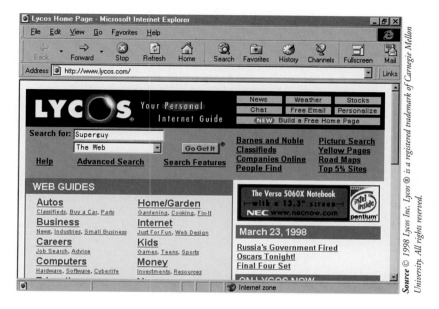

FIGURE 6.1

The Lycos Internet search engine.

Introduction

The focus of this chapter is on how the Internet works and how companies use it to streamline operations, sell products, provide customer support, or connect to suppliers. We broadly refer to the use of the Internet to support day-to-day business activities as **electronic commerce (EC)**. The Internet has become a hot topic because it is having such a broad and pervasive affect on virtually all types of organizations—from universities with distance learning programs to both large and small companies. Additionally, these influences are not limited to just the technical people. Marketing professionals focus on how to use the Internet for selling products and providing customer service. Finance professionals use the Internet to get real-time market updates. Accountants use the Internet to interconnect customer, supplier, and financial accounts. Managers must deal with employees working from remote locations using the Internet as the primary means to collaborate with colleagues. In fact, the reason so many people are excited about the Internet is that many experts feel that the Internet is the closest approximation to how most business in the very near future will be conducted.

After reading this chapter, you will be able to do the following:

1. Describe what the Internet is and how it works.

2. Explain packet switching and the TCP/IP protocol.

3. Describe the basic Internet services and the World Wide Web.

4. Explain electronic commerce and the differences between Internet-, intranet-, and extranet-based electronic commerce.

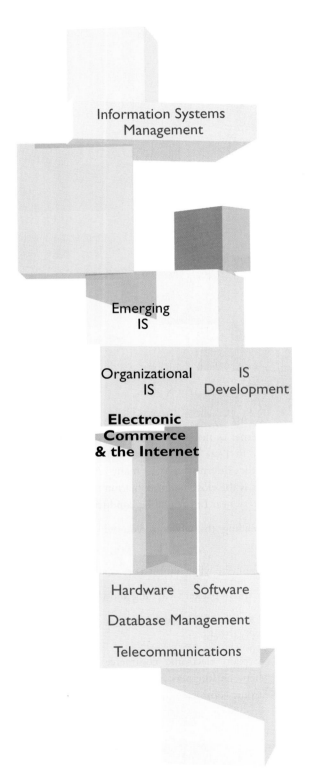

Information Systems
Management

Emerging
IS

Organizational   IS
IS   Development

**Electronic
Commerce
& the Internet**

Hardware   Software

Database Management

Telecommunications

This chapter is the first in Part 3, "Information Systems in Practice," which focuses on describing how organizations are using and applying information systems (see Figure 6.2). Although using the Internet for business is a relatively new activity, it has quickly become a key information systems issue for most organizations. As a result, organizations are trying to learn as much about the Internet as possible. If you understand the Internet and become an adept user, you will be a very valuable commodity. To help you achieve this, this chapter first provides a thorough background on how the Internet works. This section builds on the topics described in Chapter 5, "Telecommunications." After you understand the building blocks of the Internet, you can examine the application of the Internet to business, which is known as electronic commerce.

The Internet

The name "Internet" is derived from the concept of "internetworking"; that is, connecting host computers and their networks to form an even larger, global network. And that is essentially what the Internet is: a large worldwide network of networks that use a common protocol to communicate with each other. The interconnected networks include UNIX, VAX, IBM, Novell, Apple, and many other network and computer types. The Internet stands as the most prominent representation of global networking. Estimates are that a billion people will have access to the Internet by the year 2000. An easy way to show the growth of the Internet is to examine the growth in the number of Internet hosts (computers working as servers on the Internet, as shown in Figure 6.3). The networks that make up the Internet are each developed and maintained by different organizations, ranging from government agencies, to educational institutions, to private businesses, and to large commercial services such as American Online (AOL) and CompuServe. No single person or organization, therefore, owns or maintains the Internet.

FIGURE 6.2

The big picture: focusing on electronic commerce and the Internet.

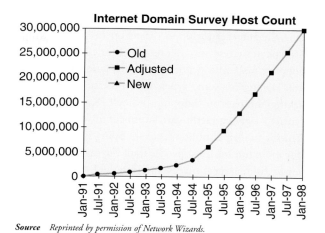

FIGURE 6.3

Growth in Internet servers (hosts).

Source   *Reprinted by permission of Network Wizards.*

Cisco Systems
A BRIEF CASE

Just as the number of users is growing, Internet-based commerce is exploding. By late 1997, Cisco Systems, a leading producer of networking technologies such as routers (see Chapter 5, "Telecommunications"), had shifted nearly forty percent of its sales to the World Wide Web (Joachim, 1997). That amounts to almost $9 million per day or more than $3 billion per year! Cisco hopes to continue this trend and projects selling more than 50 percent of its products online in 1998, and 60 percent in 1999. Additionally, Cisco is letting its biggest customers connect directly into their online inventory and product ordering system through the Internet, greatly reducing the need for sales and support personnel. As a result, Cisco is saving about $20 million per year in sales and support personnel. These huge cost savings are being pumped into the company's R&D program—far exceeding the R&D investment of Cisco's nearest competitors. What's best about this online system is that the savings are not just Cisco's. For example, a six-person department at Sprint buys approximately forty routers per week for its customers. Using Cisco's Internet-based ordering system, Sprint estimates it will save as much as $200,000 per year in labor costs.

Success at Dell
A BRIEF CASE

Another company finding great success with the Internet is Dell Computer Corporation (Cooper, 1998). Dell began selling products online in mid-1996. By early 1998, Dell was registering around $3 million in sales per day. Interestingly, Dell derives about ninety percent of its overall revenues from sales to medium and large businesses, yet more than half of its Internet-based sales have been from individuals and small businesses, who typically buy one computer at a time. As a result, Dell is experiencing big cost savings per sale by reducing the demand for phone representatives on the smaller purchases. By streamlining operations and greatly increasing sales through both online and traditional channels, Dell has grown into one of the world's largest personal computer manufacturers, with sales of more than $11 billion in 1997.

Like Cisco and Dell, countless other organizations are having unprecedented success by using the Internet to support their operations. Of course, not all companies have had this type of success. Internet retailing, for example, is having a hard time competing with shopping malls and paper-based catalogues (Resnick and Taylor, 1995). Net sales have been lagging for some types of commerce because information is often hard to find, making comparison-shopping difficult. Some individuals are also uncertain about the security of giving credit card numbers to "unknown" retailers. One other reason often cited for the lag in online retail shopping is that going to the mall with some friends is a lot more fun for most people than buying online! Nonetheless, many types of companies are finding great success in using the Internet. Additionally, as you will find out later in the chapter, companies can make or save money using the Internet in many other ways besides selling products to customers. For example, many companies are using the Internet to streamline their internal business activities and are realizing tremendous cost savings. This is discussed in greater detail later in the chapter.

What You Will Find on the Internet

You encounter information and people on the Internet. In terms of information, the Internet enables companies, groups, institutions, and individuals to share a wide range of data, including text, video, audio, graphics, databases, and other media types. The scientific and academic communities have used it for many years for information sharing and research. Recently, the largest growth segment of the Internet has been the business sector. Businesses are using the Internet for commercial purposes such as electronic commerce and marketing, global communications, customer feedback and support, and corporate logistics. For users, the Internet also provides a wealth of technical information, databases, and software services. But the Internet is more than data and information. It enables you to be in contact with people from all over the globe. Tools such as electronic mail and newsgroups assist you in communicating with other people that you may or may not know personally. In the last couple of years, there have been substantial changes in the scope of services and facilities available through the Internet. For example, recent advancements in communication technologies and increasingly high transmission speeds have made interactivity—*real time* collaboration between people— possible over the Internet.

How Does the Internet Work?

When all is working well in the networked world, many of the complexities of computers and networks are out of sight. When the communication link between your computer and the network is fast enough, cheap enough, and has virtually unlimited bandwidth, things such as applications, data, storage, and even processing become invisible. But how does the Internet really work? How do all the networks that compose the Internet communicate with each other? The following section explores these questions, describes the hardware and software of the Internet, and examines the services available to Internet users. You will see that the software that provides services over the Internet is built in two functional parts: the TCP/IP protocol, and Internet applications that provide high-level services such as electronic mail and file transfer protocol.

Inside the Internet: Underlying Technology and Basic Capabilities

As was described in the introduction to this section, no single person or organization maintains the Internet. Rather, the Internet is composed of networks developed and maintained by many different entities. The Internet follows a hierarchical structure, similar to the interstate highway system. High-speed central networks called **backbones** are like interstate highways, enabling traffic from mid-level networks to get on and off. Figure 6.4 depicts the Internet backbone in the United States. Large black lines represent major pieces of the backbone. Think of mid-level networks as city streets which, in turn, accept traffic on and off from their neighborhood streets or member networks. However, you cannot just get on an interstate or city street whenever you want to. You have to share the highway and follow traffic control signs to safely arrive at your destination. With these thoughts in mind, it's time to take a closer look at the concepts, hardware, and software underlying the Internet.

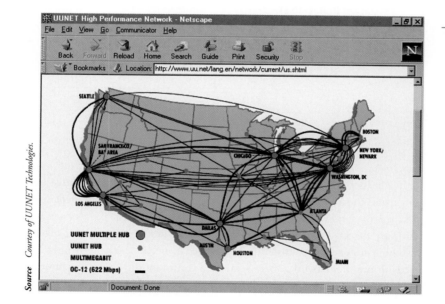

Source Courtesy of UUNET Technologies.

FIGURE 6.4

The Internet backbone in the United States.

Packet-Switching Technology

The Internet relies on **packet-switching** technology to deliver data and information across networks. Remember that the networks that comprise the Internet are shared resources. Packet-switching enables millions of users to send large and small chunks of data across the Internet concurrently. Packet-switching is based on the concept of *turn-taking*. To minimize delays, network technologies limit the amount of data that a computer can transfer on each turn. An analogy may simplify why turn-taking is important. Consider a conveyor belt as a comparison. Suppose that the conveyor belt connects a warehouse and customer storeroom. When a customer places an order, it is sent to the warehouse, where a clerk assembles the items in the order. The items are placed on the conveyor belt and delivered to the storeroom. In most situations, clerks finish sending items from one order before proceeding to send items from another order. This process works well when orders are small. But when a large order is placed with many items, sharing a conveyor belt can introduce delays for many others. Consider waiting for your one item in the storeroom while another order with fifty items is being filled.

LANs and WANs (local area networks and wide area networks, respectively)—and thus the Internet—employ packet-switching technologies so that users can share the communication channel and minimize delivery delays. Figure 6.5 illustrates how computers use packet-switching. Computer A wants to send a message to computer C; similarly, computer B wants to send a message to computer D. Network software on both A and B divides the outgoing messages into smaller packets, and then takes turns sending the packets over the transmission media. The incoming packets are reassembled at their respective destinations by network software according to packet sequence numbers.

FIGURE 6.5

Packet switching.

Source *Comer, Douglas E.,* The Internet Book. *2d ed © 1997. Reprinted by permission of Prentice-Hall, Inc., Upper Saddle River, NJ.*

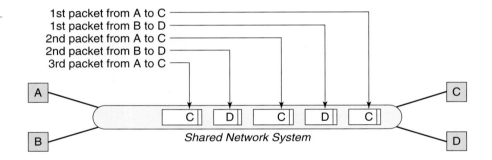

For packet-switching to work, each packet being sent across a network must be labeled with a header. This header contains the network address of the source (sending computer) and the network address of the destination (receiving computer). Each computer attached to a network has a unique network address. As packets are sent, network hardware detects whether a particular packet is destined for a local machine. Packet-switching systems adapt instantly to changes in network traffic. If only one computer needs to use the network, it can send data continuously. As soon as another computer needs to send data, packet-switching or turn-taking begins.

Connecting Independent Networks

Now that you understand how computers share a transmission path, we can examine how packet-switching networks are interconnected to form the Internet. The Internet uses special-purpose computers, called **routers**, to interconnect independent networks. For example, Figure 6.6 illustrates a router that connects Network 1 and Network 2. A router is like a conventional computer in that it has a central processor, memory, and network interfaces. However, routers do not use conventional software nor are they used to run applications. Their only job is to interconnect networks and forward data packets from one network to another. For example, in Figure 6.6, computers A and F are connected to independent networks. If computer A generates a data packet destined for computer F, the packet is sent to the router that interconnects the two networks. The router forwards the packet onto Network 2 where it is delivered to its destination at computer F.

FIGURE 6.6

Routers connect networks.

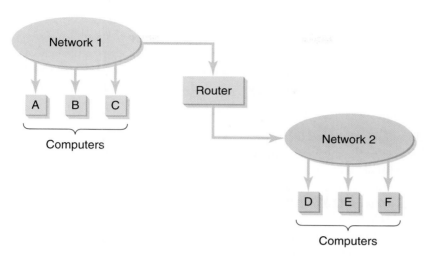

Routers are the fundamental building blocks of the Internet because they are the means by which thousands of LANs and WANs are interconnected. Typically, LANs are connected to backbone WANs, as depicted in Figure 6.7. A backbone network manages the bulk of network traffic and typically uses a higher-speed protocol than the individual LAN segments. For example, a backbone network might use fiber optic cabling, which can transfer data at a rate of 2Gbps, whereas a LAN connected to the backbone may use Ethernet cabling transferring data at a rate of 10Mbps.

FIGURE 6.7

LANs connect to wide area backbones.

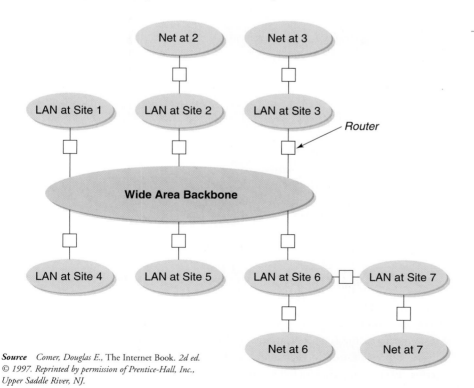

Source Comer, Douglas E., The Internet Book. *2d ed.*
© 1997. Reprinted by permission of Prentice-Hall, Inc.,
Upper Saddle River, NJ.

To gain access to the Internet, an organization generally connects a router between one of its own networks and the closest Internet site. However, most of us cannot afford a direct connection to the Internet. As described earlier, modem technology enables us to use standard telephone dial-up services to connect to a computer or network that is connected to the Internet, such as you may find at your university or business.

TCP/IP

Physically interconnecting networks is only part of the Internet story. Clearly, organizations use diverse network technologies that may or may not be compatible with the technologies of other organizations. Because so many different networks are connected, they must have a common language, or *protocol*, to communicate. The protocol of the Internet is called **TCP/IP** (Transmission Control Protocol/Internet Protocol). The first part, TCP, breaks information into small chunks. called *data packets*, that are transferred from computer to computer. For example, a single document may be broken into several packets, each containing several hundred characters, as well as a destination address, which is the IP part of the protocol. Packets travel independently to their destination, sometimes following different paths and arriving out of order. Figure 6.8 shows how routers enable packets to take different paths between two networks. This does not matter, however, because the destination computer simply reassembles all the packets based on their identification and sequencing information. As just described, routers figure out which traffic routes are best for the individual packets. Together, TCP and IP provide a reliable and efficient way to send data across the Internet.

FIGURE 6.8

Routers enable packets to take different paths between two networks.

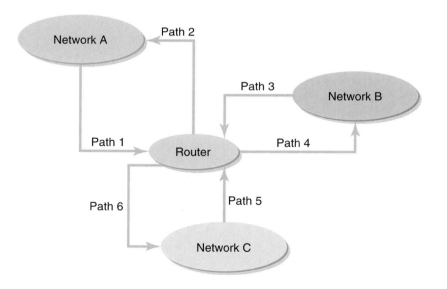

Every computer that uses the Internet must run IP software. The IP defines how a data packet must be formed and how a router must forward each packet. A data packet that conforms to the IP specification is called an **IP datagram**. Datagram routing and delivery is possible due to the unique addressing of every computer attached to the Internet. Every computer, including routers, is assigned a unique IP address. When an organization connects to the Internet, it obtains a set of IP addresses that it can assign to its computers. Remember that each computer has a different IP address and each user has a different name. The combination of these two describers is the Internet address. The IP address and the user name are separated by the @ symbol. For example, smith@cbe.wsu.edu is the Internet address of the user "smith." The IP address cbe.wsu.edu is stored internally by the computer in bytes. Fortunately, in most situations, you can enter a name in text rather than its binary representation. TCP helps IP guarantee delivery of datagrams by performing three main tasks. First, it automatically checks for datagrams that may have been lost en route from their source to destination. Second, TCP collects the incoming datagrams and puts them in the correct order to re-create the original message. Finally, TCP discards any duplicate copies of datagrams that may have been created by network hardware.

Internet Services

Many tools or applications exist for using the Internet. These applications follow the client/server model described earlier in this chapter. As a review, client programs run on the computer you are using, such as your PC, and facilitate information access by doing the behind-the-scenes work of opening connections to distant computers, sending your requests, and receiving and displaying results. The server software runs on computers that provide the information. A server is usually a very powerful computer capable of handling information requests from many clients simultaneously. A collection of Internet tools follow this approach and enable users to exchange messages, share information, or connect to remote computers. These tools are summarized in Table 6.1.

Table 6.1 Internet tools and their descriptions.

Internet Tool	Description
Email	Enables users to send messages to each other.
Telnet	Enables users to connect, or log in, to any computer on the Internet.
File Transfer Protocol (FTP)	Enables users to connect to a remote computer solely for the purpose of transferring files; either uploading (sending to the remote machine) or downloading (getting back from the remote machine) files and data.
Listserv, short for "mailing list server"	Enables groups of people with common interests to send messages to each other. Interested people subscribe to a discussion group, which is essentially a mailing list. When a subscriber sends a message to the list, the message is sent to all other subscribers.
Usenet	Enables groups of people with common interests to send messages or other binary information to each other. Unlike listserv, Usenet has no master list of subscribers. Rather, anyone with access to Usenet may use a news reader program to post and read articles from the group.
Archie	Enables users to search FTP sites for their contents. For example, you might be looking for a particular file, perhaps a software application or game. You would use Archie to search FTP sites. Using the results of the Archie search, you can determine which FTP site has the desired files, and then use FTP to download them.
WAIS (Wide Area Information Sesver)	Enables users to locate information by indexing electronic data using standard keywords.
Gopher	A text-based, menu-driven interface that enables users to access a large number of varied Internet resources as if they were in folders and menus on their own computers. Menu choices on a Gopher server include text files, graphic images, sounds, software, or even another menu.

The World Wide Web

The most powerful use of the Internet is something that you have no doubt heard a great deal about: the **World Wide Web** (WWW). More than likely, you have probably browsed the Web using Netscape Navigator, Microsoft's Internet Explorer, or some other popular browser, as shown in Figure 6.9. Browsers are fast becoming a standard Internet tool. The WWW links the various tools used on the Internet by providing users with a simple, consistent interface to a wide variety of information. Although Gopher can tie together text documents, Telnet sessions, sounds, graphics, file transfers, and more in a menu-driven format, the WWW takes Gopher one step further by using **hypertext**. A hypertext document not only contains information, but also references or links to other documents that contain related information. The standard method of formatting Web pages is to use hypertext mark-up language, or **HTML**. HTML is a language, much like a programming language, that operates through a series of codes placed within a text document. These codes are translated by your browser and result in a formatted Web page. In addition to containing HTML codes to describe how it looks, each page on the Web has a unique address called a **URL**, or uniform resource locator. Using your client software such as Netscape Navigator, when you click on a hypertext link, the document is automatically retrieved from a Web server so that you can view it right on your screen. This server may reside anywhere on the Internet.

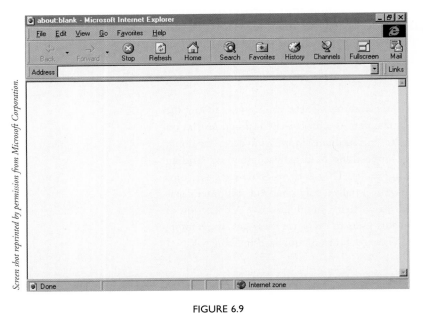

Screen shot reprinted by permission from Microsoft Corporation.

FIGURE 6.9

Microsoft's Internet Explorer.

Technologies Enabling Internet Communication

As described previously and in Chapter 5, many technologies are used to create the Internet. Many of the advancements in computer networks and telecommunications technologies center on a need for increasing bandwidth and network speed. To satisfy this need, powerful new technologies are providing networks with the bandwidth they need to handle rich and space-consuming content and the speed to support real-time interaction over the network. This section briefly describes three important technologies: ISDN, T1 Service, and Asynchronous Transfer Mode (ATM).

ISDN (Integrated Services Digital Network)

ISDN is a standard for worldwide digital—rather than analog—communications. ISDN is intended to replace all current analog systems, such as most telephone connections in the U.S., with a completely digital transmission system. Although ISDN has not been widely deployed, its greatest strength is that it can use existing twisted-pair telephone wires to provide high-speed data service. When complete, ISDN systems will be capable of transmitting voice, video, and data. Because ISDN is a purely digital network, you will be able to connect your PC to the Internet without the use of a modem. Removing the analog-to-digital conversion for sending information and the digital-to-analog conversion for receiving information greatly increases the data transfer rate. Consequently, people and organizations wanting high-speed access to the Internet are rapidly switching their phone systems to ISDN.

T1 Service

To gain adequate access to the Internet or for making EDI transmissions, organizations are turning to long-distance carriers to lease a dedicated **T1** line for digital transmissions. A T1 line is a dedicated digital transmissions line that can carry 1.544Mbps of information. In the U.S., companies selling long-distance services are often called *interexchange carriers* because their circuits carry service between the major telephone exchanges. A T1 line can carry 1.544Mbps and usually transverses hundreds or thousands of miles over leased long-distance facilities (see Table 6.2).

Table 6.2 Capacity of communication lines.

Type of Line	Data Rate (Mbps)	Equivalent Number of Voice Lines
T1	1.544	24
T3	44.736	672

For example, AT&T and other carriers charge several thousands of dollars per month for a dedicated T1 circuit spanning 1,000 miles. If you need an even faster link, a T3 link is available. T3 provides about 45Mbps of service at about ten times the leasing cost of a T1 line. Even faster lines are available if you have the money!

ATM (Asynchronous Transfer Mode)

ATM is a method of transmitting voice, video, and data over high-speed LANs. Transfer speeds of up to 2.2GBps (gigabytes per second) are possible when using this technology. ATM has found wide acceptance in the LAN and WAN arenas as a solution to integrating disparate networks over large geographic distances. ATM uses a form of packet transmission in which data is in a fixed-length, 53-byte cell sent over a packet-switched network. Although it is based on packet-switching technology, ATM has the potential to do away with routers, allocated bandwidth, and contention for communications media. Organizations in the movie and entertainment industries that need to deliver synchronized video and sound, for example, are particularly interested in ATM.

This section has described the technology behind the Internet. Now that you understand how the Internet works, you can focus on how the Internet is changing the way business is conducted.

Electronic Commerce

Perhaps no other information systems issue has captured as much attention as has electronic commerce (see Figure 6.10). **Electronic Commerce (EC)** is the online exchange of goods, services, and money within firms, between firms, and between firms and their customers. The allure of EC is that it has no geographical or time limitations; with the help of technology firms can sell 7 days a week, 24 hours a day, 365 days a year to literally anyone, anywhere. In addition, parking for customers is no problem and firms can deliver the goods right to the customer's door!

FIGURE 6.10

It has become a strategic necessity for firms to have a presence on the Internet.

©*The 5th Wave by Richard Tennant, Rockport, MA. Email: the5wave@tiac.net*

The Many Faces of Electronic Commerce

EC now takes place in a number of different ways and on a number of different technology platforms. For example, **Electronic Data Interchange (EDI)**, the on-line sale of goods and services between firms, has been happening for over a decade on proprietary networks that these firms have developed and paid for entirely themselves (described briefly in Chapter 5). However, the current trend in business today is to use the public Internet as the vehicle for EC. Giga Information Group estimates that U.S. companies buy about $500 billion worth of goods and services electronically each year via traditional, proprietary EDI networks. Estimates of the volume of Internet-based transactions for 1995 range from several hundred million dollars (source: IBM) to $15 billion (source: Simba Information, Inc.). For retail transactions, the 1997 estimate has been $3 billion and is expected to hit $6 to $8 billion by the year 2000 (Nadeau, 1997). Most experts agree that the proportion of online transactions that are Internet-based is growing quickly and may dominate very soon. This doesn't even count the trillion dollars a day that pass electronically through CHIPS, the Clearing House Inter-bank Payment System in New York. Because these are bank transfers and not really purchases, they typically are not counted in estimates of online transactions.

A Model of Electronic Commerce

Company Web sites range from passive to active. At one extreme are the relatively simple, passive Web sites that provide only product information and the company address and phone number, much like a traditional brochure would do. At the other extreme are the relatively sophisticated, active Web sites that enable customers to see products, services, and related real-time information; and actually conduct purchase transactions online. Table 6.3 shows four stages of the development of a Web site for Federal Express (www.fedex.com).

Table 6.3 The evolutionary path of Web site development for FedEx.

Stage	Activities
1. Corporate image and product information	Register a domain name and create pages providing contact information about FedEx and its products
2. Information collection and market research	Create forms with which customers can register their identity online and assign account numbers; create marketing research forms
3. Customer support and service	Link Web site to FedEx's tracking database; customers can enter a package number and view up-to-date information on package delivery or location
4. Transactions	Enable customers to request a pickup and arrange payment options

Source Adapted from Quelch, J.A. and L.R. Klein. 1996. The Internet and internal marketing. Sloan Management Review (Spring): 63.

Innovative, aggressive firms such as FedEx are finding ways to use technology to sell goods and services. Figure 6.11 shows a model of electronic commerce with five phases: information gathering, ordering, payment, fulfillment, and service and support. Firms now advertise their offerings to prospective customers through Internet email and the Web. Customers can order and pay for products and services online. If the product or service can be digitized, it can be delivered online, as in the case of information-based products, videos, and software.

A Model of Electronic Commerce

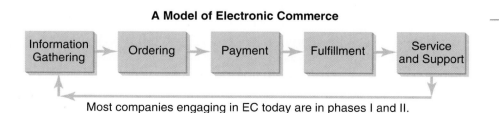

Most companies engaging in EC today are in phases I and II.

FIGURE 6.11

A model of electronic commerce.

A BRIEF CASE ─────────────────────── **Liquid Audio** ───────

Liquid Audio's Web-enabled music distribution system is changing the ways in which music is being distributed (see www.liquidaudio.com). Liquid Audio's technology enables the music industry to use the Internet as another distribution channel without fear of piracy. The system enables users to download CD-quality music that can be played on only the computer to which it was downloaded. The music is also "water-marked" so that any illegal copy—even on cassette tapes—can be traced to the original purchaser (Jahnke, 1997). Such technology works for the distribution of any type of information-based product. In the case of tangible products or ephemeral services, they can be fulfilled in more traditional, land-based methods, but any information-based components to these products or services—such as an owner's manual—can be digitized and delivered online. It is a certainty that you will see more and more digital products—music, art, video, and software—delivered over the Internet in the years to come.

Finally, some innovative firms are finding ways to provide online service and support after the sale. This can be done with online support documentation; email hot lines for customers; videoconferencing with a helpful product support technician; or, as in the case of some computer hardware vendors, the vendor can go through the Internet and diagnose and repair your computer online in real time.

The trend has been toward Internet-based EC. Figure 6.12 shows three possible modes of EC using the Internet. The term used to describe transactions between individuals and firms is Internet-based EC. **Intranet**, on the other hand, refers to use of the Internet within the same business, and **extranet** refers to the use of the Internet between firms.

FIGURE 6.12

Three possible modes of electronic commerce.

Three Possible Modes of Electronic Commerce

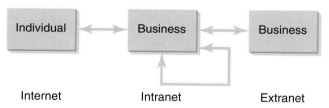

Potential EC income doesn't come from online sales transactions only. A great deal of money has been made by companies that enable other companies to advertise on their Web sites. According to Jupiter Communications, Web advertising revenue totaled near-ly $72 million for the first half of 1996, a figure that grew substantially from the previous year and is expected to continue to grow. Similarly, many firms are now beginning to collect subscription fees from Web surfers for valuable online newspapers, magazines, and other resources. Jupiter Communications estimates that subscription services on the Web were $120 million for 1996 and are still growing. The Wall Street Journal recently began collecting subscription fees for its popular online version, and many in the industry are watching closely to see whether this test case demonstrates a viable market for online subscriptions. In addition, the rapid growth in EC has created a tremendous need for skilled people to design and manage Web sites. The person most often identified as the overseer of an organization's Web site is commonly called a **Webmaster**. Specifically, a Webmaster is a diverse individual who must have strong technical and managerial skills. Webmasters manage the Internet servers and networks to assure system reliability and security. In addition, Webmasters are often responsible for working with information content providers throughout an organization. In short, Webmasters must be able to effectively communicate with a broad range of individuals and coordinate a diverse set of technical and managerial activities. Jupiter Communications can be reached on the Web at http://www.jup.com.

Exploiting Internet-based Electronic Commerce

There are two old rules of commerce:

Old Rule #1   Offer something of value.

Old Rule #2   Offer products and services at a fair price.

As with traditional commerce, the old rules still apply to EC. In other words, firms that do well have something of value to offer to people at a fair price. However, some new rules apply to EC—having a good product at a fair price may not be enough to compete in EC markets. The new rules of EC are:

EC Rule #1   The Web site must be aesthetically pleasing.

EC Rule #2   The Web site must be easy to use and FAST!

EC Rule #3   The Web site must motivate people to visit, to stay, and to return.

EC Rule #4   Advertise your presence on the Web.

EC Rule #5   Learn from your Web site.

These rules mean that the companies that were traditionally successful in the old markets won't necessarily dominate the new electronic markets. For example, many small firms have found success on the Web by offering hard-to-find goods to a global audience at reasonable prices. For example, Eastern Meat Farms, an Italian market in New York, sells hard-to-find pasta, meats, cheeses, and breads over the Internet at its salami.com Web site. Their first order was from Japan. Although the new Japanese customer paid $69 in shipping costs for the $87 order for pasta, he didn't mind; he was saving $150 by not buying the Italian delicacies locally (Rebello, 1996). Eastern Meat Farms' Web site can be found at http://www.salami.com.

EC Rule #1. The Web site must be aesthetically pleasing.
EC Rule #2. The Web site must be easy to use and FAST!

Successful firms on the Web have a site that is aesthetically pleasing. People like to visit, stay at, and return to Web sites that look good! Similarly, as with nearly all software, Web sites that are easy to use are more popular. If Web surfers have trouble finding things at the site, navigating through the site's links, or have to wait for screens to download, they are not apt to stay at the site long or to return. In fact, some early studies suggest that the average length of time that a Web surfer will wait for a Web page to download on his screen is only a couple of seconds.

EC Rule #3. The Web site must motivate people to visit, to stay, and to return.

Popular Web sites are those that motivate the user. The user is motivated to stay at the site and to return to the site again. Incentives can be useful information and links on the site, or free goods and services. One of the reasons that Microsoft's Web site is continually tops on lists of favorite Web sites is that Microsoft gives away free software, downloadable from their site. Other firms motivate visitors to come to, stay at, and revisit their Web sites by enabling users to interact at the site with other users who share common interests. In doing so, the firm helps to build an online community where members can build relationships, help each other, and feel at home (Armstrong and Hagel, 1996). For example, at GardenWeb, visitors can share problems and ideas with other gardeners, post requests for seeds and other items, and follow electronic links to other gardening resources. At this Web site, the participants communicate and carry out transactions with one another. Note that GardenWeb can be found at http://www.gardenWeb.com.

EC Rule #4. Advertise Your Presence on the Web.

The "if you build it, they will come" strategy may work for baseball fields in the heart of Iowa, but this is not a good strategy for a firm's Web site. Web sites employ more of a "pull" than a "push" marketing strategy. You must pull visitors into your site and away from the thousands and thousands of other sites they could be visiting. Smart companies are good at advertising their presence on the Internet. They do this in a number of ways.

The first way to advertise your firm's presence on the Web is to include the Web site address on all company materials, from business cards and letterheads to advertising copy. It is now common to see a company's URL listed at the end of their television commercials. Second, be sure to register the new Web site on all the search engines, such as InfoSeek, Excite, and Yahoo. In addition to the many search engines, the firm's Web site can be advertised in many electronic malls and other commerce sites. In most cases, registering with these sites is free, fast, and can be done online.

You can also advertise your Web site on other popular Web sites, such as the ESPN SportsZone (see Figure 6.13), or on one of the more popular search engines. Advertising on these sites can

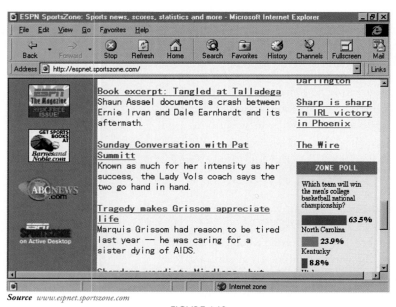

Source *www.espnet.sportszone.com*

FIGURE 6.13

ESPN SportsZone and other popular Web sites sell advertisement space.

be as much as $20,000 to $30,000 per month, but they can promise that their sites will be visited by over a million visitors a day. Given the high cost of advertising on these sites, and the fact that many of those Web surfers do not even look at the online ad, the trend in Web advertising is moving away from high, fixed, monthly charges, to a "pay by the click" scheme. Under this type of pricing scheme, the firm running the advertisement pays only when a Web surfer actually clicks on the advertisement.

Internet Advertising at Starwave

If you want to learn more about Internet-based advertising and the current fees for advertising on some of the Web's hottest sites—such as ESPN SportsZone—visit Starwave Corporation (www.starwave.com). In addition to SportsZone, Starwave is the Internet software behind ABCNEWS.COM (see Figure 6.14), Mr. Showbiz, and many other top entertainment sites (Starwave, 1998). Paul Allen (co-founder of Microsoft) and The Walt Disney Company founded Starwave in 1993. On their Web site, you can investigate the advertising rates, as well as the number and demographics of the visitors to each of their online partners. They show the size and shape of online advertisements and their associated rates. In fact, they provide all you need to place your ad, except of course, for the money to pay for it!

Companies like Starware, which hosts and manages company sites for ESPN and CBS, are generally referred to as **Internet Service Providers** (ISPs). Both individuals and companies can use an ISP to gain access to the Internet. For individuals, ISPs such as AOL, CompuServe, and countless local and regional providers can provide easy dial-up access, electronic mail accounts, and the posting of personal Web pages. For organizations, an ISP can provide total Web site hosting, design, continuous connection services, or some subset of these services. ISPs that focus on supporting organizational Web sites typically have sophisticated backup and recovery facilities, as well as redundant servers to seamlessly recover from a system failure.

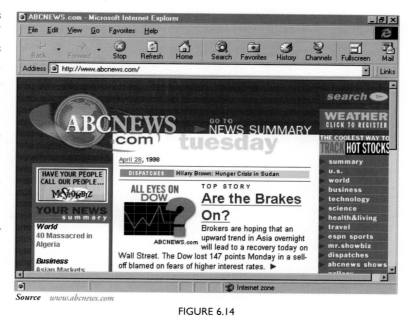

Source www.abcnews.com

FIGURE 6.14

Screen of Web site from ABCNEWS.COM.

EC Rule #5. Learn from Your Web Site

Smart companies have found that they can learn a lot from their Web sites (Bennett, 1997). Software is available to help you analyze the usage of your Web site, including the number of visitors, who is visiting your site, and how people navigate through your site.

For example, a firm can track the path that visitors take through the many pages of their Web site and record the time of day, day of the week, or times throughout the year that people visit these sites. It can then use this information to improve its Web site. If 75 percent of the visitors follow links to check the company's online posting of job opportunities within the firm or check on current pricing for a particular product, then that firm can redesign its Web site to provide that information quickly and easily for visitors.

Perhaps more importantly, this learning runs deeper than merely trying to figure out how best to redesign the Web site. You can also learn about the firm's products and services and how best to redesign the firm's offerings to better serve customers. Innovative firms provide email links on their Web sites, online guest books and suggestion forms, and even provide online forums and marketing focus groups to learn from their customers.

In short, people in organizations are finding that the Internet provides a relatively low-cost method to gain a global reach to customers. Perhaps more importantly, Web-based EC represents the closest approximation of how business will be conducted in the future. It has become a strategic necessity for firms to get their feet wet with Web-based applications so that they don't get left behind in the rush to EC.

Intranets as First Step into Electronic Commerce

Many firms have decided to utilize the Internet to support internal operations. They use the same old public Internet, but only for employees within their company. They literally block out unwanted users on the Internet from entering their Web pages and servers by using password protection, firewalls, and other technologies and techniques. Many organizations are figuring out ways to use the Internet for intranet applications.

A BRIEF CASE ——————————**U.S. Atlantic Command Intranet**——————

The U.S. Atlantic Command (USAC) recently implemented an intranet that is the first of its kind among military organizations (Finegan, 1997). The USAC is headquartered in Norfolk, Virginia and is the brain center for the U.S. military's largest joint command. The USAC includes the Navy's Atlantic Fleet, the Air Combat Command of the Air Force, the Army's Forces Command, and the Marine Corps Forces, Atlantic. In sum, it has authority over 1.2 million of the military's 1.5 million active-duty personnel, and defense responsibility for most of the U.S., the Atlantic Ocean, Europe, and the west coast of Africa. Managing such a huge organization is a challenge, to say the least. Like many organizations, the U.S. military has substantially reduced its size—from 2.2 million in 1987 to the current 1.5 million active-duty personnel—yet its responsibility has remained unchanged.

The biggest problem with USAC operations was related to the departmentalization of information. For example, the operations department, headed by an Army officer, had difficulty sharing information with logistics, headed by a Marine officer. Likewise, the strategic planning group, headed by a Naval officer, did not know the plans and information of the intelligence unit, headed by an Air Force officer. Thus, one important goal of the intranet was to break down the information-sharing barriers. A key aspect of this inability to share information was the security of the information. Although the USAC already had a secure network, getting to the point where divisions actually shared critical information was their biggest challenge. Strong leadership from the top has helped to gain the cooperation of the entire USAC, and has greatly streamlined many day-to-day activities. For example, each day, more than 40,000 messages from around the world flow into the USAC's message-handling system. Of these messages, 250 to 300 require some sort of action or response. In the past, a few officers from each of the command's eight divisions would scan and sort the entire batch of messages to assemble a file of critical information for the general or admiral heading up their respective division. In sum, about 30 officers reviewed and sorted the same 40,000 messages each day to identify the critical messages for their divisions. In addition, they were unable to route messages to the most appropriate division because no information-forwarding capabilities existed. Today, within the USAC intranet, messages are sorted by only two people and automatically forwarded to the appropriate division. Critical messages, such as news of a coup in a foreign country or notification of a natural disaster requiring military relief assistance, can be routed to top commanders. Lower-priority messages are routed to the appropriate levels. As a result, this intranet is changing the way information flows and is enabling the USAC to do more with less.

FIGURE 6.15

Aircraft carrier.

Photo by Eric Bouve © Gamma Liason

Some common uses of intranets include providing access to online, internal phone books, procedure manuals, and training materials; enabling employees to check inventories and order supplies; and enabling employees to check and modify their personal benefit plans (see Figure 6.16). Literally any internal business process can be supported, particularly those processes that involve the conveyance of information. For example, nearly every organization publishes a quarterly product pricing sheet or a policy manual. These documents are often hundreds of pages long, are published several times a year, and are copied and delivered to thousands and thousands of people. This is not only a very expensive process, but in most situations the information changes rapidly, so the shelf life of the document is not very long. The information in the document is often out-of-date by the time it arrives in the hands of the user. Putting these documents out on the Web enables employees throughout the world to quickly, easily, and inexpensively access them there. Even better, when a change is made in the document, that change is automatically reflected in the views of the document that everyone sees.

FIGURE 6.16

*Common intranet
applications.*

■ Online company phone directories

■ Online procedure manuals

■ Online training materials

■ Online product/price catalogues

■ Inventory management

■ Supply ordering

■ Benefit plan management

As you might expect, in surveys of U.S. companies of all sizes, nearly all are either already using an intranet, are planning to install one, or are evaluating their intranet options. Expenditures for Web software in 1998 are predicted to be $2 billion for standard Internet applications and a staggering $8 billion for intranet applications. Where there were almost no intranets in 1994, about 20 percent of organizations had one in 1995, almost half had one in 1996, and more than 80 percent are projected to have one by 2000.

Intranets are popular for several reasons. First, an intranet gives an organization a relatively inexpensive, easy, quick international telecommunications infrastructure. It would cost far more, and take far longer, if a firm were to develop a similar telecommunications infrastructure on their own, with dedicated phone lines rented from a telecommunications service provider. Second, intranets can help firms improve product and service quality while decreasing costs and cycle time. Third, and perhaps most important, the use of an intranet helps an organization learn more about the Internet before interacting with "real" customers. Intranets are often a wise intermediate step in preparing for full-blown EC.

From EDI to Internet-Based Extranets

In addition to intranets, many firms are also using the Internet to support their dealings with other firms. This business-to-business commerce takes many forms (see Figure 6.17). It can include ordering materials and supplies from another firm. It can include buyer/supplier/bank linkages. It can be a person-to-person electronic connection or a database-to-database communication. As we mentioned previously, the trend is toward Internet-based extranets rather than the more traditional Electronic Data Interchange using proprietary networks.

■ Manufacturer orders materials from a supplier

■ Firm makes travel arrangements with travel agency

■ Advertising firm and customer's marketing department collaborate on ad copy

■ Could be person connected to another firm's computer or could be one firm's computer working directly with another firm's computer, with no people involved

■ Could be complete vertical linkage of buyer/supplier/bank

FIGURE 6.17

Common extranet applications.

This shift makes sense. The Internet provides a global telecommunications infrastructure for which it is relatively easy and inexpensive to develop applications. Everyone uses documents based on the HTML format, packet-switching via the TC/IP network protocol, and other open, standard formats and protocols. Users have lots of good choices for browsers, HTML editors, Web server software, and other related tools. Connections to the Internet are relatively inexpensive through local and national Internet service providers. Security mechanisms on the Internet are improving every day. Why would any one firm choose to build its own global network from scratch for either an intranet or extranet application? The arguments against doing so are compelling.

American Express Retirement Services Extranet   A BRIEF CASE

American Express Retirement Services (AE), a division of American Express Financial Services, manages the retirement plans for more than 585 companies and has more than $130 billion in assets under its management (American Express, 1998). AE needed an easier way for the benefit managers of companies to access the retirement plan information for their organizations' employees. To solve this problem, AE created an extranet that enables benefit managers to access information on their desktop computers using a standard Web browser. In addition, the system is secure so that no unauthorized users can access plan information. In the past, a request for a custom report might have taken weeks to complete; the report needed to be created, printed, and then sent to the customer. Today, custom reports are just a click away. AE saves money by not having to create, print, and send reports. Likewise, companies can provide much faster responses to employee questions. Clearly, this extranet is providing a win-win solution for both American Express and its customers.

The next chapter continues with the discussion of information systems in practice by describing several contemporary information systems. This discussion describes how organizations are structured and the types of information systems used to support various activities. As you will read, organizations are organized in widely different ways and thus have differing information-processing requirements. Nonetheless, this overview will help you better understand how information systems support both large and small organizations.

ETHICAL PERSPECTIVE: ELECTRONIC PORNOGRAPHY AND THE INTERNET POLICE

The term "Internet Police" brings to mind images of "cyber-cops" searching out crimes and criminals over the Net. Actually, there is no such thing as an Internet police force or department. Yet, it is a term that has been used for several years, many times with great meaning and significance. It has been used to describe the people behind the Commu-nications Decency Act of 1996 (CDA), an important component of the broader Telecommunications Act of 1996.

Enacted into law by Congress and signed by President Clinton in early 1996, the CDA placed tight restrictions and the threat of strict punishments for people who transmit or use unacceptable subject matter over the Internet. It was an attempt to help parents protect their children and to make today's modern, electronic society a "better" place to live. In effect, its intent was to police the electronic airwaves and transmissions by making certain that people would not make available to children any indecent or illegal materials.

The CDA immediately drew fire and encountered lawsuits, claiming it was unconstitutional based on its limits of free speech. The Justice Department argued that it was in the best interest of society. It was not until June of 1996 that the U.S. District Court of Eastern Pennsylvania ruled that the act was indeed unconstitutional based on its limits of free speech. Still, Clinton stated that he feels that our Constitution allows us (the government) to help parents by enforcing this act to prevent objectionable material transmitted through computer networks.

As it stands now, very little restricts people and companies from putting pornographic material on the Internet. It has been and still is illegal to display or promote child pornography, and this includes text and pictures over the Internet. However, "mainstream" pornographic material can easily be accessed over the Internet by anyone with the time to search for it. Some sites restrict access by generating special usernames and passwords to people after their age has been verified through a service such as Net Nanny or Cyber-Patrol. Even these "restricted" sites often have preview or sample pages that show uncensored sexual activity to anyone who clicks on the link, whether 35 years old or 14 years old. Others have a pseudo-gate that merely asks that you signify you are of legal viewing age by clicking on the link to the photographs, but anyone can click the mouse.

The issue has become more complex with the development and advancements associated with the World Wide Web. Previously, Internet transmissions were textual. If a graphic was to be transmitted, it was converted to text, transmitted, and then reconverted by the recipient. Now, with the World Wide Web, graphical images, pornographic images in particular, can be transmitted as pictures relatively quickly and easily for everyone to see. No additional software or hardware is necessary to view the material when it is transmitted over the World Wide Web. To make things worse, no overall regulatory committee or enforcement agency governs or controls the content on the Internet. Host services may have their own rules, and may regulate and monitor the content on their own servers, but this is a case-by-case situation that varies from one service to the next. No Internet police exist to enforce the law or even monitor the system in general.

The CDA attempted to force all Internet sites to use age-verification programs, along with usernames and passwords, so that minors would not be able to view the material in question. It came down to a debate between the freedom of speech and the laws, beliefs, and morals of society; an age-old problem, but with new technology. An inherent problem was its enforceability. In any case, it has been blocked, and for now, individual rights are seen as more important than those of society.

Source Mendels, Pamela, 1996. Court overturns Communications Decency Act. The New York Times, June 13, A1.

Questions for Discussion

1. How is Internet pornography different from that in a magazine at the local newsstand?

2. Should there be an organization or agency with the responsibility of monitoring and enforcing laws over the Internet? Is this even possible, based on the construction of the network?

3. Should a pornographic Web site be required to have password protection on its material, similar to a bookstore owner asking for photo ID before selling a magazine?

International Perspective: INTERPOL 2000: The Net Police?

A new nation is developing, according to Business-Week, complete with citizens (or "Netizens"), its own language, and even its own boundaries (or lack of boundaries, more appropriately). This entity has additional features of a politically defined unit, including highly paid activists, militant nationalists, and a GNP expected to hit $45 billion (U.S. dollars) by the year 2000. This "nation" is Cyberspace, and, as immigrants from around the globe flock to join, governments worldwide are scrambling to find ways to control its citizens and their lifestyles.

Attempts are being made or considered to regulate everything from copyright to what passes as suitable material for Netizens. One well-known case of attempted regulation is the Communications Decency Act (CDA) of 1996, passed by the U.S. Congress, which attempted to control indecent materials online (but has since been declared unconstitutional). Netizens voted against this measure by blackening the backgrounds of their Web pages in protest. This effort at regulating the Net could not have had the intended effect of keeping pornography and other undesirable information out of the hands and off the screens of Americans; because of the nature of the Internet, this material would still be easily attainable from sites in other countries, in effect not solving the perceived problem. A more effective deterrent might be to build new border walls between Cyberspace and U.S. children; technologies such as NetWatch and NetNanny can be considered the first line of defense.

Other efforts by governments to control criminal activities in Cyberspace will probably meet with the same result as the 1996 CDA. In 1996 Germany ordered CompuServe to cut access to Germans to alt.sex Usenet discussion groups on the Internet, and China required all Net users to be registered. In August of 1996, the United Kingdom's police notified Internet service providers of a ban on 133 newsgroups. In addition, the U.S. was considering penalties for cyberfraud. However, German households can receive banned materials through sites in other countries, and Chinese citizens can get around the registration requirement in any number of ways. Cybercriminals can easily abandon land-based sites for off-shore sites or other countries without changing their mode of operation.

From these examples, it seems that the governments trying to regulate Cyberspace don't know much about the new nation or its Netizens. Perhaps they have bought into Ann Landers' claim that the main reason for Cyberspace to exist is for cybersex and other fantasy-fulfillment, as a kind of a virtual Las Vegas. A visit to Cyberspace by these foreign dignitaries may help to demonstrate that no one country or group of countries can control Cyberspace. Of course, some service providers can cut off access to some users, but as the number of service providers and the percentage of personal computers being employed as servers increases, and the number of Netizens of all kinds expands, this poses little threat to the sovereignty of Cyberspace. Without an enormous and concerted effort on an international scale (and probably not even then), the Internet can't be controlled by "foreigners." The next question is, then, should it be?

According to Internet users around the world, members of the Internet community are doing a fine job of policing themselves without interference from outsiders. Informally, transgressions against accepted norms of behavior in Cyberspace are punished by "flaming," flooding the perpetrator's electronic mailboxes with messages of outrage, refusal of service by ISPs, and even by turning lawbreakers over to the national police. Formally, the wave of the future might be something like the online "Virtual Magistrate," which provides basic arbitration services worldwide to resolve disputes based on accepted rules of Cyberspace conduct. The Magistrate project also assists in the codification of those rules.

Who eventually will control Cyberspace? Right now it's anyone's guess, but it's clear that Netizens will fight long and hard to have their voices heard.

Source *The Virtual Magistrate project can be found on the WWW at http://vmag.law.vill.edu:8080/docs/press/press.960521.html.*

Yang, C. 1996. Law creeps onto the lawless net. BusinessWeek. *May, 58–60.*

Questions for Discussion

1. Can the Internet be regulated by only its users? Why or why not?

2. Should national governments spend money and time trying to regulate Cyberspace? To what ends?

3. Who should decide what kinds of text and graphics can be displayed or sent via the Internet?

Talking with...

Wanda E. Miles, Senior Manager of Global Education Marketing at Oracle
Corporation

C&I Photography, Inc.

Educational Background

B.A. in Management, University of Redlands

Job Description

Wanda is responsible for global customer relations in the Oracle Academic Initiative.
The goal of the program is to address the critical shortage of Information Technology
professionals by identifying colleges and universities interested in incorporating
Oracle's IT into their degree programs. Her duties include developing the program
strategy, identifying academic partners, presenting the program to interested academic institutions, handling
account management and development, providing customer feedback to Oracle corporate, and attending press
events.

Critical Success Factors

Obtain varied work experience. Your career should include sales experience that develops interpersonal and public
speaking skills, gives you a skill that is always needed, and places you at the heart of the organization. Manage a large
team of people. Delegate your authority and work hard to develop the skills of your team and help them reach their
career goals. Work on visible projects and don't be afraid to publicize your accomplishments. Take responsibility for
a profit and loss center to learn the financial side of business. And finally, we live in a global economy; therefore, it
is critical to obtain international work experience and speak multiple languages.

Advice to Students

Decide what you want to do, who you want to do it for, and develop a champion within that organization to help
you get the job. Find a mentor to help you develop your career. Focus on a career in technology, and continue to
educate yourself and upgrade your skills to remain competitive in this rapidly changing field. Excel in math and science, especially if you are a woman and/or a person of color. Corporations want a workforce that reflects the diversity of its customers. Finally, share your knowledge and take pride in being a team player.

Summary

1. **Describe what the Internet is and how it works.**
The Internet is composed of networks that are
developed and maintained by many different entities, and follows a hierarchical structure, similar to
the interstate highway system. High-speed central
networks called backbones are like an interstate
highway, enabling traffic from mid-level networks
to get on and off.

2. **Explain packet switching and the TCP/IP
protocol.** The Internet relies on packet-switching
technology to deliver data and information across
networks. Routers are used to interconnect independent networks. Because so many different
networks are connected to the Internet, a common
communication protocol (TCP/IP) is used.
TCP/IP is divided into two parts. TCP breaks

information into small chunks, called data packets, which are transferred from computer to computer. The IP defines how a data packet must be formed and how a router must forward each packet. All computers, including routers, are assigned unique IP addresses. Data routing and delivery are possible, due to the unique addressing of every computer attached to the Internet. Together, TCP and IP provide a reliable and efficient way to send data across the Internet.

3. **Describe the basic Internet services and the World Wide Web.** A collection of Internet tools enable you to exchange messages, share information, or connect to remote computers. These tools include electronic mail, Telnet, file transfer protocol, listserv, Usenet, Archie, WAIS, and Gopher.

The most powerful tool today is the World Wide Web, which binds together the various tools used on the Internet, providing users with a simple, consistent interface to a wide variety of information through the use of Web browsers.

4. **Explain electronic commerce and the differences between Internet-, intranet-, and extranet-based electronic commerce.** Electronic commerce is the online exchange of goods, services, and money between firms and their customers, within firms, and between firms. Internet-based electronic commerce refers to transactions between individuals and firms. Intranet refers to the use of the Internet within the same business. Extranet refers to the use of the Internet between firms.

Key Terms

Backbones	HTML	Electronic Commerce (EC)
Packet-switching	URL	Electronic Data Interchange (EDI)
Routers	Integrated Services Digital Network (ISDN)	Intranet
TCP/IP		Extranet
IP datagram	T1	Webmaster
World Wide Web (WWW)	Asynchronous Transfer Mode (ATM)	Internet Service Provider
Hypertext		

Review Questions

1. What about packet-switching makes it ideal for the Internet, where millions of users are constantly sending to and receiving data from each other?

2. Explain the differences between the Internet, an intranet, and an extranet. What is the common bond between all three?

3. Why are companies switching from Electronic Data Interchange (EDI) to extranets?

4. What is exchanged in electronic commerce?

5. List and describe the eight major Internet services.

6. Describe some of the more common uses of intranets.

7. List the five rules of using the WWW for electronic commerce.

8. How are companies able to learn from their Web sites? Be specific.

9. How are intranets protected from outsiders who should not have access?

Problems and Exercises

◆ **Individual**   ◆◆ **Group**   ⌒ **Field**   ◯ **Web/Internet**

◆ 1. Match the following terms to the appropriate definitions:

_____ Electronic Commerce

_____ Electronic Data Interchange

_____ Extranet

_____ Hypertext

_____ Intranet

_____ Packet-Switching

_____ TCP/IP

_____ URL

a. The protocols that specify how computers communicate on the Internet

b. Online exchange of goods, services, and money between firms and their customers, within firms, and between firms

c. The use of the Internet to support processes and functions within a business

d. The online sales of goods and services between firms, transacted over proprietary networks

e. A technique used for sending information on computer networks that divides messages into small packets before sending

f. The use of the Internet between firms

g. The addressing scheme for uniquely identifying each page of information on the World Wide Web

h. Text in a Web document that is highlighted and, when clicked on by the user, evokes an embedded command that goes to another specified file or location, and brings up that file or location on the user's screen

◆ 2. Explain in simple language how the Internet works. Be sure to talk about backbones, packet-switching, networks, routers, TCP/IP, and Internet services.

◯ ◆ 3. Describe how you use the Internet today. Remember, the Internet is much more than just the World Wide Web. What technologies, hardware, and software do you utilize when using the Internet? Have you used the Internet for professional reasons? How?

◆◆ 4. The definition of electronic commerce in this chapter does not include the exchange of information. Do you feel that these exchanges are also a part of electronic commerce, in addition to goods, services, and money? Why or why not? What about some of your classmates? How do they view the definition of electronic commerce?

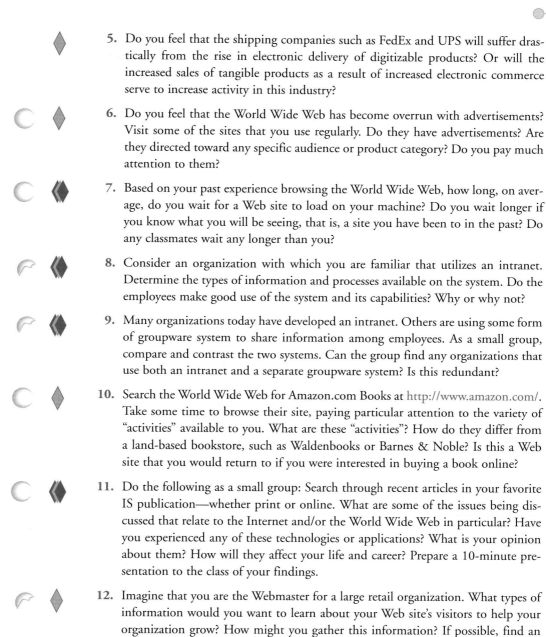

5. Do you feel that the shipping companies such as FedEx and UPS will suffer drastically from the rise in electronic delivery of digitizable products? Or will the increased sales of tangible products as a result of increased electronic commerce serve to increase activity in this industry?

6. Do you feel that the World Wide Web has become overrun with advertisements? Visit some of the sites that you use regularly. Do they have advertisements? Are they directed toward any specific audience or product category? Do you pay much attention to them?

7. Based on your past experience browsing the World Wide Web, how long, on average, do you wait for a Web site to load on your machine? Do you wait longer if you know what you will be seeing, that is, a site you have been to in the past? Do any classmates wait any longer than you?

8. Consider an organization with which you are familiar that utilizes an intranet. Determine the types of information and processes available on the system. Do the employees make good use of the system and its capabilities? Why or why not?

9. Many organizations today have developed an intranet. Others are using some form of groupware system to share information among employees. As a small group, compare and contrast the two systems. Can the group find any organizations that use both an intranet and a separate groupware system? Is this redundant?

10. Search the World Wide Web for Amazon.com Books at http://www.amazon.com/. Take some time to browse their site, paying particular attention to the variety of "activities" available to you. What are these "activities"? How do they differ from a land-based bookstore, such as Waldenbooks or Barnes & Noble? Is this a Web site that you would return to if you were interested in buying a book online?

11. Do the following as a small group: Search through recent articles in your favorite IS publication—whether print or online. What are some of the issues being discussed that relate to the Internet and/or the World Wide Web in particular? Have you experienced any of these technologies or applications? What is your opinion about them? How will they affect your life and career? Prepare a 10-minute presentation to the class of your findings.

12. Imagine that you are the Webmaster for a large retail organization. What types of information would you want to learn about your Web site's visitors to help your organization grow? How might you gather this information? If possible, find an organization's Web site that utilizes your ideas.

13. As the scenario that opened the chapter stated, many research projects can now be accomplished by using the Internet as the sole source of information. Conduct such a research project to answer the questions presented in this opening scenario: a) what is the history of the Internet, b) what are the demographics of the users of the Internet, and c) what is the historic growth and the projected growth of the Internet? Remember, use only the Internet itself to write this short paper.

Real World Case Problems

1. Electronic Commerce Bonanza: Is It Real or Imagined? The Untold Story of the World's Most Successful Web Site.

Cisco Connection Online (CCO), manufacturer of routers and switches, is considered by many to be one of the most successful electronic commerce Web sites. With the processing of almost $2 billion of customer orders over the Web since October 1996, they have entered into a new business model that takes complete advantage of the Internet. This raises a serious question: "Has this electronic marketplace actually delivered on the promise of the Internet—a new way of making money—or is it merely a clever marketing ploy by the largest vendor in the Internet-working industry to showcase what can be done on the Internet without giving much thought to its real implications?" This question is important to Cisco because they have been promoting CCO as the archetypical example of what EC should become.

Their site, with its 45,000 customers, offers real-time information on price, availability, configuration requirements, ordering, invoice status and validation, and shipping information over the Web. They also use it to forward procurement information to their own employees for possible modifications and approvals via email. It used to take days or weeks for a salesperson to complete the order; now it takes only 15 minutes to an hour to finish. Customers are able to join discussion forums, receive bug alerts and download software patches directly from the Internet. CCO currently claims 80,000 registered users and 3.5 million hits per day, and handles about 40 percent of CCO's sales estimated at $3 billion in 1998. John Chambers, CEO, states that the annualized savings to the company of $270 million is due to taking advantage of the Internet and intranet technologies.

One analyst suggests that it is difficult to measure the actual savings on the bottom line. The margins have decreased from 65.3 percent to 65.1 percent, leaving the net income basically unchanged. Administrative expenses have dropped from 21.38 percent to 20.86 percent, giving the company a total savings of less than $10 million. However, the CCO site has increased customer satisfaction and enabled the company to become more efficient. But efficiency does not always translate into a stronger business relationship or higher demand for products. Thus, CCO's has made it a point to continue the account relationship with its customers. This year CCO's best customers, such as NCR and NEC, will be offered messaging APIs. Messaging APIs allow the NCR and NEC sales forces' automation tools and purchasing systems to be directly connected into the massive CCO database and organization resource planning system. Sales personnel will have immediate feedback on their orders with these tools.

Cisco is also evaluating new application technologies for the Web. They are trying to decide whether they should continue developing their own technologies or turn to off-the-shelf software. Making these choices is difficult, and Cisco is more likely to go with what it can purchase quickly and easily off the shelf to conserve time and resources for other uses.

a. Is Cisco's Web site a success? What indicators do we have that their Web site is successful?

b. What are the causes of success for Cisco's Web site? Why is it successful?

c. Can Cisco's approach to electronic commerce be applied to other, non-technology companies? Why or why not?

Source   *Pang, Albert. 1998. Commerce bonanza: Is it real or imagined? Internet Computing. March, 70–74.*

2. Electronic Commerce Upgrades. Oracle, IBM, Others Ready New Versions of Net-Cash Products

Money transactions over the Internet are going to become easier with software being released by Oracle and IBM that enables these transactions to be more secure. Oracle is shipping Payment Server 1.0, a Java cartridge that plugs into the Oracle Web Application Server 3.0. This new software accepts credit-card payments and sends them to companies such as VeriForne and CyberCash for processing. IBM will also announce that its eTill payment server and CommercePoint Gateway are to be available on more platforms. Sonnet Financial, Inc., also has software that consolidates orders from various merchants, executes them in foreign exchange markets, and then debits and credits the appropriate customers' bank accounts. During the past year, Continental Airlines used Sonnet's existing dial-up system to convert about $15 million from one currency to another and sometimes even gets a better rate than Continental's cash manager. In addition, use of the software decreases the time that it would take an individual to make the same trade.

Internet payments were also at the center of the controversy when Open Market, Inc., received three patents for EC technology covering the secure electronic transaction protocol; this technology monitors visitors to Web sites with the concept of online shopping carts. Open Market, Inc., does not plan to use the patents as legal leverages, but rather use them for negotiating partnerships with other vendors.

a. How important is it that there be standardized, secure ways of making payments electronically over the Internet?

b. Experts argue that it is now safer to use your credit card over the Net than it is to give it to a complete stranger over the phone when ordering from a mail-order catalogue. Do you agree? Why or why not?

c. With payment mechanisms like those described in this case now available, and with safe Internet-based encryption techniques now in use, why is it that many consumers are still concerned about using their credit cards over the Net?

Source 1998. *E-commerce upgrades: Oracle, IBM, others ready new version of net-cash products*. InformationWeek. *March 9, 36.*

References

American Express, 1998. Information from: www.americanexpress.com. Information verified: February 20, 1998.

Armstrong, A., and John III. Hagel. 1996. The real value of on-line communities. *Harvard Business Review* (May–June): 134–141.

Bennett, W. D. 1997. A very public affair. *CIO Web Business*, December 1, 34–35.

Comer, D. E. 1995. *The Internet book*. Englewood Cliffs, New Jersey: Prentice Hall.

Cooper, C. 1998. Dell's cyber success story. Information from: www.zdnn.com. Information verified: February 20, 1998.

Finegan, J. 1997. Joining forces. *CIO Web Business*, December 1, 30–32.

Jahnke, A. 1997. Sound without fury. *CIO Web Business*, December 1, 30–32.

Joachim, D. 1997. Cisco and e-commerce: Like white on rice. Information from: www.techWeb.com. Information verified: February 20, 1998.

Nadeau, S. 1997. Internet shopping takes off in 1997 holiday season. Information from: http://204.71.177.76/text/headlines/971219/stories/shoptting.1.html. Information verified: February 20, 1998.

Rebello, K. 1996. Italian sausage that sizzles in cyberspace. *BusinessWeek*, September 23, 118.

Related Readings

Resnick, R. and D. Taylor. 1995. *The Internet business guide.* 2d ed. Indianapolis, Indiana: Sams.net Publishing.

Starwave, 1998. Information from: www.starwave.com. Information verified: February 20, 1998.

Armstrong, A. and J. Hagel. 1996. The real value of online communities. *Harvard Business Review* 74(3): 134–141.

Burke, R. R. 1996. Virtual shopping: Breakthrough in marketing research. *Harvard Business Review* 74(2): 120–131.

Deighton, J. 1996. The future of interactive marketing. *Harvard Business Review* 74(6): 151–166.

Detmer, W. M. and E.H. Shortliffe. 1997. Using the Internet to improve knowledge diffusion in medicine. *Communications of the ACM* 40(8): 101–108.

Foster, Rutkowski, and Goodman. 1995. Who governs the Internet? *Communications of the ACM* 40(8): 15–20.

Ghosh, S. 1998. Making business sense of the Internet. *Harvard Business Review* 76(2): 126–135.

Hiltz, S. R. and B. Wellman. 1997. Asynchronous learning networks as a virtual classroom. *Communications of the ACM* 40(9): 44–49.

Iacovou, Benbasat, and Dexter. 1995. Electronic data interchange and small organizations: Adoption and impact of technology. *Management Information Systems Quarterly* 19(4): 465–485.

Massetti, B. and R. W. Zmud. 1996. Measuring the extent of EDI usage in complex organizations: Strategies and illustrative examples. *Management Information Systems Quarterly* 20(3): 331–345.

Mukhopadhyay, Kekre, and Kalathur. 1995. Business value of information technology: A study of electronic data interchange. *Management Information Systems Quarterly* 19(2): 137–156.

Press, L. 1997. Tracking the global diffusion of the Internet. *Communications of the ACM* 40(11): 11–17.

Rayport, J. F. and J. J. Sviokla. 1995. Exploiting the virtual value chain. *Harvard Business Review* 73(6): 75–85.

Spar, D. and J. J. Bussgang. 1996. Ruling the net. *Harvard Business Review* 74(3): 125–133.

Stevens, Woodward, DeFanti, and Catlett. 1997. From the I-WAY to the national technology grid. *Communications of the ACM* 40(11): 50–60.

Upton, D. M. and A. McAfee. 1996. The real virtual factory. *Harvard Business Review* 74(4): 123–133.

Scenario: Making Better Loan Decisions

The Big Loan Bank (BLB) specializes in making loans in excess of $20,000,000 to municipalities for major construction projects. After having completed a third "Detailed Loan Study" in a year that failed to result in a loan, the president of the Big Loan Bank (BLB), George Hubman, called his chief information officer, Michelle Williams, to his office for a brainstorming session.

"Michelle, before issuing a loan, we conduct a lengthy and expensive study called a 'Detailed Loan Study.' In this study, detailed environmental and economic impact studies are performed. On average, these studies can take up to 6 months, yield a report in excess of 1000 pages, and can exceed $250,000 in costs.

"Additionally, we do not recover the costs of conducting these studies unless we actually issue the loan. In other words, the investment in the study is lost if the loan is not issued! Recently, we have conducted three studies that failed to result in a loan. Over the past year, we have had significantly fewer loans issued relative to the number of projects studied (see Figure 7.1). We must discover a better way of conducting and paying for these studies or we are going to have to get out of the big loan business.

"I wanted to come by and see whether you had any ideas on how we could use information technology to help with this problem."

"Well, George, it sounds as if you need a system to help you pick which projects to study and which projects to reject."

"Exactly!" replied George. "I need a system to help me make better choices *before* we conduct the study and spend $250,000. Is that possible?"

Michelle replied, "BLB has some of the best information systems technology in the banking industry, so options are open to us to help with this problem. For example, if we could identify some easy-to-gather factors that would help us determine which projects are good and which are bad, we could build a model that would help you make a rough prediction of good and bad projects. Such a system would at least enable you to identify the clear winners and losers. Over time we could refine our model so that eventually we could be making very reliable predictions. Are there some easy-to-identify factors that seem to distinguish good and bad projects?"

"Oh yes, there are a few factors that really make a difference," replied George. "Currently, we look at these factors only after agreeing to do the study. I guess there is no reason why we couldn't change the way we do things. It would require that we conduct a 'mini-study' to get this data, which wouldn't be free, but it would be a lot cheaper than $250,000! If we can get you this data, do you think you can build a system to help us with our decision-making?"

Introduction

The focus of this chapter is to describe several types of information systems that are widely used in organizations. Some of the systems described are relatively new, while others have been mainstays in organizations since the 1960s. Information systems have evolved with the changes in organizations and technology. To help you to better understand the various types of information systems, this chapter describes where and how each is commonly used in organizations.

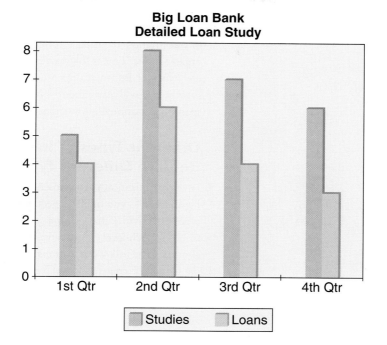

FIGURE 7.1

Detailed Loan Study summary report.

After reading this chapter you will be able to do the following:

1. Describe the characteristics that differentiate the operational, managerial, and executive levels of an organization.

2. Explain the characteristics of the three information systems designed to support each unique level of an organization: transaction processing systems, man-agement information systems, and executive information systems.

3. Describe the characteristics of three information systems that span the organizational, managerial, and executive levels: decision support systems, expert systems, and office automation systems.

4. Explain the general information system needs of various organizational functional areas.

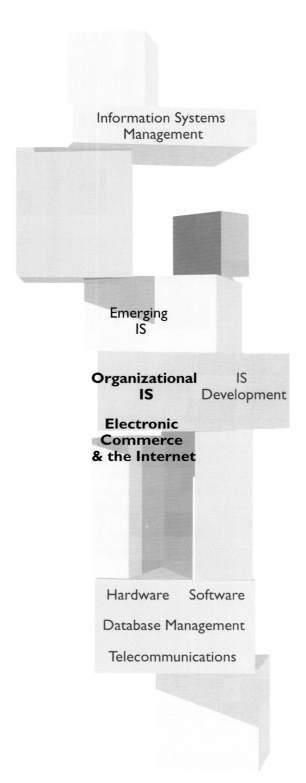

Information Systems
Management

Emerging
IS

Organizational   IS
IS   Development

Electronic
Commerce
& the Internet

Hardware   Software

Database Management

Telecommunications

Like Chapter 6, "Electronic Commerce and the Internet," this chapter focuses on describing how organizations are using and applying information systems (see Figure 7.2). The next section begins by describing the different types of information required throughout the various levels of organizations. This is followed by a discussion of the general types of information systems used in organizations. Finally, you will learn about the information systems that span organizational boundaries.

Different Types of Information Require Different Types of Systems

Every organization is composed of levels, as illustrated in Figure 7.3. As you might expect, given the vastly different types of activities that occur at different levels of an organization, each level can have vastly different informational needs. The following sections describe some of the fundamental differences between organizational levels and their informational needs. This discussion provides you with a general foundation for understanding why there are various types of information systems, each with unique characteristics.

Operational Level

At the **operational level** of the firm, the routine day-to-day business processes and interaction with customers occur. At this level, information systems are designed to automate repetitive activities, such as sales transaction processing. In short, operational-level systems are primarily designed to improve the efficiency of business

FIGURE 7.2

The big picture: focusing on organizational information systems.

processes and the customer interface. Managers at the operational level, such as fore-men or supervisors, make day-to-day decisions that are highly structured and recurring. For example, a supervisor may decide when to reorder supplies or how to best allocate personnel for the completion of a project. Given these characteristics, models can be created to help operational managers make these relatively straightforward decisions. In fact, the decisions are often so straightforward that "decisions" can be programmed directly into operational information systems so that they can be made with little or no human intervention. An inventory management system, for example, could keep track of inventory and issue an order for additional inventory when levels dropped below a specified level. Operational managers would simply need to confirm that an order was desired. Figure 7.4 summarizes the general characteristics of the operational level.

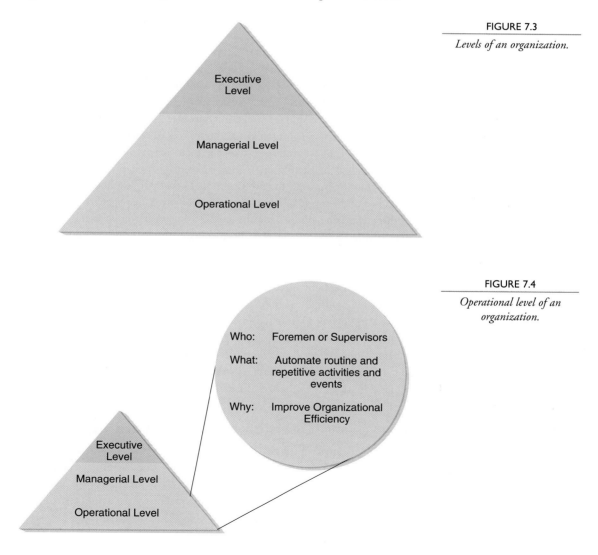

FIGURE 7.3

Levels of an organization.

FIGURE 7.4

Operational level of an organization.

── **Transaction Processing at Eddie Bauer** ──

The advent of the Internet and electronic commerce has caused Eddie Bauer, a leading retailer of casual clothing and products, to extend its transaction processing system to include Web-based sales (IBM, 1998). Based in Seattle, Washington, Eddie Bauer has more than 500 retail outlets and a very successful catalog business. In the catalog business, telemarketers enter customer orders into the company's *transaction processing system*. Unfortunately, transactions coming from their electronic commerce Web site were not integrated into their existing systems. To solve this problem, they now use a single IBM database that integrates order processing from both sources. By integrating these transactions into a single system, Eddie Bauer can more rapidly process orders and more easily manage inventory. A single transaction processing system is making operations at Eddie Bauer much more efficient.

Managerial Level

At the **managerial level** of the organization, functional managers focus on monitoring and controlling operational-level activities and providing information to higher levels of the organization. Managers at this level, often referred to as mid-level managers or functional managers (for example, marketing manager, finance manager), focus on effectively utilizing and deploying organizational resources to reach the strategic objectives of the organization. Mid-level managers typically focus on problems within a specific business function, such as marketing or finance. Here, the scope of the decision is usually contained within the business function, is moderately complex, and has a time horizon of a few days to a few months. For example, a marketing manager may decide how to allocate the advertising budget for the next business quarter or some fixed time period. Managerial-level decision making is not nearly as structured or routine as operational-level decision making. In fact, managerial-level decision making is generally referred to as *semi-structured* decision making because solutions and problems are not clear-cut and often require judgment and expertise. For example, an information system could provide a production manager with summary information about sales forecasts for multiple product lines, inventory levels, and overall production capacity. This manager could use this information to create multiple production schedules. With these schedules, the manager could examine inventory levels and potential sales profitability, depending upon the order in which manufacturing resources were used to produce each type of product. Figure 7.5 summarizes the general characteristics of the managerial level.

── **Decision Making at Sara Lee** ──

Managers within the meat division of Sara Lee—whose brands include Jimmy Dean, Hillshire Farms, Ballpark Franks, Kahn's, and West Virginia Hams—were having a tough time analyzing their retail sales data (HP, 1998). Because each brand had its own separate computing infrastructure, managers were having difficulty integrating information to make decisions related to planning and forecasting demand. To solve this problem, Sara Lee began to use the Decision Support Suite from Information Advantage, running on a Hewlett-Packard 9000 server. This system integrates information from these separate systems and provides managers with the capability to view the data in many different ways. Before, the IS department would spend three to four days each month loading and formatting the data from the prior month to create a series of management reports. Today, up-to-the-minute information is available to managers, and monthly system maintenance takes less than three hours. Using this system, Sara Lee is making much more effective decisions.

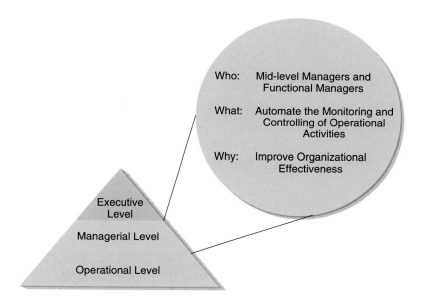

FIGURE 7.5

Managerial level of an organization.

Executive Level

At the **executive level** of the organization, managers focus on longer-term strategic issues facing the organization. Managers at this level include the president and chief executive officer (CEO), vice presidents, and possibly the board of directors. Collectively, we will refer to these managers as "executives." Executive-level decisions are often very complex problems with broad and long-term ramifications for the organization. Executive-level decision making is often referred to as being *messy* or *ill-structured* because executives must consider the ramifications of their decisions on the overall organization; understanding how a given decision impacts the overall organization makes executive decision making extremely complex. For example, top managers may decide to develop a new product or discontinue an existing one. Such a decision may have vast, long-term effects on the organization. Information systems are used to obtain aggregate summaries of trends and projections of the future to assist executive-level decision making. Figure 7.6 summarizes the general characteristics of the executive level.

FIGURE 7.6

Executive level of an organization.

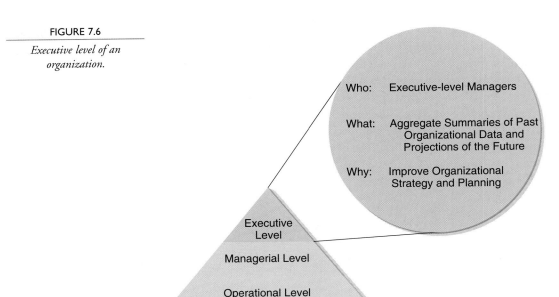

A BRIEF CASE

Executive Information at Blue Cross Blue Shield of Florida

The health insurance industry has grown to be highly complex and highly competitive. To be successful, companies must be able to change their product offerings and services rapidly based on changing market needs. Depending on the question of the moment, executives must be able to make sense of a vast amount of changing information. Information related to market segments, such as adults versus children, geographical region, aliments, and funding arrangements, must be compared and contrasted as part of the decision making process. To help manage this type of information at Blue Cross Blue Shield of Florida, executives use a special type of information system called an *executive information system* (EIS) from SAS (SAS, 1998). This EIS enables executives to examine extremely complex data easily in textual and graphical summaries. This system is helping the executives of Blue Cross Blue Shield of Florida to more easily deal with the complexities of their rapidly changing environment and achieve a strategic advantage.

In summary, most organizations have three general levels: operational, managerial, and executive. Each level has unique activities, and each requires different types of information. The next section examines various types of information systems designed to support each organizational level.

General Types of Information Systems

An easy way to understand how all information systems work is to use an input, process, and output model—the basic systems model (see Checkland, 1981 for a thorough discussion). Figure 7.7 shows the basic systems model that can be used to describe virtually all types of systems. For example, a taxi service is a "physical" system that has customers as an input, transportation provision as a process, and payment for service as an output. All types of information systems can be decomposed into the basic input, process, and output elements. For example, Figure 7.8 shows elements of a payroll system decomposed into input, process, and output elements. The inputs to a payroll system include time cards and employee lists, as well as wage and salary information. Processing transforms the inputs into outputs that include paychecks, management reports, and updated account balances. The remainder of this section uses the basic systems model to describe various types of contemporary information systems. The next section describes one fundamental type of organizational information system: the transaction processing system.

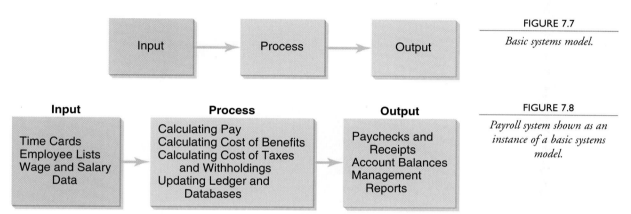

FIGURE 7.7

Basic systems model.

FIGURE 7.8

Payroll system shown as an instance of a basic systems model.

Transaction Processing Systems

Many organizations deal with repetitive types of activities. Grocery stores repeatedly scan groceries at the checkout counter. Banks repeatedly process checks drawn on customer accounts. Fast food restaurants repeatedly process customer orders. All these examples represent events in the business world, events referred to as **transactions**. In short, transactions are events that occur as a regular part of a business's day-to-day operations. **Transaction processing systems** (TPSs) are a special class of information systems designed to process business events and transactions. Consequently, TPSs often reside close to customers at the operational level of the organization, as illustrated in Figure 7.9.

The goals of transaction processing systems are to automate repetitive information processing activities within organizations to increase speed and accuracy and to lower the cost of processing each transaction—that is, to make the organization more *efficient*. Because TPSs are typically used to process large volumes of information, organizations have spent considerable resources designing TPSs to maximize the processing speed and accuracy while lowering the cost of processing each transaction. One of the easiest ways to do so is to reduce or eliminate people from the process. Reducing or eliminating people from the process not only reduces transaction costs, but it also reduces the likelihood of data entry errors. Consequently, much of the evolution of TPSs has focused on reducing the role people play in the processing of organizational transactions. The types of activities supported by TPS include:

- Payroll processing
- Sales and order processing
- Inventory management
- Product purchasing, receiving, and shipping
- Accounts payable and receivable

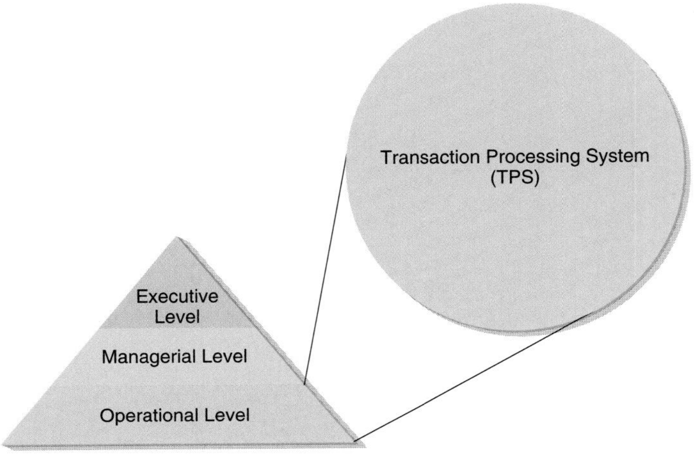

FIGURE 7.9

Transaction processing system resides at the operational level.

Architecture of a Transaction Processing System

The basic model of a TPS is shown in Figure 7.10. When a business event or transaction occurs, **source documents** describing the transaction are created. Source documents, paper or electronic, serve as a stimulus to a TPS from some external source. Source documents can be processed as they are created (known as "online processing") or they can be processed in batches (known as "batch processing"). **Online processing** of transactions provides immediate results to the system operator or customer. For example, an interactive class registration system that immediately notifies you of your success or failure in attempting to register for a class is an example of an online TPS. **Batch processing** of transactions occurs when transactions are collected and then processed together as a "batch" at some later time. Banks often use batch processing when reconciling checks drawn on customer accounts. Likewise, your university uses batch processing to process end-of-term grade reports—all inputs must be periodically processed in batches to calculate your grade point average. In general, when customers need immediate notification of the success or failure of a transaction, system designers use online processing. When immediate notification is not needed or is not practical, batch processing is the chosen system design approach. Table 7.1 lists several examples of online and batch transaction processing systems.

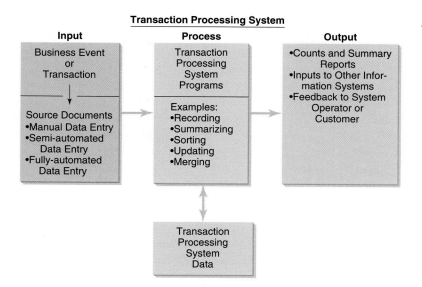

FIGURE 7.10

Architecture of a transaction processing system.

Table 7.1   Examples of online and batch transaction processing systems.

Online TPS	Batch TPS
University class registration processing	Student final grade processing
Airline reservation processing	Payroll processing
Concert/sporting event ticket reservation processing	Customer order processing (for example, insurance forms)
Grocery store checkout processing	Bank check processing

Information entry with a TPS can be manual, semi-automated, or fully automated. *Manual data entry* refers to having a person *manually* enter the source document information into the TPS. For example, when you apply for a new driver's license, a clerk enters information about you into a Driver's License Recording System, often copying the information from a form that you filled out.

A second method for system input in a TPS is *semi-automated data entry*. In a semi-automated data entry system, some type of data capture device speeds the entry and processing of the transaction. For example, a checkout scanner in the grocery store is an example of a semi-automated entry device. The checkout scanner speeds the checkout for the customer and also provides accurate and detailed data directly to many types of information systems. Another example of a semi-automated TPS would be an electronic mall on the World Wide Web. In this mall, customers enter their purchase requests, which go directly to an order fulfillment system without any additional human intervention.

Fully automated data entry requires no human intervention. In essence, two computers "talk" to each other via a communications link. For example, for automobiles built at Ford Motor Company, each part used in the manufacturing process represents a transaction in the inventory management systems. At some point in the process, the inventory management system automatically contacts a supplier's computer system to request additional raw materials. An electronic linkage between computers to share data related to business operations is referred to as electronic data interchange (EDI). Many organizations spend considerable effort with their suppliers and customers working on EDI standards so that more and more information can be exchanged without human intervention.

The characteristics of a TPS are summarized in Table 7.2. In general, inputs to a TPS are business events or transactions. The processing activities of a TPS typically focus on recording, summarizing, sorting, updating, and merging transaction information with existing organizational databases. Outputs from a TPS typically reflect summary reports, inputs to other systems, and operator notification of processing completion. People that are very close to day-to-day operations most often use TPS. For example, a checkout clerk at the grocery store uses a TPS to record your purchases. Supervisors may review transaction summary reports to better control inventory, to manage operations personnel, or to provide better customer service. Additionally, inventory management systems may monitor transaction activity and use this information to manage inventory reordering activity. This is an example of the output from the TPS as being the input to another system.

Table 7.2   Characteristics of a transaction processing system.

Inputs	Business events and transactions
Processing	Recording, summarizing, sorting, updating, merging
Outputs	Counts and summary reports of activity inputs to other information systems feedback to system operators or customers
Typical User	Operational personnel and supervisors

A BRIEF CASE ▷ ── **Transaction Processing System at Ford Motor** ── **Company**

The World Wide Web enables customers to use TPS to order products or obtain information. For example, Ford Motor Company uses the WWW to enable customers to easily obtain information about products and dealers. Figure 7.11 shows a screen from Ford's WWW site in which customers can locate their nearest dealer (Ford, 1998). The inputs to this system are zip codes entered by customers. Processing occurs back at Ford in Dearborn, Michigan, where a TPS matches the customer's zip code to one in a database containing all dealers. When a match is made, the output of the system is a report back to the customer giving the name, address, and phone of the closest dealer. In creating this online TPS, Ford has provided a valuable customer service with no human intervention. The cost for processing this transaction for Ford is virtually nil. Alternatively, if a customer calls Ford on an 800 number requesting the same information, Ford pays for the phone call and for the personnel answering the customer's question—a much higher transaction cost. Remember that the goal of TPS is to increase the speed and accuracy and lower the cost of processing for each transaction. Ford achieved all three goals with the creation of the "Dealer Locator" feature on their Web site.

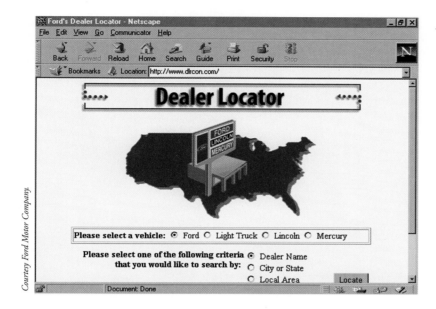

Courtesy Ford Motor Company.

FIGURE 7.11

Ford's Dealer Locator system on the World Wide Web.

Management Information Systems

Management Information System (MIS) is a term with two meanings. It is often used to describe the field of study that encompasses a variety of people involved in the development, use, management, and study of computer-based information systems in organizations. It is also used to refer to a specific type of organizational information system. These MISs are typically used to produce regular and ad hoc reports to support the ongoing, recurring decision making activities associated with managing an entire business or a functional area within a business. Consequently, an MIS often resides at the managerial level of the organization, as shown in Figure 7.12.

Remember that transaction processing systems automate repetitive information processing activities to increase *efficiency*. The basic goal of a management information system is to help mid-level managers make more *effective* decisions. In other words, MISs are designed to get the right information to the right person in the right format at the right time to help her make better decisions. MISs can often be found throughout the organization. For example, a marketing manager may have an MIS that contrasts sales revenue and marketing expenses by geographic region so that she can better understand how regional marketing promotions are performing. Examples of the types of activities supported by MISs include:

- Sales forecasting

- Financial management and forecasting

- Manufacturing planning and scheduling

- Inventory management and planning

- Advertising and product pricing

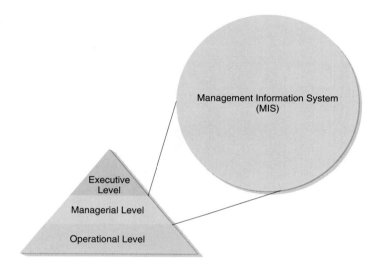

FIGURE 7.12

Management information systems reside at the managerial level.

Architecture of a Management Information System

The basic architecture of an MIS is shown in Figure 7.13. At regular intervals, managers in most organizations need to review summary information of some organizational activity. For example, a sales manager may review the weekly performance of all his sales staff. To conduct this review, an MIS summarizes the total sales volume of each salesperson in a report. This report may provide a plethora of information about each person, including the following:

- What are this salesperson's year-to-date sales totals?

- How do this year's sales figures compare to last?

- What is the average amount per sale?

- How do sales change by the day of the week?

As you can see, a manager can review much about each salesperson. Imagine the difficulty of producing these weekly reports manually if the organization has 50 salespeople, 500 salespeople, or even 5000 salespeople! It would be very difficult, if not impossible, to create these detailed reports on each sales person without an MIS. Ironically, as you can see by our example, the processing of an MIS is typically not all that complicated. In most cases, the processing amounts to combining the information from multiple data sources into a structured report.

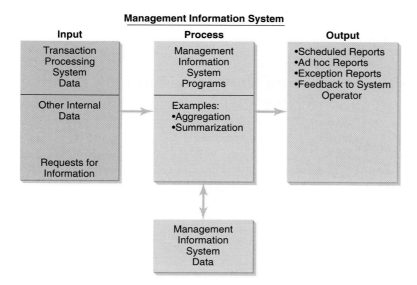

Management Information System

FIGURE 7.13

Architecture of a management information system.

Managers can also use an MIS to make *ad hoc* requests for information. For example, if a particular product is not selling as well as forecasts predicted, the manager can request a report showing which salespeople are selling the product effectively and which aren't. MIS can also be used to produce *exception reports* that highlight situations that are out of the normal range. For example, a manager with a large number of sales personnel can produce an exception report highlighting those not achieving minimum sales goals. Remember that the goal of the MIS is to help the organization be more effective. By focusing the manager's attention on the correct information, the MIS helps the organization take a first step in becoming more effective.

The characteristics of an MIS are summarized in Table 7.3. In general, inputs to an MIS are transaction processing data produced by a TPS; other internal data, such as sales promotion expenses; and ad hoc requests for special reports or summaries. The processing activities in an MIS are relatively simple. In most cases, the processing aspect of the system focuses on data aggregation and summary. Outputs are formatted reports that provide scheduled and routine information to a mid-level manager. For example, a store manager can use an MIS to review sales information to identify products that aren't selling and are in need of special promotion. The following university enrollment system example illustrates the architecture of an MIS.

Table 7.3　Characteristics of a Management Information System.

Inputs	Transaction processing data and other internal data scheduled and ad hoc requests for information
Processing	Aggregation and summary of data
Outputs	Scheduled and exception reports feedback to system operator
Typical User	Mid-level managers

A BRIEF CASE

Tracking University Enrollment with a Management Information System

All universities track class enrollments during student registration periods. An example of one such system—the course enrollment system shown in Figure 7.14—is being used by the faculty and administrators at Indiana University. With the course enrollment system, administrators can track which classes are filling up and which aren't. During a week-long registration period, more sections of a particularly popular class can be added, while courses failing to attract students can be removed. This enables administrators to move faculty resources to where the demand is and, in essence, more effectively manage university resources.

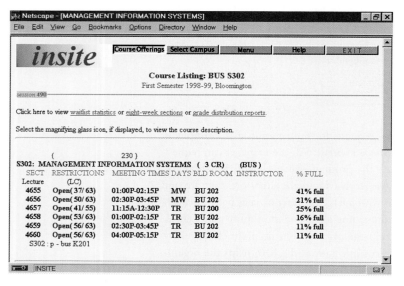

FIGURE 7.14

University course enrollment system MIS report.

Executive Information Systems

In addition to operational personnel and mid-level managers, top-level managers or executives can use information technology to support their day-to-day activities. Information systems designed to support the highest organizational managers are called **executive information systems** (EISs). As you might expect, an EIS resides at the top of the organization at the executive level, as shown in Figure 7.15. The basic goals of an EIS are to provide information to the executive in a very aggregate form so that she can scan information quickly for trends and anomalies. Although EISs are not as widely used as other types of information systems, this trend is rapidly changing because more and more executives are becoming comfortable with information technology and because an EIS can provide substantial benefits to the executive. In essence, the EIS provides a one-stop shop for a lot of the informational needs of the executive. Activities supported by an EIS include:

- Executive-level decision making

- Long-range and strategic planning

- Monitoring of internal and external events and resources

- Crisis management

- Staffing and labor relations

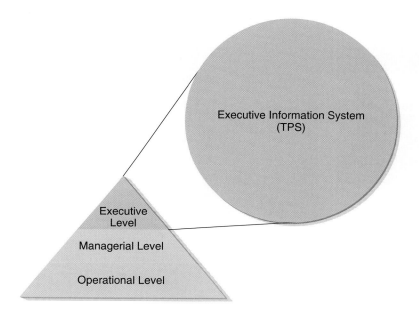

FIGURE 7.15

Executive information systems reside at the executive level.

One key element of an EIS is its capability to deliver both "soft" and "hard" data to the executive decision maker. Soft data includes textual news stories or other non-analytical information. Alternatively, hard data includes facts and numbers. Lower-level TPSs and MISs generate much of the hard data provided by an EIS. Providing timely soft information to executive decision makers has been much more of a challenge. For example, deciding how to get the late-breaking news stories and information to the system in a format consistent with the EIS philosophy was a significant challenge to organizations. Some organizations subscribe to online services such as Dow Jones as a source for their soft data; however, Dow Jones provides a relatively narrow band of information and its information is not formatted in a user-friendly manner that suits everyone's needs. People are often needed to monitor the online service to select appropriate information and to translate the information into a user-friendly format. This is clearly a time-consuming and inexact process.

A product on the World Wide Web called Point Cast Network (PCN) has radically changed how many executives can gain soft information by offering a customized and user-friendly format. PCN provides information on almost any subject or industry, virtually as it hits the news wires. Figure 7.16 shows a typical screen from PCN. Topics, arranged as separate "Channels," range from headline news, sports, and weather to the tracking of news and financial information about a specific industry or company (see Table 7.4). One of the most powerful features of PCN is that it can be customized to filter information so that only the information deemed relevant to the executive is delivered by the system. For example, if an executive is interested in the software, Internet/online, and telecommunications industries, a dialog box can be used to select these industries. Stories related to these industries will be tracked; all others will be ignored. Special versions of PCN are also created for specific industries, such as aerospace, automotive, banking, consumer markets, government, health care, legal, IT management, real estate, and telecommunications. PCN information can be updated once a day or every few minutes depending upon your Internet connection. PCN is supported by "billboard" advertisements much like television commercials, which means that one of the most exciting things about PCN is that it is free to the user!

Courtesy of PointCast, Inc.

FIGURE 7.16

Screen from Point Cast Network.

Table 7.4 Point Cast Network channels and description.

PCN Channel	Description
News	Track national, international, political, and business news.
Sports	Track news stories, team standings, schedules, and scores for professional and college sports.
Companies	Track news and stock reports for a particular company that is traded on the AMEX, NASDAQ, and NYSE exchanges.
Industries	Track news and market valuations for particular industries or for major stock markets.
Weather	Track weather information for most national and international cities as well as graphic weather maps for the continental United States, Europe, and Asia.
Lifestyles	Track horoscopes and state lottery results.
Pathfinder	Track news from Time-Warner's online daily versions of *Time*, *Money*, and *People* magazines.
LA Times	Display news from several sections of the *Los Angeles Times* newspaper.
TechWeb	Display articles on current topics in high technology.

Source PCN. 1998. *Information from:* http://www.pointcast.com/.

Architecture of an Executive Information System

The basic architecture of an EIS is shown in Figure 7.17. Inputs to an EIS are all internal databases and systems as well as *external* databases that contain information on competitors, financial markets, news (local, national, and international), and any other information deemed important by the executive in making day-to-day decisions. This suggests that an EIS could potentially "overload" the executive with too much information from too many sources. Systems designers spend considerable effort customizing the EIS so that only the most important information is provided in its most effective form. To do this, they use information filters to select information that is deemed relevant by the ex-ecutive. Also, output information is provided to executives by systems designers in a highly aggregated form, often using graphical icons to make selections and bar and line charts to summarize data, trends, and simulations. Finally, large monitors that make things easy to see are typically used. The characteristics of an EIS are summarized in Table 7.5.

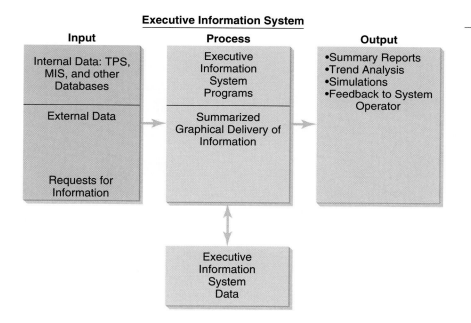

Executive Information System

Input	Process	Output
Internal Data: TPS, MIS, and other Databases	Executive Information System Programs	•Summary Reports •Trend Analysis •Simulations •Feedback to System Operator
External Data	Summarized Graphical Delivery of Information	
Requests for Information		

Executive Information System Data

FIGURE 7.17

Architecture of an executive information system.

Table 7.5 Characteristics of an executive information system.

Inputs	Aggregate internal and external data
Processing	Summarized graphical delivery
Outputs	Summary reports, trends, and simulations feedback to system operator
Typical User	Executive-level managers

Although data is provided in a very highly aggregated form, the executive also has the capability to *drill down* and see the details if necessary. For example, suppose an EIS summarizes employee absenteeism and the system shows that today's numbers are significantly higher than normal. This can be shown to the executive in a running line chart (see Figure 7.18). If the executive wants to understand the details as to why absenteeism is so high, a selection on the screen can provide the details behind the aggregate numbers (see Figure 7.19). An EIS also can connect the data in the system to the absentee employees responsible for the data in the organization through the use of the organization's internal communication network (for example, electronic or voice mail). In other words, after reviewing the detailed absenteeism figures, the executive can quickly send a message to the manager in charge of manufacturing personnel to discuss the problem she discovered in the drill-down.

FIGURE 7.18

Total employee absenteeism line chart.

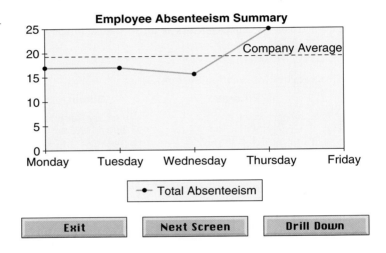

FIGURE 7.19

Drill-down numbers for employee absenteeism.

Absenteeism Drill Down

	Monday	Tuesday	Wednesday	Thursday
Manufacturing	10	11	6	19
Professional	2	2	0	1
Clerical	3	1	3	2
Sales	0	0	1	2
Support	2	3	5	1

Exit   Prior Screen   E-mail

A BRIEF CASE

Using an Executive Information System at Texaco Brazil

Texaco Brazil needed a way to easily monitor the activities of its units throughout the country. Management knew that with this capability, they could become one of Brazil's leading petroleum distributors. To support them in finding a solution, Texaco turned to

Commander EIS, produced by Comshare (Comshare, 1998). Using Commander, Texaco executives analyze company results daily. They track activity in each business unit down to the factory, branch, and service station level. Sales, purchases, cash flow, expenses, stocks, and deadlines can be monitored minute by minute. Because the information is continuously updated, management can react to even small market fluctuations, making flexible and proactive decision making possible. Since the EIS installation, Texaco Brazil attributes a lot of its success to the EIS. In fact, since installing the EIS, Texaco Brazil has become Texaco's leading operating unit in its Latin American business units.

Information Systems that Span Organizational Boundaries

The preceding section examined three general classes of information systems within s pecific hierarchical levels in the organization. Organizations also use other information systems that cannot be neatly associated with a particular level. On the contrary, these systems span all levels of the organization (see Figure 7.20). Four types of boundary-spanning systems are:

- Decision support systems

- Expert systems

- Office automation systems

- Functional area information systems

This section describes each of these in more detail.

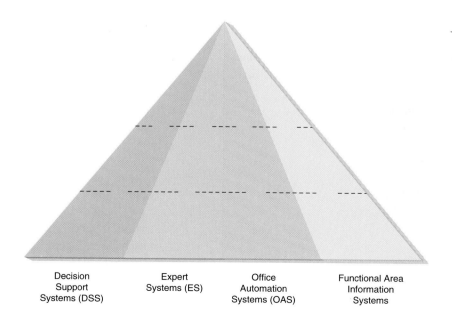

FIGURE 7.20

Organizational boundary-spanning information systems.

Decision Support Systems

Decision support systems (DSSs) are special-purpose information systems designed to support organizational decision making. A DSS is typically designed to solve a particular recurring problem in the organization. This problem may occur at the shop floor level or in the executive suite. Most often, DSSs are used by managerial-level employees to help them solve the semi-structured problems they typically address, much like the problem described in the chapter-opening scenario. That scenario described a situation in which bank managers were trying to successfully predict good and bad loans. The key distinction between a DSS and other types of previously described information systems is that with a DSS, the user actively uses decision analysis tools to either analyze or create meaningful data to address non-routine problems. In other words, a DSS is designed to be an "interactive" decision aid, whereas the systems described previously—TPS, MIS, and EIS—are much more passive.

The goal of a DSS is to augment human decision making performance and problem solving ability by enabling users to examine alternative solutions to a problem. A powerful feature of a DSS is its capability to enable you to play "what if" analyses with a problem, which means you can examine alternative problem scenarios and results. For example, a cash manager for a company could examine "what if" scenarios of the effect of various interest rates on cash availability. Results are displayed in both textual and graphical formats. The most commonly used DSS is an electronic spreadsheet, such as Microsoft Excel.

Architecture of a Decision Support System

Given that the most commonly used DSS is an electronic spreadsheet, the architecture of a DSS is relatively simple. A DSS has three main components: models, data, and a user interface (see Figure 7.21) (Sprague, 1980). **Models** are simply the ways in which the DSS allows data to be manipulated. For example, if you have some historic sales data, you can use many different types of "models" to create a forecast of future sales. One technique would be to take an average of the past sales. The formula you would use to calculate the average is the model—a relatively unsophisticated model, but a model nonetheless! A more complicated forecasting model might use time-series analysis or linear regression. Virtually countless models are used in organizations to support ad hoc decision making (see Table 7.6).

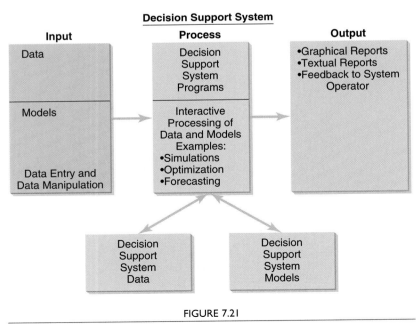

FIGURE 7.21

Architecture of a decision support system.

Data for the DSS can come from many sources, including TPS, MIS, and other information sources. The user interface is simply the way in which the DSS takes information from you and how it formats the DSS results.

Table 7.6 Common DSS models for specific organizational areas.

Area	Common DSS Models
Accounting	Cost analysis, discriminant analysis, break-even analysis, auditing, tax computation and analysis, depreciation methods, budgeting.
Corporate Level	Corporate planning, venture analysis, mergers and acquisitions.
Finance	Discounted cash flow analysis, return on investment, buy or lease, capital budgeting, bond refinancing, stock portfolio management, compound interest, after-tax yield, foreign exchange values.
Marketing	Product demand forecast, advertising strategy analysis, pricing strategies, market share analysis, sales growth evaluation, sales performance.
Personnel	Labor negotiations, labor market analysis, personnel skills assessment, employee business expense, fringe benefit computations, payroll and deductions.
Production	Product design, production scheduling, transportation analysis, product-mix inventory level, quality control, learning curve, plant location, material allocation, maintenance analysis, machine replacement, job assignment, material requirement planning.
Management Science	Linear programming, decision trees, simulation, project evaluation and planning, queuing, dynamic programming, network analysis.
Statistics	Regression and correlation analysis, exponential smoothing, sampling, time-series analysis, hypothesis testing.

The characteristics of a DSS are summarized in Table 7.7. Inputs are data and models. Processing supports interactive merging of data with models to examine alternative solution scenarios. Outputs are graphs and textual reports. DSS users are typically mid-level managers, but DSS tools can be used by virtually anyone in the organization at any level. The next section discusses an example of a DSS that you might use at home.

Table 7.7 Characteristics of a decision support system.

Inputs	Data and models data entry and data manipulation commands (via user interface)
Processing	Interactive processing of data and models simulations, optimization, forecasts
Outputs	Graphs and textual reports feedback to system operator (via user interface)
Typical User	Mid-level manager (although a DSS could be used at any level of the organization)

Using a Decision Support System to Buy a Car

When you buy a new car, one of your biggest concerns after deciding what you want to purchase is deciding how you will pay for your new vehicle. Will you pay cash? Or, if you are like most of us, will you finance most or part of the purchase price? Organizations face the same decisions every day when purchasing supplies, raw materials, and capital equipment: Should they pay cash or finance these purchases? What information do they need to know to make this decision? What tools do companies use to help in making these decisions? Interestingly, the tools that they use are relatively simple

ETHICAL PERSPECTIVE: SOFTWARE PIRACY AND INTELLECTUAL PROPERTY RIGHTS?

Have you ever gone to a friend's house with a blank disk and copied a program or a game that you wanted? Did you know that this is called software piracy? You have just "stolen" from the software producer their due profits from the sale of one unit of merchandise and you have broken U.S. copyright laws. People do it all the time, you say. The reason people do it is because it is easy and they don't get caught—not because it is the right thing to do.

When you purchase software, you are typically allowed to copy the software onto your personal computer's hard drive and make one copy of the software onto a second disk or set of disks for backup.

You're probably asking yourself how making one more extra copy of this piece of software is going to hurt the software vendor. Vendors say that it hurts plenty. Imagine that you developed a small software program and you sold 50,000 copies of it at $20.00 each, for a total of $1,000,000. Pretty good, huh? You then find out that several people who legitimately purchased the product turned right around and allowed their friends and work associates to illegally copy the program. It later turns out that you lost over 5,000 potential "sales" to these illegal copies, an additional 10% in sales volume and an additional $100,000 in revenue. Ouch! You probably could have used that additional money. To put this on a more personal level, imagine having to take a pay cut right now of between ten and fifteen percent and not being able to do anything about it. Not so simple an issue anymore, is it?

Business organizations and software vendors have expended lots of time and resources to produce the software that we now use at home and at work, and they believe that in addition to recouping their costs, they have a right to enjoy a bit of a profit for their labors. In general, software vendors and businesses have gotten tougher about illegal copying of their software. As a result, most business organizations have cracked down on illegal copying and usage of personal computer software (after some rather embarrassing public software inspections turned up many infractions). In addition, software companies such as Microsoft, IBM, and AT&T have joined forces to establish the Electronic Licensing and Security Initiative to develop software tracking "tokens" that will enable a company to track its licensed software.

Although businesses have cracked down on illegal copying of software, illegal copying in university settings in the U.S. is still fairly widespread. Most universities now have public computing sites where students and faculty have free access to many software applications. In some cases, students are able to legally download software to be used at home while they are enrolled as students. Unfortunately, many of these students continue to use the software upon graduation without ever purchasing it from the manufacturer as intended. In addition, students often freely exchange software with each other. Some people believe that software vendors are not as concerned with the illegal proliferation of software on university campuses because they see this as a potentially useful way to pre-build the market share for their software tools. Indeed, it is probably not a bad idea to have university students train on your software tools, given that they are likely to then choose to use these same tools when then enter the work world, where copies of the same software are likely to be legal purchases. In any event, this puts universities and faculty in a precarious situation (Im, J.H. & Van Epps, P.D. 1992).

The rise of the Internet has brought copying to a new level. Material on the Internet, especially the World Wide Web, is very easy to copy. This includes programming code, text, graphic images, corporate logos, pictures, and even ideas. Little protection is available to those who publish copyrighted information via the Internet. However, legislation is pending in Congress that would make it a crime to electronically copy any copyrighted material from the Internet. This bill has received support from software manufacturers and criticism from educational institutions and libraries. The criticism stems from the fact that the bill has no provision to allow such institutions fair use of the material for educational purposes. Such provisions do exist for analog material, and according to the Digital Future Coalition, this bill goes too far and fails to find a reasonable middle ground.

Questions for Discussion

1. Should people in educational institutions be allowed to copy software freely (with some restrictions, of course)?

2. How does software piracy affect the selling price of software?

3. Should software piracy be stopped? Why or why not? How could it be stopped?

Sources 1996. *Alliance seeks ways to secure software distributed on the Internet.* The Wall Street Journal, *May 8, B6.*

Jacobson, Robert L. 1996. Educators tell Congress to consider their needs in copyright law. Chronicle of Higher Education 42 (May 17): A27.

1992. Im, J.H., and P.D. Van Epps. Software piracy and software security measures in business schools. Information and Management 23: 199–203.

INTERNATIONAL PERSPECTIVE: BUSINESS INTELLIGENCE SYSTEMS IN SOUTH AFRICA

With the changing political and economic climate brought about by the recent social upheavals in South Africa, organizations are scrambling to keep up with transformations in all sectors of business and government. Managers have turned to using Business Intelligence Systems (BIS) in the attempt to "improve the flow and quality of management information" (Robertson, 1996). Software such as Impromptu and Powerplay (Cognos) and Lightship (Pilot Software) are some of the tools being chosen to help people use the flow of information more accurately and efficiently, enabling organizations to predict, for example, the potential success of specific marketing decisions.

BIS, also known as executive information systems, are used to gather key corporate and external data on factors that are critical to the success of the firm. These data are then ported to the business decision maker's desktop computer so that he can quickly see the performance of the firm on a number of key indicators. Many systems also enable the decision maker to drill down to deeper and deeper levels of data if need be.

Although BIS have been widely used in the U.S. and other countries, the use of these systems in South Africa is relatively new. One problem with this new implementation of BIS is the low availability and reliability of current data in South Africa. In the past, many businesses and government organizations employed their own isolated systems; these now must be integrated, and problems such as data overlap, incompatible data structures, and missing data must be remedied.

Robertson (1996) reports that the Department of Defense (DoD) in South Africa is one major organization that is working toward integration; the task is to bring together into a cohesive whole the seven pieces that formerly made up the armed forces of the government, the homelands, and other regions of the country. The DoD is using Pilot Software's Lightship as part of its process of gathering key performance indicators from the variety of systems involved in its shift from a typical military function-based system to a more corporate-like information structure. Robertson notes that, by employing BIS, the DoD has saved time and money and has been able to make wiser choices as it alters to fit the changing needs of South Africa.

Other South African organizations, such as Eskom Distribution (electricity) and Norwich Life (insurance), are also using BIS to "help meet the challenges of an increasingly complex South African" marketplace (Robertson, 1996). BIS are enabling these organizations to project the impacts of specific business choices, charting trends and changes, and identifying critical bits of information. For example, BIS are being used to forecast population increases and sales trends in specific regions to determine whether and when expansion into these regions is warranted.

The move toward using information systems to support business decision making in South African organizations has been difficult. Managers in business and governmental organizations have found that to deploy these systems well, they must find sources of good information, procure them, consolidate them from often incompatible systems and formats, and then present them in usable, useful ways to decision makers. Although these are formidable problems, South African organizations must solve them if they are to compete with each other and with the rest of the world.

Questions for Discussion

1. As a consultant newly appointed to assist a South African organization with the deployment of BIS, where would you start? How would you proceed in developing successful BIS in this context?

2. What does the future hold for South African organizations if they are not successful in developing their use of business intelligence? in developing their use of BIS?

3. What other ways can information technology be used to gather and manage business intelligence?

Source *Robertson, I. 1996.* Briefing Book. *Available at http://www.briefingbook.co.za/cases.*

and readily available to you. To illustrate how a DSS can be used to assist organizational decision making, we will continue with your purchasing of a new car. After going through this example, you will have a better understanding of how organizations use decision support technology to help their employees make day-to-day decisions.

Assume that you have decided to purchase a new car and have selected the year, make, model, and options for this new vehicle. Further suppose that the selling price of the car is $20,000 and that you plan to make a $2,500 down payment. You feel that you can "comfortably" make a payment of about $400 per month. Now, given these factors, you are curious about how different financing options might influence your monthly payments and cash flow. To get an idea of what is possible, you decide to contact your local credit union. As you can see from Table 7.8, interest rates vary depending upon the duration of your loan—lower rates with a shorter duration, higher rates with a longer duration. At this point, you now have all the information you need to analyze your financing options.

Table 7.8   Interest rates and loan duration.

Interest Rate	Loan Duration
7% per year	3 years
10% per year	4 years
12%per year	5 years

You decide to use Microsoft Excel to help you make your financing decision. Excel has a loan analysis template (Excel uses the term "template" to refer to models) bundled with current releases. In this template, you enter the loan amount, annual interest rate, and length of the loan (see Figure 7.22). With this information, the loan analysis DSS automatically calculates your payment, total amount paid, and the amount of interest paid over the life of the loan. With this tool, you can easily change any of the input amounts to examine "what if" scenarios—"What if I finance the loan over four years rather than five?" This is exactly how organizations examine their financing options when they make purchases. Using this tool, you decide to purchase your new vehicle over five years (see Table 7.9). Of course, you don't like the fact that your total interest payment will be almost $6,000, but you have really fallen in love with this new car and don't want to spend more than $400 per month. Happy motoring!

Table 7.9   Loan analysis summary.

Interest Rate	Loan Duration	Monthly Payment	Total Paid	Total Interest	Feasible Payment
7% per year	3 years	$540.35	$19,452.57	$1,952.57	No
10% per year	4 years	$443.85	$21,304.57	$3,804.57	No
12% per year	5 years	$389.28	$23,356.67	$5,856.67	Yes

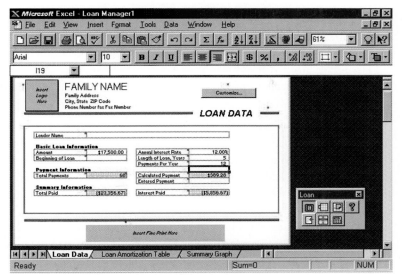

Screen shot reprinted by permission from Microsoft Corporation.

FIGURE 7.22

Loan analysis template in Microsoft Excel.

The next section discusses expert systems, a type of organizational information system that is closely related to decision support systems.

Expert Systems

An **expert system** (ES) is a special type of information system that uses knowledge within some topic area to solve problems or provide advice. Expert systems are used to mimic human expertise by manipulating knowledge (understanding acquired through experience and extensive learning) rather than simply information (see Turban, 1995, for more information). Human knowledge can be represented in an ES by facts and rules about a problem coded in a form that can be manipulated by a computer. When you use an ES, the system asks you a series of questions, much as a human expert would. It continues to ask questions, and each new question is determined by your response to the preceding question, matching the responses to the defined facts and rules, until the responses point the system to a solution. The most difficult part of building an ES is acquiring the knowledge from the expert and getting this knowledge into a consistent and complete form capable of making recommendations. ESs are used when expertise for a particular problem is rare or expensive. In this way, organizations hope to more easily and inexpensively replicate the human expertise. ESs are also used when the knowledge about a problem will be incomplete—in other words, when judgment will be used to make a decision with incomplete information. Examples of the types of activities that can be supported by expert systems include the following:

- Medical diagnosis

- Machine configuration

- Automobile diagnosis

- Financial planning
- Train and container loading
- Computer user help desk
- Software application assistance (for example, Microsoft Help "Wizards")

Architecture of an Expert System

As with other information systems described previously, the architecture of an expert system can be described using the general systems model (see Figure 7.23). Inputs to the system are questions and answers from the user. Processing is the matching of user questions and answers to information in the knowledge base. The processing in an expert system is called *inferencing,* which simply refers to the matching of facts and rules as well as determining the sequence in which questions are addressed to the user. The output from an expert system is a recommendation and possibly an explanation as to why the system made the recommendation that it did. The general characteristics of an expert system are summarized in Table 7.10.

FIGURE 7.23

Architecture of an expert system.

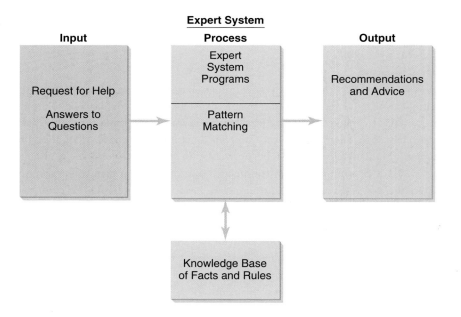

Table 7.10   Characteristics of an expert system.

Inputs	Request for help, answers to questions
Processing	Pattern matching
Outputs	Recommendation or advice
Typical User	Mid-level manager (although an expert system could be used at any level of the organization)

An Expert System on the Web

Expert systems can be designed to assist in solving a wide range of problems. Historically, expert systems have been standalone applications that ran on personal computers. Recently, MultiLogic, Incorporated, a leading producer of expert system technology, has developed a system that enables expert systems to be delivered via the World Wide Web (MultiLogic, 1998). At the MultiLogic Web site, you can test several demonstration ESs (http://www.multilogic.com). One system, for example, is designed to guide holders of restricted stock on their investment options. Restricted stock is acquired privately through corporate mergers or stock options. It is not registered with the SEC and is subject to legal restrictions on its distribution and sale. The system analyzes the investor's responses to several questions and presents personalized investment advice, much as a professional broker would do (see Figure 7.24).

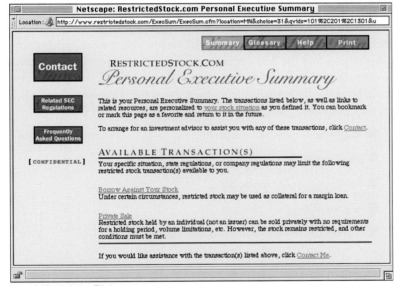

Provided by MultiLogic™, Inc.

FIGURE 7.24

MultiLogic Web-based expert system.

The second interesting feature displayed by this system is its explanation of why the system came to the conclusion that it did or why certain questions are being asked. This is a very powerful feature for training personnel and for helping users believe the system's recommendation.

Picking Better Loan Projects

A BRIEF CASE

Micro Support, Inc., a developer of expert system solutions, developed an expert system to help a bank make better loan predictions before a detailed study was performed. The system divides loans into three categories: likely to be issued, unlikely to be issued, and gray area. The bank can drop the loans that are unlikely to be issued prior to investing resources in the full study, resulting in great savings. It can pursue the loans likely to be issued with confidence that the costs will be recovered. Human experts determine whether the bank should proceed with a full study on the gray area loans. The expert system was built for a bank that specializes in very large loans, similar to the one in the opening scenario. In addition to predicting the loan study outcome, the expert system also recommends the best source of funding for the potential loan—either Ginnie Mae, Fannie Mae, Freddie Mac, or private funds—by evaluating the many requirements associated with each loan. The knowledge base created to assist in making this prediction contained 380 rules and required approximately three months to develop.

Office Automation Systems

The **office automation system** (OAS) is the third type of contemporary information system that spans organizational levels. As described in Chapter 3, OASs are technologies for developing documents, scheduling resources, and communicating. Document development tools include word processing and desktop publishing. Scheduling tools include electronic calendars that help manage human and other resources, such as equipment and rooms. For example, "smart" electronic calendars can examine the multiple schedules to find the first opportunity when all resources (people, rooms, equipment, and so on) are available. Communication technologies include electronic mail, voice mail, fax, videoconferencing, groupware, and other collaborative technologies. Examples of the types of activities supported by an OAS include the following:

- Communication and scheduling

- Document preparation

- Analyzing and merging data

- Consolidating information

- Group collaboration and decision making

Architecture of an Office Automation System

The general architecture of an OAS is shown in Figure 7.25. The inputs to an OAS are documents, schedules, and data. The processing of this information is relatively simple, focusing on storing, merging, calculating, and transporting this data. Outputs include messages, reports, and schedules. The general characteristics of an OAS are summarized in Table 7.11.

Table 7.11 Characteristics of an office automation system.

Inputs	Documents, schedules, data
Processing	Storing, merging, calculating, transporting
Outputs	Messages, reports, schedules
Typical User	All organizational personnel

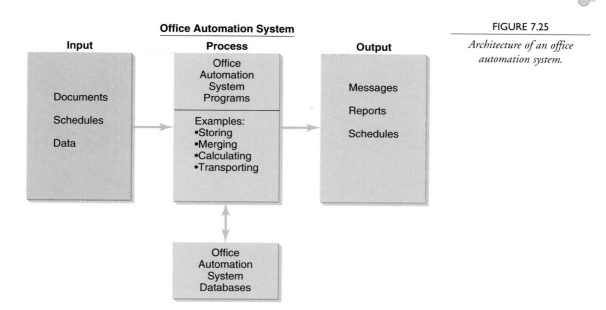

Office Automation System

Input	Process	Output
Documents Schedules Data	Office Automation System Programs Examples: •Storing •Merging •Calculating •Transporting	Messages Reports Schedules

Office Automation System Databases

FIGURE 7.25

Architecture of an office automation system.

Automating Your Daily Calendar

A powerful tool for helping you get to class on time is Microsoft Outlook's Calendar. For example, at the beginning of the semester, you can enter your class meeting times into the system. After they are entered, you can make this appointment automatically recur as long as you like (see Figure 7.26).

Additionally, you can set an alarm to notify you a few minutes before class. The alarm is a great feature to use to remind you of meetings with friends and colleagues or to notify you when your favorite TV show is on. If you live in a dorm or house with a local area network, you can enable your friends to see your schedule on their PCs. This feature enables others to quickly identify good times for meetings or to find you if you are not in your room. In short, this calendar program can truly automate your home or office.

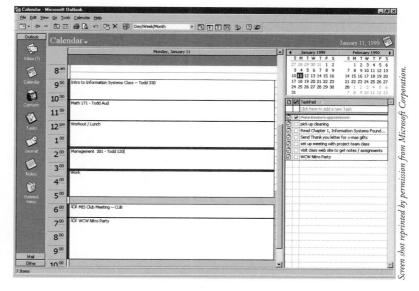

Screen shot reprinted by permission from Microsoft Corporation.

FIGURE 7.26

Coordinating a schedule in the Microsoft Outlook Calendar.

Functional Area Information Systems

A final group of cross-organizational-level information systems are those designed to support a specific **functional area information system**. These systems may be any of the types described previously—TPS, MIS, EIS, DSS, ES, and OAS—and are designed to support the needs of a specific business function (see Figure 7.27). A functional area represents a discrete area of an organization that focuses on a specific set of activities. For example, people in the marketing function focus on the activities that promote the organization and its products in a way that attracts and retains customers. People in accounting and finance focus on managing and controlling capital assets and financial resources of the organization. Table 7.12 lists various organizational functions, describes the focus of each one, and lists examples of the types of information systems used in each functional area. The systems listed in the Table are representative of the types of systems used by various organizational functions; of course, different organizations have a differing mix of systems.

Table 7.12 Organizational functions and representative information systems.

Functional Area	Information System	Examples of Typical Systems
Accounting and Finance	Systems used for managing, controlling, and auditing the financial resources of the organization.	■ Inventory management ■ Accounts payable ■ Expense accounts ■ Cash management ■ Payroll processing
Human Resource	Systems used for managing, controlling, and auditing the human resources of the organization.	■ Recruiting and hiring ■ Education and training ■ Benefits management ■ Employee termination ■ Workforce planning
Marketing	Systems used for managing new product development, distribution, pricing, promotional effectiveness, and sales forecasting of the products and services offered by the organization.	■ Market research and analysis ■ New product development ■ Promotion and advertising ■ Pricing and sales ■ Analysis ■ Product location analysis
Production and Operations	Systems used for managing, controlling, and auditing the production and operations resources of the organization.	■ Inventory management ■ Cost and quality tracking ■ Materials and resource planning ■ Customer service tracking ■ Customer problem tracking ■ Job costing ■ Resource utilization

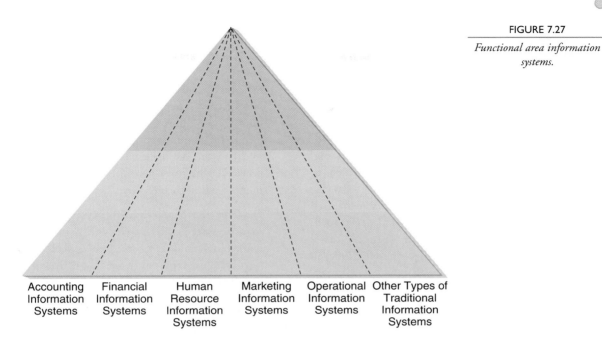

FIGURE 7.27

Functional area information systems.

Accounting Information Systems | Financial Information Systems | Human Resource Information Systems | Marketing Information Systems | Operational Information Systems | Other Types of Traditional Information Systems

Talking with...

William "Butch" Winters, Division President, EDS Corporation, Internet and New Media Business Unit

Educational Background

B.B.A. in Marketing, Southern Methodist University; B.F.A., Southern Methodist University

Job Description

Mr. Winters developed the Internet and New Media business unit for EDS. He is responsible for the Sales, Marketing, Technical, Financial, and Operations aspects of the division. He is responsible for directing this 500-person unit that targets electronic commerce opportunities within, and long-term consulting opportunities with, Fortune 100 organizations. Mr. Winters ensures that the core competencies of business strategy, technological strategy, and creativity are fully deployed among the unit's clients.

Critical Success Factors

People resources must exist to enable the three competencies of business strategy, technological strategy, and creativity. Without people, there is nothing. A strong vendor relationship is important to both understand the available technology and to gain insights into future technologies. Access to capital is vital in the information technology and electronic commerce areas.

Advice to Students

Understand the business goals and issues facing you and your organization. Know how to use technology to meet these goals successfully. Be pro-active in your use of technology; don't wait for a need to arise.

Summary

1. **Describe the characteristics that differentiate the operational, managerial, and executive levels of an organization.** At the operational level of the firm, the routine day-to-day business processes and interaction with customers occur, and information systems are designed to automate repetitive activities, such as sales transaction processing. Operational-level managers such as foremen or supervisors make day-to-day decisions that are highly structured and recurring. At the managerial level of the organization, functional managers focus on monitoring and controlling operational-level activities and providing information to higher levels of the organization. Mid-level or functional managers focus on effectively utilizing and deploying organizational resources to reach the strategic objectives of the organization. At this level, the scope of the decision is usually contained within the business function, is moderately complex, and has a time horizon of a few days to a few months. At the executive level of the organization, decisions are often very complex problems with broad and long-term ramifications for the organization. Executive-level decisions are often referred to as being *messy* or *ill-structured* because they must consider the ramifications of the overall organization.

2. **Explain the characteristics of the three information systems designed to support each of the unique levels of an organization: transaction processing systems, management information systems, and executive information systems.** Transaction processing systems (TPSs) are designed to process business events and transactions and reside close to customers at the operational level of the organization. These systems are used to automate repetitive information processing activities to increase speed and accuracy and to lower the cost of processing each transaction—that is, to make the organization more *efficient*. Management Information Systems (MISs) reside at the managerial level and are designed to produce regular and ad hoc reports to support the ongoing, recurring decision making activities associated with managing an entire business or a functional area within a business. These systems are used to help mid-level managers make more *effective* decisions. Executive information systems (EISs) are used to provide information to an executive in a very aggregate form so that information can be quickly scanned for trends and anomalies. These systems are used to provide a one-stop shop for a lot of the informational needs of the executive.

3. **Describe the characteristics of the three information systems that span the organizational, managerial, and executive levels: decision support systems, expert systems, and office automation systems.** Decision support systems (DSSs) support organizational decision making and are typically designed to solve a particular recurring problem in the organization. DSSs are most commonly used to support semi-structured problems that are addressed by managerial-level employees. A DSS is designed to be an "interactive" decision aid. An expert system (ES) is a special type of information system that uses knowledge within some topic area to solve problems or provide advice. Expert systems are used to mimic human expertise by manipulating knowledge (understanding acquired through experience and extensive learning) rather than simply information. ESs are used when expertise for a particular problem is rare or expensive. In this way, organizations hope to more easily and inexpensively replicate the human expertise. Office automation systems (OASs) are technologies for developing documents, scheduling resources, and communicating.

4. **Explain the general information system needs of various organizational functional areas.** Functional areas represent discrete areas of organizations and typically include: accounting and finance, human resource management, marketing, and production and operations management. Functional area information systems are designed to support the unique requirements of specific business functions.

Key Terms

Operational level

Managerial level

Executive level

Transactions

Transaction processing system (TPS)

Online processing

Batch processing

Management information system (MIS)

Executive information system (EIS)

Decision support system (DSS)

Models

Expert system (ES)

Office automation system (OAS)

Functional area information system

Review Questions

1. Compare and contrast the characteristics of the operational, managerial, and executive levels of an organization.

2. What is meant by "semi-structured" decision making? How does it relate to this chapter?

3. Describe the differences between online processing and batch processing. Give examples of each.

4. What are the three methods used for inputting data into a transaction processing system? Provide examples of each.

5. Differentiate the two meanings of Management Information Systems, one from Chapter 1 and one from this chapter.

6. How does a Management Information System differ from a Transaction Processing System in terms of purpose, target users, capabilities, and so forth?

7. What is an "exception report," who uses it, and how is it used?

8. How does an executive information system "drill down" into the data?

9. What are the four types of information systems that traditionally span the boundaries of organizational levels?

10. Explain the purpose of a model within a decision support system.

11. Provide some examples of functionally specific information systems and needs within an organization.

Problems and Exercises

 Individual   **Group**   **Field**   **Web/Internet**

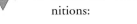

1. Match the following terms to the appropriate definitions:

   Operational level

   Transactions

   Transaction processing system

   Source document

   Online processing

   Management information system

   Decision support system

   Expert system

   a. An information system designed to process day-to-day business event data at the operational level of an organization

   b. A special-purpose information system designed to mimic human expertise by manipulating knowledge (understanding acquired through experience and extensive learning) rather than simply information

   c. The bottom level of an organization, where the routine day-to-day interaction with customers occurs

   d. A special-purpose information system designed to support organizational decision making primarily at the managerial level of the organization

   e. Processing of information immediately as it occurs

   f. Repetitive events in organizations that occur as a regular part of conducting day-to-day operations

   g. An information system designed to support the management of organizational functions at the managerial level of the organization

   h. Documents created when a business event or transaction occurs

 2. In an expert system, who is really the expert: the computer or the programmer? Why?

 3. Do you feel that, as much as possible, transaction processing systems should replace human roles and activities within organizations? Why or why not? What do some of your fellow classmates think? How much cost savings will there be if these humans are still needed to run the systems? What if you were the person being replaced? Will all errors necessarily be eliminated? Why or why not?

 4. Imagine that your boss has asked you to build an inventory transaction system that would enable the receiving and shipping clerks to enter inventory amounts for purchases and sales, respectively. Discuss the pros and cons of building this system as an online processing system versus a batch processing system. Which would you recommend to your boss?

5. The National Sales Manager for ABC Corp. is interested in purchasing a software package that will be capable of providing "accurate" sales forecasts for the short term and long term. She has asked you to recommend the type of system for this purpose. In a small group, determine the system that you would recommend. In what categories would this system fall, according to the chapter? Would you have any reservations about such a system? Why or why not?

6. Discuss the importance of the user interface of an executive information system. What issues are unique to this type of system over the others discussed in the chapter? What about the users of such systems necessitates a carefully constructed user interface? Do a search on the World Wide Web for executive information systems. What interface issues are discussed? Are these the same issues you came up with?

7. Discuss with some of your classmates the advantages and disadvantages of executives using products such as PointCast to gain information. Why might this be a bad idea? Who is ultimately controlling the information being sent through the system?

8. Explain why sometimes models do not always predict the future. Why is this important for users of decision support systems? Can these anomalies be avoided?

9. In simple terminology, explain the differences between a transaction processing system and a functional area information system? Are they necessarily different? Why?

10. Interview a top-level executive within an organization with which you are familiar. Determine the extent to which the organization utilizes executive information systems. Does this individual utilize an EIS in any way? Why or why not? Which executives do utilize an EIS?

11. Discuss the following in a small group of classmates: Based on your experiences with transaction processing systems (in everyday life and/or in the workplace), which ones used online processing and which used batch processing? Did these choices fit the system, the information, and the environment? Would you make any adjustments? Why?

12. Using any program you desire, create a template that you could use in the future to determine monthly payments on car loans. Use the situation within the chapter as an example of the kind of information that can change. Compare your template with those of several classmates. How are they different? Also, compare your group's templates with the one at http://carpoint.msn.com/LoanCalc. Would you have categorized the program you used to create this template as a decision support system before doing this exercise? Do you now?

13. Describe your experiences with expert systems to some of your classmates. In what situations were they encountered? Did you actually use the system or was it used by another individual on your behalf? Why would it be more beneficial for someone else to manipulate the expert system over yourself? What experiences have your classmates had with expert systems? (Hint: think about an automotive repair shop.)

14. Choose an organization with which you are familiar that utilizes office automation systems. Which systems do they use? Which functions have been automated and which have not been? Why have some functions not been automated? Who makes the decision of which office automation system to implement?

15. Conduct a search on the World Wide Web for "personnel management systems" using any browser you choose. Assuming that all these products perform basically the same tasks and provide the same basic functionality, what will make the difference in the purchasing decision? Personnel management is just one area in which management information systems are utilized. Do other areas have the same abundance of product choices as well?

16. Have each member of a small group interview an IS manager within an organization with which she is familiar. Of the three categories of information systems—transaction processing, management, and executive—which is utilized most in this organization? Why? Have any of these areas experienced an increase or decrease in the last few years? What predictions for the future does this manager have regarding traditional information systems? Do you agree? Prepare a 10-minute presentation to the class of your findings.

17. Imagine that you are Michelle Williams, the CIO of Big Loan Bank, as described in the scenario at the beginning of the chapter. The President of Big Loan Bank, George Hubman, wants to know whether you can help him. What do you tell him? If you are able to help, what type of information system would be appropriate for this situation? Why?

Real World Case Problems

1. Software for the Hard Sell: By Adding Functionality, Sales-force Automation Systems Are Overcoming a Bad Reputation.

The need for efficiency and increased productivity in sales has made automation a high priority with sales forces. Following years of unsuccessful implementations and lack of product acceptance, sales force automation software may be coming into use. Both Oracle and market leader Siebel Systems, Inc., are introducing major upgrades that will address traditional limitations by easing implements, improving usability, and connecting better with back-office applications, such as accounting and manufacturing systems. The SFA applications will significantly reduce selling cycles and create closer relations with customers. Applications include modules for tracking and prospecting sales, for analyzing customer data and for predicting future sales, and a sales-configuration system for helping users determine products and pricing arrangements.

When the Ritz-Carlton Hotel Co. in Atlanta started thinking about sales force automation in 1994, there was no appropriate software for them to use. Now the Ritz-Carlton plans to implement software from Sales Vision, Inc., for 700 of its sales reps by this summer. This will be the first attempt to coordinate all the hotels and salespeople on a single system. In the past, corporate customers such as meeting planners might receive phone calls from numerous Ritz-Carlton sales reps because information was not shared in the organization. This new system will help solve this coordination problem and enable the employees of the Ritz-Carlton to understand the needs of their customers.

Traditionally, this SFA software has underperformed because it had no vertical focus and because the original SFA software was more tailored to the sales manager than to the sales person. Sales people refused to use it because it didn't help them and they felt as if they were being micromanaged. Now the software has been redesigned and it focuses on different industries, such as insurance, banking, telecommunications, consumer packaged goods, and pharmaceuticals. This refocusing should dramatically decrease the implementation time.

Oracle and Onyx Software Corp. are joining the list of companies producing sales force automation software. They will also be unveiling new software designed for sales force applications and smaller companies. In late 1997, SAP bought a 50 percent stake in European Kiefer and Veittinger at the same time as they were developing their own product.

a. Should sales-force automation tools be categorized as decision support systems, office automation systems, transaction processing systems, or executive information systems? Why?

b. To which level within the organization (operational, managerial, or executive), and to which functional area of the firm are sales-force automation tools most useful?

c. Why is the use of sales-force automation tools so important to an organization such as the Ritz-Carlton Hotel?

Source *Stein, Tom. 1998. Software for the hard sell.* InformationWeek. *March 2, 18–19.*

2. Is It All a Project? Project Management Software Is Running across the Business.

Project management software, once the domain of small technical groups and highly technical industries, including aerospace, engineering, and defense, is now Web-based and easy to use, making the tools available for general business operations.

This software now runs applications such as financial and resource allocation projects. A.C. Nielson, an international marketing research company, now uses Project Planner (P3) software to plan and manage its budget. They use it to manage people working on multiple projects. With the tremendous change in organizational business, the capacity to estimate project completion is no longer enough.

The $850 million project management software market is expected to increase as much as 20 percent this year. Of this, desktop products make up almost $300 million of the market with Web-based, client-server, and mainframe products and services accounting for the rest. Of these software packages, Microsoft Project accounts for two-thirds of sales. Project 98, the newest version of MS Project, is simpler to use, has better control of project schedules, and includes Web features that allow for project member collaboration.

Web-enabled tools are enabling users who work from different computer platforms (for example, Windows-PCs, Macintosh PCs, UNIX Workstations) to access to project information. Charles Schwab & Company in San Francisco needed a Web-based project management system with cross-platform capabilities and real-time delivery and interactivity. They selected PlanView, Inc.'s Web-based software to implement consistency in how they manage their products.

Managers will have templates to guide them through the steps of the project, and to compare projects and have common expectations. With project management tools, there is a business process change that must take place. You must change the way people work, which is exactly the kind of cultural change that is the hardest to do.

a. To which level within the organization (operational, managerial, or executive) and which functional area of the firm is project management software most useful?

b. What is the pay-off to using project management software at a company like Charles Schwab & Co.? How can they justify spending up to $100,000 on project management software?

c. Why has it become so important to firms that project management software become Web-enabled?

Source *Carillo, Karen M. 1998. Is it all a project?* InformationWeek, *February 23, 100–106.*

References

Checkland, P.B. 1981. *Systems Thinking, Systems Practice.* Chichester: John Wiley.

Comshare. 1998. Information from: http://www.comshare.com. Information verified: March 12, 1998.

Ford. 1998. Information from: http://www.ford.com. Information verified: March 12, 1998.

HP. 1998. Information from: http://www.hp.com. Information verified: March 12, 1998.

IBM. 1998. Information from: http://www.ibm.com. Information verified: March 12, 1998.

MultiLogic. 1998. Information from: http://www.multilogic.com. Information verified: March 12, 1998.

PCN. 1998. Information from: http://www.pointcast.com. Information verified: March 12, 1998.

Sprague, R.H., Jr. 1980. A framework for the development of Decision Support Systems. *MIS Quarterly* 4(4): 1–26.

SAS. 1998. Information from: http://www.sas.com. Information verified: March 12, 1998.

Turban, E. (1995). *Decision Support and Expert Systems.* 4th ed. Prentice Hall: Englewood Cliffs, New Jersey.

Related Readings

Basu, A., and R.W Blanning. 1994. Metagraphs: A tool for modeling decision support systems. *Management Science* 40(12): 1579–1600.

Dutta, Wierenga, and Dalebout. 1997. Designing management support systems. *Communications of the ACM* 40(6): 70–79.

Gill, T.G. 1996. Expert system usage: Task change and intrinsic motivation, *Management Information Systems Quarterly* 20(3): 301–329.

Kasper, G.M. 1996. A theory of decision support system design for user calibration. *Information Systems Research* 7(2): 215–232.

Kendall, K.E. 1997. The significance of information systems research on emerging technologies: Seven information technologies that promise to improve managerial effectiveness. *Decision Sciences* 28(4): 775–792.

Leidner, D.E., and J.J. Elam. 1995. The impact of executive information systems on organizational design, intelligence, and decision making. *Organization Science,* 6(6): 645–664.

Mookerjee, V.S., and B.L. Dos Santos. 1993. Inductive expert system design: Maximizing system value. *Information Systems Research* 4(2): 111–140.

Rai, A., and D.S. Bajwa. 1997. An empirical investigation into factors relating to the adoption of executive information systems: An analysis of EIS for collaboration and decision support. *Decision Sciences* 28(4): 939–974.

Sharda, R., and D.M. Steiger. 1996. Inductive model analysis systems: Enhancing model analysis in decision support systems. *Information Systems Research* 7(3): 328–341.

Snead, K.C., and A.M. Harrell. 1994. An application of expectancy theory to explain a manager's intention to use a decision support system. *Decision Sciences* 25(4): 499–513.

Sprague, R. 1980. A framework for the development of decision support systems. *Management Information Systems Quarterly* 4(4): 1–25.

Vandenbosch, B., and S.L. Huff. 1997. Searching and scanning: How executives obtain information from executive information systems. *Management Information Systems Quarterly* 21(1): 81–107.

Watson, H.J., and M.N. Frolick. 1993. Determining information requirements for an EIS. *Management Information Systems Quarterly* 17(3): 255–269.

Ye, L.R., and P.E. Johnson. 1995. The impact of explanation facilities on user acceptance of expert systems advice. *Management Information Systems Quarterly* 19(2): 157–172.

Yoon, Guimaraes, and O'Neal. 1995. Exploring the factors associated with expert systems success. *Management Information Systems Quarterly* 19(1): 83–106.

Scenario: Collaboration Technologies for a Virtual Team

Assume that you work at a consulting firm that specializes in providing technical solutions for organizations. You typically work with a team of other consultants and have just begun a rather large, important project and have run into a bit of a problem. The client has asked your team to develop a new information system that pulls together data from several disparate systems. One morning your team discovers a problem in building an interface between the new system and one older system. You and your team members have never encountered anything like this and you need a solution as soon as possible.

To solve this problem, you need to talk to consultants and technical experts on other teams within your consulting firm and, perhaps, the systems staff within some of your firm's client organizations. Doing so requires multiple interactions and "question and answer" exchanges among all of these people. It would take far too long, and might be impossible, if you had to track down the people with the proper expertise using only the telephone, email, or regular mail ("snail mail"). Fortunately, your consulting firm has developed an online discussion database where you can interact with these other people and draw on the knowledge of literally thousands of other professionals within your firm (and many of your firm's clients, too). A discussion database enables multiple users around the world to post messages, documents, and file attachments to a common area. (See, for example, Figure 8.1, which shows a discussion database from Lotus Notes.) Anyone with access to the database can view the contents and participate in the discussion.

You go online and search the discussion database for topics that might provide information to help you solve your problem. Unfortunately, you find nothing that answers your question directly. Next, you pose a question to readers of the database summarizing the problem that you are having. Within hours you receive a message from a consultant describing exactly how to solve the problem. She even offers to send you a copy of the programming code used in her own similar system that will solve your problem.

You accept her offer, and within minutes receive the programming instructions attached to an email message (and also routed back out to the discussion database for others to use), along with her manager's approval to reuse the code that was intended for another client. After obtaining your own manager's approval, you integrate the code into your system. Using your firm's discussion database and email, you were able to completely solve within 48 hours a problem that, with only telephone, electronic mail, or snail mail, would have taken weeks or months to solve.

In this situation, the people collaborating to solve this problem act as members of a "virtual team," interacting quickly and remotely to solve this problem. After the problem is solved, the virtual team disbands and its members move on to other problems and virtual teams. To delay solving problems may mean angering a client, losing a current or future contract, or promoting an image of poor quality and service in the marketplace. In these situations, time really is money and teamwork is essential. Saving time and solving the problem quickly and easily reduces travel costs, helps to fulfill the contract with the client, and enhances the company's reputation for quality and service, which all directly affect the bottom line.

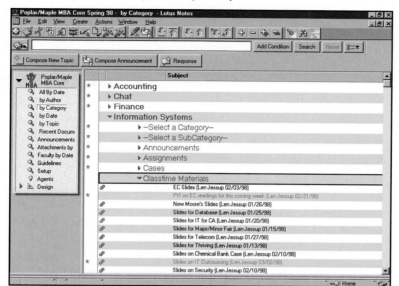

FIGURE 8.1

A discussion database enables multiple users to retrieve information from and post information to a common area.

Introduction

Customers have always hated waiting in line at the grocery store checkout counter. Not long ago, the problem was even worse because most cashiers had to manually enter the price of each grocery item using the keyboard on the cash register. Some early pioneers in this industry began using electronic scanners to very quickly and easily enter and tally the price of each item. Today, a modern grocery store would be far behind the competition if it didn't use such scanners. Similarly, early in the life of the Internet, some companies were quick to invest in interactive Web sites. These technology pioneers on the Web made it possible for their customers to get product information or even tell the company what it was doing, right or wrong. Other companies decided to wait for a while before risking any money linking to the Internet.

Grocery checkout scanners and Web sites are two common examples of information technologies that started out as innovations and soon became a more mainstream part of business. After reading this chapter, you will be able to do the following:

1. Explain why companies are continually looking for new ways to use technology for competitive advantage.

2. Describe specific examples of emerging information systems, such as videoconferencing, groupware, and group support systems for supporting collaboration and virtual teams.

3. Describe how companies are using computer kiosks, telephone interfacing, and the Internet and World Wide Web to support improved customer contact and reach.

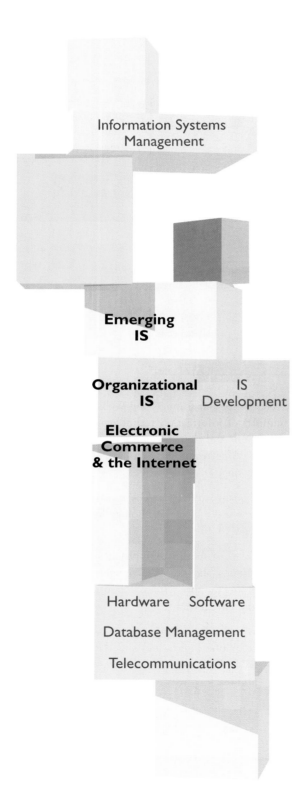

Information Systems
Management

Emerging
IS

Organizational   IS
IS   Development

Electronic
Commerce
& the Internet

Hardware   Software

Database Management

Telecommunications

This is the final chapter discussing the use of information systems in organizations and focuses on emerging types of systems (see Figure 8.2). It begins by describing the relationship between gaining and sustaining competitive advantage and emerging information systems. This is followed by a description of several types of emerging information systems.

Competitive Advantage in Being at the Cutting Edge

As discussed in the first chapter, an organization has a competitive advantage when it has an edge over rivals in attracting customers and defending against competitive forces. Competitive advantage is usually achieved when a company differentiates its product and service offerings from those of its competitors or operates at a lower cost structure than its competitors. Successful organizations typically have a strong competitive advantage, and smart organizations are continually working to either gain or sustain competitive advantage.

Why must organizations deploy "emerging" systems to gain a competitive advantage? To differentiate itself, an organization often must deploy new, state-of-the-art technologies to do things even better, faster, and cheaper than rivals that are using older technologies. Although contemporary organizational information systems, such as mainframe-based transaction processing, can be continually upgraded, these improvements can at best give only a short-lived competitive edge. To gain and sustain significant competitive advantage, firms must often deploy the latest technologies or deploy existing technologies in clever, new ways.

FIGURE 8.2

The big picture: focusing on emerging information systems.

Imagine, for example, that a manager decides to implement a local area network within a department to automate the operations of the office workers and to enable them to share peripheral devices, such as laser printers. This local area network is implemented using a Pentium-based personal computer with 32MB of RAM as a server for the network. This may seem like state-of-the-art computing to the office workers, but it is likely that rival firms have already been doing this for years. The manager might upgrade the server to a Pentium® II microprocessor and 64MB of RAM. Chances are that this would make the local area network run a bit faster than would the networks found at rival firms, but rivals can easily upgrade their own networks with faster, more powerful servers (and probably will!).

Consider another example. A firm implements a relational database management system for sales and inventory, giving it an edge over rivals in fulfilling orders faster and more accurately. Competitors soon do the same thing and it becomes necessary to improve to stay ahead. The firm could improve the system and gain a relatively small, short-lived advantage over rivals. Even better, the firm could extend this idea and implement similar database applications for all of its business processes and then integrate these applications with one another. Perhaps the firm could take one step further and enable customers and suppliers to access these systems directly. There is nearly always a better way to do thing, and new technologies to help you do things better. As they say, the best never rest.

Being at the Cutting Edge Versus the Bleeding Edge

There are limits to using emerging information systems to gain or sustain a competitive advantage. Information systems are often bought from, or built by, someone else. They are often either purchased from a vendor or developed by a consultant or outsourcing partner. In these situations, the information systems are usually not proprietary technologies owned by the organization. For example, although a soft drink company can patent the formula of a cola, or a pharmaceutical company can patent a new drug, an organization typically cannot patent its use of an information system, particularly if it was developed by someone else. The data in the system may be proprietary, but the information system typically is not.

Even in situations where an organization has developed an information system in-house, they usually do so with hardware, software, and networking components others can purchase. In short, rivals can copy emerging information systems, so this form of competitive advantage can be short-lived. Indeed, if use of the new system causes one organization to gain a significant advantage over others, smart rivals are quick to duplicate or better that use of the system.

Using emerging information systems always entails a risk. The classic example from consumer electronics is the choice of a VCR in the early days of that technology and the competing Betamax and VHS designs (see Figure 8.3). Most experts agreed that the Betamax had superior recording and playback quality, but VHS ultimately won the battle in the marketplace. People who made the "smart" choice at the time probably would have chosen a VCR with the Betamax design. Other examples in the field of consumer electronics abound today. For example, when buying a stereo today, should you invest in traditional compact disc technology (such as the read-only CD-ROM), recordable compact discs, digital audio tape, or some other technology? Many people have been stuck with huge collections of vinyl records, cassette tapes, or (gulp!) 8-track tapes. It is easy to make poor choices in consumer electronics, or to make choices that are good at the time but soon turn out to be poor choices.

Ned Matura/Gamma-Liaison International

FIGURE 8.3

Betamax tapes were shaped differently and required different technology inside the VCR than did VHS tapes.

Choosing among emerging information systems is just as difficult as choosing consumer electronics. In fact, choosing emerging systems may be far more difficult, given that the evolution of many consumer electronic technologies has stabilized while the evolution of emerging information systems is just beginning to heat up. Furthermore, it is far more devastating to choose an information system poorly due to the size of the investment and the mission-critical nature of the system. On the other hand, choosing a sub-optimal home stereo, although disappointing, is usually not devastating.

Choosing new technologies in the information systems area is like trying to hit one of several, equally attractive, fast-moving targets. You can find examples of the difficulty of forecasting emerging technologies in the experiences that many organizations have had in forecasting the growth, use, and importance of the Internet. The 1994 Technology Forecast prepared by the major consulting firm, Price Waterhouse, mentioned the word "Internet" on only five pages of the 750-page document. The next year over 75 pages addressed the Internet. In the 1997 briefing, the Internet is a pervasive topic throughout. Back in 1994 it would have been difficult, perhaps even foolish, to forecast such pervasive, rapidly growing business use of the Internet today. Table 8.1 illustrates how many people and organizations have had difficulty making technology-related predictions.

Table 8.1 Some predictions about technology that were not quite correct (Time, 1996).

Year	Source	Quote
1876	Western Union, internal memo	"This 'telephone' has too many shortcomings to be seriously considered as a means of communication. The device is inherently of no value to us."
1895	Lord Kelvin, president, Royal Society	"Heavier-than-air flying machines are impossible."
1899	C.H. Duell, commissioner, U.S. Office of Patents	"Everything that can be invented has been invented."
1927	H.M. Warner, Warner Brothers	"Who the hell wants to hear actors talk?"
1943	Thomas Watson, chairman, IBM	"I think there is a world market for maybe five computers."
1977	Ken Olsen, president, Digital Equipment Corporation	"There is no reason for any individuals to have a computer in their home."

Source   *Time 1996. The past imperfect:* Time Magazine. *July 15, 54.*

Given the pace of research and development in the information systems and components area, staying current has been nearly impossible. Probably one of the most famous metrics of computer evolution has been "Moore's Law." Intel founder Gordon Moore predicted that the number of transistors that could be squeezed onto a silicon chip would double every 18 months, and this prediction has proven itself over the past 20 years. In fact, some computer hardware and software firms roll out new versions of their products every three months. Keeping up with this pace of change can be difficult, if not unhealthy, for any organization.

The Nature of Emerging Systems

Many emerging technologies are focused on accomplishing two goals. The first goal is to support the work of **virtual teams**—people using technology to collaborate together more effectively to solve problems across time and distance. The second goal is to create more and better **customer contact** by integrating existing internal company systems for accounting, ordering, and billing, with telephones and personal computers via the Internet and enabling customers to have more direct contact with these internal systems.

One of the primary underlying technology drivers of emerging information systems is **technology convergence**. Devices that have long been separate kinds of technologies, such as telephones, computers, and video recorders, are converging. One example of the convergence of telephony and computers is in the pizza delivery business. Many pizza delivery businesses, such as Pizza Hut, Domino's, and Papa John's, now have their order entry computers linked to caller ID on the telephone line. When you call to place an order, their computer looks up the telephone number from the caller ID unit and displays the address for the clerk. This saves the customer from having to give his address every time and enables the clerks to handle more calls per hour. Another example of convergence is the capability to deliver textual, graphic, audio, or even video product literature over the Internet to customers' personal computers. Let's now discuss some of these emerging information systems for virtual teamwork and customer contact.

Requirements for Being at the Cutting Edge

Certain types of competitive environments require that organizations remain at the cutting edge in their use of information systems. For example, consider an organization that operates within an environment with strong competitive forces (Porter, 1979). The organization has competitive pressures coming from existing rival firms or from the threat of entry of new rivals. It is critical for these organizations to do things better, cheaper, and faster than rivals. These organizations are driven to deploy emerging information systems.

These environmental characteristics alone, however, are not enough to determine whether an organization should deploy emerging information systems. Before an organization can deploy new systems well, its people, structure, and processes must be capable of adapting well to change. An organization that has, say, a 10-month approval process for new information systems will probably have difficulty keeping up in an environment that forces organizations to decide on and deploy emerging information systems within a matter of weeks.

To deploy emerging systems well, people in the organization must be willing to do whatever they can to bypass and eliminate internal bureaucracy, set aside political squabbles, and pull together for the common good. Can you imagine, for example, trying to deploy a Web-based order entry system that enables customers to access inventory information directly, when people in that firm do not even share such information with each other?

Organizations deploying emerging systems must also have the human capital necessary to deploy the new systems. The organization must have enough employees available with the proper systems knowledge, skills, time, and other resources to deploy these systems. Alternatively, the organization must have resources and able systems partners available to outsource the development of such systems.

The last characteristic of an organization ready for the deployment of emerging systems is that its members must have the appropriate tolerance of risk, uncertainty, and problems to be willing to deploy and use emerging information systems that may not be as proven and pervasive as more traditional technologies. If people within the organization desire low risk and low return in their use of information systems, then gambling on cutting-edge systems will probably not be desirable or tolerable for them.

Implementing Emerging Systems

The development and use of technologies for virtual teamwork and for improved customer contact have grown considerably in the past several years. The technologies for virtual teamwork we'll discuss include videoconferencing, groupware, and group support systems. The technologies for customer contact include the Internet and the World Wide Web. We will discuss this examination of implementing emerging systems with a description of technologies for virtual teamwork, which are used to support collaboration among team members across time and distance.

Collaboration Technologies for Virtual Teamwork

To be competitive, organizations constantly need to bring together the right combinations of people who, together, have the appropriate set of knowledge, skills, information, and authority to solve problems quickly and easily. Traditionally, organizations have used task forces, which are temporary work groups with a finite task and life cycle, to solve problems that cannot be solved well by existing work groups. Unfortunately, traditional task forces, like traditional organizational structures, cannot always solve problems quickly. Structure and logistical problems often get in the way of people trying to get things done quickly.

Organizations need flexible teams that can be assembled quickly and can solve problems effectively and efficiently. Time is of the essence. Membership on these virtual teams is fluid, with teams forming and disbanding as needed, with team size fluctuating as necessary, and with team members coming and going as they are needed. Employees may, at times, find themselves on multiple teams, and the life of a team may be very short. In addition, team members must have easy, flexible access to other team members, meeting contexts, and information. Think of these virtual teams as dynamic task forces.

Traditional office technologies, such as telephones and pagers, are of some use to members of virtual teams, but are not well suited to support the types of collaboration described previously.

Telephones and pagers are not useful for rich, rapid, multiple-person team collaboration. This technology is best suited for person-to-person communication. Email is a useful technology for teams, but it does not provide the structure needed for effective multi-person interactive problem solving. Technologies that enable team members to interact through a set of media either at the same place and time or at different times and in different locations are needed, with structure to aid in interactive problem solving and access to software tools and information. A number of technologies, described in the following sections, fit the bill.

Videoconferencing

In the 1960s, at Disneyland and other theme parks and special events, the picturephone was first being demonstrated to large audiences. The phone company estimated that we would be able to see a live picture with our phone calls in the near future. It took another 30 years, but that prediction has come true within many organizations. Many organizations are conducting **videoconferencing**, and the demand for videoconferencing equipment is growing quickly. For example, sales for PictureTel, a leading videoconferencing company, grew from $37 million in 1990 to almost $500 million in 1997.

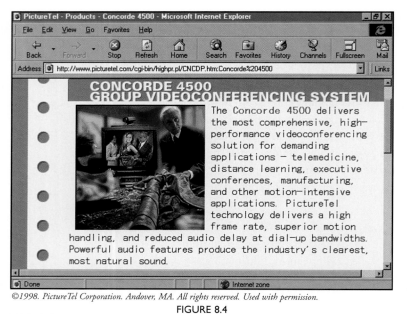

FIGURE 8.4

PictureTel's Concorde 4500 group videoconferencing unit provides television-quality video and stereo-quality sound via Bose speakers.

Figure 8.4 shows a videoconference being conducted with a textile manufacturing company.

Standalone Videoconferencing

Standalone videoconferencing products are relatively large, expensive units (approximately $30,000 and up), that have video quality similar to that of broadcast television and are used primarily to connect groups of people. For example, a conference room with three people in Washington might connect to a conference room with eight people in Indianapolis. In many cases, these systems have been built into special-purpose conference rooms, some costing hundreds of thousands of dollars to construct, but most often the systems used are portable and can be moved between rooms as needed. These videoconferencing units now have cameras that can pan left or right and zoom, user control panels, large television-like monitors, and special communications processors that connect to digital telephone lines. The units may also have document cameras to display documents remotely, or personal computer links, such as computer-based presentations, to be displayed on the monitors.

A BRIEF CASE

Videoconferencing in Singapore's Courts

An interesting application of standalone videoconferencing can be seen within the Singapore court system, in its subordinate courts, which are dispersed throughout the nation. To bring the subordinate court into the 21st century, and to enable the court system to provide a more efficient judicial process, Singapore is using videoconferencing in two innovative ways (PictureTel, 1998). First, videoconferencing is used to link witnesses to the court when testifying. This enables witnesses to be in a separate room in the same building or in some other location within the country. Judges have found that remote witnesses are more relaxed and comfortable than when in the courtroom with the defendant. As a result, people are more likely to come forward and are proving to be better witnesses. Second, subordinate courts throughout the country are linked to the country's central justice center. This enables people to appear before the courts in bail-related matters without having to be transported to the central justice center. As a result, bail hearings are now more likely to be on schedule and require less security because accused persons no longer need to be transported to the central courthouse. Videoconferencing has radically changed the Singapore court system. Likewise, organizations all over the world are using videoconferencing to change the way people work together.

Desktop Videoconferencing

Desktop videoconferencing represents a second generation of video communication that has been enabled by the growing power of personal computer processors. A desktop system usually has a fast personal computer, a small camera (often with fixed focus, though zooming and panning features are available), a speaker telephone or separate microphone, videoconferencing software, and a special video board installed inside the computer. These units typically work with special digital ISDN phone lines, available from telephone service providers in most parts of the world. One popular desktop videoconferencing product has been the Intel Proshare system, which can be purchased for approximately $1,000 per unit, plus the cost of the personal computer and the installation of the digital phone line. Installing a digital phone line usually costs about as much as installing a normal analog phone line, but the cost varies widely from region to region.

Courtesy Intel Corporation Internet & Communications Group
FIGURE 8.5

Intel Proshare units such as this one begin at about $1,000 and can be used with standard personal computers.

Most desktop videoconferencing systems, like the one shown in Figure 8.5, have three key features. First, they are easily available on a user's desk for ad-hoc meetings, so users no longer have to schedule or go to a conference room to use the group videoconferencing facility. Because these units are significantly less expensive than the larger units, many units can be purchased for the price of one dedicated standalone system.

A second feature is that desktop videoconferencing units can support software **application sharing**. Application sharing enables two people to collaborate using software on their personal computers in separate locations. For example, if I call you and we are both using desktop videoconferencing systems, I can launch a spreadsheet package from my computer and begin entering a budget with formulas. On your screen, you can drag the video window of me to the side and see in real-time the spreadsheet that I am building. Suppose that you have some of the budget information. Rather than read it to me so that I can enter it on my screen, you can take control of the spreadsheet on your screen and use the software just as if it were running on your personal computer. We can hear and see each other and everything we do on our individual computers. This form of collaboration can be a very valuable way to make meetings more effective. People can jointly work out solutions with software to support their interactions rather than work separately and send their results back and forth via mail or fax.

The third feature of desktop videoconferencing units is shared **whiteboarding software**. Just like a mark-and-wipe whiteboard in a classroom, whiteboarding software enables users to draw with a mouse or type text and display it remotely to another unit. For example, if your friend is having trouble describing to you the new floor plan for his dorm room, he can open an additional window on both his and your computer screens and sketch out a shared whiteboard space with his vision for the new floor plan. If you have a suggestion, you can draw it on the sketch provided for you on your screen, and your friend can see your additions to the sketch in real-time on his screen.

A BRIEF CASE

BMW

An example of a company using desktop videoconferencing is BMW, one of the leading automobile manufacturers in Europe (Intel, 1998). Like most automobile manufacturers, BMW gets a substantial number of its components from suppliers. In an attempt to speed the design and development of supplier-provided components, BMW used Intel's ProShare desktop videoconferencing system. For example, the supplier that provides bumpers for the Three Series automobiles is about 500km from BMW's main design facility in Munich. Despite this distance, design engineers at the two companies can work closely with each other, just as if they were in the same office, using ProShare. BMW reports that the time needed to finalize designs is being greatly reduced by desktop videoconferencing. In addition, fewer face-to-face meetings are needed; this reduction in travel equates to savings from reduced fares, accommodations, and time spent in transit. Desktop videoconferencing is accelerating the design process from BMW, resulting in substantial time and cost savings.

Limits to Videoconferencing

Although videoconferencing is a promising new technology that is growing rapidly in development and use, it has limits. One problem with desktop videoconferencing is the cost of providing digital telephone lines to many offices. It is relatively easy to pick up a standard analog telephone and place a call to most of the world, yet, most people do not have digital phone lines to support videoconferencing capabilities. As a result, videoconferencing has had limited widespread success.

Another limit to desktop videoconferencing using digital phone lines is the lack of a universally agreed upon standard, which is essential for widespread adoption of videoconferencing. Companies are understandably reluctant to invest in any unit that may not be able to communicate with units made by another company. Fortunately, the International Telecommunications Union (ITU) standards body has established a standard for videoconferencing that they have labeled H.320. A unit from any company that supports the H.320 standard can videoconference with any other H.320-compliant unit. This standard enables even desktop units to communicate with group videoconferencing systems. Because standards evolve more slowly than vendors come up with new and useful features, many of the newer features are not supported in the H.320 standard and cannot be used across different brands of units until a new standard evolves.

One other limit to most videoconferencing units is that they are point-to-point; that is, there are only two locations involved. What if you need to meet with colleagues in Vancouver, New Delhi, and Seoul simultaneously while you are stuck in Aspen? Can everyone videoconference together at the same time? Assuming that everyone has access to videoconferencing systems and digital telephone lines, it is possible to have a *multipoint* conference. One way is to use a *bridge*, a device linking multiple videoconferencing units together that is sometimes called a **multipoint control unit** *(MCU)*. Point-to-point and multipoint conferencing are depicted in Figure 8.6. Some companies own or lease a bridge, but most make arrangements with a long distance carrier such as Sprint and Deutche Telekom to rent time on one. Each colleague dials a special telephone number and the carrier's bridge connects everyone together. Some bridges can even do translation between different videoconferencing systems that might not all support the same communications standard. The bridge uses a *follow me* type of coordination. For example, if your colleague in Seoul starts speaking, the bridge activates her camera and sends her image and voice to the other three participants. When you start talking, it switches to your unit in Aspen and sends your picture to the others. Switching can sometimes take a few seconds, so the meeting has to be somewhat orderly. The bridge gets very confused if everyone talks at once!

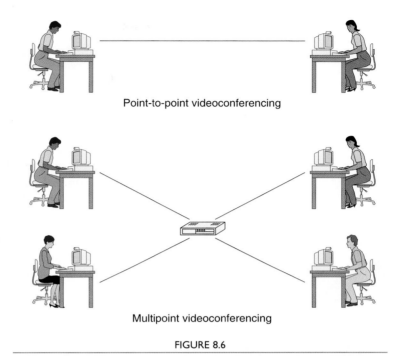

Point-to-point videoconferencing

Multipoint videoconferencing

FIGURE 8.6

Point-to-point conferencing versus multipoint conferencing. Desktop videoconferencing units have traditionally enabled only point-to-point communication, but new technology now enables multipoint desktop videoconferencing.

What you would ideally like is four tiled windows on your PC showing your three colleagues and a feedback window showing what your camera is sending. This is referred to as **continuous presence** and obviously requires more communications bandwidth to each unit. Some bridges can support continuous presence. Standard H.324 is the successor standard to H.320. The H.324 standard specifies how additional services, such as application sharing and multipoint conferencing, are to be implemented by any videoconferencing manufacturer. The standard also specifies how these services can be delivered without special digital telephone lines by using the existing POTS (Plain Old Telephone Service) lines. Videoconferencing is definitely another technology that keeps managers on the technology treadmill.

One important question that business people ask is whether videoconferencing will replace travel. Experts argue that videoconferencing, email, and other wired communication technologies will *increase* rather than decrease our demand for airline travel. They believe that these technologies will enable us to make more contacts and have more reasons for communication, setting up a spiral that requires more travel for face-to-face meetings and more videoconferencing. In fact, new airliners are even being designed to support videoconferencing services at each passenger seat. Think of it: In the not-too-distant future you could be on a plane to Singapore to meet with a new client. While enroute, you attend a meeting with the Asia sales team via videoconferencing and receive a fax from the home office in Brussels. Although such a scenario would be costly today, the time will come very soon when it is more economically feasible.

Within companies, however, videoconferencing systems available today are already demonstrating that they can be used effectively and can provide a real cost savings when compared to performing the same work without the technology. For example, managers at Royal Insurance, a multinational corporation based in the United Kingdom, use videoconferencing to deliver employee training. They have found that their use of video-conferencing has enabled them to reduce training travel costs by $250,000 a year and overall training costs by 92 percent. In addition, they have decreased their employees' time away from the office, and they now disseminate training information more effectively and efficiently. Because the training programs are now more accessible, many more employees get to participate. Like Royal, other organizations are finding clever ways to deploy videoconferencing to enable them to be better, work faster, and cut costs.

Quickcam is a registered trademark of Connectix Corporation

FIGURE 8.7

Connectix Color QuickCam.

Desktop videoconferencing now has some less expensive alternatives, although the quality of the video and audio is not as good as with the desktop units described previously. For example, for around $100 you can purchase a Color QuickCam, made by Connectix, which plugs directly into the parallel port on your personal computer (see Figure 8.7). You can then use desktop videoconferencing software, such as Microsoft's NetMeeting, available for free from Microsoft's Web site, and conduct desktop videoconferencing sessions with friends, family, and colleagues through the Internet using a standard analog phone line. If you want to have audio, you need a multimedia PC with sound card and speakers. You speak into the microphone plugged into your sound card and hear other people through the speakers that are plugged into your sound card. You pay only for your connection to the Internet, even if you're conferencing with someone halfway around the world! Although the video and audio are not as good as they are with the more expensive, ISDN-based conferencing units, the quality is acceptable for most uses. Software such as NetMeeting offers whiteboarding, the sharing of Microsoft software applications such as Word and Excel, and electronic chat. All in all, not bad for an additional investment in your PC of about $100!

Groupware

The term **groupware** refers to a class of software that enables people to work together more effectively. Lotus Development puts groupware in the mainstream when it introduced the Notes software product in 1989. In recent years, many new groupware products have emerged, several of which work through or with the Internet. At its core, groupware enables people to *communicate*, to *collaborate*, and to *coordinate* their activities. Just as Henry Ford improved the manufacturing processes with more sophisticated use of assembly lines, new tools such as groupware are needed to improve the way people work together to perform knowledge work in the information age. Figure 8.8 shows a Lotus Notes page used to organize a variety of teaching functions.

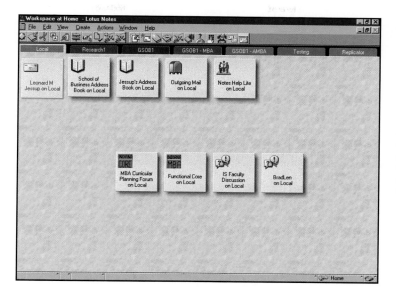

FIGURE 8.8

Lotus Notes is an award-winning groupware application with an installed base of millions of users worldwide.

©1997 Lotus Development Corporation. Used with permission of Lotus Development Corporation. Lotus and Lotus Notes are registered trademarks of Lotus Development Corporation.

One industry sector that has come to rely on groupware products quite a bit is consulting. For example, Price Waterhouse, Coopers & Lybrand, and Andersen Consulting are three of the biggest Notes users in the country. At Chicago-based Andersen, Notes is being used as the basis for Andersen's Knowledge-Xchange, an information management system that enables Andersen's consultants to exchange and share data with each other. With well over 30,000 people now working for the company all over the world in different time zones, it is much more difficult to locate and contact the experts within the company for advice. All the large consulting firms are experiencing this problem and are using groupware to help solve this problem.

Groupware at Peat Marwick
A BRIEF CASE

When KPMG Peat Marwick consultants go to a client's office, they take 75,000 professionals with them. That may sound a little cramped, but this is in virtual terms. Over the past several years Peat Marwick has been developing Knowledge Manager, an online knowledge base that enables Peat Marwick consultants to get a helping hand from their colleagues around the world (Stahl, 1994). Knowledge Manager enables employees to make use of a vast store of information and experiences about practically everything associated with the company's accounting and consulting business. From their PCs, Macintoshes, or laptops, consultants can click on a number of different folders to gain access to hundreds of gigabytes of information. Folders contain detailed information on client experiences, proposals, resumes, methodologies, best practices, vendors, demos, and more. "Help Wanted" is one of the popular folders on the system. Here, any consultant can post a request for help on a particular project. Consultants typically get feedback to their questions within an hour. Clearly, groupware is enabling Peat Marwick associates to more effectively communicate, collaborate, and coordinate.

—————— **Using Lotus Notes at Bayer Drug** ——————

Likewise, developing a new pharmaceutical drug is a long and complex process. Drug companies must take meticulous notes, run innumerable tests, and submit countless reports to pass the requirements for drug approval. Developing a new drug costs approximately $500 million and takes as long as 12 years. The amount of paperwork required by the Food and Drug Administration (FDA) over the duration of the process can fill three large trailers. Most drug companies are multinational companies that sell their products to a global market and therefore must gain approvals in each separate market. Many drug companies have separate groups in each major market working to gain approval in their local markets because the drug approval process differs substantially from country to country. Yet much of the testing information and results must be shared and coordinated. It is easy to see that to be successful in the drug approval process requires the communication, collaboration, coordination of many people, and a great deal of information. Bayer Drug Company, therefore, uses Lotus Notes to streamline their drug approval process throughout the world (Lotus, 1998). Using Notes, scientists around the world can stay informed on developments in other parts of the world and can more easily share information. The efforts of separate groups within the organization at each location, such as marketing, research and development, and engineering, are now much more coordinated. Using groupware, Bayer is significantly reducing the time and cost to develop new drugs.

Groupware to Communicate

So is groupware just a fancy name for email? Not at all. The communication part of groupware can be email that supports point-to-point messages or broadcasts to a distribution list. Email is a great way to communicate when both the sender and the recipient(s) agree that the transfer of a message in this way is both timely and useful. However, email-based communication is often misused and can be both inefficient and ineffective. To understand this, you need to first understand the difference between push and pull in electronic communication. Email is push-based. For example, I push some information into your mailbox when I think you need to know it. Unfortunately, I may push things into your mailbox that you might not want. With all of us pushing unwanted messages to each other, we clutter each other's mailboxes. In addition, we each have to keep duplicate copies of the really important messages in our mailboxes and, if we're lucky, be able to find them amidst the clutter.

For some tasks, a more effective way of communicating for the recipient is to be able to go to a centralized location for information and find and pull desired information when the recipient needs it. To enable pull-based forms of communication, an organization needs to have a place to store and index information. Groupware can provide these places, which are often called **information repositories** or **discussion databases**.

Groupware to Collaborate

Consider an example of how a consultant at Andersen Consulting used his company's groupware application. He has been invited to make a presentation to business school students regarding employment opportunities at Andersen Consulting. In the past, he would have used his personal computer and some presentation software, along with an hour or more of his time, to create a professional presentation. With groupware the process is much easier and the product much better. The consultant looks in a repository of presentations that is available to thousands of Andersen employees worldwide. He quickly finds a presentation file that had been done in Microsoft's PowerPoint, complete with speaker's notes. He downloads the presentation to his PC and makes a few edits so that it reflects the latest changes at Andersen. He then posts the updated presentation back to the repository with a note saying that it has been updated. This process would have been completely ineffective if the creator of the presentation had emailed it to thousands of Andersen employees "just in case" they ever needed it.

Think about the efficiencies for Andersen Consulting in this brief illustration. The company had already invested time and energy in addressing the problem of preparing a professional presentation. Through groupware, all employees could have access to this rather than having dozens of employees around the world each spending time to create a bunch of different and inconsistent presentations. This same process is used with software programming code, contracts, proposals, and other documents in the company.

In addition to information repositories, many companies use groupware for sharing questions and best practices. For example, similar to the discussion database described in the scenario that opened this chapter, a company that has field service technicians can maintain a repository of online technical manuals and procedures for servicing its products. The field technicians can use notebook computers and telephone lines to access the online manuals for specific problems. Most forms of groupware also support threaded discussion forums. A threaded discussion, first popularized by online bulletin board systems, shows textual conversations as continuous, chronologically ordered strings of text. If a technician cannot find a solution to a difficult problem in the manuals, he can post a question in a discussion forum, asking, "Does anyone know how to make the ABC switch work properly with the new version 3.2 of the software?" Other technicians can also monitor the discussion forum and post a response if they know the answer.

Companies that are using groupware often have many different discussion forums that build communities of expertise around specific topics. As you can imagine, some of these discussion forums or knowledge repositories can get very large over time, with thousands of postings. Some organizations have created a new job of **knowledge manager** or librarian to administer this part of groupware. The knowledge manager sets policies and makes decisions regarding the creation, retirement, and content of discussion databases.

Groupware to Coordinate

Groupware can also provide a way for people to coordinate their actions. Groupware can be programmed to support sophisticated workflow among people and departments. For example, consider how Amy, a sales representative, might fill out an online form outlining her itinerary for the next week. The itinerary requires her to fly from her home office in Phoenix to spend two days in Denver, then drive to have dinner with a customer in Boulder, and depart the next morning for a trade show in Mexico City. The itinerary can be automatically routed to the area sales manager for approval. Using groupware, the area sales manager can review and then digitally sign the itinerary, which is automatically routed to a travel agency. The travel agent searches for the best prices and times for flights, accommodations, and rental cars, and posts these back into the itinerary. The itinerary then routes back to Amy, who then knows her flight schedule and confirmation numbers. Groupware's workflow capabilities enable users to focus their time, better applying their talents and reducing the time spent playing telephone tag or chasing information from others.

Now, consider a secondary benefit of the workflow example. Suppose that the national sales manager hears by chance that a major customer will be in Denver next week. Before groupware he would have sent an email message or phoned the area managers to find out if a sales representative could be sent to Denver. With groupware, he can search the itineraries of all sales people and discover that Amy will already be in Denver during those days. Notice that he did not have to interrupt anyone else's work to get this information.

So What Is Groupware?

Now that you've seen a few examples of how groupware can be used for communication, collaboration, and coordination, what exactly is groupware? Any attempts to define groupware by its technology building blocks (for example, databases, clients and servers, agents) is not helpful because many of these same kinds of technologies are used in other categories of software. The groupware category is best defined by its capability to enable communication, collaboration, and coordination rather than by its technologies. Table 8.2 lists some of the key features of groupware.

Table 8.2   Key features of groupware.

Groupware Feature	Benefit
Rich documents	Documents can include special fonts and formatting, attachments such as a Microsoft Excel spreadsheet, a Lotus Freelance presentation, a scanned image of a written message, or even an audio recording. Groupware becomes an indexed repository for all of a group's documents.
Links	Users can build ad hoc hypertext links between documents to form a web of knowledge or information.
Replication	Replication control is critical for scaling up groupware to support many people. It helps IS managers balance the load on servers and reduce communication costs between locations. Ensures that all users are acting on the same timely information.
Full text searching	Essential for ad hoc queries, it finds all entries related to a topic of interest.
Security	Authentication ensures that the server recognizes the user as the person she claims to be. Access control can be used to give different users varying capabilities to view or add data or make changes to the structure of the database.
Messaging	Provides support for point-to-point or broadcast email.
Calendaring	Provides a shared calendar for scheduling and coordinating with others.
Workflow	Automates and allows the redesign of the steps making up business processes to streamline activities and eliminate excessive paper flow.
Connectivity	Internet connectivity and support for open standards are essential for long-term viability.

One key feature of managing groupware for many users is a process called **replication**, which is used to synchronize databases—such as discussion forums and information repositories—that are stored on multiple servers. For example, you might post a change to a product description entry on a server in your building. An associate is located in another building or another country and also has access to the same database on her local server. The servers are configured to replicate their common databases on a regular interval, such as once a day or every 10 minutes. The information that you change on your server is sent to the other server so that you both have local access to the same up-to-date information. Without replication it can be very expensive, and response times can be slow, if the remote user has to access the original database on your server every time she needs some information. Replication provides for very efficient use of communication lines between servers because it only transmits the items that have changed rather than a new copy of the database.

Groupware Products

Lotus Notes laid early claim to the groupware market, but the Internet's open standards for HTTP and HTML, along with Java scripting languages, have introduced a flurry of competitors. Following IBM's $3.2 billion purchase of Lotus in 1995, Lotus announced its technology strategy to position Notes as an integrated part of the Internet and corporate intranets. This means that people using Web browsers from Netscape or Microsoft have access to documents stored on Notes servers and that the Internet can provide the communication link between servers. In a move to offer groupware features, Netscape has integrated a threaded discussion forum in its Web server software and clients to support group collaboration. Microsoft's Exchange server also supports some of the messaging and collaboration features described previously in Table 8.1.

Hurdles to Successful Groupware Implementation

In the best-selling book, *All I Really Need to Know I Learned in Kindergarten*, author Robert Fulghum argued that as children our learning to share was probably one of our most important lessons. His argument certainly holds true for groupware implementations. When implementing groupware, the biggest hurdle isn't necessarily technical; rather, the most difficult hurdle is often convincing users to share information with each other (Stahl, 1994). Workers who have put their own blood, sweat, and tears into a project are sometimes reluctant to let others benefit from it. For example, groupware users are often reluctant to share sales information or customer leads, which is problematic given that sales applications are perhaps the most popular for groupware implementations. This does not mean that employees are necessarily stingy with their ideas; rather, they are responding to the work rules and incentives that don't reward sharing. Think back to the opening scenario, in which the consultant asked for help on the consulting firm's online discussion database. If that firm had a reward system that rewarded individual effort only and inhibited sharing, the consultant may never have received help from another employee.

In other cases employees are afraid to share information that may somehow harm their careers or their business unit. After a groupware implementation in one chemical company, management learned via information sharing that one of the company's projects seemed unlikely to gain approval from the Food and Drug Administration. They subsequently laid off the group that was working on the project. The effect on other workers was that no one wanted to continue sharing information.

Experts say that companies wishing to implement groupware should give employees incentives for sharing. For example, the sales representative who initiates the customer lead should still get credit if the sale is ultimately closed by someone else. Alternatively, salespeople could be rewarded directly for the number of customer lead "handoffs" they give to other sales people, or they could be rewarded more indirectly by being given additional bonuses for the overall sales activity of the group. Ernst & Young actually includes an evaluation of sharing in employees' performance reviews. Another consulting firm, McKinsey and Co., judges consultants' performance, in part, on how many times information they've contributed to a shared database is accessed by others. In short, an organization can promote sharing in a number of ways. Given that groupware applications are premised on collaboration and sharing, organizations should do all they can to promote these types of behaviors. Simply giving them the technology to collaborate and share is not enough.

Group Support Systems

Although many forms of groupware can be used to help groups communicate, collaborate, and coordinate, one category of groupware focuses on helping groups make better decisions. These systems are commonly referred to as **group support systems** (GSSs). A GSS is a computer-based information system used to support collaborative goal-directed work (Jessup and Valacich, 1993). A GSS is essentially a collection of personal computers networked together with sophisticated software tools to help group members solve problems and make decisions through interactive, electronic idea generation, evaluation, and voting (see Figure 8.9). Whereas a decision support system is typically used to support one user in decision making, GSSs are used to support multiple, interacting users participating in a variety of tasks.

Some typical uses for GSSs include strategic planning sessions, marketing focus groups, brainstorming sessions for system requirements definition, business process reengineering, and quality improvement. GSSs have traditionally been housed within a dedicated meeting facility, as shown in Figure 8.10. However, GSSs are also being implemented with notebook computers so that the system can be taken on the road, as shown in Figure 8.11. Additionally, Web-based implementations are supporting distributed meetings where group members access the GSS software from their computers in their offices or from home. Several different types of related systems fall under the GSS umbrella. Some of these related areas of research and development are group decision support systems, electronic meeting systems, negotiation support systems, and computer-mediated communication systems.

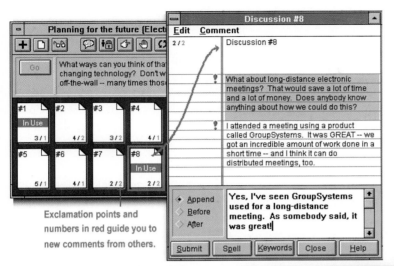

Exclamation points and numbers in red guide you to new comments from others.

FIGURE 8.9

GroupSystems users can build a meeting agenda, invite participants, and run a meeting—all online.

Courtesy Ventana Corporation

FIGURE 8.10

A computer-supported meeting facility, complete with networked PCs and GSS software.

Courtesy Ventana Corporation

FIGURE 8.11

An IBM facilitation services room in North Carolina.

Courtesy Ventana Corporation

ETHICAL PERSPECTIVE: THE ETHICS OF MARKET DOMINATION

Nearly every industry has a handful of recognized market leaders. Breakfast cereal has Kellogg's, Post, and General Mills. Household products have Johnson & Johnson, Procter & Gamble, and Colgate-Palmolive. The U.S. domestic automobile industry is dominated by the "big three." Similarly, within certain sectors of the computing industry, clear single leaders have emerged who seem to have captured the lion's share of their market.

Lotus, now part of IBM, has long dominated the groupware software category. An even stronger market domination can be found in Intel Corporation's domination of the market for semiconductor chips, motherboards, and CPUs, particularly for CPUs for personal computers. Intel has taken away from the Japanese a market that has for decades been under their control. Intel controls approximately 85 percent of its markets, and its revenues are growing exponentially as the entire world becomes computerized. Likewise, Microsoft Corporation has emerged as the dominant player in the personal computer software industry, especially for operating systems and for office productivity applications. What differentiates these technology companies from the market-leading firms listed in the previous paragraph is that they have gained greater market domination than thought possible in an extremely short period of time—only 20 years or so since they emerged onto the scene.

Ongoing controversy about monopolistic actions and unfair business practices has so far done nothing to slow the growth of both Intel and Microsoft. Intel chips are used around the world in personal and business computers. Microsoft's software is widely used in businesses and educational institutions, as well as home computing. In fact, Microsoft's designers rely on capability specifications from Intel's designers when new applications or upgrades are created, so that their software will be ensured compatibility with the computer in which it runs. Similarly, Intel wants to make sure there will be a need for its new or upgraded product, so its engineers rely on software release dates from Microsoft to ensure their chip is on the market simultaneously. The "Win-tel" Windows/Intel combination has been hard to beat!

With this worldwide usage comes the problem of compatibility with products from other companies. After a business begins using Microsoft software products, it is very easy to purchase upgrades or new applications as they are available. Little re-training is necessary for the employees and the transition is minimal. In addition, Microsoft typically offers very inexpensive upgrades to owners of previous versions of its software and it's easy to rely on Microsoft's extensive support system. When purchasing software packages, it is much simpler to choose the package of the leader, knowing that the future will bring upgrades, support, and minimal transition difficulties.

Due to its size and experience, Intel is able to develop, test, and manufacture new chips at faster rates than its competitors. The lag time is in many cases around 9–12 months, with multiple chip design teams working in parallel in a leap-frog fashion at Intel. Therefore, when Intel introduces a new product, it is often the only seller in the market. Its competition will not have a suitable product for at least six months.

Microsoft and Intel have brought us many useful, innovative products. What's wrong with their domination of these markets? Some people argue that the Win-tel stranglehold unfairly blocks other smaller companies from entering certain markets. Others add that without intense competition, Microsoft and Intel aren't pushed to make revolutionary advances, and other firms don't have the power to do so, so we're left with the evolutionary, incremental advancements that Microsoft and Intel choose to give us.

Questions for Discussion

1. Do you agree with the potential disadvantages of market domination that were described previously? Why or why not? What are some other potential disadvantages not listed?

2. What are some other benefits to having companies such as Microsoft and Intel dominate a technology market other than those discussed here?

3. Is the dominance of Microsoft and Intel just a natural artifact of the free enterprise system that should be allowed to play itself out? Are technology-related industries somehow different from other industries, and perhaps more vital to national interests? Should they therefore be dealt with (for example, monitored and/or regulated) differently than other industries?

INTERNATIONAL PERSPECTIVE: COLLABORATING ACROSS SPACE, TIME, AND CULTURE

Some people have trouble communicating effectively with other people from their own culture, even in face-to-face interaction. Individuals are probably more likely to encounter differences and potential difficulty in collaborating with someone from another culture than they are in collaborating with someone from their own culture. Assuming that the relatively easy aspects (for example, time zone differences and technological connectivity and compatibility) are taken care of, the remaining issues to consider are communication and the collaboration processes.

Imagine how much more difficult communication can be if it is mediated by technology and if, in addition, it is cross-cultural! The difficulty, and the corresponding opportunities to mangle meaning, rises dramatically. Not only are the communicators likely to speak different "first" languages, but they may not share assumptions, expectations, rules for what to say, what not to say, how to say things, to whom one can say things, and so on.

To make matters worse, these people are communicating through technology that limits the type of information that can be exchanged (not to mention the chances of cross-platform technology incompatibility!). This scenario involves not only mere communication, but untangling the logistics of actually trying to work together to complete a task, to solve a problem, and to share data, documents, and other digital resources. Although the participants may eventually learn and improve at communicating with each other in this way, the primary differences among the participants and the attendant learning curve may initially be daunting.

People on either side of the collaboration can differ from each other in many ways. In addition to differences in "first" language and communication style, individuals and groups may differ in whether or not they use information systems and, if so, in which information systems they use, how they use them, and whether these systems are compatible. Individuals and their computer systems may also differ in a number of aspects: For example, some cultures are far more polite and indirect in discourse than are individuals in some other cultures. To make matters even more difficult, colors and icons can have different meanings in different cultures. Nothing can be taken for granted.

Imagine that you are viewing both sides of a teleconference between members of a traditional Japanese business organization on one side, and members of a contemporary American business organization on the other side. The seating arrangement and behaviors of the Japanese business members would probably be such that it would be relatively easier to readily identify the person in authority there than on the American side. How should you accommodate that difference? Or, for example, suppose that you are dealing with business people from a country such as China or Saudi Arabia, where there is little or no law enforcement to protect the copyright of information—and in fact where information is believed to be owned and rightfully accessible by all. Perhaps in the cultures of your global partners women do not work in business environments. How do you decide on what role your female CEO will play?

Generally, cultural differences have many opportunities to surface, which initially presents potential difficulties and problems for collaborating effectively. What happens in each instance depends on which individuals, organizations, cultures, and technologies are involved. In addition, the effectiveness of the collaboration depends on the participants' experience in collaborating in this way and their sensitivity to potential cultural differences. In the future, individuals will use a variety of technologies to collaborate across space and time.

Questions for Discussion

1. What questions would you, as a manager, need to ask before setting up a global conference?

2. What special arrangements or considerations would need to be made?

3. What kind of training program could you develop to assist your employees with effective global collaboration?

Source *Jessup, L. 1996. April. The role of the international office worker of the future: Organizational, social, and cultural issues. Paper presented at the IFIP Conference on the International Office of the Future, Tucson, AZ.*

── **Using a GSS at Chevron Pipeline** ──

An example of where a GSS provided significant benefits can be found at Chevron Pipeline, an operating company of Chevron Corporation, which transports crude oil, refined products, natural gas, and chemicals throughout the U.S. When Chevron Pipeline established 14 teams to analyze critical business processes, such as customer order fulfillment and customer service, the first team was charged to analyze procurement services (Ventana, 1998). This team began their work by using traditional meeting tools, such as flip charts and white boards. Unfortunately, using this process for their initial meeting, the group felt frustrated by their slow progress. In an attempt to improve their meetings, the team used a GSS, GroupSystems by Ventana, for their next and subsequent meetings. Chevron feels that, by switching to GroupSystems, the team was able to complete their task of analyzing procurement services in half the time. After analyzing the procurement services process and implementing the team's recommendation, Chevron estimates that they will save more than $5 million per year. As a result of this team's success, all remaining process improvement teams used GroupSystems to support their meetings.

The Need for GSS

One powerful force in organizations that has fueled the use of GSS has been the trend toward the use of teams. There are several advantages to getting work done in groups, referred to as group process gains (Nunamaker, Dennis, Valacich, Vogel, and George, 1991). For example, a group has more information than any one member; groups are better at catching errors than are the individuals that propose them; group members can stimulate each others' creativity; and group members can learn from each other.

Unfortunately, group process gains are sometimes outweighed by group process losses. To understand these process losses and the need for GSS, think about one of the most common forms of group work: meetings. Most face-to-face meetings are very inefficient. In fact, the 3M Corporation, which conducts a great deal of research on meeting effectiveness, estimates that billions of dollars annually are wasted by U.S. companies in inefficient meetings. Table 8.3 lists several social, psychological, and structural problems that make meetings unproductive (adapted, in part, from Nunamaker, et al., 1991).

Table 8.3 Factors that lead to unproductive meetings.

Social/Psychological Meeting Problems	Structural Meeting Problems
Dominant people dominate the meeting	Not enough time for everyone to speak
Shy people do not participate	Incomplete access to necessary external information
People are intimidated by others of higher rank	Incomplete analysis and understanding of task
Politics and emotions get in the way	People get off the task
People are too polite or afraid to criticize others	Spend too much time on one agendaitem
People "free ride" on the efforts of others	Meeting runs over the time allotted
People are overloaded with information	Lack of clear agenda

Social/Psychological Meeting Problems	Structural Meeting Problems
People just want the group to agree	Agenda is not passed out well before meeting
Person forgets his idea while focusing on someone else's comments	Good notes are not kept

Group process problems that are commonly found in meetings also happen in nearly every other setting where people come together to collaborate, and many attempts have been made to improve group performance (see, for example, Van Gundy, 1988). To clearly demonstrate the problems with meetings, one organization used a simulated "clock" on a computer screen that ticked away the seconds for all to see during meetings. The interesting thing about this clock, however, was that rather than ticking away seconds it ticked away dollars, calculated with the salaries and wages of meeting participants. The clock often showed that thousands of dollars were being spent deciding on problems that of themselves were a matter of only a few dollars. The goal of GSS designers is therefore very straightforward: to design tools to maximize group process gains while minimizing group process losses.

The Benefits of GSS

Consider how a meeting would be different if the participants each had a personal computer connected to a LAN and running GSS software. The software supports interactive idea generation so that everyone can type in ideas at the same time. Everyone can see the list of ideas that has been proposed and use it to stimulate thinking about additional ideas. Usually the idea contributions are anonymous. This lets each idea stand on its own merits rather than grant the boss's idea special consideration. The GSS software also supports several ways of voting to enable the group members to express their preference for a particular solution. The voting may be by rank, ordering a list of ideas, or it might require each member to allocate 1000 points/dollars across a set of ideas. Table 8.4 summarizes the advantages to using a GSS; Table 8.5 lists some of the problems with meetings and how GSS software can help.

Table 8.4 Key GSS advantages.

GSS Advantage	Description
Process structuring	Keeps the group on track and helps them avoid costly diversions
Parallelism	Enables many people to speak and listen at the same time
Group size	Enables larger group sizes
Group memory	Automatically records member ideas, comments, and votes
Access to external information	Can easily incorporate external electronic data and files
Spanning time and space	Enables members to collaborate from different places and at different times
Anonymity	Member ideas, comments, and votes not identified to others

Table 8.5　How GSS helps manage meetings.

Some Meeting Problems	GSS Solution
Not enough airtime for everyone to talk; people dominate discussion	Parallelism via multiple simultaneous electronic communication by all
Drifting topics	Agenda and sequence of software tools can focus group's communication
Idea loss	Parallelism eliminates the wait before contributing an idea
Status barriers	Anonymous contributions stand or fall on their own merits

In GSS meetings a skilled process facilitator is often used to help the group with their communication and decision process. The facilitator does not participate in the group's content discussion, but rather provides procedural advice to help the group make the best use of the information and decision processes that are available. The facilitator may also configure the GSS to suit the group's needs and may provide relational coaching if some members are having difficulty communicating effectively. Use of a trained facilitator, although one of the strengths of a GSS-supported meeting, may be GSS's Achilles' heel. Although it is relatively easy to buy and implement GSS software, it may be more difficult to find and/or train competent facilitators.

Integrative Systems to Improve Customer Contact

The goal of technology convergence is to improve an organization's interaction with, and service to, the customer. The driving force behind this convergence is the process of **disintermediation**, or taking all the non-value-adding steps out of interacting with a customer. Think about how convenient it is for you to get cash from an Automatic Teller Machine (ATM), as shown in Figure 8.12. Before ATMs you had to go to your bank or someplace that would cash a check, wait in line to see a teller, present identification, write a check, and receive your cash. Many of these intermediate steps added to the amount of time and energy it took to get the cash from your account and, in some cases, made getting cash slow and difficult. Enter ATMs. Now this customer contact technology enables customers to quickly get cash at convenient times and locations while the bank saves money in the cost of buildings and labor. Many gasoline stations have followed this example and equipped their pumps to accept ATM and credit cards. Intermediate, non-value-adding steps have been eliminated, or disintermediated, between the customer and the product or service.

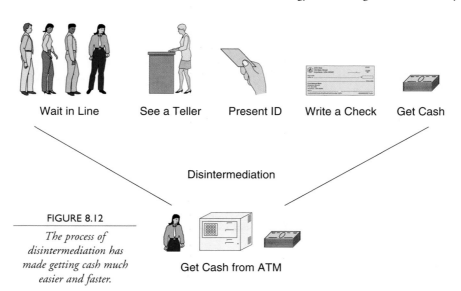

Wait in Line　　See a Teller　　Present ID　　Write a Check　　Get Cash

Disintermediation

FIGURE 8.12

The process of disintermediation has made getting cash much easier and faster.

Get Cash from ATM

Computer Kiosks

Another good example of using technology to improve customer contact is provided by Hertz, the leading car rental company in the world. Hertz uses **computer kiosks** such as the one shown in Figure 8.13 in busy airports to enable customers to quickly find a suitable car. Each kiosk provides a touch screen to guide users through the models and prices of cars available and then to direct the customer to a particular parking space number. Customers can view precise information regarding which car models, colors, and pricing packages are actually available for renting without waiting to speak with a sales agent.

Computer kiosks enable customers to quickly and easily delve directly into the organization's data and systems without an employee serving as a costly, time-consuming intermediary. Kiosks can be developed using off-the-shelf hardware and can be customized for any organization and application. Kiosk technology has progressed rapidly and far, offering links to the World Wide Web and the capability to enable users to send email, place an outgoing phone call, and print out information. In addition, kiosks can also provide an attention-grabbing self-run cycle, so that when no one is at the kiosk, graphics and animation run to attract new users to the kiosk (see Figure 8.14).

Designed and manufactured by Kiosk Information Systems.

FIGURE 8.13

Hertz uses computer kiosks such as this one to enable customers to rent from among approximately 450,000 vehicles at more than 5,400 locations in over 150 countries.

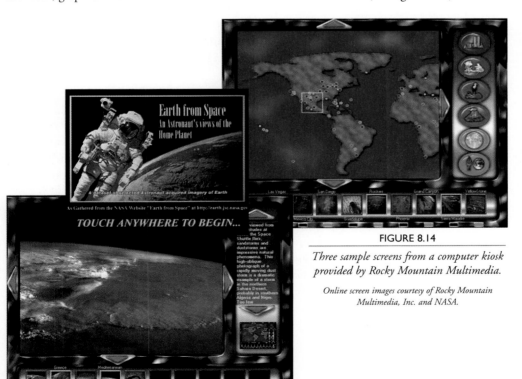

FIGURE 8.14

Three sample screens from a computer kiosk provided by Rocky Mountain Multimedia.

Online screen images courtesy of Rocky Mountain Multimedia, Inc. and NASA.

Telephone Interfacing

Another example of using emerging information systems to improve customer contact is the integration of the telephone with information systems. Telephone interfacing, also known as Interactive Voice Processing or **Computer Telephone Integration (CTI)**, is the integration of computers, fax boards, and telephone switches to the public telephone network. The purpose is to provide customers and other people with organizational information accessible through the telephone network. Users interact with the system using any regular touch-tone phone, which acts as an easy-to-use computer terminal. Voice mail is one common example of telephone interfacing. However, telephone interfacing has many other applications, which we'll discuss next.

Audiotex

One of the more common telephone interfacing applications is the **audiotex system**. These give callers pre-recorded choices organized in menus. The caller then selects the desired information from the audio menu by pressing buttons on his touch-tone phone. This is one of the most common applications that has been used to give information from stock quotes and film synopsis to government services. Such systems are often used in organizations to provide answers to frequently asked information, to direct callers to specific people or groups, and to provide support for products and services.

Automated Attendant

Automated attendant systems can be programmed to answer incoming calls and enable the caller to enter the extension to which she wants to be transferred. Alternatively, the system can ask the caller to select the person from a list and also let the caller leave a message in that person's voice mailbox. Automatic attendants can handle calls, even on multiple lines, faster than can a human, giving a caller faster access to the person she desires to reach.

Fax-on-Demand

One other form of telephone interfacing is **fax-on-demand systems**. These systems can be programmed to enable a user to select documents from a vocal menu or enter a document number and then receive the selected documents on a fax machine. These systems can be used to distribute order forms, promotional documents, technical support documents, or any other text or graphical document.

Telephone/Database Integration

Perhaps the most powerful application of telephone interfacing is the integration of telephones with computer databases. With these applications the user can remotely conduct transactions in computer databases from a touch-tone telephone. Users can check an account balance, transfer money from one account to another, check an inventory level, order from items in a database, or even request an audio or printed report of information in a database.

CDnow on the World Wide Web

The World Wide Web is one of the most exciting avenues for customer contact technologies. A site on the Web offers organizations an instant, relatively easy and inexpensive global reach to customers and partners anywhere. For example, CDnow (www.cdnow.com) is a compact disc music distributor that had no brand recognition or existing customer base before developing its Web site (see Figure 8.15). CDnow began by only providing a simple means for customers to buy a CD. As sales transactions grew, they added additional support services, such as an option to store a customer's profile so that she would not have to reenter her address and credit card numbers each time she ordered. They added online surveys for gathering marketing research and then added an audio-on-demand online clip of most CDs to provide greater product information to potential customers. In a very short time, CDnow established a global presence with high customer contact.

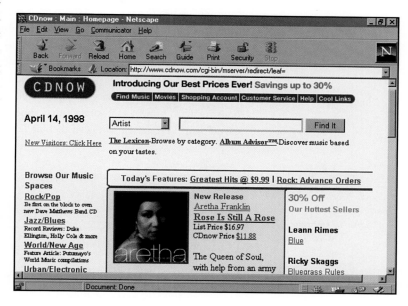

FIGURE 8.15

CDnow home page.

Limits of Customer Contact Systems

Technological advances are eliminating non-value-adding steps in the kiosk, telephone interface, and Web examples described previously. Much of the information systems development efforts in the coming years will be to link existing internal systems for ordering, inventory, and billing to customer contact technologies such as those described. However, many customers still want or need to speak with a real human rather than a machine. In some cases, customers simply prefer to interact with a human being, although in other cases they have a complex or unique question that requires the expertise of a human. By directing routine customer queries to automated customer contact systems, more employee time is freed to interact with customers who need extra attention. In addition, customer contact systems should be made to direct customers to human contact where needed. Figure 8.16 shows these models of customer contact with existing and emerging systems.

FIGURE 8.16

Models of customer contact with legacy and emerging systems.

Legacy Systems:
Internal Systems ↔ Employees ↔ Telephone ↔ Customers

Systems for Improved Customer Contact:
Internal Systems ↔ Employees ↔ Telephone/Internet ↔ Special Needs Customers

Internal Systems ↔ Kiosks/Telephone/Internet ↔ Customers with Routine Needs

Web Sites for Collaboration

Although most organizations have either passive or active Web sites, as described in Chapter 6, "Electronic Commerce and the Internet," some Web sites are interactive, enabling users to engage in real-time collaboration with other people on the pages of the Web site. At a simple level, this can be done with links from the Web pages to email and Internet Usenet newsgroups. However, some Web sites also provide online chat functions that enable participants to carry on real-time, text-based conversations with other participants. One such example is The Sports Server, Nando Sports Chat (www.nando.net/Sport-Server/), which enables net-enabled sports fanatics to converse with each other online. During a typical week, this service is accessed by millions of users (see Figure 8.17). Such chats can also include dynamic, graphical representations of participants (also known as "avatars") that appear and interact in a virtual meeting place on participants' screens, or can even include live audio/video connections.

Courtesy Worlds Inc.

FIGURE 8.17

Nando Sports Chat enables participants to interact with each other in real time on the Web.

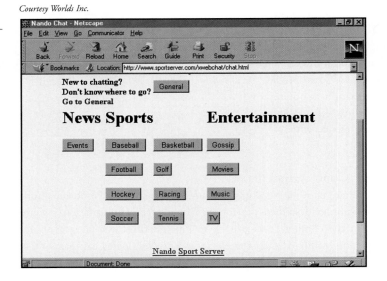

For a nice example of a fully interactive, graphical, Internet-based, virtual chat space that rivals Doom, the popular PC/LAN-based interactive game, check out World's Chat (www.worlds.net). World's Chat must first be downloaded and installed on your PC (see Figure 8.18). Examples of live, Internet-based audio/video software are Quarterdeck's WebTalk, Cornell University's CU-SeeMe, and Cybration's ICUII.

Courtesy Worlds Inc.

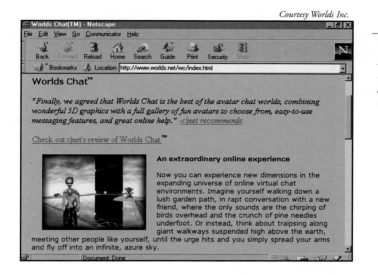

FIGURE 8.18

World's Chat enables partici- pants to interact with people from around the world in a graphical, three-dimensional virtual space, much like that in the popular PC-game Doom.

Talking with...

Joe Tooman, Webmaster at Sherwin-Williams

Educational Background

B.B.A. in Information Systems, Cleveland State University

Job Description

Mr. Tooman is responsible for the Inter/Intranet strategy, and for implementa- tion of that strategy at Sherwin-Williams. This involves the creation of, and ongoing responsibility for, functioning, security, and performance of company Inter/Intranet systems. He manages a team of Internet specialists who facilitate departments in developing intranet sites and executing the objectives in the Sherwin-Williams Inter/Intranet strategy.

Critical Success Factors

Take a business problem, develop a vision, sell that vision, and then formulate and execute a strategy. That is how I got Sherwin-Williams' intranet off the ground. Vision is very important—be creative! No problem is too big to han- dle and you should commit to constant improvement in yourself and your team. Interpersonal relationships are very important, as well as a positive and self-confident attitude.

Advice to Students

Get experience while in school! Get an internship or co-op position so that you will be more marketable and com- mand a higher price than your peers. Keep up with the industry, read trade magazines (*InfoWorld*, *WebWeek*, and *Internet Week*) to learn the players and get ideas. Take business classes as well as technical classes. Business and tech- nology are inseparable, so you need to learn both disciplines. Most colleges have much better business classes than computer classes due to the rapid pace of technology and their inability to keep up. That is another reason to get a co-op job—so you can get the up-to-date technical knowledge. Read *Awaken the Giant Within* by Tony Robbins to get rid of limiting beliefs and move to the top of your field.

Summary

1. **Explain why companies are continually looking for new ways to use technology for competitive advantage.** Organizations are finding clever ways to use new technologies to help them do things faster, cheaper, and better than rivals. Being at the technological cutting edge has its disadvantages. Given that new technologies are not as stable as traditional ones, relying on emerging systems can be problematic. Because constantly upgrading to newer and better systems is expensive, relying on emerging systems can hurt a firm financially. In addition, using emerging information systems for competitive advantage can be short-lived; competitors can quickly jump on the technological bandwagon and easily mimic the same system. As a result, many organizations find themselves on the technological bleeding edge rather than the cutting edge. Not every organization should deploy emerging information systems. Those organizations that find themselves in highly competitive environments are probably most in need of deploying new technologies to stay ahead of rivals. To best deploy these new technologies, organizations must be ready for the changes that will ensue, have the resources necessary to deploy new technologies successfully, and be tolerant of the risk and problems involved in being at the cutting edge. Deploying emerging information systems is essentially a risk/return gamble: The risks are relatively high, but the potential rewards are great.

2. **Describe specific examples of emerging information systems, such as videoconferencing, groupware, and group support systems for supporting collaboration and virtual teams.** Collaboration technologies for virtual teams include videoconferencing, groupware, and group support systems. These systems are being used to support team member communication, collaboration, coordination, and problem solving across time and distance. videoconferencing is the integration of telephone, video recording, and playback technologies by two or more people to interact with each other from remote sites. Groupware refers to computer-based information systems designed to enable group members to electronically communicate, collaborate, and coordinate their activities across time and distance. Group support systems are computer-based information systems used to support collaborative, intellectual, goal-directed work.

3. **Describe how companies are using computer kiosks, telephone interfacing, and the Internet and Web to support improved customer contact and reach.** Integrative technologies, such as computer kiosks, telephone interfacing, and the Internet and World Wide Web are being used to improve customer contact and reach. By removing non-value-adding steps from business processes and links to customers, businesses are finding ways to reach more customers and improve customer service.

Key Terms

Virtual teams	Multipoint control unit	Group support systems
Customer contact	Continuous presence	Disintermediation
Technology convergence	Groupware	Computer kiosks
Videoconferencing	Information repositories	Computer telephone integration
Desktop videoconferencing	Discussion databases	Audiotex systems
Application sharing	Knowledge manager	Automated attendant systems
Whiteboarding software	Replication	Fax-on-demand systems

Review Questions

1. What is meant by "emerging information systems"?

2. What makes emerging information systems susceptible to copying?

3. Describe the major goals that emerging technologies attempt to accomplish.

4. Describe how software application sharing can be an effective use of desktop videoconferencing.

5. Briefly explain the three major limitations to videoconferencing.

6. What are the "three Cs" of groupware?

7. Describe the major difference between push and pull technologies in relation to email and information repositories.

8. List and describe at least four benefits of groupware.

9. Compare and contrast groupware systems with group support systems.

10. Describe the differences between a traditional business meeting and a business meeting conducted with a GSS.

11. Under contemporary customer contact systems, how are customers with routine needs most often handled?

Problems and Exercises

 Individual   **Group**   **Field**   ◯ **Web/Internet**

 1. Match the following terms to the appropriate definitions:

_____ Emerging information system

_____ Customer contact

_____ Technology convergence

_____ Information repository

_____ Knowledge manager

_____ Replication

_____ Group support systems

_____ Computer telephone integration

a. A place to store and index information to enable pull-based forms of communication

b. Types of information systems that are relatively new, as opposed to types of information systems that are relatively old

c. The administrator of discussion forums and information repositories within a groupware system

d. The integration of computers, fax boards, and telephony switches to the public telephone network

e. The synchronization of databases that are stored on multiple servers

f. Computer-based information systems used to support collaborative, intellectual, goal-directed work

g. The amount and nature of interaction that an organization has with its customers and that its customers have with the organization's people, processes, systems, and data

h. The integration of previously disparate technologies, such as computer, telephone, and video recorders, into relatively seamless systems

2. Do you agree that the use of videoconferencing technologies will increase the need and demand for airline travel? Why or why not?

3. Discuss the following in a small group of classmates: Why did the Internet and the World Wide Web take as long as they did to become part of the mainstream as far as information technologies? What aspects of the Internet and World Wide Web make them appealing to companies? Did companies who held back initially make the right decision? Why or why not?

4. Describe how the new technologies described in this chapter might enable workers to work from their homes rather than the company's office. What technologies in particular might these workers utilize and how? Will companies look favorably on this use of technology? Why or why not? What experiences do you or any of your classmates have with regard to this new type of worker?

5. This chapter illustrates several examples of how groupware systems can benefit companies. What are the potential drawbacks to these systems? Under what conditions are they not effective?

6. Imagine a groupware system without the key feature of replication. What would be some of the major consequences of this? Consider situations involving spreadsheets and databases.

7. Describe the role of the facilitator of a group support systems meeting. Why is this position necessary?

8. Imagine you have just called your credit card's bank to determine your current balance before buying a new television. The bank has implemented an audiotex system for better customer service. After entering your credit card number, your expiration date, and your zip code, you receive among other things your current balance. As you hang up, your friend comments that it would have been much easier if an operator rather than the computer system had handled the call. Explain to your friend the error in his or her thinking. Be sure to mention "routine needs," "special needs," "disintermediation," and "employee contact."

9. Why shouldn't every organization deploy emerging information systems? Discuss this within a small group. What are some of the necessary characteristics of an organization that are needed to successfully deploy emerging systems? Does everyone in the group agree?

10. Consider an organization that is familiar to you. Describe the types of information systems that this organization uses. Is this organization on the "cutting edge" of information systems technology? Do their uses of information systems seem to fit their needs?

11. Using the same organization as in Question 10, does this organization have a business plan or strategy that specifically addresses the use of emerging information systems, or is the organization using its information systems for other reasons? Describe how and why the organization has selected its information systems.

12. Interview an IS Manager at an organization with which you are familiar. Determine what types of emerging systems are being used to enhance virtual teamwork. Why were these systems selected over the others? Are people pleased with the effectiveness and results of their choice of technology?

13. In a small group of classmates, describe any experiences you have had with Lotus Notes or any other groupware product. In what kind of setting were you? Was information easier or harder to obtain? How many people were using the system? What was its main purpose?

14. Based on your past work experience, describe a face-to-face meeting scenario that was not as effective or productive as possible. What social and structural problems were encountered? What aspects of a group support system would have aided in the success of this meeting? Would any of the GSS features have been detrimental to this meeting? Does this scenario repeat itself often or was this a one-time occurrence? Have any of your classmates encountered similar situations? Prepare a 10-minute presentation of your findings to the class.

15. Interview a telephone operator in a customer support center of a large organization. Does this organization utilize any telephone interfacing technologies? Which ones? Does the operator find his or her job easier because of the technology? Is the operator more effective in terms of calls handled per day than before the implementation of the technology?

16. Using the scenario at the beginning of the chapter as a starting point, search the World Wide Web for organizations that use "virtual teams" and other collaboration technologies. For starters, try Andersen Consulting at http://www.ac.com/ or Deloitte & Touche at http://www.dttus.com/. Look for other examples as well. How are these organizations creating virtual teams? What technologies are they using?

Real World Case Problems

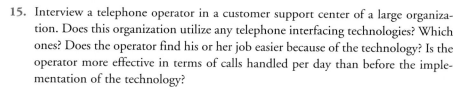

1. Ernst & Young Deploys Notes Throughout Its Large, Global Enterprise.

It is a decentralized organization of some 130 national firms around the world that work together to provide seamless cross-border service to multinational businesses. It has over 70,000 people in more than 650 locations. It is Ernst & Young International, one of the largest and leading professional services organizations, delivering leading-edge assurance, advisory, tax, and consulting services that help corporations achieve their business goals.

The capability of its people to communicate, collaborate, and share knowledge—within local and multinational teams, within service lines, and across national boundaries—has become essential to maintaining and sharpening Ernst & Young's competitive edge in the global marketplace. "We deliver our client solutions through multidisciplinary, and often multinational, teams working together in person or through connectivity to apply their combined skills and our organization's expertise to our clients' problems and needs. This is the core of our business," says John Whyte, CIO of Ernst & Young International.

In 1995, Ernst & Young member firms adopted Lotus Notes as their standard tool for collaborative working and knowledge management. This decision was made against a clean technology slate, so to speak; there were no legacy systems. By the end of 1997, there were over 100 Ernst & Young virtual teams communicating and interacting from locations around the world using their Domino/Notes Engagement Team Data Base to serve multinational clients. Even more teams were using Notes applications to manage projects and share work products and ideas within country boundaries. All but one country had migrated to Lotus Mail by the end of 1997—an outstanding achievement for a decentralized organization of Ernst & Young's size, geographical spread, and diversity. International email traffic alone (that is, excluding in-country electronic messages which, in fact, total even more) rose from 6,000 messages per month in April 1996 to 400,000 a month in September 1997, and hit 800,000 in January 1998.

"Notes enabled us to scale up to a global enterprise system that provides mission-critical connectivity among our people, within our teams, to our clients, and to internal and external knowledge stores," Whyte says. Last year (1997), Ernst & Young worldwide revenues grew by 17 percent. Whyte says, "Some of that global growth is certainly due to being able to do work without barriers and have this high level of communication and knowledge-sharing capability."

    a. How are collaboration technologies and knowledge management useful to Ernst & Young?

    b. How important is it to a firm such as Ernst & Young to use collaboration technologies such as Notes successfully? Why? How would it look if a leading IS/IT consultant wasn't deploying emerging technologies successfully?

    c. Is knowledge management using Notes useful only to consulting firms such as Ernst & Young? Why or why not?

Source *Adapted from "success story" found at http://www.lotus.com/home.nsf/ welcome/stories*

©*1997 Lotus Development Corporation. Used with permission of Lotus Development Corporation. Lotus and Lotus Notes are registered trademarks of Lotus Development Corporation.*

2. Videoconferencing Helps Savings Bank of Manchester Meet the Needs of Its Customers Now and in the Future.

For the Savings Bank of Manchester, a community bank in Connecticut, preparing for the future means implementing new technology—such as videoconferencing—today. The bank, which currently operates 23 branches and has over $1 billion in assets, has turned to a PictureTel videoconferencing solution to help it increase productivity and reduce the cost of doing business, while improving the services it delivers to its customer base and maintaining a high level of customer satisfaction.

In the past, when a customer was interested in the bank's services, a financial consultant assigned to that customer's local branch would travel from the bank's main office to the branch to meet one-on-one with the customer. Because each initial meeting with a prospective customer was often a brief session designed to examine the actual financial requirements of the customer, the bank believed that videoconferencing could replace the need for an initial face-to-face meeting.

To test out this theory, the bank decided to pilot the videoconferencing technology with Carol Comforti, a senior financial consultant. The choice of Comforti was an easy one to make because two of the branches she supports are the ones farthest away from the main office—approximately 45 miles. Three Live200 systems were used for the pilot: One was placed in Comforti's office and the other two were placed in conference rooms in each of the branches. With the installation complete, Comforti was now able to conduct the initial planning meetings with customers without leaving her office (follow-up meetings were and still are always formal one-on-one sessions). The results of the pilot have been positive: Customers have been favorably impressed with the technology, and the bank has realized cost and time savings by implementing the solution. Comforti stated:

> "In my business, time is money. So if I must drive a long distance to meet with someone, that drive uses

valuable time, time that could be better spent working with other clients. But I'm also affecting the profitability of the bank itself. And because the initial consultative meeting is used mainly to get a sense of what the client's goals are and to determine whether the financial services we offer are right for them, this meeting can often take no more than five to ten minutes to complete. With the travel time between the main office and a branch taking up to a total of two hours, we believe it isn't a cost-effective way to do business. With the videoconferencing technology, the need to travel and the cost associated with that travel are completely eliminated."

a. Describe the benefits of this use of videoconferencing technology and the potential disadvantages or downsides.

b. As best you can, quantify the benefits of this firm's use of videoconferencing. Is it worth the expense? Why or why not?

c. What other ways could Savings Bank of Manchester use videoconferencing, either internally or externally?

Source Adapted from "success story" found at http://www.picturetel.com/manchester.htm

©1998 PictureTel Corporation. Andover, MA. All rights reserved. Used with permission.

References

Dennis, George, Jessup, Nunamaker, and Vogel. 1988. Information technology to support electronic meetings. *MIS Quarterly* 12(4): 591–624.

Intel, 1998. Information from: www.intel.com. Information verified: March 15, 1998.

Jessup, L. M., and J. S. Valacich, (Eds). 1993. *Group Support Systems: New Perspectives.* Indianapolis: Macmillan Publishing Company.

Lotus, 1998. Information from: www.intel.com. Information verified: March 15, 1998.

Nunamaker, Dennis, Valacich, Vogel, and George. 1991. Electronic meeting systems to support group work. *Communications of the ACM* 34(7): 209–230.

PictureTel, 1998. Information from: www.picturetel.com. Information verified: March 15, 1998.

Porter, M. E. 1979. How competitive forces shape strategy. *Harvard Business Review* 57(2): 137–145.

Stahl, S. 1994. Groupware's culture problem—When implementing groupware, the biggest hurdle isn't technical—it's convincing users to share information. *InformationWeek*, December 23.

Time, 1996. The Past Imperfect. *Time Magazine*, July 15, 54.

Van Gundy, A.B., Jr. 1988. *Techniques of structured problem solving.* New York: Van Nostrand Reinhold.

Ventana, 1998. Information from: www.ventana.com. Information verified: March 15, 1998.

Related Readings

Alavi, Wheeler, and Valacich. 1995. Using IT to reengineer business education: An exploratory investigation of collaborative telelearning. *Management Information Systems Quarterly* 19(3): 293–312.

Anson, Bostrom, and Wynne. 1995. An experiment assessing group support system and facilitator effects on meeting outcomes. *Management Science* 41(2): 189–208.

Dennis, George, Jessup, Nunamaker, and Vogel. 1988 Information technology to support electronic meetings. *Management Information Systems Quarterly*, 12(4): 591–624.

DeSanctis, G.R., and R.B. Gallupe. 1987. A foundation for the study of group decision support systems. *Management Science*, 33(5): 589–609.

Dickson, Partridge, and Robinson. 1993. Exploring modes of facilitative support for GDSS technology. *Management Information Systems Quarterly* 17(2): 173–194.

Gowan, J.A., and J.M. Downs. 1994. Videoconferencing human-machine interface: A field study. *Information and Management* 27(6): 341–356.

Niederman, Beise, and Beranek. 1996. Issues and concerns about computer-supported meetings: The facilitator's perspective. *Management Information Systems Quarterly* 20(1): 1–22.

Nunamaker, Dennis, Valacich, Vogel, and George. 1991. Electronic meeting systems to support group work. *Communications of the ACM* 34(7): 40–61.

Sambamurthy, V., and W.W. Chin. 1994. The effects of group attitudes toward alternative GDSS designs on the decision-making performance of computer-supported groups. *Decision Sciences* 25(2): 215–241.

Turoff, Hiltz, Bahgat, and Rana. 1993. Distributed group support systems. *Management Information Systems Quarterly* 17(4): 399–417.

Warkentin, Sayeed, and Hightower. 1997. Virtual teams versus face-to-face teams: An exploratory study of a Web-based conference system. *Decision Sciences* 28(4): 975–996.

Wheeler, B.C., and J.S. Valacich. 1996. Facilitation, GSS, and training as sources of process restrictiveness and guidance for structured group decision making: An empirical assessment. *Information Systems Research* 7(4): 429–450.

Zigurs, I., and K.A. Kozar. 1994. An exploratory study of roles in computer-supported groups. *Management Information Systems Quarterly* 18(3): 277–297.

PART 4

Information Systems Development

The purpose of Part 4 is to help you understand how organizations develop and acquire information systems.

In Chapter 9, *The Information Systems Development Process*, we describe the traditional, structured process used by organizations to manage the development of contemporary information systems. We describe each major phase of the systems development life cycle: systems identification, selection, and planning; system analysis; system design; system implementation; and system maintenance. We also explain how organizations identify projects, assess feasibility, identify system benefits and costs, and perform economic analysis of a system project.

In Chapter 10, *Contemporary Information Systems Development Approaches*, we explain emerging approaches for collecting and structuring the information needed to design and construct an information system. We describe prototyping, rapid application development, and object-oriented analysis and design methods of

systems development and the strengths and weaknesses of each approach. We describe how and why to use several automated tools for supporting emerging development, including computer-aided software engineering, group support systems, and advanced programming languages.

In Chapter 11, *Alternatives to Systems Development*, we describe situations in which building a system in house is not feasible and which factors to consider making such a decision. We also explain three alternative systems development options: external acquisition, outsourcing, and end-user development.

Part 4, "Information Systems Development" is the heart and soul of the information systems field. Roll up your sleeves, turn the page, and find out what it takes to build large, complex information systems for companies.

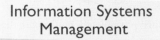

Information Systems
Management

Emerging
IS

Alternatives
to Systems
Development

Organizational
IS

Contemporary
IS
Development
Approaches

Electronic
Commerce
& the Internet

The IS
Development
Process

Hardware   Software

Database Management

Telecommunications

Scenario: Changes to the University Transcript Reporting System

Second Millennia Real Estate (SMR) is your state's largest residential and commercial real estate sales company. SMR has had a long history of providing summer internships to university business students. Internships with SMR are highly coveted due to SMR's statewide presence, offering students flexibility with location during the summer months. Most students are assigned to work within SMR's residential sales group. Interns within the residential sales group focus primarily on supporting local sales agents with day-to-day sales support activities such as staffing open houses, placing and collecting signs, and drafting advertisements and property descriptions. Within the commercial sales group, interns engage in activities similar to those of the residential group, but also focus on providing property management and investment management services to commercial customers.

Imagine that you have just applied for an internship with SMR, hoping to be selected by the commercial sales group. During the application process, you are asked to provide a copy of your academic transcripts and are told that these must be mailed to SMR within the next week. You have an older copy of your transcript that you could provide but would rather provide one that contained your most recently completed courses, given that you have made some substantial improvements in your GPA the past few terms.

To obtain a copy of your most recent transcript, you contact your school's registrar, Jackie Wang. Unfortunately, she informs you that it will take at least two weeks for you to get a copy with your most recently completed courses. Ms. Wang can, however, provide you with a copy of your transcript without the most recently completed term's grades today. You ask why transcripts with the most recently completed term's grades take an extra two weeks. She explains that student grade transcripts with the most recently completed classes are being produced by hand and are caught in a two-week backlog. Alternatively, transcripts without the

most recently completed grades can be produced by the school's Transcript Reporting System immediately. You press further and ask why the Transcript Reporting System can't include the most recently completed classes. Ms. Wang explains that when the school changed from a quarter-based to a semester-based academic calendar in the prior term, the Transcript Reporting System was not capable of supporting transcripts that had classes from both the quarter system and the semester system. "Quarter-based credit hours are two-thirds of semester-based credit hours," she explains. "Our current system just cannot handle this difference when computing grade point averages. We are having the system completely changed to support transcripts with both quarter and semester grades, but it won't be available for at least another month or so."

Frustrated at this point, you ask, "Why does it take so long to make a few changes to a system?" The registrar explains that the school has been working on this change to the Transcript Reporting System for several months and that many steps had to be performed, as outlined in Figure 9.1. She explains that she and her staff began the process by meeting with several systems analysts from the University Computing Service—a group that develops and supports computer systems at your univer-sity. "During the meeting, we described what changes were occurring in the academic calendar and how these changes were problematic to the Transcript Reporting System. After several meetings over the past few months, the analysts were able to clearly understand what was needed in the new system and were now able to design changes to the existing system. We spent most of our time discussing what we wanted and designing how it would work. Only a small part of the time will be spent on actual programming. Full implementation where they install and train us to use the new system is still at least a month away. I cannot tell you how much time and energy has gone into making the few changes to this system—much more than I have ever imagined!"

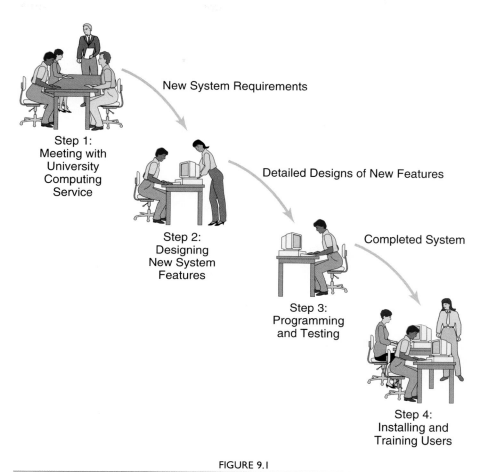

New System Requirements

Step 1:
Meeting with
University
Computing
Service

Detailed Designs of New Features

Step 2:
Designing
New System
Features

Completed System

Step 3:
Programming
and Testing

Step 4:
Installing and
Training Users

FIGURE 9.1

The steps in the changes to the system.

You explain to the registrar that you need a full transcript as soon as possible to complete your application to SMR. You also explained why you feel that a transcript containing the grades from the most recently completed semester would likely enhance your chances within SMR because of their reputation of using academic achievement as an important criteria in the selection process. Ms. Wang is sympathetic to your situation and provides you with a good compromise solution: providing a copy of your prior transcript generat-

ed by the existing Transcript Reporting System and a copy of your most recently completed report card. "Together," she says, "both provide equivalent information to an updated transcript." She also provides you with a brief letter explaining why the school could not provide a complete transcript with the most recently completed classes and grades. You thank her for all her help and for a better understanding about what even a small change to a system might entail for an organization.

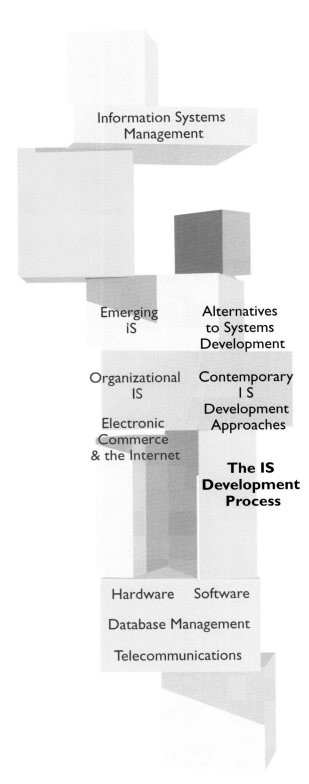

Information Systems
Management

Emerging
iS

Alternatives
to Systems
Development

Organizational
IS

Contemporary
I S
Development
Approaches

Electronic
Commerce
& the Internet

**The IS
Development
Process**

Hardware   Software

Database Management

Telecommunications

Introduction

A fairly common set of systems development methods—such as those used in modifying the Transcript Reporting System—have traditionally been used to construct and modify information systems used in organizations. For example, if you were to develop a new payroll or inventory management system for a firm, you would probably follow a contemporary development approach. With such an approach you would use a set of highly structured techniques and steps. Why use a contemporary development approach in this instance? Information systems such as transaction processing and payroll systems (described in Chapter 7, "Organizational Information Systems") typically have well-defined processes and data. Consequently, there is a natural marriage between a contemporary, structured development approach and a well-defined, structured problem such as a payroll system. Alternatively, decision support and expert systems, whose data and processing requirements are often ill defined, are usually constructed using non-traditional or emerging development methods, which are described in Chapter 10, "Contemporary Information Systems Development Approaches."

This chapter describes the process used by many organizations to design, build, and maintain several types of information systems. As you will read, different approaches have been found to be more appropriate for developing some types of systems and less appropriate for others. Learning all possible ways to develop or acquire a system, and more importantly when to apply the optimal approach, takes years of study and experience. Toward this end, this chapter has several objectives.

After reading this chapter, you will be able to do the following:

1. Understand the process used by organizations to manage the development of information systems.

2. Describe each major phase of the system's development life cycle: systems identification, selection, and planning; system analysis; system design; system implementation; and system maintenance.

FIGURE 9.2

The big picture: focusing on the information systems development process.

3. Explain how organizations identify projects, assess feasibility, identify system benefits and costs, and perform economic analysis of a system project.

This chapter is the first in Part 4, "Information Systems Development." Part 4 focuses on describing how organizations develop and acquire information systems (see Figure 9.2). Given the importance of information and technology to the success of modern organizations, the goal of this chapter is to provide you with a high-level understanding of the information system's development processes.

The Need for Structured Systems Development

The process of designing, building, and maintaining information systems is often referred to as **systems analysis and design**. Likewise, the individual who performs this task is referred to as a **systems analyst.** (This chapter uses "systems analyst" and "programmer" interchangeably.) Because few organizations can exist without effectively utilizing information and computing technology, the demand for systems analysts far outpaces the supply. Organizations want to hire systems analysts because they possess a unique blend of both managerial and technical expertise—systems analysts are not just "techies." In fact, systems analysts are in hot demand precisely due to their unique blend of technical and managerial expertise. But it wasn't always this way.

The Evolution of Information Systems Development

In the early days of computing, systems development and programming was considered an art that only a few technical "gurus" could master. Unfortunately, the techniques used to construct systems varied greatly from individual to individual. This variation made it difficult to integrate large organizational information systems. Further, many systems were not easily maintainable after the original programmer left the organization. As a result, organizations were often left with systems that were very difficult and expensive to maintain. Many organizations therefore under-utilized these technology investments and failed to realize all possible benefits from their systems.

To address this problem, information systems professionals concluded that system development needed to become an engineering-like discipline (Nunamaker, 1992). Common methods, techniques, and tools had to be developed to create a disciplined approach for constructing information systems. This evolution from an "art" to a "discipline" led to the use of the term **software engineering** to help define what systems analysts and programmers do. Transforming information systems development into a formal discipline would provide numerous benefits. First, it would be much easier to train programmers and analysts if common techniques were widely used. In essence, if all systems analysts had similar training, it would make them more interchangeable and more skilled at working on the systems developed by other analysts. Second, systems built with commonly used techniques would be more maintainable. Both industry and academic researchers have pursued the quest for new and better approaches for building information systems.

Options for Obtaining Information Systems

Organizations can obtain new information systems in many ways. One option, of course, is for the members of the organization to build the information system themselves, which is the approach described in this chapter. However, organizations can also buy a "pre-packaged" system from a software development company or consulting firm. Some information systems that are commonly used in many organizations can be purchased for much less money than what it would cost to build. Purchasing a pre-packaged system is a good option as long as its features meet the needs of the organization. For example, a payroll system is an example of a "pre-packaged" system that is often purchased rather than developed by an organization because tax laws, wage calculations, check printing, and accounting activities are highly standardized. Figure 9.3 outlines several sources for information systems.

FIGURE 9.3

Sources for information systems.

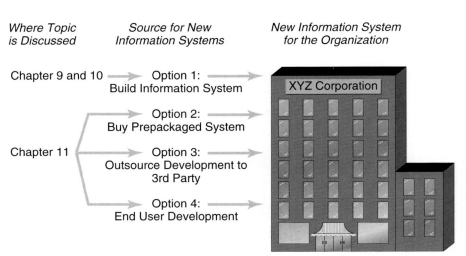

Where Topic is Discussed	Source for New Information Systems	New Information System for the Organization
Chapter 9 and 10	Option 1: Build Information System	
	Option 2: Buy Prepackaged System	
Chapter 11	Option 3: Outsource Development to 3rd Party	
	Option 4: End User Development	

A third option is to have an outside organization or consultant custom build a system to an organization's specifications. This is generally referred to as having the development outsourced. This is a good option when the organization does not have adequate systems development resources or expertise. A final option is to let individual users and departments build their own custom systems to support their individual needs. This is referred to as *end-user development*. Most organizations allow end-user development to be used to construct only a limited range of systems. For example, systems that span organizational boundaries or perform complex changes to corporate databases are typically not candidates for end-user development. Alternatively, a common application that might be constructed using end-user development is a data analysis system using a spreadsheet application such as Microsoft Excel. Regardless of the source of the new information system, the primary role of managers and users in the organization is to make sure that any new system will meet the organization's business needs. This means that managers and users must understand the systems development process to ensure that the system will meet their needs.

Information Systems Development in Action

The tools and techniques used to develop information systems are continuously evolving with the rapid changes in information system hardware and software. As you will see, the information systems development approach is a very structured process that moves from step to step. Systems analysts become adept at decomposing large, complex problems into many small, simple problems. Writing a relatively short computer program can then easily solve each simple problem. The goal of the systems analyst is to build the final system by piecing together the many small programs into one comprehensive system. This process of decomposing a problem is outlined in Figure 9.4. An easy way to think about this is to think about using Lego blocks for building a model house. When together, the blocks can create a large and very complex design. Apart, each block is a small, simple piece that is nothing without the others. When systems are built in this manner they are much easier to design, program, and, most important, maintain.

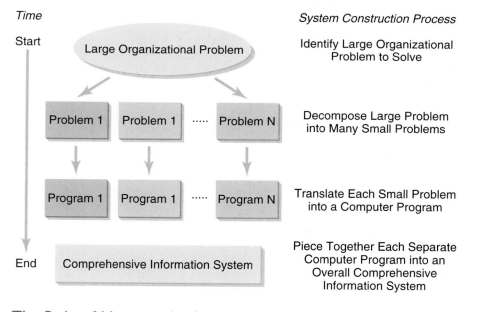

FIGURE 9.4

Problem decomposition process.

The Role of Users in the Systems Development Process

Most organizations have a huge investment in transaction processing and management information systems. These systems are most often designed, constructed, and maintained using structured development methods by systems analysts and programmers within the organization. When building and maintaining information systems, systems analysts rely on information provided by system users, who are involved in all phases of the system's development process. It is important for all members of the organization to understand what is meant by systems development and what activities occur to effectively participate in the process. A close and mutually respectful working relationship between analysts and users is a key to project success.

Now that you understand the history and need for structured systems development, it's time to consider some of the relevant techniques that are used in systems development.

Steps in the Systems Development Process

Just as the products that a firm produces and sells follow a life cycle, so do organizational information systems. For example, a new type of tennis shoe follows a life cycle of being introduced to the market, being accepted into the market, maturing, declining in popularity, and ultimately being retired. The term **systems development life cycle** (SDLC) is used to describe the life of an information system from conception to retirement (Hoffer, George, and Valacich, 1999). The SDLC has five primary phases:

1. System identification, selection, and planning

2. System analysis

3. System design

4. System implementation

5. System maintenance

Figure 9.5 is a graphical representation of the SDLC. The SDLC is represented as four boxes connected by arrows. Within the SDLC, arrows flow in both directions from the top box (System Identification, Selection, and Planning) to the bottom box (System Implementation). Arrows flowing down represent the flow of information produced in one phase as being used to seed the activities of the next. Arrows flowing up represent the possibility of returning to a prior phase, if needed. The system maintenance arrow connecting the last phase to the first is what makes the SDLC a cycle.

FIGURE 9.5

Systems development life cycle.

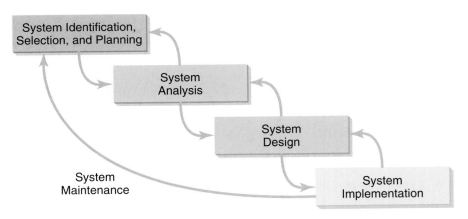

A BRIEF CASE

The SDLC at NASA

Organizations modify the basic SDLC slightly to fit their specific needs. For example, National Aeronautics and Space Administration (NASA) follows an eight-step approach (NASA, 1998). High-quality software is a key component in the success of NASA. Software is used to control countless earth-based systems such as those used to track, guide, and communicate with the space shuttles and the space-based systems that control the functioning of orbiting satellites. It is easy to imagine that a system failure could have catastrophic results! Consequently, NASA, like many other organizations, has chosen to follow a formal SDLC to help assure software and system quality and, more importantly, to help protect the lives and safety of their astronauts. The value of having standard procedures and steps such as the SDLC when building software not only speeds the development process, but it also ensures the creation of high-quality and reliable systems. As shown in Figure 9.6, the NASA SDLC contains eight phases that are essentially the same as the five-step, generic process described in this chapter. Within every step of the NASA SDLC, guidelines have been developed for accepting and ensuring the quality of work products created within a phase. These guidelines are used to make sure that all work products meet specifications and are error free before developers move to the next phase of the SDLC. The remainder of this section describes each phase in the SDLC.

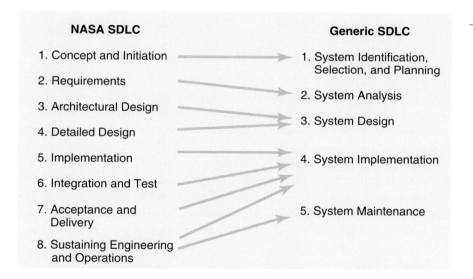

FIGURE 9.6

NASA's systems development life cycle as compared to the generic life cycle.

Phase 1: System Identification, Selection, and Planning

The first phase of the systems development life cycle is **system identification, selection, and planning**, as shown in Figure 9.7. Given that an organization can work on only a limited number of projects at a given time due to limited resources, care must be taken so that only those projects that are critical to enabling the organization's mission, goals, and objectives be undertaken. Consequently, the goal of system identification and selection is simply to identify and select a development project from all possible projects that could be performed. Organiza-tions differ in how they identify and select projects. Some organizations have a formal **information systems planning** process where a senior manager, a business group, an IS manager, or a steering committee identify and assess all possible systems development projects that an organization could undertake. Others follow a more ad hoc process for identifying potential projects. Nonetheless, after all possible projects are identified, those deemed most likely to yield significant organizational benefits, given available resources, are selected for subsequent development activities.

FIGURE 9.7

*SDLC with Phase 1
highlighted.*

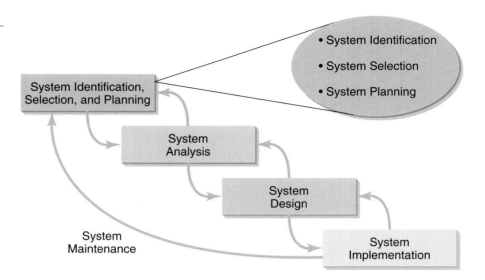

It is important to note that different approaches for identifying and selecting projects are likely to yield different organizational outcomes (see Table 9.1). For example, projects identified by top management more often have a strategic organizational focus, and projects identified by steering committees more often reflect the diversity of the committee and therefore have a cross-functional focus. Projects identified by individual departments or business units most often have a narrow, tactical focus. Finally, the typical focus of projects identified by the development group is the ease with which existing hardware and systems will integrate with the proposed project. Other factors—such as project cost, duration, complexity, and risk—are also influenced by the source of a given project. The source of projects has been found to be a key indicator of project focus and success.

Table 9.1   Sources of systems development projects and their likely focus.

Project Source	Primary Focus
Top management	Broad strategic focus
Steering committee	Cross-functional focus
Individual departments and business units	Narrow, tactical focus
Systems development group	Integration with existing information system focus
Source Adapted from McKeen, Guimaraes, and Wetherbe. 1994.	

Just as there are often differences in the source of systems projects within organizations, there are often different evaluation criteria used within organizations when classifying and ranking potential projects. During project planning, the analyst works with the customer—the potential users of the system and their managers—to collect a broad range of information to gain an understanding of the project size, potential benefits and costs, and other relevant factors. After this information is collected and analyzed, it can be brought together into a summary planning document that can be reviewed and compared to other possible projects. Table 9.2 provides a sample of the criteria often used by organizations. When reviewing a potential development project, organizations may focus on a single criterion but most often examine multiple criteria to make a decision to accept or reject a project.

Table 9.2 Possible evaluation criteria for classifying and ranking projects.

Evaluation Criteria	Description
Strategic alignment	The extent to which the project is viewed as helping the organization achieve its strategic objectives and long-term goals.
Potential benefits	The extent to which the project is viewed as improving profits, customer service, and so forth, and the duration of these benefits.
Potential costs and resource availability	The number and types of resources the project requires and their availability.
Project size / duration	The number of individuals and the length of time needed to complete the project.
Technical difficulty / risks	The level of technical difficulty involved in successfully completing the project within a given time and resource constraint.

Source   *Adapted from Hoffer, George, and Valacich. 1999. Modern Systems Analysis and Design. 2d ed. Reading, Massachusetts: Addison Wesley Longman.*

Assessing Project Feasibility

Feasibility is another factor to consider when assessing whether or not potential systems should be developed. Feasibility assessment examines the factors influencing the success or failure of a project. Different projects require different types of feasibility assessments, as summarized in Table 9.3.

Table 9.3 Types of feasibility used when assessing an information systems project.

Feasibility Type	Purpose for Assessing
Economic	To identify the financial benefits and costs associated with the development project
Technical	To gain an understanding of the development organization's capability to construct the proposed system
Operational	To gain an understanding of the degree to which and the likelihood that the proposed system solves the business problems or takes advantage of the opportunities outlined in the project request
Schedule	To gain an understanding of the likelihood that all potential timeframe and completion date schedules can be met
Legal and contractual	To gain an understanding of any potential legal ramifications of the construction of the system
Political	To gain an understanding of how key stakeholders within the organization view the proposed system

Source   *Adapted from Hoffer, George, and Valacich. 1999. Modern Systems Analysis and Design. 2d ed. Reading, Massachusetts: Addison Wesley Longman.*

Assessing schedule feasibility may uncover that a project's duration will be excessively long. Assessing technical feasibility may show that the internal development group does not possess the expertise to complete a potential project. Performing feasibility analysis is the only way for users or managers to make meaningful comparisons between rival projects.

Organizations focus most of their feasibility assessments on economic feasibility. To perform an economic assessment, an organization must first make an attempt to identify potential system benefits and costs. Analysts work very closely with potential system users and managers to identify these benefits and costs. The next few sections delve deeper into this important aspect of evaluating potential information systems projects: identifying and analyzing system benefits and costs.

Identifying System Benefits

An information system can provide many benefits to an organization. For example, a new or renovated IS can automate monotonous jobs, reduce errors, provide innovative services to customers and suppliers, and improve organizational efficiency, speed, flexibility, and morale. Some benefits can easily be measured in dollars and certainty and are referred to as **tangible benefits**. Examples of tangible benefits include reduced personnel expenses, lower transaction costs, or higher profit margins. **Intangible benefits** refer to items that cannot be easily measured in dollars or certainty. Intangible benefits may have direct organizational benefits such as the improvement of employee morale, or have broader societal implications such as the reduction of waste creation or resource consumption.

Identifying System Costs

Similar to benefits, an information system can have both tangible and intangible costs. **Tangible costs** refer to items that can be easily measured in dollars and certainty such as hardware costs, labor costs, and operational costs such as employee training and building renovations. **Intangible costs** are those items that cannot be easily measured in terms of cost or certainty such as loss of customer goodwill or employee morale. Both tangible and intangible costs can also be distinguished as either one-time or recurring. **One-time costs** refer to those associated with project initiation such as system development, new hardware and software purchases, user training, and site preparation. **Recurring costs** refer to those resulting from the ongoing evolution, use, and maintenance of the system.

Performing an Economic Analysis of a System Project

Most techniques used to determine economic feasibility encompass the concept of the time value of money (TVM). TVM refers to the concept of comparing present cash outlays to future expected returns. Because many projects may be competing for the same investment dollars and may have different useful life expectancies, all costs and benefits must be viewed in relation to their present value when investment options are compared. For example, suppose you want to buy a used personal computer (PC) from an

acquaintance and she asks that you make two payments of $1000 over two years, begin-
ning next year, for a total of $2000. If she would agree to a single lump sum payment at
the time of sale, what amount do you think she would agree to? Should the single payment be $2000 or should it be less? To answer this question, we must consider the time
value of money. Most of us would gladly accept $2000 today rather than two payments
of $1000; a dollar today is worth more than a dollar tomorrow because money can be
invested and can earn money over time. The rate at which money can be borrowed or
invested is called the cost of capital and is referred to as the discount rate for TVM calculations. Suppose that the seller could put the money received for the sale of the PC in
the bank and receive a 10% return on her investment. A simple formula can be used
when figuring out the present value of the two $1000 payments:

where PV_n is the present value of Y dollars n years from now when i is the discount rate.

From our example, the present value of the two payments of $1000 can be calculated as

$$PV_n = Y \times \frac{1}{(1 + i)^n}$$

where PV_1 and PV_2 reflect the present value of each $1000 payment in year one and
two, respectively.

$$PV_1 = 1000 \times \frac{1}{(1 + .10)^1} = 1000 \times .9091 = 909.10$$

$$PV_2 = 1000 \times \frac{1}{(1 + .10)^2} = 1000 \times .8264 = 826.40$$

To calculate the net present value (NPV) of the two $1000 payments, simply add the
present values calculated above ($NPV = PV_1 + PV_2 = 909.10 + 826.40 = 1735.50). In
other words, the seller could accept a lump-sum payment of $1735.50 as equivalent to
the two payments of $1000, given a discount rate of 10 percent.

When systems analysts perform an economic analysis of an information system, they
typically create a summary worksheet reflecting the present values of all benefits and
costs, as well as all pertinent analyses. A summary worksheet is a very powerful tool for
comparing alternative projects. For example, Figure 9.8 shows an Excel spreadsheet containing an economic analysis for a systems development project over a five-year project
life. In this analysis, benefits, one-time costs, and recurring costs were identified. The
systems analyst for this project performed three types of financial analyses: net present
value, return on investment, and break-even analysis. (See Table 9.4 for a general
description of these techniques.)

FIGURE 9.8

Economic analysis for a systems development project.

	A	B	C	D	E	F	G	H
1	Ascend Systems, Inc.							
	Economic Feasibility Analysis							
2	Customer Billing System							
3								
4								
5				Year of Project				
6		Year 0	Year 1	Year 2	Year 3	Year 4	Year 5	TOTALS
7	Net Economic Benefit	$0	$32,000	$32,000	$32,000	$32,000	$32,000	
8	Discount Rate (12%)	1.0000	0.8929	0.7972	0.7118	0.6355	0.5674	
9	PV of Benefits	$0	$28,571	$25,510	$22,777	$20,337	$18,158	
10								
11	NPV of All Benefits	$0	$28,571	$54,082	$76,859	$97,195	$115,353	$115,353
12								
13	One-time COSTS	($22,450)						
14								
15	Recurring Costs	$0	($19,750)	($19,750)	($19,750)	($19,750)	($19,750)	
16	Discount Rate (12%)	1.0000	0.8929	0.7972	0.7118	0.6355	0.5674	
17	PV of Recurring Costs	$0	($17,634)	($15,745)	($14,058)	($12,551)	($11,207)	
18								
19	NPV of All COSTS	($22,450)	($40,084)	($55,829)	($69,886)	($82,438)	($93,644)	($93,644)
20								
21								
22	Overall NPV							
23								$21,709
24								
25	Overall ROI- (Overall NPV/NPV of all COSTS)							
26								0.23
27								
28	Break-even Analysis							
29	Yearly NPV Cash Flow	($22,450)	$10,938	$9,766	$8,719	$7,785	$6,951	
30	Overall NPV Cash Flow	($22,450)	($11,513)	($1,747)	$6,972	$14,758	$21,709	
31								
32	Project Break-even Occurs Between Years 2 and 3							

Table 9.4 Commonly used economic cost-benefit analysis techniques.

Name of Technique	Description of Technique
Net Present Value (NPV)	NPV uses a discount rate determined from the company's cost of capital to establish the present value of a project. The discount rate is used to determine the present value of both cash receipts and outlays.
Return on Investment (ROI)	ROI is the ratio of the net cash receipts of the project divided by the cash outlays of the project. Tradeoff analysis can be made between projects competing for investment by comparing their representative ROI ratios.
Break-Even Analysis	This technique finds the amount of time required for the cumulative cash flow from a project to equal its initial and ongoing investment.

Source *Adapted from Hoffer, George, and Valacich. 1999. Modern Systems Analysis and Design. 2d ed. Reading, Massachusetts: Addison Wesley Longman.*

As described earlier, other criteria may also be used to evaluate a project (see Table 9.2). For example, suppose that an organization is contemplating the implementation of a new internal communication system (for example, Lotus Notes). It may be relatively easy to identify system costs. It may be very difficult, however, to quantify the potential financial benefits of this new communication environment because the organization does not have experience with this type of technology. If a financial analysis was used to evaluate the merit of a project in which only the tangible project costs could be identified, the organization may miss an important opportunity to improve their organizational communication radically. In such cases, organizations must rely on alternative evaluation criteria such as whether or not the system enables the firm to achieve its strategy.

Regardless of the criteria used to guide the decision, organizations can make a more informed decision regarding project acceptance or rejection after feasibility analysis for a project has been completed. If the project is accepted, system analysis begins.

Phase 2: System Analysis

The second phase of the systems development life cycle is called **system analysis**, as highlighted in Figure 9.9. One purpose of the system analysis phase is for designers to gain a thorough understanding of an organization's current way of doing things in the area for which the new information system will be constructed. The process of conducting an analysis requires that many tasks, or sub-phases, be performed. The first sub-phase focuses on determining system requirements. To determine the requirements, an analyst works closely with users to determine what is needed from the proposed system. Just as they did in the scenario that was used to open this chapter, analysts may interview users, develop questionnaires, or simply watch the day-to-day activities of users to gain an understanding of what the system must do. After the requirements are collected, analysts organize this information using data, process, and logic modeling tools. In short, every information system contains three key elements that must be understood by the systems analyst: data, processing logic, and data flows. These three elements are illustrated in Figure 9.10.

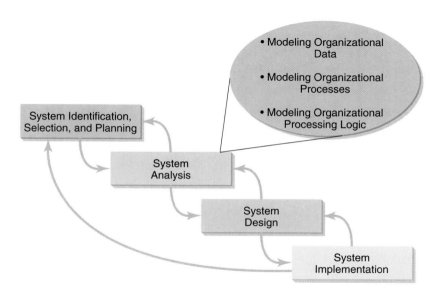

FIGURE 9.9

SDLC with Phase 2 highlighted.

FIGURE 9.10

Three key elements to development of a system: Data, Processing Logic, and Data Flows.

Data

Name	Class	GPA
Patty Nicholls	Senior	3.7
Brett Williams	Grad	2.9
Mary Shide	Fresh	3.2

Processing Logic

Data Flows

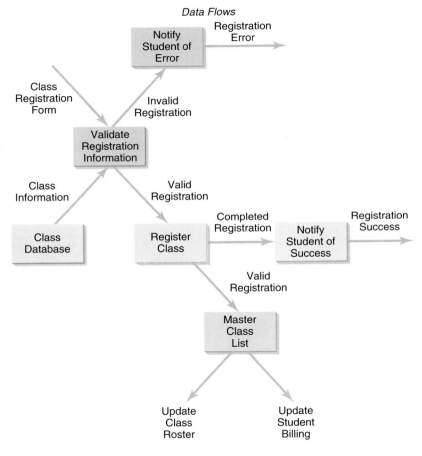

Processing Logic

```
i = read (number_of_classes)
total_hours = 0
total_grade = 0
total_gpa = 0
for j = 1 to i do
        begin
                read (course [ j ], hours [ j ], grade[ j ])
                total_hours = total_hours + hours [ j ]
                total_grade = total_grade + (hours [ j ] * grade [ j ])
        end
current_gpa = total_grade / total hours
```

Modeling Organizational Data

Data are facts that describe people, objects, or events. A lot of different facts can be used to describe a person: name, age, gender, race, and occupation. To construct an information system, systems analysts must understand what data the information system needs to accomplish the intended tasks. To do this, they use data modeling tools to collect and describe the data to users, to confirm that all needed data are known and presented to users as useful information. Figure 9.11 shows an Entity-Relationship Diagram, a type of data model, describing students, classes, majors, and classrooms at a university. Each box in the diagram is referred to as a data entity. Each data entity may have one or more attributes that describe it. For example, a "student" entity may have attributions such as: ID, Name, and Local Address. Additionally, each data entity may be "related" to other data entities. For example, because students take classes, there is a relationship between students and classes: "Student takes Class" and "Class has Student." Relationships are represented on the diagram by lines drawn between related entities. Data modeling tools enable the systems analyst to represent data in a form that is easy for users to understand and critique.

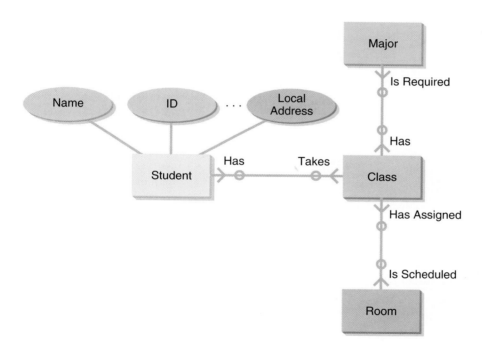

FIGURE 9.11

A sample ERD for students.

Modeling Organizational Processes

As the name implies, **data flows** represent the movement of data through an organization or within an information system. For example, your registration for a class may be captured on a registration form on paper or on a computer terminal. After it is filled out, this form probably flows through several processes to validate and record the class registration as shown as "Data Flows" in Figure 9.10. After all students have been registered, a repository of all registration information can be processed for developing class rosters or for generating student billing information, which is shown as "Data" in Figure 9.10. **Processing logic** represents the way in which data are transformed. For example, processing logic is used to calculate students' grade point averages at the conclusion of a term, as shown in the "Processing Logic" section in Figure 9.10.

After the data, data flow, and processing logic requirements for the proposed system have been identified, analysts develop one or many possible overall approaches—sometimes called "designs"—for the information system. For example, one approach for the system may possess only basic functionality, but have the advantages of being relatively easy and inexpensive to build. A more elaborate approach for the system might also be proposed, but it may be more difficult and more costly to build. Analysts evaluate alternative system approaches with the knowledge that different solutions yield different benefits and different costs. After an alternative system approach is selected, then details of that particular system approach can be defined.

Phase 3: System Design

The third phase of the systems development life cycle is **system design**, as shown in Figure 9.12. As its name implies, it is during this phase that the proposed system is designed; that is, the details of the particular approach chosen are developed. As with analysis, many different activities must occur during system design. The elements that must be designed when building an information system include

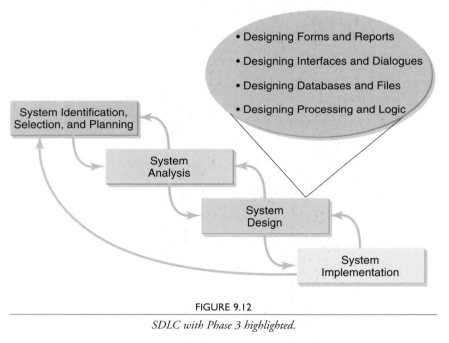

FIGURE 9.12

SDLC with Phase 3 highlighted.

- Forms and reports
- Interfaces and dialogues
- Databases and files
- Processing and logic

Designing Forms and Reports

Forms and reports represent the typical way in which information is put into or received from an information system. A **form** is a business document containing some predefined data and often including some areas where additional data can be filled in. For example, Figure 9.13 shows an employment application form with predefined information and areas where potential employees provide application information. Forms can be paper-based or computer-based. computer-based forms require that the user enter information via an input device such as a keyboard and view information via a video display device. Figure 9.14 shows a computer-based form taken from the World Wide Web home page of Novell®. Using this form, users can search for a wide variety of product and service information.

Application For Employment	Ascend Systems

Personal Information	
Name:	Date:
Social Security Number:	
Home Address:	
City, State, Zip	
Home Phone:	Business Phone:
U.S. Citizen?	If Not Give Visa No. and Expiration:

Position Applying For	
Title:	Salary Desired:
Referred By:	Data Available:

Education	
High School (Name, City, State):	
Graduation Date:	
Business or Technical School:	
Dates Attended:	Degree, Major:
Undergraduate College:	
Dates Attended:	Degree, Major:
Graduate School:	
Dates Attended:	Degree, Major:

References

FIGURE 9.13

Employment application.

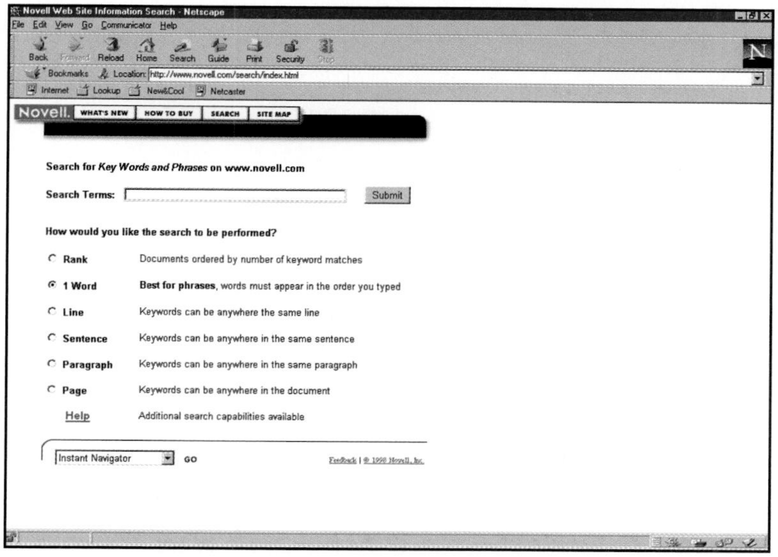

FIGURE 9.14

Novell® Web site search form.

Common business forms include product order forms, employment applications, and class registration sheets. You probably use a computer-based form regularly when you deposit or request currency from an Automated Teller Machine (ATM). On the other hand, a **report** is a business document containing only pre-defined data. In other words, reports are static documents that are used to summarize information for reading or viewing. For example, Figure 9.15 shows a report summarizing regional sales performance for several salespeople. As with forms, reports can be paper-based or computer-based.

FIGURE 9.15

Sales summary report.

Ascend Systems Incorporated
SALESPERSON ANNUAL SUMMARY REPORT 1998

REGION	SALESPERSON	SSN	QUARTERLY ACTUAL SALES			
			FIRST	SECOND	THIRD	FOURTH
Northwest and Mountain						
	Wachter	999-99-9999	16,500	18,600	24,300	18,000
	Mennecke	999-99-9999	22,000	15,500	17,300	19,800
	Wheeler	999-99-9999	19,000	12,500	22,000	28,000
Midwest and Mid-Atlantic						
	Spurrier	999-99-9999	14,000	16,000	19,000	21,000
	Powell	999-99-9999	7,500	16,600	10,000	8,000
	Topi	999-99-9999	12,000	19,800	17,000	19,000
New England						
	Speier	999-99-9999	18,000	18,000	20,000	27,000
	Morris	999-99-9999	28,000	29,000	19,000	31,000

You may be a bit confused by the subtle distinction between forms and reports, because they have many similarities. The biggest difference is that forms provide information and request new information, typically about a single record. In other words, a form would provide or capture information about a single student, a single product, or a single account. Reports, on the other hand, only provide information, and typically for multiple individuals, products, or accounts.

Designing Interfaces and Dialogues

A dialogue is a means of communication. For an information system, the interface and dialogue are the tools that enable users to interact with a system. Think about how you interact with other people. Your interface with others could be friendly and receptive, or it could be unfriendly and closed. You might give lots of non-verbal cues such as nodding your head and gesturing with your arms, or you might not give any non-verbal cues. Similarly, in your dialogue with other people you could ask simple questions that require yes/no answers, or you might describe a list of alternatives to someone else and ask him to choose the right answer.

Just as people have different ways of interacting with other people, information systems can have different ways of interacting with people. A system interface might be text-based, communicating with you through text and forcing you to communicate with it the same way. Alternatively, a system interface could use graphics and color as a way to interact with you, providing you with color-coded windows and special icons. A system dialogue could be developed such that it does nothing and waits for you to type in a command. Or it could ask you questions to which you type in commands, or present to you menus with choices from which you select your desired options. It could even do all these things.

Over the past several years, standards for user interfaces and dialogues have emerged. In the past, most systems had proprietary interfaces and dialogues. Consequently, very few systems looked or acted similarly, which left users frustrated and confused. The evolution of interface and dialogue standards helped to alleviate this problem. The first widely used standard for interacting with computers was proposed by Apple Computer in 1984 for the Macintosh personal computer. Later, Microsoft introduced a similar environment in 1990 called Windows 3.0 (Windows 1.0 was released in 1984, but found no commercial success because it couldn't run effectively on early personal computers); descendants of Windows—Windows 95, NT, and 98—are now the most widely used operating systems for personal computers. Both the Macintosh and Windows environments are generally referred to as being *graphical user interfaces.* (See Chapter 3, "Information Systems Software," for more on GUIs.) As in the Apple operating environment, information systems developed for Windows have a standard look and feel. In GUI environments, the system requests information by placing a standard window (or form) on the computer display. Menu names and the means of accessing operations are also standardized. For example, notice that for almost every Windows program the naming and placement of menus is similar (see Figure 9.16). For most Windows programs, the first menu is File and the last is Help. When systems analysts adopt a standard operating interface for the systems they design, it makes the system easier for users to learn and use. An additional benefit of using interface and dialogue standards is a reduction in the amount of software documentation and training materials needed by users.

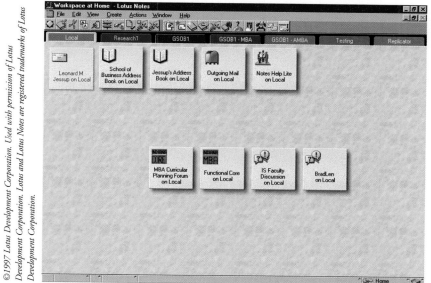

FIGURE 9.16

Most Windows-based programs follow a standard that governs the naming and placement of menus.

Designing Databases and Files

To design databases and files, a systems analyst must have a thorough understanding of the organization's data and informational needs. As described previously, a systems analyst often uses data modeling tools to first gain a comprehensive understanding of all the data used by a proposed system. After the *conceptual* data model has been completed, it can be easily translated into a *physical* data model in a database management system. For example, Figure 9.17 shows a physical data model to keep track of student information in Microsoft Access. The physical data model is more complete (shows more information about the student) and more detailed (shows how the information is formatted) than a conceptual data model. For example, contrast Figure 9.17 with the conceptual model in Figure 9.11 that contains student information.

FIGURE 9.17

An Access database.

C:\MSOFFICCE\ACCESS\STUDENT.MDB		Sunday, June 23, 1998
Table: Students		Page: 1

Properties

Date Created:	6/23/98 10:35:41 PM	Def. Updatable:	Yes
Last Updated:	6/23/98 10:35:43 PM	Record Count:	0

Columns

Name	Type	Size
StudentID	Number (Long)	4
FirstName	Text	50
MiddleName	Text	30
LastName	Text	50
ParentsNames	Text	255
Address	Text	255
City	Text	50
State	Text	50
Region	Text	50
PostalCode	Text	20
PhoneNumber	Text	30
EmailName	Text	50
Major	Text	50
Note	Memo	-

Designing Processing and Logic

The processing and logic operations of an information system are the steps and procedures that transform raw data inputs into new or modified information. For example, in the Transcript Reporting System that opened the chapter, systems people needed to calculate students' grade point averages. Calculating a grade point average would require the following steps to be performed:

1. Obtain the prior grade point average, credit hours earned, and list of prior courses

2. Obtain the list of each current course, final grade, and course credit hours

3. Combine the prior and current credit hours into aggregate sums

4. Calculate new grade point average

The logic and steps needed to make this calculation can be represented many ways. One method, referred to as writing **pseudo code**—a textual notation for describing programming code—enables the systems analyst to describe the processing steps in a manner that is similar to how a programmer might implement the steps in an actual programming language. The "Processing Logic" in Figure 9.10 is an example of pseudo code.

Other tools used by systems analysts during this activity include structure charts and decision trees. **Structure charts** are powerful tools for decomposing large problems into smaller pieces. For example, Figure 9.18 shows a high-level structure chart for a system to support student class registration at a university. **Decision trees** are helpful for designing how the actual logic of a program might be written when there are many different possibilities to consider. For example, Figure 9.19 shows a decision tree for determining undergraduate class standing by considering the number of credit hours earned and degree requirements completed.

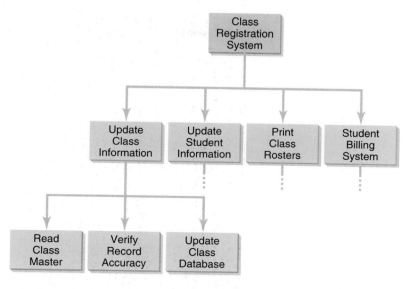

Collectively, pseudo code, structure charts, and decision trees are very powerful but easy-to-use tools for representing complex logic and processing. Converting pseudo code, structure charts, and decision trees into actual program code during system implementation is a very straightforward process.

FIGURE 9.18

Structure chart for registration system.

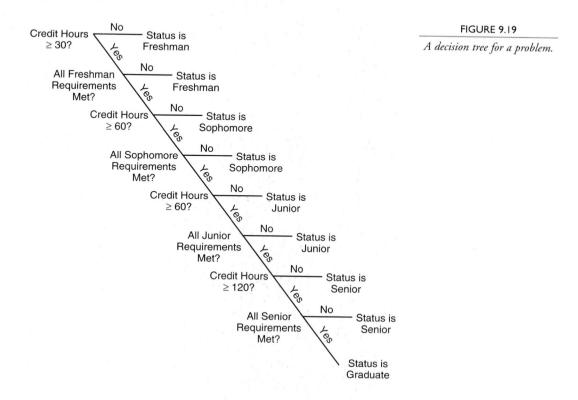

FIGURE 9.19

A decision tree for a problem.

Phase 4: System Implementation

Many separate activities occur during **system implementation**, the fourth phase of the systems development life cycle, as highlighted in Figure 9.20. One group of activities focuses on transforming the system design into a working information system that can be used by the organization. These activities include software programming and testing. A second group of activities focuses on preparing the organization for using the new information systems. These activities include system conversion, documentation, user training, and support. This section briefly describes what occurs during system implementation.

FIGURE 9.20

SDLC with Phase 4 highlighted.

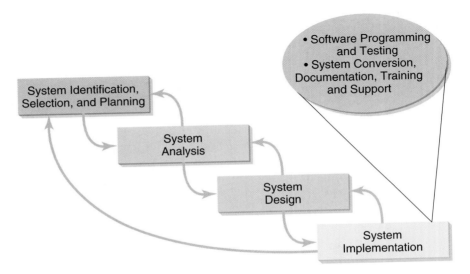

Software Programming and Testing

Programming is the process of transforming the system design into a working computer system. During this transformation, both processing and testing should occur in parallel. As you might expect, a broad range of tests are conducted before a system is complete, including developmental, alpha, and beta testing (see Table 9.5). **Developmental testing** is performed by programmers to assure that each module is error free. Develop-mental testing includes not only the testing of each separate program module but also the integrative testing of multiple modules. After all separate models of the system have been programmed and tested, **alpha testing** is performed by software testers to assess whether the entire system meets the design requirements of the users. During alpha testing, testers often force the system to fail by, for example, turning off the power to the computer or giving the system improper data. A goal of alpha testing is to determine whether the system can recover from unforeseen errors or problems. System security and performance may also be assessed during alpha testing. Finally, actual system users who test the capabilities of the system with actual data in the users' work environment perform **beta testing**. During beta testing, the development organization can also test system support mechanisms such as system help, documentation, training, and support. Testing may occur over weeks or several months, depending upon the size and complexity of the system.

Table 9.5 General testing types, their focus, and by whom they are performed.

Testing Type	Focus	Performed by
Developmental	Testing the correctness of individual modules and the integration of multiple modules	Programmer
Alpha	Testing of overall system to see whether it meets design requirements	Software tester
Beta	Testing of the capabilities of the system in the user environment with actual data	Actual system users

--- **Profile of a Software Tester** ---   A BRIEF CASE

A software tester spends most of his time trying to break software (see STI, 1998). Breaking software is referred to in the computer industry as "finding bugs." (A bug is a programming error, design flaw, or anything else that results in the computer program not running as intended.) Software testers spend countless hours trying to identify problems, typically long before the software is released to a widespread audience. Most software testers work, as you would guess, for software and computer companies such as Microsoft, IBM, or Netscape Communications. Software testers also work for companies in banking, insurance, and literally any other company devoted to developing high-quality software. In most cases, software testers are not systems developers, but many know how to program. Organizations have discovered that more errors are found if the people testing the software are separate from the development group. Many times, cash bonuses are given to testers for each bug found to give them a strong motivation for finding these pesky errors. Because testers must not only find errors, but also describe them after they are found, software testers must also have good communication skills, and be detail-oriented, patient, self-motivated, and creative. In addition to looking for bugs, software testers are also often assigned to provide customer support and training because of their intricate knowledge of how a new system works. Creating high-quality software requires a cooperative team of system designers, programmers, and testers. Good software testers are in high demand. So, if you like breaking things, and getting paid for it, maybe you would be a good software tester.

System Conversion, Documentation, Training, and Support

System conversion is the process of decommissioning the current system (automated or manual) and installing the new system into the organization. Effective conversion of a system requires not only that the new software be installed, but also that users be effectively trained and supported. System conversion can be performed in at least four ways. **Parallel conversion** is when both the old system and new system are used by the organization at the same time. After the organization is sure the new system is error free, that users are adequately trained, and that support procedures are in place, it can discontinue the old system, as illustrated in Figure 9.21a. Parallel conversion is the safest and least risky conversion strategy. Alternatively, a **direct conversion** is when the old system is discontinued on one day and the new system is used on the next, as illustrated in Figure 9.21b. Direct conversion is the riskiest conversion strategy because if the new system does not work correctly, no backup system is in place. A **phased conversion** is when parts of the system are implemented into the organization over time, as illustrated in Figure 9.21c. As each part is validated as working properly, new modules and features can be added and validated. A **pilot conversion** is when the entire system is used in one location, but not in the entire organization. After the system is validated as operating properly at one location, it can be disseminated throughout the entire organization, as illustrated in Figure 9.21d. Both phased and pilot conversion strategies have moderate levels of risk.

FIGURE 9.21

Software conversion strategies.

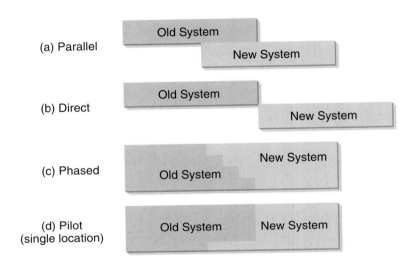

Many types of documentation must be produced for an information system. Programmers develop "system" documentation that details the inner workings of the system to ease future maintenance. Programmers develop system documentation in parallel with programming and testing activities. A second type of documentation is user-related documentation, which is not typically written by programmers or analysts, but by users or professional technical writers. The development of user documentation is a major project in and of itself for most large systems. For example, examine the documentation that accompanies a software system you have recently used or have purchased. It is likely that professional writers spent months developing these support manuals. The range of documents can include the following:

- User and reference guides

- User training and tutorials

- Installation procedures and troubleshooting suggestions

In addition to system documentation, users may also need training and ongoing support to effectively use a new system. Different types of training and support require different levels of investment by the organization. Self-paced training and tutorials are the least expensive options, and one-on-one training is the most expensive. Table 9.6 summarizes various user training options.

Table 9.6 User training options.

Training Option	Description
Tutorial	One person taught at one time by a human or by paper-based exercises
Course	Several people taught at one time
Computer-aided instruction	One person taught at one time by the computer system
Interactive training manuals	Combination of tutorials and computer-aided instruction
Resident expert	Expert on call to assist users as needed
Software help components	Built-in system components designed to train and troubleshoot problems
External sources	Vendors and training providers to provide tutorials, courses, and other training activities

IBM's Global Training Organization — A BRIEF CASE

Given the rapid pace at which software and systems are changing, more organizations are turning to outside vendors to provide user training. This is especially true for popular applications. For example, IBM provides training in more than 100 global locations on most popular PC applications; they provide more than 500 different PC-related courses (IBM, 1998). For one organization, they trained more than 10,000 employees to use Windows 95 and delivered this training in more than 60 different cities around the world. To be successful around the world, IBM offers classes in nine different languages. It is becoming much more cost effective for many organizations to use an outside organization for training employees on popular applications. Yet, for company-specific and custom applications, outside vendors are unlikely sources for training.

In addition to training, providing on-going education and problem-solving assistance for users is also necessary. This is commonly referred to as system support. The range of support activities might include the following:

- Installing the system

- Consulting on basic and advanced features

- Assisting in importing and exporting data from one system to another

- Setting up new users and accounts

- Providing demonstrations for new system uses

- Working with users on new system features and problems

System support is often provided by a special group of people in the organization who make up an information center or help desk. Support personnel must have strong communication skills and be good problem solvers, in addition to being expert users of the system. An alternative option for a system not developed internally is to outsource support activities to a vendor specializing in technical system support and training. Regardless of how support is provided, it is an ongoing issue that must be effectively managed for the company to realize the maximum benefits of a system.

Phase 5: System Maintenance

After an information system is installed, it is essentially in the maintenance phase of the SDLC. In the **maintenance phase**, one person within the systems development group is responsible for collecting maintenance requests from system users. After they are collected, requests are analyzed so that the developer can better understand how the proposed change might alter the system and what business benefits and necessities might result from such a change. If the change request is approved, a system change is designed and then implemented. As with the initial development of the system, implemented changes are formally reviewed and tested before installation into operational systems. The **system maintenance** process parallels the process used to initially develop the information system, as shown in Figure 9.22. Interestingly, it is during system maintenance that the largest part of the system development effort occurs.

FIGURE 9.22

Mapping of maintenance to SDLC.

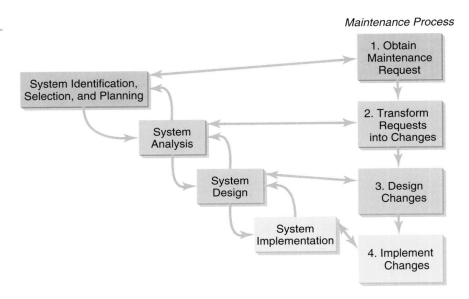

Maintenance Process

── **The Cost of Software and System Maintenance** ──

"When a company budgets $1 million to develop a new software system it is, in fact, committing to spend more than $4 million over the next five years. Each dollar spent on systems development generates, on average, 20 cents for operations and 40 cents for maintenance. Thus, the $1 million expenditure automatically generates a follow-on cost of $600,000 a year to support the initial investment. Development is in many ways the loss leader for maintenance." (Keen, 1991)

The question must be then, why does all this maintenance occur? It is not as if software wears out in the physical manner that cars, buildings, or other physical goods do. Correct? Yes, but software must still be maintained. For example, new features may be added to a system to better support changing business conditions. The Transcript Reporting System that was described at the beginning of the chapter is an example of a system being maintained because of changing business conditions (the University's change from a quarter- to a semester-based academic calendar). Maintenance may also be conducted to overcome internal processing errors not caught during programming and testing. In fact, most information systems development expenditures by organizations are on system maintenance activities. For some organizations, as much as 80 percent of their information systems budget is allocated to maintenance activities (Pressman, 1992). Interestingly, the proportion of systems expenditures on maintenance has also been rising relative to new development because many organizations have accumulated more and more older systems that require more and more maintenance. For example, Figure 9.23 shows that in the 1970s, most information systems expenditures were allocated to new development rather than maintenance. This mix has changed over the years so that the majority of expenditures are now earmarked for maintenance. Given this shift in software expenditures, building maintainable systems is critical to organizational success.

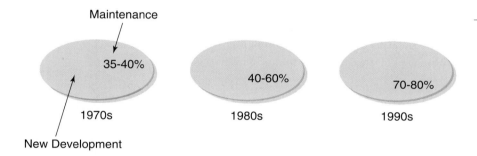

FIGURE 9.23

Pie charts show changing maintenance mix.

All maintenance requests can be classified as being one of four types: corrective, adaptive, perfective, or preventive (see Table 9.7). **Corrective maintenance** refers to making changes to an information system to repair flaws in the design, coding, or implementation. For example, if you recently purchased a used car, corrective maintenance would involve repairing things that are not working correctly. For information systems, most corrective maintenance problems surface soon after installation. When corrective maintenance problems surface, they are typically urgent and need to be resolved to prevent possible interruptions in normal business activities.

Table 9.7 Types of maintenance.

Type	Description
Corrective	Repair design and programming errors
Adaptive	Modify system to environmental changes
Perfective	Evolve system to solve new problems or take advantage of new opportunities
Preventive	Safeguard system from future problems

Source Adapted from Hoffer, George, and Valacich. 1999. Modern Systems Analysis and Design. 2d ed. Reading, Massachusetts: Addison Wesley Longman.

Adaptive maintenance refers to making changes to an information system to evolve its functionality to changing business needs or to migrate it to a different operating environment. For a car, adaptive maintenance might be adding snow tires to improve traction and handling during the winter. Adaptive maintenance is usually less urgent than corrective maintenance because business and technical changes typically occur over some period of time.

Perfective maintenance involves making enhancements to improve processing performance or interface usability, or adding desired, but not necessarily required, system features (in other words, "bells and whistles"). In the used car example, perfective maintenance might be the addition of better tires, a better stereo system, or a more efficient carburetor. Many system professionals feel that perfective maintenance is not really maintenance, but new development.

Finally, **preventive maintenance** involves changes made to a system to reduce the chance of future system failure. An example of preventive maintenance might be to increase the number of records that a system can process far beyond what is currently needed or to generalize how a system sends report information to a printer so that the system can easily adapt to changes in printer technology. In the used car example, preventive maintenance would be routine oil changes and tune-ups.

As with adaptive maintenance, both perfective and preventive maintenance are typically a much lower priority than corrective maintenance. Over the life of a system, corrective maintenance is most likely to occur after initial system installation or after major system changes. This means that adaptive, perfective, and preventive maintenance activities can lead to corrective maintenance activities if they are not carefully designed and implemented.

As you can see, there is more to system maintenance than you might think. Lots of time, effort, and money are spent in this final phase of a system's development, and it is important to follow prescribed, structured steps. In fact, the approach to systems development described in this chapter, from the initial phase of identifying, selecting, and planning for systems, to the final phase of system maintenance, is a very structured and systematic process. Each phase is fairly well prescribed and requires active involvement by systems people, users, and managers. It is likely that you will have numerous opportunities to participate in the acquisition or development of a new system for an organization for which you currently work or will work in the future. Now that you have an understanding of the process, you should be better equipped to make a positive contribution to the success of any systems development project. Good luck!

Talking with...

Jared Owens, Analyst at Procter & Gamble

Educational Background

B.A. in Mathematics, Wabash College, Crawfordsville, IN;
M.B.A. in Information Systems and Operations, Indiana University

Job Description

Mr. Owens is a database administrator (DBA) for a midrange Oracle database for Global Research and Development. He is responsible for the overall performance, capacity, and maintenance of six to seven databases on VMS (Digital Alpha machines) and UNIX (HP 9000s) operating platforms. He is also responsible for product and software upgrades and after-hours troubleshooting.

Critical Success Factors

Sell yourself in an interview. An interviewer recognizes if you feel inadequate—leverage the skills you have. A passion for new technology is important. Things are changing daily, even in conservative companies. Be adaptable. Be an effective communicator and take leadership roles on teams. Teamwork is just as important as they say in business schools. Persevere. Don't let snags or shortcomings keep you from achieving the goal you want. If you want to make a career path change, aggressively seek one. In your job, if you want to work with certain products or technologies, keep pushing the buttons until you get there.

Advice to Students

Learn as many technical skills as possible. Most likely, you will not jump straight to technology management—you need to learn it first. Sell the skills that you do have; you can be trained for those you don't. But you need something to get in the door. Learn how all things work; don't just focus on coding or hardware or project management. Try to see the big picture. Find out quickly whether you work well in open environments (consulting or technology) or more structured environments (most industry). If you don't like one or the other, you probably should not seek jobs in that area.

ETHICAL PERSPECTIVE: ACCURACY—WHO IS RESPONSIBLE?

The issue of information accuracy has become highly charged in today's wired world. With all the computerization that has taken place, people have come to expect to receive and retrieve information more easily and quickly than ever before. In addition, because computers "never make mistakes," we have come to expect this information to be accurate. A case in point is at the bank. The combination of Automatic Teller Machines, computerized record systems, and large, electronic client and transaction databases should provide customers with quick and accurate access to their account information. However, we continue to experience and hear about record keeping errors at banks.

An error of a few dollars in your banking records doesn't seem so significant. However, what if it was an error in the bank's favor of hundreds or thousands of dollars? What if the error caused one of your important payments (such as a home mortgage payment) to bounce? Bank errors can be quite important.

There are many now-infamous stories of data accuracy problems with information systems, many of which have involved banks. For example, one such case occurred in Los Angeles, but has surely been repeated many times around this country and others. The basic story is as follows. Louis and Eileen Marches had bought a house in the 1950s with financing through their local bank. Louis dutifully paid the monthly payments in person and made sure that his loan book was stamped "paid" every time, even after the bank's systems had been automated. Several years ago, the Marches were notified that their payments were in arrears. Louis went to the bank with his payment book, but because the account screen showed no payment, the teller, the head teller, and the bank manager refused to honor his stamped book. One month later the same thing happened again, but now two months were in arrears. The bank continued to refuse his proof of payment and based their decisions and actions solely on the computer system. Eventually, the bank foreclosed on the house, causing a near fatal stroke for Eileen. After a long lawsuit, the Marches recovered $268,000 from the bank and the following apology: "Computers make mistakes. Banks make mistakes, too." Similar stories abound about people who have found that mistakes in their credit reports have led to disastrous results.

Now, imagine how significant a data accuracy error might be in other settings. Hospitals use similar automation and computer-intensive record keeping. Imagine what would happen if prescription information appeared incorrectly on a patient's chart and the patient became deathly ill as a result of the medicine that was mistakenly dispensed to him. The significance of such a data accuracy error could be tremendous. Furthermore, it wouldn't be clear who was to blame. Would this be the fault of the doctor, the pharmacist, the programmer, the data entry clerk, or maybe some combination of errors by the system designer, the system analyst, the system programmer, the database administrator, and the vendor? It would be too easy to simply blame the computer; some one person would need to be found to blame.

Computer-based information systems, and the data within those systems, are only as accurate and as useful as they have been made to be. The now infamous quote that "Computers make mistakes. Banks make mistakes, too" would be better restated as, "Computers never make mistakes; only humans make mistakes." This reflects the need for better precautions and greater scrutiny when modern information systems are designed, built, and used. This means that everyone must be concerned with data integrity, from the design of the system, to the building of the system, to the person that actually enters data into the system, and to the people who use and manage the system. Perhaps more importantly, when data errors are found, people shouldn't blame the computer. After all, people designed and built it, and entered data into it in the first place.

Questions for Discussion

1. Who is responsible for the accuracy of data within information systems? Why?

2. When someone is injured, either figuratively or literally, by errors in data from an information system, who should be responsible for making the injured party whole again?

3. Have you encountered data accuracy problems such as these? If so, what was the problem? What were the consequences? How were the problems remedied?

INTERNATIONAL PERSPECTIVE: HELP WANTED: MONOLINGUALS NEED NOT APPLY

Wanted:

People with advanced degrees in engineering, computer science, or information systems. TCP/IP, HTML, C, and JAVA programming experience a plus. Will provide green card, housing, and outstanding salary. Silicon Valley location.

Wanted:

Managers who are fluently bilingual; experience managing technology projects; experience living abroad and dealing with U.S., European, or Asian clients a must. Locations worldwide.

These job ads represent the kinds of human resource needs that global companies are facing. Currently, businesses all over the world are battling fiercely to attract two sets of employees: those who have high-tech skills and those who can deal effectively in a global marketplace. Companies need people to help them build information systems worldwide using precisely the methodologies described in this chapter.

As many as a third of all Silicon Valley professionals are currently non-native; these engineers, programmers, computer scientists, and information systems specialists from Asia, India, and other countries have been granted work permits (and sometimes permanent residency) by employers, universities, and the U.S. government. There still are not enough workers to fill spots in the booming technology sector, according to Intel, Microsoft, and other technology giants. Business leaders claim that a lack of focus on science, engineering, and technology in U.S. K–12 schools and a lack of interest in the same by American university graduates has caused a major shortage of qualified workers in these areas. Recruiting at U.S. universities has intensified, and the hiring of such a diverse group of workers reflects the growing population of foreign nationals willing to take up the slack. In fact, Silicon Valley companies are lobbying the U.S. government to allow them to hire a greater proportion of foreign nationals.

This same situation is occurring in other countries, where multinational corporations are desperate to hire well-trained workers for excellent salaries. Asian companies are looking for huge numbers of managers and other workers who are able to bridge the gap between Eastern and Western cultures; business owners in Hong Kong, Malaysia, Taiwan, and Japan note that they already have an acute need that will grow as businesses expand. For those contemplating careers with these companies, it may be easier to adapt to their environments than in the past; businesses such as Fujitsu are adopting some of the characteristics of Silicon Valley businesses, such as allowing flex-time, deserting dress codes, and permitting employees to pursue creative projects.

Given that the business world is becoming much more global and electronically connected, there are and will be tremendous opportunities for those individuals who possess technological skills and information systems project management skills, as well as have proficiency in a second language, knowledge of other cultures, and/or skills in dealing with people from other cultures in business contexts. Students who think ahead and acquire these skills during their degree programs will be able to write their own (plane) tickets upon graduation!

Questions for Discussion

1. Would you be willing to work in another country? Why or why not?

2. What are some possible effects if the trend of American businesses hiring foreign nationals continues?

3. What can be done to attract students into the science and technology disciplines?

Summary

1. **Understand the process used by organizations to manage the development of information systems.** The development of information systems follows a process called the systems development life cycle (SDLC). The SDLC is a process that first identifies the need for a system and then defines the processes for designing, developing, and maintaining information systems. The process is very structured and formal and requires the active involvement of managers and users.

2. **Describe each major phase of the systems development life cycle: systems identification, selection, and planning; system analysis; system design; system implementation; and system maintenance.** The SDLC has five phases: system identification, selection, and planning; system analysis; system design; system implementation; and system maintenance. Systems identification, selection, and planning is the first phase of the SDLC, in which potential projects are identified, selected, and planned. System analysis is the second phase of the SDLC, in which the current ways of doing business are studied and alternative replacement systems are proposed. System design is the third phase of the SDLC, in which all features of the proposed system are described. System implementation is the fourth phase of the SDLC, in which the information system is programmed, tested, installed, and supported. System maintenance is the fifth and final phase of the SDLC, in which an information system is systematically repaired and improved.

3. **Explain how organizations identify projects, assess feasibility, identify system benefits and costs, and perform economic analysis of a system project.** When a potential system is identified, organizations must assess the feasibility of the project before proceeding. The types of feasibility that can be assessed are economic, technical, operational, schedule, legal and contractual, and political. A system can provide tangible and intangible benefits, as well as tangible and intangible costs. An economic assessment requires that you identify the project's potential tangible benefits and costs and calculate the net present value, return on investment, or break-even duration. Feasibility analysis helps managers determine the probability of project success and compare alternative projects. Organiza-tions can yield the greatest benefits from their investments in information technology only by following a thorough and systematic feasibility assessment.

Key Terms

Systems analysis and design

Systems analyst

Software engineering

Systems development life cycle

System identification, selection, and planning

Information systems planning

Tangible benefits

Intangible benefits

Tangible costs

Intangible costs

One-time costs

Recurring costs

System analysis

Data flows

Processing logic

System design

Form

Report

Pseudo code

Structure charts

Decision trees

System implementation

Developmental testing

Alpha testing

Beta testing

System conversion

Parallel conversion

Direct conversion

Phased conversion

Pilot conversion

Maintenance phase

System maintenance

Corrective maintenance

Adaptive maintenance

Perfective maintenance

Preventive maintenance

Review Questions

1. According to this chapter, what are the five phases of the systems development life cycle?

2. Describe the four options available to organizations for obtaining information systems.

3. Describe the four major sources of systems development projects within an organization. What is the primary focus of each?

4. What are some of the possible criteria used to evaluate possible systems development projects?

5. Compare and contrast the terms system analysis and design, systems analyst, and system analysis. How are they related?

6. What are the four major components/tasks of the system design phase of the SDLC?

7. Explain the similarities and differences between forms and reports.

8. Describe the major forms of system testing—developmental, alpha, and beta.

9. What are the four processes for system conversion? How do they differ from each other?

10. Compare and contrast the four types of system maintenance.

11. What factors are considered in an economic feasibility study of an information systems project?

Problems and Exercises

Individual   **Group**   **Field**   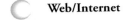 **Web/Internet**

1. Match the following terms to the appropriate definitions:

_____ Alpha testing

_____ System analysis

_____ Data flows

_____ Structure charts

_____ Parallel conversion

_____ Adaptive maintenance

_____ Tangible benefits

_____ One-time costs

a. Data in motion, moving from one place in the system to another

b. Making changes to an information system to evolve its functionality to meet changing business needs or to migrate it to a different operating environment

c. Changing over from the old to a new system by running both at the same time until the organization is sure that the new system is error free, that the users are adequately trained, and that the support procedures are in place

d. Benefits that are easily measured in dollars and with certainty

e. Testing performed by the development organization to assess whether the entire system meets the design requirements of the users

f. Hierarchical diagram that shows how an information system is organized

g. Costs that occur once during the life of a system, typically during project initiation

h. The second phase of the systems development life cycle, in which the current ways of doing business are studied and alternative replacement systems are proposed

2. A recently hired IS professional in your organization states that following a particular methodology, whether the SDLC from this chapter or any other methodology, causes development projects to take longer than necessary to implement. This person believes that projects should be developed quickly to maximize the benefits to be realized after they are in place. Do you agree? Why or why not? Explain to this person the broad goal of following methodologies for systems development. What about long-term benefits?

3. Do you agree with the assessment that the use of the systems development steps outlined in the chapter will be around for quite some time? Why or why not? Is this process appropriate when purchasing a system from an outside vendor?

4. Consider the following within a small group: Table 9.1 shows the different sources of systems development projects. Of the four listed, which do you consider the best? Why? What makes it any better than the others? Should companies use only one of these sources for their potential projects? Why or why not?

 5. Explain the differences between data and data flows. How might systems analysts obtain the information they need to generate the data flows of a system? How are these data flows and the accompanying processing logic used in the system design phase of the life cycle? What happens when the data and data flows are modeled incorrectly?

 6. Discuss why interfaces and dialogueues can make or break a new system. What are their key functions? When are they designed? Are there any conventions for producing interfaces and dialogueues? If so, what are they?

 7. When Microsoft posts a new version of Internet Explorer on the Microsoft Web site and states that this is a beta version, what do they mean? Is this a final working version of the software, or is it still being tested? Who is doing the testing? Search the World Wide Web to find other companies that have beta versions of their products available to the public. You might try Corel at http://www.corel.com/. What other companies did you find?

 8. Imagine that you have just finished developing a new system for your company. This new system, unfortunately, cannot operate on the network at the same time as the current/old system. In a small group of classmates, determine what conversion plan you would recommend for this new system. Why? What risks does this plan bring and what advantages does it have over the other options?

 9. Why is the system documentation of a new information system so important? What information does it contain? For whom is this information intended? When will the system documentation most likely be used?

10. Based on your own experiences with systems and applications, did their user documentation meet your expectations? Were you able to find the information and answers you needed? If you know, who wrote these guides, manuals, and/or procedures? Was it someone from the group that developed the system or someone from the outside?

 11. In a small group, conduct a search on the World Wide Web for "systems development life cycle" using any browser you wish. Check out some of the hits. Compare them to the SDLC outlined in this chapter and the SDLC utilized by NASA. Do all these life cycles follow the same general path? How many phases do the ones you found on the Web contain? Is the terminology the same or different? Prepare a 10-minute presentation of your findings to the class.

 12. Choose an organization with which you are familiar that develops its own information systems. Does this organization follow a systems development life cycle? If not, why not? How many phases does it have? Who developed this life cycle? Was it someone within the company, or was it adopted from somewhere else?

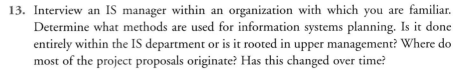

13. Interview an IS manager within an organization with which you are familiar. Determine what methods are used for information systems planning. Is it done entirely within the IS department or is it rooted in upper management? Where do most of the project proposals originate? Has this changed over time?

14. Choose an organization with which you are familiar that utilizes top-down systems planning for determining new projects to be developed. Is there any bottom-up systems planning in this organization? Why or why not? Who within the organization is most involved in this process?

15. Interview an IS manager within an organization with which you are familiar. Determine what techniques the IS department uses for analyzing the economic costs and benefits of a proposed system. Do they use only one technique? If so, why that one? If not, does one technique carry more weight if contradictory results are found? Do IS professionals conduct this analysis, or is it done by someone else? What did your fellow classmates find out from their interviews? Compare and contrast the results.

16. With a group of classmates, describe your experiences with information systems that were undergoing changes or updates (something similar to the scenario in the beginning of the chapter). What kind of conversion procedure was being used? How did this affect your interaction with the system as a user? Who else was affected? If the system was down altogether, for how long was it down? Do you or any of your classmates have "horror" stories, or were the situations not that bad?

Real World Case Problems

1. Software Gains Capital Treatment.

As of December 15, 1998, companies will be required to treat software bought or developed for internal use as an asset on their balance sheets. This rule confirms what IS managers have known for ages: Software can be as valuable as a factory. James Harrington of Coopers & Lybrand states that "Software is equivalent to the bricks and mortar of the information age."

Because the costs of large software projects will now depreciate over several years, like the costs associated with building a new factory, it is much more likely that companies will approve large, long-term IT projects. The IS managers trying to get projects approved may have to go through more red tape, however, such as forecasting a planned system's life span and its return on an investment. This is a difficult call in any environment. One overall benefit of this new rule is that IS managers will probably examine potential applications more closely for long-term solutions.

Company valuation could also change. For any company constantly investing in IT, capitalizing the software costs will increase the earnings and stockholder's equity, thus yielding an increase in the company's stock price, making it easier to borrow or prompt a higher takeover bid from a corporate suitor. Failing to capture the software's value as an asset can reduce the value of a company, especially during an acquisition or sale.

Time will tell whether it is best to record a project's costs as expenses as they are incurred or to capitalize the costs as an asset and depreciate them over the system's useful life. Some costs—such as maintenance, software coding, Year 2000 repairs, and R & D projects—will still be expressed because they do not create new functionality. The initial value of the project is the sum of the developers' salaries and the cost of the packaged software. Expensed means early pain, whereas depreciation delays it.

a. Explain the significant difference between recording an information systems project's costs as expenses as they are incurred versus capitalizing the costs as an asset and then depreciating that asset over the system's useful life. Why is this potentially important to businesses?

b. What effect will this have on the way that managers quantify the costs and benefits of information systems projects?

c. Will this make it easier for some firms to say yes to large, expensive projects? Why or why not?

Source *Hibbard, Justin. 1998. Software gains capital treatment.* InformationWeek, *January 12, 18–20.*

2. Wright Consulting Services

Wright Consulting Services, Inc. (WCS), of Portland, Oregon, provides information systems (IS) consulting services to clients in the Pacific Northwest, primarily in the Portland/Willamette Valley and Seattle/Puget Sound areas. Services include systems analysis, design, development, and implementation using Oracle Developer/2000. Clients include private sector companies of all sizes, state and local government agencies, schools and universities, and nonprofit organizations.

The purpose of WCS's systems analysis service is to gain an understanding of an organization's existing information systems. Activities include Information Gathering, Physical Process Modeling, Logical Data Modeling, and Logical Process Modeling. In the systems design phase, WCS redesigns clients' systems to more effectively match their requirements. Tasks within the systems design phase include Physical Data Modeling, Physical Process Modeling, Rapid Prototyping, Capacity Planning, and Technology Evaluation and Selection. In the systems development and implementation phase, WCS breaks down a system implementation into smaller steps and builds the system step by step, piece by piece. Activities in this phase include Technology Acquisition and/or Customization, Custom Software Development, System Testing, Data Conversion, Technical Documentation, User Documentation, and User Training.

Among its many successful engagements, WCS developed an application to manage a telecommunications company's stored value (phone/gas/merchandise) cards. Software is used by customer service representatives to view card status and transaction histories and issue manual transactions at customers' requests, by finance analysts to review transactions and issue invoices to retailers, and by merchants to review transactions. Applications were developed using Oracle Developer/2000 Forms 4.5 under Microsoft Windows.

a. How closely do the services of Wright Consulting Services parallel the methodologies described in this chapter?

b. In what ways are WCS's services different from those described in this chapter?

c. Why should companies turn to WCS to perform systems analysis and design rather than doing it themselves in-house?

Source *Wright Consulting Web site: http://www.wriconsult.com/index.html.*

References

Hoffer, George, and Valacich. 1999. *Modern systems analysis and design.* 2d ed. Reading, Massachusetts: Addison Wesley Longman.

IBM. 1998. Information from: www.ibm.com. Information verified: March 21, 1998.

Keen, P.G.W. 1991. *Shaping the future: Business design through information technology.* Cambridge, Massachusetts: Harvard Business School Press.

McKeen, Guimaraes, and Wetherbe. 1994. A comparative analysis of MIS project selection mechanisms. *Database* 25: 43–59.

NASA. 1998. Information from: www.ivv.nasa.gov. Information verified: March 21, 1998.

Nunamaker, J.F., Jr. 1992. Build and learn, evaluate and learn. *Informatica* 1(1): 1–6.

Pressman, R.S. 1992. *Software engineering.* New York: McGraw-Hill.

STI. 1998. Information from: www.ondaweb.com/sti/. Information verified: March 21, 1998.

Related Readings

Agarwal, Sinha, and Tanniru. 1996. Cognitive fit in requirements modeling: A study of object and process methodologies. *Journal of Management Information Systems* 13(2): 137–162.

Banker, R.D., and S.A. Slaughter. 1997. A field study of scale economies in software maintenance. *Management Science* 43(12): 1709–1725.

Beath, C.M., and W.J. Orlikowski. 1994. The contradictory structure of systems development methodologies: Deconstructing the IS-user relationship in information engineering. *Information Systems Research* 5(4): 350–377.

Bordoloi, Mykytyn, and Mykytyn. 1996. A framework to limit systems developers' legal liabilities. *Journal of Management Information Systems* 12(4): 161–185.

Cusamano, M.A., and R.W. Selby. 1997. How Microsoft builds software. *Communications of the ACM* 40(6): 53–61.

Fayad, M.E. 1997. Software development process: A necessary evil. *Communications of the ACM* 40(9): 101–103.

Hidding, G.J. 1997. Reinventing methodology: Who reads it and why? *Communications of the ACM* 40(11): 102–109.

McKeen, J.D., and T. Guimaraes. 1997. Successful strategies for user participation in systems development. *Journal of Management Information Systems* 14(2): 133–150.

Newman, M., and R. Sabherwal. 1996. Determinants of commitment to information systems development: A longitudinal investigation. *Management Information Systems Quarterly* 20(1): 23–54.

Rada, R., and J. Moore. 1997. Standardizing reuse. *Communications of the ACM* 40(3): 19–23.

Robey, Smith, and Vijayasarathy. 1993. Perceptions of conflict and success in information systems development projects. *Journal of Management Information Systems* 10(1): 123–139.

Sillince, J.A.A., and S. Mouakket. 1997. Varieties of political process during systems development. *Information Systems Research* 8(4): 368–397.

Vessey, I., and S. Conger. 1993. Learning to specify information requirements: The relationship between application and methodology. *Journal of Management Information Systems* 10(2): 177–201.

Scenario: Information Management at The King of Hearts Ranch

Brett Williams, owner of The King of Hearts Ranch in Great Falls, Montana, raises some of the finest cutting horses in the United States. "Cutting" has its roots in the open-range ranches of the Old West, where individual animals had to be isolated or "cut" from large herds for branding, medical treatment, or sorting. Certain horses showed an uncommon ability for separating cattle from the herd. These were the first cutting horses. Today, cutting horses are specially bred and trained. To identify the best cutting horses, special competitions are held where horse and rider have two and a half minutes to demonstrate their ability to cut a cow and keep it separated from a herd. Top cutting horses are worth more than a hundred thousand dollars. Although it comes from humble roots, cutting is big business!

At The King of Hearts Ranch, dozens of horses are cared for and trained (see Figure 10.1). Some horses are kept for breeding, some are kept for competing in cutting contests, and others—still young and unproved—are kept for training. Those not making "cutting grade" are sold off to riders who are looking for a very high-quality horse that was just not meant for cutting. For each horse, detailed information must be tracked on health, breeding, and competitions. Needless to say, managing information is an important part of the horse business. Until now, Brett has kept track of his information through the use of several ledgers. He has separate ledgers for tracking health, births and breeding, and competitions. Unfortunately, as his ranch grew, it became more and more difficult to find important information.

One night at a family gathering he talked to his nephew, a senior MIS student at the University of Montana, about his information management problems. After about an hour-long discussion, Brett summarized, "So Greg, I could hire you this summer to build a system to track all my information with a computer. This sounds great, so how would we proceed?"

"Well," replied Greg, "I would need to first interview you for an hour or so to get an idea about what you do. I will also need to get some examples of the kinds of information you use. After we do this, I could create a prototype of the system. Next, you could review this prototype and give me additional information, and suggest changes to make. We would do this until the system looked the way you wanted and provided the information you needed. The best part about building the system this way is that at the end, you have a system that does exactly what you want!"

"How long will it take to do this?" replied Brett.

FIGURE 10.1

Cutting ranch.

©Myrleen Ferguson/PhotoEdit.

CHAPTER 10

"It is not uncommon to have more than ten iterations of talking with you, refining the prototype, and then having you review my work," replied Greg. "Each iteration should take about a week to accomplish. Overall, I am confident that I could build your system over the summer, but maybe in less than two months if all goes well. I'll have a better idea of this after our first meeting; after that I'll write you a firm proposal."

Introduction

Chapter 9, "The Information Systems Development Process," talked about the information systems development process and described the systems development life cycle (SDLC). Recall that the SDLC has five phases and is most widely used to guide the development of contemporary organizational information systems such as transaction processing and management information systems. (See Chapter 7 for a review of organizational information systems). As you have read throughout this book and have experienced in your own life, information systems are of many different types, including decision support systems, executive information systems, group support systems, and Internet commerce systems. Each system is radically different from the others and from the typical system built using the SDLC. These differences are analogous to the differences among structures that could be built by a contractor. Some contractors build houses, while others build apartment buildings, warehouses, or skyscrapers.

For the building contractor, the tools and techniques needed to construct each type of structure vary greatly. Building a house is a relatively simple process using wood, nails, saws, and a minimal amount of other equipment. Of course, it is possible to build a skyscraper with the same materials and equipment, but it would probably not be constructed in the most timely and effective way. Steel girders and huge cranes speed the construction and enhance the structural quality of a skyscraper. These materials are not needed when building a house. Likewise, the tools and techniques that can be used to design and build different types of information systems vary greatly. This does not mean that you can't use the SDLC for all types of systems; you could if you wanted to. But building the best system requires that you use the right tools and techniques for the right job. Consequently, as new and different types of information systems have emerged, so too have new development approaches and tools.

This chapter describes emerging system development approaches. It first focuses on ways to identify and define system requirements—in other words, ways to get information from users on how the system should operate. Getting the system requirements correct at the beginning goes a long way toward building a high-quality system. The next section discusses emerging approaches for managing the entire development process. These approaches represent alternatives to the SDLC. Finally, the chapter describes several tools that have emerged to assist the systems development process. The goal of this chapter is to increase your knowledge of systems development methods. After reading this chapter, you will be able to do the following:

1. Explain contemporary approaches for collecting and structuring the information needed to design and construct an information system.

2. Describe prototyping, rapid application development, object-oriented analysis and design methods of systems development, and each approach's strengths and weaknesses.

3. Understand how and why to use several automated tools for supporting contemporary development, including computer-aided software engineering, group support systems, and advanced programming languages.

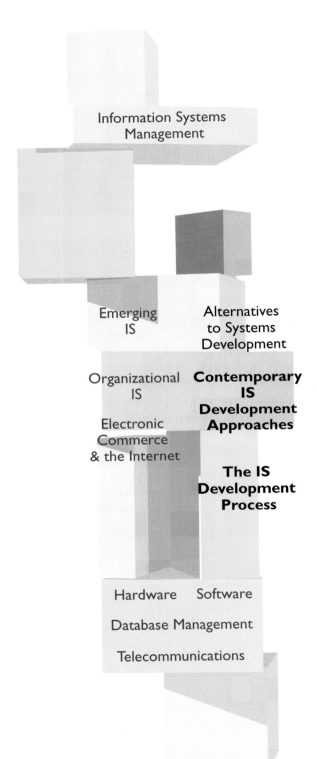

Information Systems
Management

Emerging
IS

Alternatives
to Systems
Development

Organizational
IS

**Contemporary
IS
Development
Approaches**

Electronic
Commerce
& the Internet

**The IS
Development
Process**

Hardware   Software

Database Management

Telecommunications

This chapter is the second in Part 4, "Information Systems Development," and it focuses on describing how organizations develop and acquire information systems (see Figure 10.2). In Chapter 9, we discussed the development process used to design and build most information systems. This chapter describes the various processes used to develop and build most contemporary information systems.

Contemporary Methods for Collecting and Structuring System Requirements

This section examines contemporary approaches for collecting and structuring system requirements, which are the tasks a systems professional performs during the systems analysis phase (the second phase) of the system development life cycle. The collection and structuring of system requirements is arguably the most important activity in the systems development process because all subsequent activities are influenced by how well the information system requirements are defined. The old saying, "garbage in, garbage out," very much applies to the system building process.

As you read in the preceding chapter, one purpose of the systems analysis phase is to gain a thorough understanding of an organization's current way of doing things in an area for which the new information system is to be constructed. System analysts work closely with users to determine what is needed from the proposed system. Analysts have traditionally asked users what information they need to have put into the system and what types of information they need back from the system to do their job well. This chapter describes a method for collecting system requirements that focuses the kinds of questions the analysts ask the users.

FIGURE 10.2

The big picture: focusing on contemporary information systems development approaches.

Critical Success Factors (CSF)

The **Critical Success Factor** (CSF) methodology for collecting system requirements was developed by Jack Rockart of MIT in the late 1970s as a means to help CEOs define their information system needs (Rockart, 1979). It is still quite popular today as a way to obtain a useful set of system requirements from users. A Critical Success Factor, or CSF, is something that must go well to ensure success for a manager, department, division, or organization. It was envisioned by Rockart that if CEOs—and all members of the organization, for that matter—understood and agreed upon a common set of CSFs, it would be a straightforward task to derive the informational needs of the organization.

How the CSF Approach Works

To understand an organization's CSFs, a systems analyst interviews people throughout the organization and asks each person to define her own *personal* CSFs. People asked to participate in the CSF identification process should be from a cross-section of the major functional areas of the organization. After the analyst collects these individual CSFs, he can merge, consolidate, and refine them to identify a broad set of organization-wide CSFs, as shown in Figure 10.3.

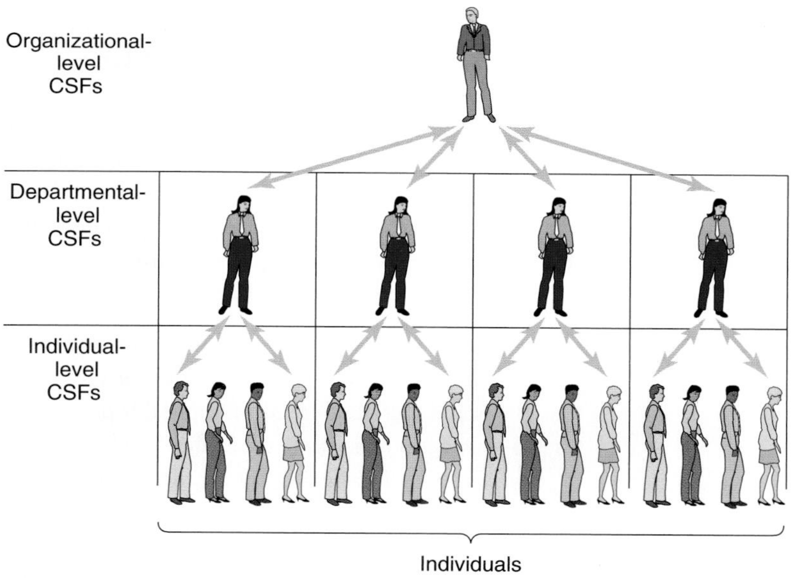

Strengths and Weaknesses of the CSF Approach

All approaches for assisting the information systems development process have strengths and weaknesses, and the CSF approach is no exception (see Boynton and Zmud, 1994). The greatest strength of the CSF approach is that senior managers intuitively understand the approach and support its usage. This is in contrast to other systems development approaches that are unintuitive and less strategically focused. A second strength is that the CSF approach provides a way to understand the information needs of the organization in order to make effective decisions. A steering or planning committee for an organization can greatly improve its effectiveness by understanding the organization's CSFs when identifying and selecting projects.

Weaknesses of the CSF approach are that the method's high-level focus can lead to an oversimplification of a complex situation. For example, people have a limited capacity for dealing with complexity and a limited capacity for keeping track of information. These limits may result in managers recalling only the most recent events, or events that are over-simplified for the complex environment in which the organization operates. As

FIGURE 10.3

Merging individual CSFs to represent organization-wide CSFs.

a result, the analyst may be left with a biased or incomplete set of information requirements. Using a broad cross-section of organizational personnel can minimize some of these problems. A second weakness centers on the difficulty of finding analysts trained to perform the CSF process that must both understand information systems and be able to effectively communicate with senior executives. Past research has found that the quality of the analyst is a key factor in the successful application of the process.

A third weakness of the CSF approach is that this method is not user-centered; that is, it relies on an expert systems analyst to glean requirements from users and to organize them appropriately. The next section explores other methods for collecting and organizing system requirements that are more user-centered.

Joint Application Requirements (JAR)/Joint Application Design (JAD)

Joint Application Requirements (JAR) and **Joint Application Design (JAD)** are methods for collecting requirements and creating system designs. Most often, people refer to both JAR and JAD as simply JAD. As with the CSF approach, JAD was introduced in the late 1970s by IBM Canada and is quite popular today as an alternative methodology within the systems analysis phase of the systems development life cycle. The defining aspect of JAD is that "joint" really means group. In other words, the JAD method is a group-based approach for collecting system requirements and for setting system design specifications. JAD was the first method for building information systems that stressed the use of groups. To understand why this is significant, recall the requirements development process within the systems development life cycle (SDLC), first described in Chapter 9.

When collecting system requirements and following the guidelines of the SDLC, a systems analyst interviews potential users of the new information system individually to understand each user's needs. During this process, the analyst may interview a large number of users. In most cases, the analyst will hear a lot of similar requests from most of the users, but will also hear many conflicting requests. The analyst will therefore spend considerable effort consolidating information and following up with users to resolve conflicting requirements and specifications. If many people are being consulted, the process of scheduling and conducting these individual interviews can be quite time consuming.

In contrast to the SDLC approach to determining systems requirements, a JAD is a special type of a group meeting in which all users meet with the analyst at the same time. During this meeting, all users *jointly* define and agree upon system requirements or designs. This process has resulted in dramatic reductions in the length of time needed to collect requirements or specify designs.

How the JAD Approach Works

The JAD meeting can be held in a normal conference room or special-purpose JAD room. Figure 10.4 shows a sample JAD room. JAD meeting rooms are often designed much like a classroom, with facilities for presenting information to the group. Most JAD rooms have overhead projectors, whiteboards, flip charts, and computers to assist in making presentations and to help in recording the ideas and deliberations of the group. Often, JAD meetings are held "off-site" to minimize the potential distractions for participants. Like all good meetings, JAD meetings have a detailed agenda with clear objectives for the session. For example, a JAD session might be used to finalize the format and content of a new report from a system.

A **facilitator** is a JAD expert who organizes the JAD meetings. The facilitator's role is to help the group work effectively during the session. A **scribe** also attends the meeting to record the *jointly* agreed-upon design information. Of course, key ingredients of a JAD meeting are the users—the people who will use the information system and know what it needs to do. Together, the team members work together to quickly identify requirements, resolve disagreements, and finalize design requirements. The objective of this "joint" approach is to involve many users early in the design of their system. Furthermore, JAD is useful across a broad range of organizations and types of information systems. JAD has been used by large organizations, such as the U.S. Army, when designing global logistics systems, and small organizations, such as small electronics companies, when designing a new manufacturing control system.

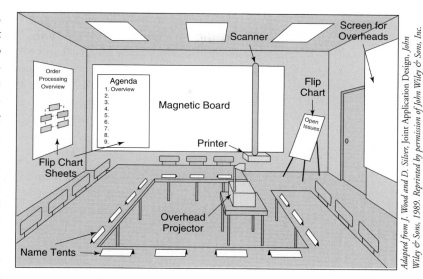

FIGURE 10.4

A JAD room.

Adapted from J. Wood and D. Silver, Joint Application Design, John Wiley & Sons, 1989. Reprinted by permission of John Wiley & Sons, Inc.

Strengths and Weaknesses of JAD

The JAD approach to systems development provides several advantages. First, the group-based process enables more people to be involved in the development effort without adversely slowing the process. This results in greater support and acceptance of the new system and can also result in a system of much higher quality. Additionally, because user involvement eases implementation (that is, users were involved in defining what the system would do and how the system would operate), training and support costs for developing the system can be significantly lower. JAD has proven the old adage that more heads are better than one!

JAD also has its weaknesses. First, it is often very difficult to get all relevant users to the same place at the same time to hold a JAD meeting. Large organizations may have users virtually all over the world; getting them all to a meeting (or a series of meetings) would be extremely difficult and expensive. Many believe that JAD requires a high-level executive sponsor pushing the process to ensure that it gets the resources (and the people) necessary to make it successful.

A second weakness of JAD relates to the inherent problems that groups may face, especially large groups. Have you ever worked in a group in which one person dominated? Probably so. Or, have you ever experienced a situation where some people in the group were shy and didn't want to talk? How about working in a group where one or more of the members simply chose not to help and let the other members of the group do the work? Consequently, the possibility of having a "bad" group is a significant potential weakness of JAD. Needless to say, many things can go wrong when groups work together. A skilled facilitator, a clear agenda, and strong management support can go a long way to remedy these problems.

The strengths and weaknesses of the Critical Success Factor (CSF) and the Joint Application Design (JAD) approaches are summarized in Table 10.1. Now that you know the contemporary methods for gathering requirements for an information system, you can consider alternatives for designing and building them.

Table 10.1   Strengths and weaknesses of contemporary methods for collecting and structuring system requirements.

Approach	Strengths	Weaknesses
Critical Success Factors	Easy for senior managers to understand; provides needed structure to the collection process	Broad focus; oversimplification of a complex situation
Joint Application Requirement / Joint Application Design	Enables more people to be involved; broad user involvement eases system implementation	Difficult and expensive to get all people to the same place at the same time; potential to have dysfunctional groups

Contemporary Approaches for Designing and Building Systems

The Systems Development Life Cycle is one approach for managing the development process and is a very good approach to follow when the requirements for the information system are highly structured and straightforward—for example, a payroll or inventory system. Today, organizations need a broad variety of information systems, not just payroll and inventory systems, for which requirements are either very hard to specify in advance or are constantly changing. For example, an organization's Web site is likely to be an information system with constantly changing requirements. How many Web sites have you visited in which the content or layout seemed to change almost every day? For this type of system, the SDLC might work as a development approach, but it wouldn't be optimal. In this section, we describe several approaches needed to develop flexible information systems: prototyping, rapid application development, and object-oriented analysis and design.

Prototyping

Prototyping is a systems development methodology that uses a "trial and error" approach for discovering how a system should operate. You may think that this doesn't sound like a process at all; however, you probably use prototyping all the time in many of your day-to-day activities, but you just don't know it! For example, when you buy new clothes you likely use prototyping—that is, trial and error—by trying on several shirts before making a selection. Likewise, when you buy a new car, computer, shoes, or even when you choose a mate, you use a trial-and-error process. When prototyping is used to design a new system, the systems designer works with users in a trial-and-error process until the system works the way the users want it to work. In our scenario at the beginning of the chapter, Greg was planning to use prototyping to build the new information system for The King of Hearts Ranch.

How Prototyping Works

Figure 10.5 diagrams the prototyping process when applied to identifying/ determining system requirements. To begin the process, the system designer interviews one or several users of the system, either individually or as a group using a JAD. After the designer gains a general understanding of what the users want, he develops a prototype of the new system as quickly as possible to share with the users. The users may like what they see or ask for changes. If changes are requested, the designer modifies the prototype and again shares it with the users. This process of sharing and refinement continues until the users approve the functionality of the system.

Strengths and Weaknesses of Prototyping

The greatest strength of prototyping is that the process helps develop a close working relationship between the system designer and users. This relationship helps build trust and acceptance for the new system. A second strength of prototyping is that it is arguably the best systems development method for identifying how a system should operate when the system's specifications are hard to define. For example, when developing an executive information system (EIS) or decision support system (DSS) (see Chapter 7, "Organizational Information Systems," for a review of these two types of systems), prototyping is often used to help the executive or manager "discover" the system requirements through the prototyping process. For many systems that are used to support individual managers and executives like an EIS and DSS, the system must be customized to the individual. In many cases the requirements cannot be defined ahead of time. We have worked with executives on these types of systems, and they literally state, "I can't tell you exactly what I want this system to do, but I'll know it when I see it." In these cases, prototyping is an excellent approach. A key to the successful application of prototyping is that each cycle of the prototyping process proceeds rapidly. In fact, it is through the rapid, iterative process that the benefits of this process are most likely to occur.

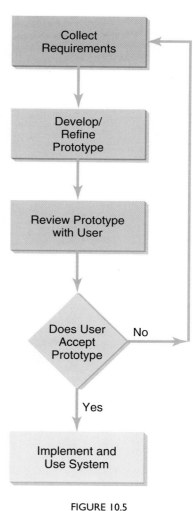

FIGURE 10.5

The prototyping process.

Prototyping also has numerous weaknesses. First and foremost, prototyping is not appropriate for developing every type of information system. For example, prototyping is very problematic in projects with a large number of users that must be consulted during the design process; requiring the systems analyst to consult with more than just a few users not only increases the complexity of the process, but also significantly slows the process. Likewise, systems with more structured requirements (that is, requirements that can be easily identified and defined—such as an inventory management or payroll system) are not good candidates for prototyping. For systems with highly structured requirements, there is little need for prototyping and the systems development life cycle approach to building the system has been found to be much more effective.

Another weakness of prototyping is that the process itself often results in not spending enough effort on important activities within the development process. Consequently, the system development process can be *rushed,* which can result in inadequate analysis and design, poor testing, and little or no documentation. Systems that lack maintainability due to inadequate documentation or some other factor cost the organization significantly more resources to maintain than do systems that are adequately documented. In other words, failing to do the job right the first time can lead to many long-term costs. For example, the quality and completeness of a system's documentation is a key factor influencing how easily a system can be changed and maintained in the future. Given that most of the costs of having a system are incurred during system maintenance, effective management of the systems development process must assure quality documentation.

Rapid Application Development (RAD)

Rapid Application Development (RAD) is a four-phase systems development methodology that combines prototyping, computer-based development tools, special management practices, and close user involvement. In 1991, James Martin conceived RAD as a methodology to develop information systems more quickly and cheaply. Others have developed their own flavors of RAD (see, for example, McConnell, 1996), yet there are some basic principles to most RAD-based methods, which are discussed here.

How Rapid Application Development Works

Martin's version of RAD has four phases: 1) requirements planning, 2) user design, 3) construction, and 4) the move to the new system. Phase 1, requirements planning, is similar to the first two phases of the SDLC, in which the system is planned and requirements are analyzed. To gain intensive user involvement, the RAD methodology encourages the use of JAD sessions to collect requirements. Where RAD becomes *radical* is during Phase 2, where users of the information system become intensively involved in the design process. CASE tools (Computer-Aided Software Engineering, discussed later in this chapter) are used to quickly structure requirements and develop prototypes. As prototypes are developed and refined, they are continually reviewed with users in additional JAD sessions. Like prototyping, RAD is a process in which requirements, designs, and the system itself are developed via iterative refinement, as shown in Figure 10.6. In a sense, with the RAD approach the people building the system and the users of that system keep cycling back and forth between Phase 2 (user design) and Phase 3 (construction) until the system is done. As a result, RAD requires close cooperation between users and designers to be successful. This means that management must actively support the development project and make it a priority for everyone involved.

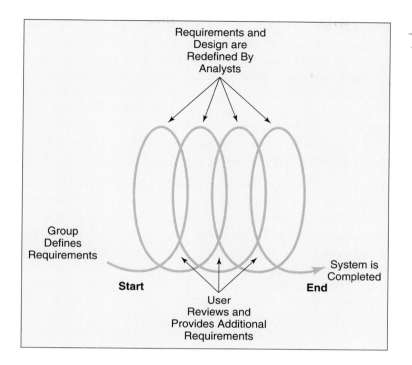

FIGURE 10.6

Iterative refinement is a key to the success of RAD.

Requirements and
Design are
Redefined By
Analysts

Group
Defines
Requirements

Start

End

System is
Completed

User
Reviews and
Provides Additional
Requirements

— Using RAD at the First National Bank of Chicago — A BRIEF CASE

An example of RAD can be found at First National Bank of Chicago. In 1994, the Internal Revenue Service (IRS) mandated the elimination of paperwork from employers' federal tax withholding payments. In the past, employers submitted a Federal Tax Deposit (FTD) coupon and a check to an authorized bank within three business days of releasing payroll to their employees. In an effort to speed processing and eliminate paperwork, the IRS mandated that employers with a tax liability in excess of $50,000 would have to begin making electronic payments by January 1, 1996. By 1999, employers with a tax liability in excess of $20,000 would also be required to make electronic payments. First National Bank was selected by the IRS to be the clearinghouse for employers in the northern tier of the U.S. Using the RAD approach and the Delphi visual programming environment (Borland, 1998), the bank developed the graphical user interface for their online tax collection system. During the RAD process, they prototyped and tested literally dozens of variations of the interface with customers to make the system very easy to use. In 1997, 1.2 million of the largest employers in the northern tier of the U.S. used the system for processing federal tax payments. By 1999, the number of employers enrolled in the system is expected to be more than 4 million. Because tax records must be maintained for seven years, more than 500 million records will be stored by the year 2000. Using Delphi and the RAD approach, the First National Bank of Chicago was able to meet contract specifications and stringent project deadlines.

Strengths and Weaknesses of Rapid Application Development

The greatest strength of RAD is the active involvement of users in the development process. With active user involvement, it is much more likely that the system being developed will actually meet their needs. Also, close user involvement eases many of the training and installation activities associated with the creation of a new system. Because the users were involved from the beginning, the new system is viewed as "their" new system. In addition, Martin claims that RAD can produce a system in a fraction of the time normally needed for a traditional SDLC approach. As a result, RAD can greatly reduce the cost associated with developing a system.

A weakness of RAD is that some people believe it may not be a good approach for developing systems that do not "need" to be developed rapidly (Gibson and Hughes, 1994). Due to RAD's accelerated analysis approach, systems built using it are often limited in functionality and flexibility for change. This may limit the use of the system in the future as the business conditions change. To develop a system for a longer-term business opportunity, it may be better to stick with the traditional (though slower) SDLC approach. With SDLC, a more thorough, slower analysis would be performed—an analysis that might make the system more robust to the broader and longer-term needs of the organization. In addition, due to the emphasis on the speed of design and development, systems developed using RAD may not be of the highest possible quality. This means that systems builders and users ought to be aware of the potential trade-offs in using the RAD approach. When systems need to be developed in an environment of rapidly changing business conditions, however, RAD is an effective tool.

In short, the RAD approach is intended to improve systems development, and ultimately improve systems quality, by enabling businesses to develop systems more quickly. The following section describes one other alternative approach to building systems—object-oriented analysis and design.

Object-Oriented Analysis and Design

As described in Chapter 3, "Information Systems Software," one key trend in programming languages has been the development of object-oriented languages such as C++. One of the major advantages of using object-oriented languages is the capability they give system designers to easily reuse commonly used modules. Systems are built more quickly and more consistently when they share common building blocks. For example, in Visual C++ it is very easy to design a user interface because the key components for developing the look and feel of the system—such as menus, buttons, and text boxes—are provided by the system, as shown in Figure 10.7. Each of these objects has a standard look and a restricted set of functions. As a result, when a designer decides to use a predefined object, he knows it will behave in the same way from system to system. Numerous object-oriented analysis and design approaches have emerged, both in response to the growth in popularity of object-oriented programming and in an effort to fully utilize object-oriented programming concepts (Booch, 1990; Coad and Yourdon, 1991; Halladay and Wiebel, 1993).

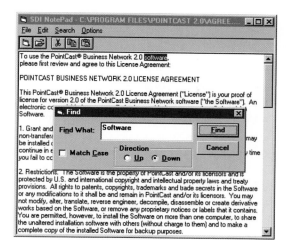

FIGURE 10.7

Building a user interface with reusable objects.

Object-Oriented Analysis and Design (OOA&D) is very similar to other analysis and design approaches. In fact, OOA&D and the traditional SDLC approach have many similarities, such as the ways in which data is modeled. OOA&D is, however, subtly different in the way that system components are thought about and used. OOA&D helps information systems users and managers think in more general terms about the various elements of an information system. The most fundamental element in OOA&D is the *object.* An object represents something tangible, such as a student, course, account, or transaction. As with data modeling (described in Chapter 4, "Database Management"), each tangible thing can have properties. For example, a student can have a name, identification number, and class schedule.

Up to this point, there is little difference between OOA&D and data modeling; however, objects can be used for more than simply defining data. Objects can also contain the operations that can be performed on the tangible thing (for example, an account) so that the data and operations are bundled together within the object. For example, the operations that can be performed with an object within a user interface are tightly coupled with the data that defines the object. Continuing with our user interface example, Figure 10.8 shows how a programmer can set the attributes for a button object on a user interface. The attributes for a button might include its shape, size, and color. When a user clicks on the button, certain pre-programmed events happen. This means that the systems analyst defines both the data describing the button and the operations—or "methods" in OOA&D terminology—that can be performed by clicking on the button. The data and the methods are bundled within the button object. This subtle difference in systems development approach equates to a big difference in how systems are designed.

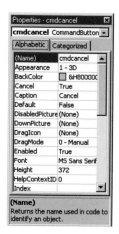

FIGURE 10.8

Setting properties on a button object.

How Object-Oriented Analysis and Design Works

When using the SDLC approach, systems analysts follow primarily a top-down process in which the system requirements are decomposed, or broken down into smaller and smaller pieces until specific programming modules can be defined, programmed, and pieced together to yield a system. Similarly, data and their interrelationships are modeled by the analysts, and these conceptual models are turned over to a programmer who actually implements these data models in a database management system. In most instances, a systems analyst develops a high-level design for the data and the processing and provides this design to programmers, who actually implement the design in programming code and databases. The analyst often never does any coding. This is different with the OOA&D approach due to the tight coupling between the methods and data and between the conceptual model of the system and its actual implementation. OOA&D can turn every programmer into an analyst and every analyst into a programmer. What this means is that the analyst using an OOA&D approach can be thinking simultaneously right from the start about the "what" (the data) *and* the "how" (the operations to be performed) as he defines all the relevant objects that the system entails. Furthermore, the design *and* implementation of the objects can happen quickly and simultaneously if an object-oriented programming language is being used. In sum, OOA&D is a more integrative prototyping process than the SDLC approach, in which data and operations on the data are modeled separately and at a conceptual level and are later implemented and brought together in a subsequent phase of the systems development process.

Strengths and Weaknesses of Object-Oriented Analysis and Design

The strengths of OOA&D are numerous. First, OOA&D forces designers to integrate their thinking to simultaneously consider both operations and data when creating a design. When analysts use SDLC, they separately model system logic, processes, and data. Because OOA&D designers use a broader and more integrated focus, advocates for OOA&D believe that system quality is improved and the duration of the system development process is reduced. Additionally, after objects are defined, they can be reused by other systems. This enables new or improved modules to be easily plugged into new systems or those being maintained.

The OOA&D approach also has some weaknesses. The most notable weakness for many organizations is the requirement that existing analysts and programmers be trained on OOA&D techniques. After they are trained in the SDLC or some other non-object-oriented method, experience has shown that it is often very difficult for people to change the way they approach the systems development process. Many organizations have had to make considerable investments in retraining programmers and analysts to adequately use the OOA&D approach. Also, although it is intuitive to believe that OOA&D will lead to lower development costs and higher-quality systems, little research exists to support this assertion. One problem, for example, is that many programmers and analysts are unwilling to search libraries for reusable code. It is unclear whether this failure to reuse standard modules is due to a lack of adequate training or just plain stubbornness. Nonetheless, one of the key benefits of OOA&D—reusability—may not be adequately utilized, which, of course, greatly limits its benefits.

This section has described some of the more popular information systems development approaches. Although each of the previously described approaches has been discussed separately, the wise organization and skilled analyst often utilize multiple methods when developing a single system. What should be clear to you is that no approach is perfect and that all have strengths and weaknesses (see Table 10.2). To put this another way, a skilled systems developer is much like a skilled craftsman, with many tools at his disposal. The skilled craftsman chooses the most appropriate tool and approach for the task at hand. Using one systems development approach or tool for all systems and problems is akin to using only a hammer to build a house. Building a house with just a hammer might be possible, but it would probably be a strange-looking house!

Table 10.2   Strengths and weaknesses of contemporary development approaches.

Approach	Strengths	Weaknesses
Prototyping	Develops close working relationship between designer and users; works well for messy and hard-to-define problems	Not practical with a large number of users; system may be built too quickly, which could result in lower quality
Rapid Application Development	Active user involvement in design process; easier implementation due to user involvement	Systems are often narrowly focused—limits future evolution; system may be built too quickly, which could result in lower quality
Object-Oriented Analysis and Design	Integration of data and processing during design should lead to higher-quality systems; reuse of common modules makes development and maintenance easier	Very difficult to train analysts and programmers on the object-oriented approach; limited use of common modules

Special types of development tools are often applied to the prototyping approach. For example, CASE (Computer-Aided Software Engineering) is a popular tool that helps to automate many aspects of the systems development process. Fourth-generation languages, object orientation, and visual programming are other tools used to assist in the rapid development of systems. Skilled designers must have a "tool kit" of powerful development tools to gain the benefits from this process. Each of these tools is described in the following section.

Tools for Supporting Contemporary Systems Development

Over the years, the tools for developing information systems have increased in variety and in power. In the early days of systems development, a developer was left to use a pencil and paper to sketch out design ideas and program code. Computers were cumbersome to use and slow to program, and most designers worked out on paper as much of the system design as they could before moving to the computer. Today, system developers have a vast array of powerful computer-based tools at their disposal. These tools have changed forever the ways in which systems are developed.

Computer-Aided Software Engineering

Computer-Aided Software Engineering (CASE) refers to automated software tools used by systems analysts to develop information systems. These tools can be used to automate or support activities throughout the systems development process, with the objective of increasing productivity and improving the overall quality of systems.

────────────────────── **Collect America** ──────────

Collect America, Ltd. (CA), a company that collects long-overdue customer and commercial debts, uses Oracle Designer/2000 and Developer/2000 CASE tools for developing their information systems (Oracle, 1998). Based in Denver, Colorado, CA tracks and monitors debtors using an Oracle database environment. To make collections, CA has franchise agreements with regional law firms in the U.S., Canada, and Mexico. As their business has grown, so too have their information management needs. As CA has used Oracle's CASE tools to design, construct, and maintain their applications, system quality and speed have improved over their previously non-CASE-developed systems. Systems developed using CASE enable applications to be moved easily from one hardware platform to another. Consequently, as the hardware infrastructure in CA has evolved, their applications have also evolved without major changes. For example, with the rapid growth and easy accessibility of the World Wide Web, CA determined they could save a lot of money if franchise offices around North America could use the Web for accessing CA's database. Using Oracle's CASE tools, system developers reconstructed applications so that they could be accessed using a standard Web browser. Today, because access to this information is through the Web, huge cost savings are being realized by CA; they no longer have to invest in routers, dedicated lines, and all the other technology needed to manage a dedicated network. For CA, CASE has really paid off.

In reference to the SDLC, the tools used to automate the first three phases of the SDLC—system identification, selection, and planning; system analysis; and system design—are generally referred to as **upper CASE** tools. For example, during system analysis activities, it is very useful to represent business processes and information flows using a graphical diagram. CASE helps you draw such diagrams by providing standard symbols to represent business processes, information flows between processes, data storage, and the organizational entities that interact with the business process. Using CASE to diagram this information greatly assists this process. For example, Figure 10.9A shows a high-level business process diagram called a Data Flow Diagram, or DFD, from the CASE system from Visible Systems Corporation called *The Visible Analyst Workbench* (VAW). This view of a business process is the highest level or the most abstract; in DFD terminology, this is called the context-level view. This diagram represents an organization's entities (in this instance, those associated with the Department of Motor Vehicles) and the process of providing licenses to potential drivers. Lower-level processes within this system are shown in Figure 10.9B, where some business processes are likely to be automated while others may not. Using a picture to represent this business process helps facilitate clear communication between the system developers and users.

Likewise, the tools used to automate the system implementation and maintenance phases are generally referred to as **lower CASE** tools. For example, one key activity during implementation is the development of the computer program code for the system. A *code generator* is a feature of lower CASE tools that produces high-level program source code by reading and interpreting the diagrams and screens used to represent the system. Many code generators can produce source code in languages such as COBOL, BASIC, and C. In addition to diagramming tools and code generators, a broad range of other tools assists in the systems development process. The general types of CASE tools used throughout the development process are summarized in Table 10.3.

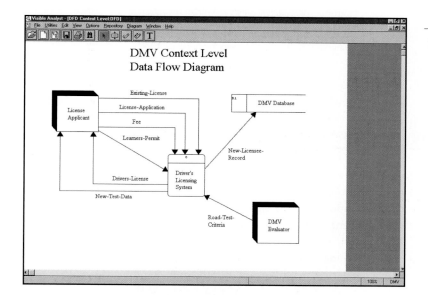

FIGURE 10.9A

High-level data flow diagram from the VAW CASE tool.

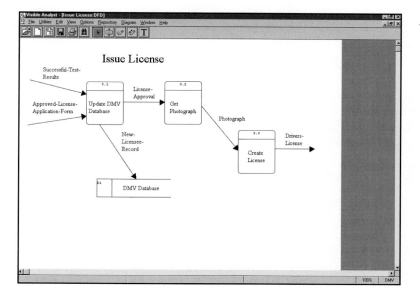

FIGURE 10.9B

Lower-level data flow diagram from the VAW CASE tool.

Table 10.3   General types of CASE tools.

CASE Tool	Description
Diagramming tools	Tools that enable system process, data, and control structures to be represented graphically.
Screen and report generators	Tools that help model how systems look and feel to users. Screen and report generators also make it easier for the systems analyst to identify data requirements and relationships.
Analysis tools	Tools that automatically check for incomplete, inconsistent, or incorrect specifications in diagrams, screens, and reports.
Repository	A tool that enables the integrated storage of specifications, diagrams, reports, and project management information.
Documentation generators	Tools that help produce both technical and user documentation in standard formats.
Code generators	Tools that enable the automatic generation of program and database definition code directly from the design documents, diagrams, screens, and reports.

Source   *Adapted from Hoffer, George, and Valacich. 1999. Modern systems analysis and design. Addison Wesley Longman: Reading, Massachusetts.*

CASE can be used to dramatically increase the speed of development and maintenance, not to mention increase the quality of the system. CASE also influences the culture of an organization in many significant ways. In fact, researchers have found that people with different career orientations have different attitudes toward CASE (Orlikowski, 1989). For example, those within the development group with a managerial orientation welcome CASE because they believe it helps reduce the risk and uncertainty in managing development projects. On the other hand, people with a more technical orientation tend to resist the use of CASE because they feel threatened by the technology's capability to replace some skills they have taken years to master. Table 10.4 lists several possible impacts of CASE on the roles of individuals within organizations. CASE is clearly a powerful technology that can have numerous and widespread impacts. Its adoption should be a well-thought-out and highly orchestrated activity.

Table 10.4   Common impacts of CASE on individuals within organizations.

Individuals	Common Impact
Systems analysts	CASE automates many routine tasks of the analyst, making the communication skills (rather than analytical skills) of the analyst most critical.
Programmers	Programmers will piece together objects created by code generators and fourth-generation languages. Their role will become more of maintaining designs than source code.
Users	Users will be much more active in the systems development process through the use of upper CASE tools.
Top managers	Top managers will play a more active role in setting priorities and strategic directions for IS by using CASE-based planning and through user-oriented system development methods.
Functional managers	Functional managers will play a greater role in leading development projects by using CASE to re-engineer their business processes.
IS project managers	IS project managers will have greater control over development projects and resources.

Source   *Adapted from 1992. Chen and Norman.*

Group Support Systems

In Chapter 8, "Emerging Information Systems," we described one type of groupware—*Group Support Systems (GSS)*—that is increasingly being used to help groups communicate, collaborate, and coordinate their activities. A key application of GSS technology is to support the collection of user requirements. In other words, it is more effective to collect user requirements for some types of systems by asking a group to collectively define these requirements through a JAD process. It is also possible to improve the processing and performance of groups by using GSS technology to structure and coordinate the group process. The marriage of GSS and JAD activities is often referred to as an electronic JAD or E-JAD.

Using GSS and JAD in the U.S. Army

A BRIEF CASE

In the early 1990s, the U.S. Army undertook a major initiative to redesign and consolidate many of the major information systems used to manage army installations around the world. At that time the army spent more than $5 billion annually and employed over 250,000 people to operate the many army, National Guard, and Reserve installations in the U.S. and around the world. Each military installation is like a small city: In addition to all the people living there, there are stores, restaurants, police and fire stations, garbage collection services, and so on. Also, at each military installation, the army needs to manage the arrival and departure of personnel (that is, collect medical records, change mailing addresses, and so on) and perform daily landlord functions (for example, rent processing), not to mention the management of military activities and equipment. Unfortunately, most people managing military installations did things their own way when it came to many of the installation support activities. This lack of consistency resulted in poor communication, redundancies, and diverse, incompatible procedures across installations. It was envisioned that if the army could increase the efficiency of installation management, significant resources could be saved and redistributed to activities such as improved personnel training and equipment. For example, a 10 percent cost reduction would yield more than $500 million per year!

To address this problem, the U.S. Congress approved a budget of $172 million to develop an army-wide system to assist in the management of the varied activities that occur at each site (Daniels, Dennis, Hayes, Nunamaker and Valacich, 1991). Because each installation has unique issues to address, any single integrated system had to consider the unique requirements of each site. For example, the procedures for "in-processing" new personnel onto a base are different in the U.S. than in Europe or Asia. To define a system for supporting in-processing that considered the needs of only the U.S. installations would be a failure. As a result, the army worked to define the most appropriate procedures to collect the system requirements correctly the first time, and used JAD as the method to collect system requirements. To make the JAD session work, user representatives of most major installations around the world flew to a central location to work on multi-week JAD sessions to define and structure the requirements for seventeen separate installation support activities. In addition to using JAD, they also combined GSS technology to automate many of the group-based discussions within the JAD sessions. As of today, most of the systems to automate the installation support process have been developed, and the army is gaining significant savings. In fact, this project has been so successful that it is being used as a model for other branches of the U.S. military.

Advanced Programming Languages

One of the greatest bottlenecks in the development and maintenance of information systems is in programming-related activities. It is no surprise that a lot has been changing to make programming faster and easier. This section describes major developments in programming languages that are helping people to effectively use the application development approaches discussed earlier in this chapter. Without these powerful programming tools, systems development (and programming in particular) would remain a slow and tedious process.

Visual Programming

Visual programming, described in Chapter 3, is a new and extremely powerful way to develop systems rapidly. A popular visual programming environment is Visual Basic by Microsoft. This language enables systems developers to quickly build new user interfaces, reports, and other features into existing systems in a fraction of the time previously required and easily links these features to countless database management systems. Rather than build a screen, report, or menu by typing crude commands (see sample commands in Figure 10.10), designers use visual tools to "draw" the design. For example, building a menu system in a visual programming environment is simple. Analysts can quickly list the order of menu commands (see Figure 10.11A) and instantly test the look of their design (see Figure 10.11B). In fact, after they are designed, these systems convert the design into the appropriate computer instructions, but all these details are hidden from the programmer. Visual development programming is also being added to more traditional programming languages, such as C, BASIC, and COBOL, as well as to special-purpose visual programming environments, such as Delphi by Borland and PowerBuilder by Powersoft.

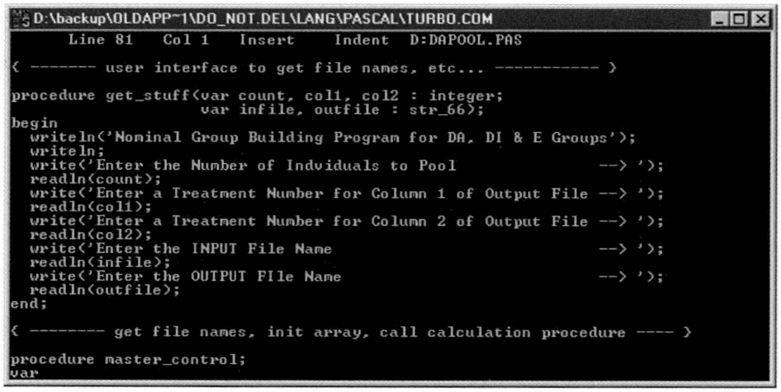

FIGURE 10.10

Sample of programming commands to build a screen.

```
D:\backup\OLDAPP~1\DO_NOT.DEL\LANG\PASCAL\TURBO.COM
       Line 81   Col 1   Insert      Indent  D:DAPOOL.PAS
{ ------- user interface to get file names, etc... ----------- }
procedure get_stuff(var count, col1, col2 : integer;
                        var infile, outfile : str_66);
begin
    writeln('Nominal Group Building Program for DA, DI & E Groups');
    writeln;
    write('Enter the Number of Individuals to Pool          --> ');
    readln(count);
    write('Enter a Treatment Number for Column 1 of Output File --> ');
    readln(col1);
    write('Enter a Treatment Number for Column 2 of Output File --> ');
    readln(col2);
    write('Enter the INPUT File Name                         --> ');
    readln(infile);
    write('Enter the OUTPUT FIle Name                        --> ');
    readln(outfile);
end;

{ -------- get file names, init array, call calculation procedure ---- }

procedure master_control;
var
```

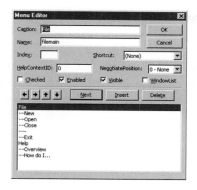

FIGURE 10.11A

Menu commands.

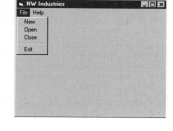

FIGURE 10.11B

Sample of a screen being drawn using visual programming tools.

—— Maintaining Ad Schedules at Fox Broadcasting —— A BRIEF CASE

The Los Angeles-based Fox Broadcasting Company is the nation's fourth largest television network. The rapidly growing network grew even faster in December 1993, when it beat CBS for the rights to broadcast the weekly National Football Conference games. With this $1.6 billion coup, Fox grew its roster of affiliate stations around the country from 138 to 199 and increased its number of broadcast hours. To accommodate this tremendous growth, Fox is using PowerBuilder to assist in its application development process (Sybase, 1998). One such system is the Sales Traffic and Billing System, which is used to automate many of the complicated tasks involved in selling, scheduling, and tracking advertising air time.

About 70 Fox sales representatives in five regional offices have a fixed pool of commercial airtime to sell. They need immediate access to information about the status of that inventory. They sell about 75 percent of their airtime up to six months before a broadcast season starts. However, deals change frequently. To be effective, reps need to be constantly aware of their colleagues' activities so that they can share the updated schedules of commercials with everyone instantly across the network. The ad programming module of the system feeds directly into Fox's automated broadcast system. The commercial scheduling module of the application automatically slates various ads and program segments into the broadcast system time slots. The application verifies that competing companies' spots don't run back-to-back or that two ads in a row don't have the same theme, such as vacation cruises. As the development process progressed, the benefits of using the visual programming environment became apparent to Fox's executives, who now believe that they could have built such a high-quality system in such a short period of time without PowerBuilder.

Although a programming language may be visual, it may not necessarily be object-oriented. The next section reviews object-oriented programming, another contemporary programming tool that can be used to better develop systems.

Object-Oriented Programming

Many organizations have had a difficult time maintaining their information systems. These systems are often huge, ranging from 100,000 lines of programming code to more than 1,000,000 in a single system. Systems of this size are hard for one person to understand and consequently often very hard to enhance or maintain. Making changes to these large-scale systems is difficult, to say the least. Making matters worse, a large organization can have hundreds of separate application systems to support common business activities such as payroll processing, inventory management, financial analysis, sales, marketing, and countless other activities. Each separate system has the potential for many redundant functions. For example, logging into a system with an approved user account or sending a report to a printer are two common functions that most business applications hold in common. For example, sending a report to a printer is a common function that most business applications hold in common. As a result, the way in which printing works in one system is often different from how it works in another. This has resulted in a system maintenance nightmare for many organizations.

Object-oriented programming (described in Chapter 3) is helping to alleviate maintenance problems plaguing organizations that have multiple systems with redundant functions. Object-oriented languages create objects that are reusable elements in a system. The idea is to make objects that can be infinitely reused and become the building blocks for all systems. Consequently, a well-designed printing object can, for example, be used in all systems. Then, when a modification needs to be made to how the print object works—suppose, for example, that you want to modify the print object to support color printing—*one* module can be changed and *all* systems can use the enhanced color printing functionality. The goal of OOP is to make software easier to create, simpler, more consistent to use, and far more reliable (Verity and Schwartz, 1994). Using object-oriented languages for building information systems is similar to using Lego blocks for building model bridges, planes, and buildings. The Lego block is reusable in an infinite number of structures. Likewise, the well-designed software object is reusable in an infinite number of systems.

Fourth-Generation Languages and Beyond

Two clear trends in the evolution of programming languages and environments used to develop information systems are increased ease and power. As described in Chapter 3, **fourth-generation languages** (4GLs) enable users to "ask" an information system to provide certain information by typing English sentence–like commands into a system. Figure 10.12 shows some sample 4GL commands. In other words, 4GLs enable users to specify what information is wanted from a system in a syntax that is relatively easy to learn and remember. In contrast, with most development environments, programmers must specify each of the minuscule steps needed to obtain this information before it can be displayed. As a result, 4GLs have given nontechnical users the capability to develop their own powerful information system applications and speed the process of obtaining information.

```
SELECT DISTINCTROW STUDENT_ID, GRADE
FROM GRADES
WHERE GRADE = "A"
ORDER BY STUDENT_ID;
```

FIGURE 10.12

Sample of 4GL commands.

A final contemporary approach to programming is to embed artificial intelligence into the development environments. For example, it is envisioned that in the near future, programmers will be able to go well beyond 4GLs and develop large-scale information systems by simply telling their computers what they want them to do. It is envisioned that intelligent agents, created by other programmers, will reside in your computer. When a user or programmer wants something to be done, a request will be made to the agent through a conversational dialogue.

Systems development tools and approaches have evolved rapidly over the past thirty years, and there appears to be no end in sight to this evolution. There is no doubt that many new approaches and tools will be proposed, with some gaining favor, and others not. Organizations and developers will have to be very selective when choosing development approaches and tools. With the selection of any approach or tool will come tremendous costs for employee training and change management. Likewise, systems developers will also find the future to be filled with uncertainty in regard to which skills to master to best equip themselves for the future. On the other hand, this evolution and change will bring a greater capability to build more powerful systems in a shorter period of time.

Talking with...

Jeanne Schaefer, Manager of Strategic Business Support at Weyerhaeuser

Educational Background

B.S. in Business Administration, University of Montana

Job Description

Ms. Schaefer is responsible for managing several project teams that are responsible for acquiring business applications in the corporate area. This includes drafting the project plan, developing the business requirements, writing requests for proposals, selecting vendors, purchasing systems, converting data, and implementing system hardware and software.

Critical Success Factors

Understand the business requirements. Agree on the scope of the project between the customer and the project manager. Complete data conversion, which includes testing the database before production. Work with dedicated people. Have a sense of humor.

Advice to Students

A career in information technology is a wonderful choice for people who enjoy variety and change at a rapid pace. Current technology has a habit of becoming obsolete very quickly in today's environment. Therefore, it is important to continually update your skills. People who are successful in information technology are creative, flexible, and able to adapt to change. IT professionals must also have a strong background in business processes to successfully recommend and implement an appropriate technology. You must develop the ability to translate the business requirements to the technology. Woe to the IT group that implements technology without sound business value.

ETHICAL PERSPECTIVE: THE ETHICS OF IS CONSULTING

Thousands of businesses, large and small, are actively participating in one of the fastest growing industry sectors of the modern world: information systems consulting services. Many large organizations have long been successful in providing IS consulting services, such as IBM, EDS, and Andersen Consulting. New companies enter this industry on a daily basis.

As with other business endeavors, IS consulting services is an area of business that puts people into situations that test their ethics. One potentially problematic area that applies to all consulting—not just IS consulting—is the fundamental conflict between needing to secure consulting contracts to bring revenue into the consulting firm and needing to not over-promise what can be delivered and/or when it can be delivered. The pressure to bring in business to generate revenue is great. New business is, after all, the lifeblood of the consulting firm. There is natural pressure to secure a consulting contract even though it may not be absolutely clear that the firm can deliver exactly what the client wants or needs by the exact deadlines that the client has set. For IS consultants, the pressure is great to promise that the job can be done quickly using "rapid" methodologies, especially given that these methodologies are in vogue. Of course, it is in the consulting firm's long-term interests not to over-promise, but the pressure is there nonetheless.

One other potential ethical dilemma facing IS consultants is the question of whom they work for and where their loyalties lie. With Joint Application Development and the use of systems development teams in which IS consultants work closely with business users, it is sometimes difficult for consultants to determine exactly for whom they work—the client or the consulting firm. On the one hand, they are servicing the client and must satisfy the client's needs. On the other hand, they work for the consulting firm. They may get pulled in two different directions, especially if the relationship between the client and the consulting firm deteriorates. The consulting firm might want the consultant to stick with the letter of the contract, to withhold certain services, or to keep her time with the client to a minimum. On the other hand, the consultant may want to go the extra distance to please the client. After all, with contemporary system development approaches the consultant probably spends more time with the client organization's personnel than with the consulting firm's personnel, and the client organization is likely to be doing the primary evaluation of the consultant's performance. In fact,

in some cases the consultants may be housed physically and semi-permanently within the client organization, may be paid directly by the client, and may enjoy other employee benefits provided by the client organization.

With increased use of Joint Application Development and other approaches to partnering with business users, comes one final, fundamental ethical dilemma that all consultants face daily. This dilemma is whether to solve problems for clients in such a way that the client learns how to solve the problems themselves or to solve problems for clients in such a way that the client needs to call the consultant back in again to solve similar problems in the future. There is a natural pressure to do the latter to ensure future business.

A useful analogy for this ethical dilemma is the way that a barber cuts your hair. A barber who wants to ensure that you will have to come back to him again would give you the best possible haircut. In addition, he would have no mirrors in the shop so that you could not see what he was doing, and he would not answer any of your questions about how he was cutting and styling your hair. On the other hand, a barber who wanted you to become self-sustaining and empowered to take care of yourself would not only give you a good haircut, but he would have mirrors all around so that you could see exactly what he was doing. He would explain exactly what he was doing at all times and answer any of your questions. Now, you wouldn't necessarily be able to cut your own hair, but you would know how to do so and could explain this to another person who could then cut your hair. You wouldn't necessarily have to come back to that same barber. Good consultants don't try to generate more business for themselves in this way. They want you to ask them back because you want to have them back, not because you need to have them back.

Questions for Discussion

1. How would you deal with an IS manager who was pushing you to develop a system in a time frame that was too rapid to enable you to do a good job? What if it was the client who was pushing you?

2. To whom should an IS consultant ultimately be loyal, to the client or to the consulting firm? Why?

3. Should IS consultants strive to not only solve clients' problems but help to teach and enable them to solve their own problems in the future? Why or why not?

INTERNATIONAL PERSPECTIVE: MANAGING CROSS-CULTURAL JAD TEAMS

Anne Masters is the leader of a systems development team that is building an inventory control system in Beijing, China, for Quality Products, a mid-sized manufacturing firm based in San Diego, California. This project is in its initial phase, and Anne is currently leading a Joint Application Development (JAD) team in fleshing out the detailed requirements and design elements of the inventory control system. Anne serves as the JAD facilitator, the key person who leads the JAD sessions. Anne has been selected as the JAD facilitator because she is a respected, skillful leader with a good reputation within the organization and excellent group facilitation skills.

The Management Sponsor for this JAD Team is Brad Wheeling, manager of the production area of the firm. He has not actively participated in every one of the JAD sessions, but he did attend the first JAD session to help get things started correctly, and he will likely attend the final session to review the results and make comments. The information specialists in this case are Sulaiman bin Daud and Hasmah binti Johann. Sulaiman and Hasmah were both born in Malaysia, are ethnic Malays, and are Muslim. Both received IS degrees from American universities and were hired right out of school by Quality Products. Their role in the JAD sessions as information specialists is to assist the end users and develop a design according to the end users' needs. Both Sulaiman and Hasmah are experienced systems analysts and good listeners. The scribe for this JAD team is Sue Brownster, who is responsible for documenting the JAD sessions. She has had to learn to accurately capture the important decisions made, who made them, and why.

The three end users participating on this JAD team include Chin Chi Chan and Me Won Huang, two local Chinese women who were hired by Quality Products as inventory control technicians, and Yu Seng Tang, a local Chinese man who was hired as an inventory control supervisor. The IS members of the JAD team know that the end users are essential to the success of the JAD team and to the ultimate success of the inventory control system they are developing. The whole point of JAD is to bring end users and IS people together in a structured environment to build a better system that meets users' needs well and helps the users to feel a sense of involvement and ownership in the system.

Anne has found that it has been much more difficult for her to manage this cross-cultural JAD team than it was for her to manage JAD teams back in the States, where the team members were typically all Americans. In that setting, JAD teams were difficult enough to manage due to conflicting personalities, goals, and expectations, as well as corporate politics thrown in the mix. In this Chinese setting, Anne has found that she must now deal with all the common difficulties of a JAD team plus some interesting new cross-cultural issues.

One such cross-cultural difficulty with this JAD team finds it roots in the historical relationship between Chinese and native Malays in Malaysia. Many argue that control by native Malays in Malaysia has been institutionalized in many ways, causing people of Chinese ancestry in Malaysia to sometimes feel like second-class citizens. Sulaiman and Hasmah certainly don't believe that people in Malaysia who are born of Chinese ancestry are second-class citizens. In any event, the team members from China sometimes feel that the two Malaysian information specialists on the team talk down to the members of the team from China. Anne knows that Sulaiman and Hasmah are not doing this, but given the history between the two ethnic groups in Malaysia, the Chinese team members sometimes perceive Sulaiman and Hasmah to be doing this. Anne has had to work hard to manage this problem by coaching Sulaiman and Hasmah to be careful about how they communicate with the Chinese team members and by continually checking with the Chinese team members to make sure that everything is going smoothly for them.

Questions for Discussion

1. What do you think of the job that Anne Masters appears to be doing thus far? What could she be doing to better manage the difficulties within her cross-cultural JAD team?

2. What other difficulties might cross-cultural JAD teams like this one encounter and how can they best be managed?

3. Would you be interested in working on a JAD team like this one? Why or why not?

Summary

1. **Explain contemporary approaches for collecting and structuring the information needed to design and construct an information system.** Two ways for collecting and structuring systems requirements are the Critical Success Factors (CSF) and Joint Application Design (JAD) approaches. Both are being used to augment other methods used to collect requirements, such as interviewing users and developing questionnaires. The CSF approach is a methodology for collecting system requirements that helps identify those few things that must go well to ensure success for a manager or organization. JAD is a group-based method for collecting requirements and creating system designs.

2. **Describe prototyping, rapid application development, and object-oriented analysis and design methods of systems development and each approach's strengths and weaknesses.** Prototyping is an iterative systems development process in which requirements are converted to a working system that is continually revised through a close working relationship between analysts and users. The strengths of prototyping are that it helps develop a close working relationship between designers and users and that it is a good approach for hard-to-define problems. Its weaknesses are that it is not a practical approach for a large number of users and that it can at times lead to a lower-quality system if the system is built too quickly. Rapid Application Development (RAD) is a systems development methodology that combines prototyping, computer-based development tools, special management practices, and close user involvement. The strength of RAD is that users are actively involved in the design process, which makes system implementation much easier. The weaknesses of RAD are that systems are sometimes narrowly focused—which might limit future evolution—and that quality problems might result if a system is designed and built too quickly (as is the case with prototyping). Object-Oriented Analysis and Design (OOA&D) is a systems development approach that focuses on modeling objects—data and operations bundled together—rather than on modeling these separately. The strengths of OOA&D are the integration of data and processing during the design, which should lead to higher-quality systems, and the reuse of common modules, which should make development and maintenance easier. The weaknesses of OOA&D are that it is very difficult to train analysts and programmers on the object-oriented approach and that analysts often re-create common modules.

3. **Understand how and why to use several automated tools for supporting contemporary development, including Computer-Aided Software Engineering, group support systems, and advanced programming languages.** Computer-Aided Software Engineering (CASE) refers to automated software tools used by systems analysts to develop information systems. These tools can be used to automate or support activities throughout the systems development process with the objective of increasing productivity and improving the overall quality of systems. Group Support Systems (GSSs) are most widely used to help groups communicate, collaborate, and coordinate their activities. In regard to information systems development, a key application of GSS technology is to support the collection of user requirements in electronic JAD sessions. Advanced programming languages, such as visual programming, and object-oriented programming languages are designed to ease programming-related activities. Visual programming enables systems developers to quickly build new user interfaces, reports, and other features into existing systems in a fraction of the time previously required to "draw" the design with visual tools. Object-oriented programming enables reusable objects to be the building blocks for all systems. Using standard objects greatly speeds development and increases system reliability.

Key Terms

Critical Success Factor

Joint Application Requirements and Joint Application Design

Facilitator

Scribe

Prototyping

Rapid Application Development

Object-Oriented Analysis and Design

Computer-Aided Software Engineering

Upper CASE

Lower CASE

Visual programming

Object-oriented programming

Fourth-generation languages

Review Questions

1. What is the major strength of the Critical Success Factor approach?

2. Describe two major weaknesses of the Critical Success Factor approach.

3. Briefly describe the Joint Application Design process of collecting system requirements.

4. What are the possible disadvantages of working in large groups that may arise with JAD?

5. What are the roles of the JAD facilitator and scribe?

6. How does prototyping differ from the traditional SDLC approach to system development?

7. What maintenance issues must be addressed when using prototyping?

8. Describe how intense user involvement strengthens the Rapid Application Development approach to system development.

9. Describe the strengths and weaknesses of the Object-Oriented Analysis and Design approach to system development.

10. How do upper CASE tools differ from lower CASE tools?

11. Describe several tools that have enabled greater programming productivity in system development.

Problems and Exercises

◆ **Individual**   ◈ **Group**   ⌒ **Field**   ◖ **Web/Internet**

1. Match the following terms to the appropriate definitions:

   _____ Joint Application Design

   _____ Prototyping

   _____ Object-Oriented Analysis and Design

   _____ Computer-Aided Software Engineering

   _____ Critical Success Factor

   _____ Visual programming

   _____ Object-oriented programming

   _____ Fourth-generation languages

   a. A programming technique that utilizes objects or modules to perform common functions within the system

   b. A methodology for collecting system requirements that helps to identify those few things that must go well to ensure success for a manager or organization

   c. A programming technique in which users "ask" a system for information using English-like commands and syntax

   d. Systems development methodologies and techniques based on objects rather than data or processes

   e. Software tools that provide automated support for some portion of the systems development process

   f. Group-based methods for collecting requirements and creating system designs

   g. A programming technique that converts drawn designs into the appropriate computer instructions

   h. An iterative systems development process in which requirements are converted to a working system that is continually revised through close work between analysts and users

 2. Discuss why Rapid Application Development is not always an appropriate development methodology. When is it an appropriate methodology?

 3. Within a small group of classmates, compare and contrast the Critical Success Factor and Joint Application Design approaches. Is one more effective than the other? Why? Does the group agree? Which approach do you think is utilized more often? Why?

 4. As part of the traditional SDLC, the development team might show the client a prototype of the proposed system at various stages of development. This is done primarily as a communication tool as well as a progress report. How is this form of prototyping different from the prototyping approach discussed in this chapter?

5. Do you agree with the statement that Object-Oriented Analysis and Design is the future for system development? Why or why not? If so, what time frame do you predict? If not, which methodology will prevail? How do your fellow classmates feel about this? Do they agree with you or do they have different opinions?

6. Describe how you would handle the resistance to implementing CASE tools by those who feel they will be replaced by technology. From whom is this resistance most likely to come? Is this fear legitimate? Why or why not?

7. With the development of advanced programming languages and code-generating CASE tools, will programming in the traditional sense become a lost art? Why or why not? If not, when and where will traditional programming remain as part of the SDLC? Search the World Wide Web for information about advanced programming languages. Be sure to check out Sun Microsystems at http://www.sun.com/. What are others saying about advanced programming languages and how are they being used?

8. Discuss among your classmates whether it is managerially possible (feasible) to employ all the techniques and methodologies discussed in this and the preceding chapter. Is that too much to handle? Why? If it is feasible, under what conditions would you advise it and under what conditions would you recommend employing only some of the methodologies?

9. After reading Chapters 9 and 10, do you have a better understanding of system development? Why or why not? Which methodologies seem the most useful? the least useful? Are there any that you, as a manager, would stay away from altogether? Why?

10. Based on your uses of information systems and applications, which programming languages were used in their creation? Can you discern this at all? Were they visual or object-oriented?

11. Choose an organization with which you are familiar that develops its own information systems. Does this organization or has this organization used CSF or JAD to determine system requirements? In what ways was this advantageous?

12. As a small group, conduct a search on the World Wide Web for "object-oriented analysis and design" using any browser you wish (Hint: Because people write differently, search using both object-oriented and object oriented.). Check out some of the hits. You should have found numerous articles regarding OOA&D's use by IS departments. Are these articles positive or negative regarding OOA&D? Do you agree with the articles? Prepare a 10-minute presentation of your findings to the class.

13. Interview an IS manager within an organization with which you are familiar. Determine whether methodologies such as prototyping, RAD, and/or OOA&D are utilized for system projects. Who makes the choice of methodology? If a methodology has not been used, is it due to choice, or is it due to a lack of need, understanding, or capability to use the methodology?

14. Choose an organization with which you are familiar that uses Group Support Systems. For what purposes are they used? Electronic JAD or electronic meetings? Do they utilize the terms GSS, JAD, or E-JAD?

15. Interview an IS manager within an organization with which you are familiar. Determine this person's feelings about the future of system development. What methodologies will be widely used? Why? Are there any emerging technologies that this person feels will make a strong impact?

16. Choose an organization with which you are familiar that uses CASE tools in system development projects. Which types of CASE tools do they use—diagramming, screen and report generators, analysis, repository, documentation generators, or code generators? Why these and not others? Was there any transition problem in the initial stages of their use? If so, how was the problem solved? Compare your findings with those of your classmates. Do CASE tools have a common use, or does everyone do something different? Why do you think this is the case?

17. Reread the opening scenario to the chapter. It seems that Greg is intending to follow the prototyping method for systems development. Do you agree with this decision? Why or why not? What other methods would work for this situation? What methods would not work?

Real World Case Problems

1. SAS's Rapid Warehousing Methodology

SAS Institute, Inc., is helping people in a variety of organizations implement data warehousing and data mining solutions. Because it needs to generate solutions quickly and efficiently, SAS uses its own Rapid Warehousing Methodology to build data warehouses. Rapid warehousing is the iterative, incremental development of data warehouse projects based on the following development phases: Justification, Requirements Gathering, Design/Prototype, Implementation, and Review. With SAS's new methodology, each iteration of the data warehouse implementation is delivered quickly, with a goal of achieving measurable results within 90 days.

In the Justification phase, the project team is formed and team members evaluate the possible impact a data warehouse can have on the business and whether it is justified to start a data warehouse project right now. In the Requirements Gathering phase, the team finds out what information users need, in what form, and how often, and they examine the site's IT architecture and strategy. A physical model of the warehouse is also defined. In the Design/Prototype phase, sample systems are built and tested and sample queries and other end-user reports are executed. In the Implementation phase, all necessary finished programs and applications are written, the data warehouse is made available to users, and users are trained. Finally, in the Review phase, the system is evaluated immediately after the system has been delivered and again after a certain amount of time has elapsed.

SAS's methodology makes extensive use of Joint Applications Development (JAD) and prototyping. With JAD, the entire data warehouse implementation team is involved in eliciting and validating requirements, reconciling business-user needs with organizational constraints, avoiding costly mistakes and unnecessary iterations, and producing the final model of the data warehouse. In addition, the prototype is shown to all the users of the data warehouse, providing an opportunity for SAS to gather further feedback before moving into final implementation. The prototype can also form the basis on which the project team can continue to build to complete the data

warehouse (that is, it doesn't necessarily have to be a throw away demo).

With SAS's use of state-of-the-art development methods—Rapid Warehousing Methodology, Joint Applications Development, prototyping—they can deliver useful data warehousing and data mining solutions quickly and efficiently.

a. How do SAS's development methods differ from traditional, structured development methods?

b. Is the goal of achieving measurable results within 90 days feasible? Why or why not?

c. Why might it be particularly useful to be able to implement data warehousing and data mining solutions quickly?

Source *SAS Institute Inc. 1998. A SAS institute white paper: data warehousing methodology. http://www.ssas.com. April.*

2. Technology Solutions Company Announces Methodology and Support Around Genesys

CTI Software: TSC to include the rapid and reliable deployment of Genesys CTI software.

Technology Solutions Company now offers a dedicated systems development methodology around the implementation and support of Genesys' Computer Telephony Integration (CTI) products. TSC will deploy, implement, and support the Genesys suite of enterprise CTI products as a component of its Enterprise Customer Management (ECM) solutions.

TSC has already successfully implemented the Genesys software within strategic ECM solutions at several of the world's largest financial institutions, pharmaceutical companies, and consumer goods organizations. By extending TSC's ECM framework to include Genesys' CTI software, TSC further enhances its capabilities to deploy and support comprehensive ECM solutions and operate as an end-to-end solutions provider to the marketplace. TSC will extend its ECM framework to include a comprehensive methodology around the rapid and reliable implementation of Genesys' CTI software. TSC will also dedicate resources within its Relationship Architecture

Design and Deployment (RADD) Laboratory to execute the implementation of the Genesys methodology, where appropriate. Representing the best practices developed by TSC, the methodology will enable an organization to implement the Genesys technology from concept to pilot in six weeks.

"By using Genesys' CTI objects, and leveraging TSC's knowledge and expertise, Zurich Kemper has been able to meet an aggressive delivery schedule for providing benefit to our customers," said Michael Goodyear, Sales Officer of Zurich Direct Insurance. "TSC's methodologies and best practices have enabled them to implement a pilot of outbound campaign management, softphone functionality, calling identification, and call center statistics within a six week time frame."

"TSC's Enterprise Customer Management framework and methodology have enabled us to quickly drive transformational change throughout organizations that seek to become customer-centric in their operations. This framework provides an end-to-end solution approach to the definition, deployment, and support of these highly complex solutions," added Kelly D. Conway, TSC's Executive Vice-President of its Worldwide Call Center and Enterprise Customer Management Practice. "We have recognized that a major stumbling block to successful ECM solutions has been the rapid and reliable deployment and support of this complex piece of technology. Our methodology and support capabilities are designed to reduce the time, risk, and cost associated with deploying these solutions. We believe that this represents a major step forward for the call center industry."

a. On which three phases of the traditional systems development life cycle is TSC's new development method focused?

b. TSC has married its alternative development method with which specific type of software and business process? Was this a good move on TSC's part? Why or why not?

c. How does TSC and its customers know that this alternative development method has worked well?

Source   1998. *Technology solutions company announces methodology and support around Genesys CTI software.* http://www.techsol.com/news/980121.htm. *January 21.*

References

Booch, G. 1990. *Object oriented design with applications.* Redwood City, California: Benjamin/Cummings.

Borland. 1998. Information from: www.borland.com. Information verified: March 22, 1998.

Boynton, A.C., and R.W. Zmud. 1994. An assessment of critical success factors. In *Management of information systems,* ed. Gray, King, McLean, and Watson, 2d ed. 293–299, 368–382. Fort Worth, Texas: The Dryden Press.

Chen M., and R. J. Norman. 1992. Integrated computer-aided software engineering (CASE): Adoption, implementation and impacts. *Proceedings of the Hawaii International Conference on System Sciences,* ed J.F. Nunamaker, Jr. vol. 3, 362–373. Los Alamitos, California: IEEE Computer Society Press.

Coad, P., and E. Yourdon. 1991. *Object-oriented design.* Englewood Cliffs, New Jersey: Prentice Hall.

Daniels, Dennis, Hayes, Nunamaker, Jr., and Valacich. 1991. GroupCASE: Electronic support for group requirements elicitation. *Hawaii International Conference on System Sciences* 3: 43–52. Los Alamitos, California: IEEE Computer Society Press.

Gibson, M.L., and C.T. Hughes. 1994. *Systems analysis and design: A comprehensive methodology with CASE.* Danvers, Massachusetts: boyd & fraser Publishing.

Halladay, S., and M. Wiebel. 1993. *Object oriented software engineering.* Englewood Cliffs, New Jersey: Prentice Hall.

Hoffer, George, and Valacich. 1999. *Modern systems analysis and design.* 2d ed. Reading, Massachusetts: Addison Wesley Longman.

Jessup, L.M., and J.S. Valacich. 1993. *Group support systems: New perspectives.* New York: Macmillian Publishing.

Oracle. 1998. Information from: www.oracle.com. Information verified: March 22, 1998.

Orlikowski, W. J. 1989. Division among the ranks: The social implications of CASE tools for system developers. *Proceedings of the Tenth International Conference on Information Systems,* 199–210.

Martin, J. 1991. *Rapid application development.* New York: Macmillan Publishing.

McConnell, S. 1996. *Rapid development.* Redmond, Washington: Microsoft Press.

Rockart, J.F. 1979. Chief executives define their own information needs. *Harvard Business Review.* (March–April): 81–93.

Sybase. 1998. Information from: www.sybase.com. Information verified: March 22, 1998.

Verity, J.W., and E.I. Schwartz. 1994. Software made simple. In *Management of Information Systems,* ed Gray, King, McLean, and Watson, 2d ed. 293–299. Fort Worth, Texas: The Dryden Press.

Related Readings

Basili, Briand, and Melo. 1996. How to reuse influences productivity in object-oriented systems. *Communications of the ACM* 39(10): 104–116.

Baskerville, R.L., and J. Stage. 1996. Controlling prototype development through risk analysis. *Management Information Systems Quarterly* 20(4): 481–504.

Finlay, P.N., and A.C. Mitchell. 1994. Perceptions of the benefits from the introduction of CASE: An empirical study. *Management Information Systems Quarterly* 18(4): 353–370.

Huh, S.Y. 1993. Modelbase construction with object-oriented constructs. *Decision Sciences* 24(2): 409–434.

Iansiti, M., and A. MacCormack. 1997. Developing products on Internet time. *Harvard Business Review* 75(5): 108–117.

Iivari, J. 1996. Why are CASE tools not used? *Communications of the ACM* 39(10): 94–103.

Orlikowski, W.J. 1993. CASE tools as organizational change: Investigating incremental and radical changes in systems development. *Management Information Systems Quarterly* 17(3): 309–340.

Parsons, J., and Y. Wand. 1997. Using objects for systems analysis. *Communications of the ACM* 40(12): 104–110.

Rai, A. and R. Patnayakuni. 1996. A structural model for CASE adoption behavior. *Journal of Management Information Systems* 13(2): 205–234.

Schmidt, D.C., and M.E. Fayad. 1997. Lessons learned building reusable OO frameworks for distributed software. *Communications of the ACM* 40(10): 85–87.

Sheetz, Irwin, Tegarden, Nelson, and Monarchi. 1997. Exploring the difficulties of learning object-oriented techniques. *Journal of Management Information Systems* 14(2): 103–131.

Subramanian, G.H., and G.E. Zarnich. 1996. An examination of some software development effort and productivity determinants in ICASE tool projects. *Journal of Management Information Systems* 12(4): 143–160.

Wang, S. 1996. Toward formalized object-oriented management information systems analysis. *Journal of Management Information Systems* 12(4): 117–141.

Scenario: Critical New Application Needed Immediately

Randy is the Manager of Systems Development at a medium-sized manufacturing organization. He has a small but adequate staff of IS professionals who are dedicated to developing new systems, maintaining existing systems, and helping end-users. The organization is implementing new information systems and updating the existing systems at a fairly rapid pace, so Randy's unit has been very busy. His staff is currently working on a new system, an inventory management application and sales lead tracking application, using contemporary and emerging methods for building systems as described in Chapters 9 and 10.

Given how busy Randy's staff has been, these two projects sat in the development "queue" for several months before his team could turn their attention to them. Now, given the complexity of these two new systems, they seem to be taking up all his developers' time—in fact, he often sees his development team working late into the evenings and occasionally on weekends.

Late one afternoon, Randy's boss, Lena, the IS department manager, calls him into her office. She explains to him that one of the organization's senior vice presidents has been pushing hard for a new system that will increase the purchasing departments' efficiency by 50%. This department has had problems in the past meeting its objectives and it seems that a new system could turn the group around. Lena explains that she has reviewed the figures and agrees that a new system should help the department reach its potential. The system would reduce mounting organizational expenses while at the same time enable the department to purchase goods and services faster and at better rates, all of which contribute directly to the organization's bottom line. Lena tells Randy that she understands that existing projects need to be completed, as they are also important; however, it quickly becomes clear to Randy that this new project is a "top priority."

What should Randy do? His development team is already in the middle of two projects that are taxing their time and energy to the limit. Adding another project to their workload does not seem to be an option. Canceling or delaying one of the projects that is currently under development would be costly and might hurt the morale of the users of that system and of those developers who have been "in" on the project from the ground floor. Furthermore, Randy has worked hard to establish some credibility for the IS department as a group that gets things done. In the past, projects were often delayed or canceled, causing managers to lose faith in the IS department's ability to deliver systems they needed. Over the past year, Randy has worked closely with the managers and has started to regain their faith. Canceling one of the existing systems would certainly hurt his and his department's credibility and might leave managers thinking it was back to "business as usual."

Nonetheless, Lena asks Randy to talk with his staff and to come back the next day with some options for getting the new system developed and running as soon as possible. Randy goes back to his office, gathers his people, and begins brainstorming on some options. His team quickly determines that they can pursue one of several options, each with unique advantages and disadvantages. They can simply take on the extra project along with their existing projects. However, without garnering extra resources such as hiring new IS employees, this option is seriously flawed. They could go out and buy one of the "canned" purchasing systems that are available. Unfortunately, these are relatively expensive, they do not provide the specific functionality that is needed, and are written in a development language with which they are not familiar. They could completely outsource the development of the new system to a third party. The downside of this option is that they would lose some degree of control over the development of the system and don't have the time necessary to find a good outsourcing partner.

FIGURE 11.1

System development options.

System Development Options

- **Option 1: In-house development by IS Group**
  - Advantages
    - Control System Quality
    - System Meets User Needs
  - Disadvantages
    - Need to Hire Additional IS Staff
    - Too Busy with Projects Already

- **Option 2: Buy System from Vendor**
  - Advantages
    - Proven System
    - Fast Deployment
  - Disadvantages
    - System Won't Meet All User Needs
    - Expensive
    - System Not Easily Changed and Maintained

- **Option 3: Hire Outside Firm to Develop Custom System**
  - Advantages
    - Little Effort to Gain System
    - System Meets User Needs
  - Disadvantages
    - Expensive
    - Time Needed to Find a Partner

- **Option 4: End-user Development**
  - Advantages
    - User Are Technically Competent
    - System Meets User Needs
    - Inexpensive
  - Disadvantages
    - IS Group Loses Control (Quality Control)
    - IS Group Needs to Support Users

They finally decide to recommend a final option: to help the employees in the purchasing department develop their own system. The purchasing department staff members are among the more technically competent in the firm and have extensive experience with PC-based databases. With some guidance, they could develop their own database application, with the IS staff serving more as consultants than as developers on the project. This option also helps to provide the much-needed "pain relief" to the IS staff and managers. They are a bit leery about relinquishing control of systems development, but they have a good relationship with the people in purchasing and trust them to do a good job.

Randy presents each of the options to Lena along with the respective advantages and disadvantages of each (see Figure 11.1). She asks which option he recommends, and he explains why he thinks that option four, guided end-user development, appears to be the best available given the current circumstances. She likes the arguments and adds that, if managed effectively, this could be exactly the solution that the organization needs for the broader problem of keeping up with the rapid pace of technology-induced change within the firm. She immediately sends an e-mail message calling together the relevant stakeholders to a meeting at which they can decide how to proceed.

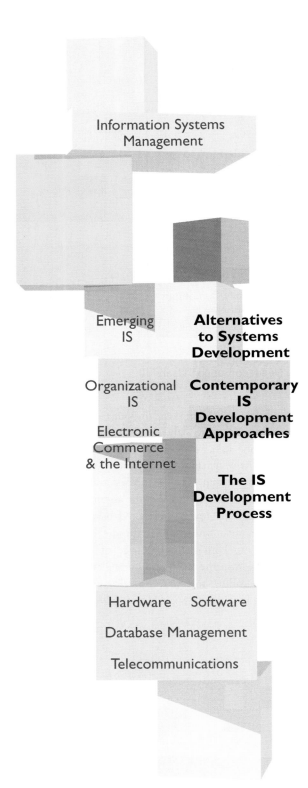

Information Systems
Management

Emerging
IS

**Alternatives
to Systems
Development**

Organizational
IS

**Contemporary
IS
Development
Approaches**

Electronic
Commerce
& the Internet

**The IS
Development
Process**

Hardware   Software

Database Management

Telecommunications

Introduction

This chapter continues the discussion of information systems development. However, the focus here is on alternatives to in-house systems development. If you are a typical business student you might be wondering why we are spending so much time discussing information systems development. The answer is simple: No matter in what area of an organization you are—such as marketing, finance, accounting, human resources, or operations—you *will* be involved in the systems development process. In fact, research indicates that more than 55% of most organizations' IS spending is controlled by specific business functions, with this number expected to jump to more than 80% by 1999 (Kutnick, 1998). What this means is that even if your career interests are something other than IS, it is very likely that you will be involved in the IS development process. Understanding all available options is important to your success.

In the preceding two chapters we discussed different methods for building information systems in-house. Under these options, systems development requests are given to the firm's IS staff, who work with others in the organization to prioritize those requests and allocate resources such as money, people, and equipment to pending projects as time allows. In many situations this option works well; the IS staff is able to deliver high-quality applications relatively quickly and at a reasonable cost. However, there are other situations where building a system in-house is not a feasible option because there may not be an adequate IS staff in-house, the IS staff may not have the required skills, or, as described in the opening scenario, the IS staff may be so overworked that it cannot possibly build a new system. Consequently, it is important to consider other options for creating and implementing new systems besides having the firm's in-house IS staff build it.

FIGURE 11.2

The big picture: focusing on alternatives to systems development.

After reading this chapter, you will be able to:

1. Understand the factors and situations where building a system in-house is not feasible.

2. Explain three alternative systems development options: external acquisition, outsourcing, and end-user development.

This chapter is the last in Part 4, "Information Systems Development." It describes how organizations develop and acquire information systems (see Figure 11.2). It begins by describing why organizations need alternatives to systems development. This is followed by a description of three alternative methods: external acquisition, outsourcing, and end-user development.

The Importance of Finding Alternatives to Building Systems Yourself

Building systems in-house with the IS staff is always an option to consider. Many times, however, this is not a feasible solution. The following are four situations in which you might need to consider alternative development strategies.

Situation 1—Limited IS staff

Often, an organization does not have the capability to build a system itself. Perhaps its IS staff is small or deployed on other activities such as maintaining a small network and helping users with problems on a day-to-day basis. This limited staff may simply not have the capability to take on an in-house development project without hiring several analysts or programmers, which is very expensive in today's labor market.

————— Outsourcing Helps Xerox Focus —————   A BRIEF CASE

With 1997 sales of approximately $18 billion, Xerox has a relatively small group of IS professionals for its size. Consequently, to allow its 700 IS professionals to focus on moving the copier giant into the flexible network computing company of the 21st century, they signed a long-term contract with Electronic Data Systems (EDS) to manage their mainframe computers and data centers (Verity, 1998). The EDS contract is enabling Xerox managers and IS professionals to focus on developing applications to support new products and services. In other words, Xerox will have its IS staff focus on adding shareholder value by supporting the creation of new products and services; routine and nonstrategic activities are being handled by EDS.

Situation 2—IS staff has limited skill set

In other situations, the IS staff may not have the skills needed to develop a particular kind of system. This has been especially true with the explosion of the World Wide Web. Many very large organizations such as ESPN, ABC News, and Walt Disney are having outside organizations manage their Web sites (Starwave, 1998). Although the existing IS staff in these and many other organizations may be highly skilled at producing traditional applications, the sudden rise in demand for new types of systems induces many organizations to seek outside help. It isn't as if the IS director can tell the boss that her department cannot build a new electronic commerce system simply because the IS staff doesn't have the necessary skills to build it! Fortunately, there are alternatives to having the IS staff build the system, which the IS director can turn to when she needs to tap into specialized skills that are not present within the IS staff.

<table>
<tr><td>A BRIEF CASE</td></tr>
</table>

Citibank Leverages AT&T's Network

In addition to needing human resources to overcome limitations in an organization's capability to develop systems, companies are creating partnerships with other organizations to gain access to infrastructure and proprietary technologies. For example, Citibank signed a five-year, $750 million partnership agreement with AT&T in 1998 to manage Citibank's data network system (Thibodeau, 1998). AT&T's global communication network will provide Citibank with greatly increased Internet bandwidth, which will enable the bank to more rapidly expand and improve its electronic commerce offerings such as home banking (see Figure 11.3). The evaluation process leading to the selection of AT&T took 12 months to complete, and the agreement will affect about 400 Citibank workers, although some of these workers will be hired by AT&T. AT&T had to beat out several other competitors to land the Citibank contract. In addition, this agreement greatly expands AT&T's networking business. In 1997, AT&T Solutions reported $650 million in revenue and is projecting to be a $4 billion company by 2002. To achieve this growth, AT&T Solutions will not only need to be successful in delivering high-quality services, but will also need to hire hundreds of new workers to staff this expansion.

FIGURE 11.3

PC-Banking at Citibank.

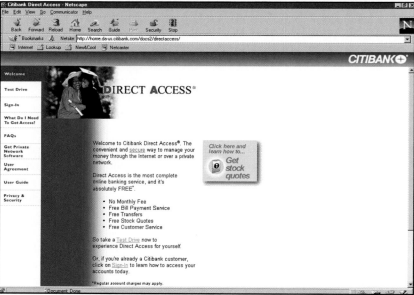

Reprinted from Citibank by permission. One-time use.

Situation 3—IS staff overworked

In some organizations, the IS staff may simply not have the time to work on all the systems that are required or desired by the organization. Obviously, the number of people dedicated to new development is not infinite. Therefore, you must have ways to prioritize development projects. In most cases, systems that are of strategic importance or that affect the whole organization are likely to receive a higher priority than those that offer only minor benefits or affect only one department or a couple of people in a department. Nonetheless, the IS manager must find a way to support all users, even when the IS staff may be tied up with other "higher-priority" projects.

Situation 4—Problems with performance of IS staff

Earlier in this book we discussed how and why systems development projects could sometimes be risky. Often the efforts of IS departments are derailed due to staff turnover, changing requirements, shifts in technology, or budget constraints. Regardless of the reason, the result is the same: another failed (or flawed) system. Given the large expenditures in staff time and training as well as the high risk associated with systems development efforts, the prudent manager tries to limit the risk of any project as much as possible. What if it were possible to see the completed system to know what it looked like before development began? Being able to see into the future would certainly help you learn more about the system and whether it would meet your needs and would help to lower the risk of a project. When building a system in-house, it is obviously not possible to see into the future. However, using some of the alternative methods described in this chapter, you *can*, in fact, see what a completed system might look like. These methods will enable you to know what you are buying, which greatly lowers the risk of a project.

If it is impossible to see the finished system before in-house development starts, how do some alternative systems development strategies enable you to know what you are buying in advance? Read on...

Common Alternatives to In-House Systems Development

Any project has at least four different systems development options. The preceding two chapters presented the first option: building the system in-house with your IS staff. The other options are

- External Acquisition

- Outsourcing

- End-User Development

The following sections examine each of these options in closer detail to see how one or more of them might fit the four situations described earlier.

External Acquisition

Purchasing an existing system from an outside vendor such as IBM, EDS, or Andersen Consulting is referred to as **external acquisition**. How does external acquisition of an information system work? Think about the process that you might use when buying a car. Do you simply walk into the first dealership you see, tell them you need a car, and see what they try to sell you? Hopefully not. Probably you've done some up-front analysis and know how much money you can afford to spend and what your needs are. If you've done your homework, you probably have an idea of what you want and which dealership can provide the type of car you desire (see Figure 11.4).

FIGURE 11.4

A prospective car buyer with a "wish list."

This up-front analysis of your needs can be extremely helpful in narrowing your options and can save you a lot of time. Understanding your needs can also help you sift through the salesmen's hype that you are likely to encounter from one dealer to the next as each tries to sell you on why his model is perfect for you. After getting some information, you may want to take a couple of promising models for a "test drive," where you actually get behind the wheel and see how well the car fits you and your driving habits. You might even talk to other people who have owned this type of car to see how they feel about it. Ultimately, you are the one who has to evaluate all the different cars to see which one is best for you. They may all be good cars; however, one may fit your needs just a little better than the others.

The external acquisition of an information system is very similar to the purchase of a car. When you acquire an IS you should do some analysis of what your specific needs are. For example, how much can you afford to spend, what basic functionality is required, and approximately how many people will use the system? Next, you can begin to "shop" for the new system by asking potential vendors to provide information about the systems that they have to offer. After evaluating this information, it may become clear that several vendors have systems that are worth considering. Those vendors may be asked to come to your organization and set up their systems so that you and your colleagues are able to "test drive" the systems. Seeing how people react to the systems and seeing how each system performs in the organizational environment can help you "see" exactly what you are buying. By seeing the actual system and how it performs with real users, with real or simulated data, you can get a much clearer idea about whether that system fits your needs. Just as you do when you take a car for a "test drive," you learn how the car meets your needs. By seeing how the system meets your needs before you buy, you can greatly reduce the risk associated with acquiring that system.

Steps in External Acquisition

In many cases, your organization will use a competitive bid process for making an external acquisition. In the competitive bid process, vendors are given an opportunity to propose systems that meet the organization's needs. The goal of the competitive process is to help the organization ensure that it gets the best system at the lowest possible price. Most competitive external acquisition processes have at least five general steps:

1. System identification, selection, and planning

2. Systems analysis

3. Development of a Request for Proposal (RFP)

4. Proposal evaluation

5. Vendor selection

You already have learned about the first two because they apply when you build a system yourself *and* when you purchase a system through an external vendor. In the first step, system identification, selection, and planning, you assess whether a proposed system is feasible. During this step, many questions are asked and answered. Can the existing technology be used for such a system? Does the organization have the funds to pay for such a system? Will such a system benefit the organization?

Assuming that the proposed system is feasible and meets your needs, a detailed systems analysis is conducted to determine the requirements of the system. As outlined in Chapter 9, the systems analysis step refines what the needs of the organization are so that a system can be built or purchased that addresses those needs. This step is critical whether building the system yourself or using external acquisition—there is no need to buy a Ferrari when a Chevrolet will do the job just as well or better. Step 3, development of a Request for Proposal, is where the external acquisition process changes significantly from in-house development.

FIGURE 11.5

Sample RFP document for information systems project.

Development of a Request for Proposal (RFP)

A **Request for Proposal**, or RFP, is simply a report that is used to tell vendors what your requirements are and to invite them to provide information about how they might be able to meet those requirements (see Figure 11.5). A RFP is sent to vendors who might potentially be interested in providing hardware and/or software for the system.

Among the areas that may be covered in a RFP are:

■ A summary of existing systems and applications

■ Reliability, backup, and service requirements

■ System performance and required system features

■ The criteria that will be used to evaluate proposals

■ Timetable and budget constraints (how much you can spend)

The RFP is then sent to prospective vendors along with an invitation to present their bids for the project. Eventually, you will likely receive a number of proposals to evaluate. If, on the other hand, you do not receive many proposals, it may be necessary to rethink the requirements—perhaps the requirements are greater than the budget limitations, or the timetable is too short. In some situations, you may need to first send out a preliminary *Request for Information* to simply gather information from prospective vendors. This will help you determine whether, indeed, the desired system is feasible or even possible. If you determine that it is, you can then send out a RFP.

Proposal Evaluation

The fourth step in external acquisition is to evaluate proposals received from vendors. This evaluation may include viewing system demonstrations, evaluating the performance of those systems, and examining criteria important to the organization and how the proposed systems "stack up" to those criteria. Demonstrations are a good way to get a "feel" for the different systems' capabilities. Just as you can go to the showroom to look over a new car and get a feel for whether it meets your needs, it is also possible to screen various systems through a demonstration from the vendor. During a demonstration, a sales team from the vendor presents an oral presentation about their system, its features, and cost, followed by a demonstration of the actual system. In some cases this may take place at your location; other times, it may take place at the vendor's facility or at one of the vendor's clients, particularly when the system is not easily transportable. Although such demonstrations are often useful in helping you understand the features of different systems being proposed, they are rarely adequate enough in and of themselves to warrant purchasing the system without further evaluation.

One of the ways you can better evaluate a proposed system is through **systems benchmarking**. For example, benchmark programs are sample programs or jobs that simulate your computer workload. You can have benchmarks designed to test portions of the system that are most critical to your needs based on the systems analysis. A benchmark might test how long it takes to calculate a set of numbers, or how long it takes to access a set of records in a database, or how long it would take to access certain information given a certain number of concurrent users. Some common system benchmarks include

- Response time given a specified number of users

- Time to sort records

- Time to retrieve a set of records

- Time to produce a given report

- Time to read in a set of data

In addition to benchmarking, workload models can be used to analyze how a given system will perform under the stress of normal daily operations. For example, if you know that you need to process 30,000 records each hour and that you have an average of 5 batch processing jobs and 20 printing requests waiting to be processed at any given time, you can build workload models that include the same mix of activities to help evaluate how a given system will perform.

In addition, vendors may also supply benchmarks that you can use, though you should not rely solely on vendor information. For smaller systems, you may be able to rely on system benchmarks published in computer trade journals such as *PC Magazine* or *PC Week*. However, in most cases, demos and benchmarks alone do not provide the only information you need to make a purchase. The systems analysis phase should have revealed some specific requirements for the new system. These requirements may be listed as criteria that the organization can use to further evaluate vendor proposals. Depending upon what you are purchasing—hardware, software, or both—the criteria you use will change. Table 11.1 provides examples of commonly used evaluation criteria.

Table 11.1 Commonly used evaluation criteria.

Hardware Criteria	Software Criteria	Other Criteria
Clock speed of CPU	Memory requirements	Training and documentation
Memory requirements	Help features	Maintenance and repair
Secondary storage	Usability	Installation
(including capacity,	Learnability	Testing
access time, and so on)	Number of features supported	Price
Video display size		
Printer speed		

Vendor Selection

In most cases, more than one system will meet your needs, just as more than one car will usually meet your needs. However, some probably "fit" better than others. In these cases, you should have a way of prioritizing or ranking competing proposals. One way of doing this is by devising a scoring system for each of the criteria and benchmarking results. For example, look back at the criteria in Table 11.1. Should all these areas be given equal weight or are some more important than others? In most cases, some criteria will be more important than others. For example, it may be very important for a system to do well on the performance benchmarks, moderately important for the system to have a printer speed in excess of 20 pages per minute, and less important for the system to have on-line help.

Some organizations create a scoring system for evaluating different systems, in which scores are assigned to each of the criteria. For example, benchmarking results might be worth 100 total points, while on-line help features are worth only 50 points. All the points for each criterion are then summed to give an overall score for each system. Then, the system with the highest score (or one of the systems among several with the highest scores) is selected. Figure 11.6 shows an example of a form that could be used to evaluate systems and choose a vendor using this method.

Criterion	Max Points (or weight)	Systems Being Evaluated (Score)		
		A	B	C
Disk capacity	20	10	17	12
Compatibility	50	45	30	25
Usability	30	12	30	20
Vendor Support	35	27	16	5
Benchmark Results	50	40	28	30
(add as needed...)				
Total	185	134	121	92

FIGURE 11.6

Sample system evaluation form with subset of criteria.

In the example shown in Figure 11.6, System A looks like the best solution because it scored highest. Using such an evaluation method, it is possible that scoring low on a given criterion might exclude otherwise outstanding systems from being purchased. You can see that Systems B and C fared very poorly on the Vendor Support criterion. It is possible that those systems do not have very good vendor support. However, it is also possible that the vendor did not adequately communicate its commitment to support, perhaps because it did not realize it was such an important issue. Therefore, it is very important for you to communicate with vendors about the evaluation process and what things you value most highly.

Other less formalized approaches to evaluate vendors may also be used. Sometimes simple checklists are used; other times a more subjective process is used. Regardless of the mechanism, eventually the evaluation stage is completed and a vendor is selected, ending the external acquisition process.

The extent to which firms use quantitative analysis such as criteria, weights, and scoring to evaluate vendor proposals varies from organization to organization. In many countries, governmental agencies are often required to perform such an analysis. Furthermore, in some situations, such agencies are required to use specific categories, weights, and scoring methods. For example, many governmental agencies, such as the Internal Revenue Service, have traditionally been required to give significant weight in their evaluation to the criteria of price. Although it is well intended, this has often led to the purchase of systems that, although they were relatively inexpensive, were less than optimal on other dimensions. Governmental agencies in the U.S. have acquired many, many systems that were "cheap" (recall our review of the Denver International Airport in Chapter 1) but in other dimensions did not fare well.

Some organizations also choose to conform to an "in use" requirement, which means that they will accept proposals from only those vendors where the technology proposed has been in actual use by a paying client for some minimum time period, such as six or twelve months. In fact, in some cases vendors are asked to prove that the technology has been in use, usually by showing a dated brochure, a sales order, or some other documentation. The "in use" criteria is meant to ensure the choice of a relatively stable system. Unfortunately, as with the tendency for governmental agencies to weight price so heavily, the "in use" criteria can also sometimes backfire. With hardware, software, and networking technologies changing so quickly, organizations with a strict, long "in use" requirement are doomed to never have new technology.

Outsourcing

A related, but different, alternative to purchasing an existing system is outsourcing. With the external acquisition option discussed above, the organization typically purchases a single system from an outside vendor. **Outsourcing** is the practice of turning over responsibility of some to all of an organization's information systems development and operations to an outside firm. Outsourcing includes a variety of working relationships. The outside firm, or service provider, may develop your information systems applications and house them within their organization, they may run your applications on their computers, or they may develop systems to run on existing computers within your organization. Anything is fair game in an outsourcing arrangement.

In recent years, outsourcing has become a very popular option for organizations. For example, the worldwide IT market for outsourcing services is growing at a rate of 20% per year and will reach a size of nearly $77 billion by the year 2000 (King, 1998). In a recent A.T. Kearney, Inc., study, 90% of the 26 multinational companies it surveyed had outsourced some function in 1995, compared with fewer than 60% in 1992 (Caldwell, 1996). Table 11.2 lists the top 20 IT outsourcing vendors. Outsourcing in the IS arena has become big business!

Table 11.2   Top 20 IT outsourcing vendors.

	Revenue Growth (%)	Revenue by Industry (% of Rev)	Sales, Pricing, & Contracting Model	Number of Regional Operations	Vertical Industry Solutions Expertise	Centers of Expertise	Total Points
1. EDS	10	2	10	10	10	10	52
2. Andersen Consulting	10	2	5	10	10	10	47
3. IBM/ISSC	10	2	5	10	10	10	47
4. CSC	10	10	5	2	10	5	42
5. Hewlett-Packard	10	10	2	5	5	10	42
6. Cap Gemini Sogeti	10	10	5	2	5	5	37
7. Digital	2	10	5	10	5	5	37
8. ICL/CFM	10	10	2	2	5	5	34
9. Sema Group	10	10	2	2	5	5	34
10. MCI/SHL	10	5	2	2	5	10	34
11. CBIS	5	5	5	2	10	5	32
12. Flserv	10	2	2	2	10	5	31
13. M&I Data Services	5	2	5	2	5	10	29
14. AT&T Solutions	5	5	5	2	5	5	27
15. Perot Systems	2	10	2	2	5	5	26
16. Unisys	2	5	2	5	5	5	24
17. Bull	2	10	2	2	2	5	23
18. Alltel IS	5	2	2	2	5	5	21
19. NTT Data	2	5	2	2	5	5	21
20. Debis	2	5	2	2	2	5	18

Source   1996. *Top 20 IT outsourcing vendors.* Information Week, *June 24, 56. Reprinted by permission.*

Why Outsourcing?

Why would a firm outsource any of its information systems services? The main reason is usually cost effectiveness. The service provider may specialize in a particular kind of service such as running payroll. Because it already has the system in place and has many companies that use its services, it is able to spread the cost out across a large number of users. These economies of scale are often not possible in smaller firms or smaller IS groups. In the payroll example, the firm simply provides payroll data such as names, hours worked, and withholding rates to the service provider. For a fee, the service provider takes that data, processes it using its payroll system, and returns paychecks, statements, and designated reports to the company. This may be much cheaper in the long run than developing and operating an in-house payroll system. Furthermore, because other companies already use the service provider for payroll, the service provider has a track record of service that the company can check and rely on. Although it is not foolproof, the fact that the service provider has been providing payroll services successfully for a period of time reduces some of the risk.

In addition to the cost-effectiveness argument, additional reasons why firms often outsource their information systems development are to avoid costs of retraining IS staff and to gain access to specialized capabilities, just as Xerox did with its decision to partner with AT&T described earlier. Avoiding retraining costs is more often used in small or low-technology organizations, where the cost of retraining IS staff to keep them "current" with existing technology is significant. Alternatively, functional business units often require specialized applications to meet unique needs. Rather than rely on in-house development to meet a specialized need, it is often easier to outsource these requirements to service providers who specialize in a particular area.

The Chicago Mercantile Exchange

A BRIEF CASE

The Chicago Mercantile Exchange is the world's leading center for financial risk and asset management (Merc, 1998). The Merc, as it is called, uses open-pit trading floors where buyers and sellers meet to trade futures contracts and options on futures through the process of open outcry (see Figure 11.7). The Merc's diverse product line consists of futures and options on futures within four general categories: agricultural commodities, foreign currencies, interest rates, and stock indexes. All over the world, pension fund and investment advisers, portfolio managers, corporate treasurers and commercial banks trade on the Merc as an integral part of their financial management strategy. In fact, when business, industry and commerce make effective use of futures markets, they help reduce the risks that are part of doing business—which means lower prices for consumers. The Merc is about commerce, but when it came time to develop an electronic commerce Web site, they selected BBN Planet (now called GTE Internetworking after being acquired by GTE Corporation in May 1997), to host their site. Hosting a Web site was not directly related to the core competencies of their IS staff. Yet, Merc officials report that using BBN Planet brought both advantages and disadvantages (Anthes, 1997). BBN offers superb security, network management, and round-the-clock response to operational problems. Additionally, they believe that outsourcing to a large service provider such as BBN Planet is much safer than hosting their own Web site, because global-class companies like BBN Planet have the resources to create huge networks with no single point of failure. A disadvantage is a loss of control. To combat this concern, Merc wrote special monitoring software—running both at BBN and at the Merc's data center—to ensure that real-time data feeds are posted correctly at the Web site.

FIGURE 11.7

Trading floor at the Chicago Mercantile Exchange.

Reprinted by permission of the Chicago Mercantile Exchange.

Unlike today, outsourcing wasn't a widely used option for most large companies until 1990 when Kodak decided to outsource its *entire* IS operation into three separate contracts with IBM, DEC, and BusinessLand. This was the first large-scale outsourcing agreement from a large international corporation. Before this agreement, outsourcing was relatively small scale, and often limited to IS groups that had suffered performance problems. Since then, the outsourcing trend has become a very important and an increasingly common development alternative. Today, firms have many additional pressures to outsource. Some of these are old reasons, but some are new to today's environment (Applegate, McFarlan, and McKenney, 1996):

- *Cost and quality concerns:* In many cases it is possible to achieve higher-quality systems at a lower price through economies of scale, better management of hardware, lower labor costs, and better software licenses on the part of a service provider.

- *Problems in IS performance:* IS departments may have problems meeting acceptable service standards due to cost overruns, delayed systems, underutilized systems, or poorly performing systems. In such cases, organizational management may attempt to increase reliability through outsourcing.

- *Supplier pressures:* Perhaps not surprisingly, some of the largest service providers are also the largest suppliers of computer equipment: IBM, DEC, and EDS. In some cases, the aggressive sales forces of these suppliers are able to convince senior managers at organizations to outsource their IS functions.

- *Simplifying, downsizing, and reengineering:* Organizations under competitive pressure often attempt to focus on only their "core competencies." In many cases, organizations simply decide that running information systems is not one of their "core competencies" and decide to outsource this function to companies such as IBM and EDS, whose primary competency *is* developing and maintaining information systems.

■ *Financial factors:* When firms turn over their information systems to a service provider, they can sometimes strengthen their balance sheets by liquefying their IT assets. Also, if users perceive they are actually paying for their IT services rather than simply having them provided by an in-house staff, they may use those services more wisely and perceive them to be of greater value.

■ *Organizational culture:* Political or organizational problems are often difficult for an IS group to overcome. However, an external service provider often brings enough clout, devoid of any organizational or functional ties, to streamline IS operations as needed.

■ *Internal irritants:* Tension between end-users and the IS staff is sometimes difficult to eliminate. At times this tension can intrude on the daily operations of the organization, and the idea of a remote, external, relatively neutral IS group can be appealing. Whether or not the tension between users and the IS staff (or service provider) is really eliminated is open to question; however, simply having the IS group external to the organization can remove a lingering thorn in management's side.

Managing the IS Outsourcing Relationship

McFarlan and Nolan (1995) argue that the ongoing management of an outsourcing alliance is the single most important aspect of the outsourcing project's success. Their recommendations for the best management are

1. A strong, active CIO and staff should continually manage the legal and professional relationship with the outsourcing firm.

2. Clear, realistic performance measurements of the systems *and* of the outsourcing arrangement should be developed, such as tangible and intangible costs and benefits.

3. The interface between the customer and the outsourcer should have multiple levels (for example, links to deal with policy and relationship issues, and links for dealing with operational and tactical issues).

Managing outsourcing alliances in this way has important implications for the success of the relationship. For example, in addition to a strong CIO and staff, McFarlan and Nolan also recommend that firms assign full-time relationship managers and coordinating groups lower in the organization to "manage" the IS outsourcing project. This means that as people within the IS function are pulled away from traditional IS tasks such as systems development, they are moved toward and organized into new roles and groups. The structure and nature of the internal IS activities change from the exclusive builds and manages systems to one that includes managing relationships with outside firms that build and manage systems under legal contract.

Not All Outsourcing Relationships Are the Same

Most organizations no longer enter into a strictly legal contract with an outsourcing vendor, but into a mutually beneficial relationship with a strategic partner. In such a relationship, the firm and the vendor are each concerned with, and perhaps have a direct stake in, the success of the other. Yet, other types of relationships exist, which means that not all outsourcing agreements need to be structured the same way (Fryer, 1998). In fact, at least three different types of outsourcing relationships can be identified:

- Basic relationship

- Preferred relationship

- Strategic relationship

A basic relationship can best be thought of as a "cash and carry" relationship where you buy products and services on the basis of price and convenience. Organizations should try to have a few preferred relationships, where the buyer and supplier set preferences and prices to the benefit of each other. For example, a supplier can provide preferred pricing to customers who do a specified volume of business. Most organizations have just a few strategic relationships, where both sides share risks and rewards.

A BRIEF CASE ── ## A Strategic Outsourcing Relationship for DuPont ──

An example of a strategic outsourcing relationship where all parties are sharing risks and rewards is among the chemical giant DuPont, Andersen Consulting, and Computer Sciences Corporation (CSC) (Verity, 1997). In this 10-year, $4 billion-plus deal, DuPont is hoping to reduce spending on IS by as much as 10%. In this agreement, CSC and Andersen will develop new products and services that will be used internally and then sold to DuPont's subsidiaries in other countries. Later, these products may be sold to competitors in the chemical and energy industries. CSC will take over 13 of DuPont's data centers and hire 2,600 of their 4,200 data processing employees. Andersen will hire 500. The fees that CSC and Andersen will receive from DuPont will be proportional to the measurable improvements in shareholder value. This relationship shares both the risks and rewards among these strategic partners.

Strategic relationships require partners to work together rather than compete against each other or point fingers at each other. They learn from each other and their pay is based in part on the success of the partners. This is a far cry from the days when outsourcing vendors competed with each other, were secretive, and were quite legalistic, adhering strictly to the letter of the contract and not willing to do or spend any more than they had to. The promise of mutually beneficial outsourcing partnerships appears to be great, both for client organizations and for vendors. It will be interesting to see where this new form for outsourcing takes us, and what the next new form of outsourcing will be. The decision of whether or not to outsource is obviously not an easy one. However, it is one option that you should be aware of and consider, depending on a whole range of different factors including organizational style, access to service providers, geographic area, or scope of operations.

We have now discussed two systems development alternatives that rely on external organizations to either completely or partially alleviate the burden of managing IS development projects in-house. In some cases, however, it may not be possible or convenient to rely on agencies outside the organization for development. In these cases, organizations may rely on another option for systems development projects.

End-User Development

In many organizations, the growing sophistication of users within the organization offers IS managers a fourth alternative for systems development. This fourth alternative is **end-user development**—having users develop their own applications. This means that the people who are actually going to *use* the systems are also those who will *develop* those systems. End-user development, then, is one way IS departments can speed up application development without relying on external entities such as vendors or service providers. However, end-user development also has risks associated with it. This section outlines the benefits of having end-users develop their own applications as well as some of the drawbacks to this approach.

Benefits of End-User Development

To help you to better understand the benefits of end-user development, you should quickly review some of the problems with conventional development that are suggested by the four situations presented earlier in this chapter:

- *Cost of labor:* Conventional systems development is labor intensive. In Chapter 3, you saw how software costs have increased while hardware costs have declined, as shown in Figure 11.8. As you can see from the figure, it becomes much cheaper for IS managers to substitute hardware for labor. By giving users their own equipment, an IS manager can significantly reduce the cost of application development simply by giving end-users the tools they need and enabling them to develop their own applications. Better yet, the various departments within the organization can purchase their own equipment, and the IS staff can simply provide guidance and other services.

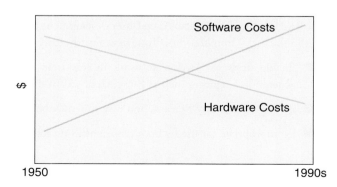

FIGURE 11.8

Rising software costs versus declining hardware costs.

■ *Long development time:* New systems can take months or even years to develop, depending on the scale and scope of the new system and the backlog of systems waiting to be developed. As a result, users' needs may significantly change between when the system was initially proposed and when it is actually implemented. In these cases, the system may be virtually obsolete before it has even been implemented! End-user-developed systems can "skip" the queue of systems waiting to be developed by the IS organization, resulting in more rapidly developed systems.

■ *Slow modification or updates of existing systems:* Related to the time it takes to develop new systems is the problem of maintaining existing systems. Often, updates to existing systems are given a lower priority than developing new systems. Unfortunately, this can result in systems that are unable to keep pace with changing business needs, becoming antiquated and under-used.

When end-users develop their own systems, the users have the responsibility to maintain and update applications as needed. Also, when systems are implemented, they often cause changes to the underlying business processes. These changes may necessitate further change or modification to the application, as highlighted in Figure 11.9. Rather than rely on IS to make these changes, users are able to modify the application in a timely manner to reflect the changed business process.

■ *Work overload:* One reason for long development times and slow modifications is that IS departments are often overloaded with work. When you leverage the talents of end-user developers, you can, in effect, increase the size of the development staff by shifting some of the workload normally handled by IS professionals to end-users, as depicted in Figure 11.10.

End-user development can radically decrease the development workload in the IS department. However, such a shift may cause other areas within IS such as a help desk, for example, to become flooded with requests for assistance. Nonetheless, end-user development can be an excellent option for organizations faced with some of the problems described above.

Encouraging End-User Development

End-user development sounds great, but how can organizations encourage and enable users to develop their own systems? Fortunately, the availability of fourth-generation tools (see Chapter 3) has enabled end-user development to become more practical today than in the early- to mid-1980s. To review, fourth-generation languages should:

■ Enable users to develop software in less time than that required by third-generation languages such as PASCAL or COBOL

■ Be easy to use, easy to learn, and easy to remember

■ Be appropriate for use by both users and IS professionals

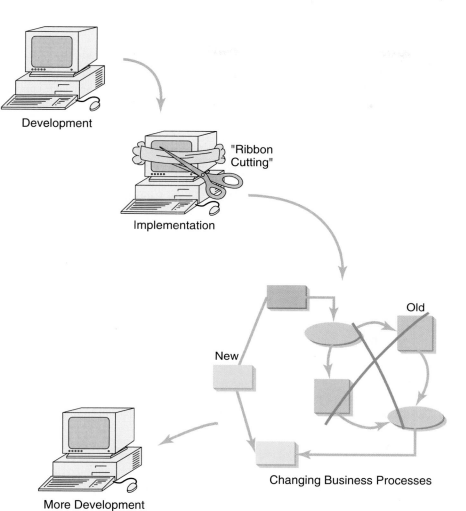

FIGURE 11.9

Continuous cycle of development: a system is developed and implemented. However, it eventually becomes inadequate, and new development takes place.

Development

"Ribbon Cutting"

Implementation

New

Old

Changing Business Processes

More Development

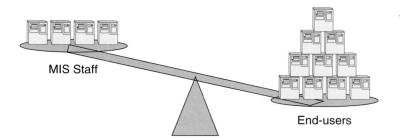

FIGURE 11.10

Shifting systems development workload as end-user development has become more prevalent.

MIS Staff

End-users

There are five categories of fourth-generation tools:

- *Personal computer tools*: Personal computer tools, including spreadsheets, database management systems, and graphics programs, are used by many users throughout an organization. Frequently, these tools enable users to build their own applications using macro languages or embedded tools within the software designed to enable users to customize their own systems.

- *Query languages/report generators*: These tools are usually associated with database systems and enable you to search a database by entering various search criteria. Structured Query Language, or SQL, is the most common query language for this purpose. For example, you may say "Give me the part numbers for any inventory that we have in stock whose quantity exceeds 30." A query language structures that query and presents the results of the query to the user. Report generators are similar to query languages and are designed to easily produce textual and tabular reports. Although query languages are often used by users alone, report generators may require some assistance from IS staff.

- *Graphics generators*: These tools can be used to extract relevant information from databases and convert that data to a graphic such as a pie chart, a line graph, or an area plot. As in report generators, users can specify many different formats.

- *Decision support or modeling tools*: Although spreadsheets can be used as decision support aids, dedicated decision support tools are often available for more complex, multi-dimensional models that may be too complex to easily be handled in a spreadsheet. These tools can enable users to develop decision support systems to aid in making decisions.

- *Application generators*: Application generators are designed to automate much of the relatively tedious programming work associated with systems development. In these tools, you can specify what you want done, then the application generator decides how to accomplish that task and generates the program code. Application generators can be used to get prototypes up and running quickly, get feedback from other potential users, and make necessary changes. Computer Aided Software Engineering (CASE) tools often include an application generator that can be used by end-users or IS professionals.

End-User Development Pitfalls

This chapter has painted a pretty rosy picture of end-user development so far. However, it is important to understand that along with the benefits come some drawbacks, as depicted in Figure 11.11.

The information systems and computer science professions have established software development standards and generally accepted practices that are used throughout different organizations and across different types of systems. Unfortunately, users may not be aware of these standards such as the need for adequate documentation, built-in error checking, and testing procedures. In small, personal applications, not adhering to the standards may not present a problem. However, if the system manages or interconnects to important business data, then lack of adherence to sound principles can quickly become a BIG problem if data becomes corrupted or is not secure.

"OK, TECHNICALLY THIS SHOULD WORK, JUDY, TYPE THE WORD, 'GOODYEAR' ALL CAPS, BOLDFACE, AT 700-POINT TYPE SIZE."

FIGURE 11.11

End-user development can sometimes be problematic.

Another problem for end-user developed systems is a potential lack of continuity. Suppose James develops a new system that meets his needs perfectly. James understands the system and uses it every day. However, one day James is transferred and is replaced by Jordan, a new hire to the company. The system that was so intuitive for James to use may not be so intuitive for Jordan. Jordan may quickly abandon James's system or may be forced to develop her own system. This example shows how end-user development can easily result in a lack of continuity among applications, leading to redundant development efforts and a lot of wasted productivity in the organization. In organizations where turnover is frequent, a lot of time can be lost "reinventing the wheel" simply because systems that are in place are undocumented and cannot be easily used by new employees.

Related to the continuity problem is the question of whether users and managers should be spending their time on IS development. That is, the organization has hired individuals to be financial managers, production managers, marketers, or salespeople. The organization expects these employees to add value to the organization based on the skills that they have to offer. If the time and energy of these individuals are diverted to developing new systems, then the organization loses out on the potential productivity these individuals have to offer in other ways. Also, individual motivation, morale, and performance might suffer if the person is unable to concentrate on her area of expertise and instead spends too much of her time worrying about developing new systems.

Fortunately, organizations that have been successful in moving to end-user development are aware of many of these problems and have established some controls to avoid them. One control mechanism is an Information Center (IC), which is charged with encouraging end users to develop their own applications while at the same time providing some management oversight. The IC staff can assist or train end users on proper development techniques or standards, prevent redundancy in application development, and ensure systems are documented properly. IC staff are often not functional-area experts, but are typically experts in using the fourth-generation tools. Working together, end users and the IC staff can develop useful systems for the organization.

Talking with...

Kraig L. Carrere, Human Resource Representative at SAFECO Insurance Co.

Educational Background

B.A. in Sociology, University of Washington

Job Description

Attract qualified applicants and interview for skills, experience, education, training, and potential to fill existing IT and non-IT openings. Develop action plans to recruit and retain employees, which include working with universities and staff, employment agencies and community-based organizations to attract a potential pool of candidates. Manage employee population to ensure general harmony and a comfortable work environment.

Critical Success Factors

Making contact and following up in a timely manner is very important to the success of hiring a candidate. In a competitive job market such as we have today, we cannot afford to let quality candidates slip by. Networking and homework are also important. Many of the people that are hired are from a referral source. You can also find out critical information on candidates and/or programs via network connections. Also, trying to stay one step ahead of the market and competition are important. Researching new ideas as well as putting a different spin on things that have worked well are important. From a recruiting perspective, the days of "if it's not broke, don't fix it" may be over.

Advice to Students

Make sure that you're looking at the entire picture of the companies with which you'll be interviewing. Focus on things such as the benefits program, opportunity for professional and personal growth, job responsibilities, and whether the people are compatible with your work style. Many students are just looking for the big payday upon graduation. There's nothing wrong with that but don't take a step back just because of the money. In today's market, the opportunities are numerous, so make the correct choice.

ETHICAL PERSPECTIVE: ETHICAL ISSUES IN A CLIENT-VENDOR RELATIONSHIP

As the demands of business grow, so do the demands on information systems. To accommodate this increased emphasis on and demand for technology, managers within many firms have chosen to purchase systems and services from outside vendors or even to completely outsource the development and/or management of entire systems to an external vendor. Just about every large organization, and many smaller ones, have some such form of client-vendor relationship either with a software or hardware vendor, a consultant, or an outsourcing partner. These relationships are typically based on a signed contract. If managed well, these types of relationships do not result in any problems or ethical breaches.

These relationships are primarily legal and contractual in nature. As with any legal, contractual relationships between two parties, problems in a client-vendor relationship can occur when one or both of the parties believe that the contract between them has been broken by the other party. One of the more common contract breaches is when the vendor is late in delivering the product or required services. Another is when the vendor's delivered product or service does meet the expectations or deliver the desired results of the client company. A contract may state that if a vendor is late in delivering computers it will incur a severe penalty, such as having to significantly reduce the price of the computers for the client.

With or without clear contracts, the relationship between vendor and client can quickly and easily deteriorate. Ernest Kallman and John Grillo recently described a case where a client believed that the vendor's software programs were not working properly. When the vendor did not satisfy the client's wishes, the client withheld further payments. However, the vendor had programmed a subroutine in these programs that when activated would stop the software from working at all. The client was unable to operate its business effectively, while the vendor merely stated that the software had been "repossessed" due to a failure to pay.

Perhaps this vendor really was at fault. For example, to provide the software by the agreed-upon date, it may be that they were forced to ship it untested. Perhaps the client was constantly changing requirements and specifications, stretching the letter of the contract and the goodwill of the vendor to the limit.

Other potential ethical issues are also involved in client-vendor relationships. For example, when a vendor creates a system for one client, it may use that same system, or some variant of it, for another similar client. The motivation for the vendor is to benefit from the labor expended and the knowledge gained in building this system and put this to use to generate revenue with other clients. The original client, however, is likely to feel that it expended resources for that system as well and may feel some ownership over it. In addition, the client is not likely to want another firm to be able to use the same system, particularly if the other client is a competitor.

Even with an appropriately worded contract, it is difficult to draw the line between outright duplication of a system and building a different system for another party that builds on knowledge from building and managing the original system. Further, it may be difficult for the original client to ever even find out that ideas or components from its original system have found their way into a different system for another client. Some vendors reserve the right to reuse their technology and systems for other clients as they see fit, while promising not to divulge important business information to competitors.

In cases similar to those described, problems regarding contractual promises made between the vendor and the client have led to requirements that future additions or modifications to the original program are to be contracted back to the vendor. For a variety of reasons the systems people within the client firm may take it upon themselves to access the code within the system and make changes and/or add features. On the one hand, the client has broken the letter of the contract and perhaps done something unethical. On the other hand, the client may have a legitimate reason to take it upon him/herself to alter the software, particularly if the vendor isn't doing its job and/or if the relationship between the client and vendor had already deteriorated. One can see how a client might feel compelled to jump in to fix a system running on its equipment in its business, especially if it feels that the vendor is not responsive or is unnecessarily restrictive. However, one can also see that the vendor might not want anyone else tinkering with its system, particularly if technically the vendor owns the system or if the vendor's head will be on the chopping block even if someone at the client firm damages the system.

Questions for Discussion

1. Do you feel that it is ethical for vendors to program subroutines into their software that can stop the client from using the software when contract disputes arise?

2. Who owns systems that are built for a client in an outsourcing arrangement? The client? The vendor? Both?

3. Should outsourcing vendors have the right to do as they wish with systems that they build for a client?

INTERNATIONAL PERSPECTIVE: THE RACE IS ON: GLOBAL OUTSOURCING

International Data Corporation predicts that the global outsourcing market will exceed $121 billion by the year 2000. IDC reports that "Fundamental business events, such as increased competition and the subsequent increasing focus on core competencies are forcing organizations throughout the world to carefully consider what tasks should remain in-house. Other more technical issues are causing agonizing support and maintenance problems for CIOs throughout the world. In many instances, outsourcing is welcomed." U.S. firms offering large-scale and worldwide outsourcing partnerships include Andersen Consulting, AT&T, Computer Sciences, Digital, EDS, Hewlett-Packard, IBM, and Entex.

The Outsourcing Institute agrees that outsourcing has benefits: "By the very nature of their specialization, outsourcing providers can bring extensive worldwide, world-class capabilities to meeting the needs of their customers... Often these vendor capabilities are the results of extensive investments in technology, methodologies, and people—investments made over a considerable period of time. In many cases, the vendor's capabilities include specialized industry expertise gained through working with many clients facing similar challenges. This expertise may be translated in skills, processes, or technologies uniquely capable of meeting these needs."

Outsourcing arrangements can be optimal for businesses around the world that have the capital but do not have the infrastructure or skills to manage, for example, a global telecommunications network or other IT functions. Companies around the world seem to agree: In the international airline industry alone, British Airways, Gulf Air, JAL, and Lufthansa have already taken advantage of outsourcing opportunities, primarily of data and telecommunications.

Experts have argued that the benefits of outsourcing are overestimated, especially as little or no empirical research is available, and companies should not outsource the management of IS. The Outsourcing Institute voices the concerns of many others when it notes that there can be problems associated with outsourcing:

"One of the most important insights gained from working with hundreds of companies looking into and implementing outsourcing is the simple but too-often overlooked fact that for outsourcing to be successful, management must have a clear set of goals and objectives in mind from the start. Outsourcing may entail significant organizational upheaval, transfer of important assets, dislocation of people, and long-term contractual relationships with an outside partner. None

of these make sense unless the benefits to be gained and the risks involved are clearly understood and managed from the outset."

They emphasize that businesses must look for long-term results rather than short-term solutions when outsourcing. In the U.S. case, much of the outsourcing specifically for software development is going to Indian and Singaporean firms, taking with it many highly-paid technology jobs.

However, U.S. firms are benefiting from a focus on global outsourcing, with companies around the world partnering with firms such as AT&T to overcome problems in "differing standards, incompatibility of communications equipment and vast up-front investments" and other problems of infrastructure and management. AT&T has targeted the 2,000 largest organizations within specific industry groups such as Utilities and Energy, Health Management, Retail and Wholesale, Transportation, and Hospitality. Its efforts are being rewarded; recently, AT&T was awarded at $1.4 million contract with the Ministry of Railways in the People's Republic of China (funded by the World Bank). One focus of its efforts to attract outsourcing is Europe, where it is expanding its employee base from 26,000. It is offering Internet and other solutions, including leased lines, Web pages and servers, Internet security, and more. Outsourcing has clearly become a worldwide phenomenon: Of the 2,000 companies targeted, 43% are headquartered in the Americas, while 27% are in the Pacific Rim, and 30% are in Europe.

Global outsourcing also means supporting U.S. multinationals. Textron, a multi-industry company, expects to generate over 1/3 of its revenues from outside the U.S. by the year 2000. Textron and AT&T signed a 10-year, $1.1 billion agreement in the fall of 1996; among the goals are assisting Textron in integrating global acquisitions and linking divisions worldwide.

Questions for Discussion

1. Does global outsourcing of information systems and technology make sense as a sound business strategy, or is it too problematic and risky to be viable in the long term?

2. If you were to make a checklist of the critical success factors for a global outsourcing partnership, what would it include? Why?

3. What do you see for the future of global outsourcing? Does it grow or subside? Why?

Summary

1. **Understand the factors and situations where building a system in-house is not feasible.** It is not feasible for an organization to build a system in house in at least four situations. First, some organizations have limited IS staffing and therefore do not have the capability to build a system themselves. Second, the organization may have IS staff with a limited skill set. Existing IS staff may be highly skilled at producing traditional applications, but not have the skills to build new types of systems or systems that require emerging development tools. Third, in many organizations, the IS staff does not have the time to work on all the systems that are desired by the organization. Fourth, some organizations have performance problems with their IS staff, where staff turnover, changing requirements, shifts in technology, or budget constraints have resulted in poor results. In any of these situations, it may be advantageous to an organization to consider an alternative to in-house systems development.

2. **Explain three alternative systems development options: external acquisition, outsourcing, and end-user development.** External acquisition is the process of purchasing an existing information system from an external organization or vendor. External acquisition is a five-step process. Step 1 is system identification, selection, and planning, which focuses on determining whether a proposed system is feasible. Step 2 is systems analysis, which focuses on determining the requirements for the system. Step 3 is the development of a Request for Proposal (RFP). A RFP is a communication tool indicating an organization's requirements for a given system and requesting information from potential vendors on their ability to deliver such a system. Step 4 is proposal evaluation, which focuses on evaluating proposals received from vendors. This evaluation may include viewing system demonstrations, evaluating the performance of those systems, and examining criteria important to the organization and how the proposed systems meet those criteria. Step 5 is vendor selection, which focuses on determining the vendor to provide the system. Outsourcing refers to the turning over of partial or entire responsibility for information systems development and management to an outside organization. End-user development is a systems development method whereby users in the organization develop, test, and maintain their own applications.

Key Terms

External acquisition

Request for Proposal

Systems benchmarking

Outsourcing

End-user development

Review Questions

1. What are the five typical steps of the external acquisition process?

2. How does the external acquisition process differ from the in-house, build-it-yourself method?

3. Describe at least five possible points that may be covered in a Request for Proposal.

4. How are software and hardware vendors able to provide a "test drive" of their system to potential clients?

5. How does systems benchmarking aid in the proposal evaluation process?

6. Describe the basic difference between systems benchmarking and workload modeling.

7. List some of the non-hardware and non-software evaluation criteria used when evaluating systems.

8. What is one of the major drawbacks of the use of a scoring system to evaluate systems?

9. What is the main reason that firms outsource information systems development?

10. What has caused much of the tension between the IS department and many end-user developers?

11. For what scale of systems is end-user development normally successful within organizations?

Problems and Exercises

◆ **Individual**   ◆◆ **Group**   ☞ **Field**   ◐ **Web/Internet**

1. Match the following terms to the appropriate definitions:

_____ External acquisition

_____ Request for Proposal

_____ Systems benchmarking

_____ Outsourcing

_____ End-user development

a. A communication tool indicating buyer requirements for a given system and requesting information from potential vendors

b. A systems development method whereby users in the organization develop, test, and maintain their own applications

c. The process of purchasing an existing information system from an external organization or vendor

d. Turning over partial or entire responsibility for information systems development and management to an outside organization

e. A standardized set of performance tests designed to facilitate comparison between systems

2. Do you believe that outsourcing will continue to be a prevalent option for systems development? What role does the increasing size of IS departments play in this? Search the World Wide Web for companies that specialize in outsourcing IS needs. You may wish to try Computer Sciences Corporation at http://www.csc.com/. What are they "selling" and how are they marketing their product?

3. Why is it so important to correctly identify the requirements of a system prior to creating the Request for Proposal? What types of problems may be encountered without this specificity?

4. During the process of external acquisition, what are the advantages and disadvantages of relying on a system that has been "proven" with a good "track record" of performance? Discus your answer with a group of classmates. How do their opinions differ from yours? Is the rapid rate of advancement within the IS field a problem?

5. It would seem that outsourcing the entire IS department is a viable option for many organizations. Pair up with a fellow classmate and decide who will present an argument for and against this notion. Take a few minutes to prepare and then debate this issue. Which parties are most affected in either situation?

6. If an organization is in the business of providing outsourced services to other organizations, what happens when these clients no longer wish to outsource? Who owns the systems? Who owns the data?

7. Discuss the following in a small group: One of the major issues with end-user development is whether users should be spending their time developing systems rather than performing their "regular" responsibilities. What do you feel is the proper balance? Why? Who is responsible for managing this systems development, their normal manager or someone from the IS department?

8. In Chapter 1 of this text, the term benchmarking was introduced as a term relevant to management information systems. Review the definition from Chapter 1, if necessary. How does benchmarking as used in Chapter 11 differ from that in Chapter 1? Are they really two distinct terms with distinct meanings?

9. Argue for or against the following. Support your answer with specific facts from this chapter. "It would be cheaper and easier to manage our information systems if we would just hire more people for our IS department than go through the hassles of outsourcing and end-user development!"

10. In a small group of classmates, use the development alternatives discussed throughout the chapter to develop solutions to each of the four situations presented at the beginning of this chapter. Provide a rationale for each solution, and describe potential drawbacks for each. Prepare a 10-15 minute presentation to the class of your decisions. Conduct this presentation as if your group were presenting your proposals to the Steering Committee in charge of IS Productivity.

11. Consider an organization that is familiar to you. Describe the method(s) of information systems development that are employed. Can you determine the reasons for the adoption of these methods over others? Who made these selections? Who determined the development alternatives?

12. Based on your past work experience, describe the relationship in your organization between end-users and the IS department. Was there substantial end-user development? Were tensions high? Did end-users feel that the IS department was unable to adequately "get things done"? Did other classmates have similar or vastly different situations? Why do you think this is so?

13. Interview an IS manager at an organization with which you are familiar. Determine what balance of systems development methods would be the most beneficial to his/her department (for example, in-house development of 50% of systems, outsource 30%, purchase 10%, and have 10% developed by end-users). What reasons were given for this particular breakdown? Is this something that can be easily quantified?

14. Interview an IS manager at an organization with which you are familiar. Determine what percentage of a typical day is spent reviewing proposals from vendors, contracting with outsourcing partners, and managing end-user development in comparison with his/her project management responsibilities for in-house projects.

15. Based on the Ethics Inset discussing some of the ethical issues of client-vendor relationships, discuss your experiences dealing with these issues within a group of classmates. Have you ever had a system delivered that did not meet expectations or pre-set requirements? What action did you and/or your company take? Was the situation resolved equitably? Were there any "horror stories" among the group? Did this system involve proprietary information from your company? Search the World Wide Web for IS vendors that provide their service agreements on their homepage. Who holds the responsibilities in these agreements?

16. Based on the scenario that opened the chapter, what would you do if you were Linda and had to make the presentation to the meeting of the stakeholders? Would you follow Steve's recommendations? Why or why not? What could you do as the IS department manager to make this project work?

Real World Case Problems

1. Ticona Chooses Andersen Consulting to Develop, Maintain Information Technology System.

Ticona, a member of the Hoechst Group, and Andersen Consulting announced an agreement under which Andersen Consulting will develop and maintain information systems designed to support Ticona's product-line extension and geographic expansion. Ticona, formerly the technical polymers division of Hoechst, is a leading supplier of engineering and high-performance thermoplastics. As part of the recent restructuring of Hoechst AG, Ticona became a stand-alone business but remains part of the Hoechst Group.

Under the contract, Andersen Consulting, combining its consulting and Business Process Management expertise, will upgrade and then maintain Ticona's SAP systems and enable the company to migrate to an information technology model that will provide improved service levels, flexibility, and cost predictability.

"As we become an increasingly independent organization, it is imperative that Ticona have an information technology system that will enable us to keep pace with expected strong growth, both in product offerings and geographic reach," said Russ Bockstedt, Ticona's information technology manager. "Based on its record of success, we are looking to Andersen Consulting to build and maintain an IT system that is in a league with our capability to develop and manufacture world-class, high-performance thermoplastic polymer products and services." Design, Build, Run, developed by Anderson Consulting, is an alternative life-cycle approach to more typical outsourcing arrangements, encompassing the development and subsequent day-to-day maintenance of information technology systems. Design, Build, Run allows clients to achieve the benefits of new systems more rapidly and affordably while mitigating risk and providing predictability for the system's entire useful life. "We are delighted that Ticona has chosen Andersen Consulting," said Charles Pisciotta, Andersen Consulting's client partner for Ticona. "Through our Design, Build, Run offering, we will help Ticona reap more strategic value from its technology investments. Additionally, this venture clearly bolsters Andersen Consulting's position within the plastics and chemical industries. It fits perfectly with our strategy to focus on our strengths, developing and managing business solutions that help our clients compete more effectively in a dynamic industry environment."

a. What, exactly, is Ticona outsourcing to Andersen Consulting, and why is it useful to Ticona to do this?

b. In what ways is this outsourcing arrangement useful to Andersen Consulting, in addition to its direct profits from the arrangement?

c. In what ways does Andersen Consulting's "Design, Build, Run" approach to building systems parallel with the emerging systems development methodologies discussed in Chapter 10?

Source *Adapted from a press release found at* http://www.ac.com/topstories/ts_frintro_1.html. *January 15, 1998.*

2. Visa Expands Outsourcing Deal: Partnership with DMR Helps Company Serve Big Customers.

Quality and on-time delivery, not cost, was the main focus of the outsourcing of Visa's customizable reporting software that is used by large corporate customers worldwide. In 1995 Visa had little choice but to outsource as its 1000 person is group lacked the expertise to develop this reporting software. It selected DMR over nine other systems integrators, but not due to the cost. Focusing on quality and delivery time won the bid. The project came in on time and on budget—something rarely heard of in the software business.

In order to win the bid DMR laid out a full-blown project methodology complete with all of the roles of the participants. Other bidders simply offered one-word answers for project descriptions to Prather, project manager and vice president of information systems at Visa's commercial card division in San Francisco. The answer was always, "Yes," but with no description of how it would be done. DMR used two project managers, Prather and one from their offices. In addition, in an unusual style, they did most of the work off-site by 40 DMR staffers paid less in Canada, in Quebec City saving Prather the money it would have cost for leasing office space.

Prather had intended for many of his staff to work on the project to learn skills that they would need for maintaining the software, but he quickly learned that his staff could not do that and keep up with their jobs. In the end they had no one who knew how to run what was developed. When outsourcing is the entire answer to the project it becomes very risky, as the outsider must understand the entire business and the competition at the same time. Still, Visa was able to maintain control of the project. Feedback from the user was constantly taken into consideration. After pulling together the project, having it delivered on time and on budget credibility gets established and Visa was able to just settle into a relationship upon which fairy tales are based.

a. How did DMR win the outsourcing deal from Visa? Why was this important to Visa?

b. Why was it important for Visa to retain some control in this arrangement? How did this pay off later?

c. Why do you suppose Visa's 1000 person IS group lacked the expertise needed to build the new client/server-based system?

d. Is this common? natural? Why or why not?

Source   *King, Julia. 1998. Visa expands outsourcing deal.* ComputerWorld. *January 26, 41–44.*

References

Anthes, G.H. 1997. Outsourcing the 'net. Information from: www.computerworld.com: Information verified: April 6, 1998.

Applegate, McFarlan, and McKenney. 1996. *Corporate information systems management: Text and cases.* Chicago, Illinois: Irwin.

Caldwell, B. 1996. The new outsourcing partnership: Vendors want to provide more than just services. *Information Week,* June 24, 50–64.

Fryer, B. 1998. Outsourcing support: Kudos and caveats. Information from: www.computerworld.com. Information verified: April 6, 1998.

King, J. 1998. Outsourcing loses stigma. Information from: www.computerworld.com. Information verified: April 6, 1998.

Kutnick, J. 1998. Shopping smart. Information from: www.computerworld.com. Information verified: April 6, 1998.

Merc, 1998. Information from: www.cme.com. Information verified: April 6, 1998.

Starwave, 1998. Information from: www.starwave.com. Information verified: April 6, 1998.

Thibodeau, P. 1998. AT&T snags $750M Citibank outsourcing job. Information from: www.computerworld.com. Information verified: April 6, 1998.

Verity, J.W. 1997. Megadeals march on. Information from: www.computerworld.com. Information verified: April 6, 1998.

Related Readings

Ang, S., and L.L. Cummings. 1997. Strategic response to institutional influences on information systems outsourcing. *Organization Science* 8(3): 235–256.

Chandhury, Nam, and Rao. 1995. Management of information systems outsourcing: A bidding perspective. *Journal of Management Information Systems* 12(2): 131–159.

Edberg, D.T., and B.J. Bowman. 1996. User-developed applications: An empirical study of application quality and developer productivity. *Journal of Management Information Systems* 13(1): 167–185.

Hu, Sanders, and Gebelt, 1997. Research report: Diffusion of information systems outsourcing: A reevaluation of influence sources. *Information Systems Research* 8(3): 288–301.

Lacity, Willcocks, and Feeny, 1995. IT outsourcing: Maximize flexibility and control. *Harvard Business Review* 73(3): 84–93.

Lawrence, M., and G. Low. 1993. Exploring individual user satisfaction within user-ked development. *Management Information Systems Quarterly* 17(2): 195–208.

Maiden, Ncube, and Moore. 1997. Lessons learned during requirements acquisition for COTS systems. *Communications of the ACM* 40(12): 21–25.

Mirani, R., and W.R. King. 1994. The development of a measure for end-user computing support. *Decision Sciences* 25(4): 481–498.

Montazemi, Cameron, and Gupta. 1996. An empirical study of factors affecting software package selection. *Journal of Management Information Systems* 13(1): 89–105.

Saarinen, T., and A.P.J. Vepsalainen. 1994. Procurement strategies for information systems. *Journal of Management Information Systems* 11(2): 187–208.

Teng, Cheon, and Grover. 1995. Decisions to outsource information systems functions: Testing a strategy-theoretic discrepancy model. *Decision Sciences* 26(1): 75–103.

Wang, Barron, and Seidmann. 1997. Contradicting structures for custom software development: The impacts of informational rents and uncertainty on internal development and outsourcing. *Management Science* 43(12): 1726–1744.

PART 5

Information Systems Management

Chapter 12:   *Managing Information Systems as an Organizational Resource*

Chapter 13:   *Making the Business Case for a System*

Chapter 14:   *Organizing the Information Systems Function*

The purpose of Part 5 is to help you to understand how best to manage information systems and to organize the information systems function within organizations.

In Chapter 12, *Managing Information Systems as an Organizational Resource,* we explain the importance of successfully managing information systems. We describe the functions of management and how they apply to information systems management. We then describe managerial roles and how they apply to information systems management. We describe sources of organizational power and the central role that information systems play in political behavior in organizations. We close the chapter by explaining technological and organizational change and ways to manage technological resistance to change.

In Chapter 13, *Making the Business Case for a System,* we explain what it means to make the business case for

a system. We describe how to formulate the business case and why it is sometimes difficult to do so. We also describe how best to present the business case for a system and to help others to understand the value that a system provides.

In Chapter 14, *Organizing the Information Systems Function,* we describe the history, evolution, and role of the IS function within firms. We explain the alternative structures and locations of the IS function within modern-day organizations and what works best under which conditions. We also describe the critical issues currently facing business managers with respect to the organization of the IS function, and we discuss the future of the IS function.

Put on your "business" hat as you read these final chapters. These chapters help you manage technology as you would any other part of the business firm.

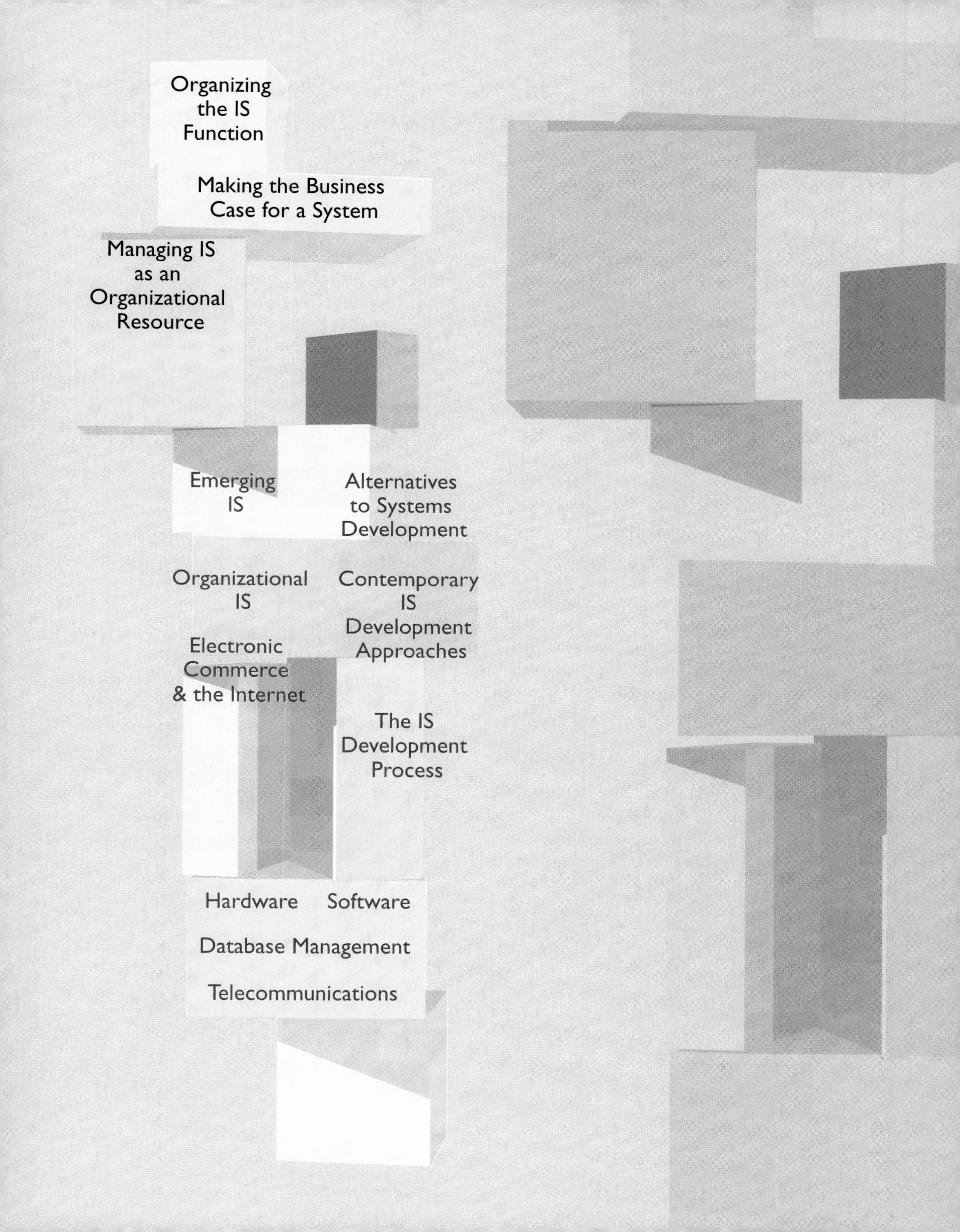

Organizing
the IS
Function

Making the Business
Case for a System

Managing IS
as an
Organizational
Resource

Emerging
IS

Alternatives
to Systems
Development

Organizational
IS

Contemporary
IS
Development
Approaches

Electronic
Commerce
& the Internet

The IS
Development
Process

Hardware   Software

Database Management

Telecommunications

Scenario: Overcoming Resistance at White Water Adventures

White Water Adventures, a company specializing in white water rafting trips and equipment, is in the midst of converting from primarily manual to computer-based operations. The company has one systems person on staff and has called in a team of consultants to help with the transition to a new, enterprise-wide, computer-based information system. People in several parts of the business began using computers some time ago, but their activities have evolved as unconnected islands of technology throughout the firm, as shown in Figure 12.1. The new system's primary goal is to integrate these islands of technology. While the mood about computers seems to be positive overall, the consultants have encountered some pockets of heavy resistance to the new system throughout the organization.

The internal systems person and the consultants discover that the strongest resistance is coming from the sales office. They cannot find out what the sales staff does not like about the new system, however, or why they are so strongly against it. The consultants therefore enlist the help of the accounting office employees, who are already using technology in their area quite intensely, are very much in favor of the new system, and seem to be aware of the attitudes toward the new system among members of the organization.

After several informal meetings, the source of the sales group's resistance becomes clearer. Over the past several years, the sales staff has slowly developed its own spreadsheet and database applications for managing sales. These staff members probably know the product and the customers better than anyone else in the organization, and they have taken a long time to develop their own applications to support the sales side of the business. While not perfect, their applications seem to work well enough, and they don't want to change them. Sales employees are afraid that much of their hard work in developing these applications may go to waste and that they will have to begin all over again with a new system.

With the help of the accounting department manager, a champion of the new system who has a good relationship with the sales employees, the systems consultants begin working with the sales manager and her staff to discover their concerns. The accounting manager begins by explaining the competitive forces and organizational problems that are pushing for the quick implementation of the new integrated system. Next, the group talks about what the new system is and is not, as well as clears up many misconceptions about the new system.

After the sales staff has become more receptive to the need for change and for the new system, the systems consultants work with them to discover the advantages of the current computer applications that can be kept in the new system, the disadvantages of their current applications that can be changed, and which data they need but are not currently getting. The sales staff quickly sees that the new system will not change much about their current spreadsheet and database applications. They realize, in fact, that the new system will help improve their existing ways of doing things.

FIGURE 12.1

Islands of technology within White Water Adventures.

CHAPTER 12

As a result, the sales staff becomes much more supportive of the new system and begins to offer ideas on how their sales data could be used by others throughout the organization to improve decision making and performance. The systems consultants learn a great deal from the sales staff about how to make the new system even better than originally envisioned. For example, the discussions with the sales staff lead the consultants to design an organization-wide system that lets the sales staff and others continue to work with the current desktop spreadsheet and database applications but runs these applications as shared, networked applications that enable people to share data quickly and easily.

The sales staff is encouraged by the new system and their entrepreneurial role in its development and use. They quickly gain a reputation throughout the firm for coming up with innovative ways to implement the new system. Several members of the sales staff serve as liaisons between the systems consultants and other groups within the organization, helping these other groups design and implement the system in their areas. Ultimately, two of the sales staff members accept promotions to work in the newly formed information systems department after the system goes online.

This example illustrates the resistance organizations often encounter when implementing new information systems or making significant changes to their existing systems. Employee concerns that could have easily been ignored or mishandled—to the detriment of the new system, the users, and the organization's performance—were transformed into a positive opportunity. Managing these types of organizational changes and handling resistance are important components of managing information systems effectively.

Introduction

In prior chapters, we showed you how and why information systems are of critical strategic importance to modern organizations. As a result of this importance, management of information systems is arguably more important than the technology itself. In this chapter, we show you how to successfully manage information systems.

After reading this chapter, you will be able to do the following:

1. Explain the importance of successfully managing information systems.

2. Describe the functions of management and how they apply to information systems management.

3. Describe managerial roles and how they apply to information systems management.

4. Describe sources of organizational power and the central role that information systems play in political behavior in organizations.

5. Explain technology and organizational change and describe ways to manage resistance to technological change.

This chapter is the first in Part 5, "Information Systems Management" (see Figure 12.2). We begin by describing the importance of successful information systems management. Next, we describe how people manage information systems. We cover the more formal and less formal managerial functions involved in successfully managing technology. We then discuss several critical issues in the management of technology—power, politics, and organizational change. Leading people through the process of technology-enabled organizational change is perhaps one of the most challenging and rewarding tasks for managers.

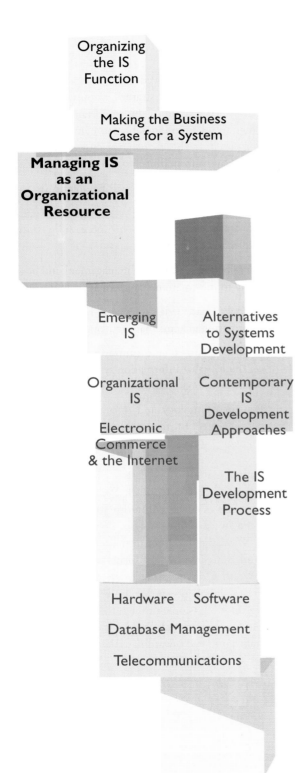

Organizing
the IS
Function

Making the Business
Case for a System

**Managing IS
as an
Organizational
Resource**

Emerging
IS

Alternatives
to Systems
Development

Organizational
IS

Contemporary
IS
Development
Approaches

Electronic
Commerce
& the Internet

The IS
Development
Process

Hardware   Software

Database Management

Telecommunications

The Importance of Successfully Managing Information Systems

As business, government, and education become more global and competition among organizations increases, no end appears to be in sight to the growing use of information systems. Over your career, you are likely to see more and more uses of technology to achieve organizational goals, compress time, and increase market share. Technology will become increasingly pervasive in organizations, and its use will become an even more natural part of doing business.

After you accept that information systems play a critical role in helping organizations be competitive today and continue to be competitive in the future, you will realize that information technology must be managed well. Just as you work hard to better manage tangible organizational resources, such as people, facilities, manufacturing equipment, cash, or trade secrets, you must also work hard to manage all information and information systems. You must plan, organize, lead, and control these resources so that they add value to the organization and help achieve organizational objectives. The effective management of information systems is perhaps the most important managerial challenge in the coming decade, whether you are a manager within the information systems unit of the firm or a manager in another functional unit. Those who manage technology well are more likely to lead their organizations to success.

Managing information systems well can help an organization save money and improve productivity. While the cost of computing power and storage is declining, the overall costs to develop, implement, and maintain organization-wide information systems are growing. Organizations are spending increasing amounts on information systems, both within the information systems budget and in the budgets of each of the various business units. After several years of cost cutting in the information systems area, information systems spending has been on the rise, as shown in Figure 12.3 (Pantages, 1996). Spending more

FIGURE 12.2

The big picture: focusing on managing information systems as an organizational resource.

on information systems does not mean that organizations are not cost conscious; most, if not all, organizations are still intensely cost conscious. If, however, an organization invests wisely in its information systems, it can cut costs in other areas of the firm while increasing productivity. In short, organizations spend a lot of money on information systems, and these expenditures can have dramatic positive results.

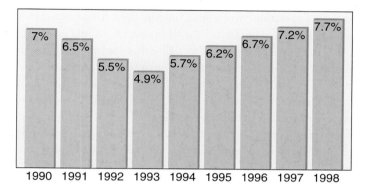

IS Budgets Continue To Rise
At what average annual rate do you expect your total IS budget to increase over the next three to five years?

FIGURE 12.3

IS budgets continue to rise.

—IS Management at Schlumberger Ltd. Saves Money and Increases Productivity

A BRIEF CASE

Such dramatic positive results are evident at Schlumberger Ltd., a New York–based manufacturer of testing and measurement equipment for oil companies (Baatz, 1997; Swanborg and Myers, 1997). SINet (the Schlumberger Information Network) began as a communication tool for the company's 60,000 employees in over 90 countries back in 1991. Schlumberger had been using a proprietary communication network to connect its many geographically dispersed research sites since 1985.

In 1991, management realized that a change was necessary, due mainly to communication costs. The Internet was chosen as the alternative means of communication. SINet has since turned into a global intranet, linking scientists, engineers, business managers, and customers with up-to-date technical information, online business transactions, academic collaboration, and file transfer capabilities. Productivity has increased, costs have decreased, and revenues have increased through new customer relationships. All of this progress has been made possible through the combination of technical know-how, solid management of systems (hardware and software), and excellent relationships with customers and suppliers. The cost of this system has not been small. Over $72 million has been invested in the system since 1991. However, the return on investment has been well over 650 percent!

The Advent of the Chief Information Officer

A number of important indications show that organizations are trying hard to manage information systems better. But perhaps nothing better demonstrates the growing importance of information systems management than the advent of the **chief information officer** (CIO) and related positions in contemporary organizations.

Evolution of the CIO

In the early 1980s, the CIO position became popular as the new title given to executive-level individuals who were responsible for the information systems component within their organizations. The CIO was charged with integrating new technologies into the organization's business strategy. Traditionally, the responsibility for integrating technology and strategy had not officially rested with any one manager. Responsibility for managing the day-to-day information systems function had previously rested with a mid-level operations manager or, in some cases, with a vice-president of information systems. Ultimate responsibility for these activities would now rest with a high-level executive, the CIO. People began to realize that the information systems department wasn't simply a cost center—a necessary evil that simply consumed resources. They realized that the information systems could be of tremendous strategic value to the organization. As a result, this new IS executive would work much like other executives, sitting at the strategy table, working right alongside the chief executive officer, chief financial officer, chief operating officer, and other chief executives and key people in the organization. When strategic decisions were to be made, technology would play a major role, and the CIO needed to participate in the strategic decision-making process.

Not surprisingly, many organizations have jumped on the CIO bandwagon and either hired or named a CIO. As a result, many people thought that the CIO boom was a fad that would soon end, as do many other popular management trends. In fact, in early 1990, *BusinessWeek* printed a story entitled, "CIO Is Starting To Stand for 'Career Is Over': Once Deemed Indispensable, the Chief Information Officer Has Become an Endangered Species" (Rothfeder and Driscoll, 1990). In this story, and in the cartoon in Figure 12.4, the authors reported statistics showing that in 1989, the CIO dismissal rate had doubled to 13 percent, which was noticeably higher than the 9 percent for all top executives. They explained that the primary reasons for CIO dismissals included tightening budgets for technology and management's overblown expectations of CIO functions. Apparently, many organizations had been caught up in the rush to have a CIO without thinking enough about why they needed to have a CIO in the first place. The authors countered, however,

FIGURE 12.4

BusinessWeek *cartoon.*

© *Dave Cutler*

that given the growing trend toward using information systems to achieve competitive advantage, the CIO could become relevant and important again. How right they were!

The CIO Today

Today, most large organizations have a CIO or an equivalent position. It is also now common for mid-sized and smaller organizations to have a CIO-like position within their organizations, although they may give this person a title such as Director of Information Systems. Even the United States Internal Revenue Service named its first-ever CIO in 1990. The current IRS CIO, Arthur Gross, manages a tremendously large, important, decade-old, $2.8-billion Tax Systems Modernization computerization project (Cone, 1996). On the industry side, Randy Mott, CIO and senior vice president for Wal-Mart, was named Chief of the Year in December 1997 by *InformationWeek* (see Figure 12.5), a magazine for business and technology managers (Wilder, 1997). Mott has been integral to Wal-Mart's success, using technology to better manage inventories, cut costs, speed operations, and help Wal-Mart remain competitive. Like many other CIOs, Gross and Mott are as critical to their organizations as the technologies that they manage.

FIGURE 12.5

InformationWeek *cover with CIO Chief of the Year Randy Mott of Wal-Mart.*

The Spread of Technology in Organizations

Another phenomenon that shows how integral and vital information systems and their proper management have become to organizations is the extent to which the technology is so firmly integrated and entrenched within the various business units (accounting, sales, marketing).

In many organizations today, you'll find that the manager of a particular information system or subsystem spends most of his time out in the business unit, along with the users of that particular system. Many times, this system manager is permanently placed—with an office, desk, phone, and personal computer—in the business unit along with the users.

In addition, it is not uncommon for this system manager to have formal education, training, and work experience in information systems *and* in the functional area that the system supports, such as finance. It is becoming increasingly difficult to separate the technology from the business or the systems staff from the other people in the organization. For this reason, how information systems are managed is important to you, no matter what career option you pursue.

Key Issues in the Management of Information System

The management of information systems will become increasingly important as you progress through your career and begin to manage or participate in information systems projects. Consequently, we review what is involved in IS management.

The Functions of Management

What does it mean to manage? Early in this century, Henri Fayol (1916), a French industrialist, wrote about the functions performed by individuals in managerial positions in organizations. Fayol's notion of the **functions of management,** while modified over the years by Koontz, O'Donnell (1955), and other management researchers is still quite useful. His notion is pervasive throughout management research, teaching, and practice today. The functions of management are now typically grouped into four categories—planning, organizing, leading, and controlling—as shown in Table 12.1.

Table 12.1   The functions of management.

Managerial Function	Description
Planning	Defining an organization's goals, establishing an overall strategy for achieving these goals, and developing a comprehensive, integrated set of subplans to integrate and coordinate activities organization-wide
Organizing	Determining what tasks are to be done, who is to do them, how the tasks can best be grouped together, who reports to whom, and where and how decisions are to be made
Leading	Motivating subordinates, directing the activities of others, selecting the most effective communication channel, and resolving conflicts among organizational members
Controlling	Monitoring the organization's performance, comparing the organization's actual performance with previously set goals, and then making any necessary changes to correct and improve the organization's performance

Some individuals, such as the chief executive officer, are responsible for the entire organization. They carry out the managerial functions from a long-term, organization-wide perspective. Other individuals carry managerial responsibility for a particular part of the organization, such as the information systems department. In addition, the managerial functions are carried out somewhat differently by higher-level executives, such as CEOs, than by lower-level managers, such as department heads or project managers. In some organizations, the higher-level managers might be more focused on a subset of the managerial functions (planning, for example), while lower-level managers might be more focused on another subset of the other functions (such as directly leading lower-level employees).

Managerial Functions Applied to IS

Let's apply the four managerial functions to the management of the information systems department within a firm. Table 12.2 describes some typical managerial functions for higher-level IS managers, such as the chief information officer, and typical, corresponding functions for mid- or low-level information system managers, such as a project manager. You can see that the higher-level IS managers are more focused on the big picture, while the lower-level IS managers are more focused on managing day-to-day operations.

Table 12.2 Some typical managerial functions for IS managers.

Managerial Functions	Higher-level IS Manager	Lower-Level IS Manager
Planning	Create high-level plans for information systems deployment and ensure that information systems plans are integrated closely with broader organizational plans. Make sure these information systems plans help achieve the organization's mission and goals.	Formulate a detailed, daily information systems project plan with a systems development team.
Organizing	Establish a clear information systems architecture for the organization, which includes hardware, software, and networking standards to be followed and supported.	Determine who will serve on a particular information systems project team and where this team will do their work.
Leading	Help define IS's new strategic role within the organization and motivate information systems personnel to focus more on the quality of the systems they develop and manage and the service they provide to others in the organization.	Direct the activities of the project team members and resolve conflicts among them.
Controlling	Coordinate the efforts of mid- and lower-level information systems managers to formally monitor and improve systems development quality and turn-around time.	Monitor the progress of the project team and work with other information systems managers to determine ways to improve systems development performance.

While the focus of their managerial duties might be different, mid- and low-level information systems managers must work in concert with the higher-level information systems managers in performing managerial functions. These high-level information systems managers must, in turn, work in concert with the high-level managers representing other parts of the organization, who in turn must work in concert with the mid- and lower-level managers in their respective areas. Coordinating the efforts of people across all levels and areas of large organizations is one of the most critical managerial tasks. In large organizations that are downsizing and eliminating layers of managers, coordinating the efforts of people throughout the organization is an even more important and difficult task.

A Day in the Life of Tom Trainer, CIO of Eli Lilly

A BRIEF CASE

These same four managerial functions—planning, organizing, leading, and controlling—apply to the CIO as well as to the CEO. In a role that relies heavily on communication skills, such as listening, strategizing, questioning, and inspiring, Tom Trainer leads the information technology (IT) efforts for Eli Lilly and Company, the Indianapolis-based pharmaceutical firm (Dragoon, 1997). A typical day at the office for Trainer begins well before 6:30 a.m. and does not end until 6:00 p.m. or later. His day consists mostly of meetings and planning sessions. Trainer might receive an update on Lilly's Year 2000 projects, move to a meeting regarding sensitive sourcing decisions, take time to plan a little IT strategy, discuss possible partnerships, meet with the Operating Committee, and at some point find time to eat lunch, check his voice mail, and respond to email. Many of these tasks may last only minutes, while others may last three to four hours. Trainer relies on his team of managers to make his job easier, a daunting task. Yet, underneath all of the tasks and relationships, Trainer is a manager who plans, organizes, leads, and controls a staff of 2,000 worldwide.

ETHICAL PERSPECTIVE: MANAGING IN A WIRED WORLD

Businesses today utilize more and faster information systems than just five years ago. The difference is even more pronounced when we compare modern, online organizations, such as Andersen Consulting, Microsoft, or FedEx, with organizations of ten or fifteen years ago. Dramatic technological and organizational changes have occurred within the careers of a generation of workers and managers, many of whom are struggling to adjust their assumptions and attitudes about work and their work styles and techniques.

One way technology has influenced us in the workplace is that it has fundamentally changed our notion of time and productivity. Tasks that once took many man hours to complete, such as inputting data from a form that a customer filled out, now take just a fraction of the time or, in some cases, are completely automated and do not involve people at all. Unfortunately, as technology enables higher and higher levels of productivity, and as we become further and further removed from paperwork and physical labor, there are potential problems in what we expect from ourselves and our employees.

It is all too easy for managers to expect too much from employees, given the capabilities for leveraging technology to work faster and smarter. These technological advances lead managers to assume that employees have more free time than they really do and that they can take on more work than they can actually complete. Similarly, some employees can do things faster and easier with technology and, in the absence of a hands-on manager, can give the impression that they are working hard and long to accomplish what are in fact simple, technology-supported tasks. Perhaps you remember the television ad for the overnight delivery service in which the sneaky young employee is bragging about his behavior. While everyone thought he was working hard, it had become so easy to ship things that all he had to do was to "just point, click, and ship!"

Another way technology influences us in the workplace is that it has changed our notions of communicating with each other. The burgeoning growth in the use of electronic mail in organizations has suddenly made everyone accessible, within and without the company. To a certain extent, this can serve to make all of us smarter, more aware, and better tapped in. Are we ready for a world in which everyone knows everything in real time?

Similarly, the rising use of Group Support Systems (GSS) has empowered employees to speak out and contribute. With GSS tools, such as electronic, anonymous brainstorming, people can voice their ideas and opinions to each other via computer in a relatively safe environment. While these systems potentially offer an incredible resource for ideas and for securing a say in important company decisions, they also pose new problems and issues for managers. The anonymity that enables open, honest exchanges of ideas and opinions can also enable caustic interaction or loafing. Furthermore, in some cases, employees might want credit for their good ideas and might not be willing to offer them anonymously for the good of the group or the organization.

Managing in a wired world is both exciting and frightening. Technology can help us do things better, faster, and cheaper, and it can make us more competitive. On the other hand, appropriate, effective technology use in the workplace calls for new ways of thinking about things and new ways of managing. Just as pilots have had to learn to "fly by wire," so too will managers have to learn to manage by wire.

Questions for Discussion

1. How can managers best be prepared to manage by wire?

2. "Workers will do the least work necessary to maximize their pay. Therefore, workers will always be less productive than technology allows." Do you agree or disagree with this statement? Why?

3. What are the organizational implications of everyone knowing everything in real time?

International Perspective: Consulting Goes Global: Price Waterhouse Inks Overseas Deals

Price Waterhouse LLP's management consulting service is turning to partnerships overseas to cope with a revenue growth rate that exceeded the 21 percent jump last year in the firm's business in the Americas. In the first two months of this year, the $1.2 billion Price Waterhouse unit struck deals in Russia and in South Korea. In January, the firm teamed up its 150 consultants in Russia with the 150 consultants and integrators of LVS, a 6-year-old Moscow firm with more than $16 million in revenue. In late February, Price Waterhouse announced a joint venture with Consulting Software Group, a 10-year-old firm in Seoul, South Korea, that has 140 professionals. Discussions are underway with two other overseas firms, including a distribution logistics consulting firm in Europe.

The Price Waterhouse unit's worldwide staff jumped 29 percent last year to 10,300 people, including 4,200 outside the Americas. The worldwide staff is likely to double by the end of the decade, says Scott Hartz, managing partner of Price Waterhouse Global Management Consulting in Philadelphia. "Our history [overseas] for many years has been growing from the ground up," Hartz says, "but we are getting very aggressive in global growth and want to supplement with transactions like LVS and CSG."

With such alliances, Price Waterhouse strengthens its ability to serve locally based companies, such as Gasprom, a $40-billion gas distributor in Moscow, and the Korean manufacturing conglomerate Samsung, as well as the local operations of other multinational clients. Because of travel, taxes, and other expenses, dispatching a U.S.-based consultant overseas is twice as expensive as using local professionals, says John Singel, head of the global IT practice at Price Waterhouse. "We have a number of very large systems-integration projects that involve worldwide rollouts of software," Singel adds, "and the economics of doing that with a roving swat team from the U.S. are not terribly good."

The opportunity for more global systems-integration projects is great, Singel says, because so far only about 30 percent of Fortune 100 companies are implementing enterprise-wide application systems.

Questions for Discussion

1. What are the pros and cons of using a local professional in a foreign country as one of your global company's IS consultants instead of sending a U.S.-based consultant overseas?

2. What might some of the difficulties be in managing a diverse international workforce that comprises consultants of many different nationalities who are based in many different countries?

3. What would you do to train these consultants consistently and ensure that the systems they build (and the advice they give to clients) are the same from project to project?

Source   Caldwell, Bruce. 1997. *Consulting goes global: Price Waterhouse inks overseas deals.* InformationWeek, *March 17. Reprinted by permission.*

The Limits of the Functional Perspective

This functions of management perspective is useful in understanding the management of information systems and in determining the purpose of IS managers. However, some managers and management researchers have criticized this perspective. Some have argued that it leaves out some of the more informal, yet important functions performed by managers, while others have argued that this perspective tells us little about what actual managers do on an everyday basis. To address these weaknesses, Henry Mintzberg (1973) observed and wrote about actual managerial behavior through the 1960s and 70s. He found that, contrary to conventional wisdom, managers were not the careful, reflective, systematic thinkers and decision makers they were assumed to be. He found that managers engaged in a large number of varied, unpatterned activities that were most often short in duration. The managers he observed had little or no time for careful reflection because they encountered constant interruptions. In fact, half of the activities of these managers lasted less than nine minutes in duration. Managers also preferred and engaged in a great deal of verbal communications, such as telephone calls, unscheduled meetings, and informal encounters.

Managerial Roles

Perhaps the most useful outcome of Mintzberg's work is his categorization scheme of **managerial roles**, which is based on the actual, day-to-day managerial behaviors he observed. This role-based perspective complements and extends Fayol's functional perspective on management. Mintzberg categorizes these managerial roles into the following three role sets:

- **Interpersonal.** The interpersonal role set includes the following three roles: figurehead, leader, and liaison.

- **Informational.** The informational role set includes the monitor, disseminator, and spokesperson roles.

- **Decisional.** The decisional role set includes the following four roles: entrepreneur, disturbance handler, resource allocator, and negotiator.

Table 12.3 describes each of these roles and applies them to the types of activities that an information systems manager might be engaged in.

Table 12.3   Managerial roles and examples for IS managers.

Managerial Role	Description	IS Example
I. Interpersonal		
Figurehead	Symbolic head; obliged to perform ceremonial, legal, and social duties	CIO cuts the ribbon draped across a new World Wide Web server at a press conference announcing the organization's new Web site for online purchasing.
Leader	Responsible for the motivation of subordinates and for staffing, training, and related duties	Mid-level IS manager recruits for new systems analysts at nearby universities and then assigns them to project teams.

Managerial Role	Description	IS Example
Liaison	Maintains a self-developed network of internal and external contacts who provide favors and information	IS project manager meets informally for lunch with her friend and confidant, the manager of the firm's accounting department, to see what can be done to smooth and speed the ongoing refinements to the accounting information system.
II. Informational		
Monitor	Seeks and receives a wide variety of information on pertinent organizational and environmental factors	Mid-level IS manager becomes the repository of all project information—knowing exactly who is working on what projects when and where.
Disseminator	Transmits information as necessary to others in the organization	Networking specialist receivesand reads various networking magazines and routes key articles to other employees
Spokesperson	Transmits information to outsiders on organization's plans, policies, actions, results, and so on	CIO gives a presentation on the state of the firm's transition to client/server computing at the next meeting of the organization's Board of Directors.
III. Decisional		
Entrepreneur	Continually looking for ways to improve and innovate, both within the information systems area and in the use of information systems throughout the organization	IS project manager champions the use of Computer-Aided Systems Engineering (CASE) tools in systems development.
Disturbance handler	Responsible for managing crises or handling conflicts within their unit	Systems manager is called in late at night to handle a team of system operators responding to the crash of a key information system.
Resource allocator	Responsible for the allocation of organizational resources of all kinds	High-level IS manager decides how much money will be spent on training, on what types of training the funding will be allocated for, and who will attend which training sessions.
Negotiator	Responsible for representing the IS department, or the entire organization, in major negotiations	CIO negotiates with vendors that the organization will purchase equipment from and with suppliers that the organization will link with electronically to conduct business.

Source   Mintzberg, H. 1993. *The nature of managerial work.* New York: Harper Row, 93–94.

Similar to the functions of management perspective, Mintzberg's managerial roles were also found to vary depending on the level of the manager. He found that the disseminator, figurehead, negotiator, liaison, and spokesperson roles were more important at the higher levels than at the lower levels. Conversely, the leader role was found to be more important for lower-level managers than for either mid- or high-level managers. What this means is that you are probably more likely to see the chief information officer than the information systems project manager presiding over ceremonies and speaking at Board meetings. Similarly, you are far more likely to see the project manager than the CIO guiding a new systems analyst or delivering a performance evaluation to a systems operator.

With the trend toward downsizing in organizations, we have seen that many of these scaled-down firms are left with fewer managers and that these managers must, therefore, take on increasing amounts of responsibility. As a result, their functions and role sets have expanded. Similarly, with the surge in workplace democratization efforts, such as self-managed work teams, it is also more common now for lower-level employees in the organization to take on some of the managerial functions and roles. For example, with self-directed work teams, in which team members manage themselves, it is common to see team members conducting their own project planning, making their own work assignments within the team, training each other, and policing themselves regarding work quality, absenteeism, and tardiness.

Effective IS Managers

We have talked about the functions information systems managers perform and the roles they play within the organization, but we have talked little about what differentiates effective, successful managers from those who are ineffective and unsuccessful. Management researcher Fred Luthans and his colleagues (1988) addressed exactly this question and found some interesting results. The managers who were effective—as defined by the quantity and quality of their performance and the satisfaction and commitment of their subordinates—were those who spent a great deal of their time on communication activities and on human resource activities, such as motivating, disciplining, managing conflict, staffing, and training. The managers who were successful—as defined by the speed at which they were promoted within their organization—were those who spent a great deal of their time on personal networking activities, such as socializing, politicking, and interacting with outsiders, and, to a lesser degree, on communication activities. These results are interesting and important because they suggest that for information systems managers, focusing on the traditional managerial functions and roles may be valuable for the organization but not necessarily for personal professional advancement. Luthans's work points to personal networking as an entirely new set of managerial activities that may be more useful to the information systems manager's career advancement.

A BRIEF CASE ———— **Information Systems Top-Job: Brewing Success at — Starbucks Coffee**

In the field of information systems, the ultimate success in terms of career advancement is the position of CIO. However, being a successful CIO is no easy task, and many obstacles block the way. Deborah J. Gillotti, senior vice-president and CIO of Starbucks Coffee Co. in Seattle, faces several immediate challenges to her success: the creation of a strategic plan for IT investment, the maximization of the utilization of new technologies, and the development of new relationships between IS and business groups (Field, 1997). In addition, while individual members of the IS staff are highly praised, the other business units have very low opinions of the IS department. The first two challenges are made evident in the following example. Starbucks has only recently moved away from Windows 3.1 and Word 2.0, upgrades long since completed in many organizations. Gillotti must convince the planning committees and her bosses that a greater IT investment and utilization of new technologies are crucial for the company. Gillotti must also forge ahead by building relationships with the other business managers who need her department's services and expertise. After these business managers get what they want and what Gillotti believes they need, she will be judged successful by her peers at the executive level. So far, she has made great strides toward the challenges that face her, but only time will tell.

IS and Organizational Power

Luthans's observations about the importance of networking in management lead to important related areas in the management of information systems—power and politics. **Power** is the ability to influence the behavior of others, and it can come from multiple sources, as described in Figure 12.6. In organizations, people often derive their power from their positions. For example, a high-ranking manager has the authority, by virtue of his position, to hire and fire, tell people what to do and not to do, and reward and punish subordinates. In addition to this common source of power, there are other sources of power that are even more relevant in the information systems context. These additional sources include expertise and information.

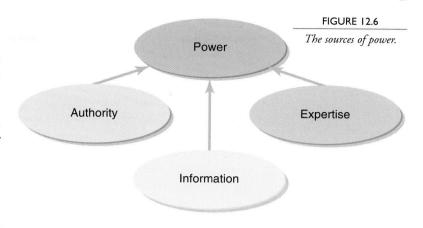

FIGURE 12.6

The sources of power.

Expertise as Power

If a person has expertise in a particular, valuable domain, he can use that knowledge or expertise to manipulate others. Just as doctors or lawyers have valuable expertise in their respective areas, so do certain employees within an organization have expertise in information systems and systems development. For example, if you are one of the few people who knows how to use a particular piece of software, say a statistical package, and other people or groups in the organization need to use that package to analyze data and make decisions but have little or no experience in using the package, you have a valuable skill and, in a sense, some power.

On a grander scale, you might be one of a few systems programmers or analysts within your organization with expertise in the World Wide Web and in building Web applications that are linked to underlying databases. If your organization has determined that it must pursue Web-based electronic commerce to remain competitive, you are valuable to your organization. If you play your cards right, you will, at a minimum, be placed on the team for this high-priority, high-profile information systems project. That alone could be useful to you. If you do well on the project, you may earn a bonus or a raise. More importantly, you may develop a reputation as a person with an emerging skill set and a can-do attitude, who has the ability to step up to the plate and deliver when called on. You would not only possess something (expertise) that other people need, but you would also be rising in the organization and garnering other sources of power.

The benefits of information systems expertise as a potential source of power in the organization have traditionally aided individuals who serve on the systems staff. However, it is becoming common for systems expertise to reside with power users, individuals who work in another area of the organization but whose use of the information systems is heavy and who have as much, and in some cases more, information systems knowledge and expertise than individuals on the systems staff. The other source of power that does not necessarily rest with individuals who have systems expertise is information. Ultimately, information rests with anyone who controls information systems within (or even outside of) the organization.

Information as Power

Controlling any valuable resource in an organization gives power to the individual or group who controls that resource. Traditionally, the more valuable organizational resources have been tangible, such as money, equipment, or space. Today, control of information has become as or more important than controlling other resources. People in organizations today are scrambling to get their hands on information that they can use to act faster and smarter than others.

Think about the various kinds of information that can exist in an organization—a database of customers or potential customers and their buying behavior, of sales divisions and sales representatives and their relative performance, of product lines and products and their relative performance, of the relative budget expenditures of the various units within the organization, of the human resource uses and needs of departments throughout the organization, or of competitors' sales and profitability. This information can be used to make decisions effectively and to help the organization do things better, faster, and cheaper—in short, to help the organization perform better. Perhaps more importantly, however, such information can be used to position one group ahead of another. If one group controls this information, the group members can use it to be more effective than other groups, and they can parcel out this valuable information to other groups in a way that benefits their own group. In essence, the group who controls this valuable information holds an incredible amount of power over others in the organization. Just as knowledge is power, information is power.

IS and Organizational Politics

As organizations are becoming more information intensive—both in terms of their recognition of information's importance and in the availability of information due to increased use of computer-based information systems—information is becoming an increasing part of organizational politics. Political behaviors in organizations, or **organizational politics**, are activities that are not necessarily required as part of one's formal job description in the organization that are aimed at influencing, or attempting to influence, the distribution of advantages and disadvantages within the organization. Essentially, political behavior is power used to influence people in ways that benefit the individual or the unit, and not necessarily the organization as a whole. Political behavior in organizations has always existed, but with scarce resources, cost cutting, and downsizing in full swing, an increased organizational anxiety can only fuel the tendency toward political behavior.

Anyone who has participated in an organization of any kind is likely to have experienced politics, whether the organization was a business, governmental agency, educational institution, religious institution, or a social club. An example of political behavior in a business setting would be when a new, high-ranking employee is about to be hired from among a pool of qualified outside candidates. Multiple individuals and groups are in the organization, each with many diverse sets of interests. Each tries to promote his favored candidate. Perhaps one employee has worked previously with one of the candidates and has a strong, positive relationship with that candidate. Perhaps one group represents the manufacturing side of the organization and is pulling for a candidate who has an engineering degree and strong technical experience and knowledge. Perhaps another set of individuals is pushing for a candidate they know is a strong proponent of radical change and innovation, as they are.

Political behavior like this happens within the information systems realm as well. An example would be when information systems proposals are being considered from outside vendors. The multiple individuals and groups within the organization have many diverse sets of interests and reasons to support their preferred information system solution and vendor. Perhaps one individual has had previous experience with a particular, cutting-edge solution and vendor and is pushing for that solution because it will make better use of her existing expertise, while other solutions will make her, in effect, a relatively inexperienced neophyte. Perhaps another group of individuals is fighting against that same cutting-edge solution precisely because they have relatively little experience with it. Perhaps another individual is pushing for a particular vendor because he plans to ultimately quit and go to work for that vendor, and the experience of helping to implement that vendor's solution is likely to provide the necessary training and opportunity for the job change.

Another common political scenario involving information systems and the control of information involves the control of sales data in an organization. Even simple sales data, such as who buys what, when, and in what quantities, is invaluable throughout the organization. Such data is necessary for effective marketing of products, for manufacturing planning and scheduling, for human resource management planning and staffing, for overall strategic planning, and for nearly every other function within the organization. Whoever collects and controls this information wields incredible power over others in the organization. In every organization there is an open, free-flowing access to and exchange of information, and employees all work for the good of the organization and want to share such information, right? Not always. It is common to find people who hoard such information and share it only when it is advantageous to them to do so. Perhaps they share information with others in the organization that they want to help, such as a friend in another unit or someone who can return the favor at some point with commensurate resources.

Consider the following example, which is typical of the "You scratch my back, I'll scratch yours" attitude in organizations. Sales information collected under the direction of the manager of the firm's sales and marketing unit might be shared only, or perhaps first, with the manager of the manufacturing unit because the two managers went to the same school together and have looked out for each other over the years. Alternatively, the sales and marketing manager might decide to share the information only with the manufacturing manager within the same division. She may decide not to share the information with sales and marketing managers or manufacturing managers within other corporate divisions. In this case, the sales and marketing manager has essentially decided that it is better to keep as much of the information to herself as possible to make her own unit look better and busier than the others, even though sharing this information across divisions would ultimately be better for the entire corporation and for each of the divisions.

Political behaviors such as those just described are all too common in organizations. If you have had any experience in an organizational setting, you have probably experienced something similar to these scenarios. Many people believe that organizations are inherently political entities—that any time you bring together two or more people who must work together to accomplish something, there will be political behavior of some sort. In any event, the political reality of organizational life is something we all must be aware of. Furthermore, information and information systems are often at the core of political behavior in organizations today. Paul Strassman (1995), who has written extensively on the politics of information management, suggests that politics and information have nearly become synonymous.

Some people argue that organizational politics is bad and that we should choose to ignore it. You do not necessarily have to engage in it, but you would be foolish to ignore its existence. The politics of the management of information systems are far too important and prevalent to ignore, particularly if you are a manager stuck in the middle of a political situation, as you undoubtedly will be in the course of developing, acquiring, or managing an information system.

IS and Organizational Change

As Benjamin Franklin noted, there are two certainties in life: death and taxes. For organizations today, there is one other certainty: change. Throughout this book, you have read about the evolution of hardware, software, applications, and development approaches. What is interesting about information change is that the pace of change is predicted to continue to increase in the future, with no end in sight. This continuous change can be a problem or an opportunity. The change can be problematic because organizations encounter problems at a faster and faster rate if change is not effectively managed. On the other hand, if change is effectively managed, organizations have the opportunity to rapidly grow and prosper. An example of a change that is a major concern to virtually all organizations throughout the world is the pending Year 2000 crisis.

This crisis relates to how programmers of business information systems have traditionally kept track of year information using only two digits. For example, 98 is used to represent the year 1998. Without making major changes, countless systems will believe that when the year 2000 rolls around, the date is 1900. If a loan system for a major bank, such as Chase Manhattan (which manages millions of accounts), doesn't recognize 00 as the year 2000, but as 1900, it will believe that accounts are past due when they are actually up-to-date. The system could print overdue notices to customers or cancel accounts.

A BRIEF CASE ─────── **Facing the Year 2000 at Morgan Stanley** ───────

Like many other large, threatened corporations, global financial services firm Morgan Stanley is spending tens of millions of dollars to change 3 million lines of information systems code to become Year 2000–compliant. Programmers are painstakingly inventorying every single piece of code and then manually fixing it. To make matters worse, programming work must be done on the weekends because most of the programs are in use during the week. As of January 1, 1997, there were only 150 or so weekends left until

December 31, 1999. The acuteness of the problem was best captured by Joshua S. Levine, a Morgan Stanley managing director, who said, "The sand is running out of the hourglass" (Nathans-Spiro, 1996). With its Year 2000 plan well underway, Morgan Stanley plans to have the problem solved well before January 1, 1999. This will enable the firm to spend 1999 evaluating the Year 2000 efforts of the thousands of organizations that have systems that interact with Morgan Stanley's systems. Fearing that they might be caught up in a systems domino effect, Morgan Stanley says that they will no longer do business with the firms that have not cleaned up their own systems.

Year 2000 at The Big Three ──── A BRIEF CASE

Just as Morgan Stanley is painstakingly fixing its Year 2000 problem, General Motors, Ford Motor Co., and Chrysler Corp. are attempting to fix theirs (*Information Week*, 1998; Kirsner, 1998). GM announced only recently that it spent $45 million on Year 2000 fixes in 1997 and expects to spend close to $500 million in the next 20 months. These three companies fear the same domino effect Morgan Stanley fears due to suppliers and customers not fixing their Year 2000 problems. In order to alleviate the fears and the potential problems, the Automotive Industry Action Group (AIAG) set up a task force to help the Big Three assist the thousands of businesses upon which each relies in fixing the Year 2000 problem. The AIAG uses seminars, surveys, an information center, and a Web database to keep track of all of these businesses and their compliance records. As Roger Buck, the Year 2000 Manager at Chrysler and chairman of the AIAG task force, states, "It's very difficult to build vehicles with missing parts and then put them in later." Due to the sheer number of businesses involved with the Big Three in one way or another, there may be enough that are not able to fix their Year 2000 problem to drastically hamper the Big Three in their production efforts. Unfortunately, GM, Ford, and Chrysler will have to wait another 20 months before they know for sure.

Despite the potential devastation, many organizations are reluctant to spend the necessary millions of dollars to fix the problem. They see companies such as Morgan Stanley and the Big Three spending tens of millions of dollars, and the spending is not contributing immediately to the firm's productivity or competitive advantage. Companies that are being proactive about the Year 2000 problem believe they will be uniquely poised to pick up business that will be lost by firms that do not adequately address Year 2000 problems. Indeed, experts predict that as some firms run out of time to fix their Year 2000 problems, they will simply discontinue certain lines of business or just let them fail. Other firms are waiting until nearly the last minute and then replacing entire systems wholescale. In any event, the next century will begin with even more anticipation and fanfare than it otherwise might have.

Managing Technological Change

The Year 2000 crisis is a specific example of change having a dramatic impact on organizations' information systems. This change is a result of not anticipating the future. When we think of change, we think of two general types: technological change and organizational change (see Figure 12.7). **Technological change** involves the rapidly evolving technologies and related skill sets that result. While incredibly difficult, technology

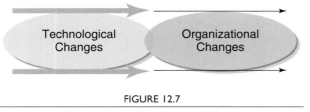

FIGURE 12.7

Technological and organizational changes.

change is probably easier to handle than organizational change. Dealing with rapidly evolving information systems hardware and software means keeping abreast of developments in the computer and telecommunications industries and participating in constant information systems training and education. In addition, managers of information systems must make smart choices about what technologies to invest in and when to do so.

A BRIEF CASE ───────── **Technological Change at Dell** ─────────

The rapidly changing face of technology has led Dell Computer Corporation to develop and implement its own business model (Magretta, 1998). Michael Dell, founder and CEO, had two key insights back in 1984: bypass the dealer network of computer retailers by building products to order, and vertical integration is not the way of the future. By bypassing the dealer network, Dell is able to offer products to its customers at substantially lower prices, as well as to reduce inventory costs through the build-to-order mentality. Dell products take advantage of the latest technology through the company's relationships with suppliers. By not vertically integrating the motherboard production, monitor production, chip production, and other hardware productions, Dell has been able to reap the benefits of the leading manufacturers through large, multiyear contracts without the worry of production facilities and their constant need for upgrading. These two philosophies have helped turn Dell into a $12-billion company.

Today, Dell is again leading the way in the changing world of technology with their *virtual integration*. Dell uses their supplier relationships and customer relationships, along with current technology, to further blur the lines between the supplier, the manufacturer, and the customer. For example, Eastman Chemical has contracted with Dell to preload their unique mix of software onto the computers as they come down the assembly line. This process takes Dell only a few seconds, through a massive internal network, as opposed to a few hours, which is what it would take if done by Eastman Chemical in the office. The same relationships exist with many of Dell's large, corporate customers. Dell Computer definitely causes technology to change, but they also take advantage of changes in technology themselves.

Managing Organizational Change

The second type of change, organizational change, is by far more difficult to manage than technological change. **Organizational change** involves designing and implementing changes in organizational processes and managing people as they attempt to deal with these changes. Organizational changes generally come in two types. One of these types is a change in information systems usage, as described in Table 12.4. For example, a company might change from a manual process to a computer-based information system (CBIS). Within many organizations today, people are foregoing the manual transfer of documents (alias "sneaker" net) and implementing local area networks to transfer electronic messages and documents. In the scenario that opened this chapter, White Water Adventures was attempting to integrate various islands of technology within their firm within one enterprise-wide network. Alternatively, there could be an upgrade to an existing CBIS or the replacement of one CBIS with another. Perhaps the company institutes an upgrade from one version of a word processing package to its most recent version, or, perhaps even more traumatic, the replacement of one word processing package with its now dominant rival. Finally, the members of the organization might be moving away from a traditional technology to a new, state-of-the-art technology, such as client/server computing. These information systems changes alone can be cause enough for fear and stress.

Table 12.4   Information systems–related organizational changes.

Some Common Types of Changes	Examples
Move from a manual system to a computer-based information system (CBIS)	Replacing "sneaker net" with Novel NetWare local area network
Upgrade to an existing CBIS	Moving from Microsoft Windows Version 3.1 to Windows 95
Replacing one CBIS with another	Replacing Netscape Navigator Web browser with Internet Explorer

Corresponding organizational and work process changes could occur as well as these systems changes, as outlined in Table 12.5. At the heart of business process reengineering lies the use of technology as the enabler of organizational change, including restructuring or downsizing.

These systems changes often accompany, and sometimes enable, important organizational changes. For example, at the heart of business process reengineering lies the use of technology as the enabler of newly streamlined and automated business processes. Similarly, organizational downsizing and restructuring often happens in tandem with changes in or new uses of information systems. Finally, changes in organizational strategy (for example, changing the firm's strategy so that getting products to customers faster now becomes the primary goal) are often made possible by new uses of information systems (for example, going online with suppliers and shippers to speed up production and delivery). One thing is clear: Systems changes are typically at the heart of major organizational changes.

Table 12.5   Other forms of organizational changes.

Some Common Types of Changes	Examples
Process improvements	Total quality management, continuous quality improvement
Process changes	Business process reengineering
Structural changes	Restructuring
Growth	New products and/or services, sales growth, mergers, acquisitions, diversification
Shrinkage	Downsizing/rightsizing, divestiture

Organizational Change Management at Oracle ——— A BRIEF CASE

As a leading developer of software applications that many organizations utilize during the implementation of organizational change, Oracle Corporation must be well versed on the intricacies and issues of organizational change management. Oracle has developed an organizational change management program based on its own experiences, with over 20,000 project implementations worldwide (Oracle, 1998). Oracle's program includes five customizable areas that adapt to each organization's culture, needs, and preferences. During business change assessment, the client begins to develop the change management plan. The client attempts to alleviate resistance and create buy-in to the change through two-way information flow during organizational communication. In the leadership development phase, the client's senior executives have the opportunity to completely understand the change. The client is assisted in meeting new performance expectations, roles, and responsibilities during the human performance and development phase. Finally, during custom training, the client's employees are given the necessary training to fully achieve the organizational change at hand. Together, these programs lead the client through the organizational change process as well as to provide support for Oracle's product.

Fear of Change

With all of these organizational and technological changes, many people tend to get nervous. Why do people get nervous when changes such as these happen? Think back to the opening scenario on White Water Adventures, in which the sales staff was resistant to the new system being implemented. Recall that the sales staff feared that moving to the new system meant they would have to give up their various "homegrown" spreadsheet and database applications. The sales staff was comfortable with the way they had been doing things and, because they didn't really know much about the new system and the opportunities it would present to them, they feared it. Common explanations of why people fear change are summarized in Table 12.6.

Table 12.6   Explanations for adverse reactions to information systems.

Explanation	Example
Comfort in the status quo	Employees may be comfortable with existing word processor and uncomfortable with giving it up.
Fear of the unknown	Employees may not know anything about the new word processing package, or, even worse, have heard incorrect, negative rumors about its functionality.
Threat to established expertise	Movement from one programming language to another poses a threat to programmers with a high investment in the older language.
Expose incompetence in or eliminate need for employees	Analysis of business process in preparation for sales order of system upgrade uncovers unnecessary or incompetent employees.
Threat to power relationships	Move to new system means that sales data is now shared and stored throughout the organization.
Poor/no fit with reward system	New, graphical order entry system replaces older, text-based system, but no incentive is given to order entry clerks to embrace new technology.

Resistance to Information Systems Changes

Fear of, and adverse reactions to, information systems changes can lead employees to resist technology and technology-related changes in organizations, such as the following:

- Won't use the system or won't allow others to do so

- Won't attend training sessions or won't allow others to do so

- Cause delays or problems in the development of a system

- Withhold needed resources for a systems project

- Speak out against a system

- Encourage others to speak out against a system

- Sabotage the system

Information systems resistance tactics can be subtle or overt. As a subtle tactic, for example, a manager might choose to make himself and his subordinates unavailable for interviews with systems analysts. If the manager strongly opposes the system and related changes, he might actually speak out against it and try to encourage others to speak out against and refuse to support the new system. This latter case may be easier to deal with than the former case because others would be able to identify the resistance.

A more problematic case would be one in which the people resisting the changes felt strongly, yet were afraid of being identified as resistant. In this situation, the opponents of the new system might actively, secretly sabotage it. For example, disgruntled users (perhaps even someone on the systems staff) might disrupt the new system or even destroy the data in the system. An ill-timed power surge or ill-placed virus could easily set back, if not doom, a fledgling new system. This kind of resistance to information systems change is by far the most difficult to contend with, particularly when those who secretly strongly resist the change openly support it.

Techniques for Successful Information Systems Management

Given the complexity of information systems management, what can you do to manage information systems well? At a minimum, those involved with information systems must participate in continual systems-related training and education. Whether you read popular press magazines such as *Computer World* or *Information Week*, attend focused training sessions on particular technologies, or go back to school for additional university course work or a degree in information systems, continued information systems training and education are essential. Training and education on the technology side are not enough, however, to ensure that you will be equipped to manage information systems well. Even more important is the ability to manage change effectively.

Effective Change Management

Kurt Lewin (1951) provided a model for organizational change, reproduced in Figure 12.8, that is still useful today. Lewin argued that successful change requires that we first "unfreeze" the status quo in the organization, then help change to a new state, and finally "refreeze" the new change so that it becomes permanent. In the unfreezing stage, those who will be changing must feel a need for change and know that the atmosphere is safe for change. In the moving stage, the information needed to make the change must be provided, and this information must be assimilated by the individuals who are affected by the change. In the refreezing stage, the new behavior must become the routine behavior. At this point, the new behavior is viewed as ordinary instead of something different and special.

FIGURE 12.8

Lewin's change model.

Source: Lewin, K. 1991. Field Theary in social science. New York: Harper Row.

Some have argued that the Lewin model of change fits only fairly calm, static organizations, which are rare in today's turbulent, sometimes chaotic business environment. In any event, Lewin's ideas are still useful in that they make us think about what it takes to change people's behaviors and how the change process ought to occur.

Overcoming Resistance to Change

Resistance can be overcome in several ways, as summarized in Table 12.7. Let's apply these methods to the information systems realm. For example, to counter opposition to systems-related changes, you must first try to look at the new system from the perspectives of other individuals and departments. Try to understand the other parties' viewpoints in order to determine where there is potential for resistance or why resistance already exists. You might then involve the opponents in the systems development process to get their input on the changes and help them feel that their voices were heard and their ideas incorporated. In this way, you might change their perspectives, and perhaps change the system, to overcome resistance. If there is no way to overcome the resistance, however, you better find a way to defend it (and perhaps yourself) from potential attacks.

Table 12.7   Methods for overcoming resistance to change.

Method	Description
Communication and education	Communicate with employees; educate them on the need and logic for change.
Participation	Enable employees to participate in the decision making process concerning the change.
Facilitation and support	Call in a professional change agent; provide employee counseling or therapy.
Negotiation	Exchange something of value for a lessening of the resistance.
Manipulation and cooptation (win people over)	Covertly attempt to influence employees who are resisting; give the leaders of a resistance group a key role in the change decision to appease them.
Coercion	Use direct threats or force to lessen the resistance.

Stakeholder Identification and Assumption Surfacing

One potentially powerful technique for preparing for a new information system or the modification of an existing system is **stakeholder identification and assumption surfacing** (SIAS) (Mitroff, 1983; Gupta, 1995). A stakeholder is any person, group, or organization affected by the proposed system or system changes. SIAS prepares you to manage people, groups, or other stakeholders in the organization.

To help you better understand SIAS, we'll apply it to a hypothetical information systems development scenario. Let's assume that a mid-sized business is implementing an integrated, computer-based order entry system to replace a manual order entry system. With the previous system, sales representatives would either call in, fax, or hand deliver sales orders to an order entry clerk, who would manually enter the orders into a database file that would be hand carried to production. With the new system, sales representatives can directly enter sales orders, which are automatically sent via computer network to all necessary recipients.

When conducting a SIAS, you need to first identify all stakeholders, their feelings about the proposed change, and the power they have to influence the outcome. For example, order entry clerks currently manually enter the orders as they come in from the sales representatives. Their current duties will be eliminated when the new system comes online, and they are worried that they will be let go. As a result, they do not support the new system. Yet, they have little or no power to influence the outcome. On the other hand, the CEO realizes that competing organizations have already moved to similar computer-based order entry systems and feels that it is time for this organization to do so as well. The CEO wants to move ahead quickly and has a lot of power in this organization. Figure 12.9 shows how you can collect and organize stakeholder information. Figure 12.10 provides a graphical representation of this data, which helps you visualize the stakeholders and their support and power relative to one another.

Stakeholder	Supports Plan	Has Power
A. order entry clerks	☐ Yes; ☒ No; ☐ ??? 1 – 2 – 3 – 4 –⑤	☐ Yes; ☒ No; ☐ ??? 1 – 2 – 3 –④ 5
B. office manager	☐ Yes; ☒ No; ☐ ??? 1 – 2 – 3 – 4 –⑤	☐ Yes; ☒ No; ☐ ??? ①– 2 – 3 – 4 – 5
C. sales representative	☒ Yes; ☐ No; ☐ ??? 1 –②– 3 – 4 – 5	☒ Yes; ☐ No; ☐ ??? ①– 2 – 3 – 4 – 5
D. sales manager	☒ Yes; ☐ No; ☐ ??? 1 – 2 – 3 –④ 5	☒ Yes; ☐ No; ☐ ??? 1 –②– 3 – 4 – 5
E. production manager	☒ Yes; ☐ No; ☐ ??? 1 – 2 –③– 4 – 5	☒ Yes; ☐ No; ☐ ??? 1 – 2 –③– 4 – 5
F. accounting manager	☒ Yes; ☐ No; ☐ ??? 1 – 2 – 3 –④ 5	☒ Yes; ☐ No; ☐ ??? 1 – 2 –③– 4 – 5
G. customers	☒ Yes; ☐ No; ☐ ??? 1 – 2 – 3 – 4 –⑤	☒ Yes; ☐ No; ☐ ??? 1 – 2 – 3 –④ 5
H. systems programmers	☐ Yes; ☒ No; ☐ ??? 1 – 2 – 3 –④ 5	☒ Yes; ☐ No; ☐ ??? 1 – 2 –③– 4 – 5
I. chief executive officer	☒ Yes; ☐ No; ☐ ??? 1 – 2 – 3 –④ 5	☒ Yes; ☐ No; ☐ ??? 1 – 2 – 3 – 4 –⑤
J. chief operating officer	☒ Yes; ☐ No; ☐ ??? 1 – 2 –③– 4 – 5	☒ Yes; ☐ No; ☐ ??? 1 – 2 – 3 –④ 5

FIGURE 12.9

List of stakeholders.

FIGURE 12.10

Graph of stakeholders.

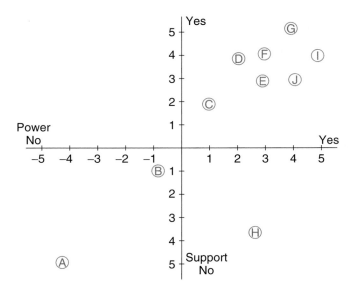

You can interpret the information from the graph shown in Figure 12.10 in many ways. The first step is to begin with the stakeholders who appear in the lower right quadrant because these are stakeholders who do not support the new system and who have the power to do something about it. The stakeholders in this lower right quadrant are the systems programmers. They represent an important stakeholder group that must be managed if this project is to be successful.

One strategy for dealing with the systems programmers is to find out more about their concerns. You learn, for example, that many of the systems programmers are not supportive of the new system because they are trained primarily in programming languages that are not used in the new system. However, you also learn that a few systems analysts may have the newer programming skills and may actually be in favor of the new system. These programmers might be instrumental in helping re-train the other, more traditional programmers to implement the new system. In any event, a coalition of stakeholders in the upper right quadrant can be built to help manage the stakeholders in the lower right quadrant. For example, given their strong support for the new system and their relatively high degree of power, the chief executive officer and chief operating officer might free resources to help quickly re-train the systems programmers.

The other group of stakeholders in this example appears in the lower left quadrant. In this example, the order entry clerks and the office manager do not support the new system, but they have little or no power. One management option is to simply ignore them because they hold little or no power and do not factor directly into the use of the new system. However, it is wrong to ignore them. These employees are likely to possess valuable information that can help in the development of the new system and the new order entry process. Furthermore, the organization may be able to find other ways to employ these workers.

This order entry system is just an example of the way that stakeholder identification and assumption surfacing (SIAS) can be used to prepare for the development of a new system or the modification of an existing system. It provides valuable information about the players involved in the systems development project and how they can best be managed.

Managing Innovation Adoption

You can evaluate and deal with people's feelings about information systems-related changes in other ways. For example, Rogers's (1983) description of the stages of the adoption process, listed in Table 12.8, is very useful in information systems settings. By thinking about systems users in terms of where they fall in the adoption process, you can strategize about how to move them along expeditiously toward successful adoption. You may have users in the interest stage who need additional information about the new system. Alternatively, you may have users in the trial stage who are ready to test and evaluate a prototype. Knowing where the users are in the adoption process and what they need in order to move to adoption is critical.

Table 12.8 Rogers's stages in the adoption process.

Stage	Description
Awareness	The individual is aware of the innovation but is not really interested in it at this point.
Interest	The individual becomes interested in the innovation and seeks additional information about it.
Evaluation	The individual is weighing the information and deciding whether or not to invest in the innovation.
Trial	The individual tests the innovation by actually using it and evaluating the benefits received from its use.
Adoption	The individual decides in favor of the innovation and adopts it for full use.

Similarly, Rogers categorized people by how quickly they adopt an innovation. We've described each of these categories in Figure 12.11. He reported that over time, diffusion of an innovation follows a bell-shaped curve. He called the first 12.5 percent the innovators and the next 13.5 percent the early adopters. The innovators tend to be adventuresome risk takers within the organization, well equipped to try out new, technical innovations. However, the innovators tend not to be opinion leaders within the organization because they are typically viewed as people who do not follow the established social norms of the organization. The early adopters, on the other hand, tend to be opinion leaders within the organization. Their actions are important within the firm, and they are viewed as role models within the

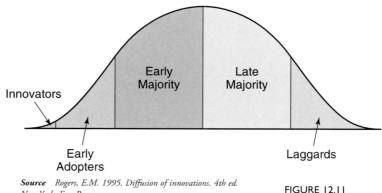

Source Rogers, E.M. 1995. *Diffusion of innovations. 4th ed.* New York: Free Press.

FIGURE 12.11

Rogers's stages of adoption.

organization. Other employees often watch the early adopters to see whether they adopt an innovation or not and then follow suit. If the early adopters adopt a new technology, others tend to do so. Alternatively, if the early adopters do not adopt, others tend to follow suit.

It is important to locate the innovators and the early adopters and to do whatever is possible (and feasible) to make their adoption successful. If their adoption is successful, you should make that success widely known throughout the organization. You might, for example, equip these people with early prototypes of the new technology and work closely with them to make the technology work. After this is accomplished, you might enlist their aid in giving demonstrations of the new technology to others throughout the organization. Similarly, information systems developers and managers will seek out a champion within the organization, a user or manager of users who is a respected, influential, opinion leader within the organization and who strongly supports the new information system or information system changes. This individual can actively help convince others to adopt the new system.

Talking with...

Ed Siegmann, Vice-President of Information Systems at Rugby Laboratories

Educational Background

A.S. in Aerospace Technology; B.A. in Computer Science

Job Description

Mr. Siegmann is responsible for the processing of 6,000,000 invoice line items and 24,000,000 EDI records per year. To accomplish this, he manages a staff of 23 associates, oversees systems design and development, manages the IS budget, prioritizes new projects based on corporate needs, establishes work standards, maintains outsourcing contracts, controls expenditures, and acts as an overall troubleshooter when necessary.

Critical Success Factors

IS is often viewed through its effort of computerization as being responsible for job elimination. While working for a growing corporation, it is important for you to keep in mind that a work effort reduction plan is not a job elimination program. IS can help employees reduce the manual effort in their day-to-day jobs, allowing them to achieve more with less effort. Be more than an administrator. As you work your way up in the organization, get to know the players, but more importantly, get to know the organization and its systems inside and out, top to bottom.

Advice to Students

Be proactive. Day-to-day activities and the status quo environment are always the first to receive service and support because that is where the cash flow is generated. However, you must always be looking to the future, constantly researching and learning new technologies that can make the business function in better ways. Also, remember your place. Although it is important to be proactive and help the organization move forward with new technologies, it is more important to know where you belong. The bottom line for an IS manager is one of support, support, support.

Summary

1. **Explain the importance of successfully managing information systems.** The effective management of information systems is one of the most important managerial challenges in the coming decade. Managing information systems well can help an organization save money and improve productivity. An organization that invests wisely in its information systems can cut costs in other areas of the firm while increasing productivity. To better manage the information systems resources, many organizations have a chief information officer (CIO), an executive-level employee who has the overall man-agement responsibility for the information systems component of the organization.

2. **Describe the functions of management and how they apply to information systems management.** The functions of management are the primary tasks performed by managers, which include planning, organizing, leading, and controlling. Planning includes defining an organization's goals, establishing an overall strategy for achieving those goals, and developing a comprehensive, integrated set of subplans to integrate and coordinate activities organization-wide. Organizing includes determining what tasks are to be done, who is to do them, how the tasks can best be grouped together, who reports to whom, and where and how decisions are to be made. Leading includes motivating subordinates, directing the activities of others, selecting the most effective communication channel, and resolving conflicts among organizational members. Controlling includes monitoring the organization's performance, comparing the organization's actual performance with previously set goals, and then making any necessary changes to correct and improve the organization's performance. IS managers perform leadership and managerial functions similar to those performed by managers from all functional areas.

3. **Describe managerial roles and how they apply to information systems management.** Managerial roles are roles fulfilled by managers in their day-to-day activities, which include interpersonal, informational, and decisional. The interpersonal role set includes the following three roles: figurehead, leader, and liaison. The informational role set includes the monitor, disseminator, and spokesperson roles. The decisional role set includes the entrepreneur, disturbance handler, resource allocator, and negotiator roles. As with the functions of management, IS managers play similar roles to those played by managers throughout the rest of an organization.

4. **Describe sources of organizational power and the central role that information systems play in political behavior in organizations.** Power is the ability to influence the behavior of others. In organizations, people often derive their power from their positions. Additional sources of power are expertise and information. If a person has expertise in a particular, valuable domain, she can use that knowledge or expertise to manipulate others. Likewise, controlling any valuable resource in an organization gives power to the individual or group who controls that resource. In essence, the group that controls important information holds an incredible amount of power over others in the organization.

5. **Explain technological and organizational change and describe ways to manage resistance to technological change.** Changes in technology concern the rapidly evolving technologies and related skill sets needed to effectively deal with this evolution. Organizational change involves designing and implementing changes in organizational processes and managing people as they attempt to deal with these changes. To manage change effectively, you must first "unfreeze" the status quo in

the organization, then help to change to a new state, and finally "refreeze" the new change so that it becomes permanent. To unfreeze the status quo, you may need to overcome resistance by using methods such as communication and education, participation, facilitation and support, negotiation, manipulation and cooptation, and coercion.

A method for preparing for a new information system or the modification of an existing system is stakeholder identification and assumption surfacing (SIAS). A stakeholder is any person, group, or organization affected by the proposed system or system changes. When conducting a SIAS, you need to identify all stakeholders, their feelings about the proposed change, and the power they have to influence the outcome. After you collect this information, it can be graphed and analyzed. This information can be used to plan your strategy for working with those who oppose your project. A final way to think about managing technological change is to identify where people fall in the adoption process—awareness, interest, evaluation, trial, and adoption. After people's positions are identified, you can find ways to move them toward adoption.

Key Terms

Chief information officer

Functions of management

Managerial roles

Power

Organizational politics

Technological change

Organizational change

Information systems resistance

Stakeholder identification and assumption surfacing (SIAS)

Review Questions

1. How does a chief information officer differ from an IS manager?

2. List some reasons why the position of CIO has arisen so quickly in the last 15 years.

3. Describe the four general functions of management.

4. How would a high-level IS manager lead differently than a low-level IS manager?

5. Describe the three managerial roles outlined in this chapter.

6. What roles do power and politics play in the management of information systems?

7. Describe how information systems expertise can be a potential source of power in an organization.

8. Describe the two types of change affecting information systems personnel and how they relate to information systems management.

9. Why are people afraid of change? List some possible explanations.

10. Define the term information systems resistance and describe some ways of handling this resistance.

11. Describe the general procedure for stakeholder identification and assumption surfacing.

Problems and Exercises

◆ **Individual**   ◆ **Group**   ⌒ **Field**   ◯ **Web/Internet**

◆ 1. Match the following terms to the appropriate definitions:

_____ Chief information officer

_____ Functions of management

_____ Interpersonal role set

_____ Decisional role set

_____ Organizational politics

_____ Technological change

_____ Organizational change

_____ Information systems resistance

a. Activities not necessarily required as part of one's formal job description that are aimed at influencing, or attempting to influence, the distribution of advantages and disadvantages within the organization

b. Includes figurehead, leader, and liaison

c. An executive-level individual who has overall responsibilities for the information systems component within the organization and is primarily concerned with the effective integration of technology and business strategy

d. Evolutionary and revolutionary advancements in information systems, systems components, and/or systems development

e. Efforts to ignore, counteract, or defeat an information system

f. Evolutionary and revolutionary alterations in people, structure, processes, and/or technology deployment and use within an organization

g. Include planning, organizing, leading, and controlling

h. Includes entrepreneur, disturbance handler, resource allocator, and negotiator

2. Imagine that you just received a telephone call from a Fortune 500 company. They have asked you to be their CIO starting next month. When you tell your best friend the wonderful news, she asks what a CIO does. Explain to her what you would be doing so that, no matter what the extent of her IS background is, she will be very clear on what your responsibilities will be.

3. Compare and contrast the implementation of information systems prior to the advent of the CIO with IS information systems implementation with a CIO. Are companies without a CIO today necessarily worse off than those with a CIO? Explain.

4. Discuss in a small group the implications of the current downsizing, reorganizing, and redefining of organizations and their functions for the three managerial roles and their division among various levels of managers.

5. In a small group of classmates, argue for *and* against the following statement: Information is the most powerful tool in business today. Divide the group into for and against sides and provide clear reasons for your arguments. Did one side have an easier time of developing their arguments? Why?

6. Are organizational politics a bad thing? Can good things result from politicking? Why or why not?

7. Do you believe that the information systems field is changing too quickly? Are there any reasons to slow down these changes? Along with several other classmates, search the World Wide Web for specific facts, stories, or circumstances to support your opinions. You may want to try sources such as ComputerWorld (http://www.computerworld.com/) or TechWeb (http://www.techweb.com/). Make sure you discuss both technology changes and organizational changes in your answer. Prepare a 10-minute presentation to the class on your findings.

8. Discuss within a group of classmates the ethical implications of the last two methods for overcoming resistance to change—cooptation and coercion. When should these be employed? Should they be employed at all? Does everyone in the group agree?

9. When using SIAS, why must the group with power and no support for a project (the lower right quadrant of the SIAS matrix; see Figure 12.10) be watched closely by management? What does this group bring to the table that is so important? Use a hypothetical situation if that helps you clarify things.

10. Consider an organization with which you are familiar. Using only the World Wide Web as a resource, describe the organization's approach to information systems management. What job positions are in existence to handle these responsibilities? You may want to draw a simple organizational chart to clarify your answer.

11. Interview an IS manager within an organization with which you are familiar. Determine what managerial roles this person handles from the discussion in this chapter. Does this person handle several roles within any one of the role sets? Is this due to the person's level within the organization or something else?

12. Using the same individual from the previous question or a different IS manager, determine the manager's perspective on the changes within the information systems field and their effect on the manager's career and organization. Find out how technological changes and organizational changes have affected this person. Does this person have a positive outlook on information systems changes?

13. Choose an organization with which you are familiar that seems to have a lot of power struggles among different departments and/or work groups. Are these power struggles related to information systems directly? Are they related to information and its control? How would you try to resolve some or all of the struggles? Discuss your findings with your classmates. How were their organizations different? (Firing everyone does not count as an acceptable solution for this question!)

14. Based on your previous work and/or professional experiences, describe instances of organizational politics that you have experienced. At what level within the organization did these situations occur? Why did these political events happen? What caused or drove them? Did any of your classmates have similar experiences?

15. Identify a situation based on your previous work and/or professional experience in which information systems resistance has arisen. Describe the situation. Why was there resistance? How was it handled? Were any of the methods listed in this chapter used to handle the situation? How would you have handled the situation?

16. In a small group, develop a stakeholder identification and assumption surfacing (SIAS) analysis for the information systems development scenario presented at the beginning of this chapter as it would have appeared before the accounting department manager stepped in to help. Be sure to include a listing of the major stakeholders and their job descriptions, support, and influence. Graph these stakeholders using the quadrants described in the chapter. What can you say about the resulting graph? Which group should be managed first? Why? What is the outlook for this scenario?

Real World Case Problems

1. Federal Aviation Administration: Crash-Landing Ahead?

On the heels of a 16-year, $7.6-billion disaster with the modernization failure of the Advanced Automation System (AAS), the FAA is about to launch the $1-billion Standard Terminal Automation Replacement System (STARS). STARS will exchange data on flight plans with air traffic automation systems, terminal control facilities, and surveillance radars across the country. However, the General Accounting Office states in a report that the FAA management structure was not effective because there was no CIO. Specifically, the report states, "No FAA organizational entity was responsible for developing and maintaining the technical Air Traffic Control architecture." Given the FAA's long-standing history of resistance to management change, many are questioning the ability of the agency to be confident about this new system's success. The FAA did not understand the complexity of the effort needed to create the system or the amount of resources required. It also did not know how to oversee the contractors' activities or control the system requirements.

A 1994 report from the Senate Committee on Governmental Affairs notes that "the Federal government continues to operate old, obsolete computer systems while it has wasted billions of dollars in failed computer modernization efforts." With the exception of the Social Security Agency, numerous governmental agencies have had systems failures. Large-scale systems projects' success is bleak to the point that budgets may be cut from the 1999 budget. On the Year 2000 problem, the government has realized that less than 30 percent of the nearly 8,600 critical systems are compliant. This problem alone will cost the government an estimated $3.9 billion. While most agencies are underway on the Year 2K problem, the FAA has only completed assessing 38 percent of its systems, not including the 245 critical systems that the agency has recently identified.

Even with all of this, the FAA is claiming that the revamping of the procurement procedures and some managerial shuffling are paying off. Zaidman, the FAA's director of architecture, says "We no longer procure systems; we acquire them." The agency has moved away from the cumbersome bidding rules that required bidding with specs to looking for functionality. They now operate more as a business and negotiate like other corporations. However, changing the procurement of systems is not the cure-all. Management must still do its job. Senior management has changed, and workers are organized into teams to help facilitate this progress.

STARS has compounded problems because FAA management and air traffic controllers are feuding. The first installation is expected in Boston in December 1998, with 172 facilities to follow through the year 2005. With the stress of the heavier air traffic, the system is not soon enough, and the air traffic controllers complain of a cumbersome interface and unclear terminal displays. Completing STARS on time would be a major success for the FAA.

a. Why has it been so difficult to implement technologies at the U. S. Federal Aviation Administration?

b. What has been done to help the FAA do a better job of implementing technologies? Has it worked?

c. What does it mean to say that instead of "procuring" systems, the FAA now "acquires" them? Why is this change significant?

Source   *Cone, Edward. 1998. Federal aviation administration: Crash-landing ahead?* InformationWeek, *January 12, 38–52.*

2. Federal CIOs Look Past Failures

Best IT Practices in the Federal Government, a report issued by the federal Chief Information Officers Council last year, cites that successes by the CIOs tend to be small and incremental. This fact alone lends one to believe that the existence of the CIOs may be an important factor in the improvement of government systems management.

Even though the government is the largest single procurer of computers and related equipment, it is not necessarily a good shopper or manager. Horror stories of computing failures abound in the federal government. Taxpayers are seeing poor returns on their money to the tune of $145 billion appropriated for IT in the federal agencies over the last 6 years. The CIO Council is attempting to rectify this by giving senior IT managers from the different federal agencies a forum and sounding board for their concerns. Each federal agency is required to have a CIO under the IT Management Reform Act of 1996 (Clinger-Cohen Act). The FAA still does not have one under an exemption rule.

The CIO Council is making some progress. They have already put a capital planning process in place. Now, they are examining return on investment, generally considered to be an alien concept for federal agencies. Responsible management is what this council is professing—to be able to report to Congress and the taxpayers that they are getting value for their investment.

The best practices report includes some successes, such as the SEC's Edgar Web site and the medical logistics system at the Defense Department, but on the whole the state of IT at the latter agency is still viewed as a disaster.

a. Will requiring U.S. federal agencies to have CIOs help solve IT problems in federal agencies? Why or why not?

b. Will the creation of the CIO Council help solve IT problems in federal agencies? Why or why not?

c. Are problems with the implementation of large IS projects occurring in corporate America as well? What is it about federal agencies and some large corporations that makes it difficult to implement large IS projects successfully?

Source   *Edward Cone. 1998. Federal CIOs look at past failure.* InformationWeek, *January 12: 44.*

References

Baatz, E.B. 1997. Net results. Information from: www.cio.com. Information verified: April 20, 1998.

Bartholomew, D. 1996. The Year 2000 problem: Time's running out. *InformationWeek*, February 5, 30–40.

Cone, E. 1996. The mess at IRS: Arthur Gross, the agency's new CIO, must save a massive systems modernization program now that Congress is threatening to cut off funds. *InformationWeek*, April 15, 38.

Dragoon, A. 1998. A day in the life. Information from: www.cio.com. Information verified: April 20, 1998.

Fayol, H. 1916. *Industrial and general administration.* Paris: Dunrod.

Field, T. 1997. Great expectations. Information from: www.cio.com. Information verified: April 20, 1998.

Gupta, A. 1995. A stakeholder analysis approach for interorganizational systems. *Industrial Management and Data Systems* 95(6): 3–5.

1998. GM names Y2K head. *InformationWeek*, April 20, 30.

Kirsner, S. 1998. The ripple effect. Information from: www.cio.com. Information verified: April 20, 1998.

Koontz, H., and C. O'Donnell. 1955. *Principles of management: An analysis of managerial functions.* New York: McGraw-Hill.

Lewin, K. 1991. *Field theory in social science.* New York: Harper and Row.

Luthans, Hodgetts, and Rosenkrantz. 1988. *Real managers.* Cambridge, Massachusetts: Ballinger Publishing.

Magretta, J. 1998. The power of virtual integration: An interview with Dell Computer's Michael Dell. *Harvard Business Review* 76(2): 72–84.

Mintzberg, H. 1973. *The Nature of managerial work.* New York: Harper Row.

Mitroff, I. I. 1983. *Stakeholders of the organizational mind.* San Francisco, Jossey-Bass.

Nathans-Spiro, L. 1996. Panic in the year zero: Can the financial world reprogram its computers in time? *BusinessWeek* August 12: 72–73.

Oracle, 1998. Organizational change management. Information from: www.oracle.com. Information verified: April 20, 1998.

Pantages, A. 1996. Enterprise computing drives IS spending. *Datamation* (42)9: 66–72.

Rogers, E. 1983. *Diffusion of innovations.* New York: The Free Press.

Rothfeder, J. and L. Driscoll. 1990. CIO is starting to stand for "career is over": Once deemed indispensable, the chief information officer has become an endangered species. *BusinessWeek*, February 26, 78.

Strassman, Paul A. 1995. *The politics of information management: Policy guidelines.* New Canaan, Connecticut: The Information Economics Press.

Swanborg, R.W., and P.S. Myers. 1997. Wise investments. Information from: www.cio.com. Information verified: April 20, 1998.

Wilder, C. 1997. Chief of the year—Wal-Mart CIO Randy Mott innovates for his company's and customers' good. Information from: www.techweb.com (*InformationWeek*). Information verified: April 18, 1998.

Related Readings

Boynton, Zmud, and Jacobs. 1994. The influence of IT management practice on IT use in large organizations. *Management Information Systems Quarterly* 18(3): 299–318.

Brynjolfsson, Malone, Gurbaxani, and Kambil. 1994. Does information technology lead to smaller firms? *Management Science* 40(12): 1628–1644.

Byrd, Sambamurthy, and Zmud. 1995. An examination of IT planning in a large, diversified public organization. *Decision Sciences* 26(1): 49–73.

Grover, Jeong, Kettinger, and Lee. 1993. The chief information officer: A study of managerial roles. *Journal of Management Information Systems* 10(2): 107–130.

Karimi, Gupta, and Somers. 1996. The congruence between a firm's competitive strategy and information technology leader's rank and role. *Journal of Management Information Systems* 13(1): 63–88.

Kim, W.C. and R. Maugorgne. 1997. Fair process: Managing in the knowledge economy. *Harvard Business Review* 75(4): 65–75.

King, W.R., and T.S.H. Teo. 1997. Integration between business planning and information systems planning: Validating a stage hypothesis. *Decision Sciences* 28(2): 279–308.

Larson, T.J. 1993. Middle managers' contribution to implemented information technology innovation. *Journal of Management Information Systems* 10(2): 155–176.

Lederer, A.L., and V. Sethi. 1996. Key prescriptions for strategic information systems planning. *Journal of Management Information Systems* 13(1): 35–62.

Lee, Trauth, and Farwell. 1995. Critical skills and knowledge requirements of IS professionals: A joint academic/industry investigation. *Management Information Systems Quarterly* 19(3): 313–340.

Levine, H.G., and D. Rossmoore. 1995. Politics and the function of power in a case study of IT implementation. *Journal of Management Information Systems* 11(3): 115–133.

Markus, M.L. 1983. Power, politics, and MIS implementation. *Communications of the ACM.* 26(6): 430–444.

Orlikowski, W.J. 1996. Improvising organizational transformation over time: A situated change perspective. *Information Systems Research* 7(1): 63–92.

MAKING THE BUSINESS CASE FOR A SYSTEM ▪

Scenario: Convincing the Boss of IT's Value

After months of preparing the proposed annual IS budget for her consumer products firm for the upcoming year, Cheri, the CIO, finally has what she considers an excellent, realistic set of projects for the upcoming year (see Figure 13.1). Despite her best efforts, however, Cheri finds herself in the CEO's office facing some tough questions. Mike, the new CEO of the firm, appears upset.

"Year after year this firm has poured thousands of dollars into new information systems—a massive data warehouse, a World Wide Web site with order entry capabilities and links to back-end databases, an enterprise resource planning system to link each of the firm's business processes…it never ends," Mike tells Cheri. "How do I know what I'm buying? Where is the payoff? We say that we're more productive—that these systems make us more effective, or more efficient, or both, but I'm skeptical. How can I be sure we're getting the best 'bang for the buck'?"

Mike further points out to Cheri that because the firm is downsizing, they all need to make sure every penny is spent wisely. If information systems do make the firm more efficient, he supports allocating the money for them. However, some people in the firm view additional IS expenditures warily, seeing them as just another excuse to eliminate more jobs, or worse, as lavish expenditures on new toys. Mike is sensitive to these concerns. He tells Cheri that they both have to be able to demonstrate beyond a doubt that these new systems are worth the money.

Mike asks Cheri to review the list of proposed projects for the upcoming year and show how each will benefit the business's bottom line. In addition, he asks for a complete review of all existing systems and figures to demonstrate what impact those systems have on organizational performance. If systems cannot be justified on these grounds, then they will be considered candidates for cutbacks, outsourcing, or worse, the scrap pile.

Cheri knows that although a couple of old legacy systems probably should be sent to the scrap pile, most of the existing systems and all of the proposed systems for the coming year are necessary for the firm's survival. She knows that these systems contribute greatly to the firm's bottom line, but it will take some work to show this conclusively. She will have to work hard to make the argument for each and every system.

Introduction

The purpose of this chapter is to show why it is vital, but sometimes difficult, for people to determine the value that a new system will provide. The same difficulties face those evaluating an existing system that is being considered for modification, continued support, scaling back, or elimination. Building the business case is necessary for making good investment decisions.

After reading this chapter, you will be able to do the following:

1. Understand what it means to make the business case for a system.

2. Describe how to formulate the business case and why it is sometimes difficult to do so.

FIGURE 13.1

Cheri's proposed projects for the current fiscal year.

1999 Fiscal Year Systems Development Projects

- New Development/Systems
  - Group Support Sytem for Electronic Meetings
  - Desktop Videoconferencing for Distributed Collaboration
- Maintenance Activities
  - Data Warehouse
  - Marketing Decision Support System
  - Inventory Management System
  - Expand/Enhance Web Commerce System
  - Product Development Tracking System

3. Present the business case for a system and help others understand the value that a system provides.

This chapter, which is the second in Part 5, "Information Systems Management," focuses on making the business case for a system (see Figure 13.2). We begin by describing what it means to make the business case and discuss why it is important that the business cases for technology-related projects be carefully developed. Next, we describe the factors you must identify and consider when building a successful business case. Finally, we illustrate important factors to keep in mind when presenting the business case to executives and other decision makers. Making the business case for a technology investment is a business decision that must help your organization achieve its strategic objectives.

Making the Case

What does making the business case for an information system mean? Think for a moment about what defense lawyers do in court trials. They carefully build a strong, integrated set of arguments and evidence to prove that their clients are innocent. In short, they build and present their case to those who will pass judgment on their clients. In much the same way, people in business often have to build a strong, integrated set of arguments and evidence to prove that an information system is adding value to the organization or its constituents. We commonly refer to this process of building and presenting this rationale as **making the business case** for a system.

It is important to know how and why to make the business case for a system for a number of reasons. As we've discussed throughout this book, information systems have become an integral part of doing business. Organizations are focused on being effective and efficient, and information systems are one vehicle for achieving this productivity. Unfortunately, information systems are expensive and difficult to buy and build. As with nearly every aspect of business, information systems must be carefully analyzed. We need to know what value the system provides, given the funding and other resources that it consumes. Does it make sense to buy, build, or continue to fund and use a particular system?

As a business professional, you'll be called on to make the business case for systems and other capital investments. As a finance, accounting, marketing, or management professional, you're likely to be involved in this process and will need to know how to make the business case for a system effectively, as well as to understand the relevant organizational issues involved. It will be in the organization's best interest, and in your own, to ferret out systems that are not adding value. In these cases, you'll need to either improve the systems or replace them.

Making the business case is as important for proposed systems as it is for existing systems. For a proposed system, the case will be used to determine whether the new system is a "go" or a "no go." For an existing system, the case determines whether the company should continue to fund the system. Whether a new system or an existing one is being considered, your goal is to make sure that the system adds value, that it helps the firm to achieve its strategy and competitive advantage over its rivals, and that money is being spent wisely.

It All Begins with Planning

Information systems planning has always been a difficult task. In many cases, the process of overall planning for information technology has not been as detailed and structured as the overall business planning process. It is possible that IT investment decisions were made more on what felt right to the IS manager or CEO than on what could be shown quantitatively to be sound investment decisions.

However, evidence indicates that this trend is changing. Recent surveys of IS executives have placed IS planning as one of the most highly rated areas of concern. The increased emphasis on planning can be seen as evidence that IS managers perceive a need to tie IS planning to overall business planning. As firms continually seek to streamline

Organizing
the IS
Function

**Making the Business
Case for a System**

**Managing IS
as an
Organizational
Resource**

Emerging
IS

Alternatives
to Systems
Development

Organizational
IS

Contemporary
IS
Development
Approaches

Electronic
Commerce
& the Internet

The IS
Development
Process

Hardware   Software

Database Management

Telecommunications

processes through reengineering and consolidation, IT investments can quickly become another area ripe for cutbacks. As a result, organizations have begun to place increasing emphasis on proper IT planning as a means to justify the business value of IT investments. In Table 13.1, we outline some of the reasons for the increased concern over IS planning.

Table 13.1   Factors driving the need for IS planning.

Factor	Description
Growth in computers, networks, and the technology use	Growth in the use of personal Internet has resulted in increased demand for advanced information technology services.
Rise in end-user computing	The rise in end-user computing has led to more systems being developed, as well as to an increased need for user support services and for ways to document or track which systems have been developed and what their payoff has been.
Importance of human resource deployment	Scarcity of human resources, particularly IS personnel, has made labor an expensive resource.
Emphasis on systems integration	The increasing integration among systems makes planning and justification for those systems more important.
Intense competition	Increased competition has led to a need to meticulously evaluate firm profitability. Investments that do not add value or increase profitability may no longer be affordable.

FIGURE 13.2

The big picture: focusing on making the business case for a system.

— The Importance of Information Systems Planning — at Hilton Hotels

Planning for the investment in and deployment of information systems is seen by many as a maze of priorities. Joe Durocher, CIO of Hilton Hotels Corporation, feels that IS planning has become so difficult that he would simply use a dartboard if he did not have the help of others (Violino, 1998). These others include managers within Hilton, the CEO, and even outside vendors. IS planning is much more than a decision about technology. It is now a business decision as well as a technology decision, and many times the emphasis is heavier on the business side. To that end, Durocher welcomes the advice and knowledge of the other senior managers at Hilton. These managers, experts in their own fields, can bring a broader business perspective to the IS planning process. Additionally, whereas decisions used to be made every six months at Hilton, IS planning now occurs on a weekly basis. Decisions are under constant evaluation and revision in order to reap the benefits of new technologies and developments within the IT industry. IS planning is an integral part of Hilton's business.

The Productivity Paradox

One of the difficulties of planning for information systems expenditures has been that it is sometimes difficult to quantify tangible productivity gains. Recently, the press has given a lot of attention to computer systems' impact or lack of impact on worker productivity. In many cases, IT expenditures, salaries, and the number of people on the IS staff have all been rising, but results from these investments have been disappointing. For example, it is estimated that technology-related spending by organizations increased five-fold from the 1980s to the 1990s (Hegendorf, 1998). As a result, justifying the costs for information technology has been a hot topic among senior managers at many firms. In particular, "white-collar" productivity, especially in the service sector, has not increased at the rate one might expect, given the billions of dollars spent on office information systems (Leibs and Carrillo, 1997).

Why has it been difficult to show that these vast expenditures on information technology have led to productivity gains? Have information systems somehow failed us, promising increases in performance and productivity and then failing to deliver on that promise? Determining the answer is not easy. Information systems may have increased productivity, but other forces may have simultaneously worked to reduce it, the end result being no visible change. Factors such as government regulation, more complex tax codes, and more complex products can all have major impacts on a firm's productivity.

It is also true that information systems built with the best intentions may have had unintended consequences—employees spending excessive amounts of time surfing the Web to check sports scores on ESPN SportZone, volumes of electronic junk mail being sent by Internet marketing companies or from personal friends, and company PCs being used to download and play software games. In these situations, information technology can result in less efficient and effective communication among employees and less productive uses of employee time than before the IT was implemented. Does this kind of employee behavior affect productivity figures? You bet it does. Still, in general, sound IT investments should increase organizational productivity. If this is so, why haven't organizations been able to show this increased productivity? A number of reasons have been given for the apparent "productivity paradox" of IT investments.

Measurement Problems

In many cases, the benefits of information technology are difficult to pinpoint because firms may be measuring the wrong things. Often, the biggest increases in productivity result from increased **system effectiveness**. Unfortunately, many business metrics focus on **system efficiency**. Although information systems may have real benefits, those benefits may not be detected. Effectiveness improvements are sometimes difficult to measure. Also, expected benefits from IT are not always defined in advance, so they are never "seen." After all, in order to "see" something, you usually have to know what to look for. Measurement problems are not limited to traditional office information systems either. All types of systems have potential measurement problems. Consider the following:

End-user development. Because end-user developed systems are often designed for individual users or individual needs, those individuals do not often meticulously track costs and benefits in order to measure impact. In addition, end users in one business unit may be tracking and analyzing systems benefits and costs in ways that are quite different from the methods used by end users in other units.

Decision support systems (DSSs). By definition, DSSs are designed to improve decision making. The problem is, how do we measure their impact? To quantify the results of DSSs, we would need to measure the differences between decisions made with the DSS and the decisions that would have been made if no DSS had been in place. This kind of comparison is difficult to make in a business setting. Furthermore, it is not clear what constitutes adding value in this context. Does adding value mean making decisions that result in better outcomes, improving the decision making process, having the capability to make more decisions, being able to justify a decision more effectively, making people feel better about the decision outcomes and/or the decision making process, or some combination of these and other factors? Until it becomes clearer how to measure easily and effectively the benefits of DSS, making the business case for DSS-like systems will continue to be difficult.

Strategic systems. Ideally, these systems are those IS managers could point to as having a tremendous impact on firm performance. However, the intent of strategic systems is to help the organization enter a new market, gain or maintain market share, and gain competitive advantage. As we've said, traditional measures of system benefits—time or money saved or return on investment—do not adequately indicate whether or not these strategic systems have been successful. Holding on to existing market share may be vitally important and yet difficult in a competitive environment. However, maintaining the *status quo* does not usually translate into impressive-looking productivity figures for an information system.

A good example of measurement problems associated with IT investment is the use of ATM machines. How much have ATMs contributed to banking productivity? Traditional statistics might look at the number of transactions or output as some multiple of the labor input needed to produce that output (for example, a transaction).

However, such statistics do not work well for the ATM example. The number of checks written may actually decrease with ATMs, making productivity statistics appear lower. Can you imagine a bank staying competitive *without* offering ATM services? The value added for the customer in terms of improved delivery of services almost dictates that banks offer a wide range of ATM services in today's competitive market. Deploying these information systems has become a strategic necessity.

Time Lags

A second explanation for why productivity is difficult to demonstrate for IT investment is that a significant time lag may occur from the IT investment until that investment is translated into improvement in the bottom line. Brynjolfsson (1993) reports that lags of two to three years are typical before strong organizational impacts of IT investment are felt.

The explanation for lags is fairly simple. At one level, it takes time for people to become proficient at using new technologies. Remember the first time you ever used a computer? It probably seemed difficult and cryptic to use. It may have taken you more time to figure out how to use the computer than it would to complete the task manually. Nonetheless, the computer probably became easier to use as you became more proficient with it. If you multiply this learning curve over everyone in an organization who may be using a given technology, you can see that until a firm has some experience in using a technology, the benefits associated with using it may be deferred. Everyone must become proficient with that technology in order to obtain the benefits from its use.

It may also take some time before the tangible benefits of a new information system can be felt. Let's return to our ATM example. It may take years from the first implementation of this new system before the benefits may be felt. The system must first be implemented, which could take years in a large, distributed financial institution. Then the system must be fine-tuned to operate optimally and must be tied into all of the necessary subsystems. Employees and customers must be trained in how to use the system properly, and it may take years before they truly become proficient and comfortable with using it.

When the system is working well, and people are using it efficiently, productivity gains may be measured. It takes time for the system to produce any labor savings within the organization and for customers' satisfaction levels to rise. Given that the ATMs have become a strategic necessity, perhaps one of their benefits is that they enable banks to gain or simply keep customers. It can take years for a financial institution to feel the effects of its deployment of ATM machines.

If time lags are the reason why IT investments do not show up in productivity figures, then eventually IS managers should be able to report some very good news about organizational return on IT investment. Still, for managers faced with the day-to-day pressures of coming up with a demonstrable impact on firm performance, such as Cheri in the chapter opening scenario, the issue of time lags may not be very helpful or comforting.

Redistribution

A third possible explanation for why IT productivity figures are not easy to find is that IT may be beneficial for individual firms, but not for a particular industry or the economy as a whole. Particularly in competitive situations, IT may be used to redistribute the pieces of the pie versus making the whole pie bigger. In other words, strategic systems may help one firm to increase its market share; however, this may come at the expense of the market share of another firm, which loses its market share as consumers transfer to the other firm. The result for the industry or economy as a whole is a wash—that is, the same number of units are being sold and the same number of dollars are being spent across all the firms. The only difference is that now one firm is getting a larger share of the business, while another firm is getting a smaller share.

While such an explanation may be feasible for some markets and industries, it does not fully explain why productivity figures would be stagnant at the firm level. Shouldn't each organization be more productive than before? Part of the problem is that our expectations of performance are somewhat biased. We tend to take for granted that technology fundamentally enables people to do things that would otherwise be nearly impossible. In effect, we continue to "raise the bar" with our expectations of what people can accomplish when supported by technology. For example, you might wonder whether the electronic spreadsheet on the PC on your desk is really helping you do your job better. To best answer this, you should think back to what it was like to create a spreadsheet by hand. It was a lot slower process, was far more likely to produce errors, and left people far less time to work on other, more important tasks.

Mismanagement

A fourth explanation is that IT has not been implemented and managed well. Some believe that people often simply build bad systems, implement them poorly, and rely on technology fixes when the organization has problems that require a joint technology/process solution. Rather than increasing outputs or profits, IT investments might merely be a Band-Aid and may serve to mask or even increase organizational slack and inefficiency.

Similarly, the rapid increase in processing time enabled by IT can result in unanticipated bottlenecks. For example, if automation has increased the potential output of a system, but part of that system is reliant on human input, then the system can only operate as fast as the human can feed input into or through that system. Spending money on IT does not help increase the firm's productivity until all of the bottlenecks are addressed. From a management standpoint, this means that managers must be sure that they evaluate the entire process being automated, making changes as necessary to old processes in order to truly benefit from IT investment. If managers simply overlay new technology on old processes, sometimes known as "paving the cow path," then they will likely be disappointed in the productivity gains reaped from their investment.

If this is the case, why do managers continue to invest in information technology? While the novelty effect of new technology cannot be ruled out, it would seem that managers know, feel, or believe that they are getting some added value out of their IT investment. Still, showing how that investment translates into *bona fide* productivity gains will continue to be a challenge for IS managers.

Mismanagement of IT Projects at Galileo

An example of poor IT management occurred in 1995 at Galileo International, a provider of global electronic distribution services for the travel industry that links customers to airlines, hotels, and car rental companies worldwide (Field, 1997). Galileo's Denver office began project Agile in order to create a stronger link between the transaction processing system in their London office and the one in Denver. Agile was scheduled to cost $400,000 and to take several months to complete. However, after many months of no results, senior management sent in the rescue team, headed by Joan Hannan, an experienced project manager. Hannan immediately realized some of the causes of Agile's failure—no definition of scope, no clear deliverables, and no customer focus. Plain and simple, the project had no management. After a seven-month rescue effort, Hannan and her team recommended that Agile be scrapped altogether and that the Denver system be retooled on its own. In six weeks, the new system was up and running. In the end, Galileo spent hundreds of thousands of dollars and an untold amount of time on a project that really only needed six weeks to complete. However, Agile was not a total loss. Galileo learned some important lessons in project management and is now aware of the symptoms of a failing or failed project.

Making a Successful Business Case

While making the business case for information systems is difficult, in most organizations today, the need to make the case is stronger than ever. Some tips for making the business case can help. In the following sections, we'll discuss several factors to take into account when making the business case for a new or existing system, including industry factors, business strategy, and implementation factors, which are shown in Figure 13.3 (Harris and Katz, 1991).

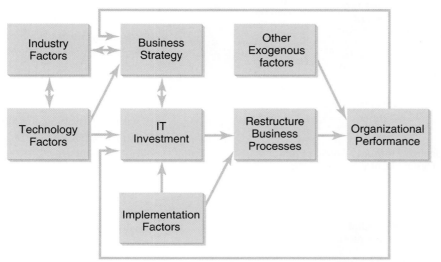

FIGURE 13.3

Factors in IT investment decisions.

Source   *Reprinted by permission. Harris, S.E., and J.L. Katz. 1991.* Organization Science 2 (August). *Copyright © 1991, The Institute of Management Sciences (currently INFORMS), 901 Elkridge Landing Road, Suite 400, Linthicum, Maryland 21090-2909 USA.*

Industry Factors

The nature of the industry can often determine what types of information systems would be most effective. Furthermore, many different types of industry factors can affect the business value of different systems. A system that may have a very positive impact on a firm in one industry may have little or no impact on a firm in another industry.

Stage of maturity. The stage of maturity for a given industry can have an important influence on IT investment. For example, in a mature and stable industry, such as the automotive industry, IT may be needed simply to maintain the current pace of operations. While having the newest IT available may be nice, it may not be needed to stay in business. However, if one is in a newer, more volatile industry, such as the cellular phone industry, it may be more important to be on the leading edge of technology in order to effectively compete in the marketplace. In fact, it may be a strategic necessity in some industries to deploy newer technologies, even though the tangible benefits of deploying these technologies may be difficult to demonstrate.

Regulation. Some industries are more highly regulated than others. In some cases, IT can be used to control processes and ensure compliance with appropriate regulations. For example, the aircraft industry is highly regulated. Information technology can provide sophisticated engineering and modeling tools to designers who can test various designs for reactions to gravity forces (G-forces) and turbulence before aircraft prototypes are even built. The designer can then understand which designs may not comply with regulatory requirements. Similar applications exist across other highly regulated industries, such as the radio and television broadcasting industries.

Nature of competition or rivalry. Probably the most important industry factor that can affect IT investment is the nature of competition or rivalry in the industry. When competition is high, as it is in the personal

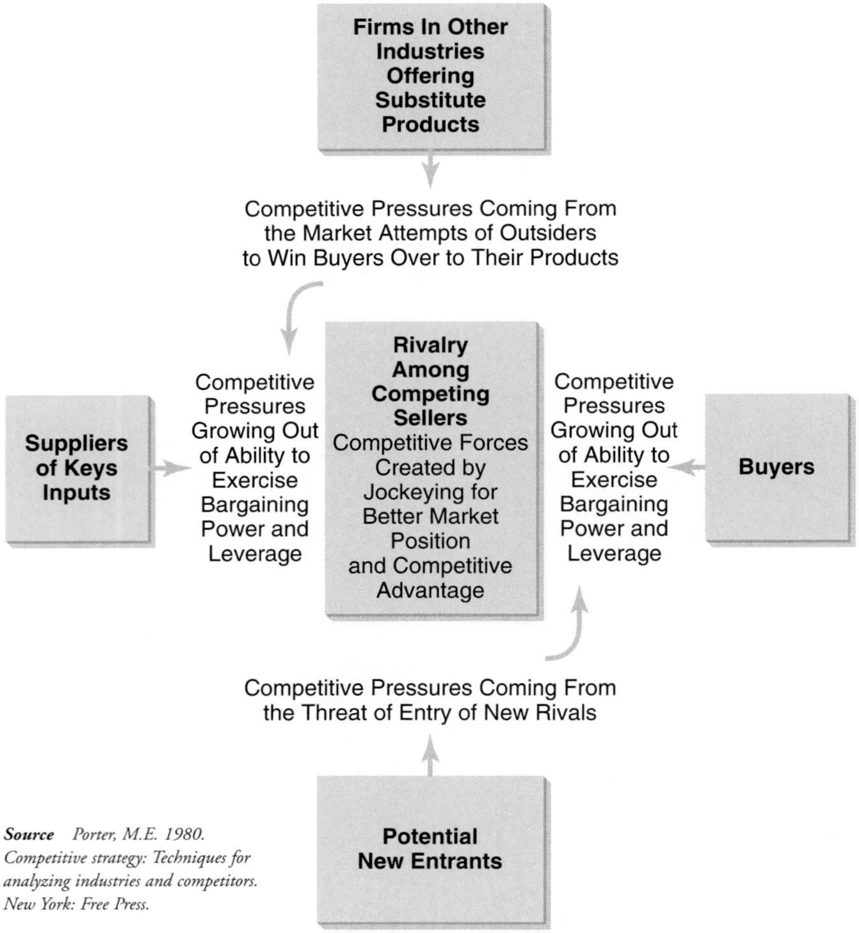

Firms In Other Industries Offering Substitute Products

Competitive Pressures Coming From the Market Attempts of Outsiders to Win Buyers Over to Their Products

Suppliers of Keys Inputs

Competitive Pressures Growing Out of Ability to Exercise Bargaining Power and Leverage

Rivalry Among Competing Sellers
Competitive Forces Created by Jockeying for Better Market Position and Competitive Advantage

Competitive Pressures Growing Out of Ability to Exercise Bargaining Power and Leverage

Buyers

Competitive Pressures Coming From the Threat of Entry of New Rivals

Potential New Entrants

Source *Porter, M.E. 1980. Competitive strategy: Techniques for analyzing industries and competitors. New York: Free Press.*

FIGURE 13.4

Porter's five forces model of competition.

computer industry, firms need to adopt a strategic, rather than a tactical, perspective. One framework often used to analyze the competition within an industry is Porter's competitive forces model, which is shown in Figure 13.4 (Porter, 1979) and Table 13.2.

Table 13.2 Elements/determinants of Porter's five forces.

Competitive Force	Elements/Determinants of Competitive Force
Potential for new entrants (entry barriers)	Economies of scale; Proprietary product differences; Brand identity; Switching costs; Capital requirements; Access to distribution; Cost advantages; Government regulation; Expected retaliation
Bargaining power of suppliers	Differentiation of inputs; Switching costs of suppliers and firms in industry; Presence of substitute inputs; Supplier concentration; Importance of volume to supplier; Cost relative to total purchases in industry; Impact of inputs on cost or differentiation
Threat of substitutes	Relative price performance of substitutes; Switching costs; Buyer propensity to substitute

Bargaining power of buyers	Bargaining leverage:
	    buyer concentration versus firm concentration,
	    buyer volume,
	    buyer switching costs,
	    buyer information,
	    and substitute products
	Price Sensitivity;
	Product differences;
	Brand identity;
	Impact on quality/performance;
	Buyer profits;
	Decision makers' incentives

Intensity of rivalry	Industry growth (stage); Fixed cost/value added; Product differences; Brand identity; Switching costs; Concentration and balance; Informational complexity; Diversity of competitors; Corporate stakes; Exit barriers

Source *Adapted from Applegate, McFarlan, and McKenney. 1996. Corporate information systems management: Text and cases. 4th ed. Burr Ridge, IL: Richard D. Irwin, Inc.*

While Porter did not originally include IT as part of his framework, his model has proven to be a useful way to analyze the value added by potential IT investments. IT managers can analyze each of the elements and determinants of the five competitive forces to gain a better understanding of the competition within their industry, as shown in Table 13.2. Perhaps the industry is dominated by suppliers or by buyers, or perhaps there is a high potential for new entrants into the markets. After you understand the competitive forces within the industry, you can begin to think about ways to use IT to add value and to mitigate competitive forces. Some uses of IT are naturally more effective and necessary than others. It is easier for you to build a case for deploying these technologies and spending money in these areas as opposed to others. Table 13.3 provides examples of how IT can impact the various competitive forces in an industry.

Table 13.3   IT impact on competitive forces.

Competitive Force	Implication for Firm	Potential Use of IT to Combat Competitive Force
Threat of new entrants	New capacity; Substantial resources; Reduced prices or inflation of firm costs	Provide entry barriers; Economies of scale; Switching costs; Product differentiation; Access to distribution channels
Buyer's bargaining power	Prices forced down; High quality; More services; Increased competition	Buyer selection; Switching costs; Differentiation; Entry barriers;
Supplier's bargaining power	Prices raised; Reduced quality and services (labor)	Selection; Threat of backward integration (establishing close electronic ties with suppliers)
Threat of substitutes	Potential returns limited; Ceiling on prices and services	Improve price/performance; Redefine products
Traditional industry rivals	Competition in price, product, distribution, and service areas	Cost-effectiveness; Market access Differentiation of product, services, and firm

Source   *Adapted from Applegate, McFarlan, and McKenney. 1996. Corporate information systems management: Text and cases. 4th ed. Burr Ridge, IL: Richard D. Irwin, Inc.*

Let's use Table 13.3 to determine which technologies have the greatest hope of adding value for a given industry when the threat of new entrants into the market is intense. An example of such a market is that for Web-based business software. While a few dominant companies aim their products at this market—Microsoft and Netscape—this industry is relatively new, there is no established leader, and it is fairly easy for other companies and entrepreneurs to enter this market with products and services. If firms in this industry don't act fast, they will find it difficult to build market share, their sales will likely drop, and their prices will have to be reduced in order to compete with existing and new competitors. Selling less and at lower prices is not a formula for business success.

Firms in the Web-based software industry must find clever ways to use technology to differentiate their products and services and, perhaps, deliver their products to customers faster. It will be critical for these firms to "wire" their employees together so that they can communicate and collaborate quickly and effectively and thus react successfully to industry forces. Email and collaborative applications, such as Lotus Notes, are likely to add value here. In addition, they may consider using the Web itself to broaden their reach to customers and, perhaps, deliver their product directly to their customers' servers. They may adopt a distribution scheme in which they deliver their Web-based business software right to the company's servers via the Internet and then conduct upgrades and system maintenance for them online.

Porter's Five Forces model of competition can be used in this way to help you determine which specific technologies will be more or less useful. Conducting this analysis will help you build the business case for technology investments. This kind of competitor-based business case might not enable you to attach specific, monetary benefits to particular information systems, but it can be used to show you and others that specific uses of particular systems are necessary to compete in your markets.

Competition and IT Investments: Domino's Pizza Delivers

A BRIEF CASE

Most of you have experienced the intense competition in the pizza restaurant industry, especially in and around college towns. This competition has forced many smaller companies to go out of business, although plenty are still around to compete with the big names of Pizza Hut, Domino's, Little Caesar's, and Papa John's. As a result, even these large companies are using technology to stay ahead of the competition. Domino's Pizza Incorporated, headquartered in Ann Arbor, Michigan, is a prime example. Domino's inventory system automatically deducts the proper quantities of toppings (based on pre-set standards) from inventory files every time an order is placed (Dragoon, 1998). A nightly report is then produced showing the store manager what to reorder. Soon, the reordering process will be online, and within the next year, distribution centers will automatically check store inventories and place orders as necessary without the involvement of management. Similar advances are occurring in the delivery market. Domino's stores employ a custom software package that combines Caller ID with their order database to display the customer's name, address, phone number, and most recent order to the employee. Even special delivery instructions can be displayed to save time. All customers need to do is call up, say they want the same order as last time, and that's it. The production and delivery processes are automatically set into motion, and the inventory system is preparing the reorder report based on the order. So, although the pizza is made in 15 minutes and the driver reaches your home in another 10, a lot more is going on behind the scenes to make the process work and to keep the restaurant competitive.

Business Strategy

The particular business strategy of the firm also plays a role in making an appropriate business case for systems. As we discussed in Chapter 1, "Information Systems Overview," the firm's strategy is its plan of how to compete in the marketplace. IT investments should be closely linked to the business strategy of the firm because these investments are becoming one of the major vehicles by which organizations achieve their strategy. In many cases, IT has become a key tool that can be used to leverage a firm's competitive position. Business strategies differ radically among firms. These differences have important implications for information systems planning and justification. Some of the most important differences are discussed next.

Scale. The scale of the business and its strategy greatly influence which type of information technology is likely to add value to the firm. Firms operating in a global marketplace have strong telecommunications requirements and may tend to need systems with significant capacity and processing power. Oftentimes, integration among subsidiaries is a difficult technical issue to solve, but it offers much opportunity for gaining efficiency if information technology can be implemented properly. On the other hand, smaller businesses may be operating on a much smaller scale. The potential of information technology for these environments is also great; however, the requirements may be somewhat different. Global connectivity is probably less important; however, adding value via quicker and more accurate service may be one way for smaller firms to take advantage of IT. Using IT to increase the speed of service may cut down on labor costs because IT can replace sizable customer service staffs.

Understanding the scale of operations suggested from the business plan helps you plan for the appropriate technology to meet your needs. Matching the appropriate technology to the business plan is critical.

Scope. Business strategies also differ in scope. Some firms have a broad scope—producing products and services across a wide range of consumer needs—while others have a more narrow, targeted focus. For example, Procter & Gamble produces dozens of household products that are consumed under various brand names—Noxzema, Folgers Coffee, Tide laundry detergent, Cover Girl cosmetics, Crest toothpaste, and Pringles potato chips, to name a few. Procter & Gamble therefore has a very broad scope. Integration across various activities might be a key goal for IT investments. Such integration might allow Procter & Gamble to streamline inventory, thus improving efficiency.

Other companies pursue a narrower scope, concentrating on well-defined niche markets. Some software companies use this strategy. For example, neither SAS nor SPSS produces word processing, spreadsheet, or database software. Instead, they both have targeted the statistical analysis sector. They market their products to a fairly well-defined set of users, primarily university, research institute, and governmental markets. The information technology that would be most useful to this type of company would be technology that helps them differentiate themselves from their competitors while adding value. Taking another example, suppose a company has a narrow focus. This company concentrates on providing customizable office furniture for organizations. IT might add value to this type of company by providing salespeople with laptops and software that allows them to draw up office designs in the office, produce a quote, and, if needed, email that quote directly back to the home office for processing. In this situation, IT is used to provide added value by producing layouts and price quotes on the spot, while the competitors might need to draw diagrams by hand and mail them back to the office for processing. In these ways, scope can affect the manner in which IT investments can add value to the organization.

Strategic potential of IT within the industry. As mentioned earlier, different forces are at play within different industries. As a result, IT has more or less strategic potential —the potential for creating competitive advantage—in different industries. The appropriate route to achieving competitive advantage is therefore very dependent on the strategic potential of IT within that industry. For example, firms with a global market have a much stronger need for telecommunications links than small regional firms.

Bakos and Treacy (1986) have argued that two factors influence whether a firm holds a competitive advantage, bargaining power and comparative efficiency, as shown in Figure 13.5. As you can see in Figure 13.5, three factors influence bargaining power: search-related costs, unique product features, and switching costs. In other words, if the costs for customers to search for alternatives to your products or services are high, your bargaining power increases. Offering unique product features can also contribute to your bargaining power. Finally, if the costs to others to switch from your firm to another firm are high, your bargaining power increases. In highly competitive industries, the three factors can be manipulated to increase a firm's bargaining power and create a competitive advantage. However, in other industries, which

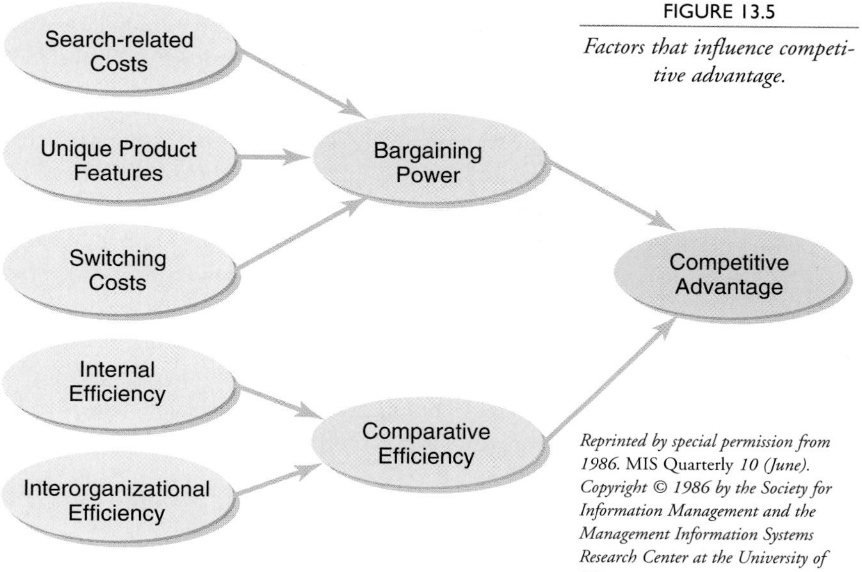

FIGURE 13.5

Factors that influence competitive advantage.

Reprinted by special permission from 1986. MIS Quarterly *10 (June). Copyright © 1986 by the Society for Information Management and the Management Information Systems Research Center at the University of Minnesota.*

may be less competitive or be dominated by a few large firms, an approach designed to create comparative efficiency might be more appropriate. The technology used to create comparative efficiency might be very different from that used to create bargaining power. Comparative efficiency can be created via internal efficiency or interorganizational efficiency. Setting up a Web site that enables customers to check on the status of their order without requiring help from a customer service representative might be one way of achieving some efficiency. However, such a technology would not necessarily increase the firm's bargaining power.

You can see how different industries have different strategic potential. Capitalizing on that potential requires the appropriate application and the selection of the most appropriate technologies, technologies that are likely to add value and for which making the business case will be natural.

Implementation Factors

Besides business industry and strategic factors, other implementation-related factors must be considered when making the business case for systems, including the type of organization, its culture, and its political environment. These are firm-specific issues that affect the firm's ability to deploy and maintain new systems.

Type of organization. Organizations differ in many different ways. Understanding the type of organization is a critical component of making a good business case for a particular technology. Some organizations are naturally conservative. For example, it is unlikely that public sector organizations will be the first to jump on a new technology. Usually, conservative organizations want to make sure that a given technology is proven before implementing it. Some even have strict in use requirements, as described in Chapter 11, "Alternatives to Systems Development." Other firms are more naturally aggressive. Firms with heavy investments in research and development, such as Nortel and Northern Telecommunications, view emerging technologies differently than do older, more traditional manufacturing firms. The type of organization can be an important consideration when evaluating the potential impact of IT and to what extent it will add value.

Another distinguishing characteristic of organizations is their **organizational culture**, the set of mutually agreed upon values and practices that define what is acceptable in the organization. Simply put, it is the overall climate or feeling one has in dealing with the organization. Whether the firm has an open, team-oriented, collaborative culture or one that fosters individual achievement can influence the appropriateness and potential impact of new technologies. For example, firms that are team-oriented and that foster and reward collaborative efforts might be expected to accept and derive great benefits from a group support system. Firms that reward individual effort and do not have a lot of collaboration would probably be less inclined to feel that group support systems would be of much benefit. Understanding these subtle differences in organizational culture can be an important part of making the right business case for a system.

Political Factors. Political agendas are an important factor in making a business case for the system. As described in Chapter 12, "Managing Information Systems as an Organizational Resource," power is not equal within organizations. Some individuals or departments have more power than others. Systems that impact the power structure will likely be controversial. On the other hand, systems viewed as beneficial to those who already have power will likely be received favorably. The point is that you must be aware of the political agendas of people and offices within the firm. In some cases, you must sell the right people on the system ahead of time. If you can gain the support of these individuals, it will be much easier to gain approval for a system. Similarly, no matter how good a given system is, if the right people are unsupportive, getting approval to develop or acquire that system will be difficult at best.

Using Cost-Benefit Analysis to Make the Business Case

In the previous section, Northern Telecommunications focused on evaluating a firm's position in the marketplace and its strategy for investing in systems that add value. The next step is to quantify the relative costs and benefits of the system. Although this step is critical, the manager must remember that there are inherent difficulties in and limits to cost-benefit analysis for information systems, as described previously.

A Web-Based System Investment

In Chapter 9, "The Information Systems Development Process," we described the nuts and bolts of conducting a cost-benefit analysis for an information system. Our purpose here is to provide an example of how cost-benefit analysis should be conducted as part of making the business case for a system. For our example, we consider the development of a Web-based order entry system for a relatively small firm.

In a cost-benefit analysis, costs can usually be divided into two categories, recurring and non-recurring. Non-recurring costs are one-time costs that are not expected to arise after the system is installed. These include costs for things such as the Web server, telecommunications equipment, Web server software, HTML editors, PERL, JAVA, PhotoShop, and other tools. One-time costs also include hiring or training a Webmaster, renovating some office space to serve as the location of the Web server, and paying analysts and programmers to develop the system.

Recurring costs are ongoing costs that occur throughout the life cycle of systems development and implementation. Recurring costs include the salary and benefits of the Webmaster and any other personnel assigned to maintain the system, upgrades and maintenance for the system components, fees paid to a local Internet service provider, and the continuing costs for the space on which the server and Webmaster's working space are located. Personnel costs are usually the largest recurring costs, and the Web-based system is no exception in this regard. These recurring expenses can go well beyond the Webmaster, to include expenses for help desk personnel, maintenance programmers, IS management, and data entry personnel.

The sample costs described previously have thus far been fairly tangible costs, which are easy to identify. Some intangible costs ought to be accounted for as well, even though they will not fit neatly into the quantitative analysis. These might include the costs of reducing traditional sales, losing some customers that are not "Web ready," or losing customers if the Web application is poorly done or not on par with competitors' sites. We can choose either to quantify these in some way (that is, determine the cost of losing a customer) or simply reserve these as important costs to consider along with the quantitative cost-benefit analysis.

Some tangible benefits are relatively easy to determine. For example, we can estimate that with the increased customer reach of the new Web-based system, at least a modest increase in sales will take place. In addition, we might also include as tangible benefits the reduction of order entry errors because orders will now be electronic and shipped automatically. We could calculate the money lost previously on faulty and lost orders and the salaries and wages of personnel assigned to fix and find these orders and then consider the reduction of these costs as a quantifiable benefit of the new system. Similarly, the new system may enable the company to use fewer order entry clerks or redeploy these personnel to other, more important functions within the company. We could consider these cost reductions as benefits of the new system.

Our Web-based system has tangible and intangible benefits as well. Some intangible benefits of this new system might include faster turnaround on fulfilling orders and improvements in customer service. Perhaps an even more intangible benefit would be improved perceptions of the firm. Customers might consider it more progressive and customer-service oriented than its rivals. Another intangible benefit might be simply that it was a strategic necessity to offer Web-based ordering to customers to keep pace with rivals. While these intangibles are difficult to quantify, they must be considered, along with the more quantitative cost-benefit analysis. In fact, the intangible benefits of this Web-based system might be so important that they could carry the day despite an inconclusive or even negative cost-benefit analysis. An example of a simplified cost-benefit analysis with tangible benefits is presented in Figure 13.6. You'll notice the fairly large investment up front, with another significant outlay in the fifth year for a system upgrade.

FIGURE 13.6

Worksheet showing simplified cost-benefit analysis for the Web-based order fulfillment system.

		1997	1998	1999	2000	2001
Costs						
Non-recurring						
Hardware		$ 20,000				
Software		$ 7,500				
Networking		$ 4,500				
Infrastructure		$ 7,500				
Personnel		$100,000				
Recurring						
Hardware			$ 500	$ 1,000	$ 2,500	$ 15,000
Software			$ 500	$ 500	$ 1,000	$ 2,500
Networking			$ 250	$ 250	$ 500	$ 1,000
Service Fees			$ 250	$ 250	$ 250	$ 500
Infrastructure				$ 250	$ 500	$ 1,500
Personnel			$ 60,000	$ 62,500	$ 70,000	$ 90,000
Total Costs		$139,500	$ 61,500	$ 64,750	$ 74,750	$110,500
Benefits						
Increased Sales		$ 20,000	$ 50,000	$ 80,000	$115,000	$175,000
Error Reduction		$ 15,000	$ 15,000	$ 15,000	$ 15,000	$ 15,000
Cost Reduction		$100,000	$100,000	$100,000	$100,000	$100,000
Total Benefits		$135,000	$165,000	$195,000	$230,000	$290,000
Net Costs/Benefit		$ (4,500)	$103,500	$130,250	$155,250	$179,500

As described in Chapter 9, we could now use the net costs-benefits for each year as the basis of our conclusion about this system. Alternatively, we could perform a break-even analysis (break even occurs early in the second year of the system's life) or a more formal net present value analysis of the relevant cash flow streams associated with the system. In any event, this cost-benefit analysis helps us make the business case for this proposed Web-based order fulfillment system. It clearly shows that the investment for this system is relatively small, and we can fairly quickly recapture the investment. In addition, there appear to be intangible, strategic benefits to deploying this system. This analysis, and the accompanying arguments and evidence, go a long way toward convincing senior managers in the firm that this new system makes sense.

— Cost-Benefit Analysis in Action: The NC Versus PC — A BRIEF CASE
Debate

Completing a cost-benefit analysis can be quite simple if you have many tangible benefits and few intangible benefits. However, the process can be very difficult if there is a large number of intangibles—costs or benefits. If the tangible benefits also drastically outweigh the tangible costs, it can be very difficult to say no to a proposed system or a proposed project. This is the case with the NC versus PC debate (Blodgett, 1998). NCs (network computers) are cheaper and provide for greater control over hardware and software than the typical PC (personal computer). Yet, the continual decreases in computer prices are keeping many potential adopters happy with PCs. In addition, the vendor wars between Oracle, Sun, and Microsoft are leaving bitter tastes in the mouths of other potential adopters. All of these intangibles add fire to the NC versus PC debate.

A cost-benefit analysis will be critical in helping Cheri (in the scenario that opened this chapter) determine whether the various systems under question are adding value. She can use cost-benefit analysis and the more strategic analysis of intangible costs and benefits to make the business case for each of the systems. Making the business case in these ways also helps diminish the skepticism that senior managers sometimes have about information systems projects and whether or not they add value.

Presenting the Business Case

Up to this point in the chapter, we've discussed the key issues to consider as you prepare to make the business case for a system. We've also shown you some tools for determining the value that a system adds to an organization. Now you are ready to actually make the case, to present your arguments and evidence to the decision makers in the firm. This task is much like that of a lawyer presenting a written and oral persuasive argument to win a judgment in her favor. Making a business case for IT really is not much different. You are simply trying to persuade the boss, steering committee, or board of directors to invest money in something you think is important to the business. Your job is to persuade them that you are right!

The Audience Matters!

Depending on the company, a number of people might be involved in the decision-making process. In the following sections, we describe the typical decision makers and their perspectives when evaluating a business case.

The IS Manager

Obviously, as the head of the information systems department, the IS manager has overall responsibility for managing IS development, implementation, and maintenance. He should be in the best position to make recommendations to decision makers, given his expertise in applying IT to business problems. The IS manager may also rely on experts in particular areas within IS to help analyze and present useful information to decision makers. For example, a networking expert may provide detailed technical information about cost, speed, and installation procedures.

Company Executives (Vice-Presidents and Higher)

Often, executives act as the decision-making body for the firm's large investment projects. They typically represent various stakeholders or interest groups within the organization, and they may have their own agendas at stake when deciding on expenses. For example, approving a large IT investment may mean that a new, expensive marketing idea gets delayed. Understanding the political implications of the approval process can be just as important as demonstrating a solid impact on the firm's bottom line.

A BRIEF CASE

Making the Most of Executive Support at In Focus

Not only do company executives make many of the decisions regarding large investment projects for the company, but many times they are also the ones the employees look to for guidance. Therefore, it is extremely important for large IT projects to have executive support. That way, IT projects have a sponsor outside of IT to keep the project on track and to rally the employees behind it if necessary. An extreme example of this occurred in 1993 at In Focus Systems Incorporated, a manufacturer of data and video projectors (Slater, 1998). In Focus competes with much larger companies such as Sony, Toshiba, and Panasonic. In order to stay competitive and to keep their jobs, the executives realized that they had to incorporate a cultural change into a learning organization that is constantly improving itself and its business processes. The executives decided that an information infrastructure was necessary to support these changes. For the project to succeed, the employees had to believe in the change and adopt it into their work. To make this happen, the executives, especially Mike Yonker (CFO) and John Harker (CEO), became active and vocal supporters of the new culture and the new information system. Employees who were quick to adopt were given salary rewards, and other incentives helped the remainder of the employees with the change. During the entire process, Yonker and Harker were staunch supporters, and everyone knew it. As it turns out, In Focus has experienced a 40-percent drop in operating expenses and an increase of 26 percent in market share. Everyone at In Focus agrees that without Yonker and Harper, the changes would have failed.

Steering Committee

Sometimes, a firm uses a steering committee made up of representatives or managers from each of the functional areas within the firm. The IS manager may make her case to this steering committee on which projects should be pursued and why. The steering committee then makes its recommendation to the CEO or corporate staff. In other cases, the steering committee may have approval authority, depending on its makeup. It may, for example, include the CEO, senior vice-presidents, or other influential people in the organization.

Steering Committee at Citizens Utilities

A BRIEF CASE

The goal of a steering committee is to get an organization's leaders, who have different interests and agendas, to share the responsibilities and risks that come with aligning IT initiatives with broader business aims. Many organizations utilize a steering committee for some aspect of their IT management. Citizens Utilities Company, a provider of natural gas, electricity, water, and wastewater treatment to 1.7 million customers in the northeast U.S., is one such example (Pearson, 1998). Citizens organizes its management into numerous steering committees. All of these committees report to the Operating Team, which is led by the president of the company. The IT steering committee, which is known as the Operating Technology Team (OTT), includes the CIO, Nicholas Ioli; the general managers of communications and public service; and the vice-presidents of finance, human resources, and regulatory affairs. A recent decision to implement an enterprise-wide Lotus Notes system had the full support of the OTT and passed through the Operating Team with no problems. Ioli notes that without the OTT's support, the implementation would have had a much lower chance of being approved. In fact, Ioli feels strongly that without the OTT, the implementation would never have happened in the first place, due to the lack of team unity and overall business support from the other leaders involved. The OTT enables Ioli to lead Citizens into the future with the necessary support and commitment from the other top-level managers.

Convert Benefits to Monetary Terms

Try to translate all benefits into monetary terms. For example, if a new system saves department managers an hour per day, try to quantify that savings in terms of dollars. Figure 13.7 shows how you might convert time savings into dollar figures. While merely explaining this benefit as "saving managers time" makes it sound like a useful benefit, it may not be considered a significant enough inducement to warrant spending a significant amount of money. Justifying a $50,000 system because it will "save time" may not be persuasive enough. However, an annual savings of $90,000.00 is more likely to capture the attention of firm managers and is more likely to result in project approval. Senior managers can easily rationalize a $50,000 expense for a $90,000 savings and can easily see why they should approve such a request. They can also more easily rationalize their decision later on if something goes wrong with the system.

Benefit:	
New system saves at least one hour per day for 12 mid-level managers.	
Quantified as:	
Manager's Salary (per Hour)	$30.00
Number of Managers Affected	12
Daily Savings (One Hour Saved *12 Managers)	$360.00
Weekly Saving (Daily Saving *5)	$1800.00
Annual Savings (Weekly Savings *50)	$90000.00

FIGURE 13.7

Converting time savings into dollar figures.

ETHICAL PERSPECTIVE: SORRY, CHARLIE—YOU BLEW IT.

I attended a meeting that got me thinking about the mores and ethics of our modern business culture. I'm not speaking about how we treat either the environment or our customers. Rather, I'm focusing very narrowly on the unwillingness of people to tell their bosses unpleasant facts. This situation hit home when I attended a strategy presentation that Charlie Adams—former planning manager for Karen Lovell and now head of a business unit—made about the potential fortunes of his new product line.

Charlie was put into his job by our president and CEO, Phil Whitestone, even though Karen, our VP of planning, had some serious reservations about his ability to implement his grand-sounding ideas. Charlie has another deficiency, one that frequently gets people promoted quickly to a certain level and then just as frequently causes their careers to crash and burn. He has real difficulty in bearing bad news to those in a position of authority.

Charlie began the meeting by touting the value of a major-league investment in technology to support his business goals, which, unfortunately, he has been failing to achieve. The overheads that he showed about the business opportunities were nothing short of brilliant. I was impressed; Karen had taught him well, and Charlie has the talent to apply the lessons skillfully. Unfortunately, the assumptions he was making about the potential of the product line were a little difficult to accept, even with a Web-based customer interface.

I couldn't understand how he could possibly achieve what he proposed. Looking over at Karen, I saw that she was fidgeting uncomfortably. I knew that she didn't want to torpedo her former subordinate, especially because it might look like she was being tough on him because he had left her employ. Karen, however, is a straight arrow, as honest as she is competent—and she is extremely competent. With a sigh, she started to probe.

Tough questions hammered Charlie like punches thrown by a heavyweight champ against a club fighter. Answers were challenged, and skepticism began its ascent in the room. Sid Gornish, our less-than-beloved chief financial officer, smelled the chum and started his own attack. Soon Charlie was sweating profusely. I have heard people use the phrase, but this is the first time I have actually seen beads of sweat break out on someone's forehead. He even began to leave wet fingerprints on the overhead projector.

What struck me was that as Charlie defended his risky assumptions, he made no move to distribute the copies of his presentation. In fact, as he talked, he moved them away from the table, clearly wanting to avoid bringing attention to them. Sid noticed, so did Karen, and so did Phil. That's what got me to thinking about ethics. Maybe minimal ethics is distributing the evidence that shows where you've glossed over the numbers.

After the search-and-destroy part of the meeting, Charlie's program was in tatters. People like Gornish smelled the fear and reacted accordingly. In retrospect, Charlie should have realized that you always hand out presentation material so that your colleagues can review your numbers. But after you are finished, never before; you want them looking at you as you talk, not at a paper. Of course, no one ever looks at a handout after a meeting. Charlie should know that. He lost points needlessly. As they said in the old tuna commercials: Sorry, Charlie.

Questions for Discussion

1. In what ways did Charlie cross the boundary into unethical behavior?

2. Why would it have been better for Charlie to be upfront and honest about the shortcomings in his proposal for a major-league investment in technology?

3. What should Charlie have done differently? Why?

Source Reprinted by permission. From Lovelace, Herbert W. 1998. *Sorry, Charlie—you blew it: First lesson in presentations: Always provide handout material—even if you've glossed over the numbers.* InformationWeek, *January 19, 174.*

INTERNATIONAL PERSPECTIVE: PROJECT OXYGEN WOULD LINK 175 COUNTRIES— GROUP LAYS OUT FIBER PLAN FOR "SUPER-NET"

Representatives of more than 250 telecommunictions carriers and regulators from 175 countries gathered in Las Vegas on December 7 for the first official technical meeting on an ambitious plan to deploy an alternative "super-Internet" over the next three to six years. Promoters say the global fiber-optic network could erase the boundaries between the Internet and traditional telecommunications, allow true connectivity from anywhere in the world, open doors to smaller carriers that could buy capacity "on-the-fly," and shift the profit model from voice service to data and video.

But critics question where the money will come from, not only for building the network, but for maintaining it. New Jersey telecom start-up CTR Group has issued a set of specifications and an invitation to submit technical proposals for the marine survey, installation, and maintenance of the proposed network under an initiative called Project Oxygen. The plan is for the first phase to be operational by 2000 and the entire network to be operational by 2003. Estimated to cost $14 billion, Project Oxygen's mostly underseas cable would extend 275,000 kilometers and transmit data at a minimum of 100 Gbps/second, with speeds eventually reaching 1 terabit/s. "Today, the Internet is a voice- and data-driven phenomenon," said Neil Tagare, CTR's president and author of the initiative. "What we are proposing here is the network of the future—a video-based Internet, which requires greater bandwidth." CTR is expected to unveil a model for buying and pricing international bandwidth at the Vegas meeting. Today's Internet, Tagare said, cannot meet the business and consumer needs of the near future. "That's why we named the project Oxygen. For carriers, it's a matter of survival."

Tagare said he believes the network will "in effect erase the dividing line between [the] Internet and traditional telecommunications," rendering distance and geography irrelevant as factors in telecom costs and tariffs. With Project Oxygen in place, said Tagare, bandwidth will be so abundant that international voice-phone calls will eventually become a free service, with international carriers instead deriving revenue from video and data traffic and from such applications as "telemedicine" and "tel-education."

The telecom model now in place requires that carriers predict the traffic they will carry for the next 25 years and then lease that capacity to third parties, such as other service providers. Alternatively, these carriers can use it themselves to provide such services as telephony. Oxygen looks to open the door to hundreds of new carriers. In light of the Internet's growing demand for capacity, the old model is now an "inflexible and inefficient system," Tagare said. CTR intends to let carriers buy capacity on-the-fly. "The cost of trivial amounts of bandwidth for individual switched international phone calls will fall so low that it won't be worth billing end users for it," said Finnie of Yankee Group Europe. The current market for international phone calls is around $90 billion. If Project Oxygen takes off, Finnie said, "this revenue stream may dry up altogether in five to seven years' time."

The initiative is gaining credibility among industry insiders, as CTR stacks up its initial cash on hand, a compelling staff, and Tagare's successful related track record. Six unidentified multinational companies from the United States, Europe, and Japan have provided capital to launch the project. CTR has signed up the former chairman of Egypt's national telephone company as the Oxygen project's rep in the Middle East and Africa.

There is, however, the question of satellites. Haven't they pretty much rendered telephone cables obsolete? "Not really," said Geoff Parr, a manager of international networks and technology at Australia's Telstra Corp. "Fiber-optic cables transmit voice and data traffic with higher reliability and security at a cheaper rate than satellites. While a satellite call must travel 27,000 miles (35,780 km) from the earth to the satellite and back, a trans-Pacific fiber-optic call need only travel about 5,000 miles point-to-point."

Questions for Discussion

1. What value will this new telecommunications infrastructure provide that justifies spending so much money to build it?

2. How can a telecommunications provider justify investing in this new technology?

3. What new capabilities will this provide to business organizations, and is it worth the expense?

Source Reprinted by permission. From Lange, Larry. 1997. Project oxygen would link 175 countries—Group lays out fiber plan for "super-Net." Electronic Engineering Times *December 1.*

Devise Proxy Variables

The situation presented in Figure 13.7 is fairly straightforward. Anyone can see that a $50,000 investment is a good idea because the return on that investment is $90,000 the first year. Unfortunately, not all cases are this clear-cut. In cases in which it is not as easy to quantify the impact of an investment, you can come up with **proxy variables** to help clarify what the impact on the firm will be. Proxy variables can be used to measure changes in terms of their perceived value to the organization. For example, if mundane administrative tasks are seen as low value (perhaps a 1 on a 5-point scale), while direct contact with customers is seen as a high value (a 5), you can use these perceptions to indicate how new systems will add value to the organization. In this example, you can show that a new system will allow personnel to have more contact with customers, while at the same time reducing the administrative workload. Senior managers can quickly see that individual workload is being shifted from low-value to high-value activities.

Alternatively, you can create a customer contact scale from 1 to 5, with 1 representing very low customer contact and 5 representing very high customer contact. You can argue that currently your firm rates a 2 on the customer contact scale and that with the new information system, your firm will rate a significantly higher number on the scale.

You can communicate these differences using percentages, increases or decreases, and so on—whatever best conveys the idea that the new system is creating changes in work, performance, and in the way people think about their work. This gives senior firm management some relatively solid data upon which to base their decision. They typically like numbers. Why not make them happy?

Develop a Work Profile Matrix

Sassone and Schwartz (1986) developed a model that has also been used to directly measure the benefits of information systems. As suggested earlier in the chapter, productivity gains have been notoriously difficult to measure with respect to information technology. Sassone and Schwartz use a two-step method to help quantify productivity benefits.

First, a **work profile matrix** is developed. The matrix, which consists of job categories and work categories, shows how much time is spent on each of the job categories and each of the different types of work. An example of a work profile matrix is shown in Figure 13.8. To design a work profile matrix, you must first have participants fill out an activity log. Every two hours over several weeks, the activity log asks participants to indicate how much time they've spent in each category over the last two hours. This information is summarized and indicated on the matrix. The results provide you with a snapshot view of how human resources are being allocated.

Second, as in Figure 13.7, the amount of money each department is spending on each type of work is calculated using salary figures. This information is compiled into a "before system" figure. An estimate is then made of how the new system will change the amount of time each job category spends on each type of activity. This can help quantify how a new system will change the balance of time spent by various workgroups on different activities and can make work shifts associated with the new system more salient to senior managers in terms of actual dollar savings or shifts.

Work Categories	Managers	Senior Professionals (or Senior Clerks)	Junior Professionals (or Junior Clerks)	Administrators & Technicians	Secretaries
Managerial	30%	2%	1%	0%	0%
Senior Professional	16	35	10	0	0
Junior Professional	13	26	50	1	0
Administrative	16	13	13	58	10
Clerical	7	12	14	27	76
Nonproductive*	18	12	12	14	14

*Necessary but not useful activities, such as walking to a meeting or waiting to use a photocopier or fax

FIGURE 13.8

Work profile matrix.

Source Sassone, P. G., and A. P. Schwartz. 1986. *Cost-justifying OA*. Datamation *Feb 15, 83–88.*

Measure What Is Important to Management

One of the most important things you can do to show the benefits of a system is one of the simplest: Measure what senior managers think is important. You may think this is trivial advice, but you would be surprised how often people calculate impressive-looking statistics in terms of downtime, reliability, and so on, only to find that senior managers disregard or only briefly skim over those figures. You should concentrate on the issues senior business managers care about. The "hot button" issues with senior firm managers should be easy to discover, and they are not always financial reports. Hot issues with senior managers could include cycle time—how long it takes to process an order—customer feedback, or employee morale. By focusing on what senior business managers believe to be important, you can make the business case for systems in a way that is more meaningful for those managers, which makes selling systems to decision makers much easier. Managers are more likely to buy in to the importance of systems if they can see the impact on areas that are important to them.

————Making a Good Business Case at Conoco ———— A BRIEF CASE

Lloyd Belcher, manager of Executive Information Systems (EIS) at Conoco, and Hugh Watson at the University of Georgia outlined a methodology that was used to establish the value of Conoco's EIS (Belcher and Watson, 1993). Conoco, based in Houston, Texas, is a global energy company with oil and natural gas refineries, as well as retail gasoline outlets. The system was initially developed in the early 1980s but has grown significantly over the last decade to include thousands of users worldwide. Much like the situation Cheri faced in the chapter opening scenario, the IS group at Conoco was charged with conducting a complete review of the existing EIS in order to determine its value for the firm.

In Conoco's case, the first step in reviewing the system was to determine the objectives of the evaluation. These included the following:

1. Identifying system users

2. Determining current requirements

3. Eliminating low-value applications

4. Identifying necessary new applications or modifications to existing applications

5. Comparing the costs and benefits of the current system

Users of the current system from all departments were interviewed, and results were summarized by department. These results were discussed with each of the respective department heads (see the interview guide in Figure 13.9 for examples of questions that users were asked). The summaries included details about the amount of usage and which applications were used by each department. A review was completed for each of the applications to determine the purpose, costs, savings, and improvements in decision making for each department, as well as any intangible improvements (shown in Figure 13.10). Costs and benefits of using the system were combined into a single worksheet to show a bottom line for each application (see Figure 13.11). When these assessments were completed for all applications and for all departments, the results were summarized across all departments into a single corporate report.

Using conservative assessments that focused primarily on tangible benefits and ignored most intangible benefits, Belcher and Watson were able to show that the benefits of Conoco's EIS were four to five times greater than the costs of the system. However, the analysis did show cases of applications that received only limited use. As a result, most of those applications were eliminated. Belcher and Watson concluded their analysis by citing 14 lessons learned about conducting EIS evaluation (although most could be used for any system evaluation). These valuable lessons are as follows:

1. A comprehensive evaluation can renew interest and support for an EIS.

2. A comprehensive evaluation can identify which applications deliver value and where enhancements or new applications are needed.

3. Both usage statistics and user interviews are needed.

4. Focus attention on mission-critical applications.

5. EIS benefits should be assessed at the level in which they occur.

6. Quantify benefits as much as possible and record intangible benefits.

7. Discount benefits by an amount commensurate to their degree of uncertainty.

8. Do not confuse the size or complexity of an application with its significance.

9. The assessment should be as open and objective as possible.

10. Keep the interview structure relatively open.

11. The interviews should be conducted by people who understand the business.

12. A comprehensive assessment requires considerable time and effort.

13. The assessment should be an ongoing process.

14. There is no single way to evaluate an EIS (or any other type of system).

EIS Interview Questions

Of all the EIS applications, which are the most important to you personally? _____

_____

_____

Which applications do you consider vital, as opposed to ancillary? _____

_____

_____

Would you replace any applications if they were no longer available? For example, If API statistics graphs were not available, would someone in your department need to assemble the data and graphs each week? _____

_____

Do you consider the EIS to be your department's information transmitter to others within or outside of your department? Would you continue to distribute this data if the EIS did not? _____

_____

Have any features in the EIS helped you eliminate data handling procedures in your own job or department? (ISD, API, Postings Bulletin, prices, etc.) _____

_____

_____

Does having the EIS at your desk give you productivity advantages you did not have before? _____

_____

_____

Does your department use Megamenu? Bulletin? EnVision? DataVision? InDepth?

_____

_____

Do you request data from the EIS database, such as spot prices, futures prices, API or DOE statistics, etc.? _____

_____

Do you foresee the EIS as a vehicle for future applications you or your department may need? _____

_____

Do you know any other system(s) in Conoco that duplicates the EIS? _____

_____

_____

Can you put a value on what the EIS means to you? _____

_____

Other comments: _____

_____

_____

FIGURE 13.9

Interview guide.

Source   *Reprinted by special permission from 1993.* MIS Quarterly *17 (September). Copyright © 1993 by the Society for Information Management and the Management Information Systems Research Center at the University of Minnesota.*

EIS Application Review

Application: *Industry Statistical Data*

Department/User Owner: *EIS*

Type of Software: *InDepth Graphics*

Maintained by: *EIS*

Basic Purpose: *Accumulate important data for quick, efficient review.*

Original Function Replaced: *Paper booklets published weekly and distributed throughout the company*

Exceptional Costs to Support this Application (Fees, etc.): *None.*

Dollar Value, Savings, Etc., Based on:
   Paper/Reproduction/Distribution: *60 weekly books at $2.00/book*

   Productivity/Time Savings/Better Information: *1 minute/access saved at employee cost savings of $1.00/minute.*

   Alternate Cost to Provide Same Benefits: *Analyst: 4 days/week = $36,000/yr. + computer clearances of $50,000/yr.*

   Improved Decision Making: *None.*

   Services Replacement Costs: *None.*

Average Accessses per Month: *108*

Noteworthy "Intangibles": *Graphics can be customized for managers (e.g., Eurostocks).*

FIGURE 13.10

EIS application review.

Source *Reprinted by special permission from 1993.* MIS Quarterly *17 (September). Copyright © 1993 by the Society for Information Management and the Management Information Systems Research Center at the University of Minnesota.*

FIGURE 13.11

EIS application benefits worksheet.

Source *Reprinted by special permission from 1993.* MIS Quarterly *17 (September). Copyright © 1993 by the Society for Information Management and the Management Information Systems Research Center at the University of Minnesota.*

EIS Application Benefits Worksheets

Application: *Industry Statistical Data*

Improved Productivity

   A. Decreased Information Creation Cost Savings: $ 41,000
   B. New Information Creation Cost Savings: 0
   C. Reduced Information Access Time Savings:

      (1) Average Access Time Reduction: *1 Minute*
      (2) Average Number of Accesses: *108/Week*
      (3) Employee Cost: *$1.00/Minute*
      (4) Savings Per Year: *1 * 108 * 1 * 52* $ 5,615

Improved Decision Making   0

Infomation Distribution Cost Savings

      (1) Cost of Document: *$2.00*
      (2) Average Number of Copies: *60/Week*
      (3) Savings per Year: *2 * 60 * 52* $ 6,240

Services Replacement Cost Savings   0

Total Tangible Benefits $ 52,856

Talking with...

Scott J. Claymon, President and Chief Marketing Officer at Pac-Van, Inc.

Educational Background

B.S. in Finance and Real Estate, Indiana University

Job Description

Mr. Claymon is responsible for long-term planning and company expansion into new geographic areas. This includes complete market analysis— from population studies, to construction activities, to competition. He is also responsible for the control, motivation, and staffing of the marketing department (sales personnel, regional/local managers, and telemarketers). In addition, he's responsible for the marketing plan, sales revenue generation, and coordination with the finance and operations departments. One of his primary tasks is to guide the company down a road that is profitable for both the employees and the shareholders and to not let barriers slow or stop growth.

Critical Success Factors

Every company is dependent upon two primary items: employees and capital. Strength comes from within. Each representative of the company is important in the long-term accumulation of customer loyalty and in the bottom line results of the operation. From the CEO to the accounting clerk, everyone has an impact on the success of the operation. Customers form their opinion of the company based upon whom they have contact with. If the receptionist does not answer the phone with a smile, the customer may formulate a poor opinion of the company. Businesses are restricted in growth by the limitations of resources. This calls for smart and strategic planning, combined with quality legal, accounting, and banking relationships.

Advice to Students

Expose yourself to as much diversity in school as possible. Not only in your classroom topics, but also in your contact with individuals both academically and socially. Whether you plan to work for yourself or with others, you are your best resource. Make yourself well-rounded; you will be able to offer your employer an invaluable asset. One of the best business-related features an individual can possess is resourcefulness. If you can solve a problem or add to a situation just by being creative, you can conquer all. Learn about information systems, accounting, and marketing even if they are not your major. Knowing all aspects of business can only help you understand your primary function in your career!

Summary

1. **Understand what it means to make the business case for a system.** Making the business case is the process of building and presenting the set of arguments that show that an information system is adding value to the organization and/or its constituents. To build the business case, you must first plan. Planning is important for making all significant business decisions, but it has become particularly important for IS investments because the rate of investment for information technology projects has skyrocketed. Factors influencing the increase in IT projects include the growth in technology use, the rise in end-user computing, the importance of effective human resource deployment of IS personnel, the increasing need for system integration, and the intensity of competition facing most organizations.

2. **Describe how to formulate the business case.** To formulate a business case for an information system, you must understand the nature of the industry—its stage of maturity, regulation, and the nature of its competition or rivalry. You must also understand the particular business strategy of your organization in order to make an effective business case for systems. In short, technology investments should be closely linked to the business strategy of the organization because these investments are becoming one of the major vehicles by which organizations can achieve their strategy. Besides business industry and strategic factors, other implementation-related factors must be considered when making the business case for systems, including the type of organization, its culture, and its political environment. These are firm-specific issues that affect the firm's ability to deploy and maintain new systems. After you gain an understanding of your organization's position in the marketplace, its strategy for investing in systems that add value, and firm-level implementation factors, you can quantify the relative costs and benefits of the system. Considering all of these factors simultaneously will help you formulate an effective business case.

3. **Present the business case for a system to help others understand the value that a system provides.** Presenting a business case for information technology investments is the process of trying to persuade the boss, steering committee, or board of directors to invest money in something you think is important to the business. In order to make a convincing presentation, you should be specific about the benefits this investment will provide for the organization. To do this, you must convert the benefits into monetary terms, such as the amount of money saved or revenue generated. If you have difficulty identifying specific monetary measures, you should devise some proxy measures to demonstrate the benefits of the system. A proxy measure is a substitute variable, such as customer contact, expressed on a five-point scale from low to high. Proxy variables are used in place of an information system's intangible benefits, which are difficult to quantify. Alternatively, you could develop a work profile matrix to help build the business case for a system. A work profile matrix summarizes the job and work categories and the time spent at each job for each type of work. A "before the system" matrix can be compared to a forecasted "after the system" matrix to identify changes in how personnel will spend their time. Convincing decision makers that a system will allow employees to spend more time on important activities, such as customer service, can help lead to a system's approval. Finally, make sure that you measure things that are important to the decision-makers of the organizations. Choosing the wrong measures can yield a negative decision about a beneficial system.

Key Terms

Making the business case

Information systems planning

System effectiveness

System efficiency

Organizational culture

Proxy variables

Work profile matrix

Review Questions

1. What does "making the business case" mean?

2. Describe several of the key factors that drive the need for IS planning.

3. In general, what is meant by the productivity paradox?

4. What is the difference between system effectiveness and system efficiency?

5. Describe some of the problems associated with measuring the productivity of decision support systems and strategic systems.

6. What are the two main reasons given to explain time lags between IT investment and IT payoff?

7. List the three factors you should consider when making the business case for an information system.

8. What is the difference between scale and scope in terms of business strategy?

9. List the different categories of costs and benefits that should be analyzed in a cost-benefit analysis.

10. How does a steering committee differ from the executives of a company?

11. What is meant by "selling to management," in regard to making the business case?

Problems and Exercises

◆ **Individual**   ◆ **Group**   ☞ **Field**   ◗ **Web/Internet**

1. Match the following terms to the appropriate definitions:

    _____ Making the business case

    _____ System effectiveness

    _____ System efficiency

    _____ Information systems planning

    _____ Organizational culture

    _____ Proxy variable

    _____ Work profile matrix

a. The set of mutually agreed upon values and practices that define what is acceptable in the organization and give the organization a unique climate or feeling

b. The extent to which the system functions or enables people to function in a way that avoids loss or waste of time, money, or other resources

c. The process of building and presenting the set of arguments that show that an information system is adding value to the organization and/or its constituents

d. Planning for the investment in and deployment of information systems that help people meet organizational strategies and objectives, given the organization's resource constraints

e. A substitute variable (such as customer contact) expressed on a five-point scale from low to high that is used in place of an information system's intangible benefit, which is difficult to quantify

f. The extent to which the system produces or is capable of producing or enabling people to accomplish desired results

g. A matrix consisting of job and work categories that is used to show how much time is spent by each of the job categories on different types of work

2. Discuss the following in a small group. After reading this chapter, it should be fairly obvious why an IS professional should be able to make a business case for a given system. Why, however, is it just as important for non-IS professionals? How are they involved in this process? What is their role in information systems planning?

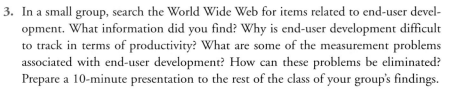

3. In a small group, search the World Wide Web for items related to end-user development. What information did you find? Why is end-user development difficult to track in terms of productivity? What are some of the measurement problems associated with end-user development? How can these problems be eliminated? Prepare a 10-minute presentation to the rest of the class of your group's findings.

4. What problems are associated with "raising the bar" of expectations for information systems? What should we really be looking at? What is the larger issue? Discuss this with a group of your classmates. Do they have the same opinions and ideas?

5. Why is it important to look at industry factors when making a business case? What effect might strong competition have on IT investment and use? What effect might weak competition have on IT investment and use? Why?

6. Argue for or against the following statement: "When making the business case, you should concentrate on the 'hot buttons' of the decision makers and gloss over some of the other details."

7. What role does the organizational culture play in IT investments? Is this something that can be easily adjusted when necessary? Why or why not? Who is in control of a firm's organizational culture? What do some of your classmates think about this? Do any of you have personal experiences with this issue?

8. Why can it be difficult to develop an accurate cost-benefit analysis? What factors may be difficult to quantify? How can this be handled? Is this something that should just be avoided altogether? What are the consequences of that approach?

9. Interview an IS manager at an organization with which you are familiar. Determine what business case for a system was the most difficult to justify to upper management. Determine what business case for a system was the easiest to justify to upper management. Why were these justifications viewed in this way? Was this manager successful with both? Why or why not?

10. Within a small group of classmates, describe any involvement you have had with making the business case for a system. To whom were you making the case? Was it a difficult sell? Why? Did you follow the guidelines set forth in this chapter? How did your business case differ from those of others in your group? Were you successful? Why or why not? Were they successful?

11. Consider an organization that is familiar to you. Of the five industry factors presented in the chapter (Porter's model), which is the most significant for this organization in terms of IT investment and development? Why? Which is the least significant? Why?

12. Discuss the following in a small group of classmates. Describe a situation from your own experience in which a system's cost-benefit analysis showed a negative result when based on tangible factors but the system was still implemented. Was the implementation decision based on intangible factors? Have these intangible factors proven themselves to be worth the investment in this system? Was it a harder sell because of these intangible factors?

13. Choose an organization with which you are familiar. Determine the length of time it has taken for various IT systems to show their productivity improvements. Was it a long time? Why did it take so long? Was it longer than expected? Why or why not? Search the Internet to find additional anecdotes about IT productivity improvements. You may want to search through CIO Magazine Online at http://www.cio.com/ to get started. How does this information compare with the organization you talked to?

14. Interview an IS manager at an organization with which you are familiar. Determine how this organization measures the productivity of end-user-developed applications and systems. Is it done at all? Is there an organization-wide procedure, or is it handled in each department? Has this issue been raised before? Does this manager feel it is a vital issue to pursue? Why or why not?

15. In the scenario that opened this chapter, Cheri's boss asked her to provide him "with some figures to demonstrate" the impact of the various systems on the performance of their organization. Why will it be difficult for Cheri to do this for all of the systems? Consider the fact that some systems are very old and that some are very new. How does this limit Cheri?

Real World Case Problems

1. Building Profitable IT

Rather than asking, "How do we create profits?" IT departments need to be asking, "How do we improve our company's performance in the areas that drive profits?" Recent articles in *Datamation* have discussed the business value of IT, focusing on linking IT projects to profit or business value. Even business managers have noted that the return on investment is too low. To make matters worse, many IT managers justify this low return based on technical terms and not on business value. Although business managers know the potential for information systems, there remains an understanding gap between knowing what can be done and what is actually done with IT. For example, in a manufacturing company, the key areas are product development, marketing, and distribution. In a medical insurance company, the key areas may be claims processing and membership services.

The Beta Group has worked with companies to make them understand that IT must directly support profit. Rarely does any IT create profit. Managers must use IT to help areas that are known to contribute directly to the profit of a company. The Beta Group suggests five principles that should be followed in making IT support profit. First, IT managers need to use a profit model to communicate with senior management. The CIO must use a model that specifies key areas of business performance measurement and IT's contribution to improving performance in these areas. Second, the IT profit model should describe the key areas of the business in terms of the profit drivers and how they are measured. Business performance measures are surrogates for financial performance. As the market share increases, the operating profit increases. Alternatively, as the service response time goes down, the operating income increases. Third, key business managers must help build the IT profit model and assess IT's impact on the profit drivers. In this case, the management team must be involved in ranking the order of projects based upon the relationship to profitability, the firm's strategies, and performance improvement objectives.

Fourth, the IT profit model should drive new project definitions. For example, when examining a backlog of projects, each should be evaluated in relation to the profitability gained from the projects. Fifth, different parts of IT will link differently to the IT profit model. The Beta Group suggests that the following model organizes IT into components for the purpose of connecting IT to business profit. The application portfolio is classified into must-have applications, without which the business cannot operate, and discretionary applications, which are intended to improve some part of the business function. Infrastructure is difficult to link to profit and operations, and support functions are generally the farthest away from the profit makers. IT profitability is a management program, not a computation. By examining the five profit model principles, we can determine the appropriate relationship between IT and profit.

a. What are some examples that demonstrate exactly how specific types of IT can lead to increased profits?

b. What is the value in involving business managers in determining how IT leads to increased profits?

c. Which is easier to link directly to profitability— new systems projects, maintenance of existing systems, improvements to the underlying network infrastructure, or IS operations and support functions? Why? Should the others be dropped or underfunded because they cannot be linked easily to profitability? Why or why not?

Source *Benson, Robert J. 1998. Building profitable IT.* Datamation *December/January, 74–76.*

2. Return on Assets: Asset-Management Software Can Cut Your Total Cost of Ownership

In a recent *InformationWeek* survey, nearly half of the companies stated that they have cut their total costs of ownership (TCO) by using tools that track software and hardware in their companies. At companies such as Florida Power and Light and Honda of America Manufacturing, the story is the same. Today, this kind of software tool is not just cutting costs, but is also tracking the physical and financial cycles of all IT assets. Even people are counted as investments.

After evaluating 30 different asset-management products, one of the big six accounting firms selected Main-Control because it had automated purchasing capabilities. Having

software that could take a company from start to finish, from the first requisition of IT assets to the disposal process, would allow for the centralization of IT buying. This new method does not come without expense. The manager estimated that the software plus the installation time cost more than $100,000.

In the days when mainframes were the only hardware, the tracking of assets was not so critical. However, today, with client/server architecture, what is on the desktop is crucial to the tracking process. Software licenses, maintenance, and support service costs need to be accounted for in addition to the hardware. The reduction of downtime is another factor in getting companies to use the software. Yet, with all of the needs and choices available in this market, the majority of companies don't use asset-management software. At Lockheed in Bethesda, Maryland, some groups do a physical inventory of property. Others outsource all workstation and desktop maintenance, including asset maintenance. To get the entire corporate picture, the departments must combine their notes.

Other reasons that companies do not use the software are that they feel they do not have the resources to commit to using it and that manual checks are sufficient. Those who use it disagree. They believe that the corporate infrastructure cannot be run effectively without it and that the financial picture would be different if it were not available.

a. Why has tracking IT assets in large firms become so complicated?

b. How are firms using asset-management software to cut their total cost of ownership of IT?

c. How would you make the case for buying and imple-menting asset-management software in a firm?

Source *Gilloly, Caryn. 1997. Return on assets.* InformationWeek *December 8, 44–56.*

References

Applegate, McFarlan, and McKenney. 1996. *Corporate information systems management: Text and cases.* 4th ed. Burr Ridge, Illinois: Richard D. Irwin, Inc.

Bakos, J. Y., and M. E. Treacy. 1986. Information technology and corporate strategy: A research perspective. *MIS Quarterly* 10(2): 107–120.

Belcher. L. W., and H. J. Watson. 1993. Assessing the value of Conoco's EIS. *MIS Quarterly* 17(3): 239–254.

Blodgett, M. 1998. NC or not NC. Information from: www.cio.com. Information verified: April 21, 1998.

Brynjolfsson, E. 1993. The productivity paradox of information technology. *Communications of the ACM* 36(12): 66–76.

Dragoon, A. 1998. Come and get IT. Information from: www.cio.com. Information verified: April 21, 1998.

Field, T. 1997. When bad things happen to good projects. Information from: www.cio.com. Information verified: April 21, 1998.

Hagendorf, J. 1998. Trying to keep pace—IT spending climbs, along with needs, costs. *Computer Reseller News.* Information from: www.techweb.com. Information verified: April 29, 1998.

Harris, S. E., and J. L. Katz. 1991. Organizational performance and information technology investment intensity in the insurance industry. *Organization Science,* 2(3): 263–295.

Leibs, S., and K.M. Carrillo. 1997. Research productivity—Replacing workers with IT doesn't guarantee maximum gains, finds a new study from Harvard: What does?: You may be surprised. *Information Week.* Information from: www.techweb.com. Information verified: April 29, 1998.

Pearson, D. 1998. Clear steering. Information from: www.cio.com. Information verified: April 21, 1998.

Porter, M. E. 1979. How competitive forces shape strategy. *Harvard Business Review* 57 (March-April): 137–145.

Sassone, P. G., and A. P. Schwartz. 1986. Cost-justifying OA. *Datamation,* Feb 15, 83–88.

Slater, D. 1998. Business line backers. Information from: www.cio.com. Information verified: April 21, 1998.

Violino, B. 1998. Here's what comes first. *InformationWeek,* April 20, 48–70.

Related Readings

Barua, Kriekel, and Mukhopadhyay. 1995. Information technologies and business value: An analytic and empirical investigation. *Information Systems Research* 6(1): 3–23.

Brynjolfsson, E., and L. Hitt. 1996. Paradox lost?: Firm-level evidence on the returns to information systems spending. *Management Science* 42(4): 541–558.

Cooper, R.B. 1994. The inertial impact of culture on IT implementation. *Information and Management* 27(1): 17–31.

Dos Santos, B.L., and K. Peffers. 1995. Rewards to investors in innovative information technology applications: First movers and early followers in ATMs. *Organization Science* 6(3): 241–259.

Earl, M.J., and D.F. Feeny. 1994. Is your CIO adding value? *Sloan Management Review* 35(3): 11–20.

Kivijarvi, H., and T. Saarinen. 1995. Investment in information systems and the financial performance of the firm. *Information and Management* 28(2): 143–163.

Kovacevic, A., and N. Majiluf. 1993. Six stages of IT strategic management. *Sloan Management Review* 34(4): 77–87.

Mahmood, Pettingell, and Shaskevich. 1996. Measuring productivity of software projects: A data envelopment analysis approach. *Decision Sciences* 27(1): 57–80.

Rai, Patnayakuni, and Patnayakuni. 1997. Technology investment and business performance. *Communications of the ACM* 40(7): 89–97.

Ross, Beath, and Goodhue. 1996. Developing long-term competitiveness through IT assets. *Sloan Management Review* 38(1): 31–42.

Weber, Y., and N. Pliskin. 1996. The effects of information systems integration and organizational culture on a firm's effectiveness. *Information and Management* 30(2): 81–90.

West, L.A. 1994. Researching the costs of information systems. *Journal of Management Information Systems* 11(2): 75–107.

Scenario: Organizing Systems at Your School

If you have a problem with one of your bills at your university, who do you contact? Alternatively, if you have a problem registering online for a class (see Figure 14.1) or checking online for the status of your accounts with the school's bursar's office, who do you speak to? What if you have a financial aid question? You might not realize it, but if you are at a relatively large school, you will probably have to speak with a different person for each of these computer-related tasks or problems.

If your organization is of at least moderate size, it probably has a relatively large staff of computing personnel who are organized in some fashion. Perhaps some of the personnel are in charge of operating and managing the school's host computers and networks. Others are probably in charge of maintaining the school's personal computer labs. Still other individuals are probably in charge of building and maintaining applications on campus, such as payroll, online registration, and fee payment.

If you are at a large university, a distinct group probably manages technology just within your particular area of the university, such as within the Business School. These individuals are likely physically separated from the computing personnel for the broader university, managed by different managers, and funded through separate budgets.

If your school is part of a larger, state-wide system, it may even have a separate computing systems and services group dealing specifically with computing needs across all campuses. Such a group might, for example, be in charge of developing an intercampus videoconferencing system for distance learning.

As schools increase in size, become more complex, and expand, their technology needs increase. As technology use grows and spreads throughout the school, the need to organize the computing facilities, information systems, and systems staffs becomes increasingly important as well. The same logic applies for business organizations.

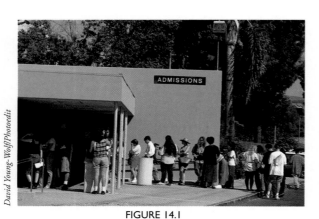

David Young-Wolff/Photoedit

FIGURE 14.1

Students waiting in line to register for classes.

Introduction

The purpose of this chapter is to discuss the proper organization of the information systems function and the proper location of the systems and systems staff within organizations. In previous chapters, we dealt with how systems are developed and acquired. In this chapter, we turn our attention to how the IS function within the firm is best organized to effectively build, acquire, and manage systems.

After reading this chapter, you will be able to do the following:

1. Describe the history, evolution, and role of the IS function within firms.

2. Explain the alternative structures and locations of the IS function within modern-day organizations and what works best under which conditions.

3. Understand the critical issues currently facing business managers with respect to the organization of the IS function.

4. Discuss the future of the IS function.

This is the last chapter in Part 5, "Information Systems Management" (see Figure 14.2). The focus is on how to best structure the IS function. How the IS area is structured in an organization greatly influences the execution of its business strategy. Additionally, given the rapid growth in technology use and the rapid pace of technological and organizational change, the management of the IS function has become an important concern for virtually all organizations. In this chapter, we describe the evolution of the IS function, how it is currently being managed, and several emerging issues that will challenge organizations to effectively organize and manage their IS resources.

The History and Role of the IS Function

Before 1950, organizations managed to function, sell, and compete without the help of computers. Indeed, "computer" was a job classification for a person who manually performed mathematical calculations. In the 1940s and early 1950s, early computers, such as ENIAC and UNIVAC, were nothing more than giant counting machines, used to automate and replace the counting and calculation tasks performed by humans. Furthermore, most organizations weren't equipped, either in structure or in spirit, to deploy and manage computers. This changed in 1952, when IBM began offering relatively affordable business computers. As computer use in businesses grew, so did the need for managing this new business resource and activity.

Management by Structure

In order to best manage resources, activities, and people in organizations, we tend to structure things. **Organizational structure**, which is typically represented in an organizational chart, includes four key characteristics (Daft, 1986):

1. Describes the allocation of tasks and responsibilities to individuals and departments throughout the organization.

2. Designates formal reporting relationships, including the number of levels in the hierarchy and the span of control of managers and supervisors.

3. Identifies the grouping together of individuals into departments and the grouping of departments into the total organization.

4. Includes the design of systems to ensure effective communication, coordination, and integration of effort in both vertical and horizontal directions.

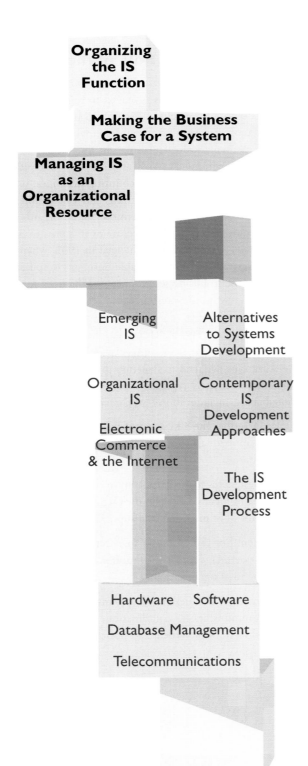

Organizing the IS Function

Making the Business Case for a System

Managing IS as an Organizational Resource

Emerging IS

Alternatives to Systems Development

Organizational IS

Contemporary IS Development Approaches

Electronic Commerce & the Internet

The IS Development Process

Hardware   Software

Database Management

Telecommunications

In the following sections, we trace the beginnings and evolution of computing in organizations from an organizational structure point of view. Recall the chapter-opening scenario, in which we discussed how schools such as the one you are attending buy computers and store them in special locations throughout the school. Similarly, these schools must hire systems personnel and organize them into groups that are placed somewhere in the organization. Business organizations must do the same thing, and these decisions about how to structure and where to place the information systems function within the firm can be very important.

An Outgrowth of the Accounting Department

Given that business computers had their beginnings as giant, electronic counting machines, they tended to be adopted in the 1950s as electronic accounting machines within the accounting and financial units of business organizations. In Figure 14.3A, we demonstrate where computers were typically placed and used within organizations with a traditional functional organizational structure. In these organizations, departments were organized along functional business lines, such as manufacturing, accounting, and personnel. Computers were placed within the accounting department.

Figure 14.3B demonstrates where computers are placed and used within organizations with a product group structure. In these organizations, people are grouped together by products or product lines. For example, for an automobile manufacturer with this kind of organizational structure, one group might be for smaller, economy cars; a second group might be for more expensive, luxury cars; and a third group might be for trucks. Each of these groups is self-contained, with its own manufacturing, accounting, marketing, and other functional departments. Under this type of organizational structure, computer use typically sprang up on its own within each of the various product divisions originally, each group controlling their own local accounting systems.

FIGURE 14.2

The big picture: focusing on the organization of the information systems function.

Early Beginnings of the IS Function

```
                    President
    ┌──────┬───────┬────────┬────────┬────────┐
Research and  Manufacturing  Accounting  Marketing and  Personnel
Development                              Sales
                               │
                          Electronic
                          Accounting
                          Machines
```

FIGURE 14.3A

A typical placement of computers within an organization with a traditional functional organizational structure.

FIGURE 14.3B

A typical placement of computers within an organization with a product group organizational structure.

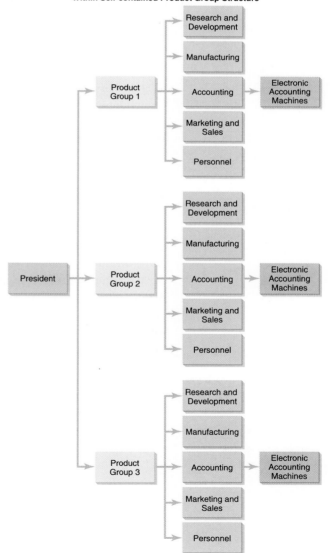

Within Self-contained Product Group Structure

In Figures 14.3A and 14.3B, which are organizational charts, we represent upper management with the sole President box, realizing that in some organizations there are often vice-presidents, chief operating officers, and other, second-level executives and managers. The same type of organizational structure and computer use origin tended to hold for organizations with a geographic organizational structure. In these organizations, separate divisions were located in different cities or countries, each self-contained, with its own business departments and its own computer use springing up within the accounting function.

The underlying theme that ran through each of these early uses of computers was that the businesses were using machines to automate accounting and other financial functions. The location, use, and control of the computing resource came under the purview of those in the accounting and financial functions of the firm.

Evolution of the IS Function

Through the 1960s, as more sophisticated mainframe systems and peripherals were developed and adopted for a variety of applications throughout organizations, the use of computers in and the spread of computer use throughout businesses increased. Computing in organizations had moved beyond merely automating human counting and calculating for accounting purposes. People in organizations began using computers throughout each of the functional areas of their firms. Because computer use was growing and spreading, it no longer made sense for the physical location and the management of the computing resource to be housed within the accounting function.

As Figure 14.4 demonstrates, new departments were created within the organizational structure for the sole purpose of managing the computing resource. In addition, because computers were being used to store and manage data for a variety of purposes, these new departments were often called data processing or electronic data processing. This change in the overall organizational structure tended to be the same whether a traditional functional structure, a product group structure, or another organizational structure was used. Although uses of computers evolved and spread throughout organizations, in many of the organizations clinging to tradition, the data processing function continued to be housed within the accounting function. Traces of this lineage still exist today. In any event, computer resources and their management tended to be fairly centralized. We'll talk more about what centralization entails, but for now we'll just say that **centralization** of computing within the firm means that the computing is located in and controlled from one place.

FIGURE 14.4

New departments were created within the organizational structure for managing the computing resource.

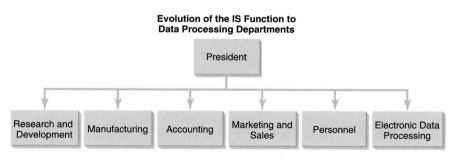

**Evolution of the IS Function to
Data Processing Departments**

Through the 1970s, the use and expansion of computing resources throughout organizations increased. Most firms stopped relying on just one central mainframe computer and began using distributed minicomputer class machines within separate functional areas or product divisions, particularly within the accounting and marketing functions. The computing resource within firms had graduated from being used to support data processing to being a complex system of mainframes, minicomputers, and dumb terminals. As a result, many organizations switched the label of the computing department from electronic data processing to management information systems or just information systems.

In Figure 14.5, we demonstrate the typical organization structure and location for the IS function during this era. The information systems department is off on its own, with the large computer hosts located and controlled by the IS department. The dotted-line relationship between the IS department and each of the other units of the firm represents the fact that these units were connected back to the IS department both literally (because their dumb terminals were connected back to mainframe and minicomputers back in the IS department) and figuratively (because the IS department had relatively centralized control of computing resources and the other business units were in a sense at the mercy of the IS department for these resources). During the 1970s, computers were most often physically located within the IS department in a central location, often called the computer center, although in some cases the computers were located within the various functional areas. In any event, the management and control of these computing resources was typically centralized within the IS department.

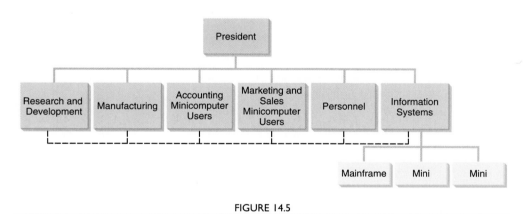

FIGURE 14.5

A typical organization structure and location for the IS function during the 1970s.

In the 1980s, organizations began using micro-, or personal, computers. In the mainframe and minicomputer markets, power and functionality grew and prices dropped. Computer use in organizations was taking off like wildfire. In addition, with the ease of use and low prices for personal computers, end-user computing spread. With telecommunications links both within and outside of organizations also growing, it was becoming even more difficult to centrally manage the computing resource, although many organizations still used a fairly centralized structure and approach to the IS function.

Figure 14.6 shows the typical location and approach to the IS function within the organization for this era of business computing.

FIGURE 14.6

A typical location and approach to the IS function during the 1980s.

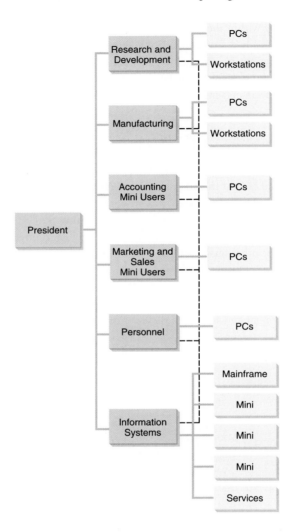

To better manage complex information systems, some larger organizations used a more decentralized structure and approach for the IS function, shown in Figure 14.7. **Decentralization** made sense given that the physical location of these computing resources was spreading throughout the firm—in many cases being deployed by the users themselves. With the continued difficulty for centralized IS functions to manage all of those systems and to please so many diverse users, we began to see the beginnings of poor relations between IS units and the other units within the firm. IS personnel simply could not keep up with so many diverse, mission-critical, quickly evolving demands for the IS department's time and resources. Ironically, while technology was increasingly being seen as an important organizational resource, most organizations still did not have a senior manager within the IS function who was of an executive rank.

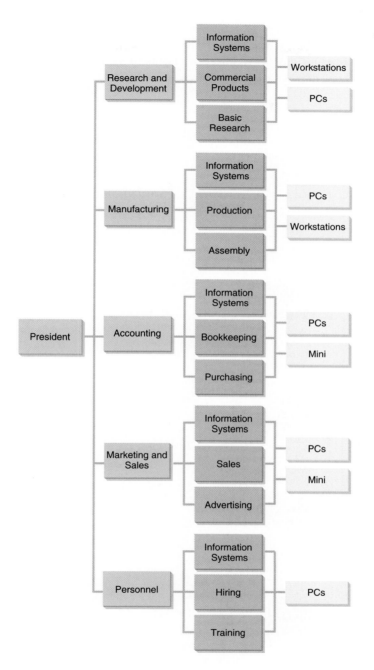

FIGURE 14.7

A more decentralized structure and approach for the IS function.

With the widespread use of and reliance on technology in the late 1980s and 1990s, organizations faced an intense need for systems integration and a solid enterprise-wide information system architecture. Organizations are now decentralizing the use of and responsibility for strategic technology throughout the organization, with greater and greater use of interconnected networks, client/server computing, and electronic connections to the outside world. At the same time, organizations are trying to centrally plan for and coordinate technology use. Now that technology is considered to be of greater strategic importance, the authority and responsibility within the IS function are being pushed up into the executive level. Figure 14.8 demonstrates the typical structure for the IS function in a modern organization.

FIGURE 14.8

A typical structure for the IS function in a modern organization.

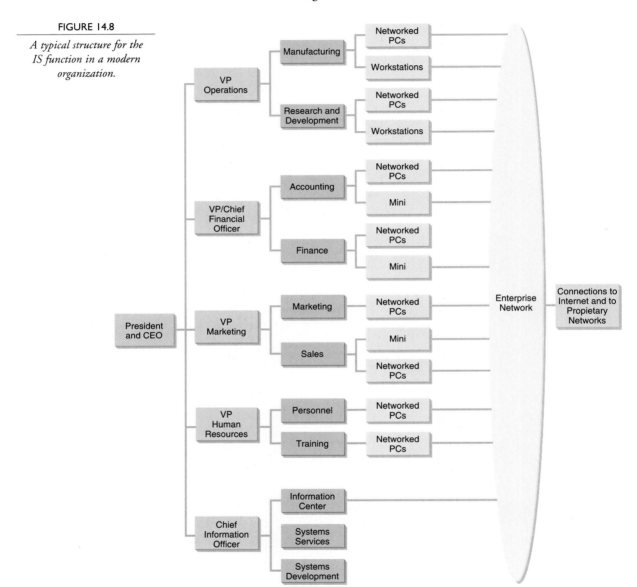

Alternative Structures for the IS Function

As Figure 14.8 shows, the use of technology has spread throughout the structure of most organizations. In the organization depicted in this figure, management of the IS resource is relatively centralized under a strong IS function with an executive-level chief information officer. The IS function, as depicted here, coordinates systems and information, provides services such as consulting and troubleshooting, and leads the development of new systems. However, in many firms today, some or all of these IS functions are pushed into each of the other functional areas of the firm. In any event, technology use is important and must be managed well one way or another, in a centralized fashion, a decentralized fashion, or in some hybrid of both.

Just as there are many different locations of the IS function within the overall firm, there are also myriad ways that the IS function itself can be structured. To a great extent, the structure of the overall organization and the centralization or decentralization of IS development, use, and management within the firm determine the nature and internal structure of the IS function itself. For example, drawing again on the scenario we used to open this chapter, if your school's computing resources and experts are spread throughout the school, it is likely that the information systems function within your school is relatively decentralized.

A Centralized IS Structure

Figure 14.9 shows a very traditional, relatively simple structure for the IS department, in which IS is centralized within the firm. In this case, the IS director is the head of the department, is a mid-level manager, and would most likely report to a higher-level manager or possibly the executive in charge of the accounting and finance arm of the firm. The IS department is primarily in the business of building and maintaining information systems for people in other functional areas of the firm. If this department were large, there would be separate managers for systems development and maintenance and for operations. Similarly, there would be project managers for new information systems and systems managers for existing systems.

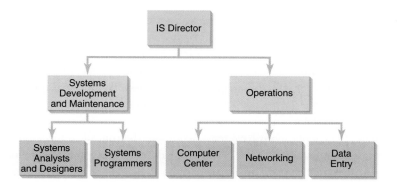

FIGURE 14.9

A traditional, simple structure for the IS department.

In Figure 14.10, we show a typical structure for a modern IS function within a firm where IS is relatively centralized. In this case, the CIO, the highest-ranking IS employee, performs duties that are strategic and long-term in nature and reports directly to the CEO. The IS director performs much of the day-to-day management of the IS function. It is also likely that there are separate managers for each of the primary and secondary units within the IS function. The IS group depicted in Figure 14.10 is responsible for building and maintaining systems, physically housing large hardware and networking equipment, providing consulting and other services to people throughout the firm, planning for new systems and for systems changes, and investigating new technologies and their potential uses.

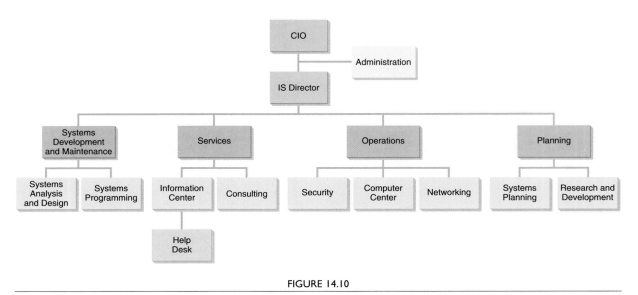

FIGURE 14.10

A more modern, centralized structure for the IS department.

(A BRIEF CASE) ─────── **Centralization at Rohm and Haas** ───────

Such a centralized approach to information systems exists at Rohm and Haas Company, a Philadelphia-based chemical manufacturer with offices and production facilities worldwide (Koch, 1998). David Stitely, CIO, has created an efficient, global IT presence that has proven to be effective. He has accomplished this presence through the creation of one corporate network, one email client, one configuration for desktop PCs, and one data center. This standardized infrastructure assures Stitely that the IT department will remain in control. In addition, it has proven to be cost effective. Decision making is also much easier now. To achieve greater effectiveness, the infrastructure has moved slightly off of the centralization model. The employees working in the various worldwide locations have their own unique styles and needs for decision support systems (DSS), so these DSS applications have remained under the control of the various business units. However, these applications must still use the corporate infrastructure for all of their data and communication. This departure from the purely centralized approach has not hindered Stitely's department. Instead, it has provided for a greater cohesiveness between the global nature of operations and the need for a unified IT architecture.

A Decentralized IS Structure

Figure 14.11, unlike Figure 14.10, shows a typical structure for a modern IS function within a firm where IS is relatively decentralized. Decentralization is more concerned with providing useful services to people throughout the firm who are deploying their own technologies by themselves; in managing the corporate network; in systems integration; in planning for systems growth, use, and change; and in helping to coordinate technology use across the firm's functional areas than the IS unit in Figure 14.10. Such a unit may not even have any serious hardware (for example, a mainframe or a mini-computer).

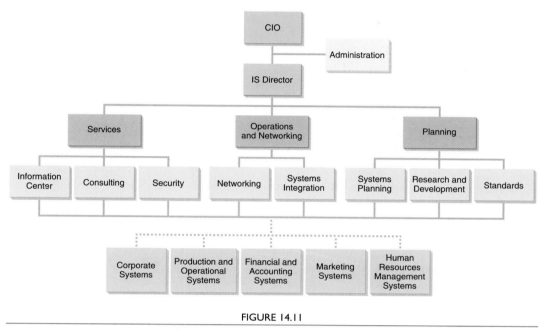

FIGURE 14.11

A modern, decentralized structure for the IS department.

Figure 14.11 depicts a manufacturing organization in which systems use is spread throughout many different functional areas of the firm—production and operations, finance and accounting, and marketing. These functional areas are shown at the bottom of the diagram with dotted-line relationships between them and the subunits within the IS function. This same model is also used for large firms with multiple divisions, for con-glomerates with multiple companies, and for firms with a product-based or geographi-cally based organizational structure. For these types of organizations, the diagram looks the same, except that instead of having each of the functional areas displayed at the bot-tom of the diagram, we would instead display each of the divisions, products, or global locations.

A Hybrid IS Structure at Nortel — A BRIEF CASE

In many companies, the IS function is organized in a **hybrid structure**, which is a mix-ture of centralization and decentralization. Northern Telecom Limited (Nortel), a man-ufacturer of telecommunications equipment, is a prime example of such a hybrid approach (Koch, 1998). Nortel wanted to create a seamless and homogeneous IT struc-ture for its global business. Yet, due to the way Nortel is organized into smaller, some-times competing business units, total IT integration just wouldn't work. Nortel's CIO, David Moores, states that they wanted to "square the circle" and have the best of both worlds—many small and independent business units working together as a global organization. The solution, which is to be completely implemented during 1998, involves the decentralization of certain functions and the centralization of others. Sales and R&D for each business unit will remain under the control of the unit, which will allow each business unit to serve itself and better enable it to bring in more business for Nortel. This is extremely advantageous in the fast-paced telecommunications industry, where quick responses and changes to meet customer demands are essential. However, all order fulfillment functions will become centralized. Under this architecture, after a business unit makes a sale, the sale will go through the centralized and global system. In the end, the centralized IT department will retain some of the control it needs, but the business units will run their own ship.

IS Personnel

In large organizations, no matter what type of organizational or IS structure is used, many different management positions are typically within the IS function. In Table 14.1, we describe several such positions. This list is not exhaustive; rather, it is intended to provide a sampling of IS management positions. Furthermore, many firms will use the same job title, but they are likely to each define it in a different way.

Table 14.1   Some IS management job titles and brief job descriptions.

Job Title	Job Description
CIO	Highest-ranking IS manager. Responsible for strategic planning and IS use throughout the firm.
IS director	Responsible for managing all systems throughout the firm and the day-to-day operations of the entire IS unit.
Account executive	Responsible for managing the day-to-day operations of all aspects of IS within one particular division, plant, functional business area, or product unit.
Information center manager	Responsible for managing IS services such as help desks, hot lines, training, consulting, and so on.
Development manager	Responsible for coordinating and managing all new systems projects.
Project manager	Responsible for managing a particular new systems project.
Maintenance manager	Responsible for coordinating and managing all systems maintenance projects.
Systems manager	Responsible for managing a particular existing system.
IS planning manager	Responsible for developing an enterprise-wide hardware, software, and networking architecture and for planning for systems growth and change.
Operations manager	Responsible for supervising the day-to-day operations of the data and/or computer center.
Programming manager	Responsible for coordinating all applications programming efforts.
Systems programming manager	Responsible for coordinating support for maintenance of all systems software (for example, operating systems, utilities, programming languages, and so on).
Manager of emerging technologies	Responsible for forecasting technology trends and for evaluating and experimenting with new technologies.

Job Title	Job Description
Telecommunications manager	Responsible for coordinating and managing the entire voice and data network.
Network manager	Responsible for managing one piece of the enterprise-wide network.
Database administrator	Responsible for managing database and database management software use.
Auditing or computer security manager	Responsible for managing ethical and legal use of information systems within the firm.
Quality assurance manager	Responsible for developing and monitoring standards and procedures to ensure that systems within the firm are accurate and of good quality.
Webmaster	Responsible for managing the firm's World Wide Web site.

As you can see from Table 14.1, the range of career opportunities for IS professionals is very broad. The mixture of skills needed to be successful differs, of course, depending upon the type of job and the job's level within the organizational hierarchy. Nonetheless, many studies have been aimed at helping us understand what knowledge and skills are necessary for a person in the IS area to be successful (see, for example, Todd, McKeen, and Gallupe, 1995). Interestingly, these studies also point out just what it is about IS personnel that makes them so valuable to their organizations. In a nutshell, good IS personnel possess valuable, integrated knowledge and skills in three areas—technical, business, and systems—as outlined in Table 14.2.

Table 14.2   IS Professional core competencies.

Domain	Description
Technical Knowledge and Skills	
Hardware	Hardware platforms, peripherals
Software	Operating systems, application software, drivers
Networking	Networking operating systems, cabling and networking interface cards, LANs, WANs, Internet
Business Knowledge and Skills	
Business	Business processes, functional areas of business and their integration, industry
Management	Planning, organizing, leading, controlling, managing people and projects
Social	Interpersonal, group dynamics, political
Systems Knowledge and Skills	
Systems Integration	Connectivity, compatibility, integrating subsystems and systems
Development Methodologies	Steps in systems analysis and design, systems development life cycle, alternative development methodologies
Critical thinking	Challenging one's and others' assumptions and ideas
Problem Solving	Information gathering and synthesis, problem identification, solution formulation, comparison, and choice

Technical Competency

These three areas of knowledge and skills—technical, business, and systems—are the core competencies that make IS professionals valuable to organizations. The **technical competency** area includes knowledge and skills in hardware, software, and networking. In a sense, this is the "nuts and bolts" of MIS. This is not to say that the IS professional must be a high-level technical expert in these areas. On the contrary, the IS professional must know just enough about these areas to understand how they work and how they can and should be applied. Typically, the IS professional manages or directs those who have deeper, more detailed technical knowledge.

The technical area of competency is, perhaps, the most difficult to maintain because the popularity of individual technologies is so fleeting. In Table 14.3, we list some technical skills areas that are currently popular. Many of these would not have appeared on this list a few years ago, and many will probably not appear on the list in a few short years.

Table 14.3   What technical skills are hot?

Languages	Development Tools
SmallTalk	PowerBuilder
Objective-C	Oracle Developer 2000
C++	JYACC JAM
C	Gupta SQLWindows
MicroFocus COBOL	Visual Basic
Java	Uniface
HTML/CGI Scripting	Lotus Domino
Operating Systems	**Networking**
Solaris	X.25
Windows NT Workstation	TCP/IP
HP-UX	
AIX	
OS/2	
MVS	
Windows	
Internetworking	**NOS LAN Administration**
Bay Networks	Banyan Vines
Cisco	Windows NT Server
3Com	IBM LAN Server
	Novell NetWare

RDBMS Administration	Systems Management and Support
Gupta SQLBase	Decision support systems
Sybase	Network management
Oracle	Project management
CA Ingres	Desktop/help desk support
Progress	
DB2	
Informix	
Applications	**Office/Email**
SAP	Lotus Notes
Oracle (applications)	Microsoft Exchange
PeopleSoft	POP Mailers

Business Competency

The **business competency** area is one that sets the IS professional apart from others who have only technical knowledge and skills. It is absolutely vital for IS professionals to understand the technical areas *and* the business and the technology/strategy fit. IS professionals must also be able to understand and manage people. These business skills propel IS professionals into project management and, ultimately, high-paying middle- and upper-level management positions.

Systems Competency

The **systems competency** area is another area that sets the IS professional apart from others with only technical knowledge and skills. Those who understand how to build and integrate systems and how to solve problems will ultimately manage large, complex systems projects, as well as manage those in the firm who have only technical knowledge and skills.

Perhaps now you can see why IS professionals are so valuable to their organizations. These individuals have a solid foundation in and integration of technical, business, and social knowledge and skills. Perhaps most importantly, they also have the social skills to understand how to work well with and motivate others. It is these core competencies that make IS professionals a hot commodity.

Critical Issues for the Locations and Structures of the IS Function

In this section, we outline three important issues that organizations face in determining where to locate and how to structure the IS unit. First, we contrast the centralized, decentralized, and hybrid organizational structures. Next, we describe the role that the IS unit often plays in organizational downsizing. Finally, we describe how the increasing focus on customer and user service is changing the structure and activities of many IS organizations.

From Centralization to Decentralization and Hybrid Models

When we say that an organization is centralized or decentralized, we are primarily talking about the extent to which decision-making authority is located toward the middle and higher ranks within the organizational hierarchy. If only the senior managers have the authority to make important decisions, then we would say that the organization is fairly centralized. If, on the other hand, decision-making authority is pushed down and throughout the organization, then we would say that the organization is decentralized. For example, consider an organization in which a salesperson or a low-level sales manager has the authority to decide whether or not to negotiate a price with a customer. In this instance, the organization is decentralized. If the salesperson or sales manager had to first get permission from a higher manager, then the organization would be fairly centralized in that instance.

Just as we can consider organizations centralized or decentralized with respect to decision-making authority, we can also discuss the relative degree of centralization with respect to the location and nature of the information systems function. As described previously, the IS function can be fairly centralized, with a strong IS unit that builds and maintains internal systems, enforces computing standards and purchases, and controls the computing resources in other similar ways. Alternatively, the IS function can be fairly decentralized, with systems development and control of computing resources located within the functional area units of the firm. The relative degree of centralization of the IS function has as much to do with the location of the IS unit and the computing resources as it does with the rules, regulations, authority, and control of those resources.

Whether or not to centralize or decentralize the IS function is a complex question with no simple answers. You can find unique advantages and disadvantages to centralization, decentralization, and hybrid models for the IS function. Which one to choose depends on many factors. Some of the primary strengths, weaknesses, and characteristics of the centralized, decentralized, and hybrid approaches are outlined in Table 14.4.

Table 14.4 Summary of centralized, decentralized, and hybrid characteristics.

	Centralized	Decentralized	Hybrid
Organizational goal	Internal efficiency, technical specialization, and quality	External effectiveness, adaptation, client satisfaction	External effectiveness and adaptation, plus internal efficiency
Operational goal	Emphasis on functional areas, including IS functional area	Emphasis on various business units	Emphasis on various business units, with some emphasis on the IS functional area
Planning and budgeting	Cost basis	Profit center basis	Varies
IS authority	IS managers	Unit managers	Shared between unit and IS managers
Strengths	■ Economies of scale ■ In-depth technical specialization development ■ Easier to coordinate, integrate, and standardize across units	■ Suited to fast change in unstable environment ■ Client satisfaction because system responsibility and contact points are clear ■ Units adapt to differences in their areas ■ Useful in large, complex, distributed organizations	■ Organization can achieve adaptability and coordination in some areas and efficiency and economies of scale in others ■ Better alignment between corporate-level and unit-level goals

	Centralized	Decentralized	Hybrid
Weaknesses	■ Slow response time to environmental changes ■ Decisions and workload may pile up, overload ■ Less innovation ■ Restricted view of organizational goals	■ Lose economies of scale ■ Poor coordination, integration, and standardization across units ■ Lose in-depth technical competence and specialization	■ Potential for excessive administrative overhead ■ Potential conflict between IS/corporate technology goals and unit-specific technology goals

Source *Daft, D. 1986. Organization theory and design. St. Paul, Minnesota: West Publishing Company.*

Centralizing clearly has benefits, whether it be the IS function, the marketing function, the accounting function, or any other business activity. Rather than having many different people throughout the firm worrying about the same things and making the same decisions independent of one another, it makes sense to coordinate and make these decisions in concert. However, too much centralization can be a bad thing. For example, in the U.S. Department of Defense, people are required to provide elaborate cost justifications and up to eight levels of signatures to buy a laptop computer costing less than $2,000.

Similarly, the benefits to a decentralized approach seem to be clear. It makes sense to let those who are down in the trenches, closest to the customer, make the decisions about how they will use computing resources. They know far more about their needs than do those far removed from the situation. However, decentralization of computing resources and decision making can cause expensive redundancies. For example, J.C. Penney & Co. managers consolidated their decentralized information systems department in late 1993, saving approximately $12 billion per year over their previous system. They created a centralized Information Technology Control Center, eliminating the previous four data centers and reducing their workforce by 288 employees, approximately 20 percent of the IS staff. The new center has approximately 100 staff members who receive very specialized training and education and are reported to be better able to manage J.C. Penney's important computing and information resources (Fox, 1995).

Which Is Better and/or More Popular?

Let's get back to the question. Which is better, centralization, decentralization, or some hybrid model? Well, it depends. Is there a trend towards centralization or decentralization of the IS function? No. Some firms are moving away from centralization, while others are moving toward centralization. The smart firms are figuring out which model works best for their particular situation and then organizing the IS function accordingly.

The centralization decision should be determined by the nature of the industry in which the firm competes, the firm's overall strategy, the overall organizational structure, the firm's IS strategy, the nature of the firm's IS function, and other factors (Brown and Magill, 1994). In the following sections, we'll talk about several of the firms included in the Brown and Magill case study, which tell us a lot about the fit between the structure of the IS function and the context in which it resides.

When a Decentralized IS Structure Fits

In their study of the structure of the IS functions within many different firms, Brown and Magill found a highly decentralized IS structure in a firm where the situation naturally called for this type of structure. This manufacturing conglomerate had a corporate strategy of unrelated diversification; recent growth, primarily via acquisition; a focused differentiation business strategy for each operating company; a decentralized line-of-business firm structure; and a culture and reward system that placed very strong emphasis on business unit autonomy. This situation naturally called for a decentralized IS structure, which the firm had. Decentralizing the IS structure made sense given this context; people within each of the business units needed to make their own decisions about technology. Indeed, people throughout the firm reported high levels of satisfaction with this approach to organizing the IS function.

When a Centralized IS Structure Fits

Brown and Magill also describe a diversified manufacturer that has a highly centralized IS structure. This firm has a corporate strategy of related diversification, related core businesses that compete in mature industries on cost and product differentiation, an overall firm structure that is less decentralized than the previous firm, and a history of strong central direction and monitoring. Given this context, the centralized IS structure fits; it makes sense to coordinate technology decisions in this situation. Overall, people in this firm were satisfied with the organization of the IS function and were happy with the economies of scale and connectivity that were achieved as a result of this approach.

When to Move Away From a Centralized IS Structure

Next, Brown and Magill describe a petrochemical firm and an insurance firm that changed from relatively centralized IS structures to hybrid structures. Both of these choices were made in response to a misalignment between the firms' new overall organizational characteristics and a centralized IS structure. At both firms, a new CEO initiated a corporate restructuring and a new corporate strategy, which included differentiation, organic (that is, informal or adaptive) decision processes, more autonomous business units, and decentralization of the locus of responsibility for many corporate functions (including responsibilities for the systems development and application planning functions). The members of the firms perceived the need to better align IS and the new operating plan for the companies. In addition, workers were dissatisfied with the old systems approval/ prioritization process, with the exorbitant amounts of money that were previously spent on the mainframe computer operation, and with the relatively little business unit control over the uses of technology resources. For this particular context, members of these organizations were ripe for a loosening of the tight, centralized grip on the IS function.

When to Move Toward a More Centralized IS Structure

Brown and Magill describe two other firms, a different petrochemical firm and an insurance firm, which abandoned hybrid forms of structure for their IS functions and recentralized the IS structures. In both firms, there was an emergent, shared belief in the strategic role of IS. In addition, people believed that some existing systems were of little strategic value to the firm. To make matters worse, members of these firms were dissatisfied with the level of progress in new system development projects, and there were deficiencies in IS performance capabilities. In one firm, some of the IS projects were out of control, and IS budgets were too high. It was decided that these firms needed to centralize the locus of control for system approval and prioritization. In addition, there was now to be greater alignment among IS plans across business units and between the IS plan and the corporate strategic plan.

The important theme that runs through these cases is that there must be a good fit, or match, between the structure of the IS function and the context in which it resides. In addition, nothing is perfect. While there may be disadvantages to the centralized approach, they may be outweighed by the advantages of this approach for a given context of organizational and environmental factors. Finding the best fit doesn't necessarily mean finding a perfect fit.

Downsizing of Organizations and IS Departments

Many organizations that are **downsizing**, or rightsizing, as some call it, are looking toward the IS function and technology as the lever for simultaneously shrinking the organization and making it more productive. In short, they are using technology to streamline business functions and, in some cases, to slash costs and replace people. Although this approach may not be fair for the people who lose their jobs, many firms are forced to do this to remain competitive and, in some cases, to continue to exist. Such uses of information systems have interesting implications for the size and structure of organizations and for the size and structure of the IS function.

One such example is provided by Motorola's General Services Sector, which moved from mainframes to distributed UNIX servers, enabling them to cut their total information technology costs in 1993 to less than 1 percent of the unit's total sales. The move has reportedly helped them remain competitive in the cellular telephone business, where prices have dropped 30 percent per year since 1989. In addition to the cost savings, Motorola managers believe that getting off mainframes has enabled people throughout the firm to access data without having to go through the IS department (Grantham, 1994).

In some companies, managers are shrinking the IS budget and department while they shrink other parts of the firm. They are asking end users to take on many of the traditional IS tasks. For example, at Sikorsky Aircraft, Senior Industrial Engineer Eric Stegman coordinates the acquisition and development of technology projects for 150 employees in the quality assurance department. Stegman estimates that he spends 60 percent of his time performing information systems-related tasks and working closely with the remaining IS staff members. In other companies that have used this approach, managers report that the new roles and relationships seem to be working out well (LaPlante, 1994).

——————— **Downsizing and Streamlining with IT at Unisys** ——

Information systems can also be used to assist management with change. Unisys Corporation, the often-troubled information systems company, has had its share of ups and downs in the last ten years (Baatz, 1995). From a high of 93,000 in 1988, the company now has fewer than 50,000 employees. At several points, the company was barely able to pay its debts and remain in business. Those employees who did remain after the layoffs, cutbacks, and downsizing were never too sure of their own future. Yet, Unisys is still around and doing quite well. CEO James Unruh attributes this to the use of technology for internal communication with the employees of Unisys. Unruh runs a monthly, interactive television program from his corporate office, in which he answers questions from employees worldwide. It is a live show, and the calls are not screened, providing a sense of openness and a more personal feeling. In addition, Unisys has begun communicating and sharing information that was previously inaccessible to the employees through their LANs. As top management has continued to share information, mid-level managers have begun sharing information with their employees as well. Therefore, the employees feel a strong connection to management and the company. They were now getting honest and quick answers to their questions and concerns. The information systems industry is volatile, and it changes quickly. Unisys still faces an unsure future, but the employees are more confident in management and believe in the company.

From Ownership and Control to a Consulting Organization and a Service Mentality

Early IS departments typically had huge project backlogs, and IS personnel would often deliver systems that were over budget, completed much too late, difficult to use, and didn't always work well. In addition, many of these old-school IS personnel believed they owned and controlled the computing resources, that they knew better than users did, and that they should and would tell users what they could and couldn't do with the computing resources. Needless to say, this wasn't a recipe for success and good relationships. Indeed, relations between IS personnel and users within the firm were often sour and were sometimes bitter.

For a long time, users were forced to put up with the poor service and the poor attitude. Then technology started to become significantly better—faster, easier to build and use, and cheaper. As a result, end users began to develop their own computing applications, as we have described in previous chapters. Disgruntled users simply said, "the heck with the IS staff; we'll build our own systems." In many cases, they did just that, and they did it well, much to the dismay of some of the IS managers.

Business managers soon became more savvy about technology and the possibilities and opportunities that it offered, and they reasoned that the possibilities and opportunities were too great to simply let the IS function whither away as end-user development took over. In addition, smart, concerned IS personnel realized that they needed an attitude adjustment. Some people believe that the changes in the nature of technology forced people to cooperate more. For example, the shift from mainframes to client/server may have forced people within the IS function to improve their operations *and* their relationships with people in other units of the firm. Client/server required a new kind of relationship between IS and other people throughout the firm (Stevens, 1994). As a result of these forces, in modern IS units that do a good job, the atmosphere, attitude, and culture are very different and much more sensitive and responsive than they used to be.

In these more responsive IS units, the personnel have taken on more of a consulting relationship with their users. The IS personnel believe that, fundamentally, they are there to help the users solve problems and be more productive. Indeed, in many cases, the IS personnel do not even refer to the users as "users." They are "clients" or "customers." This new attitude is a major change from the old days, when IS personnel didn't want to be bothered by users and thought that the techies knew better than users. It is unfortunate that this old-school mentality still exists in some organizations.

The new IS culture is much like that found in successful service organizations. Think of how customers are treated in service organizations, such as Smith Barney or Andersen Consulting, or in product-based organizations where service is also important, such as McDonalds or Nordstrom. Great service to the customer is absolutely critical, and employees do everything they can to please customers. They often live by the credo that "the customer is always right."

The same holds for IS units that have taken on this new **service mentality**. The IS personnel do everything they can to ensure that they are satisfying their systems customers within the firm. They reach out to customers and proactively seek their input and needs, rather than waiting for customers to come in with systems complaints. They modify the systems at a moment's notice just to meet customer needs quickly and effectively. They celebrate the customer's new systems ideas rather than putting up roadblocks and reasons why the new ideas can't or won't work. They fundamentally believe that the customers own the technology and the information and that the technology and information are there for the customers, not for the systems personnel. They create help desks, hot lines, information centers, and training centers to support customers. These service-oriented IS units structure the IS function so that it can better serve the customer.

The implications of this new service mentality for the IS function are staggering! It is simply amazing how unproductive it can be when the IS personnel and other people within the firm are at odds with one another. On the other hand, it is even more amazing how productive and fun work can be when people in the IS function work hand in hand with people throughout the organization. Technology is, potentially, the great lever, but it works best when people work together to use it and not against each other.

Developing a Consulting Mentality at Texas Instruments   A BRIEF CASE

The notion of a consulting mentality could not have been more appropriate than at Texas Instruments, the Dallas-based electronics manufacturer (Koch, 1998). When Pallab Chatterjee became CIO at Texas Instruments, the IT department had a very tight grip on decision making. Chatterjee soon realized that the control was so tight that the business units were literally scared to ask the IT department for anything, and they relied on "underground" IT projects without the help of the IT department. To combat this problem, Chatterjee has reorganized Texas Instruments' worldwide IT department and services into two subunits. The first, referred to as the worldwide utility, is responsible for the physical networks, the data center, the numerous local LANs, and the global WAN. This group is mainly responsible for efficiency, control, and reliability. The second subunit, the consultants, is composed of all IT staff members who are not a part of the utility group. These consultants work both at the central, corporate level as well as at the business unit level. At the business unit level, these consultants are able to work closely with the managers to develop and manage systems that do not require centralized control. The systems that do require more control are handled by the consultants at the corporate level. This model has proven to be very successful for Chatterjee and Texas Instruments because business units are no longer afraid to ask for corporate support and know that if they need the corporate support, it will be there.

The Future for the IS Function

The current emphasis on the use of technology within businesses is not a fad. Indeed, all indicators point to the increased use of technology and organizations' continued awareness of the importance of technology, both as a tool for productivity and as a vehicle for achieving competitive advantage and organizational change. In this section, we briefly discuss some likely future trends.

Continued Growth and Development

As we have discussed throughout this book, by all accounts, the future of the IS field looks very promising. All current growth indicators and forecasts for the future show that the use of information systems in organizations, the development of new technologies and systems, and, perhaps most importantly, the demand for IS personnel will continue to grow. If you had to choose a field to go into based on its growth potential and opportunities, you would most likely choose IS.

We are reminded of a classic movie line. In the 1967 Best Picture of the Year, *The Graduate*, Dustin Hoffman's character, Benjamin Braddock, arrives home after graduating from college to attend a party thrown for him by his parents (see Figure 14.12). In a now famous movie punch line, the character Mr. McGuire, a family friend, advises Benjamin on his future.

Mr. McGuire: I just want to say one word to you...just one word.

Benjamin Braddock: Yes, sir.

Mr. McGuire: Are you listening?

Benjamin Braddock: Yes, sir, I am.

Mr. McGuire:...Plastics.

The Graduate, Embassy, 1967.

Courtesy Photofest.
FIGURE 14.12

Dustin Hoffman as Benjamin Braddock in The Graduate; *will it be plastics or not?*

If the movie script for *The Graduate* were rewritten today, the punch line for that classic movie line would undoubtedly be "information systems." It is easy to predict growth and change, but predicting *exactly* what and how things will change is not easy.

The Difficulty in Predicting Technology Change ——— A BRIEF CASE

The future of information systems, information technology, and its effect on businesses can never be properly predicted (Dertouzos, 1997). Yet, that will not stop us from relaying some predictions for the future! Michael Dertouzos has been the head of MIT's Laboratory for Computer Science since 1974. He is a consultant to the White House and numerous Fortune 500 companies, as well as to many foreign governments. Some of his predictions are discussed as follows.

The future of computing will be an information marketplace, a "collection of people, computers, communications, software and services that will be engaged in the intraorganizational and interpersonal informational transactions of the future." The transactions will be based on the processing and communication of information, rather than on the more physical and material goods of today's world. A key change in the structure of the modern organization will be the increase in communication and alliances, both within and between organizations and with suppliers and customers. The result of this increase will be flatter organizational structures and a greater organizational intelligence.

A cultural change as a result of greater computing will concern telecommuting and remote work sites. If telecommuting and remote work site trends continue to grow, Dertouzos believes that the current delineations between cities and suburbs will be lost, as more personal service businesses—restaurants, cleaners, law firms, and so on—emerge in the suburbs to cater to this resident population of workers. The suburbs will slowly begin to look more like cities, and the cities will lose many of the characteristics that make them distinct from suburbs. Dertouzos does not even attempt to predict what technology will be like. Unlike organizational structures and work environments, which usually change over long periods of time, technology changes very rapidly and in many directions at once. To predict what technology will be like in 10, or even 20, years from now is extremely difficult and almost guaranteed to be incorrect because of this pace. Who knows if Dertouzos's predictions will come true? They seem logical and definitely possible, but so many other possibilities may occur instead. We'll just have to wait and see.

Pervasiveness and Spread of IS Throughout the Organization

As information systems are used more broadly throughout organizations, IS personnel often have dual-reporting relationships—reporting to both the central IS group and the business function they serve. Therefore, at least some need for centralized IS planning, deployment, and management continues—particularly with respect to achieving economies of scale in systems acquisition and development and in optimizing systems integration, enterprise networking, and the like. Even in organizations that are decentralizing technology and related decisions, a need for technology and related decisions to be coordinated well across the firm still persists. This coordination is likely to continue to happen through some form of a centralized (or at least, centrally coordinated) IS staff. Organizations are likely to continue to want to reap the benefits of IS decentralization flexibility, adaptability, and systems responsiveness, but it is equally likely that they won't want to, and will not be able to, forego the benefits of IS centralization—coordination, economies of scale, compatibility, and connectivity.

Changing Skill Set and Human Resource Planning

Given the trend toward pushing people from the IS staff out into the various business units of the firm, and given the need for people within each of the functional areas of the business to have technology skills, there is clearly a need for people who know the technology side and the business side of the business well. We suspect that the need for people to play these boundary-spanning roles will continue. Many of these people will be hired into and located within the IS departments of firms, but they are likely to spend a lot of their time working out in the business unit with their clients. Indeed, their work space is likely to be physically located out in the business unit. Staffing the IS group with these kinds of boundary spanners is and will continue to be critical to the success of the IS group and to the success of the organization.

Career Prospects and Opportunities

Although technology at some levels continues to become easier to use, there is still and is likely to continue to be an acute need for people within the organization to have the responsibility of planning for, designing, developing, maintaining, and managing technologies. Much of this will happen within the business units and will be performed by those with primarily business duties and tasks, as opposed to systems duties and tasks. However, we are a long way from the day when technology is so easy to deploy that a need no longer exists for the person wearing primarily a systems hat. In fact, many people believe that this day may never come. Although increasing numbers of people will incorporate systems responsibilities within their nonsystems jobs, there will continue to be a need for people with primarily systems responsibilities. In short, IS staffs and departments will likely continue to exist and play an important role in the foreseeable future.

While many organizations are downsizing, and while some are shrinking their IS staffs, overall hiring within IS is growing like crazy and is predicted to continue in this way through the 21st century (see Chapter 1, "Information Systems Overview"). With hiring of systems personnel in a variety of positions at a fever pitch, and with the management of technology a critical business issue, it is not likely that IS departments will go away or even shrink significantly. Indeed, all projections are for growth of IS both in scale and scope.

The future opportunities in the IS field are likely to be found in a variety of areas, which is good news for everyone. The diversity in the technology area can embrace us all. It really doesn't matter much which area of IS you choose to pursue—there will likely be a promising future there for you. Even if your career interests are outside IS, being an informed and strong user of information technologies will greatly enhance your career prospects.

Since the first computer in the early 1950s, the amazing advancements in computer-based information systems have been matched only by the radical change in perspectives toward, and increased value placed on, information systems by organizations today. In all respects, the IS field is likely to continue to be changing constantly and growing in its vital importance to organizations. We know of no other field in which you can be so intimately involved with the awesome power of technology and can experience such unparalleled growth, constant renewal, and tremendous opportunity. We, in the field of MIS, live in an exciting time, and we look forward to the future with anticipation and awe. If the next 45 years of IS are anything like the previous 45 years, we're in for a wild, wonderful ride.

Talking with...

R. W. (Rick) Ransdell, Education Executive, Midwestern Area at IBM

Educational Background

B.A. in English Literature, DePaul University

Job Description

Mr. Ransdell and his team are responsible for profitable revenue growth and (best of industry) customer satisfaction across the Midwestern education market, which includes all K–12 schools and higher education campuses across a 12-state geographical area.

Critical Success Factors

Understand your customers' industry and business. Develop and execute business strategies based upon value-added solutions that are responsive to real customer requirements. Exercise teamwork.

Advice to Students

Develop a passion for what you do. Communicate—listen more than you talk. Be adaptable and flexible—change is constant. Develop skills that customers value. Be a team player.

ETHICAL PERSPECTIVE: THE ETHICS OF RE-ENGINEERING VERSUS DOWNSIZING

In the late 1980s and early 1990s, we saw two trends emerge in the business world that have caused many debates. The first of these is downsizing. Downsizing means that a company is either making surgical cuts to their operations, such as getting rid of a division, line of business, or a specific department, or they are making across-the-board employee cuts (that is, reduction in forces, or RIFs).

There are many reasons for downsizing, including slowed business with little hope for a prolonged increase, too many workers from misguided hiring plans, declining or negative profits, new technology that reduces the need for employees through automation, or a move to become more lean and more competitive. By downsizing, a company can quickly cut costs and increase profits (or at least profit potential). Companies cannot just get smaller, they have to also become more efficient, literally becoming lean and mean firms that can do more with less.

The second trend is re-engineering, or business process re-engineering. With this approach, people in organizations rethink and redesign each of their core business processes (for example, order fulfillment), cutting out anything that does not add value, streamlining remaining processes, and finding ways to use technology to automate processes. The net effect may in fact be a downsized organization, but if the re-engineering is done well, even the downsized organization should be more efficient and effective. Oftentimes, pure downsizing activities are falsely advertised as re-engineering efforts, leaving many in the work world bitter about re-engineering.

Pure re-engineering efforts should not necessarily leave people bitter and out of work. Hammer and Champy Hammer (1993), early proponents of re-engineering, describe it as a thoughtful, inclusive process of wiping the slate clean and figuring out how to run the organization as it should be. Indeed, if done correctly, re-engineering efforts involve people in the redesign process and include the retraining of employees for different tasks, technologies, functions, and responsibilities. In some cases, re-engineering necessitates some downsizing, but probably not at the level of firms that are simply cutting thousands of jobs to cut costs.

This is not to say that re-engineering is good and that downsizing is bad. Indeed, these are just management tools or approaches. A tool or approach isn't necessarily bad per se; rather, these tools and approaches can be used in good or bad ways. What is of interest here is the role that information systems are playing in contemporary downsizing and re-engineering efforts. Information systems play a crucial, enabling role in downsizing and re-engineeering. In fact, many people see technology as the driver for downsizing and re-engineering; technology enables companies to automate and get rid of people.

It is true that technology has enabled managers to streamline their organizations, doing more with fewer people. However, it probably is not accurate to say that advances in technology and increased uses of information systems are causing downsizing and re-engineering. Environmental factors are causing business firms to become more competitive, which is forcing them to streamline and improve, and technology has enabled this to happen. In any event, technology is being used to displace people. Robotics and other manufacturing technologies are displacing "blue collar" workers, and business information systems are displacing "white collar" workers. Indeed, throughout the 1970s and 1980s, entire cadres of middle-level managers, who were primarily paper pushers, were replaced by information systems in information-intensive businesses, such as the insurance industry.

Some people take this as a great offense and argue against technology spread in organizations either in their words (for example, writing against technology adoption) or in their actions (for example, sabotaging technology in organizations). Ted Kaczynski (the Unabomber) was convicted of doing both in a very extreme, negative way. In any event, there is an interesting parallel between today's technology nay-sayers and the Luddites of the turn of the century. Ned Ludd was believed to have led displaced workers in England at the turn of the century to revolt against the increased use of automated equipment (such as looms) to replace workers. Luddites went so far as to destroy the then "modern" equipment and businesses that used it. Modern-day Luddites are fighting the same battle, but over different types of technologies.

Questions for Discussion

1. Should re-engineering always precede downsizing? Why or why not?

2. Is there too much reliance on using technology to solve what are probably just poor business practices to begin with?

3. What responsibilities to employees do organizations have?

INTERNATIONAL PERSPECTIVE: THE WORLDWIDE IT SERVICES MARKET WILL NEARLY DOUBLE IN FIVE YEARS

The shortage of technology professionals—combined with the complexity of implementing enterprise resource planning systems, the rapid pace of new technologies, and the Year 2000 dilemma—has ignited the IT services industry to reach nearly $350 billion worldwide this year.

To accommodate that growth, IT services providers are developing innovative packages, and many are beginning to penetrate the lucrative small and mid-sized business market. According to Dataquest estimates, the global IT services market will nearly double over the next five years, reaching $622 billion. These figures reflect revenue from hardware and software maintenance, consulting, systems integration, outsourcing, and education and training.

Corporate executives who want their IT organizations to work as business partners are a major force behind this growth and, as partners, they're focused on increasing revenue and profits. "Unless the IT organization figures out ways to add value," says Robert Hanson, VP of marketing for Dockers Khakis at Levi Strauss & Co. in San Francisco, "[it should] divest and outsource."

At IBM Global Services, outsourcing services for the small to mid-sized market initially were offered in the same way they were offered for large companies—through total outsourcing agreements—says Kathy Dodsworth-Rugani, director of small-to-medium business services at IBM Global Services. Then the company began catering to the demand for selective sourcing, in which management of only a few elements of a client's IT infrastructure, such as mid-range computing or help desk services, is outsourced.

Now IBM is moving to network-based offerings in which "clients can plug in without worrying about hardware, software, or access to skills," Dodsworth-Rugani says.

For example, IBM provides access to Lotus Notes for more than 1,000 lawyers in Australia and online accounting applications for new businesses in Hungary through a dedicated line to a data center in the United States. These services are offered on a per-user, per-month fee basis, so companies can quickly calculate the costs of supporting new employees, says Dodsworth-Rugani.

All told, small to mid-sized businesses worldwide will spend $141 billion on IT services in 1998, according to IBM estimates. IBM's growth rate in the segment is a healthy 22 percent per year, says Dodsworth-Rugani.

Questions for Discussion

1. Why are small to mid-sized firms around the world spending so much on IT services? Why aren't they spending this money to build their own permanent, internal IT capabilities?

2. Why would firms in Australia and Hungary use a data center in the United States?

3. How should an IT consulting firm train its consultants to provide IT services abroad? In what ways can a firm prepare its employees and IT specialists to work with external consultants from another country?

Source From Caldwell, Bruce. 1998. Technology services: The worldwide IT services market will nearly double in five years: What's behind this boom, and what does it mean for your company? Genesis of a new service area. InformationWeek, April 6. Reprinted by permission.

Summary

1. **Describe the history, evolution, and role of the IS function within firms.** Computers had their beginnings in organizations in the 1950s as electronic accounting machines. During this period, computers and computer-related personnel were typically housed in accounting departments. Through the 1960s, more sophisticated mainframe systems and peripherals were developed and adopted for a variety of applications throughout organizations. In sum, the use of computers in organizations and the spread of computers throughout organizations increased. Computing in organizations had moved beyond merely automating human counting and calculating for accounting purposes. During this period, new departments were created to manage the computing resources. These departments were commonly called electronic data processing departments. Through the 1970s, the use and spread of computing resources within organizations increased. Larger firms stopped relying on just one central mainframe computer and began distributing minicomputers into separate functional areas or product divisions. As the application of technology broadened, the name for the group responsible for managing the computing resources also changed—to information systems or management information systems. In the 1980s, organizations began using micro-, or personal, computers, and in the mainframe and minicomputer markets, power and functionality grew and prices dropped. Computers became much less expensive and much easier to use. As the numbers of users increased, so did the complexity of managing the computing resources. Many organizations struggled with finding the right way to manage their technology resources; some organizations centralized control, while others decentralized control. In the 1990s, networks and the interconnection of systems and data became the norm. As a result, many organizations have decentralized the use of and responsibility for using technology throughout the organization but have centralized the planning and control of infrastructure and databases in order to more easily deploy organization-wide systems. It is during the decade of the 90s that the top IS manager joined the executive ranks as the chief information officer.

2. **Explain the alternative structures and locations of the IS function within modern-day organizations and what works best under which conditions.** The IS function can be structured in a myriad of ways. In a centralized structure, the IS director heads the department, acts as a mid-level manager, and most likely reports to a higher-level manager or possibly the executive in charge of the accounting and finance arm of the firm. In an alternative centralized structure, the CIO reports directly to the CEO, and the IS function is a peer with other business functions, such as marketing, accounting, operations, and finance. In a decentralized structure, the IS group is linked with the functional areas of the business in order to better serve a broad and diverse user community.

3. **Understand the critical issues currently facing business managers with respect to the organization of the IS function.** Determining the structure and management of the IS function is a complex decision that many organizations struggle with. Different structures are more appropriate for some organizations than for others. The appropriate structure must match the strategy and goals of the organization. Rapid change is causing many organizations to change and evolve the structuring of the IS function. One outcome of the rapid change in the business world is downsizing of the organization and of the IS department. In fact, it is becoming very common for organizations to shrink other parts of the firm as well as the IS department. At the same time, the organizations ask end users to take

on many of the traditional IS tasks. In many modern IS departments, the IS personnel have a service orientation and play the role of consultants to end users and the functional areas of the business, while users take on broader roles. This change in orientation is helping organizations gain greater benefits from their IT investments.

4. **Discuss the future of the IS function.** The future is difficult to predict. Nonetheless, there will be broad and continued growth for IS applications. The career opportunities for IS professionals will increase at a rapid pace, making the management of the IS function and the IS human resources an important part of managing all modern organizations.

Key Terms

Organizational structure

Centralization

Decentralization

Hybrid structure

Technical competency

Business competency

Systems competency

Downsizing

Service mentality

Review Questions

1. What was the original definition of the term computer?

2. Within which business units were the first computers adopted back in the 1950s?

3. Describe the evolution of the MIS function from the 1950s to the 1980s.

4. Describe three of the modern approaches to the organization of the MIS function.

5. Identify at least five different job titles within IS management and briefly describe their respective responsibilities.

6. Which business unit holds the formal IS authority within a centralized IS management structure?

7. List at least three strengths of a decentralized IS management framework.

8. What may cause a conflict between IS/corporate technology goals and unit-specific technology goals within a hybrid IS organizational structure?

9. Who are the clients, customers, and consultants within the modern IS department?

10. Why is downsizing such an important and critical information systems issue?

11. How does the changing skill set of members of an IS department affect hiring practices?

Problems and Exercises

Individual   **Group**   **Field**   **Web/Internet**

1. Match the following terms to the appropriate definitions:

   ____ Centralization

   ____ Decentralization

   ____ Organizational structure

   ____ Hybrid structure

   ____ Business competency

   ____ Downsizing

   ____ Technical competency

   ____ Systems competency

   a. The anatomy of the firm, providing a foundation or framework within which the firm functions

   b. Using technology to streamline business functions and become more productive

   c. Computing resources and/or decision making reside within a single body or group within the organization

   d. Knowledge and skills in systems integration, development methodologies, critical thinking, and problem solving

   e. Knowledge and skills in hardware, software, and networking

   f. Knowledge and skills in business, management, and social processes

   g. Computing resources and/or decision making reside within the IS functional area, as well as in various business units throughout the organization

   h. Computing resources and/or decision making reside in various business units throughout the organization

2. In a 100 percent centralized IS department, is it necessary to have a CIO? Why or why not?

3. In your opinion, which organizational structure is better—centralization or decentralization? (Assume that this is an either-or question.) Why do you feel one is better than the other? How do your fellow classmates feel about this? Do they agree with you?

4. Given the advantages of a hybrid organization of the IS department, why don't all organizations move to a hybrid structure? Search the World Wide Web for hybrid IS department organization. Could you find any relevant information? Did this information clarify the differences between centralized, decentralized, and hybrid?

5. In an organization that promotes end-user development of applications, do you feel a centralized, decentralized, or hybrid organizational structure of the IS department is best? Why? If you choose hybrid, describe what aspects of centralization and what aspects of decentralization would exist.

6. What would happen in a decentralized structure if two or more departments wanted to purchase new hardware or equipment? Compare these purchases to those made under a centralized structure. Describe how this could affect the profitability of large organizations over the long term.

 7. In a decentralized structure, why might IS employees lose in-depth technical competence and specialization? What could an organization do to counter this?

 8. Discuss the following in a small group. How will a downsizing effort likely affect the organizational structure of the IS department within an organization? Will it likely move more toward centralization or more toward decentralization? Why?

 9. How has the shift from mainframes to client/server technologies affected the relationships between IS personnel and other employees in many organizations? Why has this happened? Discuss this with fellow classmates. Is this just a fad for the current state of technology or will it continue with future technologies? Why?

 10. Each member of a small group should do the following. Choose an organization with which you are familiar. Determine where (business unit) and when the first computers were used within this organization. When did the IS department come into existence? Is it a part of the accounting unit? Are computers currently used within all the business units? If not, why not? After gathering this information, prepare a 10-minute presentation to the rest of the class of your findings.

 11. Using the same organization from the previous question, determine the evolution of the structure of the IS department in terms of its centralization. Did it begin as centralized or decentralized? How is it organized now? If it changed, why did it? Are any changes in the works for the near future?

 12. Based on your previous work and/or professional experiences, describe your relationships with the personnel in the IS department. Was the IS department easy to work with? Why or why not? Were projects and requests completed on time and correctly? What was the organizational structure of this IS department? How do your answers compare with those of other classmates?

 13. Each member of a small group should do the following. Consider an organization that is familiar to you. Of the approximately 20 IS management job titles outlined in this chapter, how many exist in this organization? Are the responsibilities the same as those defined in this chapter? What other positions are there? Do these titles match any of the job descriptions from the chapter's list? Why are there differences, if any? Compare your answers across the group. What have you learned about the jobs within information systems?

 14. Consider an organization that is familiar to you that you feel is operating with the wrong IS structure. Why is this organization's IS department poorly structured? What changes would you make? How would this affect the organization as a whole?

15. As a small group, conduct a search on the World Wide Web for job placement services. Pick at least four of these services and find as many IS job titles as you can. You may want to try The Monster Board at http://www.monsterboard.com/. How many did you find? Were any of them different than those presented in the chapter? Could you determine the responsibilities of these positions based on the information given to you?

16. Interview an IS manager (or appropriate person) at an organization whose IS department practices a service mentality towards the other business units and personnel. When and why did this organization make the change to this approach? Alternatively, was this approach always in place? Have their been tangible benefits? intangible benefits?

17. The IS support group within the School of Business at Indiana University changed their name from "Business Computing Facility" to "Technology Services." Along with the change in name came an appropriate change in services and offerings to their clientele. Ford IT units are another example. Find an example of an organization that changed the external name of its IT or IS unit but did not change the internal structure or attitude. Why were these not changed as well? Was the name change merely to make it sound better to the outsider? Has anything been done to correct this problem?

18. Based on the scenario that opened the chapter, set out in a small group to determine how your college or university manages computing for faculty, staff, and students. Is it highly centralized or highly decentralized? Alternatively, is it a mix of the two? What is the name of this functional unit? Does the name make sense?

Real World Case Problems

1. The Education of Marc Andreessen.

Marc Andreessen, co-founder of Netscape, had led a charmed life. That is, until the fourth-quarter reports for 1997 started coming in. It was obvious that corporations were not purchasing Netscape as fast as necessary for Netscape Communications Corp. to continue on the same course of action. The $88-million loss and the firing of 400 of Netscape's 3,200 employees have caused analysts to begin to question the company's ability to survive.

Only four years earlier, Marc Andreessen, at 22 years old, had left college and arrived in California seeking fame and fortune. With his cohorts, he launched the Internet gold rush. With the initial public offering of the company, his net worth soared to $171 million. By the age of 24, he was on the cover of *Time*. He was proclaimed to be the next Bill Gates. But Gates was not going to let that happen—he also was going after the Internet business and wanted to be the king of it. Microsoft was out to crush Netscape and started giving away much of the Internet Explorer software to start this process. Andreessen now is in the fight of his life to save his company. He has learned just how fast fortunes can be gained and lost in Silicon Valley and will have to prove himself all over again.

Andreessen occupied the relatively insulated position of chief technology officer, and just as the troubles started to mount, he was promoted in July 1997 to executive vice-president in charge of Netscape's 1,000-person product-development group. This move gives him a crucial role in the fighting for Netscape's survival. He now has to make hard product choices to help Netscape regain momentum. In his past position, he felt sidelined by his absence of direct management responsibilities and deadlines and felt that quality was slipping, but he had no authority to act on these problems. By entering this new position, he became central to the company again. He is now more committed to saving Netscape from the clutches of Microsoft. Over the past few years, he has also changed his image from one of tee shirts, sandals, and sports cars to one of expensive suits and a Mercedes sedan, but this doesn't compensate for his questionable management skills. With the speed of new products on the Internet, his youth and inexperience may be hard to overcome. He now knows his earlier claim that the Internet would put operating systems such as Windows out of business was totally incorrect. On weekends he meets with CEO Barksdale to discuss issues and problems in order to become more skilled in management techniques. He knows that he has a long way to go at Netscape and is determined to see Netscape survive.

a. What are the differences between Andreessen's previous position at Netscape as chief technology officer and his new position as vice-president of product development? Why is this change important to Netscape? to Andreessen?

b. Will it be difficult for the once techie Andreessen to become more of a business manager? Why or why not?

c. Why do small high-tech companies and high-tech entrepreneurs often have trouble growing (even when there is sufficient demand for their products and plenty of cash flowing)?

Source *Hamm, Steve. 1998. The education of Marc Andreessen,* BusinessWeek, *April 13, 85–92.*

2. Chase Manhattan Names Two CIOs.

When Dennis O'Leary was promoted to deputy to Boudreau, the vice-chairman in charge of consumer activities worldwide, his position was filled by two people. Carl Morales was selected as CIO for national consumer services, reporting to O'Leary. Morales will also be responsible for development and implementation of technology strategy and the migration to enterprise technology, along with the daily operations.

Rick Mangogna became CIO for the Global Bank, reporting to Layton, vice-chairman for global markets, and to Sponholz, vice-chairman in charge of Chase Technology Solutions and the bank's administrative services. Mangogna will also continue to manage global markets and international technology, along with the Global Bank's systems architecture and developing technologies. Additionally, Chase formed a Technology Governance Board to address IT standards, architecture, and risk policies, as well as administrative matters. Sponholz chairs the 11-member board, which includes Layton, O'Leary, Morales, and Mangogna.

a. For what reasons might Chase have named two CIOs?

b. In what ways might it not be a good idea for a corporation to have two CIOs?

c. What role does Sponholz play? Is it a good idea to have him as the head of the Technology Governance Board rather than one or both of the CIOs? Why or why not?

Source   Caldwell, Bruce. 1998. *Chase Manhattan names two CIOs.* InformationWeek, *March 9, 164.*

References

Baatz, E.B. 1995. Corporate healers. Information from: www.cio.com. Information verified: April 22, 1998.

Brown, C. V., and S. L. Magill 1994. Alignment of the IS functions with the enterprise: Toward a model of antecedents. *MIS Quarterly* 18(4): 371–403.

Daft, D. 1986. Organization theory and design. St. Paul, Minnesota: West Publishing Company.

Dertouzos, M.L. 1997. *CIO Magazine,* April 15. Excerpt from *What will be: How the new world of information will save our lives.* Information from: www.cio.com. Information verified: April 22, 1998.

Fox, B. 1995. Centralized data center means efficiency for Penney. *Chain Store Age* 71(3): 157.

Grantham, T. 1994. Motorola unit slashes IS costs. *Computerworld,* July 18, 48.

Koch, C. 1998. Can federalism fly? Information from: www.cio.com. Information verified: April 22, 1998.

LaPlante, Alice. 1994. The end-user invasion. *Computerworld,* July 18, 93.

Stevens, D. 1994. Reinvent IS or Jane will. *Datamation,* December 15, 84.

Strassmann, P. A. 1995. The politics of information management: Policy guidelines. New Canaan, Connecticut: The Information Economics Press.

Todd, McKeen, and Gallupe. 1995. The evolution of IS job skills: A content analysis of IS job advertisements from 1970 to 1990. *MIS Quarterly* 19(1): 1–28.

Related Readings

Benjamin, Dickson, and Rockart. 1985. Changing the role of the corporate information systems officer. *Management Information Systems Quarterly* 9(3): 177–188.

Brown, C.V., and S.L. Magill. 1994. Alignment of the IT function with the enterprise: Towards a model of antecedents. *Management Information Systems Quarterly* 18(4): 371–403.

Brynjolfsson, E. 1994. Information assets, technology, and organization. *Management Science* 40(12): 1645–1662.

Igbaria, Parasuraman, and Badawy. 1994. Work experiences, job involvement, and quality of work life among information systems personnel. *Management Information Systems Quarterly* 18(2): 175–201.

Kumar, Ow, and Prietula. 1993. Organizational simulation and information systems design: An operations level example. *Management Science* 39(2): 218–240.

Malone, T.W. 1997. Is empowerment just a fad?: Control, decision making, and IT. *Sloan Management Review* 38(2): 23–35.

McLean, Kappelman, and Thompson. 1993. Converging end-user and corporate computing. *Communications of the ACM* 36(12): 78–92.

Nelson, R.R. 1991. Educational needs as perceived by IS and end-user personnel: A survey of knowledge and skill requirements. *Management Information Systems Quarterly* 15(4): 503–525.

Olson, M.H., and N.L. Chervany. 1980. The relationship between organizational characteristics and the structure of the information services function. *Management Information Systems Quarterly* 4(2): 57–68.

Rockart, Earl, and Ross. 1996. Eight imperatives for the new IT organization. *Sloan Management Review* 38(1): 43–55.

Tavakolian, H. 1989. Linking the information technology structure with organizational competitive strategy: A survey. *Management Information Systems Quarterly* 13(3): 309–317.

10BASE-T: A network standard (also called Twisted Pair Ethernet) using a twisted-pair cable with a maximum length of 100 meters. The cable is thinner and more flexible than the coaxial cable used for the 10BASE-2 or 10BASE-5 standards.

Adaptive maintenance: Making changes to an information system to make its functionality meet changing business needs or to migrate it to a different operating environment.

Alpha testing: Testing performed by the development organization to assess whether the entire system meets the design requirements of the users.

Application sharing: A feature of desktop videoconferencing that allows two or more people in separate locations to collaborate using software on their personal computers.

Application software: Software used to perform a specific task that the user needs to accomplish, such as entering an order for a product or composing and printing a letter.

ASCII (American Standard Code of Information Interchange): The standard for translating binary information into text and numbers.

Assembler: A type of computer program that converts software written in assembly language into machine language.

Asynchronous Transfer Mode (ATN): A method of transmitting voice, video, and data over high-speed LANs.

Attenuation: A decrease in the power of an electric signal as it is sent over increasing distances.

Audio input: Voice and sound input to a computer.

Audiotex system: A type of computer telephone integration system that uses prerecorded choices organized in menus. These choices allow a caller to select the desired information from the audio menu by pressing buttons on a touch-tone phone.

Automated attendant system: A type of computer telephone integration system that answers incoming calls. The system allows the caller to enter the desired extension, select the person from a list, or leave a message in a person's voice mailbox.

Automating: The use of technology to perform faster, easier, and/or less expensively what was previously performed manually or with different technology.

Automating mentality: Viewing information systems as a means to automate.

Backbones: A high-speed central network to which many smaller networks can be connected.

Bandwidth: The transmission capacity of a computer or communications channel. The bandwidth represents how much binary data can be reliably transmitted over the medium in one second.

Bar code/optical character reader: Special types of scanners that interpret magnetic bars or characters as input.

Batch input: A type of data input for which you enter a batch of information at one time.

Batch processing: Processing of information by collecting information (for example, transactions) until a specified time and then processing that information as a group.

Benchmarking: Comparing your organization's value chain and associated costs with those of organizations you emulate in order to improve your organization's productivity and competitive advantage.

Beta testing: Testing performed by actual system users, who test the capabilities of the system with actual data in their work environment.

Bit: The smallest unit of information in a computer—a single 0 or 1.

Browser: A software program that provides a method of navigating the World Wide Web and using Internet services via a graphical user interface.

Bus network: A network topology in which all stations are connected to a single open-ended line.

Business competency: Knowledge and skills in business, management, and social processes.

Business information systems: Software applications that are developed to perform the organization-wide operations of the firm.

Byte: A measure of information stored on a computer; one byte equals eight bits, or about one typed character.

Cache memory: A type of primary memory that the CPU uses to store information it uses often.

CD-ROM (compact disc–read-only memory): A type of secondary memory that has a huge storage capacity. CD-ROMs are small discs that have microscopic pits burned onto them for representing information.

Centralization: The extent to which authority, decision making, resources, and so on are located centrally within the firm or are distributed throughout the firm.

Centralized computing: Computing model in which all processing occurs at a large central computer and users interact with the system through the use of terminals.

Chief information officer (CIO): An executive-level individual who has overall responsibility for the information systems component within the organization. The CIO is primarily concerned with the effective integration of technology and business strategy.

Client: Any device or software application that makes use of the information or services provided by a server.

Client/server architecture: A distributed processing system in which a client application that needs data or software gets it from a server that is the source for some or all of the needed data or software.

Coaxial cable: A transmission medium (cable) consisting of a conductor surrounded by plastic insulation and an outer braided copper or foil shield.

Coding: The process of transforming a message into a predetermined set of symbols.

Collaborative computing: Computing model in which two or more networked computers are used to accomplish a common processing task.

Collisions: A condition in which two or more workstations transmit messages onto the network simultaneously.

Command-based interface: Computer interface that requires the user to enter text-based commands to instruct the computer to perform specific operations.

Competitive advantage: When an organization has an edge over rivals in attracting customers and defending against competitive forces.

Compiler: A software program that translates a programming language into machine language.

Computer-Aided Software Engineering (CASE): Software tools that provide automated support for some portion of the systems development process.

Computer kiosk: A system that provides a touch screen to users that allows them to gain information and services without the need of a human attendant.

Computer program: A set of coded instructions written in a programming language that directs the hardware circuitry to operate in a predefined way.

Computer telephone integration (CTI): The integration of computers, fax boards, and the telephone switches with the public telephone network in order to provide customers with organizational information accessible through the telephone network.

Continuous presence: The capability of a videoconferencing system to continuously show all locations in a multiparty videoconference.

Corrective maintenance: Making changes to an information system to repair flaws in its design, coding, or implementation.

CPU: The main microprocessor chip, composed of millions of tiny transistors, which is used to control the computer.

Critical Success Factor (CSF): A methodology for collecting system requirements that helps identify the things that must go well to ensure success for a manager or organization.

CSMA/CD (carrier sense multiple access/collision detection): A network access control method in which a station wanting to transmit first listens to the network and only transmits if the network is idle.

Customer contact: The amount and nature of interaction that an organization has with its customers and that its customers have with the organization's people, processes, systems, and data.

Customized application software: Software that is developed based on specifications provided by a particular organization.

Data: Unformatted information, such as words and numbers.

Data dictionary: A repository that describes data types, uses, storage requirements, and rules.

Data flows: Data moving from one place in the system to another.

Data mart: A small-scale data warehouse that contains a subset of the data for a single aspect of a company's business—for example, finance, inventory, or personnel.

Data mining: Sorting and analyzing the information stored in organizational databases, data warehouses, or data marts.

Data model: A representation of entities and their relationships in the real world.

Data type: Format for the data stored within a field.

Data warehouse: An integration of multiple, large databases and other information sources into a single repository or access point that is suitable for direct querying, analysis, or processing.

Database: A collection of related data organized in a way that facilitates data searches.

Database administrator: A person responsible for the development and management of the organization's databases.

Database management system (DBMS): A software application with which you can create, store, organize, and retrieve data for one or many databases.

Database server: The part of a client/server database system running on a server that provides database storage and access to client workstations.

Decentralization: An information systems structure in which computing resources reside within the IS functional area as well as in various business units.

Decision Support System (DSS): A special-purpose information system designed to support organizational decision making, primarily at the managerial level.

Decision trees: A graphical representation of a decision situation.

Decode: The process of transforming a set of predetermined symbols into a message so that it can be understood.

Desktop videoconferencing: The use of integrated computer, telephone, video recording, and playback technologies—typically by two people—to interact with each other using their desktop computers from remote sites.

Developmental testing: Testing performed by programmers to ensure that each module is error free.

Digitizing: The process of converting information into a digital form.

Direct conversion: Changing from an old to a new system by beginning the new system and discontinuing the old at the same time.

Direct data access: A data access method in which information is accessed by moving directly to the information.

Discussion database: A feature of many groupware systems that lets multiple users around the world post messages, post documents, and file attachments to a common area. It also allows anyone with access to the database to view the contents and participate in the discussion.

Disintermediation: The process of taking all of the non-value-adding steps out of interacting with a customer.

Distributed computing: Computing model in which separate computers work on subsets of tasks and then pool their results by communicating on a network.

Documentation: The set of books and instructions that accompanies the computer program. Documentation is designed to assist the user in successfully operating the computer program.

Dot-matrix printer: A paper-based output device that uses small dots to print text and graphics on paper.

Downsizing: Using technology to streamline business functions and to become more productive.

Electronic commerce (EC): The online exchange of goods, services, and money within firms, between firms, and between firms and their customers.

Electronic data interchange (EDI): 1. Computer-to-computer communication in which information is exchanged using previously agreed upon formats. 2. The online sale of goods and services between firms, transacted over proprietary networks.

Electronic mail: The exchange of electronic data between people via networked PCs.

Encapsulation: The grouping of data and instructions into a single object in object-oriented programming languages.

End-user development: A systems development method whereby users in the organization develop, test, and maintain their own applications.

Enterprise network: A WAN that connects all of a single location's LANs.

Entity: Things about which we collect data, such as people, courses, customers, and products.

Event-driven: Programming language characteristic that allows the development of programs to execute based on user-requested events rather than a linear sequence through the program.

Executive information system (EIS): An information system designed to provide information in a very aggregate form so that managers at the executive level of the organization can quickly scan it for trends and anomalies.

Executive level: The top level of the organization, where executives focus on long-term strategic issues facing the organization.

Expert system (ES): A special-purpose information system designed to mimic human expertise by manipulating knowledge—understanding acquired through experience and extensive learning—rather than simply information.

External acquisition: The process of purchasing an existing information system from an external organization or vendor.

Extranet: The use of the Internet between firms.

Facilitator: An expert at running JAD meetings who helps the group work effectively during the session.

Fax-on-demand system: A type of computer telephone integration system that enables a user to select documents from a vocal menu or enter a document number and then receive the selected documents on a fax machine.

Fiber-optic cable: A transmission medium consisting of a light-conducting glass or plastic core, surrounded by more glass, called cladding, and a tough outer sheath.

Field: Individual pieces of information about an entity, such as a person's last name or social security number, that are stored in a database cell.

Fixed disk: A type of secondary storage that uses direct data access and high-speed magnetic disks that are permanently installed inside a computer.

Floppy disk: A type of secondary storage that uses direct data access and removable magnetic disks.

Form: 1. A collection of blank entry boxes, each representing a field, that is used to enter information into a database. 2. A business document that contains some predefined data and may include some areas where additional data is to be filled in, typically for a single record.

Fourth-generation languages (4GLs): Enable users to "ask" an information system to provide certain information by typing English sentence–like commands into a system.

Functional area information systems: A cross-organizational-level information system designed to support a specific functional area.

Functions of management: The primary tasks performed by managers, which include planning, organizing, leading, and controlling.

Global network: A WAN spanning multiple countries that may include the networks of several organizations.

Graphical user interface: Computer interface that enables the user to select pictures, icons, and menus to send instructions to the computer.

Group support systems: Computer-based information system used to support collaborative, intellectual, goal-directed work.

Groupware: Computer-based information systems designed to enable group members to electronically communicate, collaborate, and coordinate their activities across time and distance.

Hierarchical database model: A DBMS approach in which entities are described in a parent-child relationship.

High-frequency radio: A transmission medium that uses high-frequency radio signals to broadcast data to fixed or mobile nodes on a network.

Hybrid structure: An IS function organization that is a mixture of centralization and decentralization.

Hypertext: Text in a Web document that is highlighted. When the user clicks on this text, it evokes an embedded command, which goes to another specified file or location and brings up that file or location on the user's screen.

Hypertext Markup Language (HTML): The standard method of formatting World Wide Web pages using a language that operates through a series of codes placed within a text document.

Informating: The use of technology to provide information about its own operation and the underlying work process that it supports.

Informating mentality: Recognizing that information systems can be used as a vehicle for organizational learning and change.

Information: Data formatted in such a way that it has additional value.

Information repositories: A centralized location for information.

Information systems: Combinations of hardware, software, and telecommunications networks that people build and use to collect, create, and distribute useful data in organizations.

Information systems planning: 1. A formal organizational process for assessing the information need of an organization in which the systems, databases, and technologies for meeting those needs are identified. 2. Planning for the investment in and deployment of information systems. This planning helps people meet organizational strategies and objectives given the organization's resource constraints.

Information systems resistance: Efforts to ignore, counteract, or defeat an information system.

Information technology: Machine technology (mechanical or electric devices) that is controlled by or uses information with the assistance of computing and/or networking technologies.

Infrared line of sight: A transmission medium that uses high-frequency light waves to transmit data on an unobstructed path between nodes on a network.

Inheritance: A characteristic of object-oriented programming languages that requires lower-level software, or children, to inherit the characteristics of a high-level, or parent, software.

Inkjet printer: A paper-based output device that sprays ink onto paper to form text and graphics.

Intangible benefits: Benefits that are not easily measured in dollars or with any certainty.

Intangible costs: Costs that cannot be easily measured in dollars or with any certainty.

Integrated services digital network (ISDN): A standard for worldwide digital communications.

Interface: The way in which the user interacts with the computer.

Internet: A growing network of interconnected networks that supports individual users as well as users from business, government, research, and educational institutions.

Internet service provider (ISP): A company that provides Internet access and services. For individuals, services are typically dial-up access, electronic mail accounts, and the posting of personal Web pages. For organizations, total Web site hosting, design, continuous connection services, or some subset of these services are commonly provided.

Internetworking: Communication among devices across multiple networks.

Interpreter: A software program that translates a programming language into machine language one statement at a time.

Intranet: The use of the Internet within a business.

IP datagram: A data packet that conforms to the IP specification.

Joint Application Requirements (JAR) and **Joint Application Design (JAD)**: Group-based methods for collecting requirements and creating system designs.

Joystick: A type of pointing device that works by moving a small stick that sits in a holder; selections are made by pressing buttons located near or on the holder.

Keyboard: An input device you use to enter text and data by typing.

Knowledge: A body of governing procedures, such as guidelines or rules, that are used to organize, manipulate, and integrate data and information in order to make it suitable for a given task.

Knowledge manager: A position in organizations responsible for setting policies and making decisions on the creation, retirement, and content of discussion databases.

Laser printer: A paper-based output device that uses a laser beam to burn text and graphics onto paper.

Learning organization: An organization that is skilled at creating, acquiring, and transferring knowledge and at modifying its behavior to reflect new knowledge and insights.

Light pen: A type of pointing device that works by placing a pen-like device near a computer screen; selections are made by pressing the pen to the screen.

Local area network (LAN): A group of computers at one location that share hardware and software resources.

Lower CASE: CASE tools designed to support the implementation and maintenance phases of the systems development life cycle.

Machine language: A binary-level computer language that computer hardware understands.

Magnetic tape: A type of secondary storage that uses sequential data access by magnetizing information onto plastic tape.

Mainframe: A very large computer that is used as the main, central computing system for many major corporations and governmental agencies.

Making the business case: The process of building and presenting the set of arguments that show that an information system is adding value to the organization and/or its constituents.

Management information systems (MIS): An information system designed to support the management of organizational functions at the managerial level of the organization.

Managerial level: The mid level of the organization, where functional managers focus on monitoring and controlling operational-level activities and providing information to higher levels of the organization.

Managerial roles: Roles fulfilled by managers in their day-to-day activities, which include interpersonal, informational, and decisional.

Microcomputer: A category of computer that is generally used for personal computing, for small business computing, and as a workstation attached to large computers or to other small computers on a network.

Minicomputer: A computer whose performance is lower than that of mainframes, but higher than that of microcomputers. This kind of computer is typically used for engineering and mid-sized business applications.

Models: Conceptual, mathematical, logical, and analytical formulas used to represent or project business events or trends.

Modem (MODulator / DEModulator): A device that modulates (converting analog signals into digital) and demodulates (converting digital signals into analog) signals transmitted over data communication lines.

Monitor: The hardware that displays output, such as text, numbers, and graphics, that is being entered or manipulated by users; a monitor is also called a display or screen.

Mouse: A type of pointing device that works by sliding a small box-like device on a flat surface; selections are made by pressing buttons on the mouse.

Multipoint control unit: A device that links multiple video-conferencing units together.

Network database model: A DBMS approach in which entities can have multiple parent-child relationships.

Network operating system: A group of software programs that manage and provide the network with services.

Network services: The capabilities that networked computers share through the multiple combinations of hardware and software provided by the network.

Network topology: The shape of a network and the physical and logical relationship of nodes on the network.

Networks: Groups of computers and associated peripheral devices connected by a communications channel capable of sharing files and other resources between several users.

Node: Computer or other device on a network that sends and/or receives data.

Normalization: A process of making data structures simple and clear.

Object-Oriented Analysis and Design (OOA&D): Systems development methodologies and techniques based on objects rather than data or processes.

Object-oriented database: A DBMS approach that follows the object-oriented approach of reusable objects, encapsulation, and inheritance.

Object-oriented programming languages: A programming language that groups together data and its corresponding instructions into manipulatable objects.

Office automation or **personal productivity software**: Software designed and used to support a wide range of predefined, day-to-day work activities of individuals and small groups of individuals.

Office automation systems (OAS): Information systems that span organizational levels. They are used for developing documents, scheduling resources, and communicating.

Off-the-shelf application software: Software designed and used to support general business processes. It does not require specific tailoring to meet the organization's needs.

One-time costs: Costs that occur once during the life of the system, typically during project initiation.

Online processing: Processing of information (for example, transactions) as that information occurs.

Operating system: Coordinates the interaction between users, application software, and hardware.

Operational level: The bottom level of an organization, where the routine day-to-day interaction with customers occurs.

Optical disk: A type of secondary storage device with a huge capacity—similar to a CD-ROM—that allows both writing and reading from the disk.

Organizational change: Evolutionary and revolutionary alterations in people, structure, processes, and/or technology deployment and use within organizations.

Organizational culture: The set of mutually agreed upon values and practices that define what is acceptable in the organization and give the organization a unique climate or feeling.

Organizational politics: Activities that are not necessarily required as part of one's formal job description in the organization. These activities are aimed at influencing, or attempting to influence, the distribution of advantages and disadvantages within the organization.

Organizational strategy: An overall game plan for how an organization will achieve its primary mission.

Organizational structure: The anatomy of the firm, providing a foundation or framework within which the firm functions—often depicted in an organizational chart or picture.

OSI model: A model for interconnecting heterogeneous computer networks.

Outsourcing: Turning over partial or entire responsibility for information systems development and management to an outside organization.

Packet switching: A technique used on computer networks for sending information that divides messages into small packets before sending.

Parallel conversion: Changing over from the old to a new system by running both at the same time until the organization is sure that the new system is error free, that the users are adequately trained, and that the support procedures are in place.

Peer: Two separate computers or devices on a network that may both request and provide services to each other.

Peer-to-peer networks: Networks in which computers are peers.

Perfective maintenance: Making enhancements to improve processing performance, to improve interface usability, or to add desired, but not necessarily required, system features.

Phased conversion: Changing over from the old to a new system by utilizing parts of the new system and adding new modules and features to that new system as each part is validated as working properly. This process continues until the entire system is operating and the old system is replaced.

Pilot conversion: Changing over from the old to a new system by running the entire system in one location until it is validated as operating properly and then diffusing the system into the entire organization.

Plotter: A paper-based output device that uses pens to draw information onto paper.

Pointing devices: Input devices that allow the movement of a pointer or cursor on a computer display so that you can make selections or enter information.

Power: The ability to influence the behavior of others.

Preventive maintenance: Making changes to a system to reduce the chance of future system failure.

Primary key: A field included in a database that is used to uniquely identify each instance of an entity.

Primary storage: The storage location for instructions and data currently being used by the computer.

Private branch exchange (PBX): A private telephone exchange located in a single facility that provides both voice and data communication that is usually connected to the public telephone network.

Processing logic: The steps by which data is transformed or moved, as well as a description of the events that trigger these steps.

Protocol: The set of rules used to communicate.

Prototyping: An iterative systems development process in which requirements are converted into a working system that is continually revised through close work between analysts and users.

Proxy variable: A substitute variable, such as customer contact, expressed on a five-point scale from low to high. It is used in place of an information system's intangible benefit, which is difficult to quantify.

Pseudo code: A textual notation for describing programming code.

Query: Methods used to request information from a database.

Query by example: A capability of a DBMS that enables data to be requested by providing a sample or a description of the types of data we would like to see.

RAM (random access memory): A type of primary memory for which the computer stores information until the central processing unit needs it or stores it on a secondary storage device, such as a fixed disk.

Rapid application development (RAD): A systems development methodology that combines prototyping, computer-based development tools, special management practices, and close user involvement.

Record: A collection of related fields about an entity; it is usually displayed as a row in a database.

Recurring costs: Costs associated with the ongoing evolution, use, and maintenance of a system.

Relational database model: A DBMS approach in which entities are presented as two-dimensional tables that can be joined together with common columns.

Repetitive stress injuries: Injuries caused by long periods of repetitive motion, such as typing on a keyboard.

Replication: The process of updating copies, or replicas, of a database across a system or network.

Report: 1. A compilation of data that is organized and produced in a standard format. 2. A business document that only contains predefined data used for reading and viewing, typically for multiple records.

Request for Proposal (RFP): A communication tool indicating buyer requirements for a given system and requesting information from potential vendors.

Ring network: A network topology in which all stations are connected in a closed loop.

ROM (read-only memory): A type of primary memory that you cannot erase or add to. You can only read information from ROM.

Routers: Special-purpose computers that interconnect independent networks.

Satellite microwave: A transmission medium that uses high-frequency waves to transfer signals between antennas located on earth and satellites orbiting the earth.

Scanner input: A device you use to input preprinted text and graphics.

Scribe: A person who attends a JAD meeting to record the meeting information.

Secondary storage: Storage device used for archiving data and programs for later use.

Sequential data access: A data access method in which information is accessed and stored in a sequence.

Server: A computer that stores information (programs and data) and provides services to users through a network.

Server-centric networks: Networks in which computers are either servers or clients.

Software: A program or set of programs that controls the operation of the computer hardware.

Software engineering: A disciplined approach for constructing information systems through the use of common methods, techniques, and tools.

Source document: Documents created when a business event or transaction occurs.

Stakeholder identification and assumption surfacing (SIAS): A process for identifying any person, group, or organization affected by a proposed system or system change; finding whether or not they support the system; and determining to what extent they can influence the new system.

Star network: A network topology in which all stations are connected to a central hub.

Strategic: Important in or essential to a planned series of activities for obtaining a goal or desired result.

Strategic mentality: Viewing technology as an enabler of organizational strategy.

Strategic planning: The process whereby members of an organization form a vision of where the organization needs to be headed (that is, the organization's mission), develop measurable objectives and performance targets for that vision, and craft a strategy for achieving the vision, objectives, and targets.

Structure charts: Hierarchical diagram that shows how an information system is organized.

Structured Query Language (SQL): A commonly used set of commands for requesting information from a database.

Supercomputer: The most expensive and most powerful category of computers. It is primarily used to assist in solving massive research and scientific problems.

Symbolic language: A computer programming language that uses symbols to represent binary machine language codes.

System conversion: The process of decommissioning the current system and installing a new system into the organization.

System design: The third phase of the systems development life cycle, in which all features of the proposed system are described.

System effectiveness: The extent to which the system produces or is capable of producing or enabling people to accomplish desired results.

System efficiency: The extent to which the system functions or enables people to function in a way that avoids loss or waste of time, money, or other resources.

System implementation: The fourth phase of the systems development life cycle, in which the information system is programmed, tested, installed, and supported.

System maintenance: The fifth (and final) phase of the systems development life cycle, in which an information system is systematically repaired and/or improved.

System mentality: An approach exemplified by information systems personnel doing everything they can to satisfy their systems customers within an organization.

Systems analysis: The second phase of the systems development life cycle, in which the current ways of doing business are studied and alternative replacement systems are proposed.

Systems analysis and design: The process of designing, building, and maintaining information systems.

Systems analyst: The primary person responsible for performing systems analysis and design activities.

Systems benchmarking: A standardized set of performance tests designed to facilitate comparison between systems.

Systems competency: Knowledge and skills in systems integration, development methodologies, critical thinking, and problem solving.

Systems development life cycle (SDLC): The process of identifying the need for, as well as designing, developing, and maintaining contemporary types of information systems.

Systems identification, selection, and planning: The first phase of the systems development life cycle, in which potential projects are identified, selected, and planned.

Systems software: The collection of programs that perform and coordinate the interaction between hardware devices, peripherals, application software, and users.

T1: A dedicated digital transmission line that can carry 1,544Mbps of information.

Table: A collection of related records about an entity type, in which each row is a record and each column is a field.

Tangible benefits: Benefits that are easily measured in dollars and with certainty.

Tangible costs: Costs that can be easily measured in dollars and with certainty.

TCP/IP (Transmission Control Protocol/Internet Protocol): The protocols that specify how computers communicate on the Internet.

Technical competency: Knowledge and skills in hardware, software, and networking.

Technological change: Evolutionary and revolutionary advancements in information systems, systems components, and/or systems development.

Technology: Any mechanical and/or electrical means for either supplementing or replacing manual operations or devices.

Technology convergence: The integration of previously disparate technologies, such as computer, telephone, and video recorders, into relatively seamless systems.

Telecommunications: Transmission of all forms of information, including digital data, voice, fax, sound, and video, from one location to another over some type of electronic network.

Terrestrial microwave: A transmission medium that uses high-frequency waves for earth-based line-of-sight communication.

Text recognition software: Software that interprets preprinted text that is scanned as input into actual textual letters, numbers, or words rather than just a picture of the preprinted document.

Token passing: A network access control method in which a token circulates around a ring topology and stations can only transmit messages onto the network when a non-busy token arrives.

Touch screen: A method of input in which you use your finger to make selections by touching the computer display.

Trackball: A type of pointing device that works by rolling a ball that sits in a holder; selections are made by pressing buttons located near or on the holder.

Transaction processing system (TPS): An information system designed to process day-to-day business event data at the operational level of the organization.

Transactions: Repetitive events in organizations that occur as a regular part of conducting day-to-day operations.

Transmission media: The pathway used to send a message.

Twisted-pair cable: A transmission medium consisting of two insulated wires arranged in a spiral pattern.

Upper CASE: CASE tools designed to support the system identification, selection, planning, analysis, and design phases of the systems development life cycle.

URL: The addressing scheme for uniquely identifying each page of information on the World Wide Web.

Value chain analysis: Analyzing an organization's activities to determine where value is added to products and/or services and the costs that are incurred for doing so. Results are subsequently compared with the activities, added value, and costs of other organizations for the purpose of making improvements in the organization's operations and performance.

Value-added network (VAN): A privately owned WAN whose services are shared by multiple organizations.

Videoconferencing: The use of integrated telephone, video recording, and playback technologies by two or more people to interact with each other from remote sites.

Video input: Video and image input to a computer.

Virtual team: People using technology to collaborate together more effectively to solve problems across time and distance.

Visual programming languages: Programming languages that have a graphical user interface (GUI) for the programmer and are designed for programming applications that will have a GUI.

Webmaster: A person who manages the World Wide Web presence for an organization.

Whiteboarding software: A feature of desktop videoconferencing that allows two or more people to draw with a mouse or type text and display images on an electronic work space.

Wide area network (WAN): Two or more LANs from different locations that are linked together.

Wireless media: A transmission medium that transmits and receives electromagnetic signals using methods such as infrared line of sight, high-frequency radio, and microwave systems.

Wisdom: The ability to apply concepts across different types of problems or to new situations.

Work profile matrix: A matrix consisting of job and work categories that is used to show how much time is spent for each of the job categories and different types of work.

Workstation: A category of computer, based on a very high-performance microcomputer, which is typically used to support individual engineers and analysts in solving highly computational problems.

World Wide Web (WWW): An Internet service that organizes information using hypertext.

NAME INDEX

ORGANIZATION INDEX

SUBJECT INDEX